$C

HQ 728 .G66
Goodsell, Willystine, 1870-1962.
  Problems of the family

Wed. Jan 15.   Chap 22 in text.
        Companate marriage.⎫ Know what they are
        Trial marriage.   ⎬
        Free love.   ⎭
        498 - 506 - Family as social & educational sentinel.
                                              - Goodsell
        170 - 175 Reads - Modern Family.

Friday. 17
        Laws as solution to family problems.
        Goodsell, family as social. Jnd. 536 - 550

Mon Jan 20
        Choosing life partner.
        Considerations involved. What do you say
        they should be.

Wed Jan 22.
        Justification of Monogamy & social recognition
        of Parenthood.
        Chap 24 in text.
        Reads 176 - 182
Frid Jan 24 Final examination.

PROBLEMS OF THE FAMILY

The Century Social Science Series

PROBLEMS OF THE FAMILY

BY
WILLYSTINE GOODSELL
ASSOCIATE PROFESSOR OF EDUCATION AT
TEACHERS COLLEGE, COLUMBIA UNIVERSITY

THE CENTURY CO.
NEW YORK AND LONDON

INTRODUCTION

Within the last twenty-five years there has sprung up a vital and growing interest in the institution of the family and its functioning in modern civilization. This widespread concern about the workings of marriage and the family is noteworthy in that it indicates a more or less complete abandonment of the age-old taboo upon any critical investigation in the field of sex relations, or even of any open discussion of these questions. A generation ago the frank consideration of such problems as freedom for the woman in marriage, education of young people in sex matters, birth control, divorce, and a score of other moot questions would have condemned the men and women who attempted it to social disapproval. Yet, even then, the wisdom of maintaining the ancient ban was being questioned by a few daring spirits in Europe. As early as 1892, Mrs. Havelock Ellis was delivering addresses in England which openly attacked specific evils in the marriage relation and even advocated a "novitiate for marriage"—a proposal that must have chilled the souls of all but her most "advanced" hearers. Yet, when in 1906 the American Elsie Clews Parsons threw out the suggestion that a period of "trial marriage" might prevent much unhappiness among young people, pulpits in her native land thundered their disapproval of her and her book.[1]

Obviously the relaxation of the taboo upon critical examination of our sex *mores* would not have occurred without grave cause. And this cause may be found in the fact that the ancient institution of marriage and the family is not working smoothly under modern conditions of life. The friction in the machinery has gradually become so loud and persistent that its harsh grating offends the ears of conservatives and radicals alike and can no longer be ignored. Just as maladjustment within the church or the government has led in the past to criticism and ultimately to revolution, so a similar disharmony between the family and contemporary economic, social and psychological facts is producing a volume of hostile criticism, while signs are not lacking of what has been termed a "marriage revolt."

Under these conditions it would seem that a serious and impartial

[1] The Family, p. 349.

v

study of the family institution in its historical evolution would be timely and helpful to young women and men who will probably spend the greater part of their lives within some family. Such a study should help us to understand and appreciate the enormous importance of the family in ancient and modern civilization. It should make plain the indispensable services rendered to society in the past, the important contributions of the family to present social life under transformed conditions, and the functions of the family in the society of the future. Furthermore, it should help the student to comprehend how certain marriage customs and ideas have sprung from circumstances rooted deep in ancient culture history and how, through sheer force of social inertia, they persist in contemporary life long after they have been outgrown. For instance, the restrictions still laid, in some countries, on the holding of property by married women, as well as the management of it, goes back to feudal times, when powerful overlords looked to their vassals to furnish quotas of armed men in case of war. Clearly a woman holding a fief could not be relied upon to secure and equip these forces—hence the feudal law that women could not inherit land unless there were no male heir. This situation it was, together with the widespread legal theory that a woman's separate personality was merged in that of the husband after marriage, that is chiefly responsible for the laws on the statute books of certain modern nations limiting the power of married women to hold and manage property, to make contracts, to sue and to conduct their own cases before the law. Again, the general custom among civilized nations whereby the father has superior rights in the guardianship of children goes far back in culture history to the beginnings of the patriarchal family among Aryan people. However this family type might differ in details among Greeks, Romans, Slavs and mediæval barbarians, its essential character remained the same. It was an organization in which the oldest male head was the undisputed ruler of wife, children and (in Rome) slaves. Domestic religion, control of property, the education and marriage of children, even the control of the conduct of his wife—all were in the hands of the patriarch who was thus the sole arbiter of the destinies of every member of his household. Small wonder that such vast powers, sanctioned by ages of custom, should yield tardily and grudgingly to modern conditions.

To be enlightened concerning the sources of our present-day ideas and practices with respect to marriage, the family and irregular sex relations outside the sanctioned marriage institution is to be equipped for dealing with outworn customs and ancient abuses. No scientist would attempt to solve a practical problem in chemistry or biology until he had thoroughly mastered the causes of the phenomenon and the conditions favorable to its maintenance. Likewise no one desirous of bringing about improvements in the sex *mores* can hope to work intelligently and helpfully without understanding the historic causes of modern sex and family customs. An open-minded study of the genesis and evolution of the family, together with its indispensable contributions to civilization, should induce not only an enlightened desire to work for much-needed changes, but also an appreciation of the complexity and delicate ramifications of the problem and of the peculiar difficulty of achieving reforms in folkways hallowed by daily use and wont. To attain a clear perspective with regard to those human relationships closely bound up with our deepest and most intimate feelings is a difficult accomplishment and demands ability to detach ourselves from an obscuring cloud of instinct and emotion (in the interest of clarity and truth). Once the ideal of a freer and more spiritual marriage and family life has been perceived, there is no less need for a clear recognition of realities and a patient, tactful persistence in educating the popular mind which seem the only sure methods of social change in this difficult field of social relationships. The sex *mores* of a people cannot be transformed in a day or a generation; and, even though changes in ideal and practice seem to be following rapidly upon each other, it is probable that the minds of the vast body of unthinking or conservative people remain unchanged on these questions. Witness the action of the Episcopal Church of America in its recent convention (1922) refusing to sanction divorce save for the one cause of infidelity and prohibiting clergymen from marrying any divorced person except the innocent party to a divorce on Scriptural grounds. While experiments in a more ideally satisfying sex and family life will doubtless be made from time to time by daring souls, the large majority of men and women must be won by the slow and undramatic method of education to acceptance of the freedom of men and women in marriage, of the degrading character of sex relations without love and spiritual union, of the urgent need for a sounder understanding of sex life on the part of young and old.

When the ban, laid centuries ago, upon critical examination of marriage and family customs began to be lifted, a long step was taken toward the dawn of a better social order. And when enlightened education of every youth and adult in the purposes and meaning of sex and family life has won the day, it is reasonable to hope that the present restless dissatisfaction with our sex folkways will give place to efforts (on the part of most individuals) to realize a finer sex relationship, a freer, more satisfying and at the same time more spiritually developing form of family life than any the race has known. A historical study of the family reveals the slow, upward climb of mankind from brute sex lust to romantic love, from the more or less complete subordination of women and children within the family to relative personal freedom. The strong family unit of past generations has already split up into its component individuals, recognized as separate persons before the law, with definite legal rights. But the end is not yet. The hardest lessons men and women have to learn are those of true love and of the necessity for freedom in personal development to the end that, one by one, all those fetters upon individual growth within the family inherited from the autocratic civilization of the past shall be struck off.

CONTENTS

PART ONE

HISTORICAL INTRODUCTION

PART TWO

SOCIAL CONDITIONS REACTING UPON THE FAMILY

PART THREE

INDIVIDUALISM AND THE FAMILY

PART FOUR

THE CHILD AND THE FAMILY OF THE FUTURE

PART ONE

HISTORICAL INTRODUCTION

CHAPTER I

PRIMITIVE FORMS OF MARRIAGE AND THE FAMILY

DIFFICULTIES ATTENDING THE STUDY OF THE PRIMITIVE FAMILY

THE student of social institutions who seeks to obtain clear ideas about marriage, family customs and the position of women and children among primitive peoples soon discovers that he is confronted with a mass of material dealing with a bewildering number of tribes inhabiting widely separated portions of the earth. Not only is there the greatest variety of marriage and family customs among these peoples, but the student is further confused by the fact that anthropologists explain the data at hand by contradictory theories. The earlier social writers of the last century showed a disposition to formulate too hastily a theory of the original form of sex relationships and to interpret data revealing the sharpest differences in the light of their chosen formula of explanation. Only within the last decade or two have anthropologists resolutely resolved to throw overboard all ready-made theories concerning family origins and customs and to investigate the sex *mores* of each tribe in the open-minded spirit and by the painstaking methods of science. The result has been to reduce the number of conflicting views with regard to the original forms of marriage and family organization and to increase our store of accurate knowledge of the manifold sex customs of primitive peoples. So wide a variety of types of family life makes generalization difficult and the careful writer will therefore draw general conclusions cautiously and even tentatively. Nevertheless, certain customs do emerge from the mass of conflicting facts which appear to be common to a large majority of tribes. For example, the wide prevalence of clearly defined kinship systems, of marriage prohibitions, of wife purchase and of rules of residence makes possible some general conclusions regarding the primitive family, even while these may admit of numerous exceptions.

MARRIAGE: ITS MEANING AND ORIGIN

Having cleared the ground of a few outstanding difficulties, we may next consider the question, What is the meaning of marriage and how did it originate? The word "marriage" signifies to most people a union of

3

one man and one woman based upon mutual affection and continuing to the end of life. Such, however, is not the meaning attached to the term by students of primitive life. To them, marriage means a more or less temporary union of male and female persisting beyond the act of procreation and the birth of children to the time when the offspring can care for their primary wants themselves. From this point of view, marriage is purely a biologic function, a means whereby the species is maintained. But if this be the fundamental significance of marriage, it is clear that such unions are not confined to the human race but flourish among the higher mammals, especially the apes, and even among birds. It is a fact well known to naturalists that the male gorilla, the chimpanzee and the orang-utan remain with the female and their common offspring until they are able to shift for themselves. The male not only protects his mate and their young, but he procures food for them during their period of helplessness. Here, then, is an example of the essential meaning of marriage as understood by anthropologists.

But what is the original cause of such unions, characterized as they are by some degree of permanency? Mutual affection between male and female can hardly explain the facts, since mates frequently separate for trivial causes, among both the apes and primitive man, after the young can care for themselves. Sexual desire cannot of itself account for marriage, since this impulse comes and goes fitfully and can be easily satisfied without the formation of permanent ties. The true explanation of the origin of marriage is held by most anthropologists to lie in the complete helplessness of the offspring of both apes and man, which requires the services of both parents over a long period of time. Those parents who did not develop the nurturing instinct lost their offspring through death and did not perpetuate themselves. Thus Nature "selected" for survival those species in which parental care of the young was most fully developed. If, then, the helplessness of infancy be the primary cause of a union of male and female permanent enough to be called marriage, we are led to the interesting conclusion that *the family is the true origin of marriage,* not marriage of the family. When we reflect that marriages are frequently contracted today with the definite purpose of postponing for years the rearing of a family, or of having no children at all, this well established theory of the genesis of marriage assumes peculiar significance. In an age when marriage is coming to be looked upon as the union of a man and a woman for personal motives, *i.e.,* satisfaction of love and the desire for congenial and stimulating comradeship, the biologic cause of such union is quite frequently ignored.

UNIVERSALITY OF THE INDIVIDUAL FAMILY

Although the original forms of the family were various, one characteristic seems to hold good of family organization among them all—even of the "group marriage" of Australian and Melanesian tribes, *viz.*, *the family was individual*. By this is meant, of course, that the family consisted of a separate and well defined household group composed of husband (or husbands), wife (or wives) and children, and, in some instances, of the maternal or paternal grandparents with their children. The researches of anthropologists tend to support the theory that the individual family precedes in development the sib or clan and hence is the original unit of social organization. On the prevalence of the individual family Dr. Lowie writes: We "are justified in concluding that regardless of all other social arrangements the individual family is the omnipresent social unit. It does not matter whether marital relations are permanent or temporary; whether there is polygyny or polyandry or sexual license; whether conditions are complicated by the addition of members not included in *our* family circle: the one fact stands out beyond all others that everywhere the husband, wife and immature children constitute a unit apart from the remainder of the community." [1]

MARRIAGE PROHIBITIONS

Among all primitive peoples there exist certain restrictions upon marriage. The more general of these prohibitions may be briefly treated under the following heads: (1) incest, (2) endogamy and exogamy, (3) marriage within a limited group.

Incest.

The horror of incest, or sex relationship between near relatives, is universal among primitive tribes; but the interpretation of what constitutes incest differs widely in opinion and practice. Social writers have offered numerous explanations of this widely prevalent aversion. Hobhouse regards it as instinctive while Westermarck inclines to the belief that the horror of incest is not primarily an aversion to intercourse between near relatives but rather a dislike of cohabitation between household associates. Be the reason what it may, this deep-rooted feeling has led to the formulation of incest prohibitions among all peoples. Universally sex intercourse between parent and child is forbidden. On the other hand, marriages between brother and sister were common among the ruling

[1] *Primitive Society*, pp. 66-7. Boni and Liveright, New York, 1920. By permission.

classes of Hawaii, Peru and ancient Egypt. The explanation of this custom seems to be that the chieftains and kings of these peoples had developed such pride of race that only sisters of the blood were regarded as worthy to mate with them. At the opposite extreme is the custom of some tribes of prohibiting marriage between second and third cousins and even, as in the case of the Paviotso tribe of Nevada, of the most remote cousins, who are held to be blood kin.

Exogamy and Endogamy.

Further restrictions upon marriage are seen in the customs of exogamy and endogamy. The tribal requirement that marriage be outside the clan or tribe is called *exogamy;* the requirement that mating shall be wholly within the clan is called *endogamy*. And, be it noted, these customs have all the coercive force of law. Once established, they operate as powerful prohibitions against marriage within or without the clan as the case may be. Numerous theories have been advanced by social writers to account for these prohibitions. One of the earliest views was that such arrangements prevented the marriage of kinsfolk. Tylor,[2] however, holds that exogamy did not originate in the desire to prevent marriage among kindred, since marriages were prohibited only on the mother's or the father's side, thus making unions between kin on the other side admissible. Rather does Tylor believe that exogamous marriages had a political source. They were a means of binding various clans together in peaceful alliances. This view receives support from the studies of Morgan among the Iroquois tribes, where intermarriage clearly had political significance. McLennan and others have sought to account for exogamy by the widespread practice of female infanticide, which would force men to secure wives outside their own clan. The flaws in this theory lie in the facts that (1) female infanticide is by no means a universal primitive custom; and (2) the theory does not explain the prohibition of marriage within the clan. Even if men were compelled to seek mates outside the kinship or totem group, there would seem to be no reason why they should not marry such women in the clan as had been permitted to live.

Endogamy has also been accounted for on the theory that it is a product of racial pride, class divisions and religious taboos. Thus Lowie points out that endogamy is firmly established among the Hindus, whose caste system is ironclad. Wherever the tribe is split up into groups regarded as higher or lower in rank, there the prohibition of marriage outside an individual's own group tends to prevail. The ancient Jews prac-

[2] See article "The Matriarchal Family System," in *Nineteenth Century*, July, 1896.

ticed endogamy for religious reasons, in order that the monotheistic worship of Jehovah should not be stamped out by intermarriage with their idolatrous and polytheistic neighbors.

In his well-known study of *Human Marriage,* Westermarck holds that the prohibition of marriage within the group was the result of a powerful sentiment against sexual intercourse with persons reared in the same family or neighborhood. He points out that when individuals are reared together from early youth they develop a marked indifference or even aversion to sexual intercourse with family members of the opposite sex. While this is probably true in general, it is by no means universally the case. Studies of the causes of illegitimacy among girls have plainly revealed that in not a few instances the first steps toward loose and irregular sex relations were taken by young girls who had been violated by members of their own family.

FORMS OF MARRIAGE IN PRIMITIVE TRIBES

Apart from group marriage, which is very rare, the forms of marital union most frequently found among rude peoples are polygamy, polyandry and a modified monogamy. Polygamy, when precisely used, designates *both* the marriage of a man with more than one wife and the union of a woman with more than one husband. The exact term to indicate marriage with two or more wives is "polygyny," and this term will be consistently used in that sense in this study. Polyandry designates that form of polygamy where a woman mates with several husbands.

Polygyny.

Marriage with several women is very general among primitive tribes. Probably the determining cause of this type of union is not the desire for sexual variety, although this doubtless plays its part. Far more important, however, are certain economic and social causes. The man with more than one wife has a group of workers—wives and children —more or less under his control, who can be utilized to increase his store of goods. If he works them hard enough they may add materially to his wealth. Moreover a plurality of wives greatly enhances a man's prestige within the tribe. It is an outward and visible sign of power and prosperity. Therefore it is not surprising to learn that polygyny flourishes among peoples widely scattered over the face of the earth. It is found among the Iroquois tribes of North America, the Kai of New Guinea and many native tribes of Siberia and Africa. But it is one thing to state that polygyny is a widespread form of marriage and quite another to declare that among polygynous peoples all men have more than one wife. There are certain factors bearing upon this practice which definitely restrict it to the chieftains and to a group of powerful men within each tribe. First, it should be remembered that almost universally, under natural conditions, the numerical ratio of the sexes is nearly equal. "The first thing to do," says Lowie, "on hearing of a polygamous people is to demand a census of the marriageable members of both sexes." Obviously, if the men and women in a tribe are approximately equal in numbers polygyny must be limited to a few men of wealth and prestige. Even then certain other men must go without mates or secure them by capture or purchase from another tribe.

A further restriction upon polygyny is economic in character. Wife purchase appears to be a well-nigh universal custom in primitive society. It prevails very generally among Indian tribes of North America and the natives of Asia, Africa and the Pacific Islands. Now it is clear that a man's capacity to secure wives is limited to his ability to pay the brideprice, which not seldom is large. For example, among the Kirghiz of southeastern Siberia the cost of a wife may be as high as eighty-one head of cattle. Under such conditions a man must collect the property necessary to buy a wife over a long period of time before the bargain is concluded. Unless he is well-to-do, a second wife becomes a luxury which cannot be afforded for several years, if at all.

Finally, it should be noted that the custom prevalent in some tribes whereby a man at marriage goes to live with his wife's people tends to discourage polygyny. To bring a new mate into a household composed of his wife's relatives would appear too rash an act to be performed often by any prudent man.

Polyandry.

A very few existing tribes have established that form of marriage wherein a group of men, frequently brothers, share a wife in common. With the exception of scattered Eskimo communities, polyandry is almost wholly restricted to Thibet, southern India and a few scattered islands. The custom in the latter regions is probably due to a preponderance of males. Among the Todas of southern India, female infanticide has been so freely practised that the natural proportion of the sexes is seriously disturbed. Dr. Rivers, in his interesting genealogical study of the Todas, found that, for three generations, the ratio of males to 100 females in a Toda division was 259, 202 and 171 respectively.[3] Under such conditions

[3] W. H. R. Rivers, *The Todas*, pp. 477-8. London, 1906.

it is not difficult to see why polyandry flourishes among this tribe, although the cause of the common practice of female infanticide is more obscure. On the other hand, the agricultural peoples of Thibet do not kill female infants, yet polyandry is firmly established among them, owing to a scarcity of females which has not yet been satisfactorily explained.

Polyandry among both Todas and Thibetans is usually of the fraternal type; that is a woman becomes the wife of several brothers. When a child is born, the oldest brother establishes his right to be held its legal father by going through a prescribed ceremony with a bow and arrow; but all the brothers are regarded as in a sense the child's fathers. The situation is more difficult under that form of polyandry practised by certain Toda groups where a woman becomes the wife of several men who may live in different villages. In such circumstances she divides her time among her various husbands, remaining a month or two with each. If a child is born, the man (usually the first husband) who performs the appropriate ceremony with bow and arrow is adjudged the father. In case several children are born, the first husband claims two or three and then permits the other husbands a chance to establish their rights to children.

THE THEORY OF ORIGINAL MONOGAMY

There remains for consideration the theory of a considerable group of social writers that the most widespread and persistent form of marriage has been a loose monogamy—that very generally one man and one woman remained together as mates for a considerable period, even though these unions may frequently have been temporary in character. The evidence in support of this view is briefly as follows: (1) The monogamic family is the most efficient unit in the hard struggle for existence. Such a small, mobile group, united by common interest, can secure food more readily than a larger body. This fact doubtless accounts in part for the very general existence of pair marriage among the apes and chimpanzees, while it may well be a determining factor in the practice of monogamy among many primitive tribes at present, as, for example, the Veddahs of Ceylon and the inhabitants of the Andaman Islands in the Bay of Bengal. (2) Pair marriage must, perforce, have been the more general form in all stages of civilization, because the numerical relation of the sexes is nearly equal. History makes plain that, in every social group where polygyny flourishes, the possession of more than one wife is the privilege of the well-to-do who can afford to pay for it. Of necessity, in a tribe where men and women are approximately equal in numbers, the vast majority of men must be content with one wife. (3) The instinct of sexual jealousy is so strongly developed, among both the anthropoid apes and primitive man, that it must have operated powerfully against sexual promiscuity in its precise sense. (4) Monogamy probably preceded polygyny since all evidence goes to show that the latter form of marriage is the product of rather advanced economic conditions, when private property in land and implements had developed and men could pay for the prestige of owning several wives.

These arguments have not been seriously challenged by anthropologists. Yet in themselves they hardly establish the theory that monogamy was the original form of the family among all primitive peoples. The conditions of life—climate, food supply, the existence of hunting and fishing grounds, the proximity of aggressively hostile tribes—all must have played their part in determining the type of family life among any people.

MARRIAGE CUSTOMS AND MORALITY

It need hardly be said that once any form of marriage has become thoroughly established among a people that form receives the powerful sanction of custom, while all the moral ideas of the tribe are implicated in it and lend it support. It is reported by travelers that Turkish women look with disapproval tinged with disgust upon the custom of monogamy as practised by Western nations; and no doubt Toda women would show a similar distaste if obliged to adopt monogamic marriage. In the words of Sumner: "Whatever is defined and provided for in the *mores* as a way of solving the problem of life interests is never wrong."[4] The body of moral ideas which has grown up out of the custom of monogamy is probably no more powerful than that which supports polygyny or polyandry. All marriage forms are the product of economic and social circumstances, and all, when firmly grounded in custom, are crowned with a halo of moral and religious sanctions.

KINSHIP SYSTEMS

Primitive societies are divided not only into individual families but also into kinship groups or sibs claiming descent from a common ancestor. A brisk controversy has been carried on by anthropologists with respect to the question of priority in origin of the family and the sib or clan. At present the evidence seems to show that the sib was of later origin than the family, although it made its appearance very early in culture history. The kinship systems are two in number, (1) the

[4] *Folkways*, p. 375. Ginn & Co., 1906.

maternal system — descent traced thru mother.
Matriarchate. Power i authority on maternal side

PRIMITIVE FORMS OF MARRIAGE AND THE FAMILY   11

matronymic, tracing descent through mothers, and (2) the patronymic, in which descent is traced through fathers.

The Matronymic System.

The custom of organizing tribes into matrilineal clans is very general in primitive society. The maternal kinship system flourishes among such widely separated peoples as the Malays, the Melanesians of Oceania, the Iroquois and Pueblos of North America and numerous African tribes. Several explanations have been given of the origin of the maternal sib which may be briefly summarized. (1) Its determining cause is the close physiological relationship of mother and child. (2) The custom of polygyny frequently leads to a segregation of the various wives and children in separate huts. Thus the children would be thrown into much closer association with the mother than with the father and would be held to belong to her. (3) Matrilineal descent is often linked with matrilocal residence, although not always. That is, the custom whereby a man, after marriage, goes to live with his wife's people is usually accompanied by a high development of the matrilineal system. It would be quite natural that, when a man is performing stipulated services in the household of his wife, in order to pay the purchase price demanded for her, his wife's kin should regard the offspring of the union as their own.

All these causes, and probably others, operated to bring about the development of maternal kinship groups. Under this system not only is descent traced through mothers, but property also frequently descends in the maternal line. This means, of course, that a child is held to be related only to his mother's kindred and quite commonly inherits lands and personal property from his mother's brothers or uncles—not from his father. In some tribes, however, as the Crow Indians of America, certain kinds of property are transmitted through the father's line and other kinds through the mother's. Again, among the Navahos of Arizona, where sheep-tending is the leading industry carried on by men, matrilineal descent is firmly established while property rights in the flocks descend through fathers. These are further illustrations of the endless variety of customs with regard to every institution of primitive society.

The Matriarchate and the Avunculate.

Because of the prevalence of matrilineal descent and inheritance among primitive peoples, certain social writers hold that these customs clearly indicate the predominance in primitive society of "mother-power." They argue that the relatively influential position of women in certain tribes, as the Pueblos, the Iroquois and the Wyandottes of North America, where the matronymic system is firmly established, points to a stage of culture history when women were the dominating sex within both family and tribe. This theory has been eagerly seized upon by certain writers as evidence that women, having once ruled society, are eminently fitted to do so at present and will once more become the controlling force in social life. Such a theory, however gratifying to the upholders of woman's cause, rests upon a very slender foundation of fact. Tylor, Lowie and other anthropologists who have carefully investigated the workings of the maternal system are convinced that the status of women *may* be but little improved by it. Among the Melanesian peoples of Oceania, where descent is traced through mothers, the position of women is one of marked inferiority, especially among the Fiji Islanders. The same holds true of the West Australians. Again, as anthropologists have repeatedly pointed out, even when descent and property are transmitted through mothers, women are not the ruling power within the individual household. This authority usually devolves upon the woman's brothers or uncles. Tylor has assembled valuable evidence which shows how influential is the position of the mother's brother under the maternal system.[5] He it is, rather than the father, who decides important questions concerning the training and the marriage of his sister's son; and it is quite often he who is the household head. Among the Hopi, the mother's brother instructs her children in tribal customs; among the Winnebago a nephew often serves as a servant to his uncle and formerly accompanied him on the warpath. Lowie tells us that in the Omaha tribe "the maternal uncle had full control of orphaned children and even during the parents' lifetime showed a parent's zeal in defending them or avenging an injury to which they were subjected."[6] But perhaps the most extreme case of uncle authority is reported from the coast of British Columbia, where the nephew makes his home with his uncle, works for him and finally marries his daughter and inherits his property. This widespread custom of according power and influence over children to the maternal uncle is called the *avunculate*. Manifestly where the practice exists there can be no such thing as a matriarchate. Nevertheless, there were a few tribes, as the Wyandottes of North America, where large powers were given to women. Among this people, women were once the ruling heads of households and constituted the majority in the clan and tribal councils.[7] Such instances, however, are very rare.

[5] "The Matriarchal Family System," in *Nineteenth Century*, Vol. XI, July, 1896.
[6] Lowie, *op. cit.*, p. 82.
[7] Powell, "Wyandotte Government," in Smithsonian *Miscellaneous Collections*, Vol. XXV, p. 76 *et seq.*

The Patronymic System.

Under the patronymic system, relationship is traced through the father and quite commonly property is also transmitted in the paternal line. As has been previously suggested, there is little evidence to show that the paternal system has regularly followed upon the maternal and therefore represents a more advanced culture stage. Very primitive tribes, as the West Australians and the Fuegians of South America, have developed paternal descent and inheritance. The patronymic system, like the matronymic, is probably due to a variety of causes, economic and other. Moreover, it should be always kept in mind that the customs of one tribe have frequently influenced those of neighboring peoples. Cultural borrowing has been common in primitive as in civilized society. Lowie points out that the Hopi tribes probably borrowed their maternal system from the peoples they supplanted, since no kinship groups exist among the Shoshones, to which stock the Hopis belong. On the other hand, the Yukaghir of Siberia, who have developed the custom of matrilocal residence, which usually goes hand in hand with maternal descent, have borrowed their father-sibs from a neighboring tribe.

MORALS IN PRIMITIVE SOCIETY

Just as there is the widest variety of customs among primitive tribes with respect to marriage, kinship, control of children and inheritance of property, so there are the sharpest contrasts in their conceptions of morality, especially sex morals. Whatever custom with regard to sex relations has grown out of the social conditions of a people receives the powerful sanction of tradition and popular acceptance, and thus comes to be regarded as the only right method of dealing with these matters. As Ratzel and others have pointed out, sex morality in the early stages of civilization is chiefly concerned with the *securing of private rights in women*.[8] When a husband has bought and paid for a wife he regards her as his property. Therefore adultery is generally condemned among rude peoples, not because it offends the moral sense, but because it is universally regarded as an attack upon property rights secured by purchase. As the husband's rights in his wife become more firmly established by tribal usage, adultery becomes a more serious offense, sometimes punishable by death. Under such circumstances prostitution arises as a means of satisfying man's sex impulses without endangering family ties. But, although primitive man resents any forcible infringement of his marital

[8] Ratzel, *History of Mankind*, Vol. I, p. 120.

Mores — The accepted customs of a group.
Morals, derived from this word.

rights, he may, and in some tribes often does, lend his wife to a visitor as an act of hospitality or to a chieftain as a mark of respect. In his study of the Point Barrow Eskimo, Murdoch [9] tells us that among the tribes around Repulse Bay it is a custom to exchange wives for a week or two every two months; and among the Greenland Eskimos wives are exchanged at festivals. Such customs, however, are not regarded as invalidating the husband's prior rights in his wife. It is significant, also, that among the Eskimos prostitution is uncommon.

With respect to the question of the chastity of unmarried girls and youths, tribal customs once more reveal the greatest differences. Codrington says that, in general, among the Melanesian Islanders, unchastity before marriage is not very seriously regarded and sex intercourse between boys and girls is far from rare. Yet on the island of Saa a girl found pregnant before marriage would be put to death unless her seducer were willing to pay her purchase price and marry her. Also in the Banks Islands, a Melanesian group, girls are carefully looked after and their chastity is guarded. Clearly, there is a causal relation between child betrothal and regard for chastity. Where girls are betrothed in infancy, families are careful to keep them chaste, since the suitor of a girl would refuse to marry her and would reclaim his purchase money if he knew that his rights in her person had been infringed. Ellis says that, among the negro tribes of the Gold Coast of Africa, non-virginity is a ground for repudiating a bride only when the girl has been betrothed at a tender age. Unbetrothed girls may bestow their favors as they please without restriction. In this tribe, infant betrothal of girls is customary only among the better classes, and loose sex practices are common among the unmarried of the lower class. It may be said by way of summing up the situation that at one end of the scale there are tribes which carefully guard the chastity of girls; at the other are some that sanction the father in making his daughter a prostitute for gain. But in both cases it should be clearly understood that *no ideal of chastity as a virtue has emerged and become clearly defined*. Virginity is insisted upon, if at all, because the suitor has property rights in his betrothed.

DIVORCE IN PRIMITIVE SOCIETY

Among the vast majority of primitive tribes divorce is more easily accomplished than marriage. The privilege, in most cases, is restricted to men but divorce on the initiative of the woman is not as uncommon as might be supposed. Codrington says that among the Melanesians divorce

[9] *Ninth Report*, American Bureau of Ethnology, 1892.

is easy and very general and is effected at the will of either party. The same holds true of the Slave Coast negroes, of the Eskimos and of numerous other tribes in which temporary disagreements or incompatibility are frequent causes of separation. An obstacle to complete freedom of divorce, however, lies in the property paid for the wife. Among some tribes, if a man divorces his wife unjustly, he must forfeit her purchase price. If he demands of his wife's family the repayment of the property he gave for her, on the ground that the woman is unsatisfactory, he runs the danger that a blood feud may be declared against him by the offended relatives. On the whole, however, dissatisfaction with a wife is valid ground for her divorce and the repayment of the purchase money. By no means so privileged, however, is the wife; yet among certain tribes, the Eskimos and the Melanesians for example, a woman may leave her husband at any time because of a trivial grievance. In this case, however, she must return the property paid for her. If she has "worked out" a large part of it, "a pig or two settles all claims." The same holds true of the Africans of the Slave Coast, where the wife may separate from her husband with no other difficulty than the re-payment of the "head-money" and any expenses incurred for her. In all tribes marriage tends to become more stable where children are present, and less permanent where they are lacking. Indeed, barrenness is almost universally recognized as a just cause for the repudiation of a wife.

But, although divorce is an easy matter among primitive peoples, custom usually lays down rules respecting the custody of the children and the division of the family property. Under the matronymic system the children belong to the mother and depart with her; whereas under the paternal kinship system they remain with the father who owns them. Even in this case it is not uncommon for helpless infants to be handed over to the mother, especially if they be females. Custom also prescribes how common belongings shall be divided. In some instances the husband and wife each take the property that was his or hers at the time of marriage and divide all property accumulated afterwards.

In a few scattered tribes there are evidences that divorce is not wholly a private matter between the parties concerned, but tends to be regulated in some measure by group opinion. Ellis says that among the Slave Coast negroes a wife who is grossly abused may lay the matter before the headmen of the village. If she can prove her case she is permitted to leave her husband without repaying the head-money he gave for her. In West Victoria (Australia) a man may not divorce his wife before he has summoned a council of the chiefs of her family as well as his own. The Karo-Karo tribe in Sumatra permits divorce only by mutual consent; and, strange as it may seem, two of the most primitive peoples of whom we have knowledge—the Papuans of New Guinea and the Veddahs of Ceylon— regard marriage as a lifelong union and do not recognize divorce.

THE POSITION OF WOMEN IN THE PRIMITIVE FAMILY

Educated people very generally believe that the status of women in primitive society was very low. In fact, it is held that woman was a mere chattel, bought and sold in the wife-market and held as an ill-used, over-worked drudge. Thus Herbert Spencer declares: "The only limit to the brutality women are subjected to by men of the lowest races, is their inability to live and propagate under greater." [10] This is an excellent example of the sweeping statements made by social writers in the past which a more extensive investigation of the life of primitive peoples does not support. Here, as in every other phase of primitive family customs, the widest variety exists. Needless to say there *are* many tribes in which the women are little better than beasts of burden. This is true of certain of the Kafir tribes of Africa, of most Australian tribes, of the Koreans and of many others. But among some of the most backward peoples the position of women is not far removed from that of men. Thus the Veddahs of Ceylon treat women with much consideration and such appears to be true in general of the Eskimos, the Dyaks of Borneo, and many of the North American Indians. Murdoch says of the Point Barrow Eskimo that women "seem to be on terms of perfect equality with men" and not rarely are trusted companions whose opinions are sought by their husbands.

Sex Division of Labor.

In his interesting work on *Woman's Share in Primitive Culture,* Mason paints a glowing picture of the valuable industrial work carried on by women in rude societies. Indeed as we read of the multifarious labors of primitive women we are tempted to ask whether the men did anything but hunt, fish, fight and lie indolently about the camp fire. Here as elsewhere, however, it is well to remember that the customs of primitive tribes with regard to sex division of labor vary as extensively as do their other domestic arrangements. Although women were probably the first agriculturists, employing the rude digging stick to plant their seeds, yet it was man who invented the plough and domesticated animals. Plough agriculture and stock-raising are very commonly male occupations in primitive tribes and are sometimes jealously guarded from the encroach-

[10] *Principles of Sociology,* Vol. I, Part III, p. 713 (ed. 1885).

ments of women.[11] The Todas of India forbid their wives to have any connection with cattle, even prohibiting them from cooking food containing milk; and the Bantu of Africa have developed a powerful taboo against woman's entering a corral. Yet there are exceptions to this very general custom. Among the Altaian people of Central Asia the woman tends the cattle and milks the cows, sheep and goats; and in the Hottentot tribes she regularly milks the cows.

Another widespread division of labor on a sex basis is that with respect to agriculture. Very generally, plough husbandry is in the hands of men, while gardening with the hoe is usually an occupation of the women. In Polynesia, both sexes work together in the fields; whereas among most of the horticultural tribes of Oceania, America and Africa, gardening is exclusively woman's work. Codrington tells us that among the Melanesians apportionment of sex labor is determined by custom.

When we turn to household industries the same variety with respect to the division of the work on a sex basis confronts us. Among the Eskimos, sex division of labor is fairly sharp. While the men supply the animal food, under conditions of great hardship in winter, the women care for the supplies, cook, prepare the skins brought home by the men, and make them into garments. Occasionally a woman is sent out on the ice to bring in a seal her husband has taken and is too exhausted to drag home himself. In summer the women join the men in the hunt, but at other times they ply their industries at home. The Zuñi women of New Mexico are assigned the work of finishing the building of the house after the men have laid the stone foundations and set the huge rafters in place. In every Pueblo house is a rectangular mill divided into compartments, each with its own grinding stone of different degrees of smoothness. Kneeling before these mills the squaws do all the laborious work of grinding the grain to the desired fineness. They also share in making water jars, weaving baskets of osier and making woolen and cotton blankets woven in their own looms. Curiously enough, among the Melanesians the weaving of sails for canoes and mats for floor coverings is the work of women, as is also the preparation of yams and taro for food; while the actual cooking of the food is the work of men, who dig a hole in the ground, filled with hot stones, which serves as an oven.

The Economic Contributions of Women.

It is a common fallacy, into which even trained sociologists may fall, that woman in primitive society was in a condition of economic

[11] See Lowie, *op. cit.*, pp. 74-6.

dependence in all cases where she did not provide animal food or till the ground. Even so careful a writer as Lowie, referring to the fact that the domestication of animals and plough culture were achievements of men, attributes the low status of women in China, India and Central Asia to the fact that they were "economically dependent." Yet in China the women of the poorer classes have labored immemorially in the tea and rice fields. The silk industry in China has also been carried on in considerable part by feminine labor. To class women, busy from morning to night in a round of productive home industries, as "economic dependents" seems both unfair and contrary to the facts, unless economic productivity be viewed narrowly as supplying raw materials for food and clothing. In primitive society most women were economic assets of the utmost value, even if they never plied a hoe or furnished a pound of animal food. They were, with negligible exceptions, *producers of usable household goods* in the earliest times, and have continued so to be until the revolution in domestic industry, following upon the tremendous industrial changes of the eighteenth and nineteenth centuries, deprived women of most of the productive tasks so long carried on in their own homes. It should not be overlooked, moreover, that the productive labor of women in all ages has been carried on under the tremendous handicap of continuous bearing and rearing of offspring.

CHILD NURTURE AND EDUCATION IN THE PRIMITIVE FAMILY

The birth-rate in most societies was enormously high but so, too, was the child mortality rate. When we consider the hard conditions of life in primitive society, the almost total ignorance of the simplest essentials of child care, the ever-present menace of war, plague and famine, we are not surprised at the cruelly high death rate among infants. This was raised still higher by the customs of abortion and infanticide, widely prevalent in rude societies. The cause of this ruthless practice was chiefly enonomic —an insufficient food supply or the difficulty of carrying an infant from place to place when the tribe was migratory. In his valuable book, *The Primitive Family as an Educational Agency,* A. J. Todd gives many examples of abortion and infanticide as practised by African tribes, by the Fijians, the Brazilians, the Australians, the Fuegians and other backward peoples. Parental affection, although it may be present in some degree, yields to the terrible pressure of harsh conditions of life.

Curious birth rites are practised in those instances in which the child is permitted to live. In Oceania it is customary to cut the natal cord of the boy on a club to make him brave; of the girl on the board on which *tapa*[12] is beaten out to make her an industrious housewife. Quite commonly parents observe certain food taboos in order that the child may grow well and strong. In the Melanesian Islands, the father abstains from heavy work for a month in fear that it might bring injury to the infant; and he carefully avoids all sacred places where the child could not go without harm. Among the Fijians, both father and mother give up eating fish and meat for fear of making the baby ill. The Eskimo mother refrains from eating raw meat a whole year. After each meal she puts by a little food in a skin bag— a custom called "laying up food for the infant," which is eloquent of the severe struggle of this people for existence. Among the Kafirs of Africa, a mother refrains from eating the underlip of the pig lest the lower lip of her child should grow too large, and the meat of the buck, lest the baby grow ugly.[13] In addition to food taboos, certain charms and superstitious rites are used to keep away evil spirits from the child. Quite generally childbirth, like menstruation, is regarded as an impure function among primitive peoples, and mother and child are subjected to purifying ceremonies as soon as the infant is brought into the world. The Slave Coast negroes employ priests and priestesses to conduct these rites. The Kafirs smoke new-born babies over a fire to ward off evil spirits, and hang charms about their necks as did the ancient Romans.

The Status of Children in Primitive Society.

There is abundant evidence to show that in most primitive tribes children are regarded by their parents as valuable property. Boys are very early put to work tending gardens, caring for cattle or hunting and fishing, while girls carry wood and water, tend the fire and help their mothers make garments or shoes. Panlitschke says of the Northeast African peoples: "The children of a married pair are . . . considered as scarcely higher than things. They are the property of the father, for whom they must work, from whom they must buy themselves off, who can sell them, and from whom they must be purchased. . . . Thus their labor power belongs to the father until the moment they leave the family, and become themselves the heads of families."[14] The same holds true of the Kafirs, of the Yakuts of Northeastern Siberia, the Igorots of the Island of Luzon, and many other tribes.

So widespread a tendency to regard children as chattels to be bought,

---

[12] The bark of the paper mulberry tree which is beaten into cloth.
[13] D. Kidd, *Savage Childhood: A Study of Kafir Children*, p. 8.
[14] Quoted in A. J. Todd, *The Primitive Family as an Educational Agency*, p. 102.

sold and exploited raises the question whether parental love exists at all among primitive peoples; yet, if we may believe the reports of travelers and ethnologists, affection for children is frequently seen in savage tribes, even in those parents who wring the last ounce of labor from their offspring. Probably parental sentiment is crude, fitful and irrational, as Todd would have us believe. He quotes Sutherland to the effect that the affection of savages for their children "is an instinct of race preservation analogous to that of the lower animals, and gratifying itself without restraint. The savage knows little of that higher affection subsequently developed which has a worthier purpose than merely to disport itself in the mirth of childhood, and at all hazards to avoid the annoyance of seeing its tears." [15] Yet tales are not lacking of real tenderness shown to children by savage parents, together with extreme parental indulgence. The Pueblos of New Mexico, the Indians of British Columbia, the Eskimos and many Sahara tribes are reported to be remarkably fond of children and gentle in dealing with them. Indeed the fact that savage children are sometimes badly spoiled lends support to the theory that the affection shown them by their parents is less rational than emotional and not rarely gives way to sudden bursts of uncontrolled anger and impatience when children become too noisy and annoying.

Education of Children in the Primitive Family.

As might be expected, the training given to boys and girls in primitive homes varies greatly, depending upon the stage of civilization attained by the tribe and the amount of accumulated traditions, customs, rituals and skills to be handed on to the young. So far as the primitive family had an educational purpose, it was to form in the young a body of fixed habits which would adjust them successfully to their immediate surroundings. As the life of the savage is chiefly spent in wresting a livelihood from Nature, an important part of these habits would have to do with providing animal and vegetable food, making clothing, rude implements and weapons and keeping a roof over the family. Thus home education among savages has a strongly practical character. When a tribe has climbed a little farther up the ladder of civilization and has accumulated a store of traditions about the powers surrounding man and the proper ways to propitiate these forces, education may also take on a *social and moral* character. It would then consist not only in practical training but in the formation of habits concerned with propitiatory rites, ordeals and the like, and in positive instruction in tribal beliefs and customs.

[15] *Op. cit.*, p. 96.

The sharpest differences prevail among primitive peoples with respect to (1) the existence of a *conscious* aim of educating the young and (2) the amount of instruction given. Among the Fuegians, the Brazilians, the Thompson River Indians and the natives of Guiana, children are left to grow up with little or no attention from their parents after the earliest years. The children of the Micronesian Islands in the Pacific receive almost no training of any sort. In these tribes, parents leave their offspring to pick up what they need to make or do by watching their elders, imitating them and practicing until some skill is attained.

Fortunately for civilization, all primitive parents are not as indifferent to the education of their young. Among most savage tribes some attention is given to the practical training of the young in the pursuits they must carry on when grown. Since the content of this education is simple, concrete and concerned with the arts of daily life it can best be given within the home. The father takes upon himself to train his son in the pursuits of hunting, fishing and warfare, and in such industries as are carried on by men within the tribe, while the mother familiarizes her daughter with such household skills as she has herself acquired and perhaps with gardening. Little theoretical instruction is given children by either parent. Small boys and girls are expected to observe the activities of their elders and quite early to imitate them. In some tribes children are given tiny weapons and implements and encouraged to try their skill at target-shooting or making moccasins or fishing nets.

Group Training.

The moral and social education of girls and boys seems to have been more a matter of clan than of family concern. Of course children must have picked up certain of the moral ideas and customs of their tribe within the home; but much the greater part of tribal tradition was imparted to youth in the puberty ordeals and initiation ceremonies so common in primitive society. Spencer and Gillen have described in great detail the ordeals to which Australian boys were subjected at puberty, as well as the initiatory rites by means of which they were given, in symbolic form, the religious and moral beliefs of their people. In those tribes where secret societies existed, as among the Fijians and the Torres Strait Islanders, boys were at a tender age taken from their mothers and brought up in the society "lodges" which married women were not permitted to enter. Here they were instructed in the arts and morals of their people—in the accepted ways of house-building, fishing, fighting, in the tribal rules of conduct and in religious traditions. Curious customs are found in the Hebrides Islands, New Guinea and parts of Borneo where the girls are secluded, a few years prior to puberty, in huts or cells. Here they are almost completely isolated from human intercourse and prohibited from taking physical exercise and especially from seeing the sun or touching the earth. This abnormal life was enforced upon growing girls for periods ranging from three months to seven years, until they were physically mature and ready for marriage. Then their maternal aunts or other of their female relatives (but not their mothers) came to them, took them to the sea to bathe, or carried on other rites of purification, and instructed them in such of the tribal lore as it was important for women to know.[16]

Among a few primitive tribes, for example, the Blackfoot Indians, the ancient Mexicans and the Pueblos, the parents themselves give definite moral instruction to the young. Grinnell tells us that a Blackfoot Indian who had daughters "would, as they grew large, often talk to them and give them good advice. . . . He would talk to each girl of the duties of a woman's life and warn her against the dangers she might expect to meet." The Pueblos of New Mexico also inculcated domestic and group virtues in their children by telling them tales of terror before the hearth-fire. In this direct moral instruction the parents were assisted by the elders and by the medicine men and women of the tribe. However, such deliberate and reflective family education is very rare among savage peoples.

THE SERVICES OF THE PRIMITIVE FAMILY TO CIVILIZATION

As we review the many customs and ideas that control the life of savage groups with respect to sex *mores* and family life, we must admit that primitive society has rendered very real services to civilization. It has regulated the relations of the sexes in such wise as to avoid promiscuity, which would have retarded, if not prevented, the development of a body of customary sex morals and the organization of stable family life. The primitive family itself, however unsettled by frequent divorce and divided by polygamy, yet afforded a more or less permanent refuge for men and women from the disordered conditions of life and a nursery for the helpless young who might otherwise have perished. Then, too, the family preserved and passed on to the rising generation those technical skills by means of which primitive man was fed, clothed and housed. Thus a store of knowledge indispensable to life was conserved and very slowly increased. Finally, in so far as the family upheld and inculcated the moral traditions and customs of the group, it rendered valuable service

[16] See Frazer, *The Golden Bough*, Part III, pp. 204-33 (2nd ed., 1900).

in helping to lay the foundation stones of a more idealistic conception of human relations than primitive man had even dimly perceived.

TOPICS FOR REPORTS

1. The Effect of Infancy upon Marriage.
   E. Westermarck, *The History of Human Marriage,* Ch. I.
2. Marriage by Capture and Marriage by Purchase.
   Ibid., Ch. XVII.
3. Influence of Primitive Conditions of Life upon Parental Love and Care.
   E. B. Todd, *The Primitive Family as an Educational Agency,* Ch. V.
4. Divorce among Primitive Peoples.
   Westermarck, *op cit.,* Ch. XXIII.
5. Seclusion of Girls at Puberty.
   J. G. Frazer, *The Golden Bough,* Part III, pp. 204-22.

CHAPTER II

THE PATRIARCHAL FAMILY IN ANCIENT CIVILIZATION

ADVANCE BEYOND PRIMITIVE SOCIETY

IN the long course of centuries, certain peoples of the Aryan, Semitic and Mongolian races climbed slowly from barbarism to civilization. Ages were required to transform the primitive tribes inhabiting India, China, Palestine, Greece and Rome into civilized nations possessing a rich cultural inheritance from the past. The advance of these and other neighboring peoples beyond primitive social conditions is evidenced by the development of (1) stable central governments; (2) codes of public law to some extent taking precedence of the early family and tribal law; (3) an organized religion in the hands of an educated priesthood; (4) letters and literature, making possible the transmission of invaluable social experience; (5) schools and educational systems, as deliberate means of handing on these cultural accumulations to the younger generations; and, above all, (6) some understanding of physical forces, which resulted in a satisfactory solution of man's fundamental problems of securing food, clothing and shelter. Obviously this last phase of progress—the economic— is the foundation of all the others. Only when man has learned by arduous experience how to adapt Nature's crude resources to his own needs, and to make fire, wind and water serve his life purposes, can he wrest hours of leisure for reflection from the struggle for mere existence. It is, on the whole, the man of leisure who records in literature his dreams and aspirations, his plans and achievements, and creates in art forms his conceptions of beauty.

RELICS OF PRIMITIVE CUSTOMS AND IDEAS IN THE PATRIARCHAL FAMILY

But, despite the centuries of progress that intervene between primitive and ancient society, it would be a serious mistake to assume that no traces of barbaric social customs persisted in the civilizations of the Orient, Greece and Rome. Evidences of the primitive origin of many family customs are plainly manifest. The old kinship systems in modified form were present in ancient society; relics of purchase marriage were apparent; male supremacy was fully established and reinforced by a religion of ancestor worship; the almost complete subordination of women and children was the universal custom. Of all social institutions the family has been least amenable to change because its accepted customs and ideas are worked into the very bone and sinew of the young in their most plastic period, becoming a matter of habit and surrounded with a halo of more or less tender emotions and memories. It is precisely those social *mores* closest to our daily lives that we are least capable of viewing with detachment and in due perspective.

THE GENS OR "HOUSE" AMONG ANCIENT PEOPLES

In ancient society there existed, in pure or modified form, the gens or "house"—the "great family." This kinship group consisted of all those men and *unmarried women* tracing descent to a real or mythical common ancestor. Genetic organization was more definitely developed in Greece and Rome than among the Aryan tribes of India, the Hebrews of Old Testament times, or the Mongolian race in China. Most sharply individualized was the Roman gens which, according to Morgan,[1] had the following rights and obligations:

"I. Mutual rights of succession to the property of deceased gentiles (i.e., members of the gens).

II. The possession of a common burial place.

III. Common religious rites; *sacra gentilicia*.

IV. The obligation not to marry in the gens.

V. The possession of lands in common.

VI. Reciprocal obligations of help, defense, and redress of injuries.

VII. The right to bear the gentile name (i.e., family surname).

VIII. The right to adopt strangers into the gens.

IX. The right to elect and depose its chiefs."

The members of the gens both in Greece and Rome shared in common the family burial place and worshiped the same domestic gods. In their early history these peoples were unquestionably ancestor worshipers; but certain contemporary historians are inclined to believe that crude ancestor worship gave way among the Romans of the late Republic and the Empire to the cult of domestic gods—the Lares and Penates and Vesta, goddess of the hearth.[2] Both Greeks and Romans safeguarded the gentile name; yet when a family line was threatened with extinction, adoption of sons from outside the gens was freely resorted to. By appropriate

[1] Lewis H. Morgan, *Ancient Society*, p. 285. Henry Holt & Co., 1878.
[2] See W. W. Fowler, *Religious Experience of the Roman People*, pp. 72-86.

ceremonies youths were solemnly admitted into the gens of their adoptive fathers and thenceforth worshiped his ancestors and domestic gods. Since adoption of sons was a widespread custom in ancient society, the tradition that the gentile group was descended from a common ancestor and was thus one in ties of blood was, to a considerable extent, a fiction.

Finally, something should be said of two other firmly rooted customs in the Greek and Roman gentes. Each kinship group acknowledged one chief, who was probably elected from among the oldest and most esteemed heads of individual families. In this way the gens was held together as a firmly knit whole and administered in accordance with a sacred tradition. The system of reckoning relationship was that of *agnation*, that is, the arrangement whereby all those descended *in the male line* from a chosen lineal ancestor were recognized as agnates or kinsmen within the gens, while all descendants of women were excluded. The reason for this exclusion lay in the fact that a Greek or Roman woman lost her membership in the gens of her father at marriage and was admitted to the gens of her husband, thus ceasing to be *legally* a member of her father's family. Hence the saying in ancient Rome that a woman is the terminus of the family—"*Mulier est finis familiae.*" [3]

CHARACTERISTICS OF THE ANCIENT PATRIARCHAL FAMILY

Ancestor Worship.

The family in ancient times was patriarchal in character—that is, it was ruled by its oldest male head, whose will was law. Essential to the maintenance of the patriarchal family was the institution of ancestor worship. Among Hindus, Chinese, Greeks and Romans we find this custom deeply rooted and one of the most solid supports of paternal power. It is customary for the Chinese "great families" to build temples to their ancestors and at these temples representatives of "joint families" gather periodically to prostrate themselves before the ancestral tablets which commemorate their honored dead. In every orthodox Chinese home is a shrine containing stone or wooden tablets on which are inscribed the names of deceased ascendants and twice each year, on the days of the birth and death of the departed, offerings of burning incense and eatables are spread before the shrine, while the living descendants make obeisances and protrate themselves before the tablets. Similar ceremonies in commemoration of ancestors are an ancient custom in India, where also there early appeared the sacred hearth-fire round which many religious ceremonies of

[3] See Sir Henry Maine, *Ancient Law*, p. 148 (ed. 1894). Henry Holt & Co.

a domestic nature took place. "Agni," says the Hindu Rig Veda, "must be invoked before all other gods."

In Greece and Rome, as in Oriental countries, the authority of the oldest male head of the family was enormously enhanced by the institu-, tion of ancestor worship and its observances secured the complete unity of the family organization. Fustel De Coulanges [4] maintains that the essential bond of both the Greek and Roman family "was the religion of the sacred fire and of dead ancestors. This caused the family to form a single body both in this life and the next." In the midst of the Greek and Roman home was the domestic hearth, the fire of which was carefully tended by the wife and mother. This hearth was for many centuries the very nucleus of household life among these peoples. Round the sacred hearth and the altar to the domestic gods occurred most of the solemn ceremonials that were believed to propitiate the spirits of gods and ancestors and assure the welfare of the home.

It is a noteworthy fact that in all societies where ancestor worship became deeply rooted, the patriarch, or oldest male head of the family, was the high priest in conducting the domestic ceremonies. In India and Greece the women had little or no part in the ritual save as passive onlookers. In Rome, however, the wife and children shared with the father in the worship of the hearth-gods and ancestors. Not only was it necessary that the Roman wife serve as priestess with her husband in all the sacrifices and rites of domestic worship, but the boys and girls of the family assisted in these ceremonials as *camilli* and *camillae*. Nevertheless the more important rôle played by the father did much to assure to him, in Rome as elsewhere, a degree of power and prestige that, despite some modifications, persisted almost to modern times.

Power of the Patriarch.

The vast authority of the patriarch did not rest on ancestor worship alone. Great prestige accrued to the man in ancient society, as in primitive, from the fact that he was the fighter, the protector of life and property within the nation and the family. Thanks to his physical power, he wielded tremendous social power in a world where physical force and endurance counted for much. Then, too, the economic factor enhanced his prestige and authority. Among all ancient peoples—Hindus, Chinese, Hebrews, Greeks, Romans—the male was the chief provider of food and raw materials. He was the farmer, the raiser of wool and flax, the

[4] *The Ancient City,* pp. 51, 52.

metal worker, the craftsman, the merchant. To women was assigned the rôle of transforming crude products into usable goods within the home. Although the women as spinners, weavers, makers of garments and preparers of food have, from earliest times, been indispensable contributors to economic life, the fact that they were dependent upon the outdoor labors of men for the commodities which they worked over doubtless accounts for the fact that their economic value was never justly estimated in ancient society and in consequence their economic status was almost universally one of dependence.

For all these reasons, then, patriarchal power appears to have been well-nigh absolute, especially in ancient Rome, where the *patria potestas* attained its extreme expression. In the words of Sir Henry Maine, "in all the relations created by Private Law, the son lived under a domestic despotism which, considering the severity it retained to the last and the number of centuries through which it endured, constitutes one of the strangest problems in legal history." [5] The Roman father had the power of life and death over his children as well as that of unlimited corporal punishment. He could secure a wife for his son and give his daughter in marriage. Patriarchal power also involved the right of the father to divorce his son against his will, to transfer a son by the ceremony called *emancipatio* to another family which desired to adopt him, and to hold and control all family property. This meant that even a grown son, who might hold public office as priest or magistrate, could own no property, real or personal, independently of his father, who was entitled to take all his son's belongings and to enjoy the benefits of his contracts. Probably few Roman fathers exercised these extreme rights to the full, but the law would have sustained them in such exercise, even if public opinion had been unfavorable. In the grim words of the Laws of the Twelve Tables, which date from about 450 B.C., the father has the *right during the entire lifetime of his children* "to imprison, scourge, keep to rustic labor in chains, to sell or slay, even though they may be in the enjoyment of high state offices." [6] On the other hand it can scarcely be doubted that paternal affection, together with humane public opinion, combined to make the relation between father and son endurable.

The Status of Women Under the Patriarchal System.

The subjection of children to paternal power in the ancient family was paralleled by the subordination of women. Writing of the position of

[5] Maine, *op. cit.*, pp. 137-8. By permission of Henry Holt & Co., publishers.
[6] Paul Monroe, *Source Book of the History of Education for the Greek and Roman Period*, p. 337. The quotation is a digest of fragments of the ancient laws.

women in the Roman patriarchal family, Sir Henry Maine emphasizes the institution of perpetual tutelage "under which a Female, though relieved from her Parent's authority by his decease, continues subject through life to her nearest male relations, or to her father's nominees, as her Guardians. Perpetual Guardianship is obviously neither more or less than an artificial prolongation of the Patria Potestas, when for other purposes it had been dissolved." [7] Unquestionably this custom of guardianship, even of mature married women, was in large measure due to the fact that Roman women were denied the right to absolute ownership and disposal of property. The blunt words of Gaius, the Roman jurist of the second century A. D., are worth quoting in this connection:

"In general it should be noted that those who are in another's power, whether *potestas, manus* or *mancipium,* can have nothing granted to them in law; for since they have no control over their own persons, it follows, of course, that they can claim nothing as being their own in law." [8]

In early times (prior to the second century B. C.) a Roman girl at marriage merely passed from the authority of her father (*patria potestas*) to that of her husband, called *manus.* Marriage dissolved her legal relationship to her own family, and made her a member of her husband's family. From this time forth she worshiped her husband's household gods instead of her father's and came under the authority of the patriarch of his family. In modern eyes, *manus,* or the power of the husband, seems ruthlessly absolute. Sitting in judgment upon her, the husband might condemn his wife to death for a capital offense, provided he first summoned a tribunal of her male relatives and his own and laid the question before them. He had the right to kill his wife with his own hands if he discovered her in adultery. Furthermore, the Roman husband was granted almost unlimited powers of chastisement and correction of his wife; and he could sell her labor (if not her person) to indemnify himself for any fines she had incurred, which he was obliged by law to pay.

It is all the more surprising, then, to learn that the matron of Rome was a highly respected person with considerable authority over household affairs and the upbringing of her children. Despite the harshness of the early laws, it cannot be questioned that a dignified, law-abiding Roman wife and mother held an honored place within the household over which she presided. She was looked upon as the custodian of the family honor and co-partner with her husband alike in domestic worship and in the education of their children. Lord Bryce, in his valuable study of *Marriage and Divorce under Roman and English Law,* clearly brings out the con-

[7] Maine, *op. cit.,* p. 153. Henry Holt & Co., 1894.
[8] *Institutes of Roman Law,* II, 96.

trast between the legal subordination of the Roman wife and the dignified position she held in the family:

"One can hardly imagine a more absolute subjection to one person of another person who was nevertheless not only free but respected and influential, as we know that the wife in old Rome was." [9]

BETROTHAL AND MARRIAGE

Conceptions of Marriage.

In all forms of the patriarchal family from Rome to India the prevailing conceptions of marriage and even the nuptial rites reveal striking similarities. Everywhere marriage was held in the highest esteem and regarded as a cardinal social duty. Rarely could an unmarried adult be found in ancient civilization and such an one was looked down upon as having evaded his primary obligations to society and to his gens. A man or woman in Rome, Greece or India held with intensity the conviction that the family name must not be permitted to die out; and, above all, that the ancestral spirits must be reverenced and worshiped in order that the "great family" of the living and the dead might be united by strong spiritual bonds. In these days of individual choice in marriage for personal ends and satisfactions, it is a little difficult to imagine those ancient times, when the marital relation was viewed almost solely as a means of perpetuating and unifying the family and (in Greece and Rome) of furnishing loyal citizens to the state.

Since marriage in patriarchal society was an institution of great religious and civic importance, it is not surprising to learn that its control was kept firmly within the hands of adults, that is, of the father. Although the patriarch might consult with his wife regarding the disposal of their children in marriage, the final decision rested with him. In India, Greece and Rome the fathers of marriageable youths and maidens carried on negotiations among themselves, helped by information and advice from friends. In China and Japan, however, professional "marriage-brokers" or go-betweens were (and are) employed to inform parents concerning eligible young men and women of respectable families with some property who might meet parental requirements with regard to a son-in-law or daughter-in-law. In the ancient Chinese classic called the *She-King* [10] we read:

[9] Rt. Hon. James Bryce, in *Studies in History and Jurisprudence*, p. 790 (Clarendon Press). By permission of the Oxford University Press.

[10] Quoted in Hobhouse, *Morals in Evolution*, p. 194, footnote. Henry Holt & Co., 1915.

"How do we proceed in taking a wife?
Without a go-between it cannot be done."

When son or daughter in ancient society was emerging from childhood, his or her betrothal and marriage became a matter of profound concern to parents. In India, infant betrothals and child marriages were common owing to the law of Manu which prescribed that a father was responsible for the marriage of his daughter before puberty. If her father had failed to provide her with a husband three years after she was physically mature, a woman might choose whom she would—a startling invasion of parental power that reveals the paramount importance attached by the Hindus to early marriage.

Some evidences of marriage by purchase may be found in the ancient Vedas—the sacred epics of India. Thus we read that the daughter of the Prince of Madras was purchased as a wife with gold and precious stones. Evidently the custom had persisted into later times, for the Laws of Manu seek to discourage the practice and, although recognizing purchase marriage, rank it as one of the four blameworthy forms.[11] It is quite possible, also, that purchase marriage existed among Greeks, Romans and Chinese in prehistoric times. However, with the advance of civilization, the crude custom of the sale of the wife (if it had once existed) had given way to the more civilized practice of making gifts to the bride or, as in Greece and Rome, of setting aside property as her "dower" which reverted to her family after her death. But the gifts or dower provided by the suitor were frequently more than matched by the dowry demanded of every girl whose father sought for her a husband. No custom is more strongly entrenched in ancient society than that of providing a marriageable girl with a dowry. Without it she could not hope to marry. Hence the frantic efforts of father, mother, and even distant relatives to accumulate the necessary amount before the girl reached marriageable age. No doubt this entailed much hardship upon poor families and is one of the chief reasons why, even up to modern times, the girl baby in India is looked upon as a misfortune.

It will readily be seen that the economic aspect of marriage loomed large in ancient society. Parents sought to make a good financial settlement for their children and were not at all above dickering over the amount of property that the girls should bring as dowry or that the man should set aside for his wife. Everywhere marriage was looked upon as a *private contract* between the families concerned. Our modern view that the mari-

[11] These were purchase, capture, voluntary choice in marriage, and treacherous seduction.

tal relation is a matter of such importance to society that it should be carefully regulated by the state would have met with short shrift in ancient civilization. In the earliest times neither the state nor religion attempted to curtail the power of the father to marry his children when he chose and to whom he saw fit, to arrange the marriage contract as he wished, and to conduct the nuptial rites privately within the home with or without the services of priests. Nor was there public regulation of divorce in patriarchal society until late in the culture history of these countries. Divorce, like marriage, was a private affair, and so remained for many centuries.

One further characteristic of marriage in patriarchal society deserves brief consideration. In Greece and Rome a woman at marriage lost membership in her parents' family and joined the family of her husband. The reason for this custom is not far to seek. In separating herself from the household of her father she was no longer directly under his power but had passed under the *potestas* of her husband or his father if living. The Roman word *familia,* from which our word "family" is derived, originally signified the members of a man's household (including slaves) who were under his power (*sub potestate*). Certain consequences followed from a woman's loss of family membership at her marriage. In the first place she abandoned all right to inherit a share of the family property at her father's death. Her dowry was supposed to represent her portion; therefore the estate of her father was equally divided among his widow, his sons, and his *unmarried daughters.* A further consequence of a Roman or Greek girl's marriage was that in entering her husband's family she assumed the duty of worshiping his domestic gods. Thus the young Roman or Greek bride faced the triple loss of family membership, of the familiar domestic religion of her kinsmen, and of all rights of inheritance in her father's property.

Betrothal Customs in Rome.

Within the limits of this book it is impossible to discuss betrothal and marriage practices in all the countries where the patriarchal family flourished. Since Rome was the center for the spread of Christianity, which exerted a profound influence upon the development of marriage and family relations in the barbarian nations of Western Europe, it seems desirable to select for special study the betrothal and marriage customs among the Roman people.

Let us imagine, then, that a patrician father in Rome has a young daughter of an age to be betrothed. The first concern of this father will be to find a future husband for his daughter with whom the legal marriage called *matrimonium justum* can be celebrated. This form of union carried with it the full rights of the offspring to inherit their father's property and to be granted, in due time, all the rights of Roman citizenship. On the other hand *matrimonium non justum,* although a valid marriage, was irregular and frequently worked hardship to the children. Such marriages were contracted between Roman citizens and those of lower social rank, as freedwomen, actors and gladiators. The children of these unions, although legitimate, were not admitted to the gens of the father, and took the social position of the parent of humbler degree. Thus they had no legal right to inherit the property or to fall heir to the rights of citizenship which belonged to the parent who was a full Roman citizen.

When a Roman father had found a suitable mate for his daughter, usually by inquiring among his friends, he then entered into negotiations with the young man's father on the all-important question of the amount of dowry his daughter would be expected to furnish at her marriage. No doubt some shrewd bargaining commonly preceded a Roman marriage. But, these matters once adjusted, it was customary for the betrothal (*sponsalia*) to follow in a short time. Roman girls were betrothed at a very early age; indeed, Cicero speaks of betrothing his daughter Tullia when she was ten years old, although she was not married until three years later; and this was not at all unusual. Betrothal in Rome was a formal ceremony in which the girl was promised to the man as his bride, at some future time. It is interesting to note that the promise was made, not by the young people themselves, but by their parents for them, since both the girl and the youth were probably *in potestate* and their consent was taken for granted. However, if the man were *sui juris, i.e.,* freed from paternal power and his own master, the promise of the girl's father was made directly to him. This formal betrothal agreement was not held by the Romans to be legally binding; therefore neither party could sue the other for breach of contract, although it was considered disgraceful to enter into a second engagement before the first had been broken. After the promise had been given, presents were usually exchanged. Quite often these were articles for personal use; but in Christian times it became common for the man to give his betrothed a ring, which was worn on the third finger of the left hand. Then followed a banquet in the home of the girl's father and the *sponsalia* were celebrated as a family holiday.

Marriage Rites.

Shortly after the Roman girl had attained puberty, the marriage ceremony took place on a day carefully chosen so as to avoid all evil omens. According to ancient usage, the *consensus,* or consent of the parties to the union, was the most important step in marriage; but be it noted that this consent, once more, was not given by the actual contracting parties but by their parents. Probably few youths and fewer maidens ever dared to assert their personal wishes against the will of the father which, until late in Imperial times, was absolute. The nuptial rites began in the home of the bride's father, which had been gaily decked with flowers and branches of trees for the occasion. Although historians differ on this point, it seems probable that the auspices were first taken in the bride's home. A sheep was killed and the entrails examined by the augurs. If the omens proved favorable, the bride, wearing a flame-colored veil and attended by the groom, then entered the atrium, where the wedding guests were assembled. The consent of the heads of the two families to the marriage was then formally expressed and, in the later period, the contract (*tabula*) with respect to the girl's *dos,* or dowry, was formally agreed to and sealed by those present as witnesses. On many art monuments may be seen these *tabulae* in the bridegrooms' hands. Then followed wedding festivities which continued until sundown. In the early evening it was customary for the groom to take his girl bride from her mother's arms and escort her in gay procession (*deductio*) through the streets to his own home. At the head were the torch-bearers and the flute players, and behind walked the relatives and friends of the bride and groom. Important members of this ceremonial procession were the *pronubae,* or Roman matrons only once married, whose office it was to lead the bride to the marriage couch, and the three young boys who attended the bride, two holding each a hand and the third carrying before her the wedding torch of white thorn. Behind the bride were carried the distaff and spindle, symbols of her domestic duties. Through the streets passed the brilliant procession singing marriage hymns abounding in gross jests and personal allusions, and shouting, from time to time, the ancient marriage cry whose meaning had long been lost in the dim obscurity of the past. At the door of the bridegroom's home the gathering stopped while the bride wound the doorposts with wool and anointed the door with oil. No doubt the first act symbolized her duties as mistress of the household and the second was a symbol of the plenty which it was hoped the gods would send upon this new home. These symbolic acts performed, the groom carefully lifted his bride over the threshold, thus avoiding the unlucky omen of a stumble on the part of the girl. Some writers, however, explain this act as the last survival of an age when Romans won their wives by capture. It has also been explained as a ceremonial introduction of the bride to the household gods of her husband's family. Whatever be the interpretation of the act, it was followed by a significant little ceremony. The bride turned to the groom and with quiet dignity repeated the ancient formula: *Ubi tu Caius ego Caia,* thus signifying that where he was master she was mistress.

Up to this point the nuptial rites of the Romans were much the same whatever form of ceremony was chosen. But quite early Rome had developed three marriage forms, all of which were recognized as binding. These were (1) *confarreatio,* (2) *coemptio,* (3) *usus.* Only patricians might use the first form, which was a solemn religious rite. Plebeians were never permitted to marry by *confarreatio* and if a patrician married a plebeian he forfeited the right to use this religious ceremony. The marriage form peculiar to *confarreatio* consisted in certain religious rites which were celebrated under the direction of the chief priest (*Pontifex Maximus*) and the *Flamen Dialis* [12] in the presence of ten witnesses who represented the ten gentes of Rome. The auspices were taken and were followed by two acts of solemn significance: first, a sacred cake made from the grain called *far* was given to the bride and groom, who ate it together; and, secondly, the hands of the young couple were joined by the priest. As Becker points out, the wall paintings and sarcophagi depicting marriage all show this rite of joining hands, which was probably common to all marriages. But the succeeding ceremony was peculiar to *confarreatio*. The newly married pair seated themselves for a time upon two seats covered with a sheepskin, thus signifying that they were united by a single bond, however different might be their functions within the family. These symbolic rites were succeeded by the wedding banquet—probably a gay and lengthy affair— terminated only when the *pronubae* approached the bride and led her to the marriage bed, which had been carried into the atrium on the wedding day. Long after Rome had become a highly civilized nation it was customary for the *pronubae* to stand before the door of the bridal chamber singing those hymeneal songs (*Fescennina*) that, in modern ears, sound strangely coarse and even indecent. On the morning after the marriage the young wife began her life as mistress of the household by offering a sacrifice to the domestic gods of her husband at the family altar.

In marriage under the form of *coemptio,* no religious rites were used, although the ceremonies of the wedding procession, the lifting of the bride over the threshold, the salutation, *Ubi tu Caius ego Caia,* the taking of the auspices and the joining of hands remained the same. The bride was brought *in manum* (under her husband's power) by a symbolic sale which may be a relic of purchase marriage, although this fact is not fully established. In the presence of at least five witnesses, a single coin of small

[12] Priest of Jupiter.

value was placed by the groom in the scales held by a man called the *libripens*. This little ceremony was followed by the joining of hands and the publicly expressed consent of the couple to the marriage. Probably a prayer was then recited and a sacrifice offered, after which came the banquet and the wedding festivities.

We know less of the special ceremonies characteristic of *usus* than of the other two. Probably the wedding procession, the joining of hands and the words of consent were all used. But the woman was brought *in manum* merely by living for a year in her husband's house without leaving it for three successive days. It is interesting to note that, in Imperial times, the forms peculiar to *confarreatio* and *coemptio* had largely fallen into disuse, owing to the breakdown of the custom of marriage *cum mano*. "Free marriage" became almost universal and the ancient forms that put the wife under the power of her husband finally disappeared from the Roman nuptial ceremony, save in the marriage of priests.

CHANGES IN THE PATRIARCHAL FAMILY IN ROME

The Position of the Wife.

In the long course of centuries the status of the wife changed scarcely at all in Greece and in Oriental lands. But a marked improvement in the position of women took place in Roman society after the wars with Carthage (264-249 B. C. and 219-202 B. C.). Emerging triumphant from this long-drawn-out struggle for supremacy over an ancient foe, the aggressive Romans soon embarked upon those imperialistic wars which vastly enlarged their territories and enriched their treasury at the expense of the conquered provinces. Roman fathers of the patrician class became wealthy and powerful and no longer were willing to comply with the established custom whereby all the property, both real and personal, bestowed upon their daughters as a marriage dowry became the absolute possession of their husbands. Therefore it came about, as we have seen, that the marriage ceremonies which brought a Roman girl under *manus* gradually fell into disuse in the last two centuries of the Republic and so-called "free marriage" took its place. This meant that a woman no longer passed into the family of her husband at her marriage, but remained a member of her own and thus continued under the *potestas* of her father. But this was not all. Although the husband still retained the right to administer his wife's dowry and enjoy the income therefrom, the absolute ownership resided in his wife's father. Moreover, if a Roman girl at marriage were given the life use of property in addition to the dowry, she might enjoy the income quite independently of her husband. To be sure, the management of her property remained in the hands of her father or a guardian appointed by him at his death; nevertheless the possession of an income of her own spelled economic freedom for many a Roman matron of the official class. It is not strange, therefore, that their new financial independence led them to demand larger privileges, rights and opportunities. During the first centuries of the Empire, wealthy Roman matrons were to all intents and purposes free individuals. They were often as well educated as the men; they mingled without let or hindrance in the decadent social life of the period; and they even "rooted" for their favorite candidates before an election. In the patrician class, the authority of the husband had dwindled to a mere shadow. Indeed, the wealthy married woman may, at times, have been unpleasantly domineering. "Why have I not a rich wife?" asks the Roman poet Martial. "Because I do not wish to be my wife's maid."

Economic Changes.

But the enormous influx of wealth into the public treasury and the private purses of Rome had other far-reaching effects upon Roman life, especially in the family. Gradually the lands of the small agriculturists were bought up by opulent military and civil officers and the free farming class, so respected in early Roman times, joined the growing body of the proletariat—a restless, dissatisfied mass of wage-earners who were kept quiet by free gifts of oil, wine, bread and seats at the circus, the expense of which was met by the Imperial treasury. Not only did Rome thereby lose its sturdy, hard-working and self-respecting farmers, but in their stead it had developed an idle, pleasure-loving class of landowners whose country villas were marvels of luxury. The largest of these estates were worked by thousands of slaves, whose labor was minutely specialized. In addition to those who worked on the farms were skilled gamekeepers, poulterers, gardeners, cooks, bakers, tailors and handicraftsmen of every sort whose labor made a country villa a self-sufficient economic unit. Thus, instead of a republic of small farmers, Rome became an empire sharply divided into a wealthy land-owning class, who disdained manual labor, and a body of discontented wage-earners. The middle class of traders and manufacturers was relatively small and uninfluential.

Decline in the Marriage Rate and Birth-Rate.

Such profound economic changes could not take place without a marked reaction upon social and family life. Little by little the early ideas and customs with respect to marriage underwent a transformation. By the time of Cicero (d. 53 B. C.) marriage was no longer held in high esteem; and the marriage rate was falling so rapidly that it became a matter of deep concern to the Roman Emperors of a later day. Even as early as 131 B. C., the Roman censor, Metellus Macedonicus, had publicly exhorted Roman men to marry. But his appeal clearly reflects the cynical attitude that generally prevailed with regard to the marriage relation— a cynicism in sharp contrast to the former reverence. "If we could do without wives," he declares, "we should be rid of that nuisance; but since nature has decreed that we can neither live comfortably with them nor live at all without them, we must e'en look rather to our permanent interests than to a passing pleasure." The exhortations of public men, however, and even the rewards offered by Julius Caesar to encourage marriage, had little effect in inducing Roman men to take unto themselves wives. Men and women of the wealthy patrician class were more and more absorbed in living lives of pleasure and excitement and less and less inclined to assume the responsibilities of marriage and family life. In the decadent society of the Empire sexual satisfaction could be easily secured without entailing irksome cares and duties.

Not only was there a serious decrease in the number of marriages, but there followed a corresponding decline in the birth-rate. Ignorant of methods of preventing conception, pleasure-loving parents freely resorted to abortion and infanticide as means of relieving themselves of the responsibilities of parenthood, once so highly cherished. Infants of high and low degree were ruthlessly exposed if the father declined to acknowledge them or the mother were unwilling to assume their care. Unquestionably the practice was much more common than in an earlier period, even though it had always been permitted by law. The lack of legitimate children to inherit the estates of men of the senatorial class assumed such serious proportions that they resorted to two devices to secure heirs. They either formally adopted sons, or they left their property to men called "clients," who were not above fawning upon them and playing the sycophant with an eye to a rich bequest. So open and shameless did this practice become that Ammianus Marcellinus, writing in the fourth century A. D., declares: "Some persons look on everything as worthless which is born outside the walls of the capital save only the childless and the unmarried. Nor can it be conceived with what a variety of obsequious observance men without children are courted at Rome." [13]

[13] Quoted in Davis, *The Influence of Wealth in Imperial Rome*, p. 298. The Macmillan Co., New York and London, 1910. By permission.

Such a state of affairs was deeply disturbing to the Emperor Augustus, who sought to curb these social tendencies by legal enactments. To this end he induced the Senate to enact the law called the *Lex Julia et Papia Poppaea,* passed, in final form, in 9 A. D. This law was specifically designed to increase both the marriage rate and the birth-rate by penalizing celibacy and childlessness. It decreed that men unmarried at twenty-five years of age and women at twenty were disqualified to inherit any property bequeathed to them by will. Such property reverted to the state. Moreover, childless couples were mulcted of half the amount of a bequest. On the other hand, married men with children were given the preference in appointments to public office. The *Lex Julia de adulteriis,* an earlier law enacted about 18 B. C., represented a revision of the ancient laws and practices with respect to infidelity in marriage. By the terms of this law a husband lost the right to kill his wife if he surprised her in an act of unfaithfulness, although he might kill her seducer under certain conditions, carefully laid down. The father of the wife taken in adultery might, however, kill both his daughter and her paramour, again under conditions which led to much legal hairsplitting. The law further provided that an unfaithful wife should lose half her dowry and one-third of her property and be banished to a lonely island. Likewise a husband guilty of adultery must forfeit half his property and suffer banishment.[14]

However well-intentioned these laws may have been, they signally failed of their purpose—to increase marriage and child-bearing and to decrease unfaithfulness in marriage. Many years after the *Lex Julia et Papia Poppaea* had been enacted, the historian Tacitus tells us that the law had proved worthless to encourage marriage and the rearing of offspring, "so powerful were the attractions of a childless state." In this modern age, when highly civilized nations are also confronted with a falling birth-rate, it is not without profit to consider whether legislation will settle our problem any more satisfactorily than it did that of Imperial Rome. The causes of a falling birth-rate are various and by no means always selfish; and it has yet to be proven that these causative factors are reached and prevented by legal enactments.

Family Life and Education.

When marriage is held in low esteem and when men and women are too bent upon pleasure to care much about children, family education is obviously bound to suffer. And such was the case in Rome. In the early centuries of the Republic, when life was stern and simple, parents felt

[14] See article on *Adulterium* in Smith's *Dictionary of Classical Antiquities.*

a deep sense of responsibility for the education of their children. Tacitus bears witness to the wholesome character of family education in early Rome:

"The infant, as soon as born, was not consigned to the mean dwelling of a hireling nurse, but was reared and cherished in the bosom of the mother, whose highest praise it was to take care of her household affairs, and attend to her children. It was customary, likewise, for each family to choose some elderly female relation of approved conduct, to whose charge the children were committed. In her presence not one indecent word was uttered; nothing was done against propriety and good manners. The hours of study and serious employment were settled by her direction; and not only so, but even the diversions of the children were conducted with modest reserve and sanctity of manners. Thus it was that Cornelia, the mother of the Gracchi, superintended the education of her illustrious issue. It was thus that Aurelia trained up Julius Caesar; and thus Atia formed the mind of Augustus." [15]

Having thus described the wholesome family education of children in early Rome, Tacitus reverses the picture and shows us what home influences had become in Imperial times.

"In the present age what is our practice? The infant is committed to a Greek chambermaid and a slave or two, chosen for the purpose, generally the worst of the whole household train and unfit for any office of trust. From the idle tales and gross absurdities of these people, the tender and uninstructed mind is suffered to receive its earliest impressions. Throughout the house not one servant cares what he says or does in the presence of his young master; and indeed, how should it be otherwise? since the parents themselves are so far from training their young families to virtue and modesty, that they set them the first examples of luxury and licentiousness. Thus our youth gradually acquire a confirmed habit of impudence, and a total disregard of that reverence they owe both to themselves and to others. To say truth, it seems as if a fondness for horses, actors and gladiators, the peculiar and distinguishing folly of this our city, was impressed upon them even in the womb; . . . Who talks of anything else in our houses?" [16]

The renowned teacher of rhetoric, Quintilian, living in the first Christian century, lends the support of his testimony to that of Tacitus. "Would that we ourselves did not corrupt the morals of our children!" he laments.

---

[15] Tacitus, *Dialogue Concerning Oratory,* in Monroe, *Source Book in the History of Education,* p. 362. The Macmillan Co., 1921. By permission.
[16] *Ibid.,* pp. 362-3.

"We enervate their very infancy with luxuries. . . . We are delighted if they utter anything immodest. Expressions that would not be tolerated even from the effeminate youths of Alexandria, we hear from them with a smile and a kiss. Nor is this wonderful; we have taught them; they have heard such language from ourselves. They see our mistresses, our male objects of affection; every dining room rings with impure songs; things shameful to be told are objects of sight. From such practices springs habit, and afterwards nature." [17]

DIVORCE IN IMPERIAL ROME

Such being the picture of family life in patrician homes under the Empire, it is not surprising that divorce became so frequent as to constitute a public scandal. Roman men had always had the right to divorce their wives for certain grave offenses; but divorce did not become common until the second century B. C. Thereafter men in public positions led the way in getting rid of undesired wives. Cato, Cicero, Caesar, Pompey, Antony and a score of other prominent men divorced their wives on trifling or unworthy pretexts. After Cicero's day, women exercised the same privilege, perhaps as freely as men. So numerous were the matrimonial experiences of some individuals that St. Jerome [18] in one of his writings referred to a man living with his twenty-first wife who was himself her twenty-second husband. No wonder that Tertullian, a Christian Father living in the second century, once bitterly remarked that divorce is the first fruit of marriage.

More than one Roman Emperor tried to grapple with this social problem but with small success. Their method consisted in imposing pecuniary penalties upon the guilty party in a divorce or upon the party responsible for a divorce on frivolous grounds. The law of Augustus, whereby an unfaithful wife forfeited one-half her dowry and one-third her property, was later modified so that the guilty woman lost one-sixth of the dowry, with an added sixth for each child. This property accrued to the husband upon whom fell the guardianship and support of the children of the union. If the husband were the culpable party, he was compelled to restore his wife's dowry entire.

It is highly interesting and significant that none of the Roman Emperors from Augustus to Justinian ever challenged the old theory that *divorce was a purely private matter* outside the scope of a judicial tribunal.

---

[17] Quintilian, *Institutes of Oratory*, in Monroe, *Source Book in the History of Education*, p. 460.
[18] Lived in the fourth and early fifth centuries A. D.

Nor did they seriously interfere with the prevailing view that divorce should be as free as marriage. It was many centuries before Christianity was able to enforce its contrary doctrine that marriage is indissoluble, and then only with exceptions to be noted later.

DECLINE OF THE PATRIA POTESTAS

The gradual transformation of marriage and family life had been going on for two centuries before any weakening in the power of the father over his children became apparent. During the reign of Augustus the first step was taken toward lessening the absolute authority of the paterfamilias. A law was passed at this time which authorized a son under power to dispose by will of any property he had acquired in the exercise of his duties as a soldier. The Emperor Hadrian (r. 117-138 A. D.) extended this privilege to all men under paternal power who had been honorably discharged from military service. From this time on the tendency of the Emperors to limit the authority of the father became marked. Septimius Severus (146-211 A. D.) restricted the father's right of corporal punishment to moderate chastisement and decreed that for grave offenses against the law the son must be handed over to a judicial tribunal for trial. Yet, despite these mitigations of the authority of the Roman patriarch, up to the time of the Emperor Justinian (483-565 A. D.) a father had the right to expose his child or to sell it as a slave if he were destitute. During the reign of that Christian Emperor, however, the exposure of children was forbidden under severe penalties; the killing of a grown child was declared to be a crime making the father subject to the judicial penalty for murder; and the surrender of a son to an injured party in a civil suit in order to escape responsibility for the son's fines was prohibited. Muirhead declares that the ancient conception of the *familia* as an aggregate of persons completely subject to the family head had entirely disappeared by this time. Yet, even in the code of Justinian, the ancient right of the father to sell his son was recognized under two conditions, *viz.*, if the father were destitute and the child an infant.

The humane tendency to curb the tremendous power of the Roman patriarch was probably due in the main to the advance of civilization and the spread of gentler sentiments with regard to human relationships. But two other influences were at work to further the movement when it was once begun. During the first centuries of the Empire, the theory of a "natural law" grounded on justice, which should serve as a pattern for civil legislation, was becoming widely accepted among thoughtful men, who could not fail to observe the gross disparity between their enlightened conceptions of justice and the ideas animating the old laws with respect to paternal power. Another influence serving to ameliorate the harshness of ancient law was that of Christianity, which preached the equality of all men before God and sought to develop the gentler virtues among its members.

SERVICES OF THE PATRIARCHAL FAMILY TO CIVILIZATION

Although the patriarchal family was autocratic in organization, and often harsh and repressive in its workings; although women were legally more subjected under this system than in some primitive societies, yet this family type rendered very real services to civilization. In the first place the family was a strong, well-knit, orderly institution that endured through centuries of strife and warfare, serving as a model of peace and order in times of social upheaval. It is generally admitted that family law preceded and furnished patterns for the public laws that slowly developed with the growth of nations. Religion had its chief source in the patriarchal family and it is probable that worship of the household gods was closer to the hearts of men and women than the cult of the national deities with its more elaborate ritual. Certain it is that the *sacra privata* in Rome yielded much more slowly to the advance of Christianity than the *sacra publica*. These private rites, which took place at the naming of children, at betrothals, marriages and the assuming of the toga of manhood, were associated with the most sacred events of family life and were too deeply enshrined in the affections and memories of individuals to be easily supplanted. The patriarchal family also rendered valuable economic services. In it the division of labor on a sex basis had gone much farther than in primitive society. To the woman were assigned tasks wholly within doors—the management of her household and the care of children; to the man fell the work of tilling the land and protecting the home in time of war. In a society based largely on domestic industry, such as that of patriarchal times, sex division of labor was inevitable; and its utility is shown by the fact that it persisted, with slight changes, down to modern times, when the economic organization of society was transformed by the effects of the Industrial Revolution.

The most important service of the patriarchal family was rendered as a nursery and school for the young. In most lands where this type of family flourished, the parents clearly recognized their responsibility for their offspring, although this responsibility was most seriously assumed among the ancient Hebrews and Romans. The family education of children in early Rome has already been described. The Roman home was a training school in precisely those virtues that would produce a stable and enduring society, *viz.*, reverence for the gods and for the folkways of their ancestors, loyalty to the family and the state and unquestioning obedience to those in authority. It will be seen that little room was given in these early homes for the free play of individuality. Not until far-reaching changes in economic and political conditions had occurred were family life and discipline so transformed as gradually to give larger scope to the individual to enjoy a free and meaningful life such as was difficult to achieve under the harsh restrictions of an earlier family custom.

TOPICS FOR REPORTS

1. The Influence of Marriage Customs upon the Character of Roman Women.
   J. Donaldson, *Woman: Her Position and Influence in Ancient Greece and Rome and among the Early Christians,* Book II, Chs. I, II, IV, V.
2. The Nurture and Education of Children in the Patriarchal Family.
   W. Goodsell, *A History of the Family as a Social and Educational Institution,* pp. 52, 73-6; 82, 104-7; 114-5, 125-9, 146-50.
3. Divorce and Its Regulation in Ancient Society.
   Ibid., pp. 67-71; 96-9; 139-43.
4. The Influence of Wealth upon the Roman Family.
   W. S. Davis, *The Influence of Wealth in Imperial Rome,* Ch. VII and pp. 205-17. The Macmillan Co., New York, 1910.

CHAPTER III

THE INFLUENCE OF CHRISTIANITY ON MARRIAGE AND THE FAMILY IN IMPERIAL ROME

VIEWS OF THE CHURCH FATHERS REGARDING MARRIAGE

AFTER Christianity was made a state religion by the Emperor Constantine in 313 A. D., its influence became increasingly powerful in the sphere of marriage and family relations. It is important, therefore, to have a clear understanding of the way in which the early Christian Fathers regarded marriage. Fortunately the writings of Tertullian, St. Jerome and St. Augustine contain frequent references to the marriage relation, as do those of the earlier Church Fathers. Therefore the student of social history has no difficulty in forming an adequate conception of the attitude of Christian leaders toward marriage. For the first two centuries of our era, this attitude was mildly favorable—certainly not condemnatory. By the time of Tertullian (155-222 A. D.), the views of the Church Fathers were already strongly tinctured by that distrust of marriage, that tendency to regard it as a necessary substitute for fornication, that is so conspicuous in the writings of St. Jerome a century and a half later. In Tertullian's *Letter to His Wife* he says: "We do not indeed forbid the union of man and woman, blest by God as the seminary of the human race . . . and therefore permitted. . . . What, however, is better than this 'good' we learn from the apostle who *permits* marrying, indeed, but prefers abstinence. . . . In fact in that it is written 'To marry is better than to burn,' what, pray, is the nature of the 'good' which is [only] commanded by comparison with evil, so that the reason why marrying is *more* good is [merely] that 'burning' is less? Nay, but how far better is it neither to marry nor to burn?" [1]

This passage not only shows the increasing disfavor into which marriage was falling, but also points to one source of this disapprobation in the oft-quoted statement of St. Paul, "It is better to marry than to burn." That this most influential of the early leaders of the Church more than once expressed his disfavor of marriage and appeared to hold it in low esteem proved to be a potent factor in lessening the regard in which

[1] *Ante-Nicene Christian Library*, Vol. XI, pp. 280-2.

later Fathers held the institution. Had St. Paul been a happy married man instead of a bachelor, it is possible that the Christian leaders who followed him might have adopted a more friendly attitude toward matrimony.

But other social influences were at work to lower the regard in which wedlock was held by the Fathers. From the middle of the fourth century, asceticism gained an increasing hold on the minds of Christians and exerted a profound influence in opposition to marriage. This doctrine, of course, advocated the mortification of the flesh to secure the purification of the spirit, and taught that the ruthless suppression of all natural desires was the surest way to win the favor of God and eternal happiness hereafter. Both St. Jerome and St. Augustine taught the superior purity of celibacy and placed marriage lowest in the scale of virtue, regarding it as inferior both to celibacy and to the condition of the widowed man or woman who refrained from remarriage. St. Jerome exhorts a young Roman girl who had embraced a life of perpetual virginity not to "court the company of married ladies. . . . Learn in this a holy pride; know that you are better than they." [2] And in his treatise *Against Jovinian,* this influential Father does not hesitate to say "It is good to marry simply because it is bad to burn." Likewise St. Augustine, writing to the Lady Juliana about 416 A. D., congratulated her that her young daughter Demetrias had turned from an earthly marriage to "the spiritual embrace of that Husband who is fairer than the sons of men, and in espousing themselves to whom virgins retain their virginity, and gain more abundant spiritual fruitfulness." [3]

When the Fathers of the Church themselves looked askance at marriage as a remedy for fornication it is not surprising that, with the rapid spread of asceticism in the West, the married state was regarded by many Christian teachers as a refuge for those men and women too weak spiritually to embrace the ascetic life. Yet the Church never condemned marriage; the teachings of Christ were too clearly in support of it, and even St. Paul, at times, lends marriage a somewhat doubtful sanction.[4] But the exaltation of celibacy as a holier state than matrimony and more pleasing to God dealt a blow at the dignity and purity of marriage from which it had not recovered at the close of the Middle Ages. On this point Howard writes: "History all too plainly shows that the benefits conferred by monasticism and the enforced celibacy of the secular clergy come far

[2] Letter *To Eustochium* in *A Select Library of Nicene and Post-Nicene Fathers,* Vol. VI, pp. 28-30.
[3] *A Select Library of Nicene and Post-Nicene Fathers,* Vol. I, p. 549.
[4] I *Cor.* VII, 1-17; 36-40.

short of balancing the evils flowing from the conception of wedlock as a 'remedy for concupiscence.' The influence of the church did, indeed, tend to condemn the breach of conjugal fidelity by the husband as equally sinful with that of the wife; although this righteous principle has by no means always been observed in Christian legislation. On the other hand *celibacy bred a contempt for womanhood and assailed the integrity of the family.*" [5]

In seeking to understand the social conditions responsible for the half-hearted sanction accorded by Christian leaders to marriage, the moral decadence of Roman society must not be overlooked. Although our own age tends to adopt a somewhat Pharisaical attitude toward sexual immorality in Imperial Rome, enough trustworthy contemporary evidence exists to show that it was brazen and flagrant. Gourmandizing and attendance at the brutal games of the circus but served to intensify sexual desires, already over-stimulated, and led to a laxity in the relations of men and women that more than once expressed itself in disgusting sexual orgies.[6] Under such circumstances the fear and aversion so often voiced by the Christian Fathers for all gratification of natural impulses can be better understood. An age of unrestrained license in the indulgence of bodily appetites is not infrequently followed by a period of ascetic repression of even the most innocent desires.

Holding such views with regard to marriage, it was natural enough that the Church should condemn second marriages as little better than bigamy. Tertullian refers to such unions as "detrimental to faith" and "obstructive to holiness," and declares that St. Paul would not suffer a man twice married to preside over a church or a widow to enter the order of widows unless she were "the wife of one man." "For it behooves God's altar to be set forth pure."

Likewise the church very early expressed its disapproval of a married clergy. No doubt the advice to bishops and priests not to marry was at first merely a counsel of perfection. But it is certain that the later Apostolical Canons restricted liberty of marriage after ordination to readers and singers in the lowest orders of the clergy. In 314 A. D. the Council of Ancyra permitted deacons to marry only if they had given notice of their intention to do so at the time of their ordination. Still later, in 402, a church council under Pope Innocent I ordered bishops, priests and deacons to remain unmarried.[7]

[5] *History of Matrimonial Institutions,* Vol. I, p. 331. Italics mine. University of Chicago Press, 1904. By permission.
[6] See Sienkiewicz, *Quo Vadis,* pp. 255-6.
[7] Article by Meyrick on "Marriage" in *Dictionary of Christian Antiquities,* Vol. II, p. 1098.

A fair-minded study of the writings of the *later* Church Fathers forces the conclusion that these Christian leaders with few exceptions totally failed to grasp the spiritual nature of marriage—the joys of comradeship, of mutual love and sympathy and understanding that are the most precious accompaniments of true wedlock. In their reaction against the gross licentiousness of Roman society, they tended to regard marriage as a legalized satisfaction of fleshly desire and were blind to precisely those spiritual values in the relationship of which they might reasonably have been expected to be most appreciative. This remains true even though marriage quite early came to be looked upon as a sacrament, probably owing to St. Paul's mystical comparison of the relation of husband and wife to that of Christ and his church.

ATTITUDE OF THE CHURCH TOWARD BETROTHAL AND MARRIAGE CUSTOMS

It should be remembered that for more than three centuries Christianity was seeking to establish itself in the midst of a pagan society whose marriage customs were already firmly fixed. Therefore the leaders of the Church were early confronted with the problem of acceptance or rejection of the Roman practices with regard to betrothal and nuptials. Very wisely they decided at first to accept these customs as they stood, forbidding only such sacrificial rites and prayers to the gods as were clearly opposed to Christianity. No doubt the family ceremonies connected with betrothal, marriage, naming of children and assuming the toga of manhood had far more sanctity and were more deeply enshrined in the hearts of the Roman people than the public worship of the national deities. Thus it came about that Christianity found the pagan world "more ready to give up Jupiter and Mars than the Lares and Penates." In an indulgent spirit much to its credit the early Church permitted Christians to attend the family festivals of their non-Christian friends even when pagan sacrifices were performed. It was not until 392 A. D. that Theodosius issued an edict forbidding all pagan rites in family ceremonials.

Betrothal.

It will be remembered that the Romans had regarded betrothal as a contract which might be broken without legal consequences. Therefore pagan Rome was spared the undignified suits for breach of promise that clog our modern courts. At first, Christianity accepted the Roman view of betrothal as a *private* contract voidable by either party. But in the later centuries of the Empire, when Rome came more and more into contact with the Goths, Lombards and Teutons to the North, barbarian ideas and customs regarding betrothal influenced Roman usage. Little by little the betrothal contract took on legal value, as was the universal practice among Teutonic tribes, until, in the time of Constantine, the formal exchange of a kiss gave to betrothal the character of a legal contract whose abrogation involved penalties.

So far did the Christian Church proceed in the direction of regarding betrothal as a binding contract, only a little less sacred than marriage, that, at the Council of Constantinople in Trullo, which sat in 680-81, it was decreed that marriage with a betrothed woman in the lifetime of her first betrothed constituted adultery.[8]

Since the Church Fathers made no attempt to interfere with old-established rites of betrothal and marriage, except when they were clearly idolatrous, the betrothal ceremony remained a private family festival. The parties gave their consent before witnesses to be married at some future time, and the parents signed an agreement with respect to the amount of the girl's dowry and the suitor's provision for his future wife. Then the betrothed couple clasped hands or exchanged a kiss as a symbol of formal ratification of the contract. Owing to barbarian influence, the custom grew up of giving to the girl's father a small amount of money (*arrha*) as a guarantee that the man would live up to the terms of the contract. Out of this sprang the practice, firmly established before the ninth century, of bestowing upon the girl a betrothal ring, which was always placed upon the third finger of the left hand, because of the romantic belief that a tiny vein connected this finger directly with the heart! In Tertullian's time (about 200 A. D.), it was customary for girls in Christian families to be veiled at betrothal, but this practice was later restricted to the nuptial ceremony.

Marriage.

Although the early Church sanctioned the existing Roman rites of marriage, it very early urged couples to secure the blessing of the priest upon their union. In a letter written in the first Christian century, Ignatius declares that "it becomes both men and women to form their union with the approval of the bishop that their marriage may be according to the Lord and not after their own lust." But although many good Christians did seek the priestly benediction upon their marriage, yet *such blessing was not essential to a valid marriage for many centuries*. Indeed there is a total absence of any marriage ritual in Christian manuals at least up to the seventh century. By that time it cannot be doubted that the Church was

[8] See article on "Betrothal" in *Dictionary of Christian Antiquities*, Vol. I, p. 204.

enforcing the priestly benediction as a fixed rule. Fortunately an early example of one of these marriage benedictions has been preserved to us. It runs in part as follows: "May she be a faithful and chaste Wife in Christ and may she continue a follower of holy women. . . . May she strengthen her weakness by the help of discipline! May she be modest, grave, bashful, and instructed in God by learning. May she be fruitful in child-bearing. May she be approved and innocent, and may she attain to the rest of the blessed and to the heavenly kingdom." [9]

In this ancient blessing is embodied the ideal of the married woman that had already crystallized in Christian communities. She must be a paragon of all the virtues and fully alive to the essential frailty of her nature as a woman. As the weaker vessel, she must bow at all times to her husband's will. Moreover she must meekly accept her duty, as a daughter of sinful Eve, to be "fruitful in child-bearing."

The practice of veiling the bride at marriage was not uncommon in Tertullian's day, and in the fourth century it was probably a general custom. Even then it was not obligatory, for St. Ambrose declares that "marriage itself *should be* sanctified by the priestly veil and by benediction. . . ." [10] By the ninth century, however, the Church had certainly developed a marriage ritual binding upon all true believers. As evidence, Professor Howard quotes from a letter written about 860 A. D. by Pope Nicholas to the recently converted Bulgarians who had sought his counsel with respect to the rites proper to Christian matrimony: "First of all they [the bridal couple] are placed in the church with oblations, which they have to make to God by the hands of the priest and so at last they receive the benediction and heavenly veil." [11] In the Eastern half of the Roman Empire, the practice of crowning the bride and groom with myrtle or olive leaves took the place of the veiling ceremony of the West.

MARRIAGE PROHIBITIONS

Very early the Christian Fathers began that policy of placing prohibitions upon marriage between certain individuals which was later to result in hopeless confusion. So-called "mixed marriages," *i.e.,* marriages between Christians and Jews, heretics or the unbaptized, were frowned upon from the first. In the Theodosian code of the fourth century it was enacted that marriage with a Jew was a capital crime, and later councils expanded this prohibition to include heretics and unbaptized persons. The law was

---

[9] Article on "Marriage" in *Dictionary of Christian Antiquities,* Vol. II, p. 1108.
[10] Italics mine.
[11] Howard, *op. cit.,* p. 295, footnote 6.

enforced with great difficulty because it was not in harmony with public opinion. The general disregard in which it was held is shown by the fact that St. Jerome sharply reproves the women of his day because "the greater part, despising the apostle's command, marry heathens." [12] Half a century later, St. Augustine says that mixed marriages were not held as a sin in his day nor should they preclude baptism of the parties.

Christian prohibitions upon marriage did not end here. The Church recognized three kinds of relationship which constituted impassable barriers to marriage. These were (1) consanguinity or kinship by blood, (2) affinity, (3) spiritual affinity. The second term refers to the doctrine of the church that the relatives of both husband and wife were mystically akin, since marriage made of the man and woman "one flesh." This assumed relationship barred men and women related to either husband or wife within the seventh degree from intermarriage. Matters were further complicated by the theory of the Church Fathers that all persons who had participated in the religious rites of baptism or confirmation were made spiritually akin thereby and could not intermarry. It can readily be seen how difficult it might be for any man or woman contemplating marriage to determine whether the other party were related within the forbidden degrees. So inextricable became the tangle that in 802 A. D. the Emperor Charlemagne enacted that no person could enter into matrimony until "the bishops, priests and elders of the people" had made diligent inquiry into the relationship of the parties. The records show that numerous mistakes were made, honestly and otherwise, which sometimes served as grounds for the annulment of an irksome marriage during the Middle Ages.

BENEFICIAL EFFECTS OF CHRISTIANITY UPON MARRIAGE AND FAMILY RELATIONS

From the beginning of its history Christianity set its face sternly against the low ideals and the gross abuses that were undermining family life in Rome. But at first its influence was confined to the relatively small body of believers that constituted the Christian Church. As time passed on, however, increasing numbers of cultivated pagans became attracted to the new religion and, from the fourth century on, Christianity exerted a wide influence in educating the moral sense of Rome to regard abortions, infanticide, child exposure and divorce as grave social evils. With earnest conviction the Church Fathers branded infanticide and abortion as murder.

[12] See letter *Against Jovinian* in *A Select Library of Nicene and Post-Nicene Fathers,* Vol. VI.

and punished the guilty parents with exclusion from the sacraments of the Church until the hour of death. Likewise severe penance was exacted of those who exposed their children either to death or, in case of rescue, to the terrible fate of the slave or the prostitute. Yet these practices were so deeply woven into the life of the Roman people that Christianity found them very difficult to eradicate. Centuries passed before infanticide and abortion had been stamped out in Christian Rome; and as late as the sixth century we find Justinian legislating against child exposure.

With respect to divorce the doctrine of the Church seems not to have been clearly defined for a century or two. The fact that Christ recognized no cause for dissolution of marriage in *Mark* (X, 11, 12), while in *Matthew* (XIX, 9) he sanctioned divorce for the one cause of fornication, resulted in a division of opinion among the early Church Fathers on this point. But, as the theory of the Church that marriage is a sacrament crystallized into a hard and fast dogma, the Christian leaders became more and more unwilling to sanction divorce for any cause whatever. It was this position that finally won acceptance and came to prevail throughout the Middle Ages down to the present time. Whether this unbending attitude toward the matter of divorce has been an unmixed benefit to the family may well be questioned. Nevertheless, in an age when marriage was entered into with complete irresponsibility and as lightly terminated at the whim of either or both parties, the teaching of the Church that wedlock is a sacred indissoluble relationship, in which the man and woman "become one flesh," unquestionably stabilized the family during the unsettled centuries of the Middle Ages and lent seriousness and dignity to the marriage relation. However, the process of education of the popular mind to disapproval of divorce was a very slow one. Many centuries passed before the Church had achieved complete control over this field of social relations.

Of more unmixed benefit to the development of a sound philosophy of sex relations was the doctrine of the Church that impurity of life and unfaithfulness to the marriage vow is as sinful in men as in women. With intense conviction the Christian Fathers upheld the single standard in morals and condemned adultery, in husband as in wife, in unmeasured terms. Here, again, the Church found itself opposed to popular belief and custom. Consistent as was its own teaching, therefore, it would be idle to maintain that this view was ever generally accepted in Christian lands. From the time of the Church Fathers to the present the Christian doctrine of the equal obligation of purity upon the man and woman has been regarded as an ideal but unpractical theory, while popular custom has gone quite counter to its teaching. During the first three centuries, however, when the Christian community was relatively small and closely knit, the Church *did* impartially enforce its doctrine, visiting upon guilty husband and guilty wife alike the penalty of exclusion from the Church and its sacraments.

UNFAVORABLE INFLUENCES EXERTED BY CHRISTIANITY

The influence of Christianity upon marriage and the family was not always beneficial. Reference has already been made to the theory of many of the Church Fathers that marriage represented the lowest of the three grades of purity. So deeply rooted was the idea of the essential uncleanness of the sexual act, even when an expression of love within a true marriage, that certain medieval manuals of instruction called Penitentials contained clauses forbidding married couples to take part in the sacrament of the communion if they had cohabited on the preceding night. Thus the *Penitential* of Archbishop Theodore of Canterbury, written in the seventh century, contains the following rule: *Qui in matrimonio sunt, III noctes abstineant se conjunctione antequam communicant.* ("Those who are joined together in matrimony should abstain from cohabitation three nights before receiving communion.") [13] It may readily be understood how such teachings, together with efforts to enforce them, would cast discredit upon the marriage relation as not far removed from fornication. Likewise, in its exaltation of virginity, the Church tended to encourage continence after marriage. There can be no doubt that, during the early centuries of asceticism, a considerable number of husbands and wives made the resolve to abstain from sexual intercourse. In those cases where only one partner took the vow, there must have resulted a permanent embitterment that reacted disastrously upon the happiness of married life. On this point Lecky writes: "Whenever any strong religious fervour fell upon a husband or a wife its first effect was to make a happy union impossible. The more religious partner immediately desired to live a life of solitary asceticism, or at least, if no ostensible separation took place, an unnatural life of separation in marriage. . . . The extreme disorders which such teaching produced in domestic life . . . naturally alarmed the more judicious leaders of the Church and it was ordained that married persons should not enter into an ascetic life except by mutual consent." [14]

But the unfavorable reactions of Christianity upon marriage did not

[13] Hadden and Stubbs, *Councils and Ecclesiastical Documents Relating to Great Britain and Ireland,* p. 199 (Clarendon Press). By permission of the Oxford University Press.
[14] *History of European Morals from Augustus to Charlemagne,* Vol. II, pp. 322-4. D. Appleton & Co., New York, 1903.

end here. Very early the Christian Fathers showed a disposition to thrust women back into a narrow home environment, subject them completely to the authority of their husbands and deny them the right to teach, to baptize or to preach in the Church. Probably the influence of St. Paul was in no small measure responsible for the attitude of the Christian Fathers toward women. It was this early builder of the Church who had exhorted women to "keep silence in the churches: for it is not permitted them to speak; but they are commanded to be under obedience, as also saith the law" (I *Cor.* XIV, 34). Again St. Paul reflects the Hebrew view of women, in which he had been brought up, when he declares that woman should cover her head or be shorn. "For a man indeed ought not to cover his head, forasmuch as he is the image and glory of God: but the woman is the glory of the man. For the man is not of the woman but the woman of the man. Neither was the man created for the woman but the woman for the man" (I *Cor.* XI, 7-9). These teachings were reinforced by the prevailing tendency to regard woman as the cause of the fall of Adam and responsible for the appearance of sin in the world. Tertullian is especially ruthless in his denunciation of women on this ground. "And do you not know," he exhorts them in his letter *On Female Dress,* "that you are (each) an Eve? The sentence of God on this sex of yours lives in this age: the guilt must of necessity live too." No doubt a further cause of the strict subordination of women, after the first century of Christianity, may be found in the ascetic movement itself which, prohibiting as it did even a temperate gratification of natural desires, looked askance at woman as the temptress of men to carnal acts. The writings of the Church Fathers are deeply colored by this view. It would almost seem as if the preachers of asceticism were unable to regard women in any other light than as an incitement to sexual indulgence. Therefore their teachings reveal a prurience that is more than a little distasteful to present-day readers. In consequence of the widespread acceptance of these views by the fourth Christian century, woman's place was very clearly marked off for her. She was to remain at home, serve her husband and children, be obedient and subservient to her lord and meekly accept the teachings of the Church authorities. To be sure, widows had early been employed in Christian communities to visit the sick, assist the poor and care for friendless orphans. With the advance of asceticism, however, the widow gave place to the virgin, a superior type of purity in the eyes of the Church Fathers. These single women formed the order of deaconesses that has survived to modern times. None of these women, however, was given any authority within the Church to teach, preach or baptize.

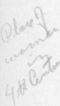

In an influential work called the *Apostolical Constitutions,* written in the fourth century, woman's position and functions are made plain: "Let the wife be obedient to her own proper husband, because 'the husband is the head of the wife' . . . Therefore, O wife, next after the Almighty . . . and after His beloved Son, . . . do thou fear thy husband and reverence him, pleasing him alone, rendering thyself acceptable to him in the several affairs of life, that so on thy account thy husband may be called blessed, . . . Look downward when thou walkest abroad, veiling thyself as becomes women." And again: "We do not permit our women to teach in the churches, but only to pray and hear those that teach; for our Master and Lord, Jesus Himself, when He sent us the twelve to make disciples of the people and of the nations, did nowhere send out women to preach, although He did not want [lack] such . . . For 'if the head of the wife be the man,' it is not reasonable that the rest of the body should govern the head." [15]

The *Clementine Homilies,* written in the third century, strike a similar note in regard to a woman's proper attitude toward her husband: "The chaste woman loves her husband from the heart, embraces, soothes, and pleases him, *acts the slave to him,* and is obedient to him in all things except when she would be disobedient to God." [16]

It is a far cry from the freedom enjoyed by the matrons of Rome under the late pagan régime to this almost Oriental subjection of women taught by the early Christian Church. The doctrine of woman's inferiority is reflected in the canon laws with respect to married women's property. Instead of allying itself with Roman law and custom, which gave comparative freedom to married women in the enjoyment of their property, independent of the dowry, and debarred husbands from the management of it, Christianity lent its powerful influence to perpetuate the practices of the barbarian tribes, who debarred women in most instances from the ownership of land and gave over the administration of all their property into the hands of their husbands. Sir Henry Maine points out that the more liberal attitude of Roman law has prevailed in Christian lands *only so far as the single woman is concerned.* Unmarried women "were relieved from the bondage of the family" and permitted to hold and administer property. But the medieval laws relating to married women should be read in the light not of Roman but of canon law, "which in no particular departs so widely from the spirit of secular jurisprudence as in the view it takes of the relations created by marriage." He adds that the

[15] *Ante-Nicene Christian Library,* Vol. XVII, p. 25 and § VI.
[16] Italics mine.

expositors of canon law, by keeping alive the property disabilities of married women, "have deeply injured civilization." [17]

THE INFLUENCE OF CHRISTIANITY ON ROMAN LEGISLATION

It is probable that the Christian Church had little effect on Roman law until Christianity was recognized by Constantine and later elevated to the position of the state religion by Theodosius (d. 395). Previous to the fourth century, Stoic influence had been powerfully exerted in behalf of more humane legislation in Rome and a mitigation of the earlier harsh laws with respect to women and children. Indeed, so careful a writer as Muirhead holds that the Stoics did more to bring about a humane spirit in Roman legislation than Christianity itself.[18] The influence of the Church made itself felt at first in the laws forbidding marriage with Jews, apostates and unbelievers. Christianity was also responsible for three changes in Roman legislation of considerable importance, *viz.*, (1) the repeal of laws penalizing celibacy, (2) legislation regulating divorce, (3) enactments depriving the Roman patriarch of most of the powers and privileges he had enjoyed under the old legal code. With regard to the first point it may be said that the Church unquestionably brought about the repeal of those clauses of the *Lex Julia et Papia Poppaea* (see p. 39) which visited severe financial penalties on men and women who were unmarried or childless. In an age when asceticism was sweeping like a flame over Western Europe, the Augustan laws making celibacy a social offense, punishable by loss of rights of inheritance, aroused strong disapproval among those Christian leaders who were upholding virginity as the highest type of life. This attitude finally led to their repeal by Constantine in 320 A. D. Quite early, also, Christian Emperors began to enact laws designed to regulate divorce by imposing financial penalties on the party responsible for dissolving a marriage on insufficient grounds, as well as on the guilty party in a divorce for recognized causes. But it is worthy of note that for two centuries none of the Christian Emperors after Constantine ever seriously attempted to interfere with divorce by mutual consent. So firmly was this custom established in Roman life and so generally accepted was the principle that divorce should be "as free as marriage and independent of the sanction or decree of a judicial tribunal" [19] that divorces by mutual consent were common up to the time of Justinian. The whirligig of time has again made of this question a live issue in the present day. Liberal men

[17] *Ancient Law*, pp. 157-8 (ed. 1894). By permission of Henry Holt & Co.
[18] *Historical Introduction to the Private Law of Rome*, p. 355. A. & C. Black, Ltd., London, 1916.
[19] See Muirhead, *op. cit.*, p. 356.

and women are maintaining, as no doubt they once argued in Rome, that the fact that *both* parties to a marriage desire its dissolution constitutes the most cogent reason for granting divorce. But the Emperor Justinian, influenced by Christian teaching, held an opposite belief. In one of his *Novels* he enacted that both parties to a divorce by mutual agreement should be required to enter a monastery. Otherwise the divorce should be null and void. However, this law was so opposed to popular opinion and custom that it was repealed by Justin the Second, his nephew and successor to the throne of the Eastern Empire.

The third point in which the Church influenced Roman legislation was in assisting to undermine the ancient supports of the *patria potestas*. From the time of Augustus Caesar laws had been passed successively tending to weaken the vast powers of the Roman husband and father. Therefore in the Justinian code almost the last relics of the old idea of the family as a body of persons absolutely under the domination of its patriarch or head had disappeared. As we have seen, *manus,* or the power of the husband over the wife, had long since been abandoned and marriage rested solely upon the consent of the parties. Roman law granted equal rights of protection to both husband and wife. Moreover, since the woman at marriage no longer became a member of her husband's family, she lost all rights of inheritance to his property until the claims of remote relatives had been satisfied. Nor could the husband inherit from the wife. To the custom of granting a *dos* or dowry to the woman for her husband's use was later added the practice of setting aside a *donatio,* or marriage settlement, for the wife from her husband's property. In the Justinian code it was laid down that, whenever a dowry was furnished by the wife's family, a *donatio* must be provided by her husband; and if one were increased during the marriage a corresponding increase must be made in the other. Furthermore, if the husband were insolvent, the wife might legally demand the transfer to herself of both her dowry and marriage settlement, on condition that the property was spent in the support of the offspring of the marriage. Likewise, in case of her husband's death or her divorce on insufficient grounds, the woman might claim both the *dos* and the *donatio.*

Perhaps the most telling blows leveled against patriarchal power consisted in the repeal of the age-old laws granting to fathers despotic powers over the persons and property of their children. Beginning with the act passed in the reign of Augustus Caesar which permitted a son to own and dispose of any property acquired by him in the active performance of his duties as a soldier, a long series of enactments stripped from the father most of his ancient authority and privileges. In the words of Muirhead: "All that remained of the *patria potestas* in Justinian's legislation is what is sanctioned in modern systems: the right of moderate chastisement for offenses, testamentary nomination of guardians, giving of the son in adoption, and withholding consent to the marriage of a child. The latter was subject to magisterial intervention if unreasonable." [20]

How much credit should be given to Christianity for the overthrow of patriarchal power? An impartial study of the Roman domestic legislation from the age of Augustus to that of Justinian shows unmistakably that a gentler spirit and a higher regard for personal rights had developed in pagan society with the advance of civilization. For example, in the first century A. D., long before Christianity became influential, a Roman father who had scourged his son to death was with difficulty rescued by Imperial officers from an angry populace bent on tearing him to pieces. The most that can be conceded to Christian influence is that it carried forward to its completion a tendency, already well advanced, toward a steady amelioration of the harsh laws of an earlier and cruder civilization.

THE MEDIEVAL PERIOD

During the long centuries of the Middle Ages, the barbarian tribes of Western Europe—the Goths, the Vandals, the Teutons, the Franks and the Saxons—were slowly learning the lessons of civilization. It required nearly a thousand years of social experience to transform these warlike, undeveloped peoples into societies with a regard for law and order, for religion and learning. Under the rude conditions of life throughout most of this period, when war was glorified and brute force exalted above the gentler social virtues, the family maintained itself in its patriarchal and autocratic form. Not only children but women were strictly subordinated to the will of the father and husband. The Christian Church strove to mitigate patriarchal power but never to undermine it. Feudalism, which was firmly established from the eleventh to the fifteenth century, denied to women the right to own land (unless there was no male heir) and did little to raise their status. During these centuries the Church established complete control over marriage and divorce, which, at the beginning of the Middle Ages, had been regarded as private matters in the hands of the male head of the family.

[20] *Historical Introduction to the Private Law of Rome*, p. 387.   A. & C. Black, Ltd., London, 1916.   By permission.

TOPICS FOR REPORTS

1. Two Views of the Influence of Early Christianity on the Roman Family.
    C. F. Thwing, *The Family,* Ch. III. Lothrop, Lee & Shepard, Boston, 1913.
    W. Goodsell, *A History of the Family as a Social and Educational Institution.* The Macmillan Co., 1915.
2. Asceticism in Its Effects upon Marriage and the Family.
    W. E. H. Lecky, *Hlstory of European Morals from Augustus to Charlemagne,* Vol. II, pp. 317-40. D. Appleton & Co., New York, 1903.
    G. E. Howard, *A History of Matrimonial Institutions,* Vol. I, pp. 324-32. University of Chicago Press, 1904.
3. Family Legislation in Rome as Influenced by Christianity.
    James Muirhead, *Historical Introduction to the Private Law of Rome,* pp. 345-426. A. & C. Black, Ltd., London, 1916.
4. Divorce in the First Christian Centuries.
    G. E. Howard, *op. cit.,* Vol. II, pp. 11-33.
5. Influence of Christianity on the Position and Social Influence of Roman Women.
    J. Donaldson, *Woman: Her Position and Influence in Ancient Greece and Rome and among the Early Christians,* pp. 148-91.

Report next Head.

Friday

CHAPTER IV

THE RENAISSANCE AND THE FAMILY

INTELLECTUAL AND SOCIAL PROGRESS OF WOMEN

THE Renaissance was a period of great intellectual energy, when men's minds were breaking loose from the bonds of dogmatic authority that had so long held them prisoners, and were escaping into the free air of inquiry, speculation and enjoyment of life in this world. The classics of Greece and Rome opened to the eager minds of the fourteenth and fifteenth centuries a new world of human interest, human aspiration, human endeavor and achievement. During this period of enlightenment, the privileged classes in Italy and France led lives of greater personal freedom of thought and action than had been known in the West since the decay of the Roman Empire.

Such an era of emancipation from customary molds of thinking and acting was bound, in time, to affect the lives of women, and such, indeed, was the case. Yet these beneficent influences, broadening, as they did, the social and intellectual experiences of women, were restricted in two ways. First, they had little or no effect upon the women of the middle and laboring classes, being limited to women of noble birth. Secondly, the liberation of the patrician woman was only partial, showing itself mainly in an improvement of her education and an enlargement of her opportunities for social intercourse.

In Italy first, and a century later in France and England, there developed alike in the palaces of royalty and the merchant-princes and in the castles of wealthy nobles, a courtly social life characterized by literary culture and much keen wit and repartee. To this brilliant company nobly born women were admitted, and contributed their share to the interest and sparkle of the conversation. From a delightful work called *The Courtier,* written by Castiglione in 1528, we may form a true and vivid picture of the larger educational and social advantages accorded to women in the princely circles of Italy. Castiglione does not hesitate to aver that all "the things that men can understand, the same can women understand too . . ." Therefore a lady's knowledge should include "Letters [*i.e.,* a wide range of literature], music, painting, and how to dance and make

60

merry." [1] Not a very comprehensive or thorough education, you may say, but it was probably much the same as that laid down for the brothers and husbands of these court ladies. Many Italian noblewomen became well grounded in ancient literature at this time; witness Cecilia Gonzaga, daughter of the Duke of Mantua, Vittoria Colonna, friend of Michelangelo, and the sisters Ginevra and Isotta d' Nogaroli, who were so thoroughly schooled in the humanities that they composed speeches and poems and were thought worthy to correspond with Guarino, most famous of the humanists of Verona.

Nor was a classical education accorded only to Italian women. History tells us of the learning of Queen Isabella of Spain, who became proficient in Latin and founded a library of priceless manuscripts at Toledo; and of her daughter Katherine of Aragon, later the unfortunate wife of Henry VIII of England, who was characterized by Erasmus as "a Miracle of her sex nor is she less to be reverenced for her piety than for her erudition." In France, too, appeared the learned woman. Margaret of France, sister of Francis I, was one of the leading intellectual spirits of her day; and her *Heptameron,* written in imitation of the widely read *Decameron* of Boccaccio, sheds a broad gleam of light on courtly ideals and manners in the France of the sixteenth century. In England, likewise, noble ladies were liberally educated. We read of the thorough classical education given to the Princesses Mary and Elizabeth and of the remarkable erudition of the Lady Jane Grey, who was said to have thoroughly mastered Greek, Latin, French and Italian at sixteen and to have had some knowledge of Hebrew, Arabic and Chaldee.

Not only were the minds of court ladies broadened and developed, but their social life seems to have been much freer than in previous centuries. Castiglione paints with glowing colors the stimulating court life at the castle of the Duke of Urbino, where lords and ladies carried on lengthy discussions of such moot and modern questions as the double standard of morals, the relations of husbands and wives, the superior chastity of women and the effect of love in making men more gentle and humane. An enthusiastic advocate of women's virtues and rights was Castiglione. Into the mouth of his spokesman, The Magnifico, he puts an ardent defense of women, relates tales of their loyalty and devotion to worthless or cruel husbands and even upholds the theory, unheard of in those days, that love should quite properly precede marriage. "If my Court Lady be unmarried and must love," he writes, "I wish her to love some one whom she can marry; nor shall I account it an errour if she shows him

[1] *The Courtier,* pp. 180-5 (ed. 1901, from the first edition, 1528).

some sign of love . . ." [2] An advanced view, truly, in an age when marriage was largely an economic bargain arranged by parents!

PROPERTY AND LEGAL RIGHTS OF WIVES

But if the education and social life of noblewomen showed marked improvement during the Renaissance, the same cannot be said of their economic status and legal rights. In theory and in fact women were economic dependents, incapable of owning land, and obliged to surrender all management of real and personal property, of which they had only the life use, into the hands of their husbands, who enjoyed the income therefrom. At the death of his wife, to be sure, the husband must surrender to her male heirs-at-law any lands of which she might have been possessed for life. But, in England at least, if a man's wife had borne him living issue he enjoyed at her death the ancient right of "curtesy," *i.e.*, the life use of all his deceased wife's real estate. Only after his death did the land revert to her legal heirs. In England also, where the laws respecting married women's property retained all the harshness of the medieval code, a woman's personal possessions, consisting of money, furniture, house linens and the like, became the *absolute* property of her husband. Only her bed, clothing and jewels [3] might be restored to a widow if her husband had not sold them before his death.

On the other hand, both France and England held to the medieval custom of granting a widow "dower," consisting usually of one-third of the deceased husband's real and personal property. This custom had never become established in Italy, where the dowry had always assumed enormous importance. No Italian girl could hope to marry without this nest egg; and ofttimes not only the immediate family, but relatives as well, struggled to assemble the necessary sum to secure a good match for the girl. The dowry was formally delivered to the husband immediately after the marriage and was his to enjoy for life. But, unlike the practice in England, he was held legally responsible to return the entire property to his wife at his death to be used for the benefit of the children. Moreover, if he mismanaged or squandered the dowry, he might be sued at law and compelled to make restitution.

No better off were married women with respect to rights of contract, suit and pleading of their own cases in the courts. At this time and for several centuries thereafter a woman at marriage lost her legal personality, which was merged in that of her husband. The current legal saying was:

[2] *Op. cit.*, p. 225.
[3] Called "paraphernalia."

"Husband and wife are one and the husband is the one." This meant that all legal action to secure his wife's rights and defend her interests was vested in the husband, who made contracts and sales, brought suit and pleaded before the law as the only person recognized by the courts in such action. These customs, of course, had their roots in the Middle Ages and, although thoroughly medieval in spirit, persisted for centuries after the Renaissance.

BETROTHAL AND MARRIAGE CUSTOMS

Owing to the influence of the Teutonic tribes of Western Europe, the old Roman theory that a betrothal was not a legal contract, and therefore could be terminated without penalty, gave way in course of time to the barbarian view that betrothal was but little less sacred and binding than marriage itself. In consequence litigation was frequently employed during the Middle Ages to bring faithless suitors to book or to force parents to carry out their part of the betrothal contract. It is unfortunate that the Teutonic and not the Roman view of betrothal has been handed down to our present age, for it has led to numberless suits for breach of promise, often resulting in heavy financial damages assessed on the party who has changed his mind, and has not rarely opened the door to blackmail.

Very little progress in ideas and practices with respect to marriage is apparent during the Renaissance, although somewhat later Luther injected into the prevailing philosophy of marriage some novel theories which will be considered later. While the Church taught that marriage was a sacrament, men in general looked upon it as a convenient economic arrangement by means of which they could secure at once keepers of their homes and wives to bear them legitimate offspring. The woman, on the other hand, looked to marriage as the only means of obtaining a respected social position and a home of her own. All the arrangements leading to betrothal and marriage were in the hands of parents who looked shrewdly into the financial aspects of the contract and did not hesitate to haggle over details of the girl's dowry or of the "marriage settlement" made by the husband in favor of the wife. Since mates were not chosen because of congeniality and affection but on grounds of economic and social advantage, and since husband and wife knew little or nothing of each other before the marriage, it is not surprising that these unions were frequently unhappy. A spirit of stoic acceptance of an evil lot or of bitter cynicism on the part of the man and woman thus mismated often appears in the literature of this period. Castiglione puts into the mouth of my Lord Gaspar the statement that there are probably many husbands who "hourly wish for death" because of "the torment of their wives"; while there are few wives "in the world who in their secret hearts do not hate their husbands."[4] About the same time Margaret of France philosophically declares: "Marriage is not a perfect state; let us be satisfied with wisely accepting it for what it is, *a makeshift but reputable.*"[5]

Among persons of rank the question of betrothing their girls and "marrying them off" at an early age seems to have been of commanding importance. Betrothals of little girls three or four years of age were not infrequent in Italy, although marriage did not take place until after puberty, in the years between fourteen and sixteen. In England, likewise, nobly born children were betrothed and even married not long after they had left the cradle. Furnivall's valuable book on *Child Marriages . . . in the Diocese of Chester* (1561-1566) is packed with evidence showing that marriages of children from four to nine years of age were far from uncommon. Fortunately for these boys and girls, thus united for life by their parents before they could understand what it all meant, they might, after reaching puberty, take their cases into the Bishop's court and refuse to consummate the marriage, if they had the courage to withstand their parents' will. One such case was that of Roland Dutton, married to Margaret Stanley when he was nine years old and she but five. As the time approached when the two would be called upon to live together as man and wife, this doughty youth steadily refused to consummate the union. Thereupon the case was carried to the ecclesiastical courts. Here the boy declared that "he would refuse to take the said Margaret to his wife; and that he would not consent to the said marriage which was solemnized in his minoritie. . . ."[6]

The custom of child betrothal and marriage is as old as social history. Savages practised it and it was common among the ancient Hebrews, Greeks and Romans, as well as in the Middle Ages. Doubtless it sprang from the desire of parents to see their children well settled in life, and, in the case of girls, safely removed from the dangers and temptations of a troubled world. Once the practice had become well established, especially among the nobility, it received all the powerful sanction of custom, and parents would then regard it as discreditable not to have married off a daughter before she was sixteen.

It must not be supposed that all marriages during this period were

---

[4] *Op. cit.,* p. 193.

[5] *Heptameron,* Tale 40. Italics mine. Quoted in de Maulde, *The Women of the Renaissance,* p. 49. George Allen & Co., Ltd., London, 1911.

[6] See Furnivall, *Child Marriages . . . in the Diocese of Chester,* Early English Text Society, Vol. CXVIII, pp. 42-51.

luckless and all husbands and wives chafing under the matrimonial yoke. Letters and diaries of Italian husbands and wives throw light on the real affection that sometimes existed between.married pairs. One Italian gentleman, Messer Donati Velluti, writes: "Bice, my first wife, was the daughter of Messer Corvone de' Covoni, and I took her in January, 1340, the year that her father died . . . She loved everybody and wished them well, and I can but extol her, for she loved me and was fain of me with all her heart." And the lady Dora del Bene writes to her absent husband that "we are all well, God be praised, but we should be still better could we be with you. Good-bye. Thy Dora commends her to thee with a thousand good wishes."[7] Written in similar affectionate vein are some of the Paston letters, the correspondence of a middle-class English family of the fifteenth century.[8]

HOUSEHOLD ARCHITECTURE AND FURNISHINGS

In its economic aspect, the Renaissance was a period of great expansion in commerce and industry which ushered in an era of prosperity. Wealth flowed into Italy first and later into Northern lands, as their trade and manufactures increased in amount and value. With the spread of prosperity there developed a leisure class eager to improve their lives alike intellectually and materially. Under the spur of desire for more beauty and comfort in their homes, the Italian princes built charming palaces to replace the gloomy castles of the Middle Ages, and furnished them with rich hangings of silk or cloth of gold, antique statues in bronze and marble, choice pictures and a variety of musical instruments. Not content with these evidences of refined taste, many nobles made collections of valuable books, the imperishable works of Greek and Latin authors, with which they enriched their libraries and quite often their minds as well. By the end of the fifteenth century most of the Italian castles had been modernized or rebuilt. Writing of these great houses, Boulting says:

"Two noble staircases . . . would lead to spacious upper chambers, where a bride would find great chests of drawers set against the walls, and an arm-chair beside a great bed tricked out with new curtains and smothered with flowers in her honor; and here she would see that her wedding-chest, filled with her rich dresses, was properly placed. Still a citadel without, the home of the wealthy noble or merchant was becoming a palace of art within. Citizens felt proud of the gorgeous private houses

[7] Quoted in Wm. Boulting, *Woman in Italy*, pp. 97-8. Methuen & Co., London, 1910. By permission.
[8] *Paston Letters* (1422-1509), ed. by John Gairdner, Westminster, 1900. See especially Vol. I, Letter 36.

that were arising in their midst. . . . Crowds of servants replaced the feudal retainers. Renée of Ferrara had, of her own separate household in 1529, four secretaries, a chief lady and seven maids of honor, an almoner, two choristers, six maids of the bedchamber, six equerries, doctors, and, altogether, about 200 attendants and servants. The greatest artists were employed in painting the walls in fresco, in designing furniture and in modeling pieces of plate. In the sixteenth century Michelangelo did not disdain to bestow his genius on a salt-cellar nor Raphael and his school on domestic pottery." [9]

To be sure, there is a darker side to this glowing picture. If the homes of the Renaissance nobles were gorgeous, they were still unsanitary and lacking in the common conveniences that we today regard as essential. Ceilings might boast priceless paintings, there might be an abundance of sculptures and tapestries, but mattresses were of straw covered with coarse cloth, combs and wash basins were far from sufficient for family needs and windows were closed with oiled linen, often torn and dirty and rarely renewed unless distinguished guests were expected!

Somewhat later, household architecture in France and England was similarly modernized and improved. Sixteenth century English nobles built lofty Gothic dining-rooms with carved wainscotings to replace the bare stone eating halls of the castles. Richly carved ceilings, solid oaken furniture, walls covered with family portraits or with carved armorial bearings became quite common in the great Tudor houses of the sixteenth century, which boasted also huge staffs of servants. Privacy, a matter of indifference during the Middle Ages, was beginning to be prized; and my lord and lady had each a lofty and comfortable bedchamber.

THEORIES OF THE PROTESTANT REFORMERS CONCERNING MARRIAGE

To the Protestant Revolt, and especially to Martin Luther, society is indebted for breaking down the taboo raised by the Catholic Church against the control of marriage by social agencies. Holding as it did in its own hands all authority over matrimony and divorce, the Church continued to teach that marriage is a sacrament and therefore subject to control only by the spiritual courts. Against this position Luther revolted, at first doubtfully, but with growing conviction. Yet Luther's statements are often ambiguous on this point, as Howard has pointed out. In certain writings he is clearly opposed to the theory of marriage as a sacrament, but in his *Bücher und Schriften* he nevertheless speaks of marriage as a "most spiritual status," "ordained and founded" by God. So holy a state

[9] Boulting, *op. cit.*, pp. 130-1. By permission of Methuen & Co., London.

does he regard it, indeed, that he finds it necessary to use the term "sacrament" in describing it in another writing. Yet in the "Preface" to his *Shorter Catechism* he distinctly states that "since weddings and matrimony are a temporal business, it becomes us clerks and servants of the church to order or rule nothing therein, but to leave to each city and state its own usages and customs in this regard." More than once he makes the same declaration, as in his *Tischreden,* where he says that marriage, being "a temporal and worldly thing, does not concern the church." [10]

Such theories, earnestly upheld by the protagonist of the Protestant Revolt, resulted in the conversion of most of the German leaders to his views, and the Protestant German states gradually assumed all authority over marriage. Nevertheless the celebration of public [11] marriages remained in the hands of the church for many years. Slowly, as the idea of marriage as a civil contract gained in popular acceptance, marriages were celebrated by public officials, as well as by the clergy, in Protestant Germany and Holland [12] and civil marriage became a firmly rooted custom. Not so, however, in England, where, although the Catholic doctrine of the sacramental character of marriage was ostensibly disavowed in the sixteenth century, the English clergy showed a disposition to compromise with this time-honored dogma. Not one clergyman of the Anglican Church took a firm stand for civil marriage during this period; consequently the religious celebration continued for centuries, with little or no change in form, except during the period of the Commonwealth.

Under the Protectorship of Cromwell a Civil Marriage Act was passed in 1653 prescribing an *obligatory* civil celebration before a justice of the peace. Banns were to be published for three Sundays in church or the marriage announcement posted for that time in the market place. At the time of marriage, a certificate stating that the publication had been duly made was to be presented to the officiating magistrate, together with proof of parental consent if the couple were under twenty-one. The ceremony itself was very simple, consisting in a public expression of consent to take each other as husband and wife "in the presence of God the Searcher of all Hearts" and before the assembled witnesses. The justice then pronounced the couple to be man and wife. The use of the ring, saturated as it was with symbolism and prominent in the Catholic ceremony, was

[10] For a thorough discussion of Luther's position and of the ambiguity of his writings on this point see Howard, *History of Matrimonial Institutions,* Vol. I, pp. 386-90, from which authority the above quotations are derived.
[11] As opposed to clandestine unions *per verba de praesenti* which were still common.
[12] In 1580.

sternly prohibited by Puritan law. Quite as important as the institution of civil marriage itself was the provision in the Act that all "matters and controversies touching contracts and marriages" were to be referred to the justice of the peace or to such officials as the "parliament shall hereafter appoint." It is noteworthy that no provision for trial of divorce cases was made during the Commonwealth and there can be no doubt that the prejudice against divorce was still strong throughout England.[13]

For seven years Cromwell's Civil Marriage Act remained in force and during this time a far more careful registration of marriages was made than had previously been known in England. Thus a sturdy blow was struck at the evil of clandestine marriages with which England was especially plagued. Unfortunately, after the Restoration the Act of Cromwell was superseded by the old laws in force before the Commonwealth. The spirit of the Act, however, lived on in the provisions made by the Puritans of the New England colonies of Massachusetts Bay and Plymouth for a civil celebration of marriages.

In two other respects Luther's teachings exercised a profound influence over Protestant conceptions of marriage, especially in German lands and in those countries most influenced by them. Although the great Reformer attempted to get away from the Scylla of the church distinction between spousals in words of the present or of the future tense, he ran against the Charybdis of a similar unfortunate distinction with regard to betrothals. That is, Luther taught that engagements to marry at some future time, when certain specified conditions were fulfilled, should be regarded as "conditional betrothals"; whereas all betrothals publicly made with parental consent, and in words of the present tense, were *valid marriages,* even though they should not be consummated until after nuptials. So binding were these contracts of future marriage (called "pre-contracts") that legal action could be taken to enforce them and severe penalties were laid upon the offender who broke them. In consequence, Luther gave the powerful sanction of his approval to actions for "breach of promise" which are still common at the present time in many Christian countries. Moreover, the tremendous importance attached by the Protestant Reformers to public betrothal led many couples thus betrothed to regard themselves as being "as good as married" and to consummate their union before the nuptial ceremony had been performed. This situation was productive of many scandals, not alone in Germany but in the New England colonies, where Luther's views about "pre-

[13] Howard, *op. cit.,* pp. 408-35.

contracts" were put into practice, sometimes with unfortunate consequences.

A third result accomplished by Luther was the breakdown in Protestant lands of the time-honored doctrine of the "celibacy of the clergy."
The literature of Luther's time and, indeed, of the centuries immediately
preceding, abounded in references to the loose lives of the priesthood.
These ballads and tales show plainly that parishioners were well aware
that many of their spiritual advisers were living almost openly with con-
cubines. With his accustomed courageous honesty, Luther "proclaimed
the natural and scriptural right of priests to marry" and led the way himself by taking to wife the escaped nun Katherine von Bora. Protestant
Germany was won over to this doctrine with comparative ease, but in
England it encountered much opposition. Although an Act of Edward VI
in 1548 expressly sanctioned clerical marriages, they did not meet with
general acceptance until after the death of Elizabeth, when the law of
Edward VI was restored.[14]

FAMILY EDUCATION AND DISCIPLINE

During the Renaissance-Reformation period, as well as in the century
preceding, many books and treatises were written exhorting parents to be
diligent in bringing up their children in the fear of the Lord, at the same
time pointing out to children the path in which they should walk with all
sobriety. In the fifteenth century there appeared in England Hugh
Rhodes's *Book of Nurture* written for the edification of parents and
children. In it we read:

> "Ryse you earely in the morning,
>   For it hath propertyes three;
> Holynesse, health and happy welth,
>   As my Father taught mee.
>
> At syxe of the cloche, without delay,
>   Use commonly to ryse,
> And give God thanks for thy good rest
>   When thou openest thyn eyes." [15]

Family government was far stronger in the sixteenth century than
it is in the twentieth; and religious education within the home was unquestionably more general than it is now. Well brought up children were
trained not only to say their prayers on rising and "to make a cross with

[14] Howard, *op. cit.*, pp. 394-9.
[15] Furnivall (ed.), *The Babees Book*, pp. 72-3. Trubner, London, 1868. Now
published by the Oxford University Press.

[their] thombe" on forehead, mouth and breast, with the words, "In nomine Patris, et Filii, et Spiritus Sancti, Amen," but to accompany their parents to morning mass before breakfast. Quite often chapels, to which the entire household repaired every morning, were built on to the castles of the nobility. So prevalent was the custom that we read of cities and towns where an early mass at four, five or six o'clock was celebrated for the benefit of those people whose occupation prevented their attendance at church at a later hour. This was known as the "Morrow Mass." After mass came the morning meal. At table "children were taught to bless themselves by the sign of the cross, and to follow the head of the family as he called down God's blessing upon what His providence had provided for them." In sober families, reading aloud at dinner or supper was sometimes resorted to in order to avoid gossip and "unprofitable talk." In a quaint book by Richard Whytford, called *Werke for Housholders,* parents are enjoined to teach their children the Lord's Prayer, the Creed and the Ave Maria, and "above all thynges (to) take heed and care in what company your chylder ben nouryshed and brought up. For education and doctrine, that is to say, bringing up and learning, done make ye manners." [16]

These were the days of stern family government and discipline. Whytford suggests that a child should be taught to ask his parents to "amende [hym] with a scourging" if he had committed any "trespace." And parents in turn are urged to "fulfil and performe theyr petition and request, and thynk it not cruelly, but mercifully done." Apparently fathers and mothers had little need of these exhortations, for the literature of the period frequently refers to the severe punishment of children and to the awe in which they were trained to hold their parents. Morning or evening they were taught to ask the parental blessing and to kneel when receiving it. We are told that Sir Thomas More, when Lord High Chancellor of England, was wont to repair to the court where his father, Sir John More, was sitting as judge to receive his blessing before hearing cases argued in his own court. The *Paston Letters,* written in the fifteenth century, throw a revealing light on the family discipline of that day. In one letter we read that the daughter of Agnes Paston, who had dared to refuse to marry the elderly man selected by her mother, had "been beaten once in a week or twice, and sometimes twice a day, and her head broken in two or three places." [17] So deeply rooted was the conviction that *parents*

---

[16] Abbot Gasquet, *Christian Family Life in Pre-Reformation Days,* p. 17 (*Educational Briefs,* No. 17, January, 1907). The Dolphin Press, Philadelphia. By permission.
[17] *Op. cit.,* Vol. I, p. 50. Westminster, 1900. By permission of Constable & Co.

owned their children and that parental authority must be maintained at any cost in the interests of family unity, that the state rarely if ever interfered to protect the rights of children. The invasion of the father's power by the super-authority of the state is a modern phenomenon.

In Luther's *Longer Catechism,* in his *Tischreden* and in other of his writings he has much to say of the importance of family government and education. Believing as he did that the basis of both Church and State is found in the family, he urges with his customary earnestness that the home is the place in which the education of children for the Kingdom of God and for good citizenship can best be carried on. Like most religious writers of the time, he makes much of the virtue of obedience to parents. Thus he writes:

"From the Fourth Commandment it is obvious that God attaches great importance to obedience to parents. And where it is not found, there can be neither good morals nor good government. For where obedience is lacking in the family, no city or principality or kingdom can be well governed. Family government is the basis of all other government; and where the root is bad, the trunk and fruit cannot be good."

Children, he declares, should not only love their parents but *honor* them and show toward them "modesty, humility and deference as though to a majesty there hidden . . ." On the other hand, parents are reminded that they are entrusted with authority by God, not to use it as they please, but to train their children for society and the Church. And for the manner in which they perform this duty they will be held to a strict account. With all his emphasis on parental authority and the reverence due to parents from their offspring, Luther does not advocate the harsh punishment of children and the frequent use of the rod so prevalent in his day. No doubt he remembered his own sufferings at the hands of a stern and autocratic father. So, while requiring the strictest obedience of children, he exhorts parents to temper their discipline with love and moderation, and even to enter joyfully into the wholesome pleasures of their boys and girls.

This brief discussion should make plain that the patriarchal family was still firmly established in Western Europe at the close of the sixteenth century. Not only children but wives were under strict family government, administered by the husband and father. Save by his advocacy of an education for girls to make them useful mothers, Luther did little or nothing to raise the status of women, within or without the family. Indeed, he declares that the "woman's will, as God says, shall be subject to the man, and he shall be her master; that is, the woman shall not live according to her free will . . . and must neither begin nor complete anything without the man; where he is there must she be, and bend before him as before her master, whom she shall fear, and to whom she shall be subject and obedient." [18] So long as these ideas persisted, the patriarchal family was bound to endure. It required a thorough-going revolution in both the economic and the political spheres to modify these ancient conceptions of the place of women and children within the family, and to grant to them certain inalienable rights *as individuals*.

TOPICS FOR REPORTS

1. Marriage and Married Life in Italy.
    R. de Maulde la Claviere, *The Women of the Renaissance*, Book I, Chs. I, II. George Allen & Co., Ltd., London, 1911.
2. Child Nurture and Education During the Renaissance.
    Ibid., Chs. III, IV.
3. Home Life and Child Care in Shakespeare's England.
    Shakespeare's England (Clarendon Press), Ch. XX. Oxford, 1916.
4. Household Economy in Renaissance Times.
    Wm. Boulting, *Woman in Italy*. Methuen & Co., London.
    W. Goodsell, *A History of the Family as a Social and Educational Institution*, pp. 271-8. The Macmillan Co., 1915.
5. The Protestant Theory of Marriage.
    G. E. Howard, *A History of Matrimonial Institutions*, Vol. I, Ch. IX. University of Chicago Press, 1904.

[18] Quoted in Wolfe, *Readings in Social Problems*, p. 475. Ginn & Co., New York, 1916.

next monday.

CHAPTER V

THE COLONIAL FAMILY IN AMERICA

THE EARLY SETTLERS

EARLY in the seventeenth century began that stream of emigration
from England to the New World which resulted in the founding of
thirteen struggling colonies on the seaboard of America. In New England,
family institutions had their source in the middle-class customs and traditions of the Puritans; while Southern family life on the plantations was
patterned largely upon that of the English manor house. In all the early
settlements, however, especially in the North, the pioneers endured cruel
hardships while establishing their new homes in a virgin wilderness.
The courage and endurance of the first settlers in Plymouth, Massachusetts Bay, New York and Pennsylvania are beyond praise. Nor were
these qualities confined to the men. Gently bred women worked shoulder
to shoulder with fathers and husbands in building and furnishing cabin
homes and securing a steady supply of food. We read, for example, of
one Elizabeth Hard who came to the shores of the Delaware with her
husband and promptly set to work with him to build a dwelling house.
"My good aunt," says Deborah Morris, in her narrative of her relative's experiences, "thought it expedient to help her husband at the end
of the saw, and to fetch all such water to make such kind of mortar as
they then had to build their chimney." Women, in the face of danger
from the Indians, learned to mould bullets and load muskets; and some,
at least, of these frontierswomen became excellent shots. Occasionally
single women came to the New World alone to open up tracts of land.
Among the first settlers of Taunton, Massachusetts, was an "antient
maid" of forty-eight named Elizabeth Poole; and the town of Haddon-
field, New Jersey, was named for a nineteen-year-old girl, Elizabeth
Haddon, who made the long journey overseas to settle a large tract of
land secured by her father.[1]

POSITION OF WOMEN IN THE COLONIES

When our Colonial forefathers emigrated from the mother country,
they brought with them not only a store of precious household goods,

[1] See J. A. Bruce, *Woman in the Making of America,* Ch. I.

73

but most of the traditional ideas about woman and woman's sphere that custom had made familiar in England. It is not surprising, then, to read that Colonial women were expected meekly to obey their husbands, to occupy themselves in household duties, to bear and rear enormous families, and not to hanker after intellectual education. In Governor Winthrop's *Journal* he states his belief that the wife of the Governor of Hartford colony had lost her mind "by occasion of giving herself wholly to reading and writing." Had she not "gone out of her way and calling to meddle in such things as are proper for men, whose minds are stronger, etc., she had kept her wits, and might have improved them usefully and honorably in the place God had set her." [2] No wonder that Anne Bradstreet, who, in the intervals of bringing up eight children and faithfully performing her domestic tasks, essayed to write verse, declares in one of these poetic ventures:

> "I am obnoxious to each carping tongue,
> Who says my hand a needle better fits,
> A poet's pen all scorn I should thus wrong,
> For such despite they cast on female wits . . ." [3]

The seventeenth-century English conception of the ideal woman was pretty faithfully reproduced in the New World. Witness this description by a Colonial writer of one Mrs. R—. She had, he says, "a round and pretty face, with gentle manners; kept her house well, her only pride to be neat and orderly. . . . The hyacinth follows not the sun more willingly than she her husband's pleasure." As in England, so in the colonies, a woman of means surrendered at marriage all her property, both real and personal, into the management of her husband, who enjoyed the income thereof. If she bore her lord a living child he was further entitled to the life use of his wife's real estate after her death. This age-old privilege of English husbands was called "curtesy," and the custom still persists in some of the states of the Union. Furthermore, the husband had the *absolute ownership* of all his wife's personal belongings, including clothing, jewels, household furnishings brought at marriage, and money. Only if the husband had not disposed of them during his lifetime could his widow reclaim her paraphernalia, *i.e.*, clothing and ornaments. If a married woman in Colonial days earned any money by her labor outside the home, she must turn every penny of it over to

[2] Entry under date of 1645.
[3] Quoted in A. W. Calhoun, *A Social History of the American Family from Colonial Times to the Present*, Vol. I, p. 85. Published by the Arthur H. Clark Co., Cleveland.

her husband, who was its rightful owner. Since she was not recognized in law as having any legal existence apart from her husband, who was her representative in the courts, the Colonial woman could neither sue nor be sued, nor could she make a contract or draw up a will without her husband's consent. It was this condition with respect to married women's legal and property disabilities that led an eighteenth-century author to declare that "she who, having laid a husband in the grave, enjoys an independent fortune, is almost the only woman among us who can be called free." [4]

But there is a reverse side of this picture that should not be ignored. In all the colonies a man was held responsible for the support of his wife according to his means and station in life; and at his death, one-third of his real and personal estate must revert to his widow for her life use. More than this, a husband was "liable to answer all such actions at law as were attached against his wife at the time of their marriage, and also to pay all the debts she had contracted previous to that period. . . ." This matter of a husband's liability for his wife's antenuptial debts led to the crude custom of so-called "smock marriages," practiced by ignorant people who believed that if a woman came to her betrothed at marriage wearing only her smock he would be relieved of all responsibility for her debts.[5] In the New World, moreover, the husband's ancient privilege of wife-beating seems to have been frowned upon, at least in the New England colonies. A law of the Massachusetts Bay Colony provided that "no man shall strike his wife, nor any woman her husband, on penalty of such fine, not exceeding £10 for one offence, or such corporall punishment as the county court shall determine." Likewise the Body of Liberties of Plymouth declared that "everie marryed woeman shall be free from bodily correction or stripes by her husband, unless it be in his own defence upon her assault."

CHILDREN IN THE COLONIES

Large families were the rule in all the colonies, since children, when well grown, could be of the utmost use in opening up waste land to cultivation and in resisting the attacks of Indian tribes, who resented the ever-widening encroachment of the white men on their lands. Women were expected to be fruitful, even to death, and were indeed, as Calhoun

[4] See W. Alexander, *The History of Women*, Vol. II, pp. 505-13. London, 1782.
[5] See Goodsell, *A History of the Family as a Social and Educational Institution*, p. 347.

declares, "the vicarious sacrifice to the peopling of a continent." Sir William Phipps was one of twenty-six children, and Benjamin Franklin could boast of sixteen brothers and sisters. There is something pathetic in the thought of the little ones, born in the early years of the settlements into frontier life, whose hardships even their parents found hard to endure.

As in England, so in the colonies, children were expected to be seen and not heard, and to submit humbly to parental authority. The view of John Robinson, the Pilgrim preacher, that "there is in all children (though not alike) a stubbernes and stoutnes of mind arising from naturall pride which must in the first place be broken and beaten down. . ." was very generally shared by Colonial parents and the birch rod was much in evidence in the home. Parental authority was firmly upheld in all the colonies, but especially in New England. The harsh law of *Deuteronomy* decreeing death to the stubborn or gluttonous son was reproduced in Connecticut in the ordinance empowering parents to bring "a stubborn and rebellious son of sufficient years and understanding . . . to the magistrates assembled in court, and testify unto them that their son is stubborn and rebellious. . . ." Thereupon "such a son shall be put to death." Thus the patriarchal ideas of Hebrew times lived on under the altered conditions of the New World family. However, it is reassuring to learn that no record exists of the actual enforcement of this law. With so much evidence at hand to show that children were required to walk the strait and narrow path of humble obedience under fear of instant punishment, it is pleasant to read that Cotton Mather preferred to rule his children by begetting in them "a high opinion of their father's love to them, and of his being best able to judge what shall be good for them. . . . I would never come to give a child a blow; except in case of obstinacy or some gross enormity." [6]

MARRIAGE AND COURTSHIP IN THE COLONIES

The institution of marriage was highly regarded in all the colonies, not only as a relationship blessed by God but as a means of peopling the vast expanse of the wilderness. It was natural enough that the handful of early pioneers, who were striving to transform forests into farmlands, to build permanent homes and establish settlements strong enough to beat off attacks by Indians, should regard it as a social obligation that every youth and maid should marry and rear a family. Everywhere

---

[6] *A Family Well-Ordered; or an Essay to Render Parents and Children Happy in One Another.* Quoted in Calhoun, *op. cit.*, Vol. I, p. 113.

celibacy met with social disapproval. Indeed, Colonial laws bore hard upon the bachelor. In some of the New England colonies, as in Connecticut, "the selfish luxury of solitary living" was taxed twenty shillings a week; and a Massachusetts act of 1630 prohibited the employment of any person for less than a year unless he were a "settled housekeeper." Also in Pennsylvania, as late as 1766, it was not uncommon to impose double taxes upon bachelors.[7] But the disadvantages of celibacy did not stop here. Very generally the New England colonies followed the example of Plymouth, which enacted that "henceforth noe single person be suffered to live by himselfe or in any family but such as the selectmen of the Towne shall approve of. . . ." A New Haven colony law of similar tenor provided that "the governor" of any family publicly licensed to receive single persons of either sex, should "duly observe the course, carriage and behaviour, of every such person, whether he or she walk diligently in a constant lawful employment, attending both family duties, and the public worship of God, and keeping good order day and night, or otherwise." [8] Clearly, our sober Colonial forefathers by no means intended that any man or "antient maid" who shirked the social duty of marriage should taste the joys of a free and independent life.

Despite the fact that family government was firmly established in the colonies, young people seem to have been allowed some freedom in the choice of a mate. In the delightful *Diary* of Judge Sewall we read that his daughter Betty refused several suitors, although her father once urged her to consider well before she dismissed a certain admirer of whom he approved. In New England, moreover, if parents unreasonably opposed a marriage, appeal could be made to the magistrate. Young people of opposite sexes were given more opportunity to mingle and to know each other in the new land than was the case in England. Even in Puritan New England we read that Boston early boasted "a small but pleasant common, where the gallants, a little before sunset, walk with their Marmalet-Madams till the nine o'clock bell rings them home to their respective habitations." And in South Carolina "at the end of the seventeenth century young girls received beaus at three o'clock expecting them to leave about six as many families retired at seven in winter and seldom sat up in summer beyond eight." [9]

In all the colonies, courtship was not expected to drag on too long and marriages at an early age were common. Madame Knight, in the

---

[7] Howard, *A History of Matrimonial Institutions*, Vol. II, p. 170.
[8] Trumbull, *True Blue Laws*, p. 258.
[9] Calhoun, *op. cit.*, Vol. I, p. 257.

racy account of her journey from Boston to New York in 1704, says of the young people of Connecticut: "They generally marry very young, the males oftener as I am told under twenty years than above." Early marriage was equally common in the Middle and Southern colonies. A North Carolina physician, writing about 1731 of the custom in his colony, says: "They marry generally very young, some at thirteen or fourteen, and she that continues unmarried until twenty, is reckoned a stale maid, which is a very indifferent character in this country." [10]

A sharp difference existed between New England and the Southern colonies with respect to their conception of marriage. In Puritan Massachusetts, marriage was held to be a civil contract, as it was in Calvinist Holland and in England during Cromwell's régime. But in the South the planters held rigidly to the conception of the Anglican church that marriage was a religious union in the nature of a sacrament. Owing to its firm belief that matrimony was a civil and temporal affair, the Massachusetts Bay colony insisted that the nuptial ceremony should be performed by a civil magistrate. Apparently the minister was not at first permitted even to preach a sermon on the happy occasion, for Governor Winthrop relates that one pastor who had been invited so to preach was forbidden by the magistrates on the ground that they "were not willing to bring in the English custom of ministers performing the solemnity of marriage which sermons at such times might induce." [11] However, Massachusetts abandoned this attitude in 1692, when fear of ecclesiastical control from England had died out. In the South, on the contrary, all marriages were celebrated by the clergy, save for a few exceptions in the Carolinas, until the period of the Revolution. The Middle colonies seem to have vacillated in this regard, although they inclined rather more toward a religious than a civil celebration. However, East and West Jersey permitted marriages by "an approved minister or justice of the peace" up to the time when they were united with New York, late in the seventeenth century; and the "Duke's Laws" for New York, issued in 1664, provided that a justice of the peace might lawfully "join the parties in marriage."

If the colonies differed as to the nature of the marriage contract they were unanimous in requiring that the marriage be duly published and registered. Publicity might be secured in three ways: (1) by reading the banns of marriage three times in some public place, preferably the church or meetinghouse on Sundays; (2) by securing a license from

[10] Vol. I, p. 245.
[11] Winthrop's *Journal*, Vol. II, p. 330. New York, 1908.

the Governor or the county court (in the South) ; (3) by posting a notice of intention to marry in some public place, as the courthouse or meeting-house door. Banns or licenses seem to have been more popular in the Southern and Middle colonies, whereas posting of a notice was very common in Pennsylvania and New England. The New Haven colony required that this notice must remain in public view for "the space of fourteen daies" and the other colonies took similar action. Publication of banns was also a general practice in New England. Needless to say, such careful provisions for publicity stand in striking contrast to the present practice in most of these United States, where a young and thoughtless couple can secure a license and enter into the bonds of matrimony on one and the same day, leaving their friends and relatives none the wiser.

The colonies further safeguarded marriage by requiring that the consent of the parents to the union be clearly expressed and that the marriage be duly recorded. Occasionally, in New England, a statement of parental consent to the future marriage was included in the banns. Registration of marriages was entrusted in New England to the town clerk, who was allowed a small fee for every person registered. Particularly stringent laws with respect to registration of marriages were enacted in Rhode Island, where a fine of five pounds was laid upon the bridegroom who failed to publish and register his marriage, as well as upon each of the offending accessories. In the South, the marriage register was kept by the clerk of the parish church and such was the custom in the Middle colonies.

COLONIAL DIVORCE LAWS

In the Southern and Middle colonies, where the Church of England was firmly established, divorce was practically nonexistent in Colonial times. The Anglican church refused to grant divorces *a vinculo* for any cause whatever, and permitted separation from bed and board only for three serious causes, namely, adultery, desertion and cruelty. Therefore no divorces were granted in the Southern colonies during the entire period that they remained under English rule; and in only a few isolated cases were divorces granted in New York and Pennsylvania, by the Governor and the colonial legislature respectively. But if the doctrine of the Anglican church respecting divorce was universally accepted in these colonies, not so was the practice of establishing ecclesiastical courts to adjudicate in questions of marriage and separation. Apparently both the Southern and Middle colonies were dubious concerning the value of these bishops' courts and fearful that they might gain an undue influence in the new country as in England. Therefore such courts were never established, even in Cavalier Virginia.

When we turn to New England we meet with a strikingly different situation. In these colonies, as we have seen, the Catholic theory of marriage as a sacrament was positively rejected in favor of the doctrine of marriage as a civil contract. Holding this view, the New England colonies generally did not hesitate to grant absolute divorce for such serious causes as adultery, desertion, cruelty and refusal to provide. In the Massachusetts Bay colony the authority to grant divorces was conferred first upon the Court of Assistants; but in 1692, by the *Acts and Resolves* it was transferred to the Governor and Council. In his valuable discussion of divorce in the New England colonies, Howard [12] gives statistics to show that between 1639 and 1692 forty cases of divorce or annulment were brought before the Court of Assistants, in twenty-eight of which women were the plaintiffs. During the period 1739-60 only three decrees of absolute divorce were issued, together with two decrees of separation. In the third period (1760-86), ninety-six petitions were presented to the Governor and Council and seventy-six absolute divorces were granted. Thirty-seven of these were given to the husband on the ground of adultery on the part of the wife. It is interesting to note that the Puritans were not yet ready to accept the principle that adultery is equally culpable in the man and in the woman. A husband could always obtain a divorce from his wife on the proven charge of infidelity, whereas a wife could secure a dissolution decree only if her husband's unfaithfulness were accompanied by desertion, cruelty or refusal to provide. During the later colonial period the practice of granting separations from bed and board, without the right of remarriage, became more common.

The colony of Connecticut was unique in that the authority to grant divorces was lodged chiefly in the courts of law, although legislative divorce was also permitted here as in Rhode Island. Connecticut was further unique in treating husband and wife with even justice in all matters concerning divorce. With respect to the advanced practices in this colony, Howard says: "In short, Connecticut, in all the more essential respects, anticipated the present policy of civilized nations by nearly two hundred years." [13]

[12] Howard, *op. cit.*, Vol. II, pp. 330-66.
[13] *Ibid.*, pp. 353-4.

HOME LIFE AND EDUCATION IN THE COLONIES

After the first generations of settlers had overcome the most serious difficulties in providing food, clothing and shelter for themselves and their families, the generations that followed found life a less strenuous and anxious affair. The well-to-do Southern families of the eighteenth century began to build those attractive plantation homes that always evoke memories of gracious and lavish hospitality. In the Middle colonies, too, the Dutch, and later the English, built substantial and sometimes beautiful homes; while in New England the charming colonial houses still standing in Concord, Salem, Litchfield and other towns bear witness to the quiet good taste of their builders, as well as to their regard for solidity. No doubt it would try the soul of a modern woman to carry on the affairs of the household with such meagre appliances as the colonial housewife made shift with. Clocks and even chairs were rare in the seventeenth century, and, until tallow became plentiful, women were forced to make candles from bayberries. Not until the early eighteenth century did forks come into general use and, since china was unknown, dishes were made of earthenware and even of wood. But if the colonists had few forks they had spoons in plenty, made of wood, of pewter and sometimes of silver. Mrs. Earle tells us that worn-out "pewter plates and dishes could be recast into new pewter spoons." Tankards were likewise made of wood, pewter and silver; and great jugs, called "black jacks," made of heavy black leather, waxed, bound and tipped with silver, were used to hold the ale and beer that our forefathers poured into these tankards for their refreshment.

Children were strictly brought up in colonial homes and their behavior was regulated by stringent rules that were sometimes printed in small books. One such book was called *A Pretty Little Pocket Book* and was published just before the Revolution. In this small manual of behavior children were enjoined never to sit down at the table until the blessing had been asked; never to speak unless spoken to, not even to ask for food; never to take salt except with a clean knife; and, above all, never to throw bones under the table! Religious training was held in high regard in colonial homes. Family prayers were offered up daily in all well-managed households and the Bible was placed in children's hands as soon as they could read. Servants were members of the family in those days and were present not only at family worship but were taught the catechism and questioned on the Sunday sermon no less than the children. But, with all this concern for the salvation of their souls, the old Adam peeped out in children and servants then as now. In 1657 a Puritan divine wrote to a brother minister:

"Do your children and family grow more godly? Much ado I have with my own family; hard to get a servant that is glad of catechizing or family duties. . . . Even the children of the godly here, and elsewhere make a woful proof." [14]

Very early, children were trained to be of use to their parents; and this practical home education of boys and girls stood by them all their lives when they were called upon to be skilful in a score of ways. In the farm and garden, children weeded flax and even helped with the spring sowing. Girls were taught when quite young to help their mothers hetchel flax, comb wool, skein yarn, wind the warp on spools and even spin. Mites of six could spin flax on the big spinning wheel, even though "they had to stand on a foot-stool to reach up." Boys also had few spare moments for play out of school hours. A round of chores awaited them both before they went and as soon as they reached home. It was their part of the family tasks to bring in fuel, water the horses, cut potatoes for the sheep, milk the cows, feed the swine, pick the vegetables and, in odd moments, weave tape and suspenders and spool yarn.[15] Life was strenuous, then as now, but in a different way; and although children received a very valuable education in coöperation and responsibility for maintaining the family comfort, there is no doubt that they lacked time for much-needed free play and were often overworked. In the eyes of the Puritan and the Quaker, idleness was the greatest of sins. We read in Bradford's *History of Plymouth Plantation* (ed. 1908) that parents, found that "necessitie was a taskmaster over them so they were forced to be such, not only to their servants, but in a sorte, to their dearest children; the which as it did not a litle wound the tender harts of many a loving father and mother, so it produced likwise sundrie sad and sorowful effects. For many of their children, that were of best dispositions and gracious inclinations haveing lernde to bear the yoake in their youth, and willing to bear parte of their parents burden, were, often times, so oppressed with their hevie labours, that though their minds were free and willing, yet their bodies bowed under the weight of the same and became decreped in their early youth; the vigor of nature being consumed in the very budd as it were."

If children were kept busy, even more so were their parents, who

[14] Alice M. Earle, *Child Life in Colonial Times*, p. 235. The Macmillan Co., New York, 1899.
[15] See Earle, *ibid.*, pp. 305-13.

were striving, against serious obstacles, to maintain a home in a new and undeveloped country, where most family needs must be met by their own effort and skill. The father labored all day at heavy tasks of lumbering, farming, building and manufacture of many of his tools and implements. As for the mother, the description given by Thomas Nelson Page of the duties of a Southern plantation lady, although written of a later period, pictures very vividly the housewife's multifarious labors, if we add those of spinning, weaving and making candles:

"She was the necessary and inevitable functionary, the keystone of the domestic economy, which bound all the rest of the structure and gave it strength and beauty. From early morn to morn again the most important and delicate concerns of the plantation were her charge and care. . . . From superintending the setting of the turkeys to fighting a pestilence, there was nothing that was not her work. She was mistress, manager, doctor, nurse, counsellor, seamstress, teacher, housekeeper, slave, all at once. She was at the beck and call of everyone, especially of her husband, to whom she was 'guide, philosopher and friend.' " [16]

This brief discussion may serve to show how firmly colonial ideas respecting marriage and family life were rooted in English law and custom. Nevertheless certain practices such as the legal protection of the wife from corporal chastisement at the hands of her husband, the freer association of girls and youths before marriage, the right of veto accorded young people with regard to the mates chosen for them by their parents, the custom of civil divorce in New England, all these are prophecies of a more equal association of the sexes and a freer family life in the United States than was known in England for centuries.

TOPICS FOR REPORTS

1. Home Life in the Dutch Colony of New Netherland.
   Washington Irving, *Knickerbocker History of New York,* Book III, Chs. III, IV, VII.
2. Courtship, Marriage and Family Life in the Southern Colonies.
   A. W. Calhoun, *A Social History of the American Family from Colonial Times to the Present,* Vol. I, Chs. XII-XV. Arthur H. Clark Co., Cleveland, 1917.
3. The Position of Women in New England and in the South.
   Calhoun, *op. cit.,* Vol. I, Chs. V, XVI.
4. Divorce in the Colonies.
   G. E. Howard, *A History of Matrimonial Institutions,* Vol. II, Ch. XV.

[16] *Social Life in Old Virginia,* pp. 37-8. Charles Scribner's Sons, New York, 1912. By permission.

CHAPTER VI

EVOLUTION OF THE MODERN FAMILY IN ENGLAND AND AMERICA

A REVIEW of family history up to the close of the eighteenth century reveals the patriarchal plan of family organization still firmly established. The family had one ruling head—the father—and the position, not only of children but of wives, was one of subordination to his will. At the present time, when certain well-intentioned persons show a disposition to bewail the departure of the good old times when family life revealed a unity and a solidarity that it no longer possesses, it is well to remember that these characteristics were secured at the expense of the free development of women and children, who lived under a rule of obedience to the family head which, while not invariably harsh and repressive, tended to become both in the hands of undisciplined men with a taste for power. Writing in 1776 to a husband of uncommonly liberal spirit, Abigail Adams urges him to make a new code of laws for Massachusetts which shall grant larger freedom to wives:

"Do not," she writes, "put such unlimited power into the hands of husbands. Remember, all men would be tyrants if they could. . . . That your sex are naturally tyrannical is a truth so thoroughly established as to admit of no dispute; but such of you as wish to be happy willingly give up the harsh title of master for the more tender and endearing one of friend. Why, then, not put it out of the power of the vicious and lawless to use us with cruelty and indignity with impunity? Men of sense in all ages abhor those customs which treat us only as the vassals of your sex. . ." [1]

Even at the time that this appeal was penned, however, the patriarchal family was beginning to be undermined by economic and social movements—movements that were to gain tremendous headway as the decades advanced and to bring about the overthrow of this antiquated system.

---

[1] *Familiar Letters of John Adams and His Wife Abigail Adams During the Revolution.* Edited by Charles Francis Adams, 1875. Houghton Mifflin Co.

The Industrial Revolution.

No doubt the paramount factor at work in the transformation of the patriarchal family into the individualized family group of the twentieth century was the economic one. In England first began the effort to improve the instruments of production which was to eventuate in revolutionizing industry. It is a striking fact that, until the second half of the eighteenth century, our forbears in Europe were using much the same plough, spindle and loom that had been employed for two thousand years and more. Not only was industry based upon handwork, but the implements in use had not materially changed since ancient times. Most of the labor required to secure the necessities of life was carried on in the household by the head of the family, assisted by his wife and children and a few apprentices. In the eighteenth century the textile industry, centered in the counties of Yorkshire, Somersetshire, Gloucestershire, Wiltshire and Dorsetshire, was carried on under the cottage system. Daniel DeFoe vividly describes this type of manufacturing, which he had observed in the course of his travels through these counties about 1745. He refers to the houses "full of lusty Fellows, some at the Dyevat, some at the Loom, others dressing the Clothes; the Women and Children carding or spinning; all employed from the youngest to the oldest; scarce anything above *four years old,* but its Hands were sufficient for its own Support." [2]

By the middle of the eighteenth century the demand for British cotton and woolen cloth and iron goods had outgrown the supply and it became imperative to find some means of increasing production. The process of spinning yarn was especially slow, eight or ten spinners being required to keep one weaver employed. Since necessity is the mother of invention, the need was met by the invention of the spinning jenny, an implement that could spin eight threads at a time. This contrivance was invented by Hargreaves in 1764. Later improvements were made by Arkwright, who invented the spinning wheel driven by water power. In 1779 Crompton invented the spinning mule, a machine which combined the best points of the other two contrivances and had the great advantage of spinning a thread fine enough to weave into a thin muslin. By means of these inventions the supply of cotton, woolen and linen yarn exceeded the ca-

[2] *A Tour Thro' the Whole Island of Great Britain,* Vol. III, pp. 137-9 (4th ed., 1748). Italics mine.

pacity of the workers to weave it into cloth. The great need of the hour was a loom operated by physical power—not man-power. This need was partially met by the invention of the power loom by a clergyman named Edward Cartwright. No doubt this machine would seem a crude affair in modern eyes, since it was operated by an ox walking round and round in a ring. Experiments with water power proved this source of energy to be not altogether reliable, and experiments began to be made with steam as a motive power. These resulted in 1785 in the invention of the steam engine by James Watt, a Scotch engineer. Within a few years steam engines were being used, not only in mines, but to work the looms in the new spinning, weaving and knitting factories that sprang up like mushroom growths in many shires of England.

With the introduction of factories equipped with power machinery, the domestic system of industry was doomed. Handicraftsmen with their families flocked to the rapidly growing towns and manned the new machines in the factories. Then began that urbanization of England which has continued to the present time. Tickner states that in 1685 only twenty percent of the people of England lived in cities; whereas in 1922 seventy-nine percent of the population was urban.[3] Following hard upon the influx of the hand-workers to the factory towns went the creation of a housing problem. Flimsy shacks were built for the thousands of workers, into which they crowded with their families, and the era of industrial slums was begun. The gardens or little farms that had occupied the craftsmen in their spare time in the country were known to them no more.

Out of these changed conditions in industry came a transformation of the lives of women and children. The early spinning machines were so simple and light that a young boy or girl could tend them. Likewise weaving machines could be operated as well by women as by men. Now, since women and children would work for much smaller wages than men, they were employed in ever-growing numbers in the factories. This threw men out of employment and caused not only a shortage of money with which to maintain families, but a marked deterioration in the character of family life among the laboring class. A mother who had been working twelve or fourteen hours in a factory had neither time nor strength for domestic tasks when she reached home at night. Deprived of the care of the mother and often of both parents, children grew up with almost no nurture or guidance; or else they accompanied their parents to the factories to be cruelly exploited there to the limit of their strength.

[3] F. W. Tickner, *Women in English Economic Life,* p. 116 (1923).

The brutality, the stupid inhumaneness of the eighteenth and early nineteenth centuries reached its peak in industry, where heartrending cruelties were practised on little children, especially paupers, to extract from them the maximum labor of which they were capable during a day that ranged from thirteen to eighteen hours. Men and women received little better treatment. Homes became places in which exhausted workers snatched a few hours of sleep before returning to labor; and meals were feverishly snatched in the brief moments of respite allowed for this purpose. It appeared as if England had produced a monster that was destroying its laboring class, once so sturdy and self-reliant.

Fortunately, State interference to improve the conditions of the workers began with the Act of 1802 which restricted the labor of pauper children to *twelve hours a day* and forced their employers to provide better workshops and sleeping places for them. From this time on public-spirited men in England strove unceasingly to write laws upon the statute books that would better the conditions of factory laborers. Acts were passed by Parliament in 1819 and in 1833 which limited the hours of labor for children; and by 1850 "no woman or child could work except between 6 A. M. and 6 P. M. in summer and 7 A. M. and 7 P. M. in winter, with no Saturday work after 2 P. M." [4]

It should not be inferred from the gloomy account above that the Industrial Revolution worked only evil to family life and to women and children. Nothing could be farther from the truth. Although this economic change wrought much hardship, especially in its first century, it has proved the most potent of all social forces in freeing married women from those feudal disabilities with respect to ownership of property and recognition before the law that had persisted into modern times. After women had abundantly demonstrated that they could earn their own livelihood outside the home and partly, at least, support their families, liberal minded men began to question the justice of depriving a woman of her wages in order to turn them over to her husband, who might be a thriftless parasite. This raised the question of whether it was fundamentally just to require that a woman at marriage should surrender all her real property into the management of her husband and all her personal belongings to his absolute ownership. After the middle of the nineteenth century, organized agitation was carried on by both men and women to secure the removal by Parliamentary action of these medieval injustices. It has frequently been remarked that "he who holds the purse wields the power"; and when women had proved their ability to achieve financial independence,

[4] Tickner, *op. cit.*, pp. 149-50.

no longer looking to father or husband for their support, one by one the old restrictive laws were altered or removed from the statute books.

To the enormous influence of the new economic movement in freeing married women must be added the effect of the novel theories disseminated during the French and American Revolutions—theories which declared the fundamental rights of man to "life, liberty and the pursuit of happiness." To be sure, the doctrine that a democracy exists to promote and secure equality of opportunity for everyone was not at first applied to women. Yet it seems highly probable that, as conditions changed, the applicability of this theory to the feminine half of humanity began to be perceived by fair-minded men.

One of the most important outcomes of the Industrial Revolution was increased leisure for women of the prosperous classes. Little by little these women saw the removal of one occupation after another from the home to the factory. Oil lamps, and later gas and electricity, took the place of candles; cotton, linen and wool were spun in the factories; and the power loom wove these threads into cloth with a rapidity that sounded the knell of hand industry. So the spindle and the loom were put into a corner, later to be transferred to the attic, and the busy housewife found herself with unemployed time on her hands. Leisure for women, together with the new points of view created by the political revolutions of the waning eighteenth century, brought about a more thorough and liberal education of middle-class women than the world had ever before seen. New schools sprang up in England and America that gave to girls a solid education such as the boarding and "finishing" schools of the eighteenth century had never contemplated. Even more revolutionary was the founding of women's colleges, first in America, a little later in England. Clearly women were not only to be made free, but intelligent in the use of their freedom.

NEW DOMESTIC LEGISLATION IN ENGLAND

Married Women's Property Acts.

Until after the middle of the nineteenth century no steps were taken in England to extend the property rights of married women. In 1857 an act was passed providing that a wife deserted by her husband might apply to a magistrate for a protection order which would safeguard from her husband's seizure any property or wages she had scraped together *after her desertion.* In 1861 another act was passed exempting a wife whose husband had been convicted of a serious assault upon her person from cohabiting with him. This early legislation, of course, benefited only deserted or abused wives. However, public opinion in England was being slowly educated to the acceptance of more liberal laws respecting married women's property. In 1870 came the first long step forward in the passage of the Married Women's Property Act which granted to wives (1) the sole and absolute ownership of their earnings and savings bank deposits; (2) the rents and profits of their real estate, which, however, must continue to be administered by the husband; (3) the ownership of any personal property not in excess of £200; (4) the right to insure their own or their husband's lives for their separate use.[5] Manifestly this act was a compromise which satisfied neither the conservatives nor those liberals who were urging the complete emancipation of married women's property from the old feudal disabilities. The final step was taken in 1882 when Parliament enacted a law granting to wives entire control over their property. The provisions of this famous act may be briefly summarized as follows: (1) The married woman was granted the absolute ownership of all property belonging to her at marriage or acquired by her thereafter, including earnings and property secured by her own labor or skill; (2) she was given the right, as an independent person before the law, to sue and be sued, to contract and to take legal action in her own name and without her husband's consent with respect to all property belonging to her *before marriage;* (3) the husband was released from liability for his wife's antenuptial debts and for the payments of fines incurred by her for torts; (4) the wife with property of her own was made liable to support her husband (if he were a pauper), as well as her children and grandchildren, out of her separate estate.[6] Thus at a blow the law struck from married women the shackles that had cramped their lives since the twelfth century.

Guardianship of Children.

In the matter of the guardianship of children, Parliament took more conservative action. Up to 1886 the English law recognized the father as sole guardian of his children, denying to the mother who bore and nurtured them any right to determine important questions such as the character of their education, their religious instruction, their medical care, and the like. A husband who was on unfriendly terms with his wife might even take her children from her into his sole custody or place them in charge of a guardian appointed by him. Moreover, he alone had the right to appoint a guardian for his children at his death. The Guardianship

---

[5] *Chitty's Statutes,* VIII, pp. 709-12.
[6] *Ibid.,* p. 713 *et seq.*

of Infants Act (1886), while still granting to the father sole rights of guardianship during his lifetime, conceded to the mother equal rights in the custody and care of her children with any guardian whom the father might appoint at his death. If the father were incapacitated the mother might appoint a guardian to act with her.[7] The inequity of this statute is obvious enough. Its gross discrimination against mothers is based not alone on custom but on economic considerations. Very possibly the discrimination may not be removed until married women are more commonly financial contributors to the family support. The fact that a man is liable in the first instance for the support of his children is held by English law to justify his privilege as sole guardian during his lifetime. That the services of the mother as home-maker, nurse and teacher have *real monetary value* and could not be replaced without a heavy drain upon the husband's purse is a fact not yet admitted by the vast majority of England's lawmakers.

Divorce.

In the matter of divorce England was likewise tardy in revising her medieval law and custom. Under the powerful influence of the Anglican church, which inherited all the prejudices of its Roman Catholic predecessor against divorce, no attempt was made to revise the divorce code until 1857. In that year the Matrimonial Causes Act was passed by Parliament. By the terms of this law, which was bitterly opposed by the clerical party, the Church lost all its ancient rights of jurisdiction in cases of marriage and divorce. These rights were removed from the spiritual courts and vested in a newly established civil "Court for Divorce and Matrimonial Causes." Although this step marked a real advance, it did nothing to rectify an ancient wrong; for the old inequality in the rights of husband and wife with respect to the causes of divorce was perpetuated in the new statute. The husband might secure a divorce if he could prove the infidelity of his wife. Furthermore, he might include in his petition for divorce a claim for damages against his wife's lover, the money to be "applied by the court for the benefit of the children of the marriage or for the maintenance of the wife." On the other hand, the wife who sued for divorce must prove not only the infidelity of her husband but in addition the fact of cruelty or desertion for two years or more. Furthermore no right to sue for damages was conceded to the wife. So inequitable a law did not fail to arouse protests from a small group of fair-minded Englishmen, of whom Gladstone was one. But it is an astonishing fact

[7] Cleveland, *Women under the English Law*, pp. 295-6.

that it was permitted to remain upon the statute books until 1923. In the summer of that year the law was amended so that the causes for divorce were equalized in the case of husband and wife. However, England has up to now refused to enact legislation increasing the causes for divorce. A Royal Commission on Divorce, appointed by Edward VII, made a majority report in favor of increasing the causes of divorce to include cruelty, desertion, insanity (pronounced incurable after a period of years), habitual drunkenness, or life imprisonment under a commuted death sentence. But this recommendation, humane as it may seem to many, was in advance of public opinion and was not acted upon. The hold of the Anglican church upon the minds of Englishmen is still too strong for them to regard this question dispassionately. However, the time is probably not far distant when they will see that divorce is purely a social problem, which can be justly solved not by application of ecclesiastical dogmas but by the principle of securing to men and women the largest possible amount of happiness and well-being consistent with the general good. It is surely a debatable question whether the refusal to release from the bonds of matrimony men and women who are chafing against an intolerable yoke does not breed more evil in the social body, in the form of secret intrigues and miserable homes, than is caused by the liberal divorce laws of America.

REVISION OF DOMESTIC RELATIONS LAWS IN AMERICA

Beginning earlier than in England, the movement to revise the domestic code in the United States has, nevertheless, labored under a serious handicap. Whereas in Great Britain a single act of Parliament sufficed to emancipate all the married women of the nation from property disabilities, in this country progressive legislation has been forced to wait upon the slow enlightenment of public opinion in forty-eight states which are autonomous commonwealths. It is hardly necessary to add that the rate of progress in the various states differs markedly, some northern, eastern and western states being far in advance of most of the commonwealths of the South.

Removal of the Property Disabilities of Married Women.

The first step toward freeing wives from the restrictions laid upon them by medieval law was in the direction of granting them the right to make wills disposing of such property at their death as their husbands might not legally claim. Prior to the Civil War at least seven states had taken such action, namely Connecticut (1809), Ohio (1835), Alabama

(1843), Pennsylvania and New York (1848), Virginia (1849) and Michigan (1850). But the states were disposed to move very slowly in the matter of granting to married women the right to own and manage their property by gift or bequest. The State of Maine, the first to accord this right to wives (in 1844), was followed by Florida in 1845, Pennsylvania and New York in 1848 and Michigan and Massachusetts in 1855.

During the conflict between North and South, progressive legislation was thrust into the background. After 1865, however, one state after another set about the reform of its domestic relations code with respect to married women's property. Curiously enough, states that were willing to give wives the full ownership of real and personal property were reluctant to grant them command of their wages. For example, in the states of North Carolina, Texas and Tennessee, married women were denied the full ownership of their wages until well into the twentieth century; and the statutes of Georgia and Washington even now (1924) declare a wife's wages to be the property of her husband unless she is living separately from him! Florida stands alone in requiring a married woman to file a petition in the Circuit Court praying for the right to control her own estate. This is referred to the Master in Chancery and if he responds favorably to the appeal the judge of the Circuit Court may grant her petition. In that large section of the far West and Southwest that once constituted the Louisiana Purchase, and in the territory acquired from Mexico after the war in 1848, a further impediment to the full ownership and control of property and earnings by married women lies in the fact that this vast domain was never governed by English common law, but by French and Spanish codes. Therefore in the states carved out from this territory the custom of "community property" exists. This means that although a married woman may own and control as freely as a *femme sole* all real and personal property that belonged to her *before marriage,* any property accumulated by either husband or wife *after marriage,* by labor, gift, devise or bequest, belongs jointly to them both, *but is administered and controlled by the husband.* At the death of either husband or wife the surviving spouse may take one-half of the community property. Consequently in the states of Arizona, California, Idaho, Louisiana, Nevada, New Mexico, Texas and Washington, by the law governing community property, a husband may not only control all property acquired by his wife after their marriage but may even demand her wages, which he is empowered to use as he pleases.[8]

[8] The facts concerning the present situation are taken from *A Survey of the Legal Status of Women in the Forty-Eight States,* published by the National League of Women Voters, March, 1924.

Removal of Legal Disabilities.

One by one the states of the Union have largely revised those ancient laws that denied legal personality to a wife and thus precluded her from making contracts, bringing suit to defend her rights or acting as surety for any person. Yet in this field much remains to be done. In only sixteen states have married women an absolute right of contract without restrictions, although in the eight community property states they may contract without limitation except with regard to community property, where the right of contract resides in the husband only. In four of the above states, however, the husband may not convey community property without his wife's expressed consent. The states of Alabama, Indiana, Minnesota, New Jersey, North Carolina, Pennsylvania, Texas and West Virginia deny to a married woman the right to convey real estate unless her husband joins with her in the conveyance. In those states, moreover, where the custom of curtesy [9] still persists, a wife may not contract to alienate real estate in such a way as to affect adversely the husband's rights of curtesy. Finally, in eight states a married woman is forbidden by statute to act as surety for any person, and there is no doubt that she is tacitly denied that right in nine other states which have failed to enact statutes giving women the general right of contract. [10] In such cases the courts have ruled that the old English common law holds good.

Guardianship Laws.

The influence of English common law in denying to the mother any rights of guardianship of her children may be clearly seen in the codes of the forty-eight states of the American Union. Very slowly has the idea gained headway that the mother should be granted equal rights with the father in the settlement of all important matters affecting the welfare of children, such as health, education, work, and the like. Nevertheless, great strides have been made within the last ten years in equalizing the guardianship rights of parents. As recently as 1912, fifteen states in the South, thirteen in the North, and four in the West ignored the mother's rights and vested all power in the father as "the natural guardian of his children." Guardianship privileges were granted to the mother only after the father's death or desertion. [11] At the present time thirty-eight commonwealths have passed equal guardianship laws. Pennsylvania, how-

[9] The right to the life use of one-half or one-third of his wife's real estate. The amount varies in different states.

[10] See *A Survey of the Legal Status of Women in the Forty-Eight States*, p. 7.

[11] Wilson, *The Legal and Political Status of Women in the United States* (1912). See laws of different states.

ever, qualifies the mother's right by the provision that she shall contribute to the support of the child, thus revealing the economic basis of the law. Only the States of Alabama, Arkansas, Georgia, Maryland, North Carolina, Oklahoma, Oregon, Texas, Virginia and West Virginia still refuse to recognize the mother's rights of guardianship in the children she has borne. And only one of this group—Georgia—still retains the barbaric law that permits a father to will away the custody of his unborn child without the mother's consent! [12] It is noteworthy that, with the exception of two border states, these backward commonwealths are all in the South. This section of the country has always been more dominated by English tradition and custom than any other. Moreover, the pre-war life of Southern gentlemen on scattered plantations like English manorial estates has not proved conducive to progressive thinking upon social questions. In recent times signs are not lacking that new economic conditions and the spread of popular education are breaking down the deep-rooted conservatism of the South.

Certain inequities still remain even in the more advanced communities: (1) In those states of the Union where equal guardianship laws have been enacted, the wife has no voice in the choice of the family home. (2) The mother shares equally with the husband in the earnings of minor children only in fourteen states: California, Colorado, Florida, Idaho, Louisiana, Mississippi, Montana, Nebraska, Ohio, Oregon, Pennsylvania, South Dakota, Washington and West Virginia. The law seems doubtful on this point in Illinois, Indiana and New York. (3) No state permits a wife to collect for services performed in the home. She is entitled to support by the husband but the extent of this support is entirely in his hands. If the matter is taken into court the support provided by the judgment is quite often meager. Moreover, support by the husband has no relation to the wife's services in the home.[13]

Divorce Legislation.

After the Revolutionary War, the commonwealths of the new American Republic began to revise their laws concerning divorce. One by one the states in the Middle Atlantic and Southern groups followed the lead of New England in permitting divorce for certain specified causes. At first jurisdiction in matters of divorce was very generally lodged in the state assembly; but late in the eighteenth century the New England states began to enact statutes transferring authority in divorce cases from the

[12] *A Survey of the Legal Status of Women in the Forty-Eight States*, pp. 52-3.
[13] *Ibid.*, p. 43.

legislative bodies to the courts. Following the example of her sister states, Maine, which had been separated from Massachusetts and constituted a state in 1820, vested jurisdiction in divorce cases in the supreme judicial court. Of the Middle States, New York and New Jersey enacted statutes after the Revolution granting authority over divorce to the courts. In Pennsylvania and Delaware, however, legislative divorce lingered on side by side with judicial divorce, until the adoption of new state constitutions, by Pennsylvania in 1874 and Delaware in 1897, finally gave the deathblow to this dual practice.[14]

In the Southern states judicial divorce was established only tardily. After the colonies had achieved independence "it was more than half a century in Virginia and Maryland, and many years in North Carolina, before the courts were granted even partial jurisdiction in divorce causes."[15] Divorces, however, were granted during this period by the state assemblies. Except for a brief period, South Carolina has up to the present time consistently refused to grant divorce for any cause whatever.[16] Georgia divided authority in divorce causes between the superior court and the legislature until 1849 when the Assembly was deprived of all jurisdiction.

It is interesting to note that, during the territorial stage of their history, and in some instances for a subsequent period, many Western states lodged authority in divorce causes with the legislative assemblies, although the statute adopted for the Northwest Territory in 1795 vested jurisdiction in the general court and the circuit courts. One by one, as the states of the Middle and far Western groups emerged from the status of territories to full statehood, each commonwealth sooner or later enacted a statute empowering the supreme court, the circuit courts, or the court of common pleas to have sole jurisdiction in divorce causes.

The further history of divorce in America is concerned with (1) increasing the causes for absolute dissolution, (2) elaborating the conditions under which a divorce may be granted, (3) making suitable provisions for alimony and the custody of children and (4) enacting decrees with respect to remarriage of the parties to a divorce. The trend toward increasing the number of causes for divorce has been very general during the nineteenth century, with the exception of the two commonwealths of South Carolina and New York. As we have seen, the former state has had no divorce law upon the statute books since the repeal of the short-lived law

[14] See Howard, *A History of Matrimonial Institutions,* Vol. III, pp. 99-101.
[15] Howard, *op. cit.,* Vol. III, p. 31.
[16] For six years (1872-78) the courts were given power to grant absolute divorces for two causes, adultery and desertion. The law was repealed in 1878.

of 1872; and New York recognizes only the scriptural cause of adultery as ground for the dissolution of marriage. On the other hand, the state of Ohio wrote six causes into her statute of 1804 and increased the grounds for divorce to ten in 1853; and the state of New Hampshire, beginning in 1791 with four causes, increased the number to fourteen in 1854. It should be noted, however, as Howard has pointed out, that "not less than seven [of these causes] have to do with absence or desertion of one or the other of the persons under various conditions." [17]

With regard to matters of alimony, property arrangements, and the custody of children, the states have enacted legislation not differing greatly save in matters of detail. In all the New England states the court is empowered to issue orders for temporary alimony during the pendency of a suit for divorce, and for the custody, care and education of the children after the decree is granted. Permanent alimony may be granted to the wife and, in the States of Vermont, New Hampshire and Massachusetts, to the husband also. The statutes of the Southern and Western states make provisions similar to those of New England. With respect to the custody of children pending the divorce, however, the Louisiana statute of 1888 provided that, in cases where they were claimed by both husband and wife, the custody belongs to the husband, whether plaintiff or defendant, "unless there shall be strong reasons to deprive him of it." [18] In cases of absolute divorce Louisiana has followed the general practice of granting the custody of minor children to the party who shall have obtained the decree, unless the court decides that he or she is not a suitable guardian.

The legislation of the forty-eight states concerning remarriage after divorce shows greater variation. The general tendency has been to permit complete freedom to both parties to remarry, except for a stipulated period subsequent to granting the decree. In Massachusetts and Maine, the early laws forbade the remarriage of the offending party to a divorce until the death of the former partner. Not until 1853 was the guilty party in the case of a divorce for desertion permitted to remarry. In both these states at the present time the offending person in a divorce suit may not remarry until two years after the decree is granted. In New Hampshire, Vermont, Rhode Island and Connecticut, no restriction is placed at present upon the remarriage of either party after the decree is granted.

During the nineteenth century the Southern states showed a tendency to be severe in granting the right of remarriage to the offending party

[17] Howard, *op. cit.*, p. 13.
[18] *Ibid.*, p. 92.

ín a divorce. But at present most of the commonwealths of the South permit remarriage of the offending person with or without restrictions. In Virginia, power is lodged with the court to decide whether or not the party guilty of infidelity may remarry. North Carolina prohibits the guilty defendant in a case of wilful desertion from remarrying within five years. In the District of Columbia a statute of 1901 denies the offending partner any right of remarriage except with his former spouse.

In the states carved out during the nineteenth century from the great Middle and far Western domain, legislation concerning remarriage showed the same lack of agreement as in the East and South. Some states, as Michigan in its territorial law of 1819, forbade the guilty defendant in a divorce suit on the ground of adultery to remarry until his former spouse was deceased. But these laws were gradually softened until, at present in most Western states, remarriage of both parties to a divorce is permitted. However, it is quite general in the states west of the Mississippi River to require that an interval shall elapse between the granting of the divorce decree and remarriage. This period varies from six months in Kansas, Nebraska, Minnesota, Oregon and Washington to two years in the case of the innocent person and three years in the case of the guilty in the State of Montana.

SUMMARY

A survey of the family history of the nineteenth century shows a gradual transformation taking place in the economic and legal position of married women and in the general character of the home. The wife was released from coverture and given the control of her property and wages. She was granted recognition by the courts as a legal person, thus abolishing the age-old submergence of a wife's personality in that of her husband. Slowly but steadily the states of the American Union have revised their divorce legislation in the direction of greater liberality, with respect to both the causes of divorce and rights of remarriage. All this means that the head of the twentieth-century family has been shorn of much of his power and prestige. The patriarchal family of ancient times can no longer be found in its pure form save in Oriental lands, in the villages and small towns of the Slavic nations and possibly in parts of Italy and Spain. The death knell of this ancient family type has been clearly sounded in every progressive country—even in Turkey. But the form that the family will assume in the coming years no careful social writer will confidently prophesy.

TOPICS FOR REPORTS

1. Study the laws governing marriage, guardianship of children, married women's property rights and divorce in the most recent code of your own state.
2. Relaxation of Family Discipline During the Nineteenth Century.
   A. W. Calhoun, *A Social History of the American Family from Colonial Times to the Present,* Vol. II, Ch. III. Arthur H. Clark Co., Cleveland.
3. Influence of the Developing Factory System on the American Family.
   Ibid., Vol. II, Ch. IX.
4. Effects of the Civil War on the Family.
   Ibid., Vol. II, Ch. XIX.

PART TWO

SOCIAL CONDITIONS REACTING UPON THE FAMILY

CHAPTER VII

THE INSTABILITY OF THE FAMILY

A LTHOUGH one social institution after another—notably the church, government and law—has been compelled by profound social changes to revolutionize its theory and procedure, the family institution has remained relatively unchanged up to recent times. Within the last two generations, however, the social and economic forces silently at work for more than a century undermining the unity of the family have come to the surface and effected transformations in the home dramatic in their rapidity and extent. From being the institution most immune to social change, the family has become the one in which change is most revolutionary and far-reaching. In the preceding chapters a brief sketch was given of the origins and character of those social movements that have transformed the unified patriarchal family of ancient times into the comparatively individualized family group of the twentieth century. And the end is not yet. With a swiftness and inevitability that appals conservative minds, the process of individualization goes on; and, within a generation or two, "father-power," even now shrunken to a mere shadow, may become little more than a name for an interesting historic phenomenon.

Such a rapid metamorphosis could not proceed without evoking gloomy prophecies from students of social change. Since the dawn of the twentieth century certain of these have foretold the doom of the monogamic family—its utter extinction or its transmutation into a form so different as to be unrecognizable. These men argue that since personal liberty is an essential condition of social progress, the disintegration of the old coercive family, with its hierarchy of authorities, is the price that society must pay for individual freedom and equality. In view of these statements, ever more confidently voiced as the evidence piles up, it behooves all thoughtful students of social institutions to consider the facts and seek to arrive at some conclusion, however tentative, with regard to the functions of the family in the society of the future. Is the monogamic family in truth an outworn institution, useful in olden times when individuals acted largely in groups governed by rigid codes, but unable to adapt itself to the unhampered individualism of the present age? Or is it possible that out of this period of flux will emerge a finer, more spiritual type of family life than any the world has yet known—one consciously providing the largest measure of individual freedom consistent with personal and social good?

EVIDENCES OF FAMILY DISINTEGRATION AND ITS CAUSES

Evidences of the increasing instability of the family, of its tendency to break up into its component units, are not far to seek. Generations ago in America began that pioneer movement into the untried wilderness of the West that was to result in the practical disappearance of what has been called the "great family," *i.e.*, the group of closely related persons descended from the same grandfather or great-grandfather and often residing in the same locality or even in the same household. The family in the hereditary meaning of the term is rapidly becoming nonexistent and with it is vanishing the hereditary homestead. How many adults in America today can point with affectionate pride to the homes of their fathers? The pioneer spirit, the love of adventurous change of a pioneer people, has dispersed the members of the old family stocks over the face of the American continent. Calhoun holds that the practical disappearance of the "great family" of olden times, which is still so strong a unit in France and Italy, has also been furthered by the American conception of marriage as a union of a single man and woman—not of two families. He cites the Frenchman Gohier's comment that in America one marries the girl, not the whole family.[1]

With the dispersion of families over the unsettled tracts of America has come about the decline not only of family unity and solidarity but also of the ancient cult of the family. Who, in this hurried, individualistic age of self-aggrandizement and self-expression, holds up before a youth the ideals and achievements of his ancestors, the honored place carved out by his family in social and political life, as did the Romans of old? Again, what has become of the religion of hearth and home?—what, indeed, of the family hearth itself as the unifying center of household activities? A variety of centrifugal forces are at work in society to reduce the lamp and hearth-fire of family life to the status of interesting historic relics and to drive the individual members of the household in different directions, each seeking his own congenial group for recreation and amusement.

To these evidences of family instability may be added others of a more disturbing character. As is generally known, the number of divorces

[1] *A Social History of the American Family from Colonial Times to the Present,* Vol. III, p. 169.

in the United States has increased ominously with every decade until the Bureau of the Census in 1925 disclosed the fact that there was one divorce to every 6.7 marriages in the country as a whole. More noteworthy still is the fact that in the states of Arizona, Idaho, Missouri, Montana, Oklahoma and Texas the proportion of divorces to marriages is *lower than one to five;* and in the state of Oregon there is actually one divorce to every 2.6 marriages! [2] It is obvious that so startling a situation is a symptom of the grave maladjustment of marriage to environing social conditions.

Another indication of family instability is the long list of "broken homes" recorded by organized social workers—homes deserted by the husband and father who lightly shifts his burdensome responsibilities to organized philanthropy and seeks to start life anew under more agreeable conditions of living. Such a simple method of breaking the chains of an irksome marriage has been dubbed the "poor man's divorce." One by one the forty-eight states of the Union have enacted laws designed to bring the deserter back and compel him to support his wife and children. Probably the recent trend in state legislation toward making desertion a felony and therefore a legal cause of extradition from another state will operate to lessen the number of family desertions. The number of desertions in New York City varies considerably from year to year. In 1921 the total number (exclusive of Brooklyn) was 470 as compared with 610 in 1912.[3]

The weakening of family ties is still further revealed by the falling marriage rate among the educated professional class and the declining birth-rate among all classes save the unskilled laboring group. Although the marriage rate for the country at large has shown a slight but steady increase since 1890, the corresponding rate for college graduates, especially women, reveals a noteworthy decline. A study of the marriage rate among 16,739 graduates of eight women's colleges and one co-educational university—Cornell—published by the Association of Collegiate Alumnæ in its *Journal* for May, 1918, shows that the *average* percent of marriages in this group is 39.1. If the recent classes (1910-1915) be eliminated and those of 1900-1910, whose graduates have been out of college from five to fifteen years, be considered alone, the percentage rises to 46.6. Obviously, this group of educated women has a low marriage

---

[2] This condition is due in part to the fact that many citizens of Oregon choose to be married in neighboring states owing to the state requirement that a physician's certificate of health must be furnished by the applicant for a marriage license.

[3] A. B. Hexter, "The Business Cycle, Relief Work and Desertion," p. 9, *Jewish Social Service Quarterly*, May, 1924.

rate, comparing very unfavorably with that of the country as a whole. The national percentage for the corresponding age-group is about 63.7.[4]

More noteworthy than the declining marriage rate among the professional group is the steadily falling birth-rate among all groups except the most ignorant and unskilled. Twenty-four years ago, when few of the states of the Union kept accurate birth statistics, the Bureau of the Census estimated, on the basis of the returns of census enumerators, that the national birth-rate was 27.2[5] But the compilers of the census declared more than once their conviction that this estimate was "much too small." If the natural rate of increase of the population were to be accounted for, the birth-rate would need to be raised to 35.1. Since 1900 one state after another has been added to the number of those keeping an accurate record of births, until in 1924 the birth registration area included thirty-three states and the District of Columbia. Within this territory the birth-rate in 1924 was 22.6—a decline, since 1915, of 2.5. The death-rate, however, has fallen even more rapidly, reaching in 1924 the low figure of 11.8. The census figures for 1924 show that the ratio of births to deaths in that year was 193 to 100, whereas in 1915 the same ratio was 178 to 100. This means that the natural increase of population in this country, *i.e.*, the excess of births over deaths, was actually greater in 1924 than a decade previous.

Not only is the number of children to a family steadily decreasing throughout the country, except in the ranks of the lowest-paid labor, but the number of childless marriages is notably on the increase. Now, if the widespread belief that dependent children hold many a family together, preventing it from splitting on the rocks of marital unhappiness, is well founded, then our sharply falling birth-rate, together with the increase of childless or one-child families, is possibly a causal factor in the instability of the twentieth-century family. Indeed, one fruitful cause of divorce is the bitterness engendered between husband and wife because one partner eagerly desires offspring while the other does not. Very generally it holds true that children prove a cementing influence within the family. Witness the fact that every year less than two-fifths of all divorces are granted to husbands and wives with children.

Certain of the reasons for the impermanence and disunity of the family deserve thoughtful consideration. They may be analyzed into the following causal factors: (1) economic and industrial conditions; (2) the

---

[4] This figure represents the *average* percentage of marriages at every age from twenty-one years to thirty-four as given by a special census report issued in 1923.

[5] The birth-rate represents the number of births per 1,000 of the population.

breakdown of paternal authority; (3) the growth of individualism; (4) bad marriage laws; (5) the lack of education for marriage and parenthood.

I. Economic and Industrial Conditions.

One determining factor in family instability at present is the virtual disappearance of the ancient land tie and the corresponding urbanization of large numbers of the population. It would be difficult to overestimate the importance of the possession of land in holding families together in olden times. Especially was this true when the land was tilled in common by the various members of the family who lived upon its proceeds. Here was a common industry in which all might share for the good of all. Mrs. Bosanquet states that in England even today, in the agricultural communities of Northumberland and Durham, where farm workers are hired by families, and wives and daughters work beside the men in the fields, "there is a definite economic inducement for the family to hold together." [6] Needless to say, the massing of people in towns and cities that followed upon the development of the factory system uprooted households from the land and shook the family to its foundations. Ever since the eighteenth century the process of urbanization has proceeded apace in every industrially advanced nation, until the city population considerably outnumbers the rural. Even in the United States, with its vast areas of arable land, the urban population increased almost five times as fast as the rural in the decade 1910-1920. In the latter year the ratio of the urban population to the rural was approximately 18 to 17. [7] Furthermore the rural population of fifteen states, showed an actual decrease during this decade. Even in those states still largely rural, tenant farming is markedly increasing, especially during the last six years, when the farmers have suffered from the acute economic depression in Europe.

If the possession of land worked in common has been a powerful cohesive influence upon the family, the opposite has tended to result from the rapid development of machine industry. As we have seen, the factory system proved at first a gigantic monster, devouring men, women and children among the poor, and bringing about the rapid deterioration of family life. Although legislation in most civilized countries has corrected some of the most flagrant abuses of the system, it still remains true that wages are frequently too low to permit the wife and mother to remain in the home. It is a commonplace to say that millions of women are at

[6] *The Family,* p. 197.
[7] The Census of 1920 (Vol. I, p. 58), gives the urban population as 54,304,603 and the rural as 51,406,017.

work in factories today, helping to increase an inadequate family income, whose services are urgently needed in the household to "make a home" for its working members and to care for helpless children. In many instances the well-being of these homes, as well as their permanency, is threatened by such conditions. Poverty is by no means solely the consequence of our present industrial system, but this system tends to breed and aggravate its evils. Whereas, under the régime of domestic industry, workers might fall back upon farming in periods of industrial depression, such an alleviation of their poverty is impossible at present. Modern industry lays off millions of laborers when times are dull, and thereby adds measurably to the difficulty of holding families together. It reduces wages in order to pay dividends, and thus sends women and children into wage-earning employments. "Most of the quarrels in married life," says a social worker, "start over money—the lack of money. It's the industrial system that's to blame at bottom rather than the husband or the wife." On the other hand, when one considers the relative stability of the family among the low-paid workers of England, Belgium, Italy, Saxony and the Ruhr —to mention only a few localities—it must be freely admitted that modern industry is by no means wholly responsible for family breakdowns.

The influences of the Industrial Revolution were not restricted to the wage-earner's family. Its effect upon the middle class has been hardly less far-reaching. It has made economic independence respectable for, if not obligatory upon, women of the professional and moderate income class. Ultimately this has spelled freedom for the entire sex—a larger degree of independence than woman has ever before known. No longer can it be said that the home is the center of all the interests of women, the focus of all their plans and endeavors. Absorbed in interesting work, women have discovered that, however dear the home may be, they can exist without it. More or less aware of this condition, some men refrain from marriage because they fear that the woman of their choice will not make the home her supreme concern and occupation.

II. The Social Process of Individualization.

Powerful as are the economic and industrial factors in bringing about family instability, they are not the sole causes of this condition. An important influence has unquestionably been the individualistic movement that has been gaining headway since the eighteenth century. Politically this tendency has resulted, in most civilized states, in extending the right of suffrage to every adult male and, recently, to women as well. Legally, the movement has operated to free women and children from the despotic authority of the father and to secure their recognition as individuals before the law. Within the family the process of individualization has perhaps gone further than in any other social organization. No longer a highly unified group, owing its character and integrity to the will of the household head, the contemporary family, as we have seen, is composed of a number of individuals, each having his or her special rights and privileges guaranteed by law, each demanding that these be respected within the home. Little by little the authority of parents over children has been curtailed, alike by law and by a powerful public opinion. Respect for the individuality of children has increased along with the general respect for personality and the growing conviction that arbitrary methods stunt personal development. Gradually the coercive ties that have bound the family together during the long course of social history have been replaced by the spiritual ties of mutual love, sympathy and daily helpful association. The father has perforce yielded much of his authority to the State, which has constituted itself an over-parent. In its legislation against child labor and in behalf of the compulsory education of children; in its efforts to protect the child against parental cruelty; in its organization of asylums, institutions for defectives, boards of children's guardians, probation systems to deal with juvenile crime and recalcitrancy, the State has gone far in the direction of paternalism. Indeed the alarmed outcries of conservatives are heard from time to time that the State has encroached too far upon the prerogatives of parents and has become an agent in the spread of family irresponsibility.

The individualizing process has not, of course, been limited to children, but has operated even more dramatically to secure the rights and develop the personalities of women. The so-called "woman-movement" of the last two generations is hardly less the offspring of the social tendency toward individualization than it is of changed economic conditions.[8] Historically speaking, individualization of the members of society is a valid mark of advancing civilization, an indication of a highly developed culture, which has abandoned subservience to custom in favor of a social life allowing freer play to the abilities and initiative of the individual. With the break-up of the feudal system, society became more fluid and social classes less rigidly separated. This gave larger freedom to the individual. Later followed the splitting up of one more unified and authoritative institution —the Holy Roman Catholic Church. In the eighteenth century came the breakdown of the domestic system of industry, and the repudiation of an

[8] Obviously the individualizing tendency is itself, in considerable measure, the product of economic circumstances.

arbitrary kingship in France and America. In all these historic events we may see the breaking up of ancient institutions that cramped and impeded individual growth. Although men were at first the chief beneficiaries of the more flexible life that ensued, with its larger freedom and multiplied opportunities for self-development, it was inevitable that the feminine half of society would increasingly share in it. When women were forced by the economic trend to enter remunerative employments outside their own homes, when they were conceded the advantage of higher education, the knell of the old order of feminine subordination was sounded. To strike from women the shackles of financial dependence on the one hand and of ignorance on the other was to start them on that long course of individuation the end of which is not yet in sight. However much conservatives may deplore the self-reliance of the modern woman, her eager desire for ever more freedom, her insistence on the right to develop her natural gifts to their fullest extent and to use them in ways that are both socially beneficial and personally rewarding, these qualities are but the marks of an irresistible individualizing process that has gone even further in the case of men. Whether this deep social trend will eventuate in the modern world, as in ancient Greece and Rome, in a general tendency toward personal development for purely personal satisfactions, accompanied by growing blindness and indifference to the essential needs of society, no student of social history can foretell.

Needless to say, the individuation of women is responsible for a conspicuous increase among them of restlessness and dissatisfaction with the home as at present constituted. Women who marry after having achieved moderate or considerable success in a congenial career find the narrowness, the restraints, the multitude of petty details of housekeeping almost unbearably irksome, especially if they belong to that large fraction of their sex who have no liking for the domestic arts. Not all families, even in the educated middle class, have incomes that make it possible to ease the drudgery of housekeeping by generous use of electrical appliances. The mechanism of the average home, with its individual cook-stove, wash-tub and broom, is hopelessly antiquated, and imposes upon a gifted and highly trained woman a severe strain. "In America," says Calhoun, "marriage can not enlarge a woman's freedom; in practice it ordinarily burdens her with house-keeping and exposes her to the risk of deterioration." [9]

III. Defective Marriage Laws.

Another condition clearly unfavorable to stable family life is found in our faulty marriage laws. Far from surrounding marriage with rea-

[9] Calhoun, op. cit., Vol. III, pp. 121-2.

sonable safeguards and preventing insurgent impulse from sweeping the young and thoughtless into matrimony, American marriage laws seem deliberately designed to make the union of the immature, the reckless and the unfit as easy as possible. Witness the fact that, in 1919, twenty-six states still recognized common-law marriages as valid; and in six other states the status of these irregular unions had not been definitely settled.[10] This means, of course, that more than half of the commonwealths of the United States are willing to accept the statement of a man and woman that they have taken each other as husband and wife (either before witnesses or not), and have been living in that relation, as constituting a valid marriage. Such laxity is striking testimony to the fact that the theory of the marriage relation which characterized the ancient world and the medieval barbarian tribes, lives on in the twentieth century. Obviously this easy-going custom may be a fertile source of unstable marriages. Again, it is a startling fact that in "17 states no marriageable ages have been fixed by law and presumably the common law ages are in force—14 for males and 12 for females."[11] Add to this the fact that, in at least eight other states and the District of Columbia, males may marry under eighteen and females under sixteen, and the reader may form some idea of the laxity of marriage legislation in this regard.[12] It would seem axiomatic that no youths, male or female, under the age of eighteen, are capable of appreciating the true meaning of marriage or of shouldering its responsibilities. Here again an ancient custom lives on, long after it has served its day, and becomes a distinct menace to happy and enduring family life.

Nor are these the only grave defects in our marriage laws. In 1919 only eight states had erected any barrier against hasty marriages. The period which must elapse by law between the application for a marriage license and its issuance is fixed in most of these eight states at five days. But in three, namely, Connecticut, Rhode Island and Vermont, the law applies only to nonresidents.[13] Therefore, in forty-three states of this Union, a young couple may secure a license and solemnize their marriage on one and the same day, thus being afforded every opportunity to "marry in haste and repent at leisure." The law requires no notice of intention to marry to be published, and furnishes no opportunity for the filing or hearing of objections to the marriage. Who can say how many unsuitable and bigamous unions might be prevented by a more enlightened procedure?

[10] F. S. Hall and Elisabeth W. Brooke, *American Marriage Laws in Their Social Aspects*, p. 14. Russell Sage Foundation, New York, 1919.
[11] *Ibid.*, p. 17.
[12] *Ibid.* See laws of the separate states, pp. 51-132.
[13] *Ibid.*, pp. 18-9; 36-7.

On this point Howard writes: "All this is contrary to sound public policy. The notice of intention should be recorded for a reasonable period, say ten days, before issuance of the license; and during this time it should be officially posted, and also published in the newspapers—not merely concealed in the register or published at the discretion of the official, as is now the usual course. Objections might then be filed, and in case of need tried in a court clothed with proper jurisdiction, before the celebration were allowed to proceed. Under the existing state legislation it would be difficult, certainly awkward, to stop a proposed marriage on the ground of alleged illegal impediments. To make an objection effective it might be necessary either to 'anticipate the notice' or to interrupt the nuptial ceremony." [14]

A further defect in our marriage laws lies in the fact that religious celebrants of marriage are not required to be licensed or registered. "In 34 states there is no official list of those authorized to solemnize marriage according to religious rites." [15] In consequence any minister of the gospel, whether he is connected with a church or not, may celebrate marriage, no inquiry being made into his character and social standing. Only fourteen states have taken steps requiring religious celebrants to file their credentials or obtain clergyman's licenses. In Kentucky, Virginia and West Virginia, the religious celebrant must give bond for the proper discharge of his duties. In view of the fact that in several states a wide variety of civil officials are permitted to celebrate marriage, ranging from higher judicial officers and justices of the peace to aldermen (eight states), police court judges (four states), any notary public (two states) and any officer authorized to administer oaths (South Carolina), it would seem well to place these officials also under bond to perform their duties with a high sense of responsibility. Most commonwealths recognize any ordained minister as empowered to solemnize marriage, but in nine states —Massachusetts, New Hampshire, Vermont, Ohio, Indiana, Michigan, Missouri, Nevada and Washington—only a minister of the gospel residing within the state may perform that office. It follows that in these nine states couples ignorant of the law may be united in marriage by a clergyman of another state, to discover later that their own commonwealth refuses to recognize the marriage as valid. [16]

Probably the most harmful defect in American marriage laws is the failure to restrict the marriage of persons suffering from mental and

[14] Howard, *A History of Matrimonial Institutions,* Vol. III, pp. 191-2. University of Chicago Press, 1904. Also quoted in Hall and Brooke, *op. cit.,* p. 18.
[15] Hall and Brooke, *op. cit.,* p. 42.
[16] *Ibid.,* p. 42.

physical disabilities. In nineteen states no attempt is made to protect either party to a marriage from the terrible consequences following from union with an epileptic, a mental defective, an insane person, or one suffering from venereal disease. Such blind indifference on the part of lawmakers seems incredible in this day and generation, when enlightenment concerning these disabilities and their devastating effects upon family life is far more widespread than ever before in social history. When we turn to the twenty-nine states whose codes do contain regulations against the marriage of persons with grave physical or mental disabilities, we are struck by the fact that in most of these states the license clerk is permitted to accept affidavits of the applicants themselves—the very persons most interested in concealing the facts—as satisfying the legal requirement! "In only six states—Alabama, North Dakota, Oregon, Wisconsin, North Carolina and Louisiana—is there any requirement that freedom from the specified physical or mental disabilities shall be established by physicians' certificates, although in New Hampshire and Virginia, certification by a physician may be required, in the discretion of the issuer of licenses, in respect to mental disorders." [17]

In two other commonwealths, Michigan and Vermont, where the marriage of persons with certain specified diseases is prohibited, the law requires that a physician's certificate shall establish the facts. But since the license clerk is not required to demand such certificates of applicants for marriage licenses, this legislation seems to be virtually a dead letter.

When the defects in American marriage laws are thus brought together and reviewed, it is easy to infer that their social consequences may be grave. In an age when marriage and family life are notoriously unstable, when the increasing volume of divorces is a cause of concern to many, it is no less than astonishing that in one-half the states of the Union common-law marriages are permitted; that young persons may assume the responsibilities of married life at a ridiculously early age; that in the great majority of states no publication of intention to marry is required before a license is issued, and thus no waiting period is enforced during which serious objections to the marriage might be brought to light; that, above all, the innocent party to a marriage is not protected, in most states, against union with a person physically or mentally diseased. Those social writers who urge that marriage laws be reformed before divorce laws are tightened clearly have much evidence on their side. In the entire code of many states it would be hard to find a body of laws more in need of drastic improvement than those concerning matrimony.

[17] Hall and Brooke, *op. cit.*, p. 40.

TOPICS FOR REPORTS

1. The Underlying Causes of Family Desertion.
   Joanna C. Colcord, *Broken Homes*, Ch. II.
2. The Influence of Social Change on the Family.
   A. W. Calhoun, *A Social History of the American Family from Colonial Times to the Present*, Vol. III, Ch. XIV. Arthur H. Clark Co., Cleveland.
3. Attitude of the Church towards Questions of Marriage and Divorce.
   Calhoun, *op. cit.*, Vol. III, Ch. XIII.
4. Problems of the Modern Family.
   G. E. Howard, *A History of Matrimonial Institutions*, Vol. III, Ch. XVIII. University of Chicago Press, 1904.

[Handwritten notes:]

Defects in Marriage laws.

1. No time limit & publicity.
2. No age limits in many states.
3. Allowing defectives to marry.
4. More than half of states allow common law marriage

Difficulties in a law to prevent defectives from marrying.

1. Expenses.
2. Fraud & bribery.

3. Civil Marriage.
   authorized by state, performed, & dissolved by state

4. Common law marriage.
   Mere living together is all that is necessary.
   State has full control of divorce.   26 states recognize the

5. Free contract marriage.
   allows parties to perform own ceremony before with
   Divorce under state authority.

6. Free love theory.
   all marriage & divorce, up to individuals, no state
   authority.   Illegal in all states

CHAPTER VIII

MODERN INDUSTRIALISM AND THE FAMILY

CHARACTERISTIC FEATURES OF MODERN INDUSTRY

THE nineteenth century has been characterized above all else by the phenomenal growth of the factory system and the supplanting of hand labor by machine industry. So far has the mechanization of industry advanced, that the labor of production has been more and more minutely specialized, until many a workman spends eight or ten hours a day performing at his machine a simple monotonous task which a boy of twelve could readily master. Another marked feature of this industrial age is the growth of huge corporations, like the United States Steel Company and the Standard Oil Company, which represent enormous aggregations of wealth and power. These monster combinations tend to supplant the more modest business organizations of half a century ago and to drive small competitors ruthlessly to the wall. Indeed the whole industrial trend seems to be in the direction of ever-expanding productive units which threaten the existence of smaller corporate groups of whatever sort. In the words of Dike: "The general movement of property has, so far, been like that of a huge glacier, breaking and wearing away into their elementary atoms all forms of corporation, whether political or economical. *Its ultimate atom is the individual;* its favorite corporation is the largest possible combination. The family has in it the greatest cohesive strength, and consequently has most successfully withstood the grinding power that has tended to crush everything subjected to it. . . . It brings the family into the labor market on the same footing as the unmarried. For small provision, at the best, will be made in fixing wages, for the rearing of children, the care of other dependents, and all those little things that make the home. *In the market of wages the family is the accident of the laborer rather than his essential.*" [1]

Together with the growth of vast accumulations of wealth in the hands of a few powerful captains of industry and finance, has gone the relative poverty of the masses of the workers. This is by no means to say that

[1] "Problems of the Family," in *Century Magazine*, Vol. XXXIX, pp. 392-3. Italics mine.

poverty is a recent social phenomenon, but only to state that our present system of industry fails to secure to a host of unskilled workers a living wage according to American standards. This is true even though real wages have shown an upward trend in the United States since 1920. In 1924 the real wages of factory workers in twenty selected industries were approximately ten percent higher than their money incomes, taking the average earnings from 1919-1922 as a base.[2]

Finally, as we have seen, modern industry has exercised a profound effect upon the growth and multiplication of cities. It has been said that contemporary industry "is almost equivalent to 'city life,' because the great industry, the factory system, builds cities around the chimneys of steam engines and electric plants." Whether urban life, together with modern industrial conditions, is compatible with health and with enduring family relations is one of the pressing social questions of the age. There is much evidence to show that in the past the combined influence of the two has been responsible for (1) high morbidity and mortality rates among adults; (2) high infant mortality rates in certain industrial centers; (3) occupational diseases leading to loss of wages and family breakdown; (4) crowded slums and unsanitary dwellings; (5) employment of women and children outside the home; (6) sweated household industries; (7) commercialized vice and commercialized amusements, almost crowding out social life within the family. On the other hand, it is well to keep in mind certain facts which indicate that city life and machine industry are not necessarily harmful to health and stable family life. For example, despite our expanding cities and industries, the 1924 Census shows that infant mortality in the United States dropped one-fifth between 1919 and 1924. The adult mortality rate is also steadily falling. Again in certain states, as New York, the urban death rate is lower than the rural. In progressive states, sweated trades carried on in the home are being legislated out of existence. Moreover, in our cities, maternity centers and child clinics are rendering valuable aid to the family. Nevertheless, conditions exist in crowded centers of population and industry that are a distinct menace to the stability and wholesomeness of family life.

FAMILY INCOMES AND WAGE RATES IN THE UNITED STATES

Recent studies of the distribution of wealth and income in the United States reveal some disturbing facts. On the basis of numerous earlier

[2] See the admirable study by W. A. Berridge, E. A. Winslow and R. A. Flinn, *Purchasing Power of the Consumer*, p. 42. A. W. Shaw Co., Chicago and New York, 1925.

studies, King estimates that in 1910 the percentage of families having an income of less than $1,000 was 69.43; and the percentage having less than $2,000 was 94.86.[3] King's estimates are supported by those of the National Bureau of Economic Research covering the decade 1909-1919. These show that the average annual earnings of laborers in various industries, in factories and in mining, fall below the minimum necessary to maintain a family of five in health and decency. The figures follow:[4]

AVERAGE ANNUAL EARNINGS OF EMPLOYEES

In Various Industries		In Mining		In Factories	
1909	$ 626	1909	$ 599	1909	$ 571
1913	723	1913	755	1913	705
1918	1,078	1918	1,283	1918	1,148

If the purchasing power of the wage in 1913 be taken as the base (100%), the indices of the purchasing power of wages in the other two years are as follows:[5]

In Industries		In Mining		In Factories	
1909	90.7	1909	83	1909	84.7
1918	94.3	1918	107.5	1918	103

The National Bureau has also estimated the personal incomes below $2,000 per annum in every year of the decade 1909-1919. The figures reveal that in 1910 there were 34,352,000 persons, or 96% of all income receivers, who had incomes under $2,000. In 1919, owing to the extraordinary prosperity enjoyed by some individuals as a result of the war, there were 34,233,000 persons, or 86%, having incomes below $2,000. Therefore in 1910 only four percent of the income-receiving citizens of this country had an estimated income of $2,000 or above; and in 1919 only fourteen percent had such an income.[6] In 1927, eighty-two percent of the population paid no income tax because their incomes fell below $2,000.[7] These figures are all the more impressive when we recall that the United States has long been regarded as the land of prosperity and opportunity. And, indeed, it is still true that the condition of the laboring class in this country is markedly better than in most European nations.

[3] Willford I. King, *The Wealth and Income of the People of the United States*, p. 228. The Macmillan Co., 1915.
[4] *Income in the United States. Its Amount and Distribution*, p. 102. New York, 1921. Condensed from statistics of the National Bureau of Economic Research.
[5] *Ibid.*, p. 102.
[6] *Ibid.*, p. 112.
[7] *New York Times*, April 4, 1927.

For instance, in 1910 more than 17,000,000 persons in Prussia lived in families receiving an income of less than 900 marks ($250) annually; and 15,123,000 persons were members of families whose income was from 1,500 marks to 3,000 marks ($375 to $750).[8] Making every allowance for the greater purchasing power of the Prussian mark as compared with the American dollar, it still remains true that the income of the lowest-paid Prussian laborer, available for the support of a family, was materially lower in 1910 than that of the American workingman of the same group.

The above statistics will serve to suggest that the distribution of income throughout the United States is markedly unequal. While 38.92% of the total income group in the country had an estimated income of *less than $700* in 1910, nearly two percent of the families received incomes of $3,600, and less than one percent had incomes ranging from $10,000 to $10,000,000.[9]

But the full import of the low incomes received by a high proportion of the adult population is not brought home to us until these incomes are compared with the amounts estimated to be necessary to bring up a so-called typical family of five on the minimum health and decency level.[10] Several authoritative budget studies of workingmen's families have been made in recent years by trained economists, by bureaus of municipal research and by the United States Bureau of Labor Statistics. These budget studies have been compiled by the Bureau of Applied Economics in Washington, D. C.[11] The minimum health and decency level, which furnishes the working basis of the following studies, should be interpreted to mean:

1. A sufficiency of nourishing food to maintain a "standard" family, consisting of husband, wife and three children under fourteen years of age, in health.
2. Housing in low-rent neighborhoods, with the minimum number of rooms consistent with decency, but with sufficient light, heat and toilet facilities for the maintenance of health.
3. Upkeep of household equipment.
4. Clothing sufficient for warmth.

[8] King, *op. cit.*, p. 233.
[9] *Ibid.*, pp. 228-9.
[10] See P. H. Douglas, *Wages and the Family*, pp. 5-6. University of Chicago Press, 1925. It should be noted that this "standard" or "normal" family is largely a fiction. Many workers have less than three dependent children and a considerable percentage have more.
[11] "Standards of Living," *Bulletin*, No. 7, 1920.

5. A surplus over expenditures which would permit a small outlay for street-car fares, a modest insurance, medical and dental care, contributions to churches and labor or benefit organizations, simple amusements (as the moving pictures) once in a while, and a daily newspaper.[12]

The first budget study considered was that made by the United States Bureau of Labor Statistics under the title "Tentative Quantity and Cost Budget Necessary to Maintain a Family of Five in Washington, D. C., at a Level of Health and Decency." The investigation was made in July and August, 1919, and the prices are as of August. The total cost of family maintenance was estimated by the Bureau to be $2,262.47. If a full working year be held to be about 300 days, allowing for Sundays, holidays and a week's vacation, it will readily be seen that this family budget calls for a wage of $7.54 a day, with no losses due to unemployment. Furthermore it has been estimated that the cost of living rose twelve percent between August, 1919, and May, 1920. This would necessitate a family budget at the latter date of $2,533.97.

Another careful budget study was made by Professor William F. Ogburn of Columbia University, at the request of the United Mine Workers of America, and was submitted to the Bituminous Coal Commission in January, 1920.[13] This budget showed in great detail that the cost of maintaining a miner's family at a level of health and decency in December, 1919, was $2,118.94. That means that if the miner with a family of four dependents were employed every day of a full working year of 300 days (which he assuredly is not) his daily wage would need to be about $7.14. Similar studies were made by the Philadelphia Bureau of Municipal Research in 1918 and by the National Industrial Conference Board in 1919.[14] The former estimated the cost of maintaining a Philadelphia workingman's family of five in "health and comfort" to be $1,636.79. The budgets estimated by the National Industrial Conference Board were prepared with reference to wage-earners' families in Fall River and Lawrence, Massachusetts. In the former city the minimum cost of living for a family of five was estimated to be $1,267.76. A more liberal standard would require $1,573.90. The corresponding figures for Lawrence gave $1,385.79 as a minimum standard; as a more liberal standard, $1,658.04.

[12] Op. cit., summarized from the "Budget for a Government Employee's Family," p. 26.
[13] Ibid., pp. 48-63.
[14] Ibid., pp. 64-81.

More recently the Family Welfare Society of Boston made a careful investigation of the wage necessary to maintain a family of five at the level of health and decency, and decided that $36 a week was the minimum. At the time this estimate was given the average wage was found to be $28 a week.

When these budgets are compared with the actual wages received by laborers in industry, in mining and in factories, as estimated by the National Bureau of Economic Research (*ante*, p. 115), the disparities are startling. Even in 1918, when the *average* wage of industrial workers reached the high level of $1,078, the worker's income fell below the costs of family maintenance as given above, by sums ranging from $189.76, for the lowest estimate, to $1,184.47 for the highest—that of the United States Bureau of Labor Statistics for the family of a government employee. At a time when many well-meaning persons are exclaiming against a wage of $5 or $6 a day as extortionate, it is salutary to face the fact that a considerable proportion of married wage-earners in this country have an income materially lower than that estimated by economic experts to be essential to the maintenance of a family of five in health and decent comfort.

Of course it should not be overlooked that a wage quite inadequate to support a standard family of five will maintain a single man or woman in considerable comfort. Moreover it should be kept in mind that the so-called standard family cannot accurately be said to exist. It has been estimated that from one fourth to one third of the 24,000,000 persons listed in the Census of 1910 as having incomes ranging from less than $600 up to $1,400 are single.[15] Paul Douglas found that only 17.7% of 11,156 families investigated had three children under fourteen. However, he also found that 11.2% of these families had four dependent children and 4.8% had five or more. In other words 16% had more than three dependent children and 17.7% had exactly three, making a total of 33.7% of the 11,156 families with three or more dependent children.[16] As yet no intelligent attempt has been made in America to distinguish between the essential needs of the head of a dependent family and those of the unmarried worker with no dependents. This fact serves to emphasize the truth of Dike's statement that in "the market of wages the family is the accident of the laborer rather than his essential."

[15] Mary W. Abel, *Successful Family Life on the Moderate Income*, p. 27. J. B. Lippincott Co., Philadelphia, 1921.
[16] Douglas, *op. cit.*, p. 35.

FACTORS IN INDUSTRIALISM AND URBAN LIFE REACTING HARMFULLY
ON THE FAMILY

I. Poverty: Unemployment.

The poverty of the group of low-paid and unskilled wage-earners
is aggravated by periodical unemployment which often results in obliterat-
ing the narrow margin that separates self-supporting families from paupers
and throws them upon the various social agencies for relief. The United
States Bureau of Labor, in a study made in 1901 of more than 25,000
families, showed that 49.81% of the heads of these families were idle
during some portion of the year.[17] The study also revealed that, on the
basis of the Census of 1900, 22.3% of all persons in gainful occupations
were unemployed at some time during the census year.[18] Nor is this condition at all unusual. "Unemployment," declares Robert Bruère, "is a
permanent feature of modern industrial life everywhere." In support of
his statement he cites the figures given by the Federal Census of Manufactures in 1910. These show that of "37,194 establishments, only forty
per cent were in operation for the full year; nineteen per cent lost a
month or more, and *eight per cent were shut down half the time.*" [19] Lest
the reader be inclined to believe that the facts cited above apply chiefly
to the pre-war years, and exist only to a limited extent at present, it is
well to note the figures given by the Biennial Census of Manufactures
recently issued by the Census Bureau for the year 1923. These show that
in the minimum month of employment (January) there were 8,421,317
workers employed as compared with 8,910,742 employed in the maximum
month (September). This means, of course, that there were 489,425
workers unemployed in January who were at work in September. And
these figures do not include the body of irregularly employed or permanently unemployed laborers.

Not only are shutdowns a common feature of modern industry, but
much employment is by its very nature seasonal. The building, painting
and plumbing trades are all more or less seasonal. Hence the high wages
demanded by skilled workers in those industries. Industrial uncertainty
is, moreover, greatly aggravated by strikes, called by the representatives
of organized labor with or without due justification. Add to these ever-
present possibilities of a curtailment of family income the further one of

[17] *United States Bureau of Labor Bulletin,* No. 109, p. 12.
[18] See J. L. Gillin, *Poverty and Dependency,* p. 74. The Century Co., New York,
1921.
[19] Bruère, "Reanchoring the Home," in *Harper's Magazine,* Vol. 124, pp. 920-1,
May, 1912.

wage decreases, which are declared whenever employers face a diminution in the financial returns of the industry that may threaten dividend payments, and the uncertainties surrounding the worker are seen to be grave realities.

The income of the laboring man is rendered still further precarious by the imminence of industrial accidents and occupational diseases. The number and extent of injuries suffered by workers over the length and breadth of the land are grim facts that state governments are only beginning to face. In the matter of legislation providing accident insurance for injured laborers the United States lags far behind European nations. Even if the worker escapes serious injury to life and limb, he still is threatened by occupational diseases. In a lengthy report on "Industrial Hygiene" prepared by Dr. Kober for the United States Bureau of Labor, a large number of occupations inimical to health are listed. Among these are the trades of the bleachers, brass founders, compositors, coopersmiths, electrotypers, gas workers, white lead workers, match workers, potters, file makers, and operatives in rubber factories. Dr. Kober's investigations show that workers in employments involving dust—metallic, mineral, animal or vegetable—have a markedly high proportion of sufferers from tuberculosis and pneumonia; while the morbidity and mortality in all occupations in which white lead is employed are notoriously high. With regard to the morbidity of the laboring class as a whole, statistics "indicate that persons habitually engaged in hard work are most frequently subject to disease and present a higher mortality than persons more favorably situated, and this is especially true of factory employees, because their work is generally more monotonous, fatiguing, and performed under less favorable surroundings, and they are too often also badly nourished and badly housed." [20]

II. Bad Housing.

One inevitable effect of low wages and unemployment is the segregation of the working class in ugly slums in which unsanitary tenement houses rub elbows with each other, leaving few open spaces for the admission of light and air. The fundamental importance of decent housing conditions to the physical and moral health of every individual—old and young—seems obvious enough and has been pointed out again and again by investigators in this field. Thus Edith Elmer Wood writes:

"No nation can rise higher than the level of its homes. Whether we approach the subject from the point of view of health, morals, child con-

[20] *United States Bureau of Labor Bulletin,* No. 75, 1908, pp. 473-7.

servation, industrial efficiency, Americanization, or good citizenship, the housing problem is fundamental." [21]

More than a generation ago Germany and Belgium attacked the crucial problem of securing decent homes for their wage-earners and England has made notable advances toward the solution of this problem. Little, however, was done in this country until the opening of the twentieth century, when numerous surveys of bad housing conditions were made in New York, Washington, Chicago, Boston, Pittsburgh and other industrial centers. The New York City Tenement House Commission was first in the field in 1900 and its admirable report led to the much-needed Tenement House Law of 1901. Needless to say all the surveys revealed unspeakably menacing and degrading conditions in those tenements occupied by the lowest-paid class of workers. Mrs. Wood sums them up as follows:

"Roughly stated, one-third of the people of the United States are living under subnormal housing conditions, conditions which fall below the minimum standard we shall presently describe, and about a tenth are living under conditions which are an acute menace to health, morals and family life, conditions which tend to produce degenerative changes in those subject to them. . . . The same conditions meet us everywhere— lot overcrowding and room overcrowding, dark rooms and inadequately lighted rooms, lack of water, lack of sanitary conveniences, dilapidation, excessive fire risks, basement and cellar dwellings." [22]

The district nurse and the social worker know only too well that tuberculosis rages in basement dwellings and dark, airless rooms. And the danger of contagion that threatens every family living under such conditions is multiplied by gross overcrowding. When the rent cannot be paid without taking in lodgers, lodgers are received into the tenements of families already indecently huddled together. Byington found an appalling situation of this kind in Homestead in 1910. In this steel city a study was made of twenty-one of the wretched courts of the Second Ward, where many of the Slavic workers were segregated. Among 239 families, 102 were taking in lodgers and in these latter families the average number of persons to a room was four. Fifty-one families were found living in one room; and two-room tenements were not rarely occupied by a man, wife, two children and two to three lodgers! [23] Such conditions are directly responsible for sexual immorality, intemperance and juvenile

[21] *The Housing of the Unskilled Wage Earner*, p. 1. The Macmillan Co., New York, 1919.
[22] Wood, *op. cit.*, pp. 7, 8.
[23] "The Family in a Typical Mill Town," in *American Journal of Sociology*, Vol. XIV, 1910, p. 654.

delinquency. And, as one writer satirically points out, we go on building hospitals, asylums and reformatories!

Particularly harmful are such home conditions in their effects upon little children. Dr. Wood quotes Luther Burbank as saying: "All animal life is sensitive to environment, but of all living things the child is most sensitive. The child absorbs environment." [24] So far as slum tenement children are concerned, it is the merest blind sentimentality to go on glorifying "the influence of the home." These dark, ill-smelling dwellings, "pestilential in winter and purgatorial in summer," are the worst possible environment for the growth of wholesome family life. Children and youth alike leave them as often as possible for the street, the movie and the dance hall, and parents are powerless to hold them. Byington says that Homestead mothers, knowing the dangers of the streets and of many commercialized amusements, "make a heroic and often pathetic effort to keep the home attractive enough to offset these temptations"; but their endeavors would in most instances seem doomed to failure from the start.

Not only the morals, but the vitality and the growth of children are menaced by the conditions prevailing in our most overcrowded tenements. Aronovici cites the results obtained by Dr. Mackenzie, of the Scottish Education Department, who in 1905-6 made a physical examination of 72,857 school children between the ages of five and eighteen. He found that Scotch boys living in one-room homes were on the average 11.7 pounds lighter in weight and 4.7 inches shorter than boys from four-room houses; and girls from one-room homes were 14 pounds lighter and 5.3 inches shorter than girls from four-room homes.[25] But stunted growth is not all. The infant mortality rate in the most crowded tenements is cruelly high. Byington found that in the wretched dwellings of Homestead's Second Ward the child death rate was double that in other wards.[26] Poverty saps the vitality of both mother and infant; and if the child grows to adult age he is unable to bear the strain of life. Low in vigor, he becomes the ready prey of occupational diseases and finds it hard to make a living that will insure to his children the health and energy which he has never enjoyed. So the vicious circle is repeated.

The conditions described above existed prior to the World War. During and for several years after that conflict, an acute housing shortage prevailed in many congested industrial centers of the United States and

[24] Wood, op. cit., p. 27.
[25] Carol Aronovici, Housing and the Housing Problem, pp. 12-3. A. C. McClurg & Co., Chicago, 1920.
[26] Aronovici, Ibid., p. 654. See also the studies made by the United States Children's Bureau on "Infant Mortality." Bureau Publications, Nos. 6, 9, 68, 112.

Europe which greatly aggravated the bad conditions already existing. This shortage of houses is now happily lessened and will probably soon disappear. But this is not to say that housing conditions have greatly improved in this country during the last decade. Most of the new houses erected in the United States since 1919 have been built for the middle and prosperous classes who could afford one-family dwellings. Slightly less than two percent of the building permits issued in 1923 were granted for "one-family and two-family dwellings with shops" and "multi-family apartments with shops" because such dwellings do not yield a high return on the capital invested.[27] When new detached homes and apartment houses are built for the relatively well-to-do classes, these buildings are promptly filled by families who have vacated inferior dwellings. It is these single or two-family houses, often run-down and sometimes lacking in modern conveniences, that are turned into tenements and occupied by laborers— the better ones by skilled workers, the less desirable by low-paid labor. According to the housing report cited above, of all families provided for by new housing in 1921, 58.3% were furnished with one-family dwellings, 2.3% with one-family and two-family dwellings with shops, and 1.3% with multi-family apartments with shops. In 1923 conditions were little better. Of all the families provided with new housing in the United States, 45.8% were furnished with one-family dwellings costing $871,704,763, while 2.3% were furnished with multi-family apartments with shops at a cost of $50,315,146.[28]

Since the World War, no attempt has been made in this country to create state or municipal housing commissions such as have existed in European countries for nearly a generation. Even limited dividend companies like the City Housing Corporation of New York, which is building on Long Island attractive homes for small-income groups, are rare in the United States, while corporations like the Bayonne (New Jersey) Housing Corporation, organized to provide homes for wage-earners at low cost, are almost unknown. The housing problem, so crucial in determining the character of family life, is left in America almost wholly to commercial companies whose chief interest is to secure generous returns on their investments. The results are not encouraging to those socially-minded persons who are interested in the improvement of the home. For example, the Philadelphia Housing Association, a voluntary organization of citizens the primary function of which "is to ascertain and to

---

[27] See "The Housing Situation in the United States," *Report of the International Labor Office*, pp. 22, 23. Geneva, 1925.
[28] *Ibid.*, p. 23.

publish the facts concerning housing conditions in the city" declared in its report of 1924 that "comparatively little of . . . new construction has as yet helped to relieve the pressure felt by the small wage-earning groups for low-cost homes." [29] In 1922 the Association described conditions in the Quaker City as follows:

"The City knows there are between 15 and 20 miles of built-up but unsewered streets within city limits, for there is a list of such streets in City Hall. . . . The City has known for over ten years that houses in wide areas of Philadelphia have an inadequate water supply; . . . that alley and court houses have no inside supply and that often their only supply, a hydrant in a court, is shared with three or four, and sometimes six neighboring families. . . . The City knows there is a teeming population in Philadelphia's narrow alleys and minor streets, approximating 60,000 persons; that in the majority of the courts and alleys, dwellings have no yards; that the children must play in long narrow passageways or in the streets where trucking and traffic dangers levy their toll in human life and in maimed bodies, or where subtle attacks on morals break down character and destroy virtue. The City knows that such places are a blight that does not improve, but rapidly becomes worse." [30]

These unfortunate conditions are not peculiar to any one locality.

Lest the reader believe that similar situations are characteristic only in congested manufacturing cities of the East, he should consult Robert E. Todd's monograph on *Housing and Good Health in Michigan*. The writer reports finding, in cities below 100,000 in population, families cooking, eating and sleeping in one room, hundreds of "dim and dark interior rooms," dark water-closets, the absence of sanitary equipment, and rooms with "practically no ventilation." [31] In 1925 the Better Housing League of Cincinnati declared that although the worst of the housing shortage had passed, the poorer families "who suffered most acutely while the shortage was at its peak are the last to feel relief." The report continues: "Even with the shortage entirely eliminated for the poorer families we would still have exactly the same problem of bad housing, only perhaps somewhat worse than existed prior to the war period. We are confronted with the gigantic task of maintaining decent conditions in some 6,500 tenements housing 30,000 families. Not all of these tenements are bad, but a large proportion of them, never intended for tenement occupancy,

---

[29] Bernard J. Newman, *Housing in Philadelphia*, p. 5. Philadelphia Housing Association, 311 South Juniper Street, Philadelphia.
[30] Bernard J. Newman, *Report of the Philadelphia Housing Association for 1922*, p. 1.
[31] Monthly publication of the Michigan State Board of Health, August, 1917.

contain or develop conditions detrimental to health, morals and general welfare." [32]

III. The Labor of Mothers and Children.

When, because of low wages, unemployment or sickness, the father is unable to earn even a minimum living wage, the mother and sometimes the children of school age are driven out of the home to seek work. This is a fact with which we are so familiar that it is accepted as a matter of course. But the consequences that follow from the all-day employment of women with young children are by no means fully understood or appreciated. Yet a week's visiting in the tenement districts would drive home to our minds the deplorable results that sometimes ensue from this practice. Obviously, if the mother is needed at home to prepare food for the family, to wash, mend, clean and care for babies or toddling children, these essential tasks are very largely neglected if she is forced to work in factory or shop from eight to ten hours. To be sure many women in these circumstances make a heroic effort to carry on two jobs. They buy cooked food at the delicatessen shop; they bravely attack the washing or cleaning after a weary day's work; they put an old mother or aunt in charge of the children, if they are fortunate enough to have such a relative available. If not, the older girl or boy is kept home from school to watch the babies; or the mother turns over part of her meager wages into a fund to pay a neighbor to take care of several families of small children. Needless to say, home care and home training suffer woefully under this régime. And the wife and mother not infrequently breaks down under the double strain, as the records of hospitals and charitable organizations all too clearly show.

A careful study of "Unemployment and Child Welfare" was recently published by the Children's Bureau of the United States Department of Labor. The investigation was made during the industrial depression of 1921 and 1922, and included an intensive study of the effects of unemployment in 356 families in two cities—Racine, Wisconsin, and Springfield, Massachusetts—where large numbers of skilled workers were commonly employed. At the time the study was undertaken, more than two-thirds of the fathers included in the investigation "had been out of work for more than a year—had gradually exhausted the resources of the families, and recourse to public and private relief as well as great changes in the family life had become necessary." [33] Not only were the savings of

[32] *The Housing Situation Today*, pp. 1, 2. Published by the Better Housing League, Cincinnati, December, 1925.
[33] *Bureau Publications*, No. 125, 1923, p. 1.

years used up in order to provide family maintenance, but sometimes "the home whose purchase represented the fulfilment of the family's ambitions (had) been sacrificed." Worse than all else was the effect of the prolonged period of unemployment on the family morale—"the father idle about the house, unsettled, disheartened; the mother going out to work if she can secure it, and using up every bit of her strength in the double task of providing for the family's maintenance and caring for the household and the children; the children suffering from the depression and uncertainty of what the future may mean, which is even more to be dreaded than the discomforts of the immediate present." [34]

In these 356 families where the father could not find work, twenty-nine percent of the mothers in Racine and thirty-seven percent in Spring-field were gainfully employed. Of the 116 working mothers in the two cities, however, twenty-two percent had been employed before the father's loss of work, leaving seventy-eight percent who had been forced to find employment because the husband was idle. No doubt many more women would have secured work had it been obtainable; but, owing to the fact that the prevailing industrial depression had reacted unfavorably upon middle-class families, which could not afford to employ the usual assistance in their homes, the employment agencies reported that it was very difficult for wage-earning women to secure work.

The effects of the employment of these mothers were far from beneficial to the families dependent upon their work at home. Under the care of the ninety-one women working away from home were 104 little children under five years of age—twelve of these being under one year, and thirty-two being between one and two years old. These little ones were cared for part of the day by the father, a neighbor, a relative, a paid caretaker, an older child or (in seven cases) by a day nursery. The family histories of several of these households have been recorded in detail by the Bureau. Perhaps this one will suffice to show the home conditions:

"The father has had blood poisoning since he lost his job, the 3-year-old girl fell and cut her face and eye while the mother was at work, and the year-old child has had a crushed hand. The family has had fewer comforts than ever before and nothing but the absolute essentials." [35]

Not alone the mother, but the older children in school are compelled to find employment when the father is out of work. In the 356 families included in the study there were 148 children fourteen to seventeen years

[34] "Unemployment and Child Welfare," *Bureau Publications,* No. 125, 1923, p. 3.
[35] *Ibid.,* p. 51.

of age. Of these, forty-five had been regularly employed at some time during the father's unemployment and forty-two made some contribution toward the family's support by working after school, on Saturdays or during vacations. Twenty-two of the children who had worked on regular permits had left school to go to work. It must not be forgotten that the Bureau's study was made of the families of *skilled workmen* making relatively high wages of from $100 to $175 a month before the period of depression. Therefore every effort would be made in these intelligent groups to keep the children in school as long as possible. Among the unskilled workers the proportion of children engaged in low-paid employments was probably much higher.

According to the United States Census of 1920 over one million (1,060,858) children under fifteen years of age were gainfully employed. Of this army of child workers 378,063 were from ten to thirteen years of age! It does not require a gifted imagination to picture the consequences of such child labor, not only to the child himself but to the family that he will establish in the future. Deprived of liberal opportunities for mental development in the years when his intellect is, perhaps, most active, deprived of enlightened moral direction when he most needs it, required to work long hours at monotonous tasks when his growing body cries out for fresh air and exercise, the child laborer discounts the future to pay for present subsistence. It is not reasonable to hope that young children who are regularly employed in factories, canneries and stores, not to mention beet sugar fields and cranberry bogs, will grow into vigorous and intelligent manhood and womanhood nor that they will escape the snares of the street and the low amusement resort that are laid for the ignorant and the untrained. These children of the nation are badly prepared to become the fathers and mothers of the next generation.

IV. Urban Life and the Family.

As we have seen, urban life is almost identical with industry, since where great industrial plants are established, there large towns and cities tend to grow up. Thousands of men and women flock to these centers for employment and, in the absence of civic housing commissions, empowered to furnish decent homes for these laborers, there follow, as inevitable consequences, dangerous segregation and unsanitary slums. In cities, where density of population is greatest, morbidity and mortality tend to increase and infectious diseases spread most easily.

The unwholesome effects of tenement-house living in our slum districts might be mitigated if there were a sufficient number of parks and playgrounds to which tenement dwellers could resort without expense and loss of time. But here, again, city life tends to react unfavorably upon individuals and families. Although much has been done in many of our large industrial centers, notably Chicago, to bring air, space and sunshine within the reach of every citizen, something remains to be done in not a few cities. In 1923 the United States Bureau of Education sought to discover, by means of a questionnaire sent to superintendents of schools, how many cities with a population of 30,000 or over were maintaining playgrounds, other than school playgrounds, out of public funds. Of the seventy cities having a population of 100,000 or more, fifty-eight replied and fifty-two of this number stated that municipal playgrounds were maintained with public funds. Of the cities having a population between 30,000 and 100,000, 128 replied to the questionnaire, and of this number ninety-seven cities were maintaining municipal playgrounds. This means that at least seventy-five percent of our largest cities and nearly seventy-six percent of our smaller cities are awake to the need of play spaces for children. Unfortunately the Bureau did not investigate the adequacy of these playgrounds in point of numbers and location to meet the needs of all the children in our centers of population. The study did, however, bring out the facts that (1) a wide disparity of standards exists with respect to the amount of play space necessary for each child and (2) marked differences exist in the provisions for a trained director of sports and games.[36]

The special report on "Birth, Stillbirth and Infant Mortality Statistics" issued by the United States Bureau of the Census for 1923, gives the birth-rates in cities and in rural districts over a period from 1915 to 1923 inclusive. These show that in every year of this period the rural birth-rate per 1,000 population has fallen *below* the urban, probably because the age composition in rural sections is unfavorable to fecundity. The rates for 1922 and 1923 follow:

1922		1923	
Cities	22.7	Cities	22.7
Rural districts	22.3	Rural districts	21.8

It would seem then, that, in the United States at least, fecundity is not adversely affected by city life.

The question as to whether divorces are more numerous in urban centers than in rural districts is of interest to the student of social prob-

[36] J. F. Rogers, "Municipal and School Playgrounds and Their Management," pp. 5, 9. *School Health Studies*, No. 6, 1924, United States Bureau of Education.

lems. The latest census figures available [37] show high divorce rates in agricultural states in which few large cities are located. Thus Kansas has one divorce to every 5.9 marriages; Iowa, one to every 5.3; Texas, one to 4.6; Nebraska, one to 6; and Missouri, one to 4.12. These are high rates when compared with the country at large. Probably much more intensive research must be undertaken, however, before a reliable conclusion can be reached concerning the effect of urban life on divorce.

One important outcome of city dwelling remains to be briefly considered. It can hardly be doubted that our "modern Babylons," with their huge populations, develop *mass habits* which insidiously undermine family life. It has been said that "men work in crowds, eat in crowds, seek recreation in crowds, and satisfy sex impulse in public brothels." Among the wealthy in our largest cities, such as New York, Chicago, Detroit and San Francisco, meals are more and more often eaten in hotels and fashionable restaurants; dinners, bridge parties, dances and even marriages take place in public resorts with ever increasing frequency. A great metropolitan daily recently published a racy article on the theme "Dining Out with Kitchenless New York." After describing the disappearance of the old-fashioned kitchen from the homes of all but the prosperous, the writer continues:

"How often do you hear in New York of big dinners, fashionable dinners, at private homes? Even the luncheons and suppers are given at public or semi-public places. A single New York hotel, aware of this demand, has forty-two private dining rooms and banquet halls, and others are hardly less amply supplied; in addition and supplementary to which there are scores of descendants of Delmonico's." [38]

Needless to say life *en masse* is even more general among the poor. In the ranks of the unskilled laborers, homes are places in which to snatch a hasty meal, to find a corner of bed or floor or table not preëmpted by family members or lodgers on which to sleep—and then to get away from it to the street, the factory, the cheap amusement place. Even the middle-class home in our largest cities is being profoundly affected by the trend toward public mass living and eating. To quote once more from the *Times* article:

"On every hand apartment houses and apartment hotels spring up with amazing speed, sometimes to amazing proportions. Old houses are being remodeled by the thousand into small suites, and in them not even the kitchenette is to be found.

[37] Census Report on Marriage and Divorce, 1925.
[38] *New York Times,* Magazine Section, January 25, 1925.

"Here, in dwellings that once sheltered families of means, and probably of size, with a cook for each family and a minor tribe of servants, even 'light housekeeping' is forbidden. The law requires expensive and unsightly fire-escapes front and back if there be more than one kitchen apparatus on the premises. The tenant is forbidden to enjoy so much as the modest comfort of an electric toaster. But the real estate agent and the 'superintendent,' meaning the janitor, seldom incline to take the rule too seriously. It is tacitly understood that breakfast and perhaps lunch will be prepared at home. Everybody does it. The economies effected by enduring the cramped quarters of a suite would be dissipated were it necessary to take all the meals at a restaurant. And so New York, the heaven of the bootlegger, is coming to be also the haven of the 'cooklegger.'

"Canned food and the delicatessen do the rest. The living room is also the dining room and the kitchenette. But as a rule the 'familette' goes out to dinner, and as a consequence there has come into existence here a kind of restaurant specially dedicated to the kitchenless, an asylum for those who will never know the kind of pie mother used to make.

"It is an institution indigenous to New York, and apparently peculiar to it. Other cities have their counterparts of Sherry's and Pierre's, their likenesses to the chain restaurants which besprinkle this island; and everywhere will be found lunch rooms for the business man of all degrees, from the clerk to the corporation executive; but where else will be found places calculated solely to catch the dinner trade of the kitchenless middle-class family? Where but in New York?

"So uptown, anywhere uptown from the West Sixties to the Hundreds, this singular establishment is to be found on every hand. Enter between 6 and 7 of an evening, scan the menu and observe the guests. From the bill of fare you will find that a table d'hôte dinner may be had for 85 cents or $1, and that a meal may be ordered à la carte within the bounds of middle-class Manhattan salaries. You must remember that most New Yorkers pay half their income for rent nowadays, instead of the good old domestic-science maximum of one-fourth. The rapacious landlord takes this toll despite the abolition of the kitchen.

"Enter now the children of Father Knickerbocker—a floor manager in a department store, his idle and discontented wife; their daughter, who is a filing clerk in a downtown warren of concrete and steel; and their son, from whose chaff a dispirited Columbia Faculty is trying to winnow a grain of usefulness. They scan the bill of fare with varying degrees of intensity or distaste, and eat amid a monosyllabic silence. The girl pays her own check.

"The four are a slice of that vast people, New York's middle class. It was said once that the English were like a keg of their own ale, mostly froth at the top and dregs at the bottom, but thoroughly sound in the middle. The population of this town is more like a bottle of fermented buttermilk, an artificial product throughout but advertised as healthful. If the kitchenette spreads over the country, as the Playgrounds and Recreation folk fear it will, and then tends to vanish as it is doing here, what is to be the fate of a nation founded upon the family?"

What will be the psychological and social outcomes of such continuous mass living? asks the student of social conditions. What the effect upon marriage and the family? The most resolute advocate of the *status quo* will hardly maintain that the intimate family associations of bygone times can be so metamorphosed in our huge cities without profoundly affecting the family institution. Unquestionably the rising generation is destined to see a further transformation of family life brought about, in part, by the widespread development of mass habits of living and thinking in congested centers of population. Nor can it be asserted too casually that such changes will prove either disastrous or beneficial. Neither the dark prophecies of the reactionary nor the easy optimism of the advocates of social change should determine the judgment of intelligent men and women with regard to this many-sided question. We need not only more concrete evidence concerning the social causes of family change, but we need also to develop still further an objective attitude toward the study of family problems. Whether the family of the future succeeds or fails depends in no small measure upon a far more general spread of exact knowledge with respect to the social conditions that impede its functioning.

TOPICS FOR REPORTS

1. The Unemployment Problem and the Home.
    Robert Bruère, "Reanchoring the Home," in *Harper's Magazine,* Vol. 124, pp. 918-24, May, 1912.
2. The Distribution of the Income among Families.
    Willford I. King, *The Wealth and Income of the People of the United States,* Ch. IX. The Macmillan Co., New York, 1915.
3. Effects of a Surplus on the Worker's Family.
    Simon N. Patten, *The New Basis of Civilization,* pp. 41-61. The Macmillan Co., New York, 1907.
4. How to Get Better Houses.
    Edith Elmer Wood, in *Journal of Home Economics,* Vol. XVI, No. 1, January, 1924.

CHAPTER IX

THE IMMIGRANT FAMILY

THE IMMIGRANT STREAM

LIKE a deep-moving tide the flow of immigration to this "promised land" has swelled with every passing year since the end of the nineteenth century. The stream reached its peak in 1907, when 1,285,349 foreign-born men, women and children entered the gates of America; and that height was again almost reached in 1914 when 1,218,489 immigrants were admitted at our ports. Since that time the tide has never risen so high, owing first to the World War and later to the restrictive legislation enacted by Congress in 1921, which reduced the army of incoming potential citizens to 304,488 in 1925-26.[1] Two important changes may be noted in the character of the immigrant stream since it first flowed strongly toward the New World: (1) a change in the dominant motive for immigration, and (2) a change in the racial elements involved. Until well past the middle of the nineteenth century the motives driving men and women to leave their home lands for a new start in America were religious and political as well as economic. These immigrants were a group selected, more or less, by their pioneer spirit and their unwillingness to submit to tyrannical institutions. But for many years past immigrants have come to our shores for almost purely economic motives—to make a better living for themselves and their children than it was possible to make in the country of their birth. However, it should not be overlooked that "a better living" in the minds of many a Russian, Rumanian, Polish or Italian parent has meant not alone securing material necessities and comforts, but obtaining for their children those educational opportunities that were all but denied them in their native land.

The second change has to do with the racial composition of the immigrant body. Since 1883 the falling off in the proportion of immigrants from western Europe and the increase in the ratio of those coming from southern and southeastern Europe has startled those sociologists who hold the theory of "Nordic superiority" and supremacy. Prior to 1883

[1] The Report of the Immigration Commissioner for 1926 has reference to a year running from June 30, 1925, to June 30, 1926.

132

about ninety-five percent of our immigration came from the United Kingdom, Belgium, France, Germany, Denmark, Norway, Sweden, the Netherlands and Switzerland;[2] whereas in 1907 no less than eighty-one percent of European immigrants were natives of Russia, Bulgaria, Rumania, Serbia, Poland, Greece, Italy, Spain, Turkey and Syria.

A change has also taken place with regard to the occupations the foreign-born are fitted to carry on in their adopted country. During the decade 1899-1909 the immigrants from western Europe—the so-called "old immigration"—showed a relatively high percentage of skilled laborers (19.5) when compared with the "new immigration," which contained only 8.9% of skilled labor. On the other hand, the old immigration contained only 6.1% of experienced farm laborers, as against 23.1% in the new immigration.[3] This disparity assumes significance when we recall that America's supply of unappropriated land had shrunk by 1922 to less than one-third the area of 1890.[4] These farming peasants of Poland, Hungary, Bulgaria and the other Slavic countries, skilled in intensive agriculture, find that the most active demand for their labor comes from the textile manufacturing cities of New England, the great steel and iron towns, the mining centers of Pennsylvania, West Virginia and Illinois. If that man is most happy and efficient who performs the work he is trained to do and enjoys doing, this last change can hardly be regarded as beneficial, either to the individual laborer or to industry.

In the decade preceding the World War, immigration to the United States reached such proportions that assimilation of the new races became increasingly difficult. Over one million immigrants were entering the port of New York every year. Diverse in languages, customs and national traditions, this enormous army of peoples could not be readily incorporated into the body of American life. Many of the immigrant groups were illiterate peasant farmers who found adjustment to New World conditions difficult and the language of their adopted country hard to acquire. Therefore the vast incoming army split up into "colonies" dwelling in sections of our large industrial cities, especially New York and Chicago, and striving to maintain, so far as possible, their own language and national customs. Economists are apparently agreed that unrestricted immigration in the years before 1914 was responsible not only for the presence in our midst of large bodies of only partially assimilated aliens, but

[2] See the graphs in E. A. Ross's *The Old World in the New*, pp. 45, 66, 92. The Century Co., New York, 1914.
[3] Jeremiah W. Jenks and W. Jett Lauck, *The Immigration Problem*, p. 32. Funk & Wagnalls Co., New York and London, 1922 (5th edition).
[4] See *Statistical Abstract of the United States* (1922), p. 17.

for the depreciation of wages in the ranks of unskilled labor. It is highly questionable whether real wages would have risen approximately ten percent since 1920 (see *ante*, p. 114) had not the army of immigrants seeking access to America after the World War been drastically reduced.

IMMIGRANT BACKGROUNDS

If the student of social conditions would understand the strange and difficult situation in which the immigrant family from Poland or Italy finds itself on entering the gates of America, he should acquaint himself with the social heritage of these family groups. These people have a cultural background that is always interesting, sometimes colorful and not rarely superior at certain points to our own. Many of the immigrants from southeastern Europe, as we have seen, are farm laborers whose families have for generations cultivated intensively tiny farms of four to eight acres. Only the impossibility of feeding a family group numbering anywhere from five to twelve souls on these farms has driven the peasant farmers to abandon their family acres and seek their fortunes across the sea. Among all these races inhabiting the European countries from Russia and Poland on the east to Italy and Portugal on the south, familial and communal solidarity is very strong. The family comprises not alone the individual family or *Länderfamilie,* comprising father, mother and children, but all the members of a family group in the ascending and descending lines—the joint family. Thus there may be found under one roof three generations or more, from the grandparents, or great-grandparents, to the newest grandson. Such a familial group has a common interest in the land, which all the able-bodied members till, and on the fruits of which they live. In a joint family of this type, the individual may well be submerged in the group and his personal growth sacrificed to it. On the other hand, family life has a solidarity, a community of interest and of labor, that is rarely seen in the New World.

The familial group is reproduced in the large in the communal group. These peasant families live in compact villages, where everyone knows his neighbors and is under strong social pressure to conform to group custom and take part in group life. Village dances and festivals are common, and are participated in by whole families. Ancient folk songs are known and sung by all. Life in southern lands is largely spent out-of-doors in the warm sunshine, and is filled with wholesome labor on the land. Here is a description given by an Italian of village life in his native land:

"In his home village the Italian slept with his family crowded in one room. That did not hurt him or his family, for they did not live in the room, as they are compelled to do here by the bitter climate; they just slept there for a few hours. During the short, cool Italian nights only were they inside. Life was spent working, eating, and resting in the open air. The sturdy peasant in Italy ate the fruits of his *orto,* drank the wine of his vineyard, wore the wool of his sheep. . . . Early in the morning he called out to his friends across the street as he went to the field. No one was disturbed by it. People were up early in the village. He sang as he crossed the village going to work and coming back; the *stornello* of his friend answered his song." [5]

With a few changes in detail, this picture would serve equally well to depict communal life in the Slavic villages in Poland, Rumania or Serbia, which is characterized by simplicity, solidarity and a high degree of sociability. When milk is wanted, the family cow or goat supplies it, fresh and warm, to children and adults. No public control is exercised over the milk supply or over the disposal of garbage and refuse. That is a family matter. The garbage may be fed to the pig and the refuse may be burnt; or it may all be thrown out near the house. With this important matter the community does not interfere.

In the towns and larger villages of certain European countries, cultural opportunities are probably more numerous and more generally utilized than in America. The great music of the nation and something of its art and literature are known to very humble folk who swell our immigrant tide. A Swedish colony settled in Kansas, mindful of the musical traditions of the mother country, have for thirty years given Handel's "Messiah" during Easter week with a chorus of 500 voices. The chorus is recruited from the farmers, artisans, merchants and housewives of the town and countryside. This joyful community tribute to the Muses was surely not learned in Kansas; it must have been brought from music-loving Sweden. [6]

One more picture may be added to help the reader to piece out this meager sketch of social backgrounds. An Italian tailor, living on the East Side of New York, is speaking:

"In Italy I live in small town—six, seven thousand. It take not much money to live. We pay the rent once a year, only little money. We have fine garden, we live healthy, happy. I obey my mother's word, which is

[5] Michael M. Davis, *Immigrant Health and the Community,* pp. 113-4. Harper & Brothers, New York, 1921. Now published by the Carnegie Corporation of New York. By permission.

[6] Robert E. Park and Henry A. Miller, *Old World Traits Transplanted,* pp. 12, 13. Harper & Brothers, New York, 1921. Now published by the Carnegie Corporation of New York.

like the God. . . . We work little bit, then we take the leisure. We love very much the music, art, poetry. We love the poetical life—poetry today, and tomorrow we take what's coming with the good patience. The way I mean is not only to read the books of the great poets, of Dante that we love more than a father, or Petrarcha, Ariosto, Tasso, Alfieri, and so many others down to Mangoni, Carducci, Giusti, D'Annunzio, but the poetry of the beautiful scenery in the country, the poetry of the music, the poetry of the friendship. Even in the small town we have band and philharmonica. Not to know the musical works of Rossini, like 'Barbiere di Seviglia' and 'Guglielmo Tell' is not to know anything." [7]

FIRST IMPRESSIONS OF AMERICA

Reared thus in a simple, communal society, scores of thousands of immigrants enter the ports of America every year and find themselves in an environment bewilderingly different from anything they have known. A fraction of this host of men, women and children comes singly, hoping to earn enough in the new land to send for a near relation, or perhaps for the whole family except the grandparents. Many, however, come in families, and it is with this group that we are specially concerned. How does America receive these potential citizens, dazed by the noise, hurry and strangeness of our port cities, ignorant of the language and perhaps knowing not a soul? Sophonisba Breckinridge, who has studied the immigrant problem at first hand, tells us:

"With few exceptions no provision by native Americans has been made for their reception in their new places of residence. Communities of kindly-intentioned persons, because of their lack of imagination and their indifference, have allowed the old, the young, the mother and infant to come in by back ways, at any hour of day or night. Frequently they have been received by uncomprehending or indifferent railroad officials or oversolicitous exploiters. . . . Their reception, however, need not be an impossible task. On their arrival they are formally admitted, and information as to their origin and destination must be supplied. Methods could be devised for receiving them in such a way as to make them feel at ease, and for interpreting to them the changed surroundings in which they must find a home and a job in the shortest possible time." [8]

The outcome of our method of receiving these immigrant families, our apparent indifference to their forlorn ignorance of what to say, what

[7] Quoted in Park and Miller, *op. cit.*, pp. 11, 12. By permission of the Carnegie Corporation of New York.
[8] S. Breckinridge, *New Homes for Old*, pp. 1-2. Carnegie Corporation of New York, 1921. By permission.

to do, where to go, is the beginning of that alienation of the foreign-born from the native-born, that failure to understand each other that is so characteristic of American social life. It results in the newcomers huddling together with those who speak their own tongue and are familiar with their own social heritage. Thus we have "colonies" in our large industrial cities, in our steel towns, in our mining camps, made up of Russians, Poles, Italians, Hungarians and all the other peoples who flock here— those of each nationality in their own section, speaking the language of their country and striving to preserve, more or less, its folkways. Not until the Great War did the American people awake to the evils of this system, to the disunity of interest, of standards and of social habits that it implies. There followed a nation-wide effort toward "Americanization" of the immigrant—an attempt to instruct him in the language, the customs and the traditions of the American people, which has not met with a notable degree of success.

LIVING CONDITIONS IN THE NEW WORLD

Most of our immigrants settle in the territory east of the Mississippi and north of the Potomac and Ohio rivers, although there are large immigrant colonies in the coal-mining districts of Alabama, Oklahoma, Arkansas and West Virginia. As we have seen, foreigners tend to form communities of their own in the poorer quarters of industrial cities; or, as in the bituminous and anthracite coal-mining regions, they establish new settlements composed wholly of Slavs, Magyars, Italians around mines or industrial plants.

Let us imagine an immigrant family seeking to establish itself in one of our great industrial centers—New York, Detroit, Pittsburgh or Chicago. Its first problem will be to find shelter. What homes are available for these newcomers? In general they are of two types: (1) the old family homes once occupied by prosperous citizens and now remodeled into tenements accommodating several families, or (2) tenements specially built for wage-earners. The first of these quite commonly provide miserable living conditions. The spacious, light, airy rooms of the old family house are divided and subdivided into small rooms, frequently dark and without proper ventilation. Toilets for the common use of several families are provided in the hallways, and running water is furnished likewise in the dark halls for the use of all the tenants on the floor. "Into these patched-up structures," says Davis, "crowd the immigrants, accustomed to the outdoors and agricultural life, ignorant of urban sanitation and toilet facilities." [9] Since the Tenement House Law of 1901 was enacted,

[9] Davis, *op. cit.,* p. 77.

New York's more recently built tenements are an improvement on these improvised flats; but they, too, have semi-dark rooms, opening on narrow, foul-smelling courts, and quite inadequate ventilation, washing facilities and toilets.

In 1919 the Reconstruction Commission of the State of New York made a tenement house survey in New York City and issued a preliminary report in the form of an address delivered by its chairman, Abram I. Elkus, before a meeting of the Commission. Extracts from this report are worth quoting:

"By the time this work is completed we will have visited 1700 houses, consisting of about 34,000 apartments, accommodating between 175,000 and 200,000 persons.

"In innumerable instances families are crowded together in dark, ill-smelling apartments and are unable to find other quarters. . . . To a great extent vacancies exist in Italian and other foreign districts. . . . Thus it is evident that the immigrants who have once known better quarters than the slums cannot be induced to live in them again. It is in the regions occupied by the newly arrived immigrants that the most miserable tenements are found. . . . All of these apartments have interior, dark rooms, but these exist in practically every neighborhood that was investigated by the committee. In a block in the East Forties vacancies existed in houses of a similar type. Very often they were caused by a lack of proper sanitary and toilet facilities. These were situated very often in the yards and were used by a number of families. The rooms in the vacant apartments are dark and in many cases damp. Practically all the houses were in need of repair. . . . A study of a block in the East Forties gives some very good examples of conditions difficult to remedy. The thirty-six tenement houses in this block are all old brick houses built before 1901 and showing all the evils of the 'old law' tenement construction. The lighting is particularly bad. Of some 1,200 rooms in the block, 600 have indirect lighting—that is, they have no windows opening to the outer air, only the so-called windows opening on to another room. Of the other 600 rooms, only half have windows to the street. The others open on a back yard or on a court. Of course, these 600 dark rooms must be used. It is evident that at least 600 people and probably a great many more, since at least, often two, three, and sometimes four people sleep in these dark bedrooms, are compelled to sleep under unsanitary conditions, no matter how well they keep their apartments." [10]

[10] Quoted in Davis, *op. cit.*, pp. 79, 80. By permission of the Carnegie Corporation of New York.

Into these dingy, unsanitary tenements crowd families of Polish peasant farmers and their children, and sun-loving Italians and Portuguese. Bewildered in their strange surroundings, unacquainted with the conveniences of running water, bathtubs (in a few "model apartments"), gas fixtures, garbage and waste removal by city agencies, it is no wonder that these simple people make mistakes. Some of the housewives probably have (as in the oft-told tale) used a rare bathtub for storing coal. They have been accustomed to wash both children and clothing in the running streams near their village homes. Italians no doubt have thrown refuse into the small yards back of the tenements; that has been the common practice under less crowded conditions in the villages of the mother country. Many an immigrant mother has blown out the gas to the imminent danger of her family. In our American impatience with these "stupidities" we have lost sight of their causes. Habit, daily custom, in adults is the most powerful determinant of their actions. This is as true of cleanly, educated Americans as it is of uncleanly, ignorant Poles, Lithuanians and Serbs. We approve of and cling to those folkways in which we have been born and bred. Education in the forming of new habits is what is needed. It would seem possible, as Miss Breckinridge suggests,[11] for "the rent collector or a sanitary inspector with a social point of view to establish friendly relations on their regular visits to the families. With confidence gained and tact displayed, much in the way of education could be accomplished." But if this seems too wild a dream, surely it is feasible for the city to organize a system of immigrant home visiting carried on by trained and sympathetic agents who understand the language of the immigrants as well as their home conditions in the old country. Such visitors, if they were endowed with tact and monumental patience, could do wonders in helping immigrant housewives to adjust to the unfamiliar living conditions of their adopted land.

The problem of these housewives is, of course, greatly complicated if the husband's wages are too low to support the family. In such a case, only too frequent, the wife has one of two alternatives—she may take in lodgers or she may go to work. The consequences of keeping lodgers have already been briefly described in a previous chapter. Overcrowding, the utter absence of privacy for adults and children and sometimes sexual promiscuity are the outcomes. Overcrowding, to be sure, frequently exists in immigrant homes even when no roomers are received into the family. The report of the United States Immigration Commission made in 1910 showed that 32.8% of immigrant families had at least three persons sleep-

[11] Breckinridge, *op. cit.*, p. 81.

ing in one bedroom, while among the Slovenians 13.8% had *five or more* in one sleeping room and 5.2% had actually *six or more* sleeping in one room. A recent study of more than 15,000 immigrant households revealed the fact that 32.9% kept lodgers or boarders. The Serbs showed the highest percentage, 92.8, and the Rumanians and Croatians came next with percentages of 77.9 and 59.5 respectively.[12]

It is not reasonable to suppose that strangers are permanently received into immigrant families, already crowded, for reasons of hospitality or gregariousness. The all-powerful motives, it can hardly be doubted, are economic necessity or the urgent desire of the parents to save for a home of their own at some time in the future. But, whatever the motive, the results are the same—the break-up of any real family life, disorder, the massing of human beings together, and an enormous increase in the already heavy labors of the housewife. With reference to this last point, the Children's Bureau Publication on "Infant Mortality in Johnstown, Pennsylvania," describes the exhausting work of the Serbo-Croatian woman who "makes up the beds, does the washing and ironing, and buys and prepares the food for all the lodgers. . . . In a working man's family, it is sometimes said, the woman's work-day is two hours longer than the man's. But if this statement is correct in general, the augmentation stated is insufficient in these abnormal homes where the women are required to have many meals and dinner buckets ready at irregular hours to accommodate men working on different shifts." [13] The report adds that the infant mortality rate among the Serbo-Croatian women, who carry on more of this laborious work than any other foreign-born women, is 263.9, as compared with a rate of 171.3 for all the immigrant women. Should the babies of Serbo-Croatian mothers be excluded, the infant mortality rate for these groups would fall to 159.7.

PROBLEMS OF FOOD AND CLOTHING

Difficult as must be the adjustment of immigrant families to industrial life after that of farming, and to the novel housing conditions that meet them in our industrial cities, their difficulties are by no means at an end after these adaptations have been more or less successfully made. The purchase and preparation of food and clothing call for a large number of new adjustments. The housewife is confronted with a confusing array of unfamiliar foods of the value of which she is quite ignorant. Changes in the family diet are forced upon her by circumstances and these changes

[12] See Jenks and Lauck, *op. cit.*, pp. 141-2.
[13] *Bureau Publications*, No. 9, p. 29.

are by no means always for the best. The family soup-kettle gives way to the coffee-pot, left on the stove all day; and its stimulating contents are fed even to babies. In the home lands of many immigrants, vegetables, fruits, milk and cheese were produced on the farm and were plentiful and fresh; whereas meat was almost prohibitive in price and was rarely used. In America, meat is much more freely eaten and fresh vegetables, not always easy to get and rather expensive, are less staple articles of diet. No doubt an unbalanced dietary is only too often the result of these new circumstances; and canned food or delicatessen products come to play a large part in feeding the immigrant family, especially if the mother is working outside the home.

When the foreign-born housewife goes out to buy food for the family, she is apt to seek a store in her neighborhood where she is reasonably certain of finding someone to serve her who speaks her own language. An astonishing number of grocery stores, delicatessen shops and meat markets may be found within an area of a mile or so, serving the needs of Poles, Russians, Slovaks, Italians and other races who may inhabit that district. As the housewife has little or no storage space in her apartment, she buys food to last from meal to meal, or at most for one day. This is expensive buying, as every experienced housekeeper knows. Then again, as she has little ready money, she buys on credit, presenting to the salesman her small account book, in which he enters the amount of the purchase but not the thing bought. Breckinridge points out that under this system there is "every chance for inaccurate entry" as well as for extravagant buying. The quality of food in many of the neighborhood stores that serve the foreign-born is poor, as well as expensive. Fresh vegetables are hard to secure, except in the Italian quarter, where the stores have a surprising variety of fruits and fresh vegetables, notably salad greens, all the year round.

No doubt Professor Breckinridge is correct in her belief that one ill effect of organizing these neighborhood stores on a nationality basis "is to prevent the members of one group from gaining the advantage of dietetically better practices followed in other groups." [14] For instance the Lithuanians eat much meat, canned goods and rye bread, but little or no fresh vegetables. Although a Lithuanian store may be in the same block with an Italian, the former does not borrow from its neighbor the excellent custom of offering fresh vegetables in abundance, largely because of national barriers in language and tradition. Breckinridge deplores the fact that although the food demands of a family in most instances require

[14] Breckinridge, *op. cit.*, p. 128.

an expenditure of forty percent of the income, little aid if any is given to the foreign-born housewife "in the matter of adapting the diet of her family to American or dietetic requirements."

"It is clear," she writes, "that the retail trade, being unstandardized, gives no help to the immigrant woman in the matter of efficient buying. There is as yet no fine art of service in this field based on careful accounting of cost and service. Obviously there is great waste in the number of stores, in the number of persons engaged in conducting them, in the needless duplication of even such meager equipment as is found in them. This waste will reflect itself in needlessly high prices which, while they mulct the buyer, bring the seller little gain." [15]

Difficulties in the matter of purchase of clothing also bristle in the path of the housewife. Most of our immigrants are accustomed to a distinctive type of dress by which they may be known as Czecho-Slovakian, Polish and the like. On reaching America they soon discover that everyone dresses as much alike as possible in the latest prevailing mode. Durability in textiles is sacrificed for flimsiness, and the old-country dress, still with plenty of "wear" in it, is speedily thrown aside for the newest American fashion. This is especially true of the young sons and daughters in foreign-born families, who are not slow to learn that if they would not be stigmatized as queer and alien they must conform in dress to American standards, which quite often are beyond the meager family income. Probably the question of dress causes more friction between parents, with old-country standards, and children, who are rapidly acquiring the extravagant notions of the new, than any other subject. The mother usually capitulates and buys for her girls showy gowns and shoes that are poor but by no means cheap imitations of similar articles of apparel in that uptown district of fashion which she has never dared to visit.

NEW ADJUSTMENTS WITHIN THE FAMILY

In most of the lands of southern and eastern Europe from which, prior to 1921, the great majority of our immigrants came, the patriarchal family system is still firmly established. As a matter of course the father dominates the household, meting out punishment to both wife and children when they act counter to his will. If any money comes into the family through the labors of any of its members he appropriates it, as he does any little property his wife may have brought in marriage.

When the Poles, Jews, Lithuanians and Italians who hold to these patriarchal ideas and customs have lived but a little while in America they

[15] Breckinridge, *op. cit.*, pp. 128-9.

become dimly aware of other standards of family relationships than any they have known. Sooner or later—sometimes very late—foreign-born husbands and wives learn that in most American states the separate rights of the married woman are carefully protected; that a man may not beat his wife or deprive her of her property or earnings. They learn, too, that protection is given to the children against cruelty and exploitation. It must be a matter of bewildering surprise to immigrant parents when they first are brought face to face with the fact that in their adopted country the State constitutes itself an over-parent, reserving the right to protect children from unreasonable discipline, to ensure a minimum of proper care for them, and to enforce a law, quite unfamiliar to these parents, compelling them to send their children to school and keep them there. Every one of these regulations encroaches upon the age-old authority of parents to care for and train their children as they see fit. Furthermore it prevents, at least in part, that early exploitation of children for the benefit of the parents, so common among the Poles, who look forward to stopping work before they are old in order to live on the wages of their children.

Not only is the foreign-born father in America restricted in his authority by the State, he is also compelled by the law to support both his wife and children. Uninstructed in the family law of his new country, he may learn to his cost that desertion or refusal to support his family constitutes an offense punishable by fine or imprisonment. In the old country, where the well-being of the family as a whole counts for more than the personal development of the individuals who compose it, a father may deny his children an education and keep them at hard work in the fields to support a household including dependent grandparents and unmarried or widowed aunts. Not so in the new land. On every hand parents learn that their authority is curbed and that they must adjust themselves to a new and perplexing situation which demands larger freedom and fuller opportunity for minor children. Sometimes these adjustments are made gradually and without too much bitterness and conflict. Sometimes, as Breckinridge points out, the parents, ignorant of the law and confusedly aware of only one thing—that they cannot rule their children in America as they did in Russia or Italy—remove all restraints and let their boys and girls go very much their own away, without either the old arbitrary control or any intelligent help from their parents in acquiring a sense of responsibility for their actions. This latter group, fortunately, is in the minority. Another method of dealing with the problem of parental authority is the uncompromising one adopted by the Italians and Jugo-Slavs, who are said very generally to enforce upon wives and children the same repressive discipline with which they are familiar in the mother country. It is notorious that Italian girls are strictly brought up and guarded in America, and are married off by their parents at an early age quite in the manner of the sixteenth century.

Whatever the policy adopted, the problem of intra-family adjustments is rendered more difficult by the fact that the children in immigrant families learn the language and acquire the new attitudes and habits of America far more readily than do their less plastic parents. This gives boys and girls a tremendous advantage within the family council, and not rarely induces them to believe that they are more intelligent than their parents, upon whom they look down at times with conscious superiority. Such a situation is more apt to develop in the relations of children with the mother than with the father. The latter is forced by the exigencies of his work to learn enough English to get about freely, whereas the mother, tied to the home and the neighborhood by her tasks, rarely if ever meeting native-born Americans of more than a generation back, is living under precisely the circumstances that would make the learning of a new language most arduous and most unlikely. "She doesn't understand," is a phrase very often on the lips of children when referring to their mothers, who persist in wearing the dress, carrying on the customs and speaking the language of their native land. This attitude of scornful superiority is strengthened in some children by the fact that they are called upon to serve as interpreters when the truant officer, the district nurse or the rent collector visits the home. It is not surprising that these boys and girls should jump to the conclusion that, since they have more knowledge of the language of America, they know more about everything that is worth knowing. But if the situation is not surprising, it is sometimes poignantly pathetic. Park and Miller quote from the *Forward* of July 9, 1917, an account of the unhappiness of two Jewish parents whose sixteen-year-old daughter emigrated to America two years ahead of them. The mother speaks:

"My husband began to earn little by little. We fixed up a nice home and I was happy because I could see my daughter. But soon I realized that my big pretty daughter is not the girl I knew; she has changed entirely. During the few years that she was here without us she became a regular Yankee and forgot how to talk Yiddish. I talk to her in Yiddish and she replies in English. . . . So I ask her: 'Daughter of mine, talk Yiddish to me and I will understand you.' She says that it is not nice to talk Yiddish and that I am a greenhorn. And that is not all. She does worse things. She wants to make a Christian woman out of me. She does not like to have me light the Sabbath candles, to observe the Sabbath. When I light the candles she blows them out. She does all the things that I do not want, that cause me the greatest heartache. And she argues with me. She says that because I and my husband are pious and have a Jewish home, she can never invite a boy acquaintance to her house; she is ashamed. She makes fun of me and her father. She calls us greenhorns and is ashamed of us." [16]

Here is tragedy—the dumb suffering of two parents, who love their old-world ideals and folkways, inflicted on them by a beloved daughter whom every passing day in the freer air of America alienates more completely from the habits and beliefs of her people. To the tension that is present in greater or less degree in every home where adolescent youth and settled age come into conflict, is added the far greater strain caused by a sharp divergence in fundamental attitudes and ideas between immigrant parents and their children. Such parents need help from wise, understanding social workers, preferably chosen from among their own people, who are successfully adapted to American life, and who could assist them to make some necessary adjustments to new-world conditions; while their children are no less in need of enlightenment with regard to the confusion of mind, the feeling of helpless ignorance in the presence of so much that is strange and untested, that makes life so perplexing for their parents. Breckinridge deplores the fact that "some of the agencies from whom the most help might have been expected have deliberately passed over the mother to educate the child, hastening the process by which the child becomes Americanized in advance of his parents. Both the church and the school seem inclined to regard the parents as too advanced in years to assimilate new ideas or, as one principal of a Chicago public school asserted, 'so incorrigibly stupid' that it is a waste of time to educate them." [17]

When the conflict within the home has reached its height, open rebellion of the older children is apt to follow. Nor is this revolt altogether to be wondered at, when we recall that in many immigrant homes well-grown girls and youths must turn over to the parents every penny of their earnings, receiving back only car-fare or a very meager weekly allowance. Or they must submit to arbitrary commands and unreasonable restrictions laid on them by fathers and mothers who have only the dimmest notion of what American freedom means. Juvenile delinquency

[16] Quoted in Park and Miller, *op. cit.*, pp. 63-4. By permission of the Carnegie Corporation of New York.

[17] Breckinridge, *op. cit.*, pp. 180-1.

is far higher among the foreign-born than among the native population of our country. A study of 14,183 delinquent children brought before the Cook County Juvenile Court between July 1, 1899, and June 30, 1909, revealed that 72.8% of these delinquents had foreign-born parents.[18]

HOW MAY IMMIGRANT FAMILIES BE ASSISTED IN ADJUSTING TO NOVEL CONDITIONS?

The above sketch has perhaps made plain the genuine need of the foreign-born within our gates for enlightened help in adjusting themselves to the strange new ways of America. This assistance rendered to immigrant families might well take two forms: (1) improvement in housing conditions, and (2) development of a variety of agencies for helping and educating the immigrant.

Plans for Improving Homes.

Probably no one is more accurately and widely informed concerning the housing situation in our industrial cities than Edith Elmer Wood. She has not been content to paint a dismal picture of the shocking tenement house conditions that still exist, but has given earnest attention to the constructive aspect of housing reform. Like social insurance, housing reform in America is far more backward than in certain European countries, notably Holland. However, experiments of a philanthropic or semi-philanthropic nature have been made from time to time in this country ever since the Workmen's Home Association was launched in 1854. Of these the City and Suburban Homes Company of New York, organized in 1896, is one of the most successful, and owns tenement properties accommodating over 11,000 people. The aim of the company "is to provide at current market rents for ordinary tenements, a wholesome and superior type of accommodation." Apartments are only two rooms deep, all rooms are light, and there is a toilet in each apartment. Repairs are also well looked to. Unfortunately, however, baths are provided in few of these tenements.[19]

Beside these attempts to provide decent and comfortable homes for industrial workers, the employers of labor have themselves made numerous efforts to house their employees. Perhaps the home-owning enterprise of the Goodyear Tire and Rubber Company at Akron, Ohio, for the benefit of its highly paid employees is one of the best known. Since 1917, several

---

[18] Breckinridge, op. cit., p. 184.
[19] Edith Elmer Wood, The Housing of the Unskilled Wage Earner, pp. 98-100. The Carnegie Corporation of New York, 1919.

projects have been launched for furnishing good houses on easy terms to working people. Two of these were undertaken by the Chambers of Commerce of Flint (Michigan) and Cleveland. Wood sums up the conclusions that seem warranted by these early private experiments in home-building as follows:

1. The trend of opinion is away from multiple dwellings (tenements) toward single family houses in garden suburbs.

2. Philanthropy can set standards but it cannot supply the need for cheap, sanitary homes for workingmen. It never has met this demand adequately at any time in any place.

3. Housing by employers "is at best a makeshift. It can never furnish the final solution unless we are to go back to feudalism."

4. Housing conditions exist "all over the United States which cannot be tolerated in civilized communities." Restrictive housing laws "ameliorate bad conditions but cannot cure them." [20]

How then is the problem of building simple, decent homes for unskilled wage-earners to be met? All social workers who come in contact with our immigrant population testify to the yearning of these people for detached homes with small garden plots attached. Peasant farmers from Poland, Italy and other lands will save every cent they can squeeze from their meager wages and live under conditions that would horrify a native-born American workman, in order to build up a little fund with which they can buy homes of their own in the suburbs or the country. The widespread desire for a separate home with a plot of land is, then, a good starting point for housing reform among immigrant wage-earners.

Interesting experiments in state housing made in Massachusetts, California and Oklahoma are indices of a growing trend of public opinion away from philanthropic effort to state and municipal enterprise and control. The Massachusetts Homestead Commission, established in 1909, "is now conducting the first state housing enterprise in continental North America and it established in 1913 the first state-wide system of town planning boards." [21]

Housing experiments by the Federal Government during the World War were just getting under way, with eighty-nine projects decided on and fifty-five only slightly advanced or not yet under way when the Armistice was declared. These hopeful beginnings "were at once abandoned, and fourteen more curtailed, leaving (in 1919) twenty projects

[20] Wood, *op. cit.*, pp. 131-2. By permission of the Carnegie Corporation of New York.
[21] *Ibid.*, p. 222.

which the Housing Corporation will carry out as planned if Congress will permit it to do so." [22] A comparative study of national housing efforts in England and these war-emergency experiments in America will show how far the latter lags behind the former in the formulation of a national housing policy to meet the needs of unskilled as well as skilled laborers.

In a valuable last chapter giving an "Outline of a Comprehensive Housing Policy" for America, Wood favors the following constructive measures:

1. Provision by Congress of a National Housing Commission, whose functions should include (a) the allotment of funds to the several states and (b) the imposition of standards by means of the power to grant or withhold funds.
2. Postal Savings Deposit Loans and housing loans by national banks to individual workmen.
3. State legislation, including a restrictive housing law, a constructive housing law and a town planning law.
4. Local housing and town planning boards.

Such a well-considered national, state and local policy, if sincerely carried out, would do much within a decade or two to provide for the laboring class, and especially for the immigrant families in our midst, wholesome, comfortable homes at low rental, each with its small garden patch for which the immigrant longs. This reform in itself would accomplish a great deal in making the foreign-born feel at home and contented in the new land, as well as more self-respecting. What the reform would effect in the way of beneficent changes in the character of family life, by doing away with dirt, disorder, dark, unsanitary rooms and overcrowding can hardly be exaggerated. It seems a foolish optimism, if not downright insincerity, to expect wholesome, happy family life to develop under the conditions that exist in the tenements where our immigrants are huddled. That such family life does sometimes go on in those surroundings only testifies to the strength of the bonds that unite those of the same blood and daily associations.

Agencies to Assist Adjustment.

But America has not done all that needs to be done when it has provided decent homes for immigrant wage-earners; there still remains the herculean task of helping them to understand American standards and habits of living, with regard to household management, sanitation, diet,

[22] Wood, *op. cit.*, p. 236.

education. As a result of her study of immigrant families Breckinridge holds that certain community services should be rendered foreign-born family groups that would prevent much waste, suffering and isolation and facilitate their adjustment and assimilation to American social life. She classifies these social services into three groups:

"(1) the exercise of hospitality; (2) supplying information and opportunities for instruction; (3) assistance in the performance of household tasks." [23]

The Immigrants' Protective League of Chicago, organized in 1907, has already performed notable services in assisting immigrants entering Chicago in their industrial relations and in protecting them against exploitation or violation of their civic rights. The experience of the League has made plain the necessity for a national system of agencies which shall (1) give out much-needed information to individuals and families at ports of entry and (2) assist them when they reach their destination in securing the kind of help they need. Until the Federal Immigration Service is prepared to take on that responsible work, Breckinridge holds that existing private agencies could undertake the task of organizing National Reception Committees, if their financial resources could be enlarged. Such committees should not only give the immediate service that is needed, but should also develop an educational technique. This would provide regular instruction in their own language to the foreign-born with regard to American family law—the rights of the wife and children, the curtailment of the powers of the husband and father, his new duties of support of wife and offspring. Instruction might also be given in the sanitary and hygienic practices of the new country, in wise spending for food and clothing, in well-balanced dietaries and in child care—physical, mental and moral. This information might be given to housewives individually or in groups as seemed most helpful. But always the teachers must be those who have first-hand knowledge and sympathetic understanding of the problems of these hard-worked and bewildered women in a totally unfamiliar environment, bristling with difficulties. Nor should they overlook the fact that many of the housewives' habitual ways of doing things have distinct value and should be respected. The school, the church, the settlement, the district nursing service, the visiting home teacher may all coöperate usefully in this great work if they will. In view of the disunity in American social life today, as evidenced by the "colonies" of unadjusted immigrants in our midst, it would seem that this important task should appeal powerfully to public-

[23] Breckinridge, *op. cit.,* p. 222.

spirited men and women, if once they fully understood the urgent need that it be undertaken.

TOPICS FOR REPORTS

1. Maternity Care for Immigrant Women.
    Michael M. Davis, *Immigrant Health and the Community*, Chs. IX-XI. Harper & Brothers, New York, 1921.
2. Adjustment of Immigrant Diets to American Food.
    Davis, *op. cit.*, Ch. XII.
3. A Constructive Housing Policy for Immigrants and Others.
    Edith Elmer Wood, *Housing of the Unskilled Wage Earner*, Ch. VIII and Appendices B and C.
4. How Immigrant Organizations and Social Agencies Help in Solving Family Problems.
    Sophonisba P. Breckinridge, *New Homes for Old*, Chs. VII, VIII. Harper & Brothers, New York, 1921. Now controlled by the Carnegie Corporation of New York.

CHAPTER X

MOTHERS WHO MUST EARN

WOMEN IN GAINFUL EMPLOYMENT

A MONG the many economic and social changes that mark the course of the nineteenth and early twentieth centuries none is more arresting to the student of social history, or more far-reaching in its effects, than the influx of women into gainful occupations outside the home. It is a commonplace to say that women have followed their ancient employments of food preparation, weaving, garment making, nursing and teaching into the factory, the hospital and the school—a commonplace so trite that we may easily overlook the enormous import of the facts. Beginning in the late eighteenth century, there has been a steady infiltration of women into paid employments, until, in the second decade of the twentieth century, the body of women in gainful work had swelled to a mighty army in Germany, France, Great Britain and America.

In the United States the number of women ten years of age and over who were gainfully occupied in 1920 is reported in the Census as 8,549,511. This number represents an increase of nearly half a million over the figures for 1910. The census statistics for 1920 are misleading for purposes of comparison, however, owing to the fact that the census of 1910 was taken in April, whereas the last census returns were secured in January. The result was that the number of women working on farms showed a very slight increase in 1920 when compared with the agricultural workers in 1910. Furthermore, there were actual decreases of 50,000 or more in the number of women employed as farm laborers, as domestic servants, as milliners and as dressmakers in 1920. "If the women in these four occupations had shown an increase in number commensurate with that of the female population, then 25.4 percent of all women 10 years of age and over would have been gainfully employed in 1920, as compared with 23.4 per cent so occupied in 1910."[1]

The decrease in the number of women in domestic and personal service occupations is significant, and it has already shown a marked reaction

[1] "The Occupational Progress of Women," p. 3. *Bulletin of the Women's Bureau,* No. 27, 1922. United States Department of Labor.

upon the character of home life in cities. During a decade or more, detached, private homes requiring a staff of servants for their maintenance have been abandoned for apartments that could be managed with from one to four servants. Offsetting the trend away from domestic employments is the ever-swelling stream of women pouring into clerical occupations, into trade and transportation, into manufacturing and mechanical industries. In clerical occupations, women were nearly two and one-half times as numerous in 1920 as in 1910; in trade, their number increased 42.7%; in transportation, their number was doubled; in mechanical industries and manufacturing, their number increased more than 100,000. Perhaps the most surprising increment in the last group was in the division of automobile industries, where women operatives increased 1,408 percent—from 848 in 1910 to 12,788 in 1920. But this is not the whole story. In by far the majority of occupations employing 1,000 or more of both men and women, the rate of increase of the women exceeded that of the men. While the men still greatly outnumber the women in these employments, the enormous percentage increases shown by the women indicate a growing demand for their labor and an accelerated movement of women from domestic pursuits into industry.[2] This remains true even though the numerical increase of gainfully employed women in the decade 1910-20, as shown by the census, was not as great as had been expected by many social writers.

MARRIED WOMEN IN INDUSTRY

A very significant fact brought out in the census statistics of 1920 is the number of *married women* (fifteen years of age and over) in paid employments. This division of women toilers numbers 1,920,281. Twenty-three percent of all women fifteen years of age and over employed in gainful occupations were married in 1920, as compared with 4.6% in 1890 and 5.6% in 1900. In 1910 the percentage was even higher, being 25.4. The census of 1920 records that 33.5% of women workers of the age-group twenty-five to forty-four years were married—slightly more than one-third of the number!

A bulletin recently published by the Women's Bureau of the United States Department of Labor entitled "Family Status of Breadwinning Women in Four Selected Cities" brings to light some facts that stimulate thought. In the four selected cities—Jacksonville, Wilkes-Barre and Hanover Township, Butte (Montana) and Passaic—the number of gainfully employed women (38,446) "constituted over 38 per cent of the

[2] *op. cit.*, pp. 4-11.

entire female population 14 years of age and over reported in these communities." In Jacksonville and Passaic, the percentages were respectively forty-five and forty-six. Of this army of employed women, approximately fifty-five percent were or had been married; and of this group (21,000), over sixty-one percent were living with wage-earning husbands! This circumstance bears witness to the fact, well known to social workers, that these women cannot hold their homes together on the low wages paid their husbands, and are perforce driven into gainful employment. The Bulletin declares further that it "was not chiefly the childless women from whom the married breadwinners were recruited, for nearly 53 percent of all the gainfully employed matrons had children, *and 40 percent of these mothers had babies under 5 years.*" Nor were these women boarding; almost four-fifths of the women breadwinners who were or had been married were maintaining homes. Nearly one-half of this married group were engaged in gainful employments that took them outside their own homes.[3]

Causes of Entry of Married Women into Gainful Occupations.

When the question of married women's work outside the home is under discussion, it is surprising how frequently well-meaning persons, not in close touch with the actual situation, will blandly ignore its real causes and ascribe the gainful employment of married women to the desire for unnecessary comforts and a sociable life. With many people this is a pet theory, accepted on the evidence of one or two cases, which enables them to adopt a censorious attitude toward these "erring wives and mothers" whose place so obviously is in the home. But trained social workers and observers know better. Their long experience, as well as their special investigations, both lead to the conclusion that the primary reason why married women work in unskilled occupations for low wages is economic pressure. It is poverty that sends the mother from the home at seven o'clock in the morning, after she has washed and fed her children, to labor for a full or part-time day in order to supplement an income that no amount of "stretching" will make adequate to house, feed and clothe the family. In England and America alike, careful investigations, carried on by trained workers, reveal the same causes. The British *Report of the Interdepartmental Committee on Physical Deterioration,* made to Parliament in 1904, states the reasons for the labor of English wage-earning mothers as being (1) death of the father or lack of employment, or inadequacy of the father's wage; (2) desertion of

[3] "Family Status of Breadwinning Women in Four Selected Cities," pp. 7-11. *Bulletin of the Women's Bureau,* No. 23, 1922. United States Department of Labor.

the father; (3) fear on the mother's part of loss of future work in the factory; (4) preference for factory over domestic work. The report adds that the "great majority of cases may be said to fall under one or other of the three sub-divisions in class (1)." [4] Among 120 cases of married women at work in Manchester, England, only six could be discovered in which the wife's wage-earning occupations were explained on the ground of preference. In Liverpool, the wives were reported to be at work because their husbands were "often casual labourers or drunkards." From Newcastle came the report that wives were wage-earners from necessity and not from choice. Their work was unattractive and often exhausting, "and not one of them seems to take the slightest pleasure in it." [5]

When we turn to America, similar conditions are found to prevail. Katherine Anthony's committee made a house-to-house study of 370 working mothers living in the Middle West Side district of New York which disclosed the following facts regarding their conjugal condition and the ability of their husbands to support the family: [6]

Group	Conjugal Condition	Number	Percent
I	Widows	125	33.8
II	Deserted wives	40	10.8
III	Separated wives	9	2.4
IV	Wives with incapacitated husbands	21	5.7
V	Wives with idle husbands	12	3.2
VI	Wives with husbands at work	163	44.1
	Total	370	100.0

It will be noted that considerably less than half of these women had husbands who contributed to the family support, and nearly one-third were widows. In every family where the husband was at work (163) he earned *less than $500 a year* and the earnings of the mother, or both mother and children, were essential to the support of the family. In ninety-six of these families the mother's earnings constituted thirty-one percent of the family income; in sixty-seven families, 18.8%. [7]

Commenting on these facts, Miss Anthony says:

"Too often we hear these women spoken of as if some perversity of instinct drove them to neglect their homes and go to work at the

[4] P. 48.
[5] See Clementina Black (editor), *Married Women's Work*, pp. 161, 183, 203. George Bell & Sons, Ltd., London, 1915. By permission.
[6] Anthony, *Mothers Who Must Earn*, p. 128. Russell Sage Foundation, New York, 1914.
[7] *Ibid.*, p. 128.

expense of their homes and children. It is for the sake of their children that they work, as mothers have done from time immemorial. The last penny of their earnings is absorbed by their homes. Visit one of them on Saturday night and see how they spend their wages. The money which the woman has earned on her hands and knees is spent in the Tenth Avenue stores and comes back into the home in the form of meat for Sunday's dinner and warm new clothing for the children. She buys little for herself but the bare necessities and even these she often foregoes." [8]

A recent study made by the Women's Bureau of the United States Department of Labor of men and women wage-earners in the shoe industry in Manchester, New Hampshire, disclosed that, in the great majority of families where married women were wage-earners, there were one or more dependents to be supported, and the women's wages were of real value. In eighty-five percent of the 113 families investigated, where the wife was contributing to the family income, the husband's wages were $1,500 or less—in the great majority of cases less. In twenty-one families, the father earned less than $1,000. The investigators concluded their study of the contributions of these married women to the family income with the statement: "The fact that the inclusion of the wives' earnings raises the median of *per capita* earnings from $438, which is considerably below the median for all families, to $641, which is considerably above, leaves little doubt that the earnings of the married women in the majority of these cases were important in keeping up the standard of living for their families." [9]

Over the heads of most wage-earning wives and mothers hangs the fear that on any day the husband may come home with his overalls and bag and announce that he has been "fired." Unemployment is the bogy of the laboring class, especially of the unskilled group. At any time the mother may find herself the sole support of the family. Miss Anthony vividly describes the curse of unemployment that visits the families of unskilled wage-earners in the Middle West Side district of New York:

"Sometimes it strikes a man without a word of warning. His wife sees him coming home in the middle of the morning and she knows what has happened even before he speaks. If she is apt at nothing else, she is quick to read the signs of this particular misfortune. Sometimes it strikes the family just when they have begun to entertain hopes and

---

[8] Anthony, *op. cit.*, p. 129.
[9] "The Share of Wage-Earning Women in Family Support," p. 84. *Bulletin of the Women's Bureau*, No. 30, 1923. United States Department of Labor. Italics mine.

to make plans. The Gurneys had just moved into a four-room flat with rent at $16. They had formerly lived in a rear tenement, but Mr. Gurney, who was a cab driver, thought he was 'in steady' for awhile. Then one day Mrs. Gurney, coming home in the afternoon, 'saw his boots and his bandbox with his hat in the middle of the room.' Mr. Gurney was nowhere about. He had gone out again after leaving these silent witnesses of misfortune. Mrs. Gurney threw herself on the bed and wept despairingly. The Gurneys were soon living in a basement." [10]

MOTHERHOOD AND WAGE-EARNING

A high proportion of married women in gainful employments are mothers; and, indeed, this fact, as we have seen, is a most powerful motive impelling them to work outside the home. A study made by the Women's Bureau in 1922 of nearly 10,000 women breadwinners in Passaic, New Jersey, showed that one-half of them were or had been married, and nearly three-fourths of the married or once-married group were mothers. Of these mothers, 1,800 were employed outside the home; and nearly sixty percent had children under five years of age.[11] Similar conditions have been disclosed by the Children's Bureau in its studies of "Infant Mortality" in Manchester, New Hampshire, and New Bedford, Massachusetts. In the textile manufacturing city of Manchester, during a selected period—November 1, 1912, to October 31, 1913—1,643 mothers were investigated, all of whom had borne children during that year. Of these, 722, or 43.9%, were gainfully employed within or outside the home after the birth of the child. In New Bedford, 2,662 similar cases were studied, in 1,242 of which (nearly forty-three percent) the mothers entered paid employment after childbirth.[12] These facts and figures could readily be reproduced in most of the great textile manufacturing centers of New England and the South.

Effects of the Employment of Mothers.

What are the reactions of the employment of these breadwinning mothers upon the home and the nurture of children under school age? The consequences have been repeatedly summed up as harmful with respect to home management, child care and training and infant mor-

---

[10] Anthony, op. cit., p. 41.
[11] "The Family Status of Breadwinning Women," p. 4. *Bulletin of the Women's Bureau*, No. 23, 1922. United States Department of Labor.
[12] See *Bulletin of the Children's Bureau*, No. 20 (Manchester), p. 50; and No. 68, (New Bedford), p. 42.

tality—not to mention the large number of abortions that are brought about through the necessity of the mother's employment. Let us examine each of these counts in the light of such facts as are well substantiated; for assuredly no progress will ever be made in solving these tangled social questions by the easy method of wholesale acceptance of unexamined opinions, especially when these opinions are more often than not grounded upon emotional prejudice. Since a high infant mortality rate is asserted to be directly attributable to the gainful employment of mothers and prospective mothers, let us begin our examination with this social condition.

Infant Mortality among Employed and Non-employed Mothers.

Owing to the indications in the Federal Census of inordinately high infant death rates in the textile and shoe manufacturing cities of New England, the Children's Bureau began a series of detailed investigations of the facts, the conditions and the causes of this social phenomenon. As stated above, the studies in Manchester and New Bedford revealed that many hundreds of mothers with infants less than a year old were employed in these industrial centers, whereas a greater number of mothers were not engaged in gainful work. Such a condition made possible some interesting and highly significant comparisons of the infant mortality rate among wage-earning and non-wage-earning mothers. In Manchester, 1,643 mothers were included in the study, to all of whom children had been born in the selected year (1912-13). Of these women, 864 were not gainfully employed during the year preceding the birth of the child and 776 were gainfully employed. The infant mortality rate [13] for the unemployed women was 133.9; for the breadwinning mothers, 199.2. Another striking fact brought out by the study was the smaller infant death-rate among women engaged in wage-earning occupations *at home* before the birth of the child when compared with those going out into the factories to work. The rates follow: [14]

WOMEN EMPLOYED AT HOME		WOMEN WORKING AWAY FROM HOME	
Type of Work	*Infant Mortality Rate*	*Type of Work*	*Infant Mortality Rate*
Keeping lodgers	149.8	Textile mill	227.5
Other home work	153.8	Other factories	240.5

[13] The infant mortality rate represents the number of infant deaths, during the first year of life, per 1,000 live births.
[14] Infant Mortality: The Results of a Field Study in Manchester, N. H.," p. 50. *Bureau Publications*, No. 20, 1917.

It will be readily noted that, although the women carrying on paid employments in their homes show a higher infant death-rate than women not so employed, the rate of this group is conspicuously lower than that of the women factory operatives. Stillbirths were also less numerous among the home workers.

The study made three years later in New Bedford, Massachusetts, shows similar findings:[15]

	Live Births	Infant Mortality Rate
Mothers not gainfully employed prior to child-birth, 1420	1370	108.8
Mothers gainfully employed prior to childbirth, 1242	1217	154.5
Employed at home, 360	353	121.8
Employed away from home, 882	864	167.8

Employment of mothers *after* the birth of the child also results in a high infant death-rate. In Manchester, this rate was 220.9 for employed mothers, as compared with 122 for mothers not gainfully employed. In New Bedford, 475 mothers resumed work away from home who left infants under one year of age. "If the average infant mortality rate for the city for the remainder of the year had prevailed among them, a total of 29 deaths would have occurred; but actually 43 of these infants died. The ratio of 43 to 29 expresses the extra mortality among these infants of gainfully employed mothers."[16]

The primary cause of the high infant mortality rates among wage-earning mothers appears to be the artificial feeding of the child. Breast-fed children showed a uniformly lower death-rate in both Manchester and New Bedford. The younger the baby, the more marked the harmful effect of the mother's absence, both in depriving the infant of her care and in depriving it of breast-milk. Of 119 babies in Manchester whose mothers began working away from home before the baby was four months old, thirty-three died before the end of the first year—a mortality rate of 277.3, as compared with the rate of 121.7 for the remainder of the group, namely 1,389 babies.[17] As might be expected, a much higher proportion of gainfully employed women resort to artificial feeding of infants

[15] "Infant Mortality. Results of a Field Study in New Bedford, Mass.," p. 42. *Bureau Publications,* No. 68, 1920.
[16] "Infant Mortality. Results of a Field Study in New Bedford, Mass.," p. 44. *Bureau Publications,* No. 68, 1920.
[17] "Infant Mortality: The Results of a Field Study in Manchester, N. H.," p. 53. *Bureau Publications,* No. 20, 1920.

than is true of non-wage-earning women. In New Bedford, 45.9% of women gainfully employed away from home were feeding their babies artificially at the age of three months, as compared with 24.3% of unemployed mothers. In Manchester 65.5% of the babies of mothers employed away from home were artificially fed, as compared with 28.5% of the babies of women not gainfully employed.

Not only is artificial feeding less beneficial to infants, when the mother has an ample supply of good milk, but it is rendered virulently harmful by the careless methods of preparation and sterilization used by ignorant and hurried mothers. If all the women included in these two studies had received careful instruction in the preparation of modified milk for their babies, the infant death-rate from gastric and intestinal diseases would no doubt have fallen sharply. As evidence of the truth of this statement the following fact will serve. More native-born than foreign-born women in New Bedford used artificial feeding of their infants; but the infant mortality rate among the native-born group was considerably lower than among the ignorant Portuguese mothers who fed their babies artificially. "There are many different types of artificial feeding," writes Jessamine Whitney in the New Bedford Report; "the mother who gives her baby modified milk in accordance with a physician's prescription, and who observes carefully all the rules for cleanliness and sterilization, is classed as giving artificial feeding as well as the mother who is ignorant of the necessity of providing pure, clean milk or one who gives her baby condensed milk, solid food, coffee or tea. The contrast is well illustrated in the following descriptions of the feeding of two infants both classed as artificially fed. When Baby A cried, his milk bottle was picked up from the dirty floor, partly filled with condensed milk from the can, then placed under the faucet and filled up with water. The nipple was also recovered from the floor and Baby A was fed. For Baby B the bottles were kept sterilized; the milk, the best obtainable, was modified in accordance with a physician's directions and the ingredients of the formula were carefully measured; the temperature' was properly regulated. Baby B was fed at regular intervals; he was seen at least once a week by a doctor, and the milk formula was changed when necessary. Both these babies were 'artificially fed.' "[18]

The fact that stands out clearly from the above excerpt is that artificial feeding *in itself* need not be harmful to babies. In New York City, for example, the sharp fall in the infant death-rate in recent years

[18] *Op. cit.*, p. 35. *Bureau Publications*, No. 68, 1920.

is due not only to better prenatal care of mothers in maternity centers and by visiting nurses, but also to improved methods of artificial feeding due to the careful instruction given to mothers who are as ignorant as their own babes of the paramount importance of cleanliness, sterilization and food formulas adapted to the child.

Even if it be granted that breast-feeding of infants is, on the whole, superior to the best of artificial feeding, this need not constitute an insuperable barrier to the employment of nursing mothers. In France, where many married women are gainfully employed, the law of 1917 requires that "for one year after the birth of the child, nursing mothers shall be allowed one hour a day during hours of work for the purpose of feeding their infants." This hour is divided into two periods of thirty minutes each, one during the morning and one during the afternoon. "The mother shall always be allowed to nurse her infant on the premises." Nursing rooms must be set up in or near any establishment where more than 100 women over fifteen years of age are employed; and "the conditions as regards construction, hygiene and supervision" of these nursing rooms "shall be. determined by public administrative regulations. . . ." [19] Thus France, mindful of her low birth-rate, protects the infants of her working mothers. When will the United States be moved to follow her example?

Some striking facts have emerged from recent studies of infant mortality rates in the group of gainfully employed mothers in England. In Manchester, England, the infant mortality rate was 267 per thousand in the cases where the mothers were not employed outside the home and 210 in cases where they were so employed.[20] The same condition was found to exist in Birmingham, where the infant death-rate in 1910, in the case of mothers employed before or after confinement, was found to be 153 per 1,000 births; among mothers who remained at home it was 161 per 1,000 births.[21] Obviously some factors are at work determining infant mortality other than the gainful employment of mothers in factories. Dr. Ashby does not hesitate to declare that *the chief of these is "poverty* which, together with ignorance, perhaps, more than anything else dominates the situation." [22]

These and other factors responsible for high infant death-rates will be considered below; but the question of the causal relationship of the

[19] *Bulletin of the International Labour Office*, October, 1919, p. 47. London.
[20] Clementina Black (editor), *Married Women's Work*, p. 176.
[21] Hugh T. Ashby, M.D., *Infant Mortality*, p. 68. Cambridge University Press, 1915.
[22] *Ibid.*, p. 68. Italics mine.

gainful employment of mothers to infant mortality should not be left without consideration of an important contributory fact. Mothers employed outside the home are carrying a dual job—a full day's work and the manifold duties of housekeeping and child care. No fair test of the effects on infant mortality of extra-domestic employment of mothers can possibly be made until this condition is eliminated. A mother tired out by an eight-hour or ten-hour day in a factory is in no condition to give careful, intelligent physical care to a six-months' baby. But that is not to say that the baby would not flourish if it received that care in a neighborhood nursery at the hands of specialists in child rearing. If mothers are forced out of the home by economic pressure to augment the family income, it would seem that more intelligent measures for meeting this situation could be devised than wringing our hands and censuring the neglect of their offspring by the aforesaid delinquent mothers. One such measure (not the only one) would be to organize an adequate number of social agencies for the proper care of the children of employed mothers. At present many of these women know not where to turn for help. It is only the fortunate woman who has an aging mother or mother-in-law with whom the child may be left. Others are obliged to leave the infant with a neighbor, whom they pay for a service often inefficiently performed. Still others rely on the older children, out of school hours, for the essential care, or on an unemployed husband. A few are forced to leave the baby with its food tied round its neck— and hope for the best! Such conditions are a comment on the backwardness of society in ameliorating the conditions which it creates. Humane feeling exists everywhere, but organized and effective social aid lags behind.

The employment of mothers up to the time of confinement is generally believed to be a harmful practice. The Commonwealth of Massachusetts has on its statute books a law prohibiting the employment of a woman "knowingly" within two weeks before or four weeks after childbirth. Such laws are hard to enforce unless a matron is appointed in each factory to see that the provisions are complied with. In England, where no prohibition exists regarding employment *before* confinement, Dr. Ashby has given attention to the question of the effect upon the offspring of the mother's employment up to the day of confinement, especially where she works hard "and has only the bare necessaries in the way of food." He finds that such conditions affect the weight of the child adversely. Of 500 babies whose mothers worked up to the day of their birth, the average weight at birth was 3,010 grams. Of 500 babies whose mothers spent ten days in a pre-maternity home, the average weight was 3,290 grams. Of 500 infants whose mothers spent more than ten days in the home, the average weight was 3,366 grams.[23]

Influence of the Father's Earnings.

Reference has previously been made to the fact that the extra-domestic employment of mothers is by no means the only cause of high infant mortality rates. Obviously the social phenomenon of bread-winning mothers is clearly related to that of low-paid fathers. An interesting and suggestive graph is produced in the Manchester report on infant mortality which shows conclusively that the employment of mothers fell sharply as the wages of the fathers rose. When the fathers were earning *less than $450 a year,* then nearly seventy-five percent of the mothers were forced into gainful employment. And there were 225 such cases in the selected families studied! When the men's wages had risen to from $540 to $649, the percentage of mothers employed had sunk to fifty-five. In the group in which the fathers were earning $1,050 and over, only ten percent of the mothers were breadwinners. This situation tells its own tale.[24]

In New Bedford conditions were very similar. A father's wage below $450 meant that over sixty percent of the wives and mothers entered gainful occupations. When the husband's earnings had mounted to $650, the percentage of mothers employed was cut almost in half. In the more adequately paid group, in which the father's wages were $1,050 or over, only slightly more than fifteen percent of mothers were gainfully employed.[25]

Grim and conclusive is the evidence as to the close correlation between a high infant mortality rate and low wages earned by fathers. In Manchester, when the wages of 225 fathers fell below $450, the infant mortality rate rose to the appalling figure of 242.9—almost one infant death to every four births! When the relatively high wage-group $850 to $1,049 is reached, the death-rate of babies has fallen to 125 —only slightly over half the first figure. In the highest wage-group of $1,250 or over, the infant mortality rate has dropped to the very low figure of 58.3—about one infant death to 18 births.[26] New Bedford shows much the same conditions—an infant mortality rate of 201.9 when the

[23] Ashby, *op. cit.,* p. 62.

[24] "Infant Mortality: The Results of a Field Study in Manchester, N. H.," p. 49. *Bureau Publications,* No. 20, 1917.

[25] "Infant Mortality. Results of a Field Study in New Bedford, Mass.," p. 40. *Bureau Publications,* No. 68, 1920.

[26] "Infant Mortality: The Results of a Field Study in Manchester, N. H.,' p. 45. *Bureau Publications,* No. 20, 1917.

father earns less than $450, and a rate of 59.9 when his earnings reach $1,250 or over.[27] In the lowest earning group one live-born baby in every five died before reaching its first birthday.

The low earnings of fathers react unfavorably upon the infant death-rate in at least two ways: they are chiefly responsible for the high percentage of employed mothers, unable to give their infants proper care or breast feeding; and also they are responsible for the bad housing conditions and overcrowding that are the inevitable accompaniments of poverty. Again, the densest ignorance of the principles of child care and feeding is most commonly found in the lowest wage-groups; and the foreign-born mothers in this group, being often illiterate and unable to speak or understand English, can profit least by the printed pamphlets issued by boards of health and by the instructions of public health nurses. In Manchester, with its very high infant mortality rate of 165, the rate for babies of literate mothers, exclusive of French connections, was 94.6. In the case of illiterate mothers the rate rose to 198.8. "Poverty nullifies in part the advantages of breast feeding," says the Manchester report, "while an ample income mitigates the disadvantages of artificial feeding. The reason for this may be, as before noted, that poverty usually means low standards and ignorance on the part of the mother, while ample income makes possible the attainment of higher standards, better medical attention, and greater knowledge in the care of the baby." [28]

So-called "immaturity" or inability to meet the demands of bare physical existence, is responsible for a large number of infant deaths during the first month of life. There is good reason to believe that this condition is largely due to the malnutrition and overwork of the mothers in the poorer class—whether they are employed outside the home or not. Dr. Ashby, a well-known English authority on this subject, declares:

"My own experience in the out-patient room entirely confirms the opinion that nutrition of the mother has a very important bearing on the nutrition of the foetus, and that the statement that the percentage of unhealthy births among the poor is small is not justified by facts. We constantly see fully developed infants a day or two old . . . clearly ill-fitted, as the event proves, to withstand the conditions of external existence. . . . There is no question of syphilis; they are the children of poor mothers who have lived hard lives of wear and tear during

[27] "Infant Mortality. Results of a Field Study in New Bedford, Mass.," p. 41. *Bureau Publications,* No. 68, 1920.
[28] "Infant Mortality: The Results of a Field Study in Manchester, N. H.," p. 71. *Bureau Publications,* No. 20, 1917.

pregnancy,[29] are themselves badly nourished and weakly, and have felt the pinch of poverty, though often perhaps poverty of the secondary sort." [30]

Bad housing, congestion and unsanitary conditions, such as defective sewerage, dirty streets and impure water supply, were fortunately not widespread in either New Bedford or Manchester. Nevertheless the investigators reported that acute conditions of this description were discovered here and there in both cities. In the central portion of Manchester "were some bad housing areas and congested sections and in the tenement houses agents found many dark rooms as well as dark unventilated toilets." It is difficult, of course, to apportion the exact degree of responsibility that these conditions must bear for the high infant mortality in Manchester, although the investigators declare that "to bad housing conditions belongs some share at least in the responsibility for the high infant death-rates which accompany them." [31] Babies whose homes were in multiple dwellings, housing a large number of families, had a decidedly higher death-rate than those whose homes were in single family houses. Also, as might be expected, the infant mortality rate rose *pari passu* with the average number of persons per room. Where the average was less than one person, the mortality rate was 123.3; where the average was under two persons, the rate was 177.8; and where the average was less than three, the rate rose to 261.7.[32]

In New Bedford, large numbers of foreign-born families were living in the so-called "unfavorable area," on low ground near the river. Here were found small, damp, gloomy rooms and much congestion, with water occasionally standing in the cellars. Forty-six percent of the total births in New Bedford occurred in families having less than one person to a room; and, in this favored group, the infant mortality rate was 146. "Six percent of the families lived in congested conditions, viz., with an average of from two to five persons per room; the infant mortality rate for this last group was 222." [33] It should be understood that, in reckoning the number of persons per room, *all the rooms* (not merely the bedrooms) are included. This means that, under the best conditions,

---

[29] It should be remembered that women employed outside the home also carry on heavy domestic tasks.

[30] Quoted in *Maternity Letters from Working Women*, p. 11. George Bell & Sons, Ltd., London, 1915. By permission.

[31] "Infant Mortality: The Results of a Field Study in Manchester, N. H.," p. 109. *Bureau Publications*, No. 20, 1917.

[32] *Ibid.*, pp. 111, 112.

[33] "Infant Mortality. Results of a Field Study in New Bedford, Mass.," p. 61. *Bureau Publications*, No. 68, 1920.

four or five persons were living in tenements of that number of rooms; and, under the worst conditions, fifteen or more persons might be housed in a five-room house.

It would seem from the above discussion that any impartial attempt to appraise justly the influence of the extra-domestic employment of mothers upon infant mortality must give due attention to factors, often lightly passed over, which are not the consequence of the gainful work of mothers, but of an economic situation that is characterized by the prevalence of low wages.

Still-births, Abortions and Miscarriages.

Apparently not much is known of the effect of the gainful employment of mothers upon the number of still-births. Of 2,662 births in New Bedford, seventy-five were still-births, giving a still-birth rate of 2.8% of total births. It is noteworthy that, in New Bedford, the percentage of still-births in the group of non-employed mothers was 3.5, as compared with a percentage of two among gainfully employed women. In Manchester, on the contrary, the percentage of still-births was 5.5 among gainfully employed mothers, and only 4.1 among the group not so employed. The percentage was highest among the wage-earning mothers working away from home, where it rose to 7.5—a rate of seventy-five per thousand.

Whether the number of miscarriages among wage-earning mothers is higher than among those not gainfully employed is not apparent from a study of the reports. Abortions are far from uncommon among breadwinning mothers, who know full well that each new baby means illness, loss of work and wages and one more mouth to feed. Anthony reports that among the 370 wage-earning mothers included in her investigation "abortions are common and unsuccessful attempts are even commoner. Patent medicine vendors and certain classes of doctors and midwives carry on an illicit business in the district. A practice which the women know to be so common they can scarcely regard as immoral; and, in any case, they feel that it is justified by their necessities." [34] From England come similar reports concerning gainfully employed mothers. In the anonymous "Introduction" to a volume of *Maternity Letters from Working Women,* the writer says: "There are many facts which go to prove that the habit of taking . . . drugs [to procure abortion] has spread to an alarming extent in many places among working women. Several of these letters confirm that conclusion. The practice is ruinous to the health of women,

[34] Anthony, *op. cit.*, pp. 154-5.

is more often than not useless for procuring the object desired, and probably accounts for the fact that many children are weakly and diseased from birth. But here again the cause of the evil lies in the conditions which produce it. Where maternity is only followed by an addition to the daily life of suffering, want, overwork, and poverty, people will continue to adopt even the most dangerous, uncertain, and disastrous methods of avoiding it." [35] Persons who are opposed to birth control on moral grounds should be brought face to face with this situation and squarely confronted with this question: Which is more immoral, to prevent conception by scientific methods, or to take the life of an unborn infant at grave risk to its mother's life and health?

No working mother in her senses, who is striving with all her strength to feed and clothe a family already numbering three or four children, sometimes more, can possibly desire an addition to her family so long as these conditions exist. Therefore, when the children of these women die, the mothers do not grieve long. The mortality rate among the children of the poor is notoriously high. Anthony states that to the 370 gainfully employed mothers whom her committee personally investigated, 1,758 children had been born. Of these, 437 had died—almost twenty-five percent! "They are strangely apathetic toward the loss of their children by death," she writes. "Almost as soon as the first pang of sorrow is past, the bereaved mother is ready to say that the little one 'is better off' and to speak of death as a merciful release from a life of hardships. One never hears from them the mourning cry of the mother in happier circumstances, 'So much love and pain and all for nothing.' " [36] Nor should we be surprised and repelled at this situation. It is well known that grinding poverty and a bitter daily struggle for mere existence blunt the finer sensibilities. These same mothers, who mourn their dead offspring so briefly, will work long hours to keep up a home for their children, and will show real heroism in the fight against poverty.

Effect of Extra-domestic Employment of Married Women on Home and Child Care.

There is a widespread conviction that the homes and children of wage-earning mothers suffer from neglect, and there is some evidence to support this theory. Obviously a woman cannot be employed nine hours a day in a factory, or shaking clothes in a laundry, and at the same time maintain a clean, well-ordered home and give intelligent care and

[35] P. 15.   [36] Anthony, op. cit., p. 155.

oversight to her children. Yet it is surprising to read the accounts of social investigators concerning the decent home conditions they found among breadwinning women. Although the small flats or multiple houses in which many of these women live are cramped and lacking in conveniences, they are by no means always dirty. Wage-earning women will come home, tired out from a heavy day's work, and, after eating and resting a little, will start in washing the day's accumulation of dishes, sweeping or doing the family wash. Anthony says that the women she investigated usually spend three or four evenings in the week washing and ironing. One mother of two spotless little girls, on being asked how she managed to do it, replied, "I wash and iron every day." Hard as this labor is, it is not so discouraging in its results as is the struggle to keep the home in order. The flats occupied by the poorer working class in New York consist usually of three or four rooms—a sitting-room, a combination kitchen and dining-room and one or two bedrooms. Closets do not exist, and clothing must be hung on hooks in the walls or thrown over chair-backs, unless the mother is fortunate enough to own a wardrobe and a bureau. The kitchen has no space for storage other than a shallow cupboard, thus necessitating the purchase of food from day to day. The space under the stationary tubs quite often is utilized to store the kindlings that children have dragged home from warehouses and stores, in the form of packing boxes, and have chopped up on the sidewalk. The family's entire stock of coal is kept in a box or sack in the kitchen. "Housekeeping in these cramped quarters is exceedingly difficult," writes Anthony. "Such a home absorbs an endless amount of labor without making much return in the way of tidy appearance; the housekeeper can overcome the dirt more easily than the disorder. 'It looks as if the place was upside down,' they would sometimes say, 'but it's clean anyway.' " [37]

Apparently little cooking and sewing are done in these homes. There is no time. The breadwinning mother soon learns the entire stock of canned foods at her disposal in the neighboring grocery stores. Anthony found "only occasional survivals of old-fashioned methods of preparing food . . ." among her 370 employed mothers. Not only are these methods time-consuming, but they use up precious fuel. Theorists are not lacking who maintain that the wage-earning mother expends and wastes more than she earns by not staying at home and looking thriftily to its management. But there is some evidence opposed to this view. In 1910, Rose

[37] For this entire subject, see Anthony, *op. cit.*, pp. 141-5; also see Gwendolyn Hughes, *Mothers in Industry*, Chs. IX, X. New Republic, Inc., New York, 1925.

Otto made a thorough inquiry into this question with reference to the factory-working married woman in Munich, Germany. Her conclusion was that without the wife's wage the family's necessities could not be met. "The size of the deficits," she declares, "disproved the assertion that the women could accomplish as much by thrifty housekeeping as by increasing the family income with their own earnings. On a merely pecuniary basis, this was seen to be impossible." Very interesting are Miss Otto's statements that "the domestic arrangements of families with mothers at work did not differ materially from those where the mother was not employed. Lowering the cost of food in families without a maternal wage-earner was only accomplished by lowering the quantity of food without making up the loss by the substitution of more nutritious values. Contrary to the general assumption that the women who do not work secure with the same expenditure a relatively better nourishment, it was shown that *the same kind and amount of foodstuffs were used in both types of families. . . ."* [38]

The causes for this similarity in housekeeping methods are not far to seek. As Miss Otto points out, the question uppermost in the minds of both the factory-working mother and the woman who spends a day at the family wash-tubs is the same: "What costs the least?" Of course a lack of training in household management and ignorance of food values is as true of the unemployed as of the gainfully employed mother. Neither knows how to make the most of the little she has to spend. Certainly, this careful German study suggests that further comparative studies of the differences in the home conditions and daily diet in households where mothers are wage-earners and in those where they remain at home are greatly needed before any sweeping statements can be made concerning the quality of housekeeping in each group.

But if there is room for opposing opinions regarding the question of home management among employed and unemployed mothers, there can, it would seem, be none about child care. Even when a mother is busy at the stove or ironing-board, she can leave these tasks to perform essential services for a helpless baby or a toddling mite. Not so the mother working for wages away from home. She must leave the house early in the morning and perhaps not revisit it until her day's work is done. At best she has but an hour at noon. The day nurseries are at present quite inadequate in number to meet the need, and are often far

---

[38] *Über Fabrikarbeit Verheirateter Frauen*, p. 288 ff. *Münchener Volkswissenschaftliche Studien*. Cottasche Buchhandlung, 1910. Quoted in Anthony, *op. cit.*, p. 149.

distant from the working mother's home. Anthony found that of 221 children below school age, only forty were placed in day nurseries. The others shifted for themselves at home. Indeed, only two day nurseries were established in this entire West Side District, extending from Thirty-Fourth Street north to Fifty-Fourth, and from Eighth Avenue west to Eleventh. These two nurseries could accommodate only 120 children. Probably the small fee usually charged proved prohibitive for some mothers; and no doubt there was a certain amount of ignorant distrust of nursery methods of feeding and bathing. Then, too, the managing personnel of these nurseries, as the writer has more than once observed, are not always tactful and willing to show due regard for the views of mothers.

What happens to the hundreds of babies left at home when mothers start for the day's work? As we have seen, some receive intermittent care from sisters or brothers in school; some are left with a neighbor who takes charge of several at once; occasionally the father, out of employment or engaged only in night work, will take care of the little ones. Somehow these mothers manage, and surely not only at the expense of the babies, but at the cost of wearing anxiety on the part of women during their hours of absence.

The Health of the Wage-Earning Mother.

Whether the health of the wage-earning women in low-paid employments is markedly worse than among their sisters who stay at home, but also struggle to make both ends meet, is not known. It would seem reasonable to infer that, if the first group carries two heavy jobs instead of one, this double burden must be borne at a physical cost more or less serious, depending upon the physique of the worker. After hours of scrubbing in private homes or public buildings, or after a long day in a laundry or factory, these women, who rose very early to get breakfast, care for the baby and prepare the older children for school, often come home in a pitiful condition of fatigue. Among the reports of social investigations we read accounts of the "shocking state of exhaustion" in which some of the laundry and factory workers reach home, when they have been working overtime, as they quite often do. And there are no hours of leisure for these women before bedtime and the next day's work. A score of neglected household tasks cry out for their attention, even when the older children assume their share of the work.

This continuous grind of toil must surely have its reaction upon the health of overburdened mothers. Katherine Anthony found hernia and varicose veins common among them, and could not estimate how much they suffered from bad teeth and aching feet. Certainly many of them were almost toothless before the age of fifty. Owing to the small income on which the family must be supported, most of these mothers neglect their health until they are really ill. Then, too, continuous pregnancies and confinements in the thoroughly unsanitary conditions that prevail in many homes of the poorer working class do much to sap the health of many breadwinning mothers. Of 386 women who wrote the *Maternity Letters* previously referred to, 348 had had 1,396 live children, 83 still-births, and 218 miscarriages—an average of almost five pregnancies per mother! One woman had had eleven children and two miscarriages in twenty years; another had had five children and one miscarriage in nine years; still another had had five children and five miscarriages in twelve and one-half years. These are conditions that would undermine the health of the most vigorous human beings.

State Responsibility.

Perhaps the above discussion has served to make plain that the extra-domestic work of wage-earning women cannot be dismissed with a reprimand. Its roots lie deep in economic and social conditions that force the mother from the home to swell the ranks of the untrained wage-earners. Society provides neither her husband nor herself with a living wage; nor does it give either one the training that would enable him or her to enter the more adequately paid ranks of skilled labor. Through the entire duration of their married life, these couples are engaged in an arduous struggle to keep a home and to drive the wolf from the door. Probably the vast majority of these employed mothers would gladly abandon factory work, scrubbing, washing and ironing in laundries and in private homes, if they were assured of an income adequate to support their families.

But there is another aspect of this many-sided question. Although there is much evidence to show that child mortality is higher among gainfully employed mothers than among those not working away from home, it has not yet been clearly demonstrated that this evil is inseparable from the gainful employment of mothers. Rather does it appear that a considerable part of this high mortality among babies under one year could be prevented by (1) laws forbidding the return of mothers to work after childbirth for a considerably longer period than four weeks; (2) by enacting legislation providing maternity insurance and nursing benefits for mothers; (3) by public provision of neighborhood nurseries, adequate in number and equipment to furnish excellent care to the babies (and children under school age) of employed women; (4) by a further extension of maternity centers, hospital facilities for expectant mothers whose cases are difficult and visiting nurse service. It should not be forgotten that infant mortality rates among mothers who do not engage in gainful occupations are also high—in a few cases higher than among employed mothers—due, no doubt, to ignorance and poverty. The infant mortality rate among unemployed mothers in New Bedford was 108.8 —nearly one death to every nine births. In Manchester, the rate in the case of mothers not working away from home was 122—almost one infant death to every eight births. Public agencies for the prenatal care of mothers and postnatal care of both mothers and infants, together with systematic home visiting and instruction of women in the principles of child nurture and hygiene, are as much needed by unemployed as by breadwinning mothers.

In these years of rapid social change, the State is being called upon more and more to aid in righting social conditions demonstrably unfavorable to wholesome, happy, effective living—living that seems worth while to human beings. In the words of an English writer:

"The State has first to realize that if it wants citizens, and healthy citizens, it must make it possible for men and women to have families while living a full life themselves and giving a full life to their children. At the present moment this is not possible from top to bottom of the working class, unless the economic position of the working-class family be improved. The first requisite is, then, the improvement of the economic position of the family." [39]

TOPICS FOR REPORTS

1. The Share of Wage-Earning Women in Family Support.
    Bulletin of the Women's Bureau, No. 30, 1923, pp. 25-35, 67-86. United States Department of Labor.
2. A Study of Breadwinning Mothers in Passaic, New Jersey.
    Bulletin of the Women's Bureau, No. 23, 1922, pp. 16-23, 35-43. United States Department of Labor.
3. Occupations and Income of Unskilled Wage-Earning Mothers.
    Katherine Anthony (editor), *Mothers Who Must Earn*, Chs. III, V. Russell Sage Foundation, New York, 1914.
4. Housework and Child Care in Homes of Working Mothers.
    Gwendolyn Hughes, *Mothers in Industry*, Chs. IX, X. New Republic, Inc., New York, 1925.

[39] *Maternity Letters from Working Women,* Introduction, p. 16. George Bell & Sons, Ltd., London, 1915.

CHAPTER XI

PUBLIC AID TO MOTHERS AND DEPENDENT CHILDREN

THE MODERN TREND TOWARD PUBLIC AID FOR MOTHERS

AMONG all the contemporary movements concerned with the strengthening of family life, none is of more interest to the student of social institutions than the trend toward state aid of mothers and dependent children. Not only is it significant in itself, as representing a powerful means of family rehabilitation and improvement, but it marks a complete reversal of the age-old policy of society by which each family was left to struggle on by itself. Only when the home was actually broken up, or the parents were demonstrably unfit to rear their offspring, did the public authorities intervene to protect the children. Little by little during the nineteenth and the first quarter of the twentieth centuries, this public policy of "hands off" has been undermined by repeated acts of the State in behalf of dependent children. The compulsory education laws, the acts designed to protect children from industrial exploitation and cruelty as well as to secure for them proper nourishment and care and training from their parents, under penalty of their removal from the home, are, of course, merely so many instances of the direct intervention of the State in family affairs which, in the past, were left wholly to the determination of parents. With the decline of the patriarchal family there has developed a social conviction that the State must assume further responsibilities for the well-being of helpless children, especially when it is apparent that the family is unable to meet those responsibilities. Needless to say, the ancient philosophy of *laissez faire* individualism has by no means released its hold upon the minds of men, despite these new ventures; witness the recent outcry raised by intelligent citizens against the proposed Child Labor Amendment as an invasion of family rights. Nevertheless, the present trend is in the direction of rendering increased public aid to families to hold them together and secure their more succssful functioning.

This tendency has received a powerful impetus from the fact that our present industrial order makes it exceedingly difficult for the large group of unskilled wage-earners to hold their families together. As we

172

have seen, the labor of hundreds of thousands of mothers in factories, laundries and office-buildings is necessary to enable the home to continue. The very large increase in the number of juvenile offenders in recent years, and the fact that many of these youthful law-breakers have been deprived of parental care and guidance all day, year in and year out, have been brought to public attention by the press and the published reports of trained social workers. Slowly the conviction has taken root that, in self-protection, if for no more humane reasons, the State must strive to secure for all children so far as possible the benefits of a mother's nurture and training, even if that mother be only a moderately deserving and efficient person.

This enhanced appreciation of the virtues of a good home has been accompanied by increasing dissatisfaction with public institutions as places for the up-bringing of children. For more than a decade physicians, educators and social workers have expressed more and more vigorously their criticisms of public homes for children as places which tend to adopt the lock-step procedure of reformatories and to crush the budding individuality of boys and girls. Indeed there is evidence that these institutions leave their ineffaceable mark upon children in the form of a permanent stultification of initiative and self-confidence. Then, too, the mortality rate among babies committed to institutions is notoriously high, suggesting that these newcomers into a troubled world are vitally in need of a mother's affection and coddling.

Other forces have been at work impelling modern states toward a policy of public aid to mothers and families. Among these may be noted the inadequacy of private agencies to meet the enormous social need. Although many philanthropic organizations in the United States were aligned solidly against the policy of State relief, when it was first discussed, yet their own inability to grapple with the situation could not be denied. It is gratifying to note that, in recent years, much of the opposition of private agencies to such measures of family relief as the various states of the Union have set up has died down.

Another condition that has led governments to grant aid to mothers is the falling birth-rate in well-nigh all civilized countries. In France, where the low birth-rate has recently caused something like a panic among the official class, maternity benefits may be traced directly to fear of national decline and racial extinction. Although the birth-rate in other advanced countries has not fallen at a rate sufficient to arouse general alarm, yet statisticians and eugenists in England and America have uttered repeated warnings to the public, pointing out the danger of a loss of national power and prestige if the birth-rate continues to fall. It is probable that the publicity given to this subject has had an effect, more or less conscious, on the minds of legislators in both countries, disposing them more favorably to public measures designed to secure to the nation healthy, well-trained children. There is another aspect of this question that should not be overlooked. For years certain social writers have been asserting that *if the family continues to be regarded by the State as an independent and self-sufficient unit,* then the State has no right to demand large families, criticize small ones or, indeed, intervene at all to influence the size of families. Mr. H. G. Wells has vigorously presented this point of view:

"If having and rearing children is a private affair, then no one has any right to revile small families; if it is a public service, then the parent is justified in looking to the State to recognize that service and offer some compensation for the worldly disadvantages it entails. He is justified in saying that while his unencumbered rival wins past him he is doing the State a most precious service in the world by rearing and educating a family, and that the State has become his debtor." [1]

Another factor that has influenced governments in granting aid to mothers is a more thoroughgoing realization of the economic importance of child conservation. Vital statistics and morbidity statistics alike have shed revealing rays upon the waste of human life and vigor for which the slums and the industrial system must share the responsibility. Gradually it is being driven home to the minds of lawmakers that, if healthy children are an asset to the nation and to productive industry, those children must be assured of decent home life and the nurture and oversight of a mother. Instead of leaving parents to flounder on in a morass of poverty while the State invokes the sacred tradition of family independence, one nation after another is taking measures to conserve the mother, the child and home life such as would never have been contemplated a generation ago.

HISTORICAL DEVELOPMENT OF PUBLIC AID TO MOTHERS

It is well known to sociologists that the United States has been one of the most backward of civilized nations in enacting legislation designed to protect laborers against sickness, accident, unemployment and old age. With respect to all these forms of social relief legislation, Europe has taken the lead in passing laws that are more comprehensive and more easily enforceable than those enacted by a few commonwealths of the United States. Likewise in the field of State aid to mothers, European

[1] *Social Forces in England and America,* p. 271.

countries have led the way. The strongly individualistic spirit of the pioneers who colonized America, and who hewed out their homes and settlements in the wilderness, lives on in the America of today. This temper has, of course, been fostered by the enormous natural wealth of the country, and by the abundance of free land. Now that the nation's wealth is concentrated in the hands of relatively few and the supply of free land is almost exhausted, conditions are developing in the United States similar to those of older European nations. Germany was the pioneer nation to provide maternity aid on a national scale by including such relief in a compulsory sickness insurance act passed in 1883. Austria followed her lead in 1888, and at present almost every European country has provided for some form of maternity insurance or maternity grants to assist working mothers at the time of childbirth. In 1912 Australia passed a Maternity Allowance Act which will be considered later. In 1913 New Zealand took action providing a state system of widow's pensions; and in the same year France enacted a law providing public grants to mothers for a fixed period before and after childbirth.[2] In the United States, the first step toward providing any kind of public aid to mothers was taken in the state of Missouri in 1911. It took the form of public grants payable to mothers with dependent children, under carefully pre-scribed conditions. During the last fourteen years the so-called "mothers' pension movement" has spread over the country and legislation establish-ing a state system of mothers' pensions has been enacted in nearly all the states of the Union.

Much diversity exists in the systems of public aid granted to mothers. They range from national sickness insurance schemes, including ma-ternity benefits, to grants made outright to mothers from state funds under legally prescribed conditions. A brief consideration of the systems in operation in certain leading countries will serve to make plain their extent, variety and importance.

MOTHERS' PENSIONS

The countries in which pensions from public funds are granted to certain classes of mothers with dependent children are Great Britain, New Zealand, Canada, Denmark and the United States. In all these lands, the mothers' pension movement marks a reaction against the institutional care of dependent children and a healthy recognition of the fact that even a moderately good home, presided over by a decent and fairly efficient

[2] See H. J. Harris, "Maternity Benefit Systems in Certain Foreign Countries." *Bureau Publications*, No. 57, United States Children's Bureau.

mother, is a vastly better place in which to bring up children than a public institution, where boys and girls are reared and trained *en masse* with scant attention to individual differences.

Mothers' Pensions in the United States.

The origin of mothers' pensions in the United States may be traced to the White House Conference called by President Roosevelt in 1909 to consider problems connected with dependent children. Out of this conference emerged the conviction, expressed as a fundamental postulate, that children should not be deprived of home care except for urgent and weighty reasons. However, it is interesting to note that the disapproval of *public* relief to the needy which then prevailed was revealed in the conclusion that aid to mothers who are caring for dependent children should be administered by private agencies. Two years later, in 1911, the Missouri legislature made legal provision for the payment of public funds to mothers of dependent children. Because of a population limitation, the law at first applied only to Jackson County, in which Kansas City is situated; but in the same year the State granted to the city of St. Louis the power to establish a board of children's guardians with authority "to board out children to their own mothers." A storm of protest from the opponents of public relief to mothers greeted this new departure in legislation. Fortunately this did not prevent the state of Illinois from taking similar state-wide action in the enactment of its "fund to parents act" in July, 1911. This law—the first in the country applying to an entire state—contained the following provisions:

"If the parent or parents of such dependent or neglected child are poor and unable to properly care for the said child, but are otherwise proper guardians and it is for the welfare of such child to remain at home, the court may enter an order finding such facts and fixing the amount of money necessary to enable the parent or parents to properly care for such child, and thereupon it shall be the duty of the county board, through its county agent or otherwise, to pay to such parent or parents at such times as said order may designate the amount so specified for the care of such dependent or neglected child until the further order of the court." [3]

The State of Colorado next fell into line, early in 1913, with a "mothers' compensation act" which was framed in harmony with the provisions of the Illinois law. By the end of 1913, eighteen states had

[3] Laura A. Thompson, "Laws Relating to Mothers' Pensions," p. 7. *Bureau Publications*, No. 63, United States Children's Bureau.

enacted mothers' pension or aid to mothers laws. In two of these states, California and Wisconsin, certain counties had previously granted funds to needy mothers of dependent children, under a liberal interpretation of existing laws, but without specific state enactment. After 1913 the movement to grant public aid gained powerful headway in this country. In 1914, Arizona passed a mothers' pension law. In 1915, eight states were added to the list—Montana, Kansas, New York, North Dakota, Oklahoma, Tennessee, West Virginia and Wyoming. Maryland fell into line in 1916 and was followed in the next year by Arkansas, Delaware, Maine, Texas, Vermont, Alaska and Missouri, which last commonwealth passed a state-wide law completing the work of her earlier statute. In 1919, Connecticut, Florida, Indiana and Hawaii enacted similar laws; and between 1920 and 1922, Louisiana, North Carolina and Rhode Island did likewise. By 1924, forty-two states, together with Alaska and Hawaii, had enacted laws aiding mothers of dependent children from public funds. Only the southern commonwealths of Kentucky, South Carolina, Georgia, Alabama, Mississippi and New Mexico have failed thus far to put such laws on their statute books.[4]

Needless to say, this legislation has not been enacted without weighty opposition. It was urged that mothers' pensions would pauperize the families receiving them; that the law represented the inauguration of a vicious policy of state paternalism; that money should not be given to needy persons to spend in their own homes, but rather to organizations to spend for them; that new machinery for relief would have to be established which would duplicate the work of private relief agencies and conflict with it; that no proper supervision could be instituted over the ways in which the state's money was spent by private individuals. Happily, a great deal of this opposition has ceased, and those who are most deeply concerned in the successful operation of the laws are at present bending every effort to their improvement by means of carefully framed amendments.

The earlier name *widows' pensions,* applied to this form of public aid to mothers, is already becoming obsolete both in theory and in usage. In a pamphlet containing recent pension laws issued by the Children's Bureau in 1924 this statement is significant:

"The emphasis is being placed on providing home care for children, with a constantly broadening inclusion of the classes of children for

[4] See "State Laws Affecting Working Women," chart and map, pp. 50, 51. *Bulletin of the Women's Bureau,* No. 16, 1921. United States Department of Labor.
See also "Laws Relating to Mothers' Pensions in the United States, 1920-23," p. III. Government Printing Office, Washington, 1924.

whom grants for this purpose may be made. Aid is being administered, not as a 'pension' but in accordance with the methods of social case work, including thorough investigation of the needs and resources of each family, attention to the physical and mental condition of each member of the family, and such assistance as will promote the welfare of each child receiving this form of public aid."

Owing to the experimental nature of the greater part of the early legislation outlined above, many of the state laws have been drastically revised since 1913. Most of these amendments have aimed to make the law more inclusive in its application, to improve its administration and to increase the state appropriations available for the payment of grants in aid. The pioneer laws tended to restrict public aid to *widows* with dependent children, thus denying relief to deserted mothers, or to those with incapacitated husbands. Little by little, public opinion has undergone a "sea-change" with respect to this policy, and in 1919 only six states limited the grant to widows. The early laws of Illinois and Colorado provided for state aid to needy *parents* with dependent children, thus making the grant payable to fathers as well as mothers. However, Illinois has revised its law to apply only to dependent children whose fathers are dead or wholly incapacitated. Deserted mothers may be granted aid in seventeen states, divorced mothers in six states. Eighteen states help mothers whose husbands are totally incapacitated; fifteen grant aid in cases where the father is feeble-minded or is in an institution for the insane; and twenty states pay grants if the father is in a state penitentiary. North Dakota's law is unique in granting aid to any "women who have one or more children dependent upon them for support." Nebraska and Michigan stand alone in providing that public aid shall be granted to unmarried mothers.[5]

Mothers' pension laws in the United States reveal wide variations with respect to the age-period during which children are regarded as dependents, the amount of aid granted and the administration and supervision of relief. Briefly it may be said that the age-period coincides rather closely with the minimum age at which a child may legally engage in gainful employment. West Virginia is the only state setting the age-limit as low as thirteen years. In nine states, the grants are made to children up to fourteen years; in seven states, up to fifteen years; in nineteen states, up to sixteen years. The State of Indiana grants aid up to the age of sixteen for boys and seventeen for girls; Michigan extends its

[5] Emma Lundberg, "Aid to Mothers with Dependent Children," in *Annals of the American Academy*, November, 1921, pp. 98-9.

grants to the age of seventeen years; while in Vermont and Ohio, no age-limit is stated in the laws.[6]

The diversities in the *amount of state grants* to mothers are no less marked than those regarding the age of child dependents. Not all states specify the amount that may be given. But in those commonwealths where the law prescribes maximum grants for three children, these vary from $19 to $20 a month to $50 to $55 monthly. It requires very little knowledge of the cost of boarding out children in private homes to reach the conclusion that at least the first payments are quite insufficient. The boarding homes which receive dependent or neglected children probably have some other income, whereas the families receiving mothers' pensions are much less likely to have other resources. Referring to this fact, Lundberg says: "Yet the standard set in mothers' pension laws is approximately from one-third to two-thirds the amount ($4.50 weekly per child) found requisite by agencies for boarding children in family homes. Local economy and inadequate appropriations set a minimum entirely insufficient for the proper maintenance and safeguarding of the children who are by this legislation recognized as being in special need of aid and protection by the state. . . . Not infrequently the public funds known to be required must be supplemented by private charity or ordinary poor relief grants. Or, as seems to be the situation in a very considerable proportion of localities, the allowances must be eked out by the mothers' earning. If proper arrangements can be made for the care and safeguarding of the children while the mother is away from the home, this may work out satisfactorily. But it requires very careful attention to the situation in each home aided to make sure that the assistance given is such that the welfare of the children is conserved." [7]

No uniformity exists throughout this country with respect to the *agency* that administers aid to mothers. In twenty states, the power is lodged in the juvenile court; in eleven states, county, town or city boards for dispensing poor-relief add the administration of mothers' pensions to their duties. New York, Pennsylvania and Delaware have created special county boards to administer aid to mothers. State boards already functioning in other capacities are given the administration of mothers' pensions, or supervision over the work of town or county boards, in New Jersey, Vermont, California, Arizona, New Hampshire and Florida. Unfortunately, state supervision of the administration of aid to mothers

---

[6] Lundberg, *op. cit.,* p. 99.
[7] *Ibid.,* pp. 103, 104. Emma O. Lundberg is Director of the Social Service Division of the Children's Bureau in Washington.

is not as fully developed as it should be. In 1921, only eighteen states exercised careful oversight of the administration of grants.

Unquestionably, administrative agencies are not doing nearly enough systematic advisory work with mothers and children, by way of discovering their special needs or deficiencies and helping them to meet these. It would seem the part of wisdom to teach mothers how to keep itemized household expense accounts, which would be of the utmost service to administrators of state aid in their struggle to secure adequate appropriations. The investigators of the various boards that administer mothers' aid have an unequaled chance to find out the peculiar needs and ambitious interests of the children of each home which they visit and render valuable assistance to these boys and girls, wards of the state. In New York City, for example, the visiting investigators pay particular attention to the problems of children soon to take out their working papers, and report their findings to the Employment Bureau of the Board of Child Welfare. The Bureau calls in the mother and child and talks over with them the whole question of the child's employment. It also keeps in touch with the school authorities, and obtains from them their judgment regarding the child's capabilities and his need of further schooling. If it is discovered that the child would profit by another six months or a year of more specialized education, fitting him to secure better-paid employment, the Board obtains a scholarship for him or her, or continues the child's allowance for a longer period. Consultation hours with employed children are held weekly during the first months of their employment, and opportunity is given them to discuss their difficulties and their future plans. At the end of three months, and again at the end of six, the children are followed up and valuable data are secured which point to the crying need of supervision of children in the first years of their contacts with industry. Such advisory work should be carried on in all states which have enacted mothers' pension laws. Obviously the usefulness of the money grants could be tremendously enhanced by wise counsel and aid adapted to the needs of particular families and individuals.

Although, during the past decade, scores of thousands of mothers with dependent children have been assisted by the State to keep their homes together and give personal care and training to their children, much remains to be done before the relief granted these mothers is adequate either in amount or in kind. The recommendations made by a special committee on mothers' pensions in the Proceedings of the Conference on Mothers' Pensions held in Providence, Rhode Island, June 28, 1922, illumine the deficiencies that still exist, not only in the administration of aid to mothers, but in the provisions of the laws granting that aid. The committee urgently recommended first, that "mothers' pension agencies make it their policy to grant aid sufficient to meet the deficit in the family budget, so far as the maximum grant under the law permits." Clearly if the mother is not to work regularly in outside employment she must be given a sufficient sum to make it possible for her to remain at home at least four days a week and rear her family with proper attention to their physical well-being and moral training. To this end, the committee might well have added a corollary to the first recommendation, urging that mothers' pension agencies bend every effort to secure such changes in the various state laws as will make possible the payment of allowances sufficient to meet essential needs. The committee's second recommendation was to the effect that a budget should be made out for each family receiving aid, which should be based on a standard budget schedule as well as on the mother's estimate of family requirements. Such a budget should include housing, food, fuel and light, household supplies, health and incidentals. The latter item comprised recreation, education, emergencies, car-fare, insurance and spending money. A system of granting aid to mothers which takes careful account of actual, reasonable family needs, as determined by a standard budget schedule subject to revision from time to time, would seem to be the only intelligent and adequate method of deciding the amount of family allotments. Any other method is haphazard, undiscriminating and probably inadequate in the relief it affords.

Third, the committee recommended that "all mothers' pension agencies require at intervals itemized household expense accounts from families receiving assistance." This appears to be a thoroughly reasonable requirement, and might well prove to be a valuable means of educating mothers in economical and businesslike administration of the household, as well as of revealing the inadequacy of the family allowance. Fourth, the committee recommended that literature on health, food values, menus, school lunches and the like, such as are issued by the United States Bureau of Education, the extension departments of the state colleges and other organizations, be distributed by mothers' pension agencies directly or through other sources. The fifth recommendation was to the effect that "some form of State supervision be adopted in those States not yet having it, for the accomplishment of effective administration of the mothers' pension laws." Finally it was recommended that "careful consideration be given to the formulation of general minimum standards of living, including housing, food, clothing, heat, light, education, recreation, health, household equipment, etc.," such as those worked out by Florence Nesbitt in her book *Household Management*.[8]

No doubt much water will flow under the mill before the changes embodied in these recommendations are realized in this country. Nevertheless, the fact that nearly every State in the Union has awakened to the need of helping mothers to maintain good homes, in which their children may be suitably and happily brought up, is a most significant reversal of the historic policy of "let alone" where the family is concerned, and a hopeful augury that mothers' aid in the future may be both more generous in amount and more effective in administration. The first step in any departure from deep-rooted custom is always the most important. That step once taken, others in the direction of the goal are bound to follow if the reform meets with popular approval.

Mothers' Pensions in Canada, New Zealand and Denmark.

Space forbids anything more than a brief account of the laws of certain foreign countries which also grant aid to mothers of dependent children. In 1916, Canada took the first step, when the Province of Manitoba passed a mothers' allowance act. Saskatchewan and Alberta took similar action in 1917 and 1919, respectively, and since then the matter has been under consideration in British Columbia, Nova Scotia and Ontario. In the Canadian provinces, the aid is granted by the authorized provincial authority—in Manitoba by a special commission, and in Alberta and Saskatchewan by the superintendent of neglected and dependent children. The allowances are paid from the funds of the province which, however, levies a tax on the municipalities to cover part of the cost. In Saskatchewan, the sum to be paid the mother is fixed at three dollars weekly for each dependent child; but in Manitoba and Alberta, the amount given is left to be determined by the needs of the family. The result is that the mothers' allowances in Manitoba in May, 1919, averaged $61 a month in the cities and $49.16 in the rural districts—amounts considerably in excess of those paid in the United States. Owing to the greater flexibility in the financial provisions of the laws of Alberta and Manitoba, mothers' aid grants can be adapted to the vital needs of the growing children and to the fluctuations in the cost of living.[9]

New Zealand passed its first widows' pension act in 1911, amended that law in 1912 and the following year enacted the New Zealand Pensions

[8] "Proceedings of Conference on Mothers' Pensions," *Bureau Publications*, No. 109, p. 16. United States Children's Bureau.
[9] See Laura A. Thompson, *op. cit.*, pp. 237-47.

Act, which supersedes the earlier widows' pension law. This later act of 1913 applies to old-age and military pensions as well as widows' pensions, bringing them all under the administration of one department. Under this law, public aid is granted to widows (not to mothers with incapacitated husbands) who have dependent children under the age of fourteen. Applications must be made to the registrars of pensions and a hearing before a magistrate must precede the grant or refusal of public aid. The law provides that the magistrate must be satisfied that the widow "is of sober habits and of good moral character, and that the pension will be properly used for the support of her children." For one child, the amount payable as pension is twelve pounds a year; for each additional child, the pension is increased six pounds a year. But these amounts are "subject to a deduction of one pound for every pound by which the annual income of the widow and her children . . . after deducting personal earnings to an amount not exceeding one hundred pounds, exceeds the sum of thirty pounds." [10]

It will readily be seen that the New Zealand law contains two of the defects found in certain of our own state laws: (1) the pension is restricted to widows, thus denying to worthy mothers of dependent children who have been deserted, or who are struggling to maintain a home after their husbands have become physically or mentally incapacitated, any aid from public funds; (2) a fixed amount is paid for each child, making it impossible for the amount of the pension to be adapted to the needs of the family. Obviously the grants made under the New Zealand law are quite inadequate. Sixty dollars a year (£12) for the first child, and thirty dollars additional for each other child, would amount, in the case of a family with three children under fourteen, to approximately $120 a year —a sum too small to support even one child in decent comfort.

The Danish law, enacted in 1913 and effective January 1, 1914, provides that widows "who are considered indigent shall, provided they are entitled to support in cases of continuous need, have the right to a public contribution toward the support and education of their legitimate children or children adopted under marriage, without the disabilities attaching to poor relief." Indigency is defined as a condition in which the widow's property does not exceed 4,000 kr. ($1,072), with the addition of 500 kr. for each child under fourteen years. Moreover, the income of the widow must not exceed the amount exempt from state taxation in the commune concerned. The allowance provided by the original law is 100 kr. ($26.80) yearly until the child is two years old; 80 kr. ($21.44) yearly until the

[10] Thompson, op. cit., pp. 256-7.

child is twelve years; 60 kr. ($16.08) yearly until the child reaches the age of fourteen. These amounts were materially increased during the lean years of 1918 and 1919, but have been at all times quite inadequate. Because of this fact, many widows have been forced to refuse the grants and seek relief from the poor funds. Indeed, a temporary law of October, 1915, permitted widows to supplement their meager allowances by applying for aid from the poor-relief funds—thus defeating the essential purpose of the Widows' Pension Law, namely, to make grants to widows from public funds which should bear no stigma of poor-relief.

Under exceptional circumstances, the Danish act of 1913 permits public grants to be made to a child up to the age of eighteen years. It also provides that after the death of the widow the allowance for the support and education of the child may be paid to the guardian of the child or to the person who "exercises the right of rearing the child." Half the expense of the allowance is borne by the State, the other half by the commune in which the widow (or after her death, the child) has her permanent abode. The administration of the public grants rests upon the communal authorities, who are required to investigate carefully the economic conditions of the home in question, as well as "other circumstances" determining aid, and "to exercise supervision in order that the subsistence allowance shall be expended in a proper manner for the benefit of the children concerned." [11]

Thus the Danish law, like that of New Zealand, restricts its aid to the limited group of mothers who are widows. It will be interesting to note, in the years to come, whether or not these two countries will follow in the path of most of the commonwealths of the United States and extend public aid to all needy and deserving mothers with dependent children.

THE WIDOWS, ORPHANS AND OLD AGE CONTRIBUTORY PENSIONS ACTS OF GREAT BRITAIN

In 1925, the conservative government of Great Britain enacted important legislation securing to widows (or widowers) with dependent children and to orphans the payment of weekly allowances. The pensions are classified into contributory and non-contributory. Contributory pensions are payable to (1) the widow of a man insured under the National Health Insurance Act who had paid 104 contributions prior to his death after January, 1926, when the Act went into effect; (2) the children of an insured man; (3) orphan children, *i.e.,* those who have lost both parents and are offspring of an insured man or an insured woman. The

[11] Thompson, *op. cit.,* pp. 249-52.

word *child* is interpreted to include a stepchild or the illegitimate child of a man or his wife, who was living with him at the time of his death; or the illegitimate child of an insured widow, who was living with her at the time of her death. Non-contributory pensions will be paid to widows, children and to orphans of men or widows who die before the commencement of the Act, but who would have been insured persons if the law had been in force. It is estimated that approximately 196,000 widows and 386,000 orphans will benefit by the Act.

The amounts of pensions paid are ten shillings per week for widows, five shillings for the eldest child of a widow and three shillings for subsequent children, 7s. 6d. for orphans or for children who are removed from the custody of their mother. In the case of children these allowances are paid only until the children are fourteen and one-half years of age, or up to sixteen years in cases where the child is in full-time attendance at a day school. To these pensions men and women in employment will be required to contribute at the rate of 9d. for a man (4½d. paid by the employer and 4½d. by the employee) and 4½d. for a woman (2½d. paid by the employer and 2d. by the employee). These rates include payments toward old-age pensions after sixty-five years. No widow may receive a pension if she remarries or cohabits, nor will pensions be paid to persons in poor-law institutions, lunatic asylums or prisons (without the option of a fine).

The Act provides that the authorities empowered to administer it shall be the county borough, borough council, or county council or any non-county or urban district which is both a local education authority and authority under the Maternity and Child Welfare Act, 1918. These powers may be delegated to local committees, either to the education committee or to the maternity and child welfare committee.

To the fund required to meet the expense of this national pension system, the government of Great Britain will pay £4,000,000 annually for ten years. The pensions are paid through the Post Office. Contributions by employers and employees are paid as under the Insurance Act, a stamp combining health and pension contribution being provided by the government to be attached to the necessary document.[12]

An examination of this Act, which has been in effect only two years, reveals some interesting facts. All workingmen and women who are compelled to take out insurance under the National Health Insurance Act are also compelled to be insured for widows', orphans' and old-age pensions, with the exception of a few exempted persons who will not be required

[12] Facts taken from *Woman's Leader,* August 21, 1925—an English publication.

to contribute to the old-age allowance. Thus Great Britain is committed to the principle that all wage-earners, except the very poorest, should be required to coöperate with the government and the employer in providing for future contingencies such as are bound to arise when the chief provider of a family dies leaving a widow and young children. It is a fair question whether such a system of contributory payments by workers is not a sounder one than that in use in the United States, where the pension is a gift of the State. The British method would, it seems, better ensure the independence and self-respect of the pensioner. Further, it should be noted that the British Act does not discriminate against illegitimate children, thus taking an important step toward the righting of an ancient wrong—the hardships wrought, by the attitude and customs of Christian nations, upon innocent children born out of wedlock. Finally it should be noted that, by this national Act, Great Britain has established a uniform widows' and orphans' pension system throughout England and Wales; whereas in the United States each commonwealth enacts its own separate laws, some of which are markedly inferior to those of the more progressive States.

MATERNITY BENEFIT SYSTEMS IN EUROPE AND THE UNITED STATES

Long before the awful carnage of the World War had aroused the governments of Europe to the importance of conserving the lives of mothers and infants, Germany, Austria and Hungary had developed maternity benefit systems.[13] The compulsory sickness insurance laws of Germany, Austria-Hungary and Denmark provided for maternity aid on a national scale between the years 1883 and 1892. The early example of these European countries was followed by Belgium in 1904; Switzerland and Great Britain in 1911; Russia, Sweden and Rumania in 1912; France and the Netherlands in 1913; and Norway in 1919. Since the close of the World War, most of the smaller European states have enacted some form of maternity benefit legislation. To these nations should be added the new-world countries of Australia, New Zealand and the United States, which have provided forms of aid to mothers at childbirth differing markedly from the systems developed in Europe.

Forms of Maternity Aid.

A glance at the laws of the various nations that have provided a statewide system of maternity benefits serves to reveal the bewildering diversity

---

[13] The facts in the following account are derived from the admirable study by H. J. Harris for the United States Children's Bureau entitled "Maternity Benefit Systems in Certain Foreign Countries." *Bureau Publications*, No. 57, 1919.

that exists among them. However, it is possible to classify the systems under the following heads: (1) *compulsory* sickness insurance, including maternity insurance, to which employers, employees and sometimes the State contribute; (2) maternity insurance in connection with *voluntary* sickness insurance, subsidized and controlled by the State; (3) compulsory maternity insurance in the absence of a national sickness insurance system; (4) maternity benefits without insurance in the form of straight grants to mothers from public funds; (5) the provision to mothers of medical attendance, nursing service and helpful advice during pregnancy and confinement furnished by voluntary organizations. The first two systems are by far the most general, being in operation at present in twenty-five states of Europe.[14] The third method is restricted to Italy and Spain. The fourth system is established in Australia and France; the fifth in New Zealand and the United States.

Maternity Benefits in Connection with a National Insurance System.

In those European countries that have adopted some form of national insurance against sickness, maternity benefits are included in this scheme. As we have seen, however, the insurance system may be compulsory or voluntary. Among the more important European countries that have made provision for compulsory sickness insurance, including maternity insurance, are Germany, Austria, Hungary, Great Britain, the Netherlands, Norway, Poland, Rumania, Jugo-Slavia, Switzerland (in cantons electing this system), Czechoslovakia and Greece. Maternity insurance in connection with voluntary sickness insurance, subsidized and controlled by the State, prevails in Belgium, Denmark, Finland, Sweden and Switzerland (in certain cantons). With respect to financing the scheme, two methods are in general use. (1) The income of the sickness and maternity insurance funds is derived wholly from an assessment on wages, of which the employer and the employed pay fixed proportions, the State contributing nothing. Such is the method in Austria, Germany, the Netherlands and several other countries. (2) The insurance funds are obtained by contributions from the employer, the employee and the State. State grants or subsidies to insurance funds are made in Great Britain, Norway, Sweden, Denmark, Switzerland and Italy.

The *benefits* enjoyed by those eligible to maternity aid under the insurance systems reveal considerable diversity. Those of Austria, Germany, Norway, Czechoslovakia, Luxemburg, Poland and certain Swiss cantons are, perhaps, most generous and comprehensive. In these countries, the

[14] Stencilled sheet of information prepared by the United States Children's Bureau and dated March 27, 1925.

sickness (including maternity) funds provide for two or more of the following forms of benefit:

1. Medical benefit. This consists of free medical attendance and midwife service, free medicines and appliances. If the expectant mother's condition before confinement is not satisfactory, she may be given medical treatment and maintenance in a maternity hospital. In such cases a fixed proportion may be deducted from the daily cash benefit described below.[15]

2. Maternity benefit. Women who have paid sickness insurance for a period varying from six to nine months may receive, in addition to medical and nursing care, a maternity benefit. This consists of a sum of money paid daily over a period of six to eight weeks after confinement, which is designed to recompense the mother in part for the wages she has forfeited. In Austria the maternity benefit amounts to sixty percent of the standard rate of the wage-class to which the woman belongs, and may be increased to ninety percent. A nursing benefit equal to half the maternity benefit is paid for twelve weeks to mothers who nurse their children at the breast. In Germany, a lump sum of twenty-five marks is granted to the mother outright. In addition, she is entitled to a maternity benefit, which is computed on the actual daily earnings of the insured, and normally is equivalent to half the basic wage. To this payment is added a nursing benefit equal to half the sick benefit, which may be granted for twelve weeks and extended to twenty-six weeks.

The maternity benefit in Great Britain is limited to the payment of a lump sum of £2 derived from the dues paid by an insured husband, and an equal amount from dues paid in to the fund by the wife, if she herself is insured. Both these payments are given to the wife and constitute her property. The second payment, made only to insured married women, imposes upon them the obligation to abstain from gainful employment for a period of four weeks after childbirth, under penalty of a fine for infraction of the regulation. No provision is made in the act for any free medical benefits at confinement such as those described above. Not only does the law specifically provide that the medical benefits granted to insured persons in case of sickness *do not include any right to medical attendance in respect of a confinement, but ordinary sickness benefits may not be paid after childbirth unless the sickness is not connected, directly or indirectly, with the confinement.* However, section 14 of the amended law of 1913 provides that the insurance society shall pay the maternity benefit "in cash or otherwise." In consequence many societies have adopted

[15] The information contained in the United States Children's Bureau study of maternity benefit systems has been revised by reference to the summary of laws concerning the "Protection of Women in Industry before and after Childbirth," issued by the International Labour Office, Geneva, 1926.

the rule that a woman eligible for the benefit must be attended by a duly qualified physician or midwife. If the society so elects, therefore, the benefit may be paid partly in cash and partly in kind "by placing at the disposal of members the services of qualified midwives and physicians." Under a subsequent act of 1918 the National Government "practically assumes the cost of the sickness benefit for women during pregnancy."

Within the brief compass of a chapter it is impossible to give more than the barest outlines of the insurance systems in operation in Europe to assist wage-earning mothers at the crucial period of confinement and thereafter. But perhaps enough has been written to indicate that, among the States that have established national sickness and maternity insurance systems, there exist marked differences in the kind and amount of benefits received by the insured. Germany and Austria appear to have the most comprehensive plans, with Norway and Switzerland coming next. Italy's system provides only for the payment of a lump sum of forty lire to the insured woman, one half to be paid within one week after childbirth, the other half within one week after the mother has returned to work. No medical or nursing attendance is provided. As we have seen, Great Britain, also, has adopted the method of paying outright a specified amount to a wage-earning mother. Criticisms of the British system have not been lacking from socially-minded Englishmen. At a conference on national health held in England in 1917, Mr. Broadbent, vice chairman of the National Association for the Prevention of Infant Mortality, declared that of the approximately 4,500,000 married women of child-bearing age in England and Wales, as many as 1,250,000 were not entitled to maternity benefit at all, being neither themselves insured nor insured through their husbands. Even if many of this group were too well off to need state assistance, Mr. Broadbent ventured the supposition "that some hundreds of thousands of the most needy mothers in the land are left outside the range of the maternity benefit altogether." [16] The speaker further deplored the absence of medical, midwife and nursing attendance from the provisions of the law, and, above all, the lack of any helpful supervision or skilled advice given to the pregnant mother. He scored the inadequacy of the cash benefit of thirty shillings (60s. if the mother were also insured), pointing out that "a confinement in an ordinary working-class household means an outlay of at least £5, and where there are a number of other children and home help is required £7 10s. is not too much." [17]

[16] H. J. Harris, "Maternity Benefit Systems in Certain Foreign Countries," p. 118. *Bureau Publications*, No. 57, 1919, United States Children's Bureau.

[17] *Ibid.*, p. 119.

State Benefits to Mothers without Insurance.

Australia and France are the two countries which make state grants to *uninsured* mothers on the occasion of childbirth. The Australian law of 1912 provides for a substantial grant of £5 ($25) to be paid for each case of childbirth in the Commonwealth, without requiring any contribution whatever from the beneficiary. The prime minister, in presenting the bill, declared that great care had been exercised to avoid any stigma of charity attaching to the grant. He characterized the measure as providing "a maternity allowance for the protection and care of the mother, which is tantamount to the care and protection of the unborn child." In his vigorous defense of the proposed bill he declared that it "is the duty of the community, and especially the duty of a national parliament, to protect every possible life." Such measures, he argued, were justified on economic grounds as "a provision for the safety of the State." With the exception of natives and Asiatics, the allowance is paid to all mothers who are inhabitants of Australia, *whether married or unmarried*. Only one allowance is paid for a confinement, and if the child is not alive within twelve hours after birth, the claimant must present a medical certificate to the effect that the infant was a viable child, *i.e.,* capable of living. In 1912-13, the total claims presented amounted to 83,094; in 1916-17, these claims had risen to 132,866, involving an expense to the government of $3,221,793.

It would appear from these facts that Australia has the distinction of being the first State in the family of nations to regard the birth of every child as a public service, and on that ground to accept the obligation of assisting *every* mother with financial aid during the difficult and expensive period of childbirth. On the other hand, it is doubtful if a lump sum, paid directly to the mother after confinement, is of such real service as the provision of skilled medical advice, supervision and treatment, together with the care of trained nurses or midwives. The Australian system of maternity aid is easy to administer, but its value, when compared with that of certain European systems, is questionable.[18]

Maternity Aid in France.

Unlike her neighbors, Germany, Italy and Austria, France has developed no system of insurance providing funds for aid to mothers during and after childbirth. Quite early, however, she began enacting laws designed to provide some measure of aid or protection for mothers during

[18] H. J. Harris, "Maternity Benefit Systems in Certain Foreign Countries," pp. 17-9. *Bureau Publications,* No. 57, 1919, United States Children's Bureau.

maternity. These laws regulated the training and licensing of child nurses (1874), codified the laws regulating midwifery (1892), created a commission to distribute State subsidies to institutions providing maternity care and care of infants in the first years of life (1900), and provided a system of temporary aid for children of tender years in cases where the parents were unable to care properly for them and might be tempted to abandon them (1904).

On June 17, 1913, France went a step further and passed a law granting to any woman dependent on her earnings a daily allowance from the public funds of not less than half the pre-war franc ($0.096) during a period of eight weeks at childbirth, with an additional grant of fifty centimes daily if the mother should nurse her child. The law also prohibited any employer in a commercial or industrial establishment from employing any woman within four weeks after childbirth. There can be no doubt that the controlling motive for the adoption of this measure was the possibility of reducing the high infant mortality in France, especially in the first four weeks of life. During the debate on the bill, the attention of senators was called to the fact that, owing to the enlightened instruction and aid rendered by the Mutual Maternity Society of Paris (Mutualité Maternelle de Paris) to mothers and their new-born infants, the mortality of infants thus aided had been reduced from ten percent in 1892 to 3.08% in 1909. In 1910 the mortality of all infants in Paris (most of whom were not aided by the Société) was fifteen percent, or 150 per thousand—a high infant death-rate, comparing most unfavorably with that of the maternity societies. To encourage a higher birth-rate, the law of 1913 further provided for pensions to be paid to families dependent on their earnings if they have four or five children under the age of thirteen years.

Only women of French nationality, without means, who work for remuneration, either within or outside the home, either as wage-earners, salaried employees or domestic servants are entitled to the benefits of the law. Later the law was amended to include wives of men in military service entitled to separation allowances. The words "without means" have been interpreted by the authorities to designate persons dependent on their earnings. Since few women in rural districts are wage-earners, that important group, who are in as real need of public aid as their city sisters, are excluded from the benefits of the act.

TOPICS FOR REPORTS

1. Study the question of the adequacy of pension grants in Cook County, Illinois. What are your conclusions?

    Edith Abbott and Sophonisba P. Breckinridge, "The Administration of the Aid-to-Mothers Law in Illinois," pp. 47-71, 59-64. *Bureau Publications*, No. 82, 1921, United States Children's Bureau.

2. Supervision of Pensioned Families: The Arguments for State Control.

    Ibid., pp. 150-71.

3. Compare the maternity benefit systems of Germany and France. Which seems the more satisfactory and why?

    H. J. Harris, "Maternity Benefit Systems in Certain Foreign Countries," pp. 37-47, 49-65. *Bureau Publications*, No. 57, 1919, United States Children's Bureau.

4. The Voluntary Insurance System of New Zealand: Advantages and Disadvantages.

    Ibid., pp. 149-52.

CHAPTER XII

PUBLIC AID TO MOTHERS AND DEPENDENT CHILDREN
(*Continued*)

THE ACT TO PROMOTE MATERNITY AND INFANT WELFARE AND HYGIENE
IN THE UNITED STATES

ALTHOUGH American physicians, nurses and social workers had been urging for years the importance of better health protection of motherhood and infancy, it was not until November 23, 1921, that the United States Congress passed the law entitled "An Act for the Promotion of the Welfare and Hygiene of Maternity and Infancy." By the terms of the act, (1) Federal financial aid is furnished to the States complying with the conditions laid down by the law; (2) the administration of the aid is given over to the Children's Bureau; (3) such aid is to be applied to the reduction of maternal and infant mortality and to the protection of the health of mothers and infants; (4) the States are vested with complete authority to initiate and administer their own plans to achieve these ends, subject only to approval by the Federal Board of Maternity and Infant Hygiene.[1]

Beginning June 30, 1923, the Act provides for a Federal appropriation of $1,240,000 annually for five years. Of this amount, $240,000 is to be equally apportioned among the States and granted outright; $240,000 additional is to be equally apportioned and granted if matched dollar for dollar by state funds; and $710,000 is to be apportioned to the States on the basis of population, and granted if matched by an equal state appropriation.

The States may secure the benefits of the Act by (1) the formal acceptance of the provisions of the law by the state legislature; (2) the designation of a state agency to coöperate with the Children's Bureau in carrying out the purposes of the Act. Those states having a child welfare or child hygiene division of the board of health must designate that department. (3) The designated agency must submit detailed plans for carry-

[1] See the pamphlet on "The Promotion of the Welfare and Hygiene of Maternity and Infancy." *Bureau Publications*, No. 137, 1924, United States Children's Bureau.

193

ing out the purposes of the act to the Children's Bureau for approval by the Federal Board of Maternity and Infant Hygiene, and also make such reports to the Children's Bureau concerning its operations and expenditures for the purposes of the Act as the Bureau may prescribe.

By June 30, 1923, the legislatures of all the States had convened and forty commonwealths out of the forty-eight had accepted the provisions of the Act, commonly called the Sheppard-Towner Act. Since that time, three other States have fallen in line, leaving in April, 1926, only five States —Maine, Massachusetts, Connecticut, Illinois and Kansas—still holding out against the policy of accepting Federal aid in the administration of social benefits.[2] The Federal grants available to the coöperating states range from $11,311.12 in the case of Wyoming, with a population in 1920 of only 194,402 souls, to $89,041.78 in the case of New York, with a population of over 10,000,000. Although these grants may seem small, in view of the scope and importance of the undertaking, they are sufficient to stimulate the states to match the Federal grants and engage in a much-needed crusade to save the lives of mothers and new-born infants.

The report of the Federal Board for the year ended June 30, 1923, states that educational activities in the form of lectures, demonstrations, exhibits and educational films have played a prominent part in state programs. This is as it should be, since the success of the enterprise in any state is dependent upon the intelligent coöperation of the general public. Information concerning the hygiene of pregnancy is given in two ways, (1) by the distribution of literature and (2) by consultations with expectant mothers. In 1923, twenty-five states reported using booklets, pamphlets or letters wholly or in part devoted to the subject of prenatal care. Only a few states have prepared their own pamphlets on this subject, preferring to use the excellent bulletin on "Prenatal Care" issued by the Federal Children's Bureau. In many states, sets of five to twelve prenatal letters were sent monthly to expectant mothers whose names had been furnished by their physicians to the state child hygiene division. Another educational effort took the form of infant health conferences, held by thirty-six states; and maternity conferences, held by thirty-one states. In 1925, the state reports showed that 18,154 child health conferences had been held throughout the country by the various state agencies administering Federal funds.

Excellent as these educational plans may be, they should be reinforced and extended by the establishment of *permanent* child health and ma-

<hr>

[2] "The Promotion of the Welfare and Hygiene of Maternity and Infancy," footnote, p. 1. *Bureau Publications*, No. 78, United States Children's Bureau.

ternity consultation centers. Only twelve States had organized such centers up to June 30, 1923. The report issued by the Children's Bureau for 1924, however, declares that an "objective in most of the States is state-wide establishment of permanent, locally supported children's health centers and prenatal centers, accessible to all the population in need of such assistance and instruction. . . . [These centers] are everywhere recognized as the best teaching agencies." [3] Up to June, 1924, 1,084 children's health centers had been established by the forty-three coöperating States. The report for 1925 records the opening of 506 new centers during that year, as well as sixty-five additional prenatal centers. A successful device employed by several Southern commonwealths takes the form of an automobile outfitted as a center. Such a "healthmobile" has been "found to be of especial advantage in initiating a maternity and infancy program in areas where the nature of the work is little understood. Since it attracts attention all along the route it has great educational value." [4]

In all the States, special efforts were made in 1924 to launch a program for prenatal care. Investigations have disclosed that in many rural sections of the country women do not have medical supervision during pregnancy, nor medical care during confinement and the lying-in period. Failure to appreciate the importance of prenatal care is far more general than many persons realize. In Wyoming, the director of this work reported that in some counties "40 percent of the women were not attended by doctor, nurse or midwife during childbirth." In view of these conditions, the Federal Board states that "the prenatal program is still fundamentally educational for the general population as well as for the individual woman who is reached through the conference." [5]

Midwife surveys have been undertaken in recent years in many states and steady "progress has been made in acquiring definite information on the number and character of midwives practicing legally or illegally, also in registering, supervising and instructing the best of these women and eliminating those who seem unscrupulous as well as wholly untrained." [6] An encouraging result of these state efforts are reports to the effect that midwives unwilling to comply with state laws are ceasing to practice.

Since the Sheppard-Towner Act has been in operation only four years, it is not surprising that the state programs for maternity and infancy welfare have not been fully realized in a single commonwealth. In some States where the ground was prepared before Federal funds became avail-

[3] *Bureau Publications,* No. 146, p. 4, United States Children's Bureau.
[4] *Ibid.,* p. 5.
[5] *Ibid.,* pp. 9-10.
[6] *Ibid.,* p. 11.

able, progress has been made along many lines, particularly in the direction of education of public opinion, extension of facilities for maternity and infant care to localities where none have existed, establishment of community public health nursing service, provision of hospital facilities for complicated pregnancies and confinements, and increased local appropriations to cover all public maternity and infancy activities. On the other hand, in not a few States only the preliminary work of educating public opinion has been attempted, since this foundation must of necessity be laid before organized activities can successfully be attempted. When the student considers the many aspects of this social problem—educational, medical, administrative and financial—he will not be unduly critical when he learns that in "no State can the whole field be said to have been plowed the first time."

THE THEORY OF A "STANDARD" FAMILY WAGE

During the past decade a significant movement has originated in several European countries which bids fair to result in a firmly established policy of a novel character. The movement had its source in the heightened appreciation on the part of a few employers of labor of the bitter struggle for existence waged by many of their employees, especially those with families of small children. Perhaps the perception of itself would not have availed much in stimulating employers to ease the heavy burdens of their married workers, but it was reinforced by a clearer understanding of the unfavorable reaction of the struggle against poverty upon the productivity of adult workers and upon the health and vigor of their children, who will be the industrial laborers of the next generation. In France, where the movement has gained much headway, it has received a powerful impetus from a declining birth-rate and a high infant mortality rate. For these reasons, employers have been compelled "to allow the question of the human needs of workers and their families to intrude itself into discussions on wages." Out of these discussions has emerged the concept of a "living wage"—a sum sufficient to maintain not only a full-time male worker, but his family also. This family has come to be regarded as conforming to a general type in numbers, that is, to a purely hypothetical "normal family" of five—father, mother and three children. Miss Rathbone, in her admirable study of *The Disinherited Family*, has boldly challenged the existence of this supposititious "normal" or "standard" family and has brought into prominence some interesting facts. She cites the investigation made by Dr. Bowley of a large number of working class households in five English industrial towns in order to ascertain their marital conditions and the number of dependent children in each family. This was supplemented by a scrutiny of the British Census reports (1911) for seven other manufacturing cities and towns. The number of working-men about whom family particulars were thus obtained was 13,475. The facts brought out by the investigation with reference to men workers over twenty are as follows:[7]

> "27 percent are bachelors or widowers without dependent children.
> 24.7 percent are married couples without children or with no dependent child below fourteen.
> 16.6 percent have one dependent child.
> 13 percent have two dependent children.
> 8.8 percent have three dependent children.
> 9.9 percent have more than three dependent children (i.e. 5.5 percent have four children; 2.8 percent have five; 1.1 percent have six; 4 percent have seven; and .1 percent eight or nine)."

These figures are highly significant and could probably be pretty closely duplicated in other countries. Needless to say, if the sampling of the working population is large enough to be typical—and it would seem that it is—the existence of a normal or standard family of five is a myth, like so many other easy generalizations about social questions. It some-what rudely upsets one of our well-rooted convictions to learn that, in England at least, nearly fifty-two percent of the male workers at any given time have no dependent children under fourteen, and an additional 29.6% have only one or two. But it should not be overlooked that, although slightly less than ten percent of the workers have more than three dependent children, these children constitute about forty percent of all the child dependents. A "normal" family wage would be obviously inadequate for this group of from four to nine children to a family. Moreover, as Miss Rathbone does not fail to point out, Mr. Rowntree's investigations in York "indicated that 33 percent of workingmen have more than three children simultaneously dependent on them during part of their married life and that if only three children were allowed for, in fixing minimum wages, 62 percent of the children of men in receipt of such wages would be in a condition of privation for varying periods, and 54 percent would remain in such condition for five years or more."[8]

But this is only one aspect of the question. On the basis of the figures

[7] Rathbone, *The Disinherited Family: A Plea for the Endowment of the Family,* p. 16, Edward Arnold & Co., London, 1924.
[8] *Ibid.,* pp. 17-8. The quotations are by permission of the author.

given in the British Census of 1911, Miss Rathbone estimates that there were in the working class approximately 8,360,000 adult workingmen, but only 5,300,000 wives and about 9½ or 10 million children. To assume that every one of these 8,360,000 men workers had a wife and three children would mean that there were 8,360,000 wives and 25,080,000 children. Therefore, if every adult male worker was paid on the basis of the "standard" or five-member family wage, "provision would be made for 3 million phantom wives, and for over 16 million phantom children in the families containing less than three children, while on the other hand, in families containing more than three children, those in excess of that number, over 1¼ million in all, would still remain unprovided for." [9]

Miss Rathbone's study of the problem of the family wage in Europe was followed within a year by a similar work prepared by Professor Paul Douglas of the University of Chicago.[10] On the basis of an extended investigation made by a group of Parisian manufacturers in 1919, Professor Douglas declares that the family of three children was characteristic of only 6.4% of the married workers, who constituted sixty-three percent of all the workers. A similar investigation made in 1923 disclosed that only 24.7% of several hundred thousand French workers were fathers. However, this result was somewhat vitiated by the fact that women and children were included as workers. Only eleven percent of the group had three children, while the average number of children in families having any at all was 1.65.[11]

Three investigations recently made in the United States furnish valuable material concerning the composition of workingmen's families in our own country. The first, made by the United States Bureau of Labor, showed that, of 11,156 workers' families classified as "normal," [12] the family of three children characterized only 17.7% of the entire number. Somewhat over two-thirds of the group had less than three children and sixteen percent had more. In 1918, the Illinois Health Insurance Commission made another important investigation of the members of working class homes in thirty selected blocks in Chicago. Although the basis of the investigation was "members" rather than children, it was found that 65.2% of the families consisted of less than five persons, while only 13.1% had precisely that number. However, nearly twenty-two percent

[9] Rathbone, *op. cit.*, p. 20.
[10] *Wages and the Family.* University of Chicago Press, 1925.
[11] *Ibid.*, pp. 32-3.
[12] This was defined to mean a family where the husband was at work, where there was a wife and not more than five children under fourteen, and where there were no dependent lodgers, boarders or servants.

of the families investigated included more than five members. Obviously the value of this study for our purposes was lessened by the fact that it was not strictly limited to the dependent children under fourteen in each family. A third very extensive investigation of miners' families was undertaken by the United States Coal Commission in 1923. Data were secured for 128,853 miners, of whom more than half were of foreign birth. Of this large number, 83,877 or 65.1% were heads of households. The investigation revealed that *only 15.9%* of these families had exactly three children, while 44.3% had less, and 39.2% had more. The latter percentage is unusually high, and is accounted for by the fact that foreign-born immigrants from southern, eastern and southeastern Europe have large families. Fortunately Miss Obenauer, who conducted the investigation, made a comparison of the families of native-born and foreign-born miners which brought to light some significant differences. Of the native-born families, 58.2% had fewer than three children, while only 36.2% of the foreign-born had less. Furthermore, only 27.1% of the native-born had more than three children, as compared with 47.6% of the foreign-born.[13]

Not content with the results of these investigations, Professor Douglas consulted the United States Census figures for 1920. These showed that approximately 28,200,000 males were gainfully employed in 1920. If it were assumed that each of these workers had a wife and three dependent children, in accordance with the theory of the "normal" family, Professor Douglas estimated that wage payments on this basis "would have been made for 35,000,000 fictitious wives and children, even were the males to be considered as the sole supporters of the people of the country. But there were no less than 6,200,000 adult women and 6,300,000 juveniles from sixteen to twenty who were also employed. . . . To pay each of these adult males enough to maintain a family of five, while continuing to pay women and children as before, would amount to paying for approximately 48,000,000 people that did not exist." [14]

It need hardly be said that these figures do not constitute an argument against paying workers a living wage, but only against the assumption that every adult workman is supporting a family of five. The conclusion seems inescapable that any wage system which is not intelligently adjusted to the size of families is on the one hand wasteful, and on the other so inadequate as to work serious hardship. Not only is it true that in a considerable percentage of married workers' families there are fewer

[13] See Douglas, *op. cit.*, pp. 34-7.
[14] *Ibid.*, p. 38. By permission of the University of Chicago Press.

than three dependent children; it is also true that in a percentage, varying greatly in Europe and America, there are more than three.

But the question of the "standard" family wage should be viewed from another standpoint. Recent investigations have demonstrated beyond per-adventure that national income could not bear the strain of paying single men, widowers and married men with no children the same wage that is paid heads of families with four dependents. Statisticians in England and America have estimated that if the total amount of national income, over a small fixed amount, were pooled and evenly divided among all the families of the country, each would receive a very small weekly or annual increase. In the case of England, Sir Joshua Stamp, an eminent British statistician, estimates that if all incomes in excess of £250 ($1,250) were distributed, the increase per family would be only £14 (approximately $70) annually, or about 5 shillings weekly.[15] In the United States, where prosperity is far greater than in the war-exhausted countries of the Old World, there are probably localities where it is possible that a "normal family wage" could be paid to all adult male workers twenty years of age and over, as well as a living wage to adult females and to juvenile workers. For example, Douglas shows that in 1919 the city of Philadelphia could have paid such wages and still have received a return of 4.5% upon the invested capital. But he is careful to point out that these facts indicate a greater capacity to pay high wages in the Quaker City than is shown by the country as a whole.[16] Furthermore, he believes that the balance left employers and the investing public is "scarcely sufficient, under capitalism, to compensate people for their savings and to reimburse businesses for losses in such less prosperous years of the business cycle as 1921 and 1922, or, under socialism, to satisfy the annual requirement for saving." [17]

No doubt some questions rise in the mind of the reader at this point. Some there are who will ask whether, if *under the capitalist system,* two-thirds of 356 manufacturing industries in the United States could not have paid $1,600 a year to their workers, after deducting for costs, con-tract work, depreciation, wages, salaries, advertising and the like, these facts do not indicate grave defects in the system of capitalism itself. For one thing, would it not be wise to investigate the repeated statements of industrial engineers that there is enormous wastage, amounting in some instances to fifty percent, in the conduct of most industries? Moreover, is it not pertinent to inquire whether an *increase in production of the essen-tial goods and reasonable comforts of life and the elimination of produc-*

---

[15] See Rathbone, *op. cit.,* pp. 29-38.   [16] Douglas, *op. cit.,* pp. 19-21.
[17] *Ibid.,* pp. 18-9.

tion of useless luxuries would not raise the level of living of most workers —single or married—from the minimum-of-subsistence level, as defined by Professor Douglas,[18] to the minimum-of-comfort level? It is, perhaps, not so much an increase in wages that is required as an increase in the goods necessary to healthful, comfortable living, bringing them within the reach of all. Whether this reform can be accomplished under capitalism remains to be seen. It is an ironical fact that, coincident with the efforts of most States to maintain a high birth-rate and decrease infant mortality, there are tendencies in the industrial system, largely unregulated by the State, to keep down wages, thus penalizing those workers with decent standards of living who have more than one or two children.

The Minimum Wage Investigation in Australia.

Australia was the first country to demonstrate that, under the present system of production, it is impossible to meet essential family needs by means of a "standard" family wage *paid to the worker as an individual.* Owing to the widespread dissatisfaction with the wage rates prevailing at the close of the war, which had not been adjusted to the tremendous rise in the cost of living, the government in 1919 appointed a commission "to inquire into the cost of living in relation to the minimum or basic wage." After a year of painstaking and thorough work, the commission made its report to the effect that the actual cost of living for a "standard" family of five varied from £5 17s. per week in Sydney to £5 6s. 2d. in Brisbane. These figures were arrived at by carefully making out family budgets, based upon existing prices, which covered the needs of a working-man, his wife and three children. The principle governing the commission in preparing these budgets was "that even the humblest worker ought to receive a wage which will afford him 'reasonable standards of comfort' in regard to 'all matters comprised in the ordinary expenditure of a household'. . . ." [19]

The report of the commission was printed in November, 1920, and immediately thereafter the Prime Minister called upon the Commonwealth Statistician, Mr. G. H. Knibbs, to render a judgment as to the feasibility of paying a wage corresponding to the commission's findings, *i.e.,* not less than £5 16s. weekly, to every adult male employee. The reply of Mr. Knibbs was both prompt and discouraging. He declared:

"Such a wage cannot be paid to all adult employees because the whole produced wealth of the country, including all that portion of produced

[18] Douglas, *op. cit.*, p. 5.
[19] Rathbone, *op. cit.*, p. 173.

wealth which now goes in the shape of profit to employers would not, if divided equally amongst employees, yield the necessary weekly amount." [20]

In the face of this pronouncement, the government naturally refused to attempt the scheme of putting into force a basic wage of £5 16s. Three weeks later, the Prime Minister, Mr. Hughes, announced that a minimum wage of £4 a week for married men in the public service, with an additional allowance of 5s weekly for each child, would be sponsored by the government. Single men in the service of the commonwealth were to receive the same advance, minus, of course, the allowance for children. Shortly after this announcement, however, the Prime Minister departed for Europe, and no further action in this direction was taken by the Australian Parliament.[21]

As suggested above, the significance of this effort on the part of Australia is not at all in its positive accomplishment, which was nil, but in its demonstration of the truth of the theory, for some years known to economists and statisticians, that, under our present system of production, the amount of national income available for distribution in any country— even if profits be wholly wiped out—is insufficient to raise the wage of every workingman to the level essential to maintain a worker's family of five.

THE SYSTEM OF FAMILY ALLOWANCES IN FRANCE

However disheartening the facts discussed above may appear to those of us who desire to see the standard of living raised for many wage-earners, it should not be assumed that nothing can be done by way of relieving the economic stress in workingmen's families. France was the first nation to point out that the problem may be attacked in another way than by State action, and can be at least partially solved without abandoning the pet principle of labor—"equal pay for equal work." This method is the system of making grants to married workers in proportion to the number of dependent children in the family.

Although family allowances in a rudimentary form were initiated by the railroad companies in France as early as 1890, and by the State in 1919 for its lower-paid employees, the first important movement by private employers in industry was inaugurated in 1916 by M. Romanet, managing director of a large iron manufacturing establishment in the city of Grenoble. A man of intense piety, fervent idealism and broad vision, M. Romanet had influenced the owner of the factory, M. Joya, to attempt some experiments in industrial welfare as early as 1905. It was not until

---

[20] Rathbone, *op. cit.,* p. 178.   [21] *Ibid.,* p. 184.

the spring of 1916, however, that the experiment of paying family allowances was launched. At a meeting of workingmen's associations, several men had complained of the heavy family burdens they were forced to carry. This led to an investigation of the households of eight employees of Maison Joya. M. Romanet was convinced by his inquiries that the economic situation in families with dependent children was one involving genuine hardship and often debt. Moreover this clear-sighted idealist perceived that a rise in the wages of all employees would not meet the difficulty, since previous rises had been followed by an increase in the cost of living which, in the case of a workman with several dependent children, had considerably outrun the advance in wages. His reflections on the problem led M. Romanet to the conclusion that the payment to workingmen's families of an allowance for every child under thirteen was the only wise solution. Without much difficulty, he persuaded M. Joya to try the novel plan of family allowances (*allocations familiales*). The payments at first were on a very modest scale—7.50 francs per month for one child, eighteen francs for two children, 31.50 for three and forty-eight for four. The new scheme aroused much discussion among employers and workers, and resulted in agitation on the part of employees in other metal working establishments for similar privileges. Conferences were soon arranged at which M. Romanet set forth his ideas; and in the end all the firms belonging to the engineering and metal working industries in the locality decided to pay family allowances on a scale to be agreed upon. At first a very low scale of payments was adopted, but this has been several times raised, until in 1921 it reached twenty francs per month for the first child, twenty-five francs for the second, and thirty francs for subsequent children.[22] Owing to the depreciation of the franc it will readily be seen that these payments are at best very small in amount. Nevertheless they help in some measure to bridge over the difference between a very low standard of living, together with debt, on the one hand, and a minimum standard of decent living on the other.

This original scheme had not long been in operation when it became evident to the keen intelligence of M. Romanet that the employers would probably be tempted to discriminate against married men in order to avoid the cost of the allowances. He therefore hit upon the plan of inducing the employers to pool the cost of family allowances and form a general compensation fund. According to this scheme, the expense of the grants is divided among the employers according to some agreed principle— either in proportion (1) to the total number of their employees, men or

[22] Rathbone, *op. cit.*, pp. 195-6.

women married or single; or (2) to the total amount of their wages bill. By means of this shrewd device, no employer is benefited by discriminating against married workers.

The compensation fund for family allowances (*Caisse de compensation pour allocations familiales*) began its useful work in Grenoble in May, 1918. It was anticipated by a similar experiment started at Lorient in January by the President of the Chamber of Commerce, under the control of the Alliance of Industry and Commerce. This *Caisse* was organized as a result of agitation by workers for an increase of wages. From 1918 to the present time *Caisses de compensation* have sprung up like mushroom growths from one end of France to the other. In general they have originated not with the workers, but with federations of employers or with chambers of commerce, who have become convinced of their useful function, and have advocated their establishment with enthusiastic conviction. At the third annual congress of the *Caisses,* held in June, 1923, "the President, M. Mathon, claimed that there were affiliated to the Committee 120 *Caisses,* including 7,600 firms, and distributing in family allowances over 92 million francs annually for the direct or indirect benefit of 880,000 wage-earners. Including the great public and private bodies which administer allowances individually, he reckoned that the allowances paid amount to over 300 million francs annually and affect over 2½ million wage-earners." It has been calculated further that "the system of family allowances already covers about half the industrial wage-earners of France." [23]

More recent figures concerning the extension of the system of family allowances in France were given by M. Mathon at the meeting of the Central Committee of Family Allowances on December 19, 1924. There were at that time 159 *Caisses de compensation,* with others in process of organization. These comprise nearly 10,000 business organizations. "Including independent firms, railways, mines and State payments, the allowances amount to 900 million francs per annum, covering three million wage-earners (two-thirds of those engaged in French industry)." [24]

The French government has recently set the seal of its approval on the system of family allowances by requiring that all tenders for government work shall contain a clause obliging the contractor to pay family allowances and to belong to a *Caisse.* The only exception admitted by the government is in the case of a contractor employing at least 2,000 persons

[23] Rathbone, *op. cit.,* pp. 197-8.
[24] *Monthly Notes,* January, 1925. Family Endowment Society, 50 Romney St., London S. W. I.

who has already developed his own approved scheme for payment of allowances. The rates of allowances to be paid, as well as other conditions, are prescribed by the Minister of Labor. Thus France has taken a long stride toward government regulation of the system of family allowances. Perhaps it is not unduly rash to predict that the whole system will eventually fall under State control.

Such rapid growth and success of a new movement, which represents a somewhat radical departure from custom, seems extraordinary. It may be in part explained by the serious alarm of government officials and employers of labor alike at the steady, long-continued fall of the French birth-rate, rendered more disturbing by the existence of a high infant mortality rate. But successful as has been the movement for the payment of family allowances, it has not proceeded without encountering difficulties and even opposition. One question, difficult of settlement, has been whether the allowance should be paid to the mother or the father. In a land where the patriarchal family is still firmly entrenched, and where the father is the unquestioned head of the family, it is a delicate matter to pay the allowance to the mother. Yet many employers believe that this is the only way to insure that the money will be spent exclusively for the benefit of the children, thus realizing the fundamental purpose of the plan —a lower mortality rate and healthy, well nourished children. In 1924, the majority of the *Caisses* paid the allowance to the father; but an encouraging number of funds, including those at Paris, Lille, Tours, Dijon and Amiens, are making the payment direct to the mother. In August, 1925, the Permanent Commission of the French Central Committee of Family Allowances declared its preference for payment of the children's allowances to the mother.

Another delicate question the *Caisses* have had to settle is concerned with the payment of allowances to unmarried mothers. Some employers argue that, since the *Caisse* is organized to recognize parenthood within marriage as deserving of social aid, it is a mistaken policy to make grants to women who bring children into the world irregularly and without responsibility. Others—and these are probably in the majority—reason that a refusal to grant allowances to illegitimate offspring merely penalizes the innocent child whom the system is organized to benefit.

The attitude of organized labor in France toward the system of family allowances, initiated and controlled as it is by the employers, is too long and intricate a subject to be adequately considered in this chapter. The early hostility of the trade unions seems to have given place, in some cases, to indifference; in others, to a definite demand that the system be taken from the control of the employers and placed under that of the State. At the Annual Congress of the General Confederation of Labor (*Confédération Générale du Travail*) held in January, 1923, the present system of family allowances was denounced on the ground that, if the grants are paid by individual employers, there is risk of discrimination against married workers; if they are paid by the *Caisse*, "this gives the employing class an unwarrantable power of interference in the workman's household, and enables them by means of objectionable regulations to keep the workers in tutelage and to counteract their efforts of emancipation." [25] For these reasons the Congress passed a resolution declaring that "the service of family allowances, premiums at birth [26] and allowances to nursing mothers should be under the control of the State (*la collectivité*), managed by officially appointed committees, including representatives of the various interests concerned, and financed by subsidies from the public purse. The allowances should be completely separated from the question of labour, and should not be affected by its fluctuations, or by unemployment or illness."

Even more downright is the statement of M. Lapierre, one of the secretaries of the General Confederation of Labor, who, in a public address, declared:

"I demand the immediate transformation of the present system because I consider it to be a grave danger to the organizations of workers and their beneficiaries. In its existing form, the institution of family allowances is aimed at undermining the freedom of the workers." [27]

The hostility of the French labor unions to the control of family allowances and maternity benefits by federations of employers is, of course, entirely natural and by no means without grounds. Intelligent labor leaders fear that the system may make the worker so content with his lot that he will lose zeal for the great objectives of organized labor—shorter hours, higher wages and, above all, an increasing control of industry by the workers, culminating in complete socialization. Then, too, they fear the potential power which the payment of family allowances confers upon the employing class, and point as evidence to the fact that, when the workers in Roubaix were planning a one-day general strike, the mothers of families were visited by representatives of the employers and warned of the consequences to their families of the projected strike. Another reason for the antagonistic attitude of many trade unions to the private admin-

[25] Rathbone, *op. cit.*, p. 213.
[26] Many *Caisses* make these special grants to mothers in addition to family allowances.
[27] Rathbone, *op. cit.*, p. 214.

istration of family allowances is the fact that they are completely excluded from a voice in the management of the scheme. This resentment would largely evaporate if the State should assume control of the system.

On the other hand, the employers of labor are strongly opposed to State legalization and administration of family allowances on the grounds that such action would constitute an invasion of their private rights and freedom. Also the employers are quite well aware that a State law compelling all industrial concerns to pay allowances, and fixing the amount of the grants, would add materially to the expense of administration and to the size of the allowances. At present, owing to the small amount paid for each child in every *Caisse* outside of Roubaix, the cost of family allowances to the individual employer does not exceed two percent of their wages costs. In 1920, a bill was presented to the Chamber of Deputies which proposed that the organization of *Caisses* be made compulsory, and that the scale of payments for allowances, birth premiums and nursing premiums be at least five percent of the wages cost. The bill failed of passage, but it indicates unmistakably that State control of the administration and finance of the *Caisses* would eventuate in greatly increased costs to employers.

THE SYSTEM OF FAMILY ALLOWANCES IN OTHER EUROPEAN COUNTRIES

In Germany, as in France, the custom of paying grants to families with dependent children originated before the war. However, in Germany such payments were made only to civil service employees of the national and local governments, to agricultural workers and to the employees in an occasional industrial organization like the Zeiss optical works. During the war the practice became much more general, especially in private firms engaged in government work. Owing to the antipathy of the labor unions, however, the payment of family allowances seems to have been largely abandoned for a short period after the war. But the deplorable economic conditions in Germany soon forced a return to the practice, and for the last few years most collective wage agreements have contained clauses providing for family allowances. Early in 1923, the Ministry of Labor divided these agreements into three classes with respect to the payment of allowances: (1) those in which allowances are universally recognized, as in mechanical engineering, textiles, coal-mining, paper manufacturing; (2) those about equally divided between acceptance and non-acceptance of the new scheme; (3) those where the system is not recognized.

Germany has not yet developed the compensation fund on the pool system to nearly the extent it has reached in France. Most allowances are paid by individual firms, and are thus open to the objection that the payments, made openly to married workers with dependent families, frequently arouse jealousy and ill-feeling on the part of unmarried employees. The first fund on the French plan for payment of family allowances was organized in Berlin by the Union of Metal Industries in 1920. Since that time such funds have been instituted in Cologne, Berg, Münster and a few other industrial cities. Only eight were in successful operation at the end of 1923.[28] The basis of assessment for the pool is either the wages bill or the numbers employed; but several important industries have abandoned the latter for the former method.

Several firms in Germany pay allowances, not alone to children under fourteen, but to dependent wives or relatives, or even to women acting as heads of households. The amount of the allowance is pitifully small, however, and quite inadequate for the entire support of the beneficiary. A few of the more skilled and highly paid occupations continue the payments to the sons and daughters of employees who are students in secondary schools and even in universities.

The same controversies have been waged in Germany as in other countries with regard to the virtues or defects of the system of family allowances. The German trade unions and Socialist unions have been consistently opposed to the scheme, at least in theory. It has been urged in Germany, as in France, that the system encourages discrimination against married workers, while it works injustice to the unmarried by paying higher wages for the same work to men with families. The Socialists advocate the abandonment of family allowances and the substitution for them of a kind of communal paternalism, consisting of the provision to children not only of free schooling, but free meals, books and even clothing. Yet, in spite of the adverse criticisms openly expressed by labor unions, the system of family allowances has become widely extended in Germany. Whether the severe economic stress in that country at the present writing and the wretched condition of many of the wage-earners, who have lost nearly all the benefits they had acquired by organized effort before the war, will militate against the further successful development of the system remains to be seen.[29]

Influenced, perhaps, by the example of her neighbor, France, Belgium has also instituted the system of family allowances. First introduced in

[28] Douglas, *op. cit.*, p. 114.
[29] For the development of family allowances in Germany see Rathbone, *op. cit.*, pp. 219-23. Also see Douglas, *op. cit.*, Ch. VIII.

1915, it developed slowly until after the War, when several funds were formed in the mining districts. The most important *Caisse* was founded in Liège in 1922. This fund is on a regional basis and is open to all the commercial and industrial establishments in the provinces of Liège, Limbourg and Luxembourg. Allowances are made on behalf of dependent children under fourteen, the amounts being graded from ten francs for the first child to forty francs for the fourth and subsequent children. Like the French *Caisse,* after which it is modeled, this Belgian fund pays birth premiums of 250 francs at the birth of the first child and 150 francs for each succeeding child. In most of the other Belgian funds the amounts paid are smaller. State employees receive allowances for dependent children up to the age of twenty-one. In 1926, equalization funds had been established in 800 firms, which paid family allowances to 400,-000 workers. In addition, the State system of allowances benefited 230,000 State employees, including teachers and railway workers.

The trade unions and Socialist unions in Belgium show much the same distrust of the system of family allowances as is revealed in France and Germany. While asserting the necessity of assistance for large families, the National Committee of the Belgian Syndicalist Commission declares that this aid should be extended by the State, and "repudiates what it considers the false philanthropy and degrading charity of employers, who aim only at further enslavement of the workers." [30]

During the War, the practice of making provision for the families of workers was instituted in Holland, although it was confined to certain State departments and a limited number of industrial firms. In 1920, Holland adopted the policy of paying children's allowances to all State civil servants, including all branches of the army, railway workers, postmen and teachers. The grants vary from fifty florins to 200 florins per child per year and are continued in the case of children of civil servants up to the age of eighteen. The example of the national government has been followed by most of the provincial governments and by some of the municipal authorities. Some commercial and industrial establishments have also adopted the system of family allowances. In 1920, twenty-two collective agreements had been concluded, affecting 756 firms employing 34,000 workers. The grants are very small, varying from 0.20 florins to 1.30 florins [31] weekly for each child, and are sometimes paid only for the third or fourth child.

---

[30] Rathbone, *op. cit.,* p. 225.
[31] From eight cents to fifty-two cents. A florin was worth forty cents before the War.

It is interesting to note that the system of family allowances has met with organized opposition in Holland, where a committee formed to combat it has found support, not only from the Democratic and Social Democratic parties, but from feminist organizations. These groups take the position that the principle of "equal pay for equal work" is violated by the system of children's allowances. Despite the fact that the uniform living wages, if high enough to support a family of three or four children in reasonable comfort, would enable a single worker to live in comparative luxury; and despite the further important consideration that statisticians have demonstrated the economic impossibility of paying such wages indiscriminately to all workers, the Social Democrats and the feminists continue to advocate the policy of a high, uniform wage.[32]

In Austria, children's allowances had been paid by the employers in the metal working and engineering industries for a few years prior to 1921. In that year an act was passed requiring all establishments to pay to their workers bonuses, for themselves, their wives and their children, proportioned to the price of bread. This act was to continue in force until a children's insurance act should be passed. Such a bill was prepared by the Social Democratic party in February, 1923, under the name of the Children's Bonus Bill. The bill has been introduced by the government and provides for "the inclusion of an allowance clause in all collective agreements, and for the formation of Compensation Funds on a district basis, the Funds being administered by Joint Committees of employers and employed. . . . Owing to depreciated currency the rates are very inadequate." [33]

The latest recruits to the system of family allowances are the Commonwealths of New Zealand and New South Wales. In 1926, a bill providing for an allowance of 2 s. per week per child under fifteen years of age, after the second child and up to the ninth, passed both Houses of the New Zealand Parliament with little opposition. Payments are restricted to families whose income from all sources does not exceed £4 per week. In the case of children physically or mentally incapacitated, the allowance may be continued beyond the age of fifteen. The act stipulates that all allowances shall be paid to the mother and "applied for the children's benefit." It is estimated that from 55,000 to 60,000 children will be benefited by the new legislation.

[32] Rathbone, *op. cit.*, pp. 225-7.
[33] Pamphlet on "Foreign and Colonial Experiments in Family Allowances," issued by the Family Endowment Society, London. Revised to January, 1925.

THE SITUATION IN ENGLAND

In England, owing to the marked trade stagnation prevailing since the War, wages have steadily fallen in some industries to even below the pre-war level. For several years past the Family Endowment Society, located in London, has been active in its attempts to educate public opinion and the minds of legislators to the importance of the movement for granting family allowances, and to the necessity for establishing the system in England. Particularly persuasive and convincing have been the efforts of Miss Eleanor Rathbone, whose book on *The Disinherited Family* has so frequently been cited in this chapter. In a letter to the *London Times* of March 5, 1925, Miss Rathbone suggested the appointment of a government commission "to investigate the whole vexed question of the proper basis of wages—whether it should be influenced by or based on cost of living, and if so, whether the cost should be that of an imaginary 'normal family' or should provide for actual families through the allowance system." [34]

The endeavors of the Family Endowment Society have not been wholly in vain, if we may judge by the "maiden budget" of Mr. Winston Churchill, Chancellor of the Exchequer, presented to the House of Commons on April 28, 1925. This eagerly anticipated budget plan included a "scheme of contributory insurance for the working classes, which next year will give the widows of insured men 10 shillings weekly for life, with 5 shillings weekly for the eldest child and 3 shillings for each other child under the age of 14. . . ." [35] The Chancellor estimated that the scheme would entail little expense to the taxpayers until the third year of its operation, when the charge on the State would be £4,000,000, rising to £24,000,000 in the twentieth year. As we have seen in the previous chapter (*ante,* p. 184), the bill was promptly enacted into law. The scheme will bring enormous relief, no doubt, to widows with young children, who are striving to hold the home together; yet it seems unfortunate that the even greater body of mothers whose husbands' wages are insufficient to support the family should receive no recognition in the plan. However, the law may prove to be merely a pathfinder to a more comprehensive act providing family allowances for all married wage-workers.

THE POLICY AND EFFECTS OF PUBLIC AID TO MOTHERS

When the reader passes in review the long series of laws granting varying degrees and kinds of aid to mothers of dependent children, he cannot

[34] *Monthly Notes,* March, 1925. Family Endowment Society.
[35] *New York Times,* April 29, 1925.

fail to be impressed with the strides made by modern States in the direction of open acknowledgement of their responsibility to provide the conditions for wholesome family life. At least, the way is opened for public recognition of maternity and child rearing as services to the State and to industry, which are entitled to financial aid as well as the skilled assistance and instruction of physicians, nurses and midwives.

What will be the outcome of the virtual abandonment by the State of its time-honored tradition that each family is an independent unit, free to do as it pleases, and at the same time left alone to wage its fight against the industrial forces that are often too strong for it? What will be the effect of the new policy on the future of married women? Will it in time guarantee to *all mothers* such sufficient aid in the bearing and nurture of children as to lift from their shoulders heavy financial and physical burdens, and enable them to live fuller lives in which self-development and self-expression find some place? Or will the payment of children's allowances be restricted to wage-earners and be always insufficient for the support of the child, thus forcing the working class mother to carry on two jobs at once? Again, what influence will the whole system of public aid to expectant mothers and to dependent children have upon the birth-rate in countries where it has been declining for several generations? The latest figures show that the almost nation-wide system of family allowances in France, to which birth premiums have been added, has had no effect in raising the birth-rate, although this has been the chief purpose of all schemes for maternity and child aid in that country. The number of births in the ten largest towns of France has fallen steadily in the last four years, from 105,129 in 1921 to 92,369 in 1924.[36] Nor is this decline confined to these localities. The birth-rate for the whole of France showed a decline from 194 per 10,000 in 1923 to 192 in 1924. The death-rate rose from 170 in 1923 to 173 in 1924, while the excess of births over deaths was 72,216 in 1924, as compared with 95,000 for the preceding year.[37]

Finally, what will be the effect of the various forms of maternity and child aid in different countries upon the influx of married women into industry? Conceivably, if the financial aid is substantial enough, it may stem that ever-swelling tide of mothers into gainful occupations, put them back into the home, and set them once more to work at domestic tasks. Would this be pure gain? It is difficult to say. Certainly nothing can be more crushing than the load of toil borne by those mothers who are carry-

[36] *Monthly Notes,* February, 1925. Family Endowment Society.
[37] *New York Times,* March 27, 1925. Also *Monthly Notes,* April, 1925. Family Endowment Society.

ing on two occupations—wage-earning and home work. To relieve working women of that double burden would be a humane accomplishment. On the other hand, the testimony of social workers and nurses should not be ignored to the effect that in any considerable group of wage-earning mothers there is always a percentage of women, usually rather small, who actively dislike housekeeping and the physical care of children and perform these tasks very indifferently, if not badly. These women languish in the unsocial atmosphere of the home, and go about their duties with a sense of lonely distaste. As they well know, in the factory, the store, the laundry, they would meet other women and have some opportunity for the social interchange that they crave. Moreover, these women value the sense of economic independence that is the result of earning their own money, and also enjoy spending their earnings in buying comforts and necessities for the children. The payment of family allowances might in time have the effect of holding these women down pretty closely to the performance of household tasks as a condition of receiving the grant, and thus unduly restricting their freedom to choose an occupation. For this group, the only way out seems to lie, not in the payment of allowances, but in the establishment of a much greater number of day nurseries and community kitchens, under private or public management, than now exists. This is only to say that society, having embarked upon the course of helping mothers with dependent little children, may be compelled by the course of events to become more and more responsive to a variety of different needs, inhering in diverse groups. He would be a bold prophet who would venture to foretell with confidence what will be the future outcome of this policy of social aid to the family upon which the State has embarked, tentatively and doubtfully at first, but which, in all probability, it will carry forward with increasing confidence and vision.

TOPICS FOR REPORTS

1. The Case of the Opposition to Family Allowances: Can Their Arguments Be Met?
    Eleanor Rathbone, *The Disinherited Family: A Plea for the Endowment of the Family,* Ch. VI. Edward Arnold & Co., London, 1924.
2. Conditions of a Workable National Scheme of Family Allowances.
    Ibid., Ch. VII.
3. Wages and the "Typical" Family of Five.
    Paul Douglas, *Wages and the Family,* Chs. II, III. University of Chicago Press, 1925.
4. State and Federal Administration of the Sheppard-Towner Act.
    See *Bureau Publications,* No. 137, 1924, of the United States Children's

Bureau, entitled "The Promotion of the Welfare and Hygiene of Maternity and Infancy."

5. Pros and Cons with Regard to the Payment of Family Allowances.

Mary T. Waggaman, "Family Allowances in Foreign Countries," pp. 52-105. *Bulletin of United States Bureau of Labor Statistics*, No. 401, 1926.

CHAPTER XIII

PROSTITUTION AS A FAMILY PROBLEM

PROSTITUTION may be defined as the act or business whereby a woman offers sexual favors to men for material recompense in the form of money, clothes, trinkets or amusements. Flexner has analyzed three elements that he believes are present in every form of prostitution, *viz.*, barter, promiscuity and emotional indifference.[1] All prostitution involves selling the body for hire; it almost universally implies the absence of personal choice on the part of the woman who indiscriminately barters her favors; and, finally, it is very rarely accompanied by any emotional urge or satisfaction so far as the prostitute herself is concerned.

This social institution—if we may so call it—appears to be as old as civilization. It may be found today in some, but not all, savage tribes. Although prostitution requires the active support of both men and women, no shameful name is applied to the man who buys sexual satisfaction, but always to the woman who sells it. Much has been written of that mournful figure who "appears in every age as the perpetual symbol of the degradation and sinfulness of man," and whose existence has been defended as essential to the purity of the home. In the absence of that outlet to the passions of men which the prostitute affords, it has been maintained that no woman would be safe from their demands. In the oft-quoted words of Lecky: "She remains, while creeds and civilizations rise and fall, the eternal priestess of humanity, blasted for the sins of the people." [2] Only within the last generation has this ancient belief been seriously challenged. But, although belated, the challenge has been flung down in recent years and the attack on this age-old theory has been waged with vigor and intelligence. Few indeed are the informed men and women today who believe that thousands of girls and young women must be offered as a living sacrifice to protect "virtuous" women in the enjoyment of happy homes. With the advance of knowledge regarding the possibility and beneficent effects of the control and sublimation of the sexual impulse, with increased enlightenment as to the social conditions out of which prostitution grows, medical men and

[1] Abraham Flexner, *Prostitution in Europe*, p. 11. The Century Co., New York, 1914.
[2] *History of European Morals*, Vol. II, p. 283.

laymen alike have relegated to the scrap heap that unsavory doctrine which served as a sanction to the unbridled passions of men.

Prostitution as an Urban Problem.

There can be little doubt that prostitution is a far more difficult problem in a large city than in a small town, and the difficulty increases in almost exact proportion to the size of population. As Abraham Flexner has pointed out, "thirty lewd women in a town of 3,000 inhabitants and 5,000 in a town of half a million represent precisely the same proportion —one per cent in both cases—nevertheless the quantitative increase makes an enormous difference in the feasibility of measures designed to deal with one aspect or another of the situation. A device that might conceivably be effective on the smaller scale would probably break down completely if applied on the larger." [3] The huge size of many modern cities adds to the difficulty, since prostitutes are not so readily discriminated and known as they almost invariably are in small communities. In these "latter-day Babylons," as Flexner terms them, the family is often unstable, and family ties are weak. Young people early go out from the home to earn their livelihood and are thrust ignorant, untrained, sometimes irresponsible, into the scramble of the market-place. The conditions under which they work and eat and travel to and from their dwellings may be, and often are, of a sort to disintegrate character. In our monstrous industrial centers of today, no one knows his neighbors, and thus few boys and girls have the tremendous deterrent from immoral living which is furnished by public opinion. Add to this the fact that the temptations and allurements of a large city are opened up to youth at the very time that restraints are loosened, and the problem of urban prostitution will be more clearly apprehended.

Public Measures for Dealing with Prostitution.

Sporadically, for many centuries, public authorities have sought to control prostitution—rarely, to stamp it out. The favorite policy in European cities has been regulation; that is, an attempt is made to compel prostitutes and keepers of houses of prostitution to submit to definite rules. These regulations govern the location of houses of ill-fame, the age at which girls may become inmates, the sale of liquor on the premises, the maintenance of order, the appearance of prostitutes on the streets and in public resorts, and, above all, the medical inspection of inmates. Houses of prostitution ("Bordells") are licensed and tolerated in France,

[3] Flexner, *op. cit.*, p. 8. The Century Co., New York, 1914. By permission.

Belgium, Austria-Hungary and Italy; they are forbidden in the German Empire, Holland, Switzerland, Denmark, Norway, Sweden and Great Britain. Nevertheless, in Germany, at least, and probably in other countries refusing to license these houses, establishments exist through the connivance of the police, "which are bordells in everything but name."[4]

Unlike certain European countries, the temper of the American people has always been averse to public regulation of prostitution, on the ground that such a policy accepts and legalizes it. According to Woolston, prostitution in earlier times "was not an offense either in English or American common law."[5] Prior to the twentieth century, in many states a prostitute could not be punished *as such,* but must be arrested and held under laws governing fornication, adultery or night-walking. A system of toleration, if not of regulation, actually existed at that time in most states of the Union, and an ostrich-like refusal to face the conditions was very general from one end of the country to the other. But the ignorance and indifference of the American people was rudely jolted by the shocking facts revealed in 1902 at the Conference on Commercialized Vice held in Paris. Although the United States was not represented in the conference, its published findings were widely read in this country and served to arouse public opinion to the necessity of investigating the conditions in our midst and of setting our own house in order. Between 1910 and 1917, forty-three vice investigations were conducted in various states and cities, and the revolting details that were published led to the passage of laws by well-nigh every state "punishing those guilty of forcing girls and women into prostitution, those guilty of pandering, and those living off the earnings of prostitution." In 1921, only three states—Georgia, North Carolina and Mississippi—had failed to enact such laws.[6]

Largely owing to the facts laid bare by the vice investigations, a healthy and vigorous public opinion was developed against the segregation of prostitutes in the so-called "red-light districts," and many of these sections were closed. In every state save five, statutes have been enacted prohibiting the maintenance of houses of prostitution. Furthermore, the system whereby the keepers of these disorderly places were haled into the criminal courts, fined and then dismissed, to return to their resorts of vice, has practically disappeared. In 1909, Iowa led the way in the adoption of a more efficient method, by the enactment of an Injunction and Abatement Law which aims to get rid of houses of prostitution without

---

[4] Flexner, *op. cit.,* pp. 166-9.
[5] H. B. Woolston, *Prostitution in the United States,* p. 25. The Century Co., New York, 1921.
[6] *Ibid.,* p. 32.

appeal to the criminal courts. This act, which has served as a model for many other states, empowers any responsible citizen *to prevent by injunction* the continued operation of disorderly houses as nuisances, without being compelled to prove that the complainant has himself suffered special damages.

America, then, has clearly embarked upon a policy of non-toleration of commercialized vice, which was considerably accelerated by the widely felt need for protecting soldiers in training camps and at the front during the World War. But let it not be imagined that this ancient evil has been fairly well stamped out in these United States. Woolston has estimated that perhaps 200,000 prostitutes, including street-walkers, operated in this country in 1910;[7] and although the number has unquestionably been greatly reduced by the public measures since taken, it is quite possible that the amount of *clandestine* illicit intercourse may actually have increased.

Who Are the Recruits?

The girls and women that drift or are thrust into prostitution are predominantly of foreign birth or foreign parentage. Miner says that over three-fifths of a group of 1,000 prostitutes in New York were of foreign parentage. Only one-fifth had been born in America of American parentage. The remainder had one native and one foreign parent or were ignorant of their parents' birthplace. The daughters of native-born parents had drifted to the city from poor homes in small towns and communities. Some had come to "see New York," animated by the spirit of adventure that burns so high in youth; others had joined circus troupes or theatrical companies that visited the city in their travels from place to place. None of these unfortunate girls had come from good homes, and most of them were receiving low wages before they adopted the life of the prostitute. Miss Miner's investigations brought to light the fact that sixty-five percent of these girls who had worked in factories had received six dollars a week or less; and the average wage of 354 girls who had been employed in stores, offices, factories and laundries in 1916 was $6.35.[8]

Most prostitutes are young—in their early twenties—and few are over twenty-eight, as shown by Kneeland in his study of commercialized vice in New York.[9] Indeed, there is some evidence to show that girls

---

[7] Woolston, *op. cit.*, p. 38.

[8] Maude Miner, *Slavery of Prostitution*, p. 37. The Macmillan Co., New York, 1916.

[9] *Commercialized Prostitution in New York*, p. 107.

become sexual delinquents at an earlier age than formerly, probably due, in considerable measure, to the breakdown of home influences. Dr. Miriam Van Waters, in her admirable study of juvenile delinquency,[10] describes several cases of girls from thirteen to sixteen who have had irregular and sometimes indiscriminate sex experience. Kneeland found, after a study of 2,700 cases, that the most frequent age for committing the first offense is sixteen. Thomas quotes from testimony of a young prostitute of English parentage: "Nowadays girls go wrong younger. Today there are girls on the Common (Boston) at night, thirteen and fourteen, who know everything there is to know." [11] Here is a problem for all socially-minded men and women to investigate: What are the conditions in contemporary urban life that encourage little girls of fourteen to start upon a course that leads almost inevitably to prostitution?

CAUSES OF PROSTITUTION

The Personal Factors.

One most important element in maintaining and extending prostitution is "the unregulated desire of men." Powerful as is the sex urge in men, especially in the years between sixteen and thirty, devastating as are known to be the social and individual consequences of giving it free play, little has yet been done, either within the home or without, to help young men to hold this driving impulse in leash. Although signs are not lacking of the awakening of public opinion to the urgent need of well-planned sex education in home and school, it is still true that millions of boys and young men go through life without it. Sex education should begin in early childhood, and aim to develop in both boys and girls not only ideals of sex love and sex relations, but *habits of self-control* that will stand by them in hours of storm and stress when every other bulwark falls away. "The type of personality that loves its neighbor as itself, that lives rather than talks the square deal, that is tender, chivalrous, loyal and generous, possesses a margin of sexual safety for which there is no prophylactic substitute. Make a *man* first; teach him honor, make his word his bond, his first thought for the other fellow—then let him love, and there will be little cause for fear." [12] Despite the fact that the dual

[10] *Youth in Conflict.* New Republic, Inc., New York, 1925.
[11] Edith L. Smith, "A Study in Sexual Morality," in *Social Hygiene*, Vol. II, p. 538. Quoted in W. I. Thomas, *The Unadjusted Girl*, p. 138. Little, Brown & Co., Boston, 1923.
[12] Dr. John H. Stokes, *Today's World Problem in Disease Prevention*, p. 124. United States Public Health Service. Italics mine.

standard of morality that condones sexual irregularities in men while it sternly metes out social condemnation and ostracism to women, is no longer allowed to pass unchallenged, it nevertheless remains true that many intelligent men and women do not yet fully realize that *"prostitution is a concept involving two persons,"* one of whom is an undisciplined man.

Another vital factor in bringing about prostitution is the craving for fuller life, for luxuries and pleasure on the part of girls whose daily experience is a drab routine. Working girls, with little joy in their lives, yearn for comfortable lodgings, good food, pretty clothes and ornaments and above all "a good time." They find an easy market for their physical charms if they are willing to capitalize them; and so self-respect, moral and physical health, are exchanged for gay companionship. Adults are only too prone to forget that amusement, adventure, freedom to come and go in a world that seems filled with allurement, are the very breath of life to youth. Somehow virtue must be made rewarding, since only to the noble does it bring its own reward. Youth should be shown that a life of self-control in the interest of worthy ideals may be also a life worth living.

After examining 3,000 girl delinquents, Thomas declares that these girls usually become "wild" before sex feeling has awakened. With them sexual intercourse is submitted to, sometimes with embarrassment and reluctance, rarely with pleasure, in order to satisfy a driving desire for "vagabonding tours," showy clothes, night life in restaurants, cabarets and moving picture houses.[13]

Social Factors in Prostitution.

Important as are the personal factors involved in prostitution, no less so are the social elements. Investigators are thoroughly in agreement concerning the social conditions that promote vice and start the girl on a career of sexual delinquency. Bad home conditions, undue severity of parents, economic pressure, total lack of training for gainful work, dangerous forms of recreation and dangerous types of employment, such as those of waitresses in cafés, chambermaids in hotels, chorus girls, manicurists, masseuses—these are some of the salient conditions that make it easy for girls to "go wrong." One thousand prostitutes, studied over a period of nine years by Maude Miner, gave the following reasons for adopting prostitution:[14]

[13] *The Unadjusted Girl,* p. 109.
[14] Miner, *op. cit.,* pp. 2-7.

Influence of procurers	25.6%
Bad home conditions	21.0%
Amusement and bad companions	18.7%
Economic or occupational factors	17.0%
Personal reasons	17.0%

To these causes should be added those of bad heredity and lack of education and training. Nearly one third of 577 delinquent women at Waverley House (New York) were so retarded as to be considered feeble-minded. A study of their heredity disclosed disease, drunkenness, prostitution and feeble-mindedness in their parents.[15] Fifty percent of the delinquent women at the Connecticut State Farm, who were given intelligence tests three years ago, were found to have the intellectual ability of a child of ten years or under. Moreover, when the educational opportunities of delinquent young women are investigated, it often appears that they have been pitifully meager. Woolston states that of nearly 11,000 cases investigated in New York, twelve percent were found to be illiterate, and less than five percent of the entire number had finished the work of the grammar school.[16]

This army of girls, uneducated, untrained for gainful employment, was thrown on the market to secure what wages they might and more often than not to move from job to job in the hope of bettering themselves. Not a few had responsibilities for contributing to family support. After a day of heavy, monotonous work, they seek the streets and the "movies" for warmth and light and gayety. At many burlesque theatres and moving picture houses, immoral men and women are stationed with the definite purpose of influencing unattended girls to go with them "for a good time." The theatrical exhibitions themselves often make a brazen appeal to the sex impulse. Add to these danger spots the cheap cabarets with their women entertainers and "bootleg" liquor, and the public dance halls, too often unsupervised and sometimes literally dens of vice, and it is not difficult to understand why young girls, quite unprepared to resist these cheap allurements, choose what seems the easiest way. Dr. Van Waters denounces the methods by which youth's natural love of pleasure is taken advantage of by cold-minded adults who deliberately use it to coin money. Our tawdry commercialized amusements are the outward and visible sign of the exploitation of youth by age.[17] No less should be denounced the indifference—greater or less—of the public authorities who permit this exploitation to go on unchecked and unregulated.

[15] Miner, *op. cit.*, p. 45.   [16] Woolston, *op. cit.*, p. 62.
[17] Van Waters, *op. cit.*, pp. 118-9.

PROSTITUTION IN ITS RELATION TO THE FAMILY

The foregoing discussion has been merely introductory to a consideration of the incidence of prostitution on the family. A study of the social evil soon reveals that it touches the home at two points—in its causes and in its effects. Testimony of probation officers and protective associations is unanimous that bad or "broken" homes stand first among the factors responsible for vice. And the youths and girls, men and women, who frequent houses of prostitution pass on its toll of disease to innocent married women and to children yet unborn, thus ruining the marriage relation and not rarely breaking up the family.

Bad Homes as Factors in Prostitution.

Wretched, poverty-stricken homes, especially those that have lost father or mother, are potent factors in driving girls into commercialized vice. Miner declares that of 878 homes of young prostitutes, about which definite information was secured, over sixty percent were "broken"—by desertion, divorce or death.[18] Overcrowding of large families in tenement homes of two or three rooms is a grave menace to boys and girls, who have never known what decent privacy is, and who very early become acquainted with sex relationships. Conditions are made worse when mothers, anxious to make both ends meet, and failing to understand the danger to their daughters, take in lodgers into the already overcrowded rooms. "Girls have admitted frankly," says Miner, "that they were seduced or assaulted at the age of twelve or thirteen years by boarders who shared the crowded rooms."[19] Not only are young people squeezed together with adults and babies in these homes, but they are sometimes expected to carry on sweatshop work long hours before and after school. Home becomes in their minds an intolerable place of herded human beings, foul smells and language, and the heartbreaking struggle to pay the rent and buy food. The account given by Sophonisba Breckinridge and Edith Abbott of the homes from which delinquent girls in Chicago come is the result of many years' investigation of this problem:

"These children come in many instances from homes in which they have been accustomed from their earliest infancy to drunkenness, immorality, obscene and vulgar language, filthy and degraded conditions of living . . . Among the 157 girls in the State Training School from Chicago, for whom family schedules were obtained, 31 were the daughters of drunken fathers, 10 at least had drunken mothers, 27 had fathers who

[18] Miner, *op. cit.*, p. 54.   [19] *Ibid.*, p. 55.

were of vicious habits, 16 had immoral, vicious or criminal mothers, while 12 belonged to families in which other members than the parents were vicious or criminal. In at least 21 cases the father had shirked all responsibility and had deserted the family. . . .

"The worst cases of all are those of the delinquent girls who come from depraved homes where the mother is a delinquent woman, or from homes still more tragic where the father has himself abused the person of the child. . . . In families of this degraded type it is found, too, not only that the girl is victimized by her father but that she is often led to her undoing by her mother or by the woman who has undertaken to fill a mother's place." [20]

Dr. Katherine Bement Davis's study of 647 prostitutes committed to Bedford Reformatory shows that very few came from homes where there were economic security, wholesome family life, sound moral standards and educational opportunity.

But wretched home conditions are not the only disadvantage in the family life of delinquent girls. Parents, even mothers, frequently show a total inability to understand their daughters or to influence them. Bringing with them to the new country the ideas of parental discipline to which they were accustomed in the old, they show unwise severity in dealing with their girls. Many parents demand of a young working girl every cent in her pay envelope except the next week's car-fare. If the girl seeks amusement on the streets or in the movies she is soundly rated and even beaten when she comes home. Parents are often too busy eking out a bare living to give any moral guidance other than harsh warnings to their daughters; and they seem quite incapable of making virtuous living seem anything but a drab deprivation. When their wayward daughters make the first misstep, not a few parents have unthinkingly pushed them further down the road toward prostitution by refusing to forgive them and take them back into the home. In their determination to avert disgrace from the family at any cost, they have made themselves in part responsible for the moral degradation of their daughters.

Bad homes, then, are in a very real sense nurseries of the delinquent girls and boys, the prostitutes and panderers of society. And the two most fruitful causes of bad homes are poverty and ignorance. To be sure, defective family life may be found all around us, among rich and poor. In these homes, fathers and mothers fail to give boys and girls the love and understanding that is essential in their formative years; they neglect or do not know how to build up those ideals and habits of living that

[20] *The Delinquent Child and the Home*, pp. 74, 105.

determine character. But, although bad homes are not restricted to the poor, it will not be denied that poverty is a fertile source of family degradation; and the deterioration in standards and habits of life may safely be said to be in close ratio to the degree of impoverishment. The same holds true of ignorance. Poverty breeds ignorance and this in turn is the mother of poverty. So the vicious circle is complete. And in it are enmeshed young boys and girls who are, in the poet's phrase, literally "angering for life."

It is sheer hypocrisy to tell these young people to work hard, keep away from evil and lead a virtuous life, when the conditions are all against them. Until society has found a way to pay working parents a wage that guarantees decent conditions of living and some economic security, we shall have bad homes. And until schools and educational associations have grappled more seriously with the problem of *educating parents,* we shall have children growing up like Topsy, with no intelligent help in the upbuilding of character from the fathers and mothers who brought them into the world. There are encouraging signs at present that our old attitude of horror and lamentation when confronted with the fact of prostitution is giving way to an honest effort to understand its contributing causes. But when we investigate, we find the roots of the evil in our very homes, and are once more impelled to examine the economic and educational conditions that are responsible for such travesties of family life. "We were told nearly two thousand years ago that 'the wages of sin is death,' but we also know that too often 'the wages of virtue is dust,'" says the *Report on Social Hygiene* submitted by a committee of the women's clubs of Chicago. And these women urge that a proposed minimum wage law be passed as one means of strengthening the wage-earning girl against temptation.

The Effects of Prostitution on the Family.

The "wages" of prostitution are by no means always death, but they are more likely than not to be disease. The so-called "social diseases," of which syphilis and gonorrhea are the most virulent, are spread by prostitution among innocent victims who have never knowingly seen a house of ill-fame. Usually infected early in their careers, prostitutes become active mediums for the spread of infection to their male patrons. Very few prostitutes escape infection, as is shown by the careful studies of physicians working in connection with Protective Associations and Social Hygiene Laboratories. From coast to coast, the report is the same. Dr. Guibard at the social hygiene laboratory in Bedford Hills, New York, after a very searching examination of 200 delinquent women, found only 13.5% entirely free from taint of venereal disease—27 out of 200! In San Francisco, Dr. Ball obtained positive Wassermann reactions [21] among seventy-four percent of San Francisco prostitutes.[22] Since gonorrhea has been until recently more prevalent than syphilis, it is safe to say that nearly every prostitute has been or is infected with that disease.

These unfortunate women, then, are an active menace to the men who consort with them. On returning to their homes, the men in turn spread the infections they have acquired among those who come into close contact with them. It is probably not profitable to speculate very much concerning the prevalence of venereal diseases among the community at large. Accurate and complete records for such estimates do not exist, and the tendency has unquestionably been to exaggerate the number of sufferers. Nevertheless, data enough exist to show that the problem of disease prevention and cure is a very serious one.

It is, of course, the incidence of prostitution on homes and family life with which we are most concerned. A man who visits a house of prostitution, once or many times, may marry in ignorance of his own infection, and transmit a loathsome disease to his young wife. Even worse, he may, despite the verdict of his physician that he is diseased, decide to "take a chance" and marry the girl to whom he is engaged in the hope that she may not contract his infection. Owing to the ethics of the medical profession, such a dastardly act is made easy. The obligation laid upon every physician to maintain as a profound secret any information concerning a patient's condition that has been confided to him in the exercise of his profession prevents many a medical man from revealing to the parents of a pure-minded, wholesome girl that her fiancé is suffering from a virulent disease. Such is the so-called "medical secret," which is really the patient's secret. Wise as may be the ethics that lies behind professional secrecy *when no other life is endangered,* it has been demonstrated to be a maleficent influence in depriving the physician of his liberty of action in a situation where gross wrong may be worked upon the innocent. The difficulty that any physician would experience should he seek to break through this ancient ethical law is enhanced enormously by the fact that the legal codes of many nations and states enforce professional secrecy by statute. Thus Article 834 of the Code of Civil Procedure of New York State declares: "A person duly authorized to practice physic or surgery shall not be allowed to disclose any information acquired

[21] The blood test announced by Wassermann in 1904 for the detection of syphilis.
[22] Woolston, *op. cit.,* pp. 53-4.

in attending a patient in a professional capacity, and which was necessary to enable him to act in that capacity." [23]

With regard to this question, both law and ethics seem to place the interest of the individual above that of the social group. Instances are by no means rare in which a man, fully informed regarding the infectious character of his disease, refuses to delay his marriage until a complete cure is effected. In such cases, Dr. Morrow seriously raises the question whether the physician does not by his "silence and inaction" make himself "an accomplice, a *particeps criminis.*" [24] For many years this disturbing dilemma has been thoughtfully considered by medical men, and as yet they have reached no definite solution. Certainly it must not be overlooked that, if professional secrecy were no longer imposed, and a person suffering from venereal disease could not confidently rely upon the silence of his physician, he would probably seek the advice of a medical quack, or treat himself, or let his disease run its course without treatment. Nevertheless, Dr. Morrow is of the opinion that, while "the obligation of the medical secret is in the general interest of the social order, and should be maintained as a fixed principle of professional conduct, it may be admitted that a situation of a peculiarly aggravating character may present itself when the patient shows himself an exceptional sort of brute by the obstinacy with which he adheres to his criminal purposes after he is assured that he will almost certainly infect his wife—in such a case the physician, knowing all the circumstances and fully appreciating the tragic significance of such a step, must be guided by his own lights and conscience." [25]

The devastating effects of marriages ignorantly contracted under these circumstances can hardly be exaggerated. Writing with the wise caution of an experienced physician, Dr. Stokes admits that some wives do escape infection, and others do not progress "step by step to the worst possible outcome." Nevertheless, he adds that while "one may rejoice that many escape the worst, it is impossible to ignore the fact that enough women are wrecked by gonorrhea in one way or another to maintain an entire specialty in medicine—gynecology, which would become relatively a side issue in surgery if the effects of gonorrheal pelvic inflammation and of abortion or miscarriage could be eliminated. Few have been found to dispute the opinion of Noeggerath, who first recognized gonorrhea in women as a definite and distinct condition, when he stated that 80 to 90 percent

[23] Quoted in Dr. Prince Morrow, *Social Diseases and Marriage,* p. 48. Lea & Febiger, Philadelphia, 1904.
[24] *Ibid.*, p. 51.
[25] *Ibid.*, p. 61. By permission of the publishers, Lea & Febiger, Philadelphia.

of pelvic inflammatory disease and 50 *per cent of absolute and one-child sterility in women is due to gonorrhea.*" [26]

Added to her own bitter scourge of disease, the married woman must face the fact that she can have but one child, or that motherhood is forever denied her by no fault of her own. While not more than half the cases of sterility are due to gonorrhea, there can be no doubt that many a woman who has suffered in the past from the stigma of barrenness (once so shameful) was rendered sterile by the pre-nuptial adventures of her husband.

Nor do the evil consequences of pre-nuptial infection end here. Once more the innocent baby suffers from the sins of the father. Gonorrheal ophthalmia, or infection of the eyes, is more common in children than in adults, and usually occurs at birth. The mother, herself a sufferer from the disease (often unknowingly), is thus made the infector of her own child. It should be said at once that gonorrhea of the eyes can be prevented by proper treatment immediately after birth; and in enlightened countries most physicians and nurses do so treat the eyes of all new-born infants, taking no chances.

The effects of syphilis on the race are, if possible, more terrible than those of gonorrhea. The latter, it is true, renders men and women childless; but the awful scourge of syphilis destroys outright "75 percent of the children of syphilitic parents before they are born or during the first year of life." Of those that survive, a considerable proportion are crippled or weakened.[27] Who shall say how many abortions and miscarriages, "repeated again and again whenever the woman becomes pregnant," are due in the last analysis to a syphilitic infection of the wife by her husband? Jeans estimates that thirty percent of the pregnancies of a syphilitic mother terminate in death at or before delivery—a waste three times greater than in nonsyphilitic families.[28]

Married Men and Prostitution.

Hitherto we have considered only the unmarried man as the patron of the prostitute. And, indeed, the evidence shows that the younger, single men form by far the largest group in maintaining prostitution. Nevertheless, it is unwise to overlook the fact that a by no means negligible body of men with wives and children seek the haunts of the prostitute from time to time. No doubt there are various reasons for such a

[26] Stokes, *op. cit.*, pp. 37-8. Italics mine.
[27] *Ibid.*, p. 82.
[28] "Syphilis and Its Relation to Infant Mortality," in *American Journal of Syphilis,* January, 1919, p. 122. Quoted in Woolston, *op. cit.*, p. 190.

situation, but Woolston inclines to think that one important cause is "the failure of the family to develop a strong and restraining affection." Certainly a man who meets with indifference or friction in his home, and who has ceased to care deeply for his wife, has lost a powerful influence in holding him loyal to his family and his ideals.

The question has frequently been raised by social writers whether our present laws and customs with respect to marriage are such as to satisfy the deepest needs of men and women. The spread of clandestine intercourse has led radical thinkers to assert that present-day exclusive monogamy carries as its necessary complement a system of prostitution or of free love with birth control. These writers point out that one vital reason why men seek illicit sexual gratification and why women, living lonely, independent lives, are ready to form sex relations outside the law, is precisely the fact of deferred marriage, due to the high standard of living. A social order in which monogamic marriage is the only form of sexual relationship sanctioned by public opinion, and in which at the same time legal unions are rendered difficult, if not impossible, for many young persons by reason of economic factors, is bound to work itself out in ways harmful to society and the individual unless the problem is resolutely grappled with by all our resources of intelligence and good will. The dilemma has been vigorously set forth by Dr. Stokes:

"Early marriage of all things is the most completely out of harmony with the existing economic order, while it seems the only available solution within existing conventions, of the problem of sexual life. When a man's sexual ardor and value are greatest, he should marry; but to do so, too often chains himself and the girl to the treadmill of economic bondage. The advice has so little of practicality in it under present conditions that those who undertake to follow it today are regarded as painfully and even questionably romantic." [29]

The above statement applies with peculiar force to the small-salaried middle and professional classes in which the marriage rate is low, even while it has steadily risen in the country at large since 1890.

Psychological Effects of Prostitution on Family Life.

The evil consequences of prostitution are felt not only in the ruin of health and the production of sterility, but in the destruction of the spiritual relationships of husband and wife. The love of the woman for her mate, her trust in him and joy in his society may receive such a prostrating blow from the knowledge that he is responsible for the infection of herself and her children that they will never recover. Permanent aliena-

[29] Stokes, *op. cit.*, p. 113.

tions, separations and divorces are not rarely the outcome of such discoveries by the wife. More especially is this true in modern times, when women have been set free from the bondage of ancient laws, and are recognized in law and economic life as independent persons. Deep injuries, to body and to spirit, women were once expected to endure uncomplainingly. Indeed, a father occasionally warned his daughter, as did the Marquis of Halifax, in 1700, that, since the age "hath rendered some kind of Frailties so habitual that they lay claim to large grains of allowance, . . . next to the danger of committing the fault yourself, the greatest is that of seeing it in your Husband. Do not seem to look or hear that way." But it is a far cry from 1700 to 1927, and the women who meekly accept grievous wrongs, not alone to themselves but their helpless offspring, grow fewer with the passing of the years.

HOW COMBAT PROSTITUTION?

Few social workers can be found who believe that closing up the "red-light districts" and driving prostitutes and panderers from the city, or into temporary seclusion, will put an end to so ancient a social evil as prostitution. Such a policy may, and probably will, lessen its extent, but, on the other hand, it may increase the amount of clandestine prostitution. To a direct frontal attack on prostitution, by way of legislation, the police and the courts, should be added other measures, even more important.

1. *Strengthening of Home Influences.*

It is a commonplace to declare that the contemporary home fails deplorably to measure up to its possibilities as a character-building agency; but the triteness of the statement should not blind us to the unhappy consequences of the situation. Now that a bewildering variety of occupations essential to its maintenance have been withdrawn from the home into the factory, the family is not so interesting and absorbing a place as formerly. Children and parents alike are not engaged in common tasks of benefit to all. If the father's wages are low, the mother goes out to work to eke out the family income, thereby removing the influence of both parents from the home when the boys and girls most need it. In families where the income is sufficient for comfort, and perhaps luxury, the parents are very often absorbed in their own interests and fail utterly to understand that food, clothing, warmth and school instruction do not embrace all the essential needs of their children. Much has been said and written of the tragic gulf of misunderstanding that yawns between youth and age. Each accuses the other with bitterness of *failure to understand*—and each is right. But upon adults, because of their maturity and experience, must be placed the chief responsibility for bridging this gulf. If well-to-do parents devoted a fraction of the time given to business, bridge, club work or the theatre to a serious study of child nature and its needs, of the momentous changes in impulses and interests that accompany adolescence, they could keep in more sympathetic touch with growing girls and boys and preserve that most precious thing—their children's confidence. Youth needs sympathy, understanding, and not too tight a curb. Adventure is the very breath of its nostrils; and settled-down parents, who have drifted into a dull and aimless routine of comfortable living, have thereby lost the most vital means of keeping in spiritual comradeship with their children. Age will not be able to guide youth unless it comprehends its eager search for more life, more challenge, effort, joy. When parents fully appreciate this fundamental antithesis between themselves and their children, they may be willing to abandon their slothful ease once in a while to take up new interests, develop new skills in skating, dancing, outdoor games that will lessen the difference between themselves and their young, and introduce a new spirit of activity and even adventure into the home.

Then, too, if parents are vitally concerned in the new conceptions of human relationships that are abroad in the world today—the interdependence of labor and capital, war and peace, international relations, the place of women in society, the community church and religion of the future—if they discuss these issues in the home with informed intelligence, they will open up to their children a world of large interests and social standards of living that will stand them in good stead in the years to come. The narrow stuffiness and self-complacency of too many modern homes, the failure of adult conventions and standards to seem in the least worth while to eager youth, these are some of the basic reasons for delinquency in girls and boys. Dr. Van Waters has finely described the family life that shapes character:

"Within the adequate home there should be tolerance, flexibility and scope for new departures. Life should be viewed as a perpetual conflict; a spiritual and biological venture that deserves our utmost. Child and adult go together up the same trail. One departs a little sooner than the other. There should not be strife between them." [30]

2. The Need for Sex Education.

Although no system of school instruction will ever be a substitute for the right kind of family life, and although it is true that to find the cause of most sexual offenses we must go back to the home, yet there is a

[30] Van Waters, *Youth in Conflict*, pp. 86-7. New Republic, Inc., New York, 1926. By permission.

growing appreciation of the fact that the influence of the family must be supplemented by that of the school. Sex education should begin early in family and school and continue up to maturity, meeting the needs and curiosity of youth at every stage of growth. Eighteen out of twenty-five vice commissions recommend such instruction as one important means of checking prostitution. Yet the ancient taboo still holds in most communities, and scientific sex instruction, given in connection with nature study, biology, hygiene, literature and the social sciences, is in its infancy. Such indirect information has been proven far more valuable than a single course labelled "Sex Education." The planning of sound sex instruction, from the elementary school through the university, is no simple problem. Nor is it an easy task to awaken parents to the fact of their own shortcomings in this matter and give them the scientific information of which they are almost as much in need as their children. No sudden spurts of sex instruction given to young people at puberty can possibly take the place of a thoughtfully planned scheme of education through childhood and youth, in which parents and teachers intelligently coöperate. The United States Public Health Service urges that a broader conception of sex education be adopted, one which includes "the whole process of reproduction and nurture of children, the meaning of marriage, prostitution, venereal diseases, illegitimacy, and the hygiene of sound recreation. These cannot be taught at one time or place. *They must be given at appropriate periods from early childhood to mature manhood and womanhood.* And to be thorough, this education must be accomplished through the coöperation of the homes, the churches, the schools, the press, clubs and societies." [31]

Mere information cannot, of course, make men and women moral; nor can an appeal to their fear of contamination by vile diseases keep them from "taking a chance." Information must be supplemented by wise, sympathetic, firm guidance in the habitual control of the most insurgent impulse of human nature. "The 'Everlasting No' in the sexual life must be bred in the bone, not merely put on as a garment." Here parents and teachers of understanding minds and a firm conviction of the value of voluntary continence in early years—a faith which is the fruition of their own struggle for self-control—can be of the utmost help to youth.

3. Sublimation.

It is important that sexual morality should not be taught negatively as mere repression, but with positive idealism as the expression of the best

[31] *The Problem of Sex Education in Schools,* p. 7. Pamphlet issued by United States Public Health Service, 1919. Italics mine.

in human nature. A physician of long experience in treating venereal diseases deprecates an over-emphasis on the negative side of sex life: "The sexual life of humanity needs inhibitions to be sure—but too often the negations have been substituted for the outlets and expressions, and dwarfing without ennoblement has been the result. . . . It is an essentially evolutionary and stimulating view of the possibilities of the sexual life which teaches a self-control that expresses itself in noble action rather than in the negative virtue of frigid ultra-restraint." [32] Youth can be taught by those who have found the way that there are altruistic outlets for sex energy, indirect channels for its expression that will enrich not only society but themselves. Adolescent boys and girls should be helped to find some form of social activity—Scouting, community improvement schemes, the Big Brother and Big Sister movements—into which they can throw themselves with enthusiasm. "Sublimation" of instinct may be an overworked term, but it expresses a reality. Society should not, however, expect this sublimation to go on indefinitely, but should bestir itself to discover and, so far as possible, remove the obstacles that lie in the way of early marriage.

No doubt genuine sublimation is an achievement of years. Other outlets for the sex urge must be provided in an abundance of wholesome recreation *for all youth*, not alone the privileged. More playgrounds are needed, with trained leaders to organize games and sports; more carefully supervised dance halls, since youth *will* dance; more moving pictures which are stirring without being demoralizing. There is no problem more worthy the whole-souled attention and effort of public-spirited men and women than that of extending the facilities for healthy recreation in our towns and cities and bringing them within reach of the humblest girl and boy.

4. *Health Certificates for Marriage.*

For some years past there has been developing in America a body of public opinion favorable to the enactment of statutes requiring a health certificate of all applicants for a marriage license. However, only six states of the Union have thus far passed laws requiring that freedom from certain specified mental and physical diseases shall be established by a physician's certificate. These states are Alabama, North Dakota, Oregon, Wisconsin, North Carolina and Louisiana. The remaining forty-two commonwealths are content merely to prohibit the marriage of diseased persons, or to forbid the issuance of a license to applicants afflicted with

[32] Stokes, *op. cit.*, p. 123.

specified diseases, thus throwing the burden of determining the facts upon an ignorant and overworked clerk.

It is frequently argued that the requirement of marriage health certificates is impossible to enforce; that long-continued, searching and expensive tests are necessary to determine the presence of venereal disease in persons exposed to infection, tests that few individuals can afford. Dr. Prince Morrow opposes the certificate requirement on the ground that among "other abuses, offices would be opened for the sale of certificates destined only to dupe those they are ostensibly designed to protect." [33] While it may be admitted that, in the states where medical certification is required, the examination of applicants is too often brief and perfunctory, this does not militate against the principle that the State should throw safeguards around all persons entering the marriage relation. When this responsibility of the State is clearly envisaged and seriously accepted, boards of medical examiners, carefully chosen for their task, will make honest and searching tests of physical fitness for marriage; and the cost will be borne by the State in all cases where the applicant cannot meet the expense. Such a reform seems urgently necessary, if marriage and motherhood are to be protected from pollution.

TOPICS FOR REPORTS

1. Study the cases reported in W. I. Thomas, *The Unadjusted Girl* (Little, Brown & Co., Boston, 1923).
   What causes for the delinquency of girls do you deduce from these cases?
2. The Conflict of Youth in the Home.
   Miriam Van Waters, *Youth in Conflict*, Chs. I, II. New Republic, Inc., New York, 1925.
3. Conflict of Youth in the School and the Community.
   Ibid., Chs. III, IV.
4. Benefits to the Community from Public Repression of Prostitution.
   Abraham Flexner, *Prostitution in Europe*, Ch. XI. The Century Co., New York, 1914.

[33] Morrow, *op. cit.*, p. 64. Lea & Febiger, Philadelphia.

CHAPTER XIV

ILLEGITIMACY AS A PROBLEM IN CHILD WELFARE

SOCIAL AND LEGAL HISTORY OF ILLEGITIMACY

ILLEGITIMACY, like prostitution, appears to be well-nigh as old as organized society. However, it is probably true that in ancient society the child born of irregular sexual unions was not so harshly stigmatized and outlawed as was the case among Western nations after the establishment of Christianity. In its desire to uproot licentiousness and exalt monogamic marriage, the Christian Church encouraged stern social condemnation, not only of erring unmarried mothers but of their innocent offspring. Therefore, in nominally Christian lands, the illegitimate child has borne the full weight of social disapproval and ostracism for the sins of his parents.

The heavy penalty exacted of women who bore children out of wedlock, together with economic difficulties, resulted in the prevalence of infanticide and child exposure during the Middle Ages. Disturbed by these conditions, the Church took steps to care at least for the helpless infants exposed at its very doors. As early as the sixth century of the Christian era, foundling asylums were established in Italy, and in course of time they were founded in all the large cities of western Europe. The first "tour" or turnbox, a sort of rude cradle, one side of which was left open to the street to receive an infant, was fixed in the wall of a foundling hospital in Rome at the end of the twelfth century. Any mother wishing to leave a baby placed it in the box, rang a bell and slipped away undiscovered, knowing that her child would be received in the foundling hospital. "Tours" were quite generally established in Spain, Portugal and Italy during the centuries that succeeded, but they were not officially introduced into France and Belgium until 1811. In both countries, they were abolished after a period of fifty years' trial, because it had become clearly evident that this supposed preventive of infant deaths in reality resulted in an enormously high mortality rate among these abandoned babies.

Foundling hospitals, however, lived on in Europe and the United States until recent times. Indeed, these institutions are still numerous in

234

Austria, Italy and in this country, but they have fallen under a ban in France and Germany. The Foundling Hospital of London, established in 1739 "to prevent the frequent murders of poor miserable children at their birth," was granted public funds by the House of Commons until the evils connected with its administration became so scandalous that the support was withdrawn.[1]

Illegitimacy Laws in England and the United States.

The old common law of England, which was transplanted to the American colonies and became the basis of the laws of the forty-eight states of the Union, was ruthless in its denial of rights to the child born out of lawful wedlock. The "bastard," the term applied to the illegitimate child in English law for many centuries, is described as *filius nullius*—nobody's child—and this designation clearly describes his status. Common law recognizes no *legal* relationship even between mother and child, far less between the father and his offspring. Furthermore English law departed from the legal systems of the Continent in refusing to allow the legitimation of the child by the subsequent marriage of his parents, although canon law in England recognized such legitimation. The natural claims of the mother were, however, recognized by the common law to the extent of granting to her the custody of her child. But the illegitimate child in England had no rights of inheritance from mother or father.

Such remained the legal situation in England with respect to illegitimacy until the reign of Queen Elizabeth. In 1576 a law was enacted compelling support of a bastard child by its father if his identity could be established. This legislation has been the outstanding feature of the bastardy law of England to this day, and its provisions have been incorporated in the laws of the American states. In 1918 the Elizabethan law requiring support by the father was amended and improved by Parliament; but in all other respects the present illegitimacy laws of England bear as heavily on the illegitimate child as was the case in the Middle Ages.

American legislation has fortunately been more progressive, even though it is true that, in most of the states, the humanizing of illegitimacy laws has been slow and halting. Three important changes in the common law inherited from England have been rather generally adopted in the American commonwealths: (1) the issue of certain annulled marriages have been declared legitimate; (2) the subsequent marriage of the parents

[1] Lundberg and Lenroot, "Illegitimacy as a Child Welfare Problem," Part I, pp. 43-5. *Bureau Publications*, No. 66, 1920, United States Children's Bureau.

of an illegitimate child is recognized as legitimating the offspring in every state save four;[2] (3) rights of inheritance between the illegitimate child and the mother who dies intestate have been created by law in many states. These alterations in the common law began to be made at the close of the Revolutionary War, and accessions to them have been made from time to time. In sixteen states, the issue of void or annulled marriages are declared legitimate, with certain restrictive clauses.[3]

As we have seen, the statute law of England takes cognizance of the relation between the father and his illegitimate child only in its legislation regarding bastardy support. In general, the laws of the American states follow English precedent in this regard, but there are a few exceptions that should be noted. At least sixteen states permit the legitimation of a child *by judicial proceeding,* as well as by the marriage of his parents. In California, moreover, the law provides that the father of an illegitimate child, by publicly acknowledging it as his own and receiving it into his family,[4] treating it as if it were legitimate, "thereby adopts it as such; and such child is thereupon deemed for all purposes legitimate from the time of its birth." This is an informal method of legitimation. In states where no such provision is made for legitimating a child, virtually the same effect can be accomplished by legal adoption of the child.

With respect to rights of inheritance from the father, the legal practice of the American states varies. In several Western states, illegitimate children are permitted to inherit from the father if they have been publicly acknowledged by him or, as in the case of Iowa and Wisconsin (1917), if paternity has been proven during the lifetime of the father. Rarely, indeed, do the American states recognize the father's right of custody of the child. Illinois, however, does concede this right to the father when the child is ten years of age, and, in case the mother is an unfit guardian, at an even earlier age.

As previously stated, the bulk of legislation in the United States (as in England) regarding the relation between father and "natural" child, is concerned with compulsory support. In England, the bastardy law of 1575-6 was designed to relieve the parish of the burden of support of illegitimate children. It provided that two justices of the peace might "take order for the keeping of every such bastard child by charging such mother or reputed father, with the payment of money weekly or other sustentation for the relief of such child, in such wise as they shall think meet and

---

[2] See "Illegitimacy Laws of the United States," p. 12, *Bureau Publications,* No. 42, 1919. United States Children's Bureau.
[3] *Ibid.,* p. 13.
[4] If he is married, with the consent of his wife.

convenient. . . ." If father or mother failed to observe such an order, he or she was to be confined in the "common gaol," there to remain until surety was given for the performance of the order, or at the discretion of the justices. This legislation remained on the statute books of England without important change for more than two centuries. In 1914, an act was passed providing for the appointment of a collecting officer whose duty it is to enforce the payments the law demands from the father. It is pleasant to note that the grim old word "bastardy" in proceedings for support has given place in English legal verbiage to the term "affiliation."

Early in their history, the American colonies enacted bastardy support laws similar to those of England. It is a striking fact that, in many instances, these laws have undergone no radical alteration until recent times. "The most striking feature of bastardy legislation," declares Professor Ernst Freund, "is its stationary character, indicative of a lack of thought or movement as regards the relation of the father to the illegitimate child, or perhaps to a certain extent also of an extreme conservatism of sentiment." [5] Bastardy proceedings in most states have these features in common: A woman pregnant with or delivered of a bastard child brings complaint against the putative father to a justice of the peace; this magistrate issues a warrant against the man named in the complaint, directing him to appear at a hearing; a preliminary hearing takes place at which the accused may prove his innocence, if possible; an order is issued binding him over for trial if he fails to exculpate himself, the said trial to take place after the birth of the child; a trial follows, at which the defendant may demand a jury; judgment, if adverse to the defendant, provides for his maintenance of the child; periodical payments for support are made; the court is empowered to enforce these payments and demand security for the same. In those states, ten in number, where non-support and abandonment laws are made to apply to illegitimate as well as to legitimate children, the duty of maintenance can be enforced by criminal prosecution. It is a deplorable fact that no bastardy support legislation has been enacted in six American states and the territory of Alaska. Such laws were not put on the statute books of the District of Columbia until 1912; and of Oregon, until 1917.

The amount of the support is usually in the discretion of the court or sometimes of the jury. The order of judgment commonly demands not one lump sum but annual, monthly or weekly payments. Great variety is shown in the amounts exacted by different state laws, ranging from $1 to

[5] Freund, "Illegitimacy Laws of the United States," p. 29. *Bureau Publications*, No. 42, 1919. United States Children's Bureau.

$3 a month in Arkansas, and $40 a year in Tennessee, to $200 for the first year and not exceeding $150 per year for the next succeeding seventeen years in Utah.[6] These niggardly sums, fixed by the laws of a few states, probably fairly well reflect popular sentiment with respect to the needs of an illegitimate child, for Freund notes that the allowances fixed by courts and juries in several cases are no more generous. The length of time during which the support is to be given likewise varies in state laws. Where no age-limit is stated, the minority of the child would be the maximum period. Several states have set the age limit at eighteen; others fix the age at sixteen; and in the states of Delaware, Florida and Illinois the age is actually set at ten years!

PREVALENCE OF ILLEGITIMACY

There can be little question that illegitimacy is more prevalent on the continent of Europe than in most states of America. The average percentage of illegitimate births for the period of 1910-14 in selected European countries follows:[7]

Austria	11.9	German Empire	9.4
Hungary	9.	England and Wales	4.2
Belgium	6.3	Italy	6.9
Denmark	11.3	Sweden	15.1
France	8.7	Switzerland	4.7

The Netherlands 2.1

With very few exceptions these are high illegitimacy rates when compared with the percentages found in sixteen American states in the registration area, where births are carefully registered. The percentage of illegitimate births in these states, exclusive of negroes, for the year 1915 will be found on the following page.[8]

As might be expected, the economic and social conditions in congested areas of large cities are responsible for a sharp rise in percentages of illegitimate births in urban centers. Thus it was found that Berlin, in the period 1905-09, showed 18.1% of illegitimate births; Munich, 27.8; Paris, 25.5; Petrograd, 20.2; Rome, 16.5; Stockholm, 33.4; and Vienna, 30.1. London was the only city that showed a lower rate than the country as a whole, namely 3.5, as against 4 for England and Wales in the same period.[9]

[6] Freund, op. cit., p. 42.
[7] Lundberg and Lenroot, op. cit., p. 13.
[8] Ibid., p. 23.
[9] Ibid., p. 14.

State	Percentage Reported as Illegitimate
Alabama	1.0
Connecticut	1.1
Indiana	1.4
Maryland	2.4
Massachusetts	2.3
Michigan	1.7
Minnesota	2.0
Missouri	2.1
Nevada	.9
New Hampshire	.8
Pennsylvania	2.0
Rhode Island	1.5
South Dakota	.8
Utah	.8
Vermont	1.9
Wisconsin	1.4

American cities, with some exceptions, also reveal a rise in illegitimacy when compared with state figures, although the discrepancy is not nearly so great. The percentages of selected cities, exclusive of negro births, are given below: [10]

City	Percentage Reported as Illegitimate
Baltimore	3.1
Boston	4.6
Cincinnati	3.8
Denver	2.8
Detroit	2.6
Kansas City	6.1
Milwaukee	2.6
Minneapolis	4.3
New York	1.2
Philadelphia	2.7
Providence	2.1
St. Louis	3.7

On the basis of the illegitimacy figures for sixteen states, Lundberg and Lenroot estimate that about 32,400 illegitimate white births occur each year in the United States.[11]

CAUSATIVE FACTORS IN ILLEGITIMACY

With almost complete unanimity, social investigators agree upon a variety of causes, both personal and social, for the prevalence of illegiti-

[10] Lundberg and Lenroot, op. cit., p. 25.   [11] Ibid., p. 26.

macy. Mangold,[12] while giving due weight to other factors, holds that the chief causes of illegitimacy in the United States are "ignorance and low ideals." To these he adds defective home life, overcrowding, unwholesome amusements, evil companions, lack of moral training, broken homes and alcoholism. This enumeration corresponds closely to that of Kammerer, who has made an intensive analysis of the case records of 500 unmarried mothers.[13] Kammerer lists the causes and conditions responsible for illegitimacy as follows: no home protection, as in the case of girl immigrants who have preceded their families to America; vicious neighborhood conditions, evil companions, bad employment conditions, demoralizing recreation, educational disadvantages, bad home conditions, early sex experience, abnormal physical condition (not apparently an important factor), sexual suggestibility and mental abnormality. By far the most powerful factor in all the melancholy array of causes Kammerer found to be bad home conditions. In 194 cases out of the 500, such conditions proved to be a major cause of immorality; and in 158 cases, a minor factor. Thus demoralized family life played an important part in causing illegitimacy in 352 instances out of 500, or in seventy percent of the cases.[14]

A detailed examination of the records of these 500 unmarried mothers disclosed overcrowding in their homes, greatly aggravated by taking lodgers. Often quarreling, abuse and nagging in the family circle created irritating conditions from which girls strove to escape. All too evident was the lack of parental control, due to ignorance, indifference or inability. Then, too, the parental demand that the girl help support the family is sometimes harshly enforced. Not rarely have girls reported that, under stress of poverty, made more heavy by the girl's loss of position, they were told by mother or father that they need not return home at night if they had not found a job during the day. Such a situation has its source in patriarchal ideas and customs with regard to the exploitation of children brought by parents from foreign lands.

On the basis of the records, Kammerer declares that the "very heart" of family deterioration centered in the character of the parents. The father was often impersonal, "liking to boss"; sometimes he was cruel, especially when drunk. His daughters were exploited for the wages they could earn, at the same time that their freedom was unduly restricted and they were prohibited recreation and the privilege of receiving their

[12] G. B. Mangold, "Children Born Out of Wedlock," p. 41. University of Missouri Studies, Vol. III, No. 3, 1921.
[13] Percy G. Kammerer, *The Unmarried Mother, A Study of Five Hundred Cases.* Little, Brown & Co., Boston, 1918.
[14] *Ibid.*, p. 320.

friends at home. On the other hand, the mothers were frequently quite outside the range of their daughters' interests, curiously indifferent to their conditions of employment, their work companions and their recreation, so long as they regularly turned over their pay envelopes. Pressure of poverty not rarely made family life rasping and sordid, and had the effect of sending girls to work at the earliest possible age, while the boys hardly ever assumed a fair share of responsibility for the younger children. Kammerer cites the findings of the Philadelphia Municipal Court, in its report of 1915, which indicated that in only thirty-one cases out of 129 did the data about the home conditions of unmarried mothers merit the application of the term "normal" to these homes.[15]

In some cases, the homes of these 500 unmarried mothers were "broken" by the death of the father, which entailed financial hardship and compelled the mother to leave the home to work. Sometimes the deterioration of the family was due to the death of the mother, whose influence may be of supreme importance in the life of the adolescent girl. Again, father and mother had separated in some instances, and to the disadvantages mentioned above was added in such cases a sense of disgrace in the minds of sensitive girls, together with the development of a warped and hostile attitude toward marriage, due to the abuse they had heard freely heaped by one parent upon the other. Finally, there were several cases in which both parents were dead, "one of the most dangerous occurrences that could happen to an adolescent girl." [16]

However important bad home conditions unquestionably are in bringing about immorality and illegitimacy, they are not the only causative factors. Among the 500 cases of unmarried mothers, Kammerer found "bad environment" a major factor twenty-nine times, and a minor cause fifty-six times. This classification is meant to include demoralizing employment conditions, especially in hotels and restaurants. Vicious companions were a major factor eight times, and a minor cause 136 times. Recreational disadvantages proved a minor factor twenty-two times, and educational disadvantages twenty times. Sexual suggestibility, i.e., marked readiness to yield to sexual suggestions, with weak inhibition, was the chief cause of illegitimacy in twenty-seven cases, and a minor cause in sixteen. There were, moreover, thirty-eight cases in which girls proved easily suggestible by one individual, although not suggestible in general. Finally there were fourteen cases in which illegitimacy had been brought about by assault, rape and incest.[17]

When we reflect upon these findings, we are forced, it would seem, to the conclusion that society does not as yet properly protect adolescent

[15] Kammerer, *op. cit.*, pp. 105-10.   [16] *Ibid.*, pp. 164-74.   [17] *Ibid.*, p. 320.

girls. The fact that in 352 cases out of 500, home conditions were so bad as to constitute a determining factor in illegitimacy—either major or minor—and furthermore that poverty and drink were prime causes of the sordid character of these homes, should challenge right-minded men and women to give more thought to the conditions in our society that are the source of these evils.

But this is not all. It is equally clear that society has not accepted responsibility for demoralizing neighborhood environments and for employment conditions in hotels, restaurants, stores and offices, which are notoriously bad, especially in the two former. In 1912, the Juvenile Protective Association of Chicago made an investigation of the girls employed as waitresses and chambermaids in hotels and cafés. Wages were found to be low; the sleeping accommodations inadequate and very inferior; food "second-hand" and served in uncleanly, ill-ventilated rooms. Bad as were the physical conditions, they were far less hazardous than the moral dangers to which these girls were daily exposed. Housekeepers in many of the hotels advised the investigators not to permit girls to enter this occupation, since the immoral overtures of the men guests were winked at by the management, and no oversight of the girls was maintained during their free time. The Association went on record to the effect that the largest proportion of these girls whose sexual habits had become lax, were impelled to immorality first, because of lack of wholesome recreation; second, because of immoral surroundings; third, because of the indifference of people to them and their consequent loneliness; and fourth, because their work, involving much standing and carrying of heavy trays, was so fatiguing that any means of recreation was gladly seized upon.[18] It is encouraging to note that the Juvenile Protective Association made definite recommendations to the effect that (1) a Registration Bureau be established in Chicago where country girls might register and secure advice from socially minded individuals; (2) that a staff of investigators examine the conditions under which girls are working in hotels; (3) that Welfare Secretaries be appointed by social agencies, whose work it would be to understand the difficulties and temptations of these girls and give them friendly help and counsel.

Popular opinion is also not fully awake to the need for public supervision of places of amusement, parks and steamboats. One of the ugliest features of our modern civilization is the callous way in which youth's love of pleasure is exploited by age. Social workers are a unit in declaring that indecent movies; unsupervised dance halls, where procurers fre-

[18] See Kammerer, *op. cit.*, pp. 51-7 for a more complete account of the report of the Association.

quently may be found seeking to induce girls to earn "easy money" by prostitution; cheap cabarets and vaudeville houses, with flaunting signs advertising "shows" sometimes grossly salacious, are potent means of weakening sexual inhibitions in girls with a natural craving for "a good time." A deep conviction of the responsibility of society to regulate and supervise these places is driven home to the minds of social workers, although popular opinion is not sufficiently informed by actual acquaintance with the conditions to demand prompt public action.

UNMARRIED MOTHERS: AGE

It is a disturbing fact that illegitimacy exists among very young girls. A high percentage of unmarried mothers are under twenty-one years of age, and many a girl fifteen to seventeen years old has become an unmarried mother. Mangold finds the modal year is 18-19. He has classified the unmarried mothers reported in three large American cities and in the Registration Area of the United States into two age-groups—those under and those over twenty-one years of age. In Washington, D. C., the percentage of single girls under twenty-one who became mothers in 1912 was 37.17; in Philadelphia in 1915, the percentage was 52.9; and in St. Louis in 1912-13, it was 55.7. In the Birth Registration Area in 1918, 45.2% of unmarried mothers were under twenty years of age.[19] Bingham found that the median age of 500 sex delinquents in Waverley House was seventeen years and three months.[20] Of 465 unmarried mothers in Boston, Parker gives the age distribution as follows:[21]

Age	Number	Percentage
Less than 15 years	4	.9
15 years	4	.9
16 years	17	3.6
17 years	29	6.2
18-20 years	135	29.0
21-24 years	164	35.3
25-29 years	68	14.6
30-34 years	23	5.0
35-39 years	12	2.6
40-44 years	8	1.7
45 and over	1	.2

[19] Mangold, op. cit., p. 60.
[20] Ann T. Bingham, "Determinants of Sex Delinquency in Girls," p. 518, in Journal of the American Institute of Criminal Law and Criminology, Vol. XIII, No. 4, February, 1923.
[21] Ida R. Parker, A Follow-Up Study of 500 Illegitimacy Applications, p. 21. Research Bureau on Social Case Work, Boston, 1924.

It will be seen that the modal age in this group is twenty-one to twenty-four years; yet since this is a three-year group, and the preceding classification (18 to 20 years) is a two-year grouping, it is quite possible that the age-group where the greatest number of cases fall is the 18-20 year class.

PARENTAGE OF UNMARRIED MOTHERS

It seems fairly well established that a high percentage of the parents of unmarried mothers are of foreign birth. Bingham found that in 65.2% of 500 cases, both parents of sex delinquents in Waverley House were foreign-born; and in twelve percent of the cases, one parent was of foreign birth.[22] Does this mean that foreign-born parents, ill adjusted to American conditions of living, and handicapped by inability to speak English, lose authority over their daughters? Or does the fact point to a different moral code in the countries from which the parents emigrate?

Alcoholism and vicious moral conditions frequently exist in the homes from which unmarried mothers come. Kammerer cites instances in which father or mother or both were alcoholic, immoral or criminalistic, exercising a vicious influence upon their daughters, and declares that in "many cases this constitutes a direct causative factor in their pregnancy."[23] In their study of "Illegitimacy as a Child Welfare Problem," Lundberg and Lenroot found that one or both parents of nearly one-third of the 840 mothers of children born out of wedlock in Boston in 1914 were dead, divorced, separated or not living in the United States. This means that 261 of the homes from which these unmarried mothers came were "broken homes," crippled in their primary task of rearing the young under wholesome conditions. Moreover, one or both parents of one-eighth of the 840 unmarried mothers "were reported to be alcoholic, immoral or otherwise of poor character."[24] Of 2,178 illegitimate children in the care of Boston agencies in 1914, it was reported that sixty-five had maternal grandparents (one or both) who "were insane or mentally below normal." The social histories of 408 of the 2,178 children (nineteen percent) revealed "a heritage in which there was known to be insanity, feeblemindedness, or other subnormal or abnormal mental conditions, or probably subnormality or feeblemindedness. In 195 cases—9 percent of the total reported— there was definite feeblemindedness or insanity in the family history."[25]

Further evidence that the parentage of many unmarried mothers is of such a character as to develop anti-social conduct in their children is

[22] Bingham, *op. cit.*, p. 505.
[23] Kammerer, *op. cit.*, p. 122.
[24] Lundberg and Lenroot, *op. cit.*, Part II, p. 49.   [25] *Ibid.*, p. 196.

furnished by Bingham.[26] Her investigations disclosed that alcoholism was common among the parents of the 500 sex delinquents in Waverley House. Both parents were alcoholic in nineteen cases; the father, in 159; the mother, in thirty-one; the brothers, in seventeen; and the sisters, in three cases. Sexual immorality existed in both parents in fourteen cases; in the father, in fifty-two; in the mother, in sixty. Thirty-seven of the fathers of these girls had criminal records, nine of the mothers, nineteen of the brothers and five of the sisters.

Healy and Bronner, in their recently published study of juvenile delinquents,[27] each took 1,000 cases of repeated offenders and investigated the homes. Their conclusion was as follows:

"Specifically, if we ruled out the families in which there were such clearly unfortunate features of home life, poverty, great crowding, or very unsanitary surroundings, extreme parental neglect or extreme lack of parental control, excessive quarreling, alcoholism, obscenity, immorality or criminalism, mother away working, mentally diseased parent in the home, how many had we left? Enumerating the good homes thus by elimination, we found . . . the figures for Boston to be 10.3%, for Chicago 5%, numerically only a small difference. Among 2,000 young repeated offenders, then, there were living under reasonably good conditions for the upbringing of a child, only 7.6%."

When bad heredity and home conditions such as these furnish the background of life of young, impressionable girls from early childhood, the wonder is not that they go wrong, but that so many of them remain moral and self-respecting.

PHYSICAL CONDITION OF UNMARRIED MOTHERS

Apparently, abnormal physical conditions in unmarried mothers are not an important causative factor in illegitimacy. Physical conditions weakening the bodily functions or causing irritation would tend to break down the resistance of an individual to sexual influences or pressure. In only six cases did Kammerer find physical abnormality a major factor in illegitimacy; and in fifty-three cases, a minor factor. In five of the six cases where physical conditions were a primary cause of illegitimacy, the disease was epilepsy, long known to be a powerful factor in anti-social behavior.[28] Lundberg and Lenroot report that of 473 unmarried mothers in Boston, whose records had been carefully taken, twenty-four percent

[26] Bingham, op. cit., p. 510.
[27] Delinquents and Criminals: Their Making and Unmaking. Studies in Two American Cities, p. 129. The Macmillan Co., New York, 1926. By permission.
[28] Kammerer, op. cit., pp. 184-6.

(or fourteen percent of the total 840 mothers) were in poor physical condition and eight percent of these were venereally diseased.[29] On the other hand, Bingham states that the 500 sex delinquents examined by her were on the whole remarkably free from organic defects and showed only slight deviations from the standards for their age and sex.[30]

MENTAL ABNORMALITY

Not so favorable are the records regarding the mental condition of unmarried mothers. Parker states that 111 out of 550 unmarried mothers in Boston investigated by her in 1920-21 had been given psychological or psychiatric tests. Although the classification of these tests on the basis of intelligence was vague and incomplete, she says that "it can be stated with certainty . . . that 43.2% (48) of those examined . . . were feeble-minded. Another 17.1% (19) of those examined may be considered normal and dull normal, while still another 9% (10) grade in intelligence somewhere between normal and feeble-minded. Twelve mothers (10.8%) were reported to be suffering from a psychic disorder, 4 of them from a psychosis, 8 from some psychopathic condition."[31] Of course it should be borne in mind in drawing conclusions from these records that only those were selected for examination who showed some mental defect or disorder.

Even more unfavorable are the reports of Bingham. She groups the 500 sex delinquents in Waverley House in terms of mental status as follows:[32]

Normal intelligence	28.0%
Mental defectives	37.2%
"Constitutional psychopathic inferiors"	26.5%
Mentally diseased	5.8%
Epileptics (without mental deficiency)	2.6%

On the basis of these findings, Bingham declares: "There has been abundant proof from our material that mental defect and neuropathic traits, both presumably inherited, have stood in the way of satisfactory social adjustments."[33]

Mangold believes that a large proportion of illegitimate children have feeble-minded mothers, and points as evidence to Miss Jean Weidensall's studies at the Bedford Reformatory for Women in New York. This investigator found only twenty percent of the sex delinquents clearly normal,

---

[29] Lundberg and Lenroot, *op. cit.*, p. 39.
[30] Bingham, *op. cit.*, p. 535.
[31] Parker, *op. cit.*, pp. 28-9.
[32] Bingham, *op. cit.*, p. 496.
[33] *Ibid.*, p. 502.

and forty to forty-five percent so subnormal as to need institutional care.[34] This agrees with the results of investigations in England which show that about forty percent of illegitimate mothers are feeble-minded.

On the other hand, there is some reason to believe that more cautious and scientific studies of the mental status of unmarried mothers might support the theory that mental abnormality as a cause of sex delinquency has been overstressed, important as this factor doubtless is. For instance, Healy and Bronner's study of juvenile delinquents and criminals (2,000 in Chicago and 2,000 in Boston), which involved use of objective standardized tests and careful mental diagnosis, showed seventy percent of Chicago girls and 73.2% of Boston girls mentally normal. Of Chicago girls, 18.1% were clearly feeble-minded, as were eighteen percent of Boston delinquents. Subnormal mentality was shown in 6.4% of Chicago cases and five percent of Boston cases. Psychosis existed in the case of 5.5% of Chicago girls and one percent of Boston girls. In addition, 2.8% of the Boston group were classified as "psychopathic personalities." [35]

Obviously, this is a much better showing with respect to mental normality than Bingham's findings. Likewise, Wallin's study of 1,363 delinquent school children sent for mental testing showed that delinquents are, in a majority of cases, mentally normal. This writer warns us to beware of figures showing a very high percentage of feeble-mindedness among juvenile delinquents, and holds that cautious investigators of sober judgment and wide experience do not put the ratio of mental abnormality above twenty-five or thirty percent.[36] But if there exists even thirty percent of feeble-mindedness among illegitimate mothers, this condition constitutes in itself a grave social problem which will be considered later.

[34] See Mangold, *op. cit.*, p. 46.
[35] Healy and Bronner, *op. cit.*, p. 273.
[36] "Feeble-mindedness and Illegitimacy," in *Mental Hygiene,* Vol. I, pp. 585-90, October, 1917.

CHAPTER XV

ILLEGITIMACY AS A PROBLEM IN CHILD WELFARE
(Continued)

CARE AND PROTECTION AFFORDED UNMARRIED MOTHERS

OBVIOUSLY, the burden and the shame of bringing into the world an illegitimate child, for whom there is no home, falls unequally upon the two parents. The father usually escapes unpenalized, while the mother, who must carry and bear the child, cannot evade the consequences of the social offense in which both were involved and in which, not rarely, the male was the chief offender. What facilities in the way of care, before and after confinement, does society furnish the unmarried mother? What help does it give her in securing employment and if possible, winning back her independence and self-respect?

Among the institutions and agencies that care for unmarried pregnant women, are (1) private maternity homes; (2) maternity hospitals, both private and municipal; (3) so-called "rescue homes," such as those founded by the Florence Crittenden League and the Salvation Army; (4) social agencies that render assistance to the unmarried mother and her child, such as children's aid societies, home-finding societies, the Society for the Prevention of Cruelty to Children and the like.

There can be little doubt that many of the private maternity homes in all of our large cities, managed as they are on a purely commercial basis, and avoiding publicity as much as possible, are "a distinct social menace." Mangold quotes certain of the advertisements inserted in the newspapers by these homes which show clearly enough that these institutions seek to serve unmarried mothers with as much secrecy as possible. The rates charged are "as high as the traffic will bear," but in some instances the mother is permitted to pay part of her expenses in work. Private maternity homes usually have little interest in the rehabilitation of the mother and are often quite willing to dispose of the child by adoption or placing in a home for a fee ranging from $15 to $50.[1] Indeed, it is probable that such institutions sometimes make a special effort to separate mother and child, and to this end discourage breast-feeding. Moreover, there is evi-

[1] See Mangold, "Children Born Out of Wedlock," p. 85. University of Missouri Studies, Vol. III, No. 3, 1921.

dence to show that very little care is exercised by some of these maternity homes, when placing babies in foster families, to discover the character of either the home or the future care-takers of the child. Gross neglect is shown in keeping track of babies thus disposed of, and mothers often lose all knowledge of their whereabouts. Adoption papers are rarely made out and filed by the less responsible managers of maternity homes, for their all-controlling desire is secrecy and avoidance of all connection with courts or legal processes.

It can hardly be doubted that babies thus separated from their mothers and "farmed out" to strangers, or placed in so-called "baby farms," die in appalling numbers; but unfortunately the public is not yet aroused to the need of more adequate inspection and regulation of commercial maternity homes and "baby farms." Mangold states that, after the Indiana Board of State Charities had been empowered to license and control maternity homes, it began an investigation which resulted in refusing licenses to many of these institutions and raising the standards of those permitted to continue.[2]

Confinement facilities for pregnant single women are also furnished by private and municipal hospitals which maintain maternity wards. Few of these institutions have adequate social service departments. Therefore little is done to supervise the unmarried mother after she leaves the hospital, to return her to her home and family, if they will receive her, or to find work that will enable her to support herself and baby and, if at all possible, to keep the child with her. Nor is much accomplished in the direction of reaching the putative fathers of illegitimate children and compelling them to render support and assistance to mother and child by court action.

The social agencies that deal with illegitimacy cases have until recently done little in the way of securing adequate records concerning unmarried mothers and their children. There can be no enlightened constructive program for dealing with this problem until far more complete data are secured. Nor can much be accomplished by social agencies to rehabilitate unhappy mothers who have borne children out of wedlock until our illegitimacy laws are thoroughly amended, and until society is willing to undertake the establishment of institutions where unmarried mothers may go, not only for immediate aid, but for such prolonged supervision and wise assistance as they may need in order to face the world once more with hope and serious purpose. "An important need, for successful work," says Mangold, "is a 'mothers' and babies' home,' a place where

[2] For this whole topic see Mangold, *op. cit.,* pp. 83-90.

a woman can live and where her baby can be cared for while she is at work during the day. . . . Without such a home, the agencies have no propositions to make which a woman will consider, and, therefore, their reconstructive efforts collapse, with the frequent result that the woman returns in a year or two with a second illegitimate baby, or joins the ever present body of prostitutes in the city." [3]

LEGAL AID TO UNMARRIED MOTHERS: PUBLIC GUARDIANSHIP OF ILLEGITIMATE CHILDREN

As stated above, most American commonwealths have enacted laws to enforce support of the illegitimate child by the father, if paternity is established by a court trial. The law usually provides that the mother shall institute proceedings against the putative father of her child, but many states also authorize the poor-law authorities to act, or any agencies that would be charged with the support of the child. Apparently, few actions are brought against putative fathers, and fewer still are vigorously pressed. In 550 cases of illegitimacy investigated by Parker, information was secured about 384 men, 70.4% of the total number of fathers. Of this number, 127 had been prosecuted—thirty-three percent of those about whom information was given, or 23.3% of all fathers. "In most instances," says Parker, "an agency had assisted the mother in the prosecution." Out of the 127 cases, twelve men were found not guilty, the cases against three others were dismissed because not prosecuted, thirteen cases were pending and seven were not reported. This left ninety-two men who were adjudged fathers of illegitimate children, and were compelled by the court to pay sums for their support ranging from $2.50 to $12 per week. Frequently the court order included the expenses for confinement. It is significant that 257 putative fathers—sixty-seven percent of the 384 about whom information was secured—were not prosecuted. In explanation it may be said that nearly one-third of these men were not located. In seventy-three instances, the mother or her relatives were opposed to prosecution for fear of publicity. Several women disappeared before prosecution could be begun.[4]

Similar conditions with respect to the prosecution of putative fathers were disclosed by Lundberg and Lenroot in their analysis of the results of the Massachusetts law of 1913, making the father of an illegitimate child liable for reasonable contributions to its support during minority.

[3] Mangold, *op. cit.*, p. 107. By permission of the author.
[4] Parker, *A Follow-Up Study of 550 Illegitimacy Applications*, pp. 40-1. Research Bureau on Social Case Work, Boston, 1924.

In 1914, the number of cases initiated under the act was 256—less than one-third of the illegitimacy cases for that year. At the close of 1915, less than half the cases had resulted in a legal arrangement for support of the child or for confinement expenses or both, by which a man could be held to his obligation. Moreover, the money collected was as a rule less in amount than that required for the support of dependent children who are wards of the State.[5]

It seems from the evidence at hand that the proper authorities are not sufficiently active in themselves initiating proceedings against putative fathers or in bringing steady pressure to bear upon unmarried mothers to prosecute. The conditions suggest that the whole responsibility might well be centered in a state authority, whose primary duty it should be to protect illegitimate children and secure for them the full measure of support, education and general welfare for which the law makes provision. The Minnesota child welfare laws, enacted in 1917, are the most liberal and enlightened in the entire country in their provisions for safeguarding the rights and well-being of illegitimate children. The statutes (Ch. 194, sec. 2) provide that:

"It shall be the duty of the board of control when notified of a woman who is delivered of an illegitimate child, or pregnant with child likely to be illegitimate when born, to take care that the interests of the child are safeguarded, that appropriate steps are taken to establish his paternity, and that there is secured for him the nearest approximation to the care, support and education that he would be entitled to if born of lawful marriage. For the better accomplishment of these purposes the board may initiate such legal or other action as is deemed necessary; may make such provision for the care, maintenance and education of the child as the best interests of the child may from time to time require, and may offer its aid and protection in such ways as are found wise and expedient to the unmarried woman approaching motherhood."

In this law may be seen the first example of the public guardianship of illegitimate children that has long existed in many cities of Germany and in Sweden.[6]

Of the thirty-five child welfare laws enacted in Minnesota in 1917, those dealing with "the supervision of maternity hospitals and children's homes, the adoption laws, the statutes concerning such sex offenses as abortion, assault and carnal knowledge, the law regarding penalties for

[5] "Illegitimacy as a Child Welfare Problem," Part II, pp. 47-8. *Bureau Publications,* No. 66, 1920, United States Children's Bureau.
[6] See "Illegitimacy as a Child Welfare Problem," Part I, pp. 50-2.

the abandonment of minor children may be considered as supporting illegitimacy legislation." [7]

Probably the most progressive feature of the Minnesota laws is the act providing that large powers of guardianship shall be conferred on the Minnesota State Board of Control. Under the terms of this act, not only dependent, defective and delinquent but illegitimate children may be committed to the Board by the courts. The Board may make such disposition as seems best for each child, except that it may not place a child in an institution for delinquents who has not been adjudged a delinquent by the proper authorities. The wisdom of such a provision for public guardianship of illegitimate children becomes apparent when it is realized that such children are often in need of the protection of the State because the mother has deserted them or is an unfit person to care for them. Where the mother herself is a young girl with a wretched home environment, in which she cannot be left without harm, the statute makes it possible for her also to be committed to the Board of Control and removed from the debasing surroundings in which her mistake was made.

An interesting feature of the law consists in the fact that these public guardianship powers are an example of centralized responsibility and decentralized administration. Although the State Board of Control is held accountable for 1,000 or more illegitimate children born every year in Minnesota, each of the counties in the State is expected to care for the illegitimate children within its own confines. Before any action is taken by the State Board, the county commissioners must take formal action requesting the Board to appoint a child welfare board within the county. Individuals or agencies who see the need for child welfare work frequently bring pressure to bear on the commissioners to pass such a formal resolution. The funds for financing the work of the child welfare boards come from the counties themselves.

Under stimulus from the child welfare board, if necessary, the mother brings complaint against the putative father before a justice of the peace, and a warrant is issued which may be executed anywhere in the State. A preliminary hearing is held and, if the evidence indicates the guilt of the putative father, the judge binds him over under security of from $300 to $1,000 for trial in the district court. If the man is adjudged the father of the child, judgment may be entered against him on behalf of the county for the confinement expenses of the mother, the support of the child up

[7] Mildred D. Mudgett, "Results of Minnesota's Laws for Protection of Children Born Out of Wedlock," p. 183. *Bureau Publications*, No. 128, Part III, United States Children's Bureau.

to the time of judgment (if the expense has been borne by the county) and the costs of prosecution. If the man fails to pay, he may be jailed for ninety days, after which he may be discharged if he proves that he has no property. Finally, an order for support of the child is made by the judge, requiring monthly payments of amounts varying from $10 to $25. The usual amount demanded is $15 a month. Unfortunately, in Minnesota as in other states, actions for establishment of paternity lag far behind the number of illegitimate births. In 1921, only thirty-three percent of the total cases were prosecuted.

The procedure does not differ greatly from that prevailing in other states. But with respect to the guardianship of the child after judgment, the Minnesota law is unique. The State Board of Control discourages the appointment of the mother or a relative as guardian, since, if a lump-sum settlement of his financial obligations is permitted the father by the court, the money paid over may not be expended for the child. "The procedure permitted by law and urged by the State board of control is to make the board the guardian of the child, or to order that the money be paid to the local child welfare board, leaving it to the latter to advise the mother regarding the expenditure." [8]

Minnesota makes abandonment of a minor child a felony punishable by five years' imprisonment. As soon as a man is adjudged father of an illegitimate child, the provisions of the abandonment law become applicable to him. Moreover, a special statute provides that if a putative father of an illegitimate child leaves the State during the pregnancy of the mother or within sixty days after the birth of a living child, provided that he left "with intent to evade proceedings to establish paternity," he is adjudged a felon and may be imprisoned two years. The weakness of this law obviously consists in the fact that, since paternity of an illegitimate child is not itself a felony, it is a difficult matter to prove that the man left the State to evade illegitimacy proceedings, and not on lawful business.

This brief exposition of the Minnesota laws of 1917 should serve to make clear that this State is the first in the Union to assume public responsibility and guardianship of children born out of wedlock and even of very young mothers, to the end of reducing to a minimum the hardships of the illegitimate child and of diminishing the ever increasing expense for delinquents and dependents that every state is forced to carry. In the words of a recent investigator: "The assumption by the State of responsibility for the welfare of illegitimate children has a sound economic basis. Each

[8] Mudgett, *op. cit.*, p. 187.

year in Minnesota 1,000 or more children are born out of wedlock. Handicapped from the start by being deprived of normal home life, this group
in succeeding years adds thousands of individuals to the already heavy
burden of dependents maintained by the State. The fact that a remedy has
not been sought earlier is doubtless due to the close association of the
problem with a double standard of morals and a traditional reluctance to
discuss sex problems." [9]

THE CHILD BORN OUT OF WEDLOCK: HANDICAPS

Harsh and condemnatory as the traditional attitude of society to the
unmarried mother has been, it has not been so crushing as the treatment
meted out to the illegitimate child by its parents and by society. Few
individuals, outside of social workers, fully realize the handicaps under
which an illegitimate child begins its life struggle. With a heritage often
gravely defective, borne under detrimental conditions of a mother worn
by anxiety and fear of exposure, the child born out of wedlock is menaced
by serious hazards to life and health. He is frequently deprived of a
mother's care as well as of the care and support of his father; he is shifted
about from place to place and from one type of care to another—both too
often defective; finally he labors under hampering legal and social disadvantages. In most states, the illegitimate child can inherit from the mother,
but not from the father; even if his paternity is established, as it infrequently is, he commonly receives no care and insufficient support from
his father; his birth record discloses the fact of his illegitimate birth, if
not specifically, yet by implication; and since this record is more often
than not open to public inspection, it may be maliciously used against
him; the circumstances of his birth may become known in school, or
when he takes out his working papers, through the medium of his birth
certificate. Add to these disabilities the cloud under which the child
lives, the social stigma too often fixed upon him by the cruel and the
thoughtless, and it will be appreciated that he is gravely handicapped from
his birth.

Little is definitely known of the mental effect upon a sensitive child
of the knowledge of his illegitimate birth. Lundberg and Lenroot state
that the stories of several children who were public charges in Boston
indicated mental suffering occasioned by ignorance or uncertainty in regard
to the life histories or the whereabouts of their parents. They quote a few
pitiful letters unveiling this distress. One boy of fourteen, who had not
heard from his mother for thirteen years, during which time he had been

[9] Mudgett, *op. cit.*, pp. 183-4.

under the care of the state, suddenly received a letter from her. His delight was touching and he wrote the following reply:

"I was very glad to hear from you. I was so surprised to hear from my mother I didn't know what to do. I didn't know I had a mother. Have I any father, sisters or brothers, aunts, uncles, cousins? I am well. I am almost 14. How old are you? I hope you are well the same as me. Write to me and tell me more about you—what you are doing. From your son." [10]

Infant Mortality among Illegitimate Children.

The unfavorable environmental conditions surrounding illegitimate children, especially the early separation from the mother of a large proportion of babies, is responsible for a shockingly high infant mortality among them. This is true in every country of the world where vital statistics are kept. Frequently, the deaths under one year of illegitimate infants are almost double in number those of legitimate children. A few statistics of European countries will make this plain.[11]

COUNTRY	ANNUAL AVERAGE NUMBER OF DEATHS UNDER ONE YEAR PER 1,000 LIVE BIRTHS		
	Illegitimate	*Legitimate*	*Ratio of Illegitimate to Legitimate Deaths*
Austria	247	188	1.3
Belgium	213	136	1.6
Denmark	167	90	1.9
England and Wales	208	104	2.0
Finland	175	106	1.7
France	221	111	2.0
German Empire	250	187	1.3
Italy	223	134	1.7
Norway	122	62	2.0
Scotland	223	120	1.9
Sweden	109	66	1.7
Switzerland	169	99	1.7
The Netherlands	233	102	2.3

When we turn to the United States, we are confronted by the fact that no figures on comparative mortality rates of illegitimate children are available, either for the country as a whole or for the states. The backwardness of this country in securing vital statistics is striking in comparison with European nations. In 1920, the only published sources of

[10] Lundberg and Lenroot, *op. cit.*, Part II, p. 61.
[11] *Ibid.*, Part I, p. 28.

information concerning mortality among illegitimate infants, so far as the Children's Bureau investigators could discover, were the figures for the Boston Health Department in 1915, similar data in reports of the Newark, New Jersey, Health Department and the report of the Health Officer of the District of Columbia for 1912. In Boston, it was found that in 1914 the infant mortality rate among legitimate children was ninety-five, among illegitimate, 261 per 1000. Obviously, in that year the death rate of illegitimate babies in Boston was nearly three times greater than that of legitimate babies. This goes far beyond European disparities. In Baltimore, conditions were worse, for the infant mortality rate for illegitimate white children was 3.3 times that for legitimate infants. The Health Officer of the District of Columbia reported that the infant mortality of legitimate children in the District in 1912 was 79.7 per 1,000, whereas the rate for illegitimate infants was 302.7—almost four times as great![12] Mangold cites figures for Cincinnati in 1912 which show an illegitimate infant mortality of 20.9% (209 per 1,000), compared to 10.3% in the case of legitimate babies.[13]

PROVISIONS FOR CARE AND PROTECTION OF ILLEGITIMATE CHILDREN

A large proportion of illegitimate children are cared for by private agencies or become charges of the State or the city. In our times, the foundling hospitals keep children only until homes can be found for them. If children are in poor physical condition when received into foundling hospitals, they are cared for until they are well before being boarded out. In addition to these institutions are orphanages for dependent children, which sometimes receive illegitimate children, keep them for a while and then find homes for them. For some years past there has been developing a powerful trend in the United States in the direction of supplying family care for children who have been deprived of their homes or who have never known home life. Numerous societies have been formed with this end in view. Some of these place children only in free homes, where there is a chance of their being legally adopted. Other agencies pay stipulated sums for the care of dependent illegitimate children in boarding homes. Most readers will agree that this movement is in the best interests of children, who are known to pine and die under a régime of institutional life. Yet there are serious hazards involved in placing children in homes unless there is regular public supervision of these places, and of the children themselves over a period of years.

[12] Lundberg and Lenroot, *op. cit.*, Part I, p. 35.
[13] Mangold, *op. cit.*, p. 119.

In the United States, with the exception of Minnesota, the supervision of the State over illegitimate children appears to be merely incidental to state control of agencies or institutions caring for dependent or delinquent children. In many states, although not in all, organizations which care for or place out children in homes are subject to state supervision, as are the homes themselves. But there are no special boards or public guardians to care for the interests of illegitimate children as such. It is to be hoped that, in the future, other states will follow the lead of Minnesota in surrounding the illegitimate child with the protection that apparently only a specially constituted public board can give.

Of the 847 children born out of wedlock in Boston, in 1914, 230 died in the first year of life—more than one-fourth. Sixty-two percent (522) of the total number of illegitimate children received prolonged care from child-caring or child protective agencies, maternity homes or the Commonwealth public infirmary.[14] In addition to these babies, there were in 1914 a total of 2,863 illegitimate children under the care of Boston agencies, 1,721 under the care of the division of State minor wards of the Massachusetts State Board of Charity; 102 under care of State institutions for delinquents; and seventy-three under care of State institutions for the feeble-minded, with sixty-seven more illegitimate children waiting admission. In addition, 204 cases of adoption of illegitimate children were pending in four county courts.[15] This record will serve to show the amount of care and expense involved in illegitimacy in one state only.

THE BURDEN CARRIED BY SOCIETY

By this time the reader will have gained some conception of the heavy burden carried by the public with respect to illegitimacy. In a large majority of cases, a child born out of wedlock, with no home to receive him, becomes a public charge because his mother is unable or unfit to care for him and his father was not prosecuted and compelled to furnish at least part of the support of the child he thoughtlessly brought into the world. The obligations not assumed by the parents must be taken up by the public if the child is not to be left to die. Consequently, society carries a heavy load of responsibility and expense for maternity and infancy care, and later for child dependency. In the majority of cases, all or part of the expenses for confinement and after-care of mother and child are borne by private and public agencies; and a by no means negligible proportion of child dependents are of illegitimate birth.

[14] Lundberg and Lenroot, *op. cit.*, Part II, pp. 135-6.
[15] *Ibid.*, Part II, pp. 36-8.

This, however, is not all the public burden entailed by illegitimacy. The Children's Bureau study of illegitimacy in Boston and Massachusetts refers to the restlessness, the morbid outlook on life or the anti-social conduct of many children born out of wedlock. A comparison of dependent children of legitimate and illegitimate birth, fourteen years old and over, who were under state care, showed that twenty-eight percent of the illegitimate children were troublesome, as compared with sixteen percent of the legitimate children. Furthermore, a study of delinquent children in state institutions in Massachusetts indicated that the proportion of illegitimate children in these reformatory schools is high when compared with the percentage of illegitimate births in the State. In partial explanation of this disproportion, the investigators state that, although the figures were too small to justify positive conclusions, "the findings suggest that children handicapped by birth out of wedlock, and therefore frequently deprived of care by their own parents, are turned over to the care of correctional institutions at an earlier age and for less serious offenses than children whose home ties are more nearly normal." [16]

The expense entailed in caring for children born out of wedlock is no inconsiderable item of a city's budget. It is estimated, on the basis of agency reports and those of the Massachusetts Board of Charity, that Boston spent more than $123,500 for its care of illegitimate children in 1914.[17] The appropriation for maintenance of the Minnesota Children's Bureau was, in 1921-22, $35,000—an inadequate amount when the importance and extent of the work is considered. Minnesota, however, is a farming state which, like the rest of the Middle West, is struggling in the trough of prolonged agricultural depression. Moreover, it should be kept in mind that this appropriation is but a drop in the bucket in the total costs of illegitimacy borne by county welfare boards and private social agencies throughout Minnesota. In no single state of the Union are figures available for estimating the expenditures involved in caring for unmarried mothers and illegitimate children, but they must mount into enormous sums over a period of years.

PROPOSALS FOR REFORM IN LEGISLATION AND ADMINISTRATION

It is encouraging to note the pronounced tendency in the United States, during the past decade, toward making the child the central figure in the social problem of illegitimacy and in safeguarding his interests. But in every country much remains to be done before the illegitimate child is

[16] Lundberg and Lenroot, *op. cit.*, Part II, pp. 65-6.
[17] *Ibid.*, Part II, p. 153.

secured opportunities for survival, for normal development, for even moderately happy childhood, for education and preparation for life work at all equal to those enjoyed by children born in wedlock. Society as a whole still tends to apply with more or less literalness the grim saying of the Hebrew Decalogue that "the sins of the fathers shall be visited upon the children even unto the third and fourth generation."

Numerous proposals for reform of illegitimacy laws, and of the work of social agencies dealing with illegitimate mothers and their children, have been made in recent years. It is possible to touch only very briefly upon a few of these. Mangold suggests a program for prevention of illegitimacy [18] by controlling the mentally and morally unfit. The United States has, as yet, by no means seriously grappled with the problems of its appalling army of defectives—men, women and minor children. It is estimated that two-thirds of them are at large to propagate their kind. Not only are these unfortunates weak in inhibition, and lacking in foresight of consequences, but they are almost incapable, at least in the lower levels, of *learning from experience*—the distinguishing mark of the intelligent individual. It is idle to talk of giving moral training to genuine defectives, while they are left at the mercy of environmental influences that tempt to irregular sex relations. Mangold holds that the social hazards of allowing feeble-minded persons at large (especially women, who are the easy prey of men of all social stations) are so great that every state should promptly take steps to segregate these persons and provide facilities for their employment under wholesome and, so far as possible, happy conditions. He believes that the enormous cost to the State involved in a program of public care of thousands of feeble-minded girls and women can be greatly reduced by making "colonies" of feeble-minded persons self-supporting. In time such a thoroughgoing measure of prevention will, he believes, greatly reduce the public burden of illegitimacy, delinquency, poverty and crime.

The second type of individual which Mangold would have segregated at public charge, or rendered harmless by sterilization, are so-called sex perverts of both sexes. These are the highly sexed men and (occasionally) women who are guilty of serious and continued sex offenses, and appear to be sexually irresponsible. Several states have already made provision for the sterilization of male sex perverts [19] but, as Mangold points out, public opinion is not sufficiently enlightened to support vigorously the enforcement of these laws.

[18] Mangold, *op. cit.*, pp. 184-8.
[19] By means of a harmless operation.

In a Children's Bureau publication,[20] issued in 1919, Professor Ernst Freund of the University of Chicago suggests possible changes in the illegitimacy laws of the states that would render them more favorable to the illegitimate child. The first suggestion is concerned with the payments demanded by state courts from the father. These are notoriously inadequate and sometimes are not long enough continued. Freund suggests that these payments should, normally, be extended until the child is sixteen years of age, and that the amount of payment should be governed by the father's standard of life.

With regard to legal provisions for guardianship and permanent care of the child, he holds that any "comprehensive scheme of reform should consider the creation of an official guardianship, in order to do full justice to the varying and developing circumstances of each case, and to standardize the legal duties of fathers toward the illegitimate offspring." [21] In his opinion it is to legislation of the type enacted in Minnesota that society must look for the most effectual enforcement of laws for illegitimate support.

Professor Freund further believes that, although everything possible should be done by legislation to mitigate the hardships of illegitimacy, the practical consequences of attempts to assimilate the status of the illegitimate child to that of the child born in wedlock are limited. Nevertheless he regards it as desirable that the following provisions be adopted in all states: [22]

1. A declaration that the issue of null marriages are legitimate.
2. A proceeding to establish legitimacy or illegitimacy.
3. Legitimation by subsequent marriage of the father and mother, where the father acknowledges the child.
4. The possibility of voluntary legitimation after the death of the mother, or where marriage or adoption is impossible.
5. The possibility of adoption by the father.
6. A declaration that the relation of mother and child is the same whether the child is legitimate or illegitimate.

These are cautious measures, but Freund holds that the North Dakota law of 1917, which declares every child to be "the legitimate child of the natural parents," entitled to inherit from the parents and their kindred, and to dwell with the father's family unless the father be married to some other woman, would be difficult of enforcement. Likewise he believes that

[20] "Illegitimacy Laws of the United States and Certain Foreign Countries," pp. 52-8. *Bureau Publications*, No. 42, 1919.
[21] *Ibid.*, p. 54.
[22] *Ibid.*, pp. 55-6.

adoption by the states of a law providing that the illegitimate child shall be given the name of the father, if paternity is established, might entail embarrassing consequences to the child by advertising his illegitimacy when he is living with his mother.

The resolutions adopted by the New York Regional Conference on Illegitimacy, held in 1920, represent pretty clearly the state of progressive opinion at present in regard to public care and protection of illegitimate children. A few of the resolutions may profitably be summarized.[23] The Conference went on record as favoring the creation of state departments responsible for child welfare, "which should include among their duties the assisting of unmarried mothers and of children born out of wedlock." However, it was the sense of the conference that "State guardianship should be exercised only over those children who are neglected or dependent or in danger of becoming dependent." Clearly, public sentiment in this country is not yet ready to sponsor the "public guardian" of illegitimate children provided for in the laws of Sweden and Germany. "The State should license and supervise private hospitals which receive unmarried mothers for confinement and all private child-helping and child-placing agencies, to the end that unfit hospitals and agencies may be sufficiently improved or eliminated." The registration of all births should be compulsory, but the father's name should be recorded on the birth certificate only if paternity has been established. All records of births out of wedlock should be confidential, open to inspection only upon court order. The names of parents should be omitted from all transcripts for school and employment purposes.

"The mother should be persuaded, by case work, to start proceedings (against the father) whenever possible. *Otherwise the State department above mentioned should assume this responsibility.*" When paternity has been adjudicated, the father should be obligated to support an illegitimate child *in the same manner as a legitimate child.* The States should enact uniform laws making desertion of an illegitimate child an offense as serious as abandonment of a legitimate child, *and such offenses should be "readily extraditable."* The jurisdiction of the court with respect to custody and support of the child should continue *during minority.* "After an adjudication of paternity or an acknowledgment in writing by the father, the child born out of wedlock should have the *same rights of inheritance* as the child born in wedlock." After paternity is established, the "child's right to the name of the father should be permissive. . . . The mother

[23] "Standards of Legal Protection for Children Born Out of Wedlock," pp. 17-9, *Bureau Publications,* No. 77, United States Children's Bureau.

should be persuaded, by good case work, to keep her child at least during the nursing period whenever possible. When necessary, steps should be taken to secure for mother and child the benefits of the so-called mothers' pension acts." [24]

NEED FOR A PROGRAM OF PREVENTION

A careful consideration of the proposals outlined above will convince the reader that they are purely remedial measures, designed to alleviate a bad social situation after it has developed. If society is not forever to carry the burden of illegitimacy on its shoulders, it behooves its leaders to work out a program that goes to the source of the evil and seeks to eliminate so far as may be the social causes of illegitimacy. Paramount among these will be found poverty and ignorance, and the ills that go hand in hand with these—overcrowding, bad housing and degraded family life. What can be done to secure for every worker a decent living wage, and, if he is married, such "family wages" as will be of vital assistance in rearing his children in decent comfort? This is the crucial question to which social workers, in their fight to remedy grave social evils, return again and again.

But the attack upon poverty and bad housing is not enough. There must be a recognition on the part of the public of its responsibility for providing better facilities for recreation for the youth of our towns and cities. All wholesome forms of recreation, outdoor and indoor, including dancing, should be provided in sufficient amount to meet the needs of youth thirsting for pleasure and fullness of life. A comprehensive plan for recreation should be worked out and put into operation in crowded industrial centers, *under careful public supervision*. It will prove an excellent social investment in the end, although it will entail large expense in the beginning.

Another preventive measure consists in public supervision of employment agencies for girls and also of such employments as those of waitresses and chambermaids in hotels, of girls in department stores and offices, of domestic servants. It has been abundantly proved that these occupations, especially those of hotel, café and domestic workers, are peculiarly hazardous for young girls and furnish an unduly large proportion of illegitimate mothers and prostitutes. Shall society continue to sidestep its manifest responsibility to safeguard the employments that have been proved to be demoralizing to girls?

The schools likewise have their part to play by discovering feeble-

[24] Italics mine.

minded children of the lower levels and making possible their segregation, at least after puberty, a policy which it would seem wise for every state to adopt. Nor does the responsibility of the school stop here. Somehow, despite the handicaps of overcrowding of class and curriculum under which the public schools labor, more must be done to discover the worthwhile interests and enthusiasms of youth, and develop tastes and hobbies that will make leisure time enjoyable and profitable. Finally, a thoughtful, well-planned program of sex instruction, in connection with regular school studies and with the coöperation of parents, should be worked out in every public school system—urban and rural. It is not an idle dream to believe that youth can be educated to greater respect for sex functions if they are given clearer understanding and idealistic appreciation of the part these functions play in personal and social life. The most gifted teachers of the best scientific training, combined with dynamic idealism and sympathetic comprehension of the problems and stresses of adolescent youth, are the only individuals who should be allowed to undertake this sex instruction. For upon it hangs, in no small degree, the issue of enlightened sex control on the part of the public in general.

TOPICS FOR REPORTS

1. Analyze and criticize in detail the Minnesota Laws for the protection of illegitimate children.

    Mildred D. Mudgett, "Results of Minnesota's Laws for Protection of Children Born Out of Wedlock," *Bureau Publications,* No. 128 ("Illegitimacy as a Child Welfare Problem"), Part III, United States Children's Bureau.

2. A Study of the Family Conditions, Physical and Mental Status and Marriage of Delinquents.

    William Healy, M. D., and Augusta F. Bronner, *Delinquents and Criminals: Their Making and Unmaking,* pp. 103-63, 179-82. The Macmillan Co., New York, 1926.

3. The Unmarried Mother in Different Countries of Europe and America.

    P. G. Kammerer, *The Unmarried Mother, A Study of Five Hundred Cases,* pp. 265-83. Little, Brown & Co., Boston, 1918.

    E. O. Lundberg and K. F. Lenroot, "Illegitimacy as a Child Welfare Problem," pp. 50-6. *Bureau Publications,* No. 66, Part I, 1920, United States Children's Bureau.

4. Analyze Parker's study of 550 illegitimacy cases in Boston and report your own conclusions.

    Ida R. Parker, *A Follow-Up Study of 550 Illegitimacy Applications.* Research Bureau on Social Case Work, 400 Boylston Street, Boston, 1924.

PART THREE

INDIVIDUALISM AND THE FAMILY

CHAPTER XVI

THE WOMAN MOVEMENT AND THE FAMILY

THE "WOMAN MOVEMENT" IN ITS LARGER SOCIAL ASPECTS

THE "woman movement" represents one aspect of that great libertarian impulse which from time to time has stirred the souls of mankind and united them in an effort to attain a larger freedom. Through the long progress of social history man is seen engaged in a struggle, sporadic but intense, to overcome obstacles to his own best development and to fight his way up to higher levels of expression. Those very customs, institutions and socially current ideas that once represented man's highest range of achievement seem destined to become, in the course of time, prison houses of his spirit. History makes plain that the *élan vital,* the life force that dwells in human beings, cannot be permanently confined within the rigid barriers of any social system. Not only does this energy break out in the form of strivings for political and economic liberty, but it likewise expresses itself in rebirths of the human spirit, when groups of men, animated by the vision of a more generous and stimulating domain of the mind than any they have known, throw off the shackles of outworn intellectual systems and draw deep breaths of freedom on higher plateaus of thought and action.

Until the eighteenth century, however, little had been accomplished by way of setting the woman free from those age-old responsibilities and duties which must be assumed if the race is to "carry on." Indubitably these social demands were answerable for woman's high degree of specialization on the biological side of her nature, together with her retarded development of an integral personality. To be a good wife and mother was above all else what man required of woman—and, indeed, is probably what the majority of men today desire of women. But this dedication of one-half the members of the human race to the specific task of bearing and rearing the new generation has arrested the development of their power to think rationally, to understand the conditions of their own lives and, in some degree at least, to control them. Consequently in all societies, in all ages, man has regarded woman as emotional, impulsive, intuitive and irrational. He has quite failed to apprehend that these qualities have in large measure been evoked by the character of woman's limited experience as bearer and rearer of the young and keeper of the home; whereas her capacity for clear, straight thinking in the service of a more adequate control of external circumstances has been meagerly stimulated, if at all. Now, since man, in the course of centuries of civilization, has evolved into a being who yearns to idealize his mate, he seizes upon her obvious virtues as a mother and glorifies these in artistic and literary forms. The exaltation of woman as mother and her corresponding abasement as an individual—these are ancient facts sending their roots deep down into social history. At an earlier period, such an attitude toward women was no doubt socially serviceable in securing the maintenance of the race and the home under conditions of warfare and hardship. But in an age in which the environing circumstances of life have been revolutionized, many men still ignore the fact that their life partners are individuals with all that this implies of special tastes, abilities and interests. If woman is ever to achieve an integrated personality, she must develop those capacities of her ego that will give her a firmer grip on social conditions, the ability to create in art and science and the power to build a character in successful adjustment to reality.

Maladjustment of the Modern Woman to Social Conditions.

The economic and social transformations of the past century have brought about a serious maladjustment of woman to her social environment. The old love of husband and offspring, the tenderness lavished on the young, the practical skills essential in an age of hand industry, the utter subordination of self to family—these are not enough to ensure her adaptation to the conditions of the modern world. On every side, the educated woman of broad interests and developed powers finds herself ill adjusted to one or more of the aspects of her life. If she has become accustomed to the regular hours, the intelligent organization, the skilled procedure of a business or profession, she discovers after marriage that these form a sharp and agreeable contrast to the endless, heterogeneous, unorganized details of housekeeping as at present conducted. As the manager of a household, the educated woman comes to perceive that she is in reality an "untrained consumer" living in a thoroughly organized and specialized world demanding intelligence and efficiency of a high order. If she is thoughtful enough, she will likewise perceive that the semi-cloistered character of her life and education, as well as the social expectation that her days will be spent largely in the peaceful oasis of the home, make her wholly unfitted to understand the great industrial machine that is furnishing her family with the necessities and comforts of life. Not understanding its operations, she cannot, of course, exercise any control over them, and in the end she is forced to accept the quality of output, the prices and the conditions of manufacture dictated by those in control of the means of production.

Not only on the social and economic side is the modern woman ill-adjusted to her world, but on the ethical and intellectual side as well. The girl is taught one code of moral principles in the home, and discovers later that a different code prevails in society. The strict chastity always held before her as the controlling ideal of her life is brought into clear relief in her mind against the license of considerable numbers of men. In consequence, she is called upon to make within marriage a difficult and delicate adjustment for which she is not prepared. How reconcile her own yearning for a finer expression of sex impulse, a truer appreciation of its function in the individual life, with the crude expressions of sex on the part of many men? Needless to say, not a few marriages go on the rocks at this point.

Again, a large number of educated women discover after marriage that the home affords too meager a stimulus and outlet to their intellectual abilities. In the difficult period of transition from the old order to the new, woman is perhaps the chief sufferer. Public opinion has advanced to the point of conceding to women the right of higher education, but denies to them opportunities for the full exercise of their developed powers. At some time in their lives, most individualized women stand at the parting of the ways, compelled to choose between the satisfaction of their emotional natures through love and children and the free development of personality in congenial work. If they choose the path of marriage and homes of their own, too many discover that they have grasped one great good of life at the sacrifice of another, viz., the continuous growth and enrichment of the self, and of its capacity for wide social usefulness. If, on the other hand, they elect to turn their backs upon love and accept the challenging opportunities of a career, those women will be self-reliant indeed who do not in some hours regret their "barren chastity" and loneliness, even though they do not regret their choice.

As yet, society has done little or nothing to help woman solve this fundamental problem of her life—how to reconcile the demand of society that she be a contented mother and homemaker with the demand of the self for ever fuller expression of native abilities in a stimulating environment. That woman is dissatisfied with the alternatives presented to her, as well as with the consequences of accepting one or the other, is merely an indication that she is an intelligent human being. No organism that passively yields to basically unsatisfying conditions of life can long survive without deterioration. The impatience conservative persons feel with the restless discontent of many married women betrays a superficial comprehension of a crucial situation. In this age of machine industry and rapid social changes, the "woman problem" is but one phase of the wider social problem, common to all mankind, of meeting new situations with satisfactory adaptations. "The cry of the uneasy woman," says Jessie Taft, "is not merely the reprehensible expression of her own personal restlessness. Consciously or unconsciously it voices her share in the protest of the age against the impossible situation in which humanity finds itself today, and her struggles, even though they seem to be but a vain beating against the righteous and inevitable order of things, are a real part of that larger conflict which society as a whole is waging in its effort to combine modern industry and modern individualism." [1] The struggles of men to escape the deadening influence of simple, mechanical tasks, to be something more than cogs in the vast industrial machine, find their counterpart in the efforts of women to escape in part from domestic routine into a sphere of work that stimulates the peculiar talents which mark them as individuals.

"Feminism's Awkward Age."

Critics frequently comment upon the self-consciousness and aggressiveness of the feminist movement. The indictment is probably just. However, the judges have in most instances failed to take account of the fact that few, if any, conflicts against circumstances have been carried on with self-forgetful grace and poise. As John Dewey has pointed out, maladjustment is itself a primary condition of self-consciousness. Moreover, struggle is by its very nature an aggressive affair. The battle to overcome hampering conditions and win through to a larger life is not recruited from the weak, the supine and the "ladylike." It is not surprising that the "woman movement" has developed some vigorous personalities, engrossed with the problems of women, and inclined to carry a chip on their shoulders. Such characters are often found among men who espouse causes—personal or social. But society finds these qualities peculiarly exasperating in a woman, whose historic rôle has ever been meek acceptance of her lot. Self-consciousness and self-assertiveness are not likable characteristics in any individual, and those women who reveal them become the special mark

[1] "The Woman Movement and the Larger Social Situation," in *International Journal of Ethics*, Vol. XXV, April, 1915, pp. 328-9.

of satire, ridicule and dislike. Yet, when viewed in relation to the situation that has produced them, these traits must fairly be admitted to be signs of striving to achieve a more satisfying life. When the end that evoked them has been achieved, they will tend, as in the case of men, to weaken or disappear.

Quite often intelligent men, observing the preoccupation of certain able women with the problems of their sex and their instant resentment of the slights and rebuffs of a society unfriendly to their purposes, charge women with suffering from an inferiority complex. And this is quite probably the case. The widespread opinion, whether expressed or not, that women's mental endowment renders them on the whole incapable of sustained thought, constructive organization or creative achievement furnishes excellent soil for growing inferiority complexes and these, in turn, may lead to reactions on the part of their possessors that appear to the detached onlooker as mere silly sensitiveness, unpleasant self-absorption or stupid belligerency.

All this is only to say that the woman movement is in its "awkward age." As Elizabeth Breuer has pointed out, feminism "has passed its adolescence, passed the unthinking hurrahs of its first youth, and now is tackling the problems of maturity." [2] If women, in the midst of the struggle of their lives to find a way of harmonizing their love needs with their needs as individuals, become "assertive and angular" and "get in everybody's way," that is only to be expected. In course of time they will come to closer grips with their problem, will think it through and find satisfactory ways of meeting it. Probably the solution will not be the same for all. Each individual woman must find her own way out of her personal dilemma. In so doing, she blazes a trail for other women with less initiative to follow and wear into a broad, well-traveled highway. This is by no means to say that groups of women may and will not combine to experiment and find a solution of their common difficulties, but only to maintain that each woman's solution must be her own, in the sense that it is clearly apprehended and freely accepted as her way of overcoming the cramping restrictions of her own life. In course of time, feminism, which as Elizabeth Breuer truly suggests, *is not an end in itself, but an attitude toward life,* will have surmounted the chief obstacles in the path of women and will thereupon cast off its assertiveness and solemn self-consciousness like a garment. But the end is not yet.

[2] "Feminism's Awkward Age," in *Harper's Magazine,* April, 1925, p. 545.

HISTORY OF THE WOMAN MOVEMENT

Since French women have not yet attained that political enfranchisement which most progressive modern states have granted to women, it is an arresting fact that feminism may be said to have had its birth in France. As early as 1604, Marie de Gournay, *protégée* of Montaigne and herself a gifted author, wrote her daring work *L'Egalité des Hommes et des Femmes,* which secured for her the title of the "mother of modern feminism." But her demand for equality as between men and women fell on deaf ears, and no more was heard of it for a century. Then these ideas were once more espoused by certain of the French Encyclopedists of the eighteenth century, notably by D'Holbach and Condorcet. In his *Système Social,* published in 1773, Baron D'Holbach brought to the light the medieval disabilities laid upon women, and urged that the feminine half of society be accorded more respect. He even referred approvingly to the theory of Plato, set forth in the famous fifth book of the *Republic,* that women be given an equal education and equal opportunities with men, so far as their natures fitted them for these advantages. More definite and courageous were the views of Condorcet, expressed in his article *Sur l'Admission des Femmes au Droit de Cité* which was published in the *Journal de la Société de 1789.* In this vigorous polemic, Condorcet advocated not only the political equality of men and women, but the concession of absolutely the same rights to both sexes. Unfortunately for the successful development of feminism in France, however, the leaders of the Revolution were far too much absorbed in realizing their theories of human rights for men to accord much attention to women. Their hour had not yet struck. Then, too, Napoleon was notoriously hostile to an enlargement of the liberties and educational opportunities of women. Therefore, the seeds first planted in France were destined to be harvested in other lands.

In 1791, Mary Wollstonecraft, who had been a visitor in France in the first years of the Revolution, returned to England profoundly impressed with the ideas of the Encyclopedists. In her fertile mind the theories of Condorcet germinated and brought forth fruit in that ringing denunciation of the whole European theory and practice regarding women entitled *Vindication of the Rights of Woman.* This vigorous book, published in 1792, is in very truth the gospel of feminism. Over-long and repetitive as it may be, its pages shine with sincerity and make plain that its author had placed her finger on the dominant causes of women's inferiority and subordination, namely, their economic dependence and lack of sound education. "How many women," she exclaims, "waste life away, the prey of discontent, who might have practiced as physicians, regulated a farm, managed a shop, and stood erect, supported by their own industry, instead of hanging their heads surcharged with the dew of sensibility . . . How much more respectable is the woman who earns her own bread by fulfilling any duty, than the most accomplished beauty! . . . I . . . would fain convince reasonable men of the importance of some of my remarks . . . I entreat them to assist to emancipate their companions, to make her a *help-mate* for them." And again, "If marriage be the cement of society, mankind should all be educated after the same model, or the intercourse of the sexes will never deserve the name of fellowship; nor will women ever fulfill the peculiar duties of their sex till they become enlightened citizens, till they become free by being enabled to earn their own subsistence. . . ."[3]

It would hardly be true to say that Mary Wollstonecraft was successful in convincing English men and women of the truth of her strictures and the justice of her demands. On the contrary she was promptly dubbed by conservatives "a hyena in petticoats." Yet her penetrating common sense and her courageous honesty did not fail to make occasional converts, even in her own age. The last hours of an outworn social order were striking as she wrote, and the strong current of events was flowing with her social philosophy. The Industrial Revolution basically altered the age-old activities of women, thereby transforming their lives. Once women had fully demonstrated their ability to be self-supporting, the old feudal chains were struck off, one by one. No doubt also, the emancipation of women was hastened by the new gospel of liberty and equality which was first preached in France and first realized, in part at least, in the new world of America.

An important factor in securing more thorough education for women was the new leisure that ensued when the industries they had so long carried on were removed to the factory and the mill. In consequence there were opened up almost the first opportunities for intellectual education that middle-class and lower-class women had enjoyed since civilization began. Schools and even so-called colleges for "the fair sex" began to be popular in America during the first half of the nineteenth century, and somewhat later in England. Little did their founders reck of the spiritual outcomes of the higher education of women. With it began that *individualizing* of women which was to eventuate in their struggle for a larger life. For higher education has revealed to women as to men their possibilities as individuals, as well as the need of society for their trained serv-

[3] *Humboldt Library of Popular Science Literature*, Nos. 140-7, pp. 156-7, 171.

ices. In a social order demonstrably ugly, crude and inhumane in certain of its aspects, there is ample room for the talents of trained women to exercise themselves. Society will be indeed the gainer if women's profound interest in human life and its values can find free play in helping to increase the beauty and joy of living and to eradicate ancient social wrongs that cry aloud to be righted.

Anglo-Saxon and Teutonic Feminism.

In one of his brilliant social studies, Havelock Ellis has pointed out the marked contrast presented by the "woman movement" in English-speaking and in Teutonic lands.[4] No reader can follow the evolution of feminism in Germany and in English-speaking nations without being struck by the sharp antithesis in the goals pursued by the two movements. In England and America, educated women have been struggling to achieve for their sex entire equality with men, not alone in the political sphere but in the social (including the family), the educational and above all the economic. They have tilted with a good will against every unjust disability which cramps the freedom of the modern woman. In pre-war Germany, on the other hand, women were "spending very little energy in waving the red flag before the fortresses of male monopoly." They were concentrating their efforts to secure protection for the mother and the child, on the theory that if woman's sphere is the home, woman should shape the laws that are to govern that sphere. Out of this view grew the *Mutterschutz* movement in Germany, which, even before the World War, had become a powerful force in behalf of mothers married and unmarried. "The Mutterschutz idea," says Katherine Anthony, "was the natural historical corrective of an exclusively theological and proprietary marriage."[5] In 1905, the views of its proponents had made such headway that there was organized the society known as the *Bund für Mutterschutz*. The campaign gallantly waged by this organization has had three ends in view: (1) the acceptance by society of new moral ideals; (2) the establishment of novel social customs with respect to sex; and (3) the enactment of humane laws protecting mothers and children. Among the leaders of the movement stand out two German women of marked ability who have recently lectured in the United States—Dr. Helene Stöcker and Frau Adele Schreiber, member of the Reichstag.

It is a striking fact that, since the foundation of the German Repub-

[4] *The Task of Social Hygiene*, pp. 109-10. Houghton Mifflin Co., Boston, 1912.
[5] *Feminism in Germany and Scandinavia*, p. 88. Henry Holt & Co., New York, 1915. By permission.

lic in 1918-19 and the conferring of full political rights upon women, more German women have been elected members of the highest governing body of the land—the Reichstag—than any other country can boast. Their interests are various, as are those of the men members, but deep underneath them all burns the determination to free women from the tyrannies of proprietary marriage and to secure some measure of happiness and well-being to unmarried mothers and their luckless offspring.

THE INCIDENCE OF THE WOMAN MOVEMENT ON THE FAMILY

So deep-flowing and extensive a movement for the liberation of women inevitably makes itself felt in many aspects of family life. The outstanding obstacles in the path of woman's fullest self-development at present are her family responsibilities as child-bearer and keeper of the home. It should at once be added that these functions of women unquestionably contain within themselves possibilities of deep satisfactions, as well as real opportunities for self-education. Indeed, it is possible that no woman can attain her highest levels of development unless she has known the profoundly moving joys of love and motherhood. But this is not to say that one capacity of her nature, the emotional, should be permitted to submerge all the others; that love and service of husband and children should be accepted as the whole of life-experience for educated women. No longer should an integrated personality—one that has achieved expression of all its worthy potentialities, and has coördinated them into a harmoniously working whole—be the sole prerogative of men. Somehow women, too, must find a way to reconcile impulses driving them toward mating, motherhood and home with those impelling them to the development and active expression of their special talents.

At present it must be admitted that little has been accomplished to remove obstacles from the path of the married woman who desires to find her own field of activity. Public opinion and the rigid organization of business and professions on the basis of a full day's work or no work have done their best to shut out married women from gainful employment. With regard to the question whether professionally trained married women have special talents and interests that should be set to work in the interests of society, the public reveals, on the whole, supreme unconcern. Far from helping these women, society expatiates on the social obligation of women to bear and rear children, and on the beauty of the sacrifices made by the mother. Certain astute writers have not failed to point out that in these exhortations the emphasis on *sacrifice* demonstrates clearly enough that woman's restless dissatisfaction with her present situation is no vain illusion. Society unquestionably exacts from women so large a surrender of individuality after marriage as seriously to raise the ethical question whether such surrender, carried at times to the point of self-stultification, is either morally justifiable or socially serviceable. Probably it can never again be a generally accepted moral ideal in highly civilized societies. In this age, the ancient principle of self-immolation, always held before women, is brought squarely into conflict with a newer ethical conception that the highest duty of every individual is to develop all his talents, for his own good as well as for the benefit of humanity. "We are afraid," writes Jessie Taft, "to face the fact that the home in its present unrelated, individual form does demand of women, and men too for that matter, a sacrifice so great as to have lost a great part of its value for spiritual growth, an overwhelming and crushing sacrifice of the possibilities of motherhood and fatherhood that defeats its own end." [6]

In the generation to come, it must be the work of forward-looking women, and such men as believe in women's possibilities for larger social usefulness, to convince public opinion by the slow method of education that society has need of the services of trained women, married and unmarried. This will be no easy task. For all human strivings toward ends that involve a fundamental change in the *mores* inevitably encounter a solid wall of social inertia, dislike or fear of novelty. Especially is this true of family customs and ideas, around which the emotions and instinctive preferences of mankind are firmly twined. Yet the battle must be fought not alone with intellectual and moral, but with practical weapons, if women are ever to count for much in the larger life of society. As Jessie Taft so clearly shows, society's favorite method of dealing with human wants, the satisfaction of which means change of the social order, is first, to deny that the want exists; second, to brand it as foolish, wicked and harmful to both the individual and society; third, to suppress it by force—the force of an aroused public opinion or even that of law. Needless to say, society does not so meet the demand of any considerable group which wants to fly in the air or talk with people of other lands or harness water power in the service of human needs. Here no basic change in the *mores* is involved, and experts can at once set to work to solve these scientific problems. But the type of human wants the fulfilment of which can only be secured by a transformation of social custom can be realized solely by continuous effort to enlighten and convince the popular mind. "The chief task of all social movements, then, must be at first to impress upon the rest of society the right of unsatisfied and unexpressed

[6] Taft, *op. cit.*, p. 343.

human impulses to constitute a real problem worthy of the same amount of expert attention whether they demand a new way of crossing the Atlantic Ocean or a new combination of work and social expression in the lives of men and women. This they will never bring about until there is a sufficient number of people who are so socially sensitive and adaptable that they feel within themselves as their own the impulses and points of view of all classes and both sexes." [7] When this goal has been attained even approximately, then experimentation on the part of the courageous vanguard will not be penalized by hostile social criticism. Already there are clear signs that here and there persons are seeing the light and shedding it abroad as did Ibsen in "A Doll's House." The reader will recall that the young wife, Nora, who had been expected to be nothing more than an affectionate mother and a pretty plaything for her husband, Helmer, suddenly revolts against her rôle in life and decides to leave her home. She tries to explain to her husband that she is inadequately equipped for the task of educating her children. The conversation that follows between husband and wife is illuminating.

"*Nora* . . . There is another task I must undertake first. I must try and educate myself—you are not the man to help me in that. I must do that for myself. And that is why I am going to leave you now . . .

"*Helmer.* It's shocking. This is how you would neglect your most sacred duties.

"*Nora.* What do you consider my most sacred duties?

"*Helmer.* Do I need to tell you that? Are they not your duties to your husband and to your children?

"*Nora.* I have other duties just as sacred.

"*Helmer.* That you have not. What duties could those be?

"*Nora.* Duties to myself.

"*Helmer.* Before all else you are a wife and a mother.

"*Nora.* I don't believe that any longer. I believe that before all else I am a reasonable human being, just as you are—or, at all events, that I must try to become one." [8]

TOPICS FOR REPORTS

1. Psychological Aspects of Women's Struggle for Individuality.
    Beatrice Hinkle, M. D., *The Re-Creating of the Individual*, pp. 318-35. Harcourt, Brace & Co., New York, 1923.
2. Social Aspects of the Woman Movement.
    Jessie Taft, "The Woman Movement and the Larger Social Situation," in *International Journal of Ethics*, Vol. XXV, April, 1915, pp. 328-45.

[7] Taft, *op. cit.*, pp. 344-5.
[8] By permission of Charles Scribner's Sons, New York, 1916.

3. Obstacles in the Way of Professions for Married Women.

Eleanor R. Wembridge, "The Professional Education of Women and the Family Problem," in *Journal of Social Hygiene,* Vol. VI, April, 1920, 181-96.

4. The Danger of Parasitism in Women.

Olive Schreiner, *Woman and Labor,* Chs. III, IV. F. A. Stokes Co., New York, 1911.

CHAPTER XVII

MARRIED WOMEN AND CAREERS

THE PROBLEM OF THE PROFESSIONALLY TRAINED WOMAN

THE individualization of women, which has been proceeding apace for two generations or more, has raised one of the knottiest social problems of our age, a problem already outlined in the chapter preceding. How shall educated and professionally trained women satisfy deep-rooted desires for mating and children and at the same time "carry on" in a chosen occupation which enlists their whole-hearted interest and energies? Needless to say, this problem hardly existed in an earlier age, when household economy loomed large, and the higher education of women was undreamed of. But in an era when the demands upon the housewife have shrunken to a shadow of their former proportions, and when colleges and professional schools are sending out each year thousands of eager, alert, highly trained young women who, in ever-increasing numbers, enter the professions and skilled business posts and make good therein, it must be admitted that the old order has been transformed. How to reconcile maternity with a career becomes an urgent question, intruding itself more and more insistently into the consciousness of the housewife and mother who has abandoned congenial work for marriage.

The discontent of many trained women with their domestic lot is not difficult to understand. As suggested above, it is but the outward and visible sign of a sense of frustrated capacity. These women feel their trained abilities rusting with the passage of the years, their costly mental equipment steadily deteriorating. These wives, like their husbands, feel the urge to use their skill and to taste the joy of achievement. No one knows better than the housewife who, before her marriage, was absorbed in interesting work, that her performance in the home lags far behind her abilities. And, in the case of some married women, at least, the resulting sense of frustration eats deep into contentment and joy of living.

It may be urged at this point that a properly conducted home will furnish opportunity for the exercise of all an educated woman's powers. This dogma is still intensely believed in by probably the majority of men and women, in whose minds it is as sacrosanct as the ark of the covenant. Nevertheless, if the theory be as dispassionately examined as it is passionately proclaimed, it is found to rest on a flimsy foundation. If—and this is a big if—a woman has had special training in nutrition, household sanitation, child hygiene, child psychology and other of the valuable subjects taught in our schools of home economics and child welfare, these sciences will unquestionably be of the utmost value in managing her household and rearing her children. But this is not to say that these activities constitute a full-sized job for a lifetime or that, *at any time*, they furnish adequate outlets for the interests and skills of trained women. Who would ever think of urging an architect, a physician, a college professor, a chemist or an electrical engineer, who happened also to be a father, to restrict the practice of his profession to the limits of his household, on the theory that the situations arising in the home would furnish ample scope for his abilities? And yet that is precisely what we do in the case of women, with sublime unawareness of its absurdity. Dr. Ethel Puffer Howes should have punctured that theory once for all in the minds of those men and women who have read her stimulating article in the *Atlantic Monthly* five years ago:

"When I imagine trained and able women I have known, or known about, seeking *within the home* the proper exercise of their abilities,—the auditor, the patent lawyer, the astronomical computer, the palæontologist, the insurance statistician, the specialist on the lymphatic system, the microscopist in electro-metallurgy, the archæologist for prehistoric Greeks, the consulting entomologist attached to an agricultural experiment station,—well, 'the sense faints picturing them'!" [1]

It would seem as if the dissatisfaction of so many highly educated women with their domestic job should, in itself, constitute valid evidence against the soundness of the theory that the home furnishes ample intellectual opportunities for all women. The dilemma of the modern woman has become a favorite theme for fiction and the drama. No doubt it is responsible for nervous strain and downright ill health in some women. There is a body of medical opinion, by no means negligible, to the effect that the frustration of the desire of housewives to secure a preferred and satisfying mode of living results in nervous strains and pathological conditions. A few years ago Dr. Myerson, Visiting Physician of the Nervous Department, Boston City Hospital, became so concerned about this problem that he published a book called *The Nervous Housewife,* in which he made some disturbingly unconventional statements. "It is," he declares, "the main thesis of this book that the neurosis of the housewife has a large

[1] "Continuity for Women," in *Atlantic Monthly*, Vol. 130, December, 1922, p. 733.

part of its origin in the increasing desires of women, in their demands for a fuller, more varied life than that afforded by the lot of the housewife. The nervousness of the housewife is first a medical problem and then a social, psychological one." [2] The writer then goes on to discuss the "segregation, the isolation of the home"; its monotony and the effects of such monotony; its sedentary and indoor character which "tends quite definitely to lower the vigor of the entire organism." And he does not hesitate to declare that "A man would be a wreck morally, physically, and mentally if he coped with his wife's burdens for a month. Either that or the housekeeping would get down to bare essentials." [3] To complete the gloomy picture, Dr. Myerson does not hold out much hope that the restlessness of the housewife will disappear with time; rather, he records it as his conviction that "we may look to an increasing individuality of woman; an increasing reluctance to take up life as the traditional housewife." [4]

Perhaps a concrete instance of the situation in which the trained woman often finds herself after marriage may serve to make the problem more real in the minds of the indifferent or the unsympathetic. In one of the issues of the *Journal of the Association of Collegiate Alumnæ*,[5] there appeared a few years ago a brief article entitled "Reflections of a Professor's Wife." With her husband, the writer had spent several years in the graduate school of a university where both had earned their doctors' degrees. Then the equality in work and the delightful companionship ceased. The man was appointed assistant professor in a state university at a small salary; and the woman, who had eagerly looked forward to a similar appointment in the same institution, was brought face to face with the ruling, by no means uncommon, which prohibited wives of faculty members from teaching in the university. The comments of the professor's wife, after years spent in housekeeping, are worth quoting, for they reflect the feelings of many other women caught in a similar net of circumstance:

"After an expenditure of several thousand dollars and the devotion of some of the best years of my life to special study, I was cut off from any opportunity to utilize this training. And unless I could earn enough money to pay some one else to do the housework, I was doomed to spend a large part of my time in tasks which a woman with practically no education could do. However, accepting the situation, I put on my apron and

---

[2] Dr. A. Myerson, *The Nervous Housewife*, p. 75. By permission of Little, Brown & Co., Boston, 1920.
[3] *Ibid.*, pp. 86-7.   [4] *Ibid.*, p. 246.   [5] January, 1921.

went into the kitchen, where for six years I have cooked a professor's meals and pondered over the policy of our university. Can it be in the divine order of things that one Ph.D. should wash dishes a whole life time for another Ph.D. just because one is a woman and the other a man?" [6]

The Social Background of the Problem.

Needless to say, the web of "a thousand Lilliputian threads" in which many married women find themselves enmeshed has been spun from materials furnished by the larger social situation. On the whole, public opinion still holds to the ancient saw that "woman's place is in the home." The great majority of men and women are either indifferent or hostile to the demand of the housewife for a fuller, more satisfying life which shall not require the sacrifice of home and children. "Society," says Jessie Taft, "no more makes a thoughtful attempt to give the maternal interests the most complete development and employment possible than it makes any pretense at all of using the natural impulse of woman to be of economic value in the world. Much less does it offer a rational scheme for combining both motives within a possible form of living for the average normal woman." [7] The home is still feudal in its individualism, still unconnected at many essential points with the organized economic activities of the community. The intelligent housewife, pursuing her ancient tasks in the home, cannot fail to be conscious of her detachment from the larger social life and, above all, of her almost complete helplessness to control the conditions of production in such wise as to benefit the family for which she works. She "carries on" by herself in semi-isolation from that great industrial and social world whose products she uses and by whose customary ideas her life is governed.

The attitude of popular opinion toward extra-domestic work for married women is probably rather faithfully reflected in the replies made by 354 men to the following questions embodied in a questionnaire submitted to them by Lorine Pruette:

"Question I.

"What view do you most favor?

"A. The married woman should devote her time to the home.

"B. The married woman should work outside if she desires, except when the care of young children demands her time.

---

[6] Pp. 90-1.
[7] Taft, "The Woman Movement and the Larger Social Situation," in *International Journal of Ethics*, Vol. XXV, April, 1915, p. 34.

"C. It should be expected that the married woman shall earn part of the family income, the husband assisting her with household duties and the care of children.

"D. Housework and the care of children should be done by specialists or coöperative methods, the time of the married woman thus set free like her husband's, to be used in outside work." [8]

When the responses to this question were examined, it was discovered that 11.2% of the 354 men were too indifferent to reply. If we classify the remainder under the headings *conservative* (in favor of A), *liberal* (favoring B) and *radical* (favoring C or D) we get the following results:

Conservative	57.6%	(204 men)
Liberal	27.7%	(98 men)
Radical	3.5%	(C, 7 men; D, 5) [9]

The replies reveal that over fifty-seven percent of the total group were opposed to the work of married women outside the home. If to this number be added the 11.2% (forty men) who were too "apathetic" to answer the question, and who would very likely have been found in the conservative group had they responded, we find 68.8% of the men definitely or probably antagonistic to extra-domestic employment for wives. If the forty men who did not respond be excluded, sixty-five percent of the 314 men remaining favored A. On the other hand thirty-one percent of the smaller group were disposed to favor such work if it did not interfere with the care of children. This is probably a far higher proportion than would have been found in a similar group in any earlier epoch of social history, and reflects the profound changes in economic conditions that have taken place during the last century. It may also indicate the slowly growing appreciation on the part of men that women are individuals, with individual abilities, tastes and preferences. That ninety-eight men out of 314 should have been willing to accord to wives the right to work outside the home, so long as children did not suffer thereby, may be a sign of promise that the age-old custom of massing all women of diverse interests, capacities and training under the caption "Woman," and then generalizing about them, is very gradually becoming a thing of the past. Half the battle of the trained woman who longs for both a profession and a home with husband and children will have been won when men (and women also) are ready to admit that no such entity as "Woman" exists.

[8] Lorine Pruette, *Women and Leisure*, p. 100. Copyright by E. P. Dutton & Co., New York, 1924.
[9] *Ibid.*, p. 101.

The fact that only twelve men out of 354 were in favor of wives earning part of the family income as a matter of course, the housework and child care to be undertaken by husband and wife together or left to coöperative agencies, is no more than is to be expected. The march of economic events, as well as the progress of experimentation in coöperative methods, must go much farther and be reinforced by daily education of the popular mind before this tiny group of "radicals" will be greatly increased.

But an unconcerned or antagonistic public opinion is not the only obstacle in the path of those married women who seek to use their talents in some chosen field of the world's work. The economic situation at present is notoriously inelastic and unaccommodating to the desires of married women seeking employment. Even for the woman who gives up all idea of plunging into the tremendous current of driving effort and concentrated interest necessary to the successful pursuit of a career, and is content to find congenial part-time work as an outlet for her trained abilities, the path is beset with difficulties. As Elsie Clews Parsons pointed out long ago, the economic demand is very largely for a whole day's work or no work. Not only is this true, but probably no inconsiderable number of business and professional organizations discriminate against married women on the ground either that they should remain at home, or that they would be more irregular in attendance than single women. A limited investigation of this question by a student, residing in a large Eastern city, revealed that of thirteen business firms employing married as well as single women, most had formulated no policy about such employment, except that married women must be prepared to meet exactly the same conditions as single women, and show as good results. One great corporation, however, employing thousands of single women, declared through its Vice-President that "the Company did not desire to be a party to aid in the drive which seems to be going on against the American home." [10] More extended research would probably disclose that managers of other corporations, banks, department stores, telephone companies, business offices and the like hold similar views; and it is to be hoped that a thorough investigation of this question will be undertaken before many years.

Social Consequences of the Policy of Keeping Trained Women in the Home.

The social pressure which is unquestionably being exercised to hold women of talent and trained capacities to household tasks has, of course,

[10] Data collected by Miss Kathleen Crowley, formerly a student of Teachers College, Columbia University, New York.

its inevitable results, both individual and social. The thwarting of personal desires for activity, for "a preferred way of living" always reacts unfavorably upon the individual. As we have seen, it is chiefly responsible for the dissatisfaction of many married women of education and training with the kind of lives they are expected to live. Most husbands find this discontent, this restive seeking for more rewarding outlets for activity, irritating and hard to bear. "Why can't they be content to take care of their homes and their children?" they ask, only dimly aware of the tumult of questioning and revolt that is going on in the minds of their mates. Now this blindness may be genuine bewilderment in the case of some men; but in many instances it is due to an exasperated refusal to face squarely the difficulties with which their wives are confronted in the natural human attempt to achieve a satisfying life. As one writer has suggested, it is difficult to believe that if men had devoted to the problem of their wives' discontent a tithe of the heart-whole attention they lavish upon the matter of aviation or taxes, husbands and wives would have gone far toward reaching a solution, at least of their own individual problem. As it is, the unquiet strivings of women and their patent dissatisfaction with this "sorry scheme of things entire" too often eventuate merely in domestic friction. The spiritual atmosphere of the home, far from being one of mutual understanding and coöperation, is replete with tensions and conflicts and thus furnishes the worst possible environment for the rearing of sensitive young children.

It is idle to attempt to solve the difficulty by pointing to the advances made in the scientific theories of home economics and child care. In most homes, women's tasks are "casual, unsupervised, unstandardized" and probably, in consequence, more or less inefficiently performed. Moreover, even if the latest scientific knowledge and inventions *were* applied to the activities of the home, these would still fail to satisfy the cravings of gifted women who long to use their talents in what to them is a wider, more challenging, more interesting and absorbing type of work. The time-honored custom of fitting the talents of women to the Procrustean bed of household tasks is failing to justify itself and must make way for other methods of meeting the situation.

But this is not all. As Lorine Pruette has so convincingly shown, a large number of trained women are utilizing only a part of their capabilities in a half-time or quarter-time household job. Most men are desirous to secure for their wives as much paid assistance in maintaining the home and caring for children as their income will permit. Hence the large number of semi-parasitic married women who, when their home tasks are performed, throng the streets "window-shopping," or become theatre and movie "fans" or "bridge fiends." The faces of these women "are marked by the strain of too much leisure. . . . They are a mark, not only of their husbands' ability to keep them in comfort, not only of 'vicarious consumption,' but of social inefficiency, of society's failure adequately to make use of its human material." [11]

At this point, no doubt, some readers will say, "Why can't these women take up club work or church work or serve as volunteer workers in connection with philanthropic or political organizations? Surely there is enough to do in these fields to satisfy any reasonable woman." Of course, many married women do find these outlets. Witness the number of matrons who are leaders in all these spheres of activity. But there are numerous housewives who do not find in these activities the kind of work they crave. This may be deplorable, but it is none the less both true and natural. Those who insist that women *ought* to find these outlets attractive simply do not take into account the facts of human nature well known to psychologists. Interests and talents are as various as individuals. Moreover, they reveal themselves spontaneously, and cannot be made to order at the demand of captious individuals or societies. To require all trained women to throw themselves into club or "uplift" activities when they are craving the chance to work as artists, economists, scientific research workers, architects or deans of women is to shut one's eyes to the fundamental truths of psychology. Married women who force themselves to engage in philanthropic or social work for which they are not adapted not only do not lessen, but may appreciably increase, the tension which springs from the thwarting of their spontaneous desires.

The harmful effects of refusing to married women congenial work outside the home are not restricted to the domestic circle. It seems scarcely open to question that this policy results in enormous social wastage. In our present stage of social development there is urgent need of the contribution of every trained human being in the solution of problems of economic production, of social well-being and happiness, of political justice, of a truer democratization of society, of scientific research, of the heightening and extension of aesthetic enjoyment. Who can say that our tens of thousands of educated wives and mothers have nothing to offer by way of meeting these human needs; or that their work in managing a small household and rearing two or three children constitutes the full job of a life-time, enlisting all their capabilities? A little unprejudiced reflection should convince most intelligent men and women that the social waste involved in this state of affairs is deplorable.

[11] Pruette, *op. cit.*, pp. xii, xiii. By permission of E. P. Dutton & Co.

As Pruette has pointed out, human material has been very cheap in the past, plentifully produced and not easily destroyed—even when cruelly exploited. But signs are not lacking that the sharp fall in the birth-rate, characteristic of every highly civilized country, will bear fruit in a truer appreciation of human life, in a realization that society is the loser when it sanctions "the wrecking of some by industrial strain and overwork, of others by leisure-strain and underwork." [12] What is urgently needed today is a new kind of "social engineering," applied not only to industrial workers but to women, with a view to discovering and training their special talents and furnishing opportunities for their exercise. A program of social engineering would frankly accept at the outset a "selective motherhood," while it developed ways and means of solving the cruel dilemma of the woman who longs to be both a mother and a worker. If increasing prosperity results for a time in making more and more women non-producers, or part-time workers, society in the end will be forced to undertake such measures for utilizing women's efforts as it was unwilling to institute at the beginning. For with the steady increase in population, due to the fact that the death-rate is falling faster than the birth-rate, the time is not very far distant when every nation will be confronted with urgent problems growing out of density of numbers. Economists tell us that man's control over nature is based upon production of a surplus, a surplus not only of material goods but of scientific knowledge, useful inventions, initiative and energy. When populations become dense over the earth, the problem of maintaining millions of semi-idle or non-productive women will assume menacing proportions. Even now, economic pressure is forcing millions of women into gainful employments, and the percentage of these women workers who are married is steadily increasing. Almost two million married women are working outside the home at present; and the social current has set strongly in that direction. It is probable that the pressure of events will accomplish what education of the popular mind may fail to do, namely, make the contribution of the married woman to the production of material and spiritual goods appear a matter of course even to the plain man and woman on the street. Only when this miracle has been wrought can women be said to have won their struggle for a home and a chosen vocation.

Do All Women Desire Careers?

Years of observation and questioning of women have gone far to convince the writer that by no means all educated women long for a career

[12] Pruette, *op. cit.*, p. xiii.

after marriage. Probably the majority of wives find satisfying outlets for their special capacities in home management and the care and guidance of small children. Certainly, when these tasks are expertly performed, arousing interest, stimulating study and consuming much of the time of the housewife, they constitute a profession in themselves. But in those cases where domestic help is adequately provided, the housewife by no means has a full-sized job. The wives and mothers of this group, half-time or even quarter-time workers, have just enough to do to give them the comfortable conviction that they are not mere idlers, while they command no little leisure to spend in agreeable social intercourse or in amusement. Still another body of women, by no means negligible in numbers, are frankly parasitic. They are the mates of prosperous business men whose boast it is that their wives need "never lift a hand." From morning to night it is doubtful whether these women perform a single important task within the home or out of it. They inherit and continue the tradition of the idle "lady," smooth of hand and too often empty of head, whom some men delight to maintain in unproductive luxury. In neither of these last two groups is there any dynamic interest in a career.

If it be admitted that probably the majority of women would even now choose to make a home and rear children rather than to carry on a profession, it should at once be added that this does not fully state the case. In the present social situation, two sharply separated alternatives are commonly presented to young women, namely, love, home and children on the one hand, and a profession on the other. When women are confronted with these alternatives and asked to choose one, most of them will yield to the imperious demands of racial impulses and elect the former. This is by no means to say that they have no desire to work after marriage; but only that their emotional urge, reinforced by social suggestion and pressure, proves too strong for their professional interest. This view receives support from the replies to a questionnaire which Lorine Pruette received from 347 young women. The median age of this group was 16.5 years. Two hundred of the cases fell within the years fifteen to seventeen, while thirteen were women above thirty. On the whole, then, the group was composed of young adolescents. Less than fifty of the number had not enjoyed the benefits of high school, college or graduate study. Question I submitted to this group was as follows: "If you could choose anything in the world, what would you most like to be? (doctor, lawyer, teacher, actress, artist, business woman, stenographer, household expert, wife, mother or anything else)." The replies showed that 238 votes (sixty-one per cent) were cast for careers and 149 votes (thirty-nine percent) for home (wife or mother). In estimating the significance of these responses, however, two facts should be kept in mind. First, the alternative of home *or* career was not clearly presented to the young women in this question; second, although the total number of those who chose various careers exceeded the number who elected to be wives or mothers, yet the highest number of votes for any single vocation were cast for the two latter. Sixty-two girls chose to be mothers and eighty-seven chose to be wives, as against, for example, one who chose to be an interior decorator; three, to be doctors; fifteen, to be writers; and thirty-five, to be artists.[13]

Question III of the questionnaire presented clearly the alternative with which most trained women are faced. "If you had to choose which would you rather have:

"A. A career (that is, work outside the home with independent income but without a husband and children)?

"B. A home of your own, with husband and children to care for but without an independent income and outside work?" [14]

In response to this question, 118 girls (thirty-five percent) chose the career; 212 (sixty-three percent), the home; and nine wrote that they wanted both. Miss Pruette comments on the frequency of erasures throughout the schedules, which were most noticeable on this question, and revealed a shifting in many girls from one side to the other. No doubt, considerable hesitation was evoked when the group was faced with this clear-cut division of the ways. Miss Pruette further ventures the opinion that had B included with home, husband and children an independent income and outside work, more than sixty-three percent would have chosen it; whereas if A had combined the prospect of a career with the possibility of love expression outside of marriage, more than thirty-five percent would have elected it.[15]

Although no doubt this questionnaire was a more or less crude measure of the choices of young women, and the inquiry would need to be supplemented and extended before it could furnish reliable grounds for generalization, it is interesting as far as it goes in revealing a trend among girls to substitute a career for marriage, or to hesitate when called upon to choose between them. It is a safe assumption that, if these questions had been put to 347 young women only a generation ago, the votes for home and husband would have mounted far higher than they did, while those for a career would have shrunk to small proportions.

[13] Pruette, *op. cit.*, pp. 120-3.
[14] *Ibid.*, p. 131. By permission.
[15] See pp. 131-2.

The Need for Experimentation.

All social writers who have come to grips with this woman problem, with something of the unbiased detachment of the scientist, are agreed that no easy, ready-made solution will meet the complexities of the situation. The generations to come will unquestionably be a period of experimentation, of publishing results, of more or less deliberate education of public opinion. More and more women must be prepared to be adventurers, willing to explore unknown regions of possibility, to tap new sources of help. By their courage, their inventiveness, their persistence, they will in time bring about a considerable degree of social toleration of their experiments—the first step toward general acceptance of a new economic order for women. The growing pressure of social needs will be on the side of these adventurers; and they will be assisted, as they always have been, by a handful of forward-looking men in every land who are sympathetically concerned with the predicament of the modern woman. No doubt, the outer bastions of prejudice will require a lengthy siege. Women must resign themselves to "a protracted period of ventilating the question and arguing it through"; they must be willing to "explore, experiment, educate, agitate," as Dr. Howes has so convincingly shown.[16] In the end they will find a way out of the morass in which they are held at present.

Obstacles Confronting Married Women Who Seek Careers.

It is safe to prophesy that experimentation, once begun, will take more forms than one, depending upon the attitude of the individual experimenters toward the question of motherhood, the most serious difficulty in the path of professional married women. Whether there be a maternal instinct or not, and this question has already divided psychologists into warring camps, certain it seems that some women have only the feeblest desire for offspring, and are far from successful in their relations with children. Indeed, there are men who seem much more spontaneously interested in children, more happily sympathetic and imaginative in dealing with them than are some women. This is a not uncommon situation and has been interestingly portrayed in fiction.[17] In a more flexible society, the right of these women to select or reject motherhood would be fully recognized. If Western civilization ever becomes more responsive to the needs of many women of many minds, a place will be found for these married professional women who insist on rejecting what Pruette calls

[16] Howes, *op. cit.*, p. 737.
[17] See Dorothy Canfield Fisher's novel, *The Homemaker*. Harcourt, Brace & Co., New York, 1924.

"the dogma of the child" in order that they may throw all their energies of mind and body into the engrossing demands of a profession. In course of time, society will probably reconcile itself to "selective motherhood," not only because free choice in this regard would appear to be an inalienable personal right, but also because these sterile professional women may be rendering valuable service in many socially useful fields of work and, perhaps, expending their nurturing and aesthetic impulses, their dynamic interest in human life and its values, in ways that will make society more humane and beautiful. The social organism is surely not the loser if a proportion of married women elect to be "social mothers" rather than physiological parents.

This is, of course, not to say that these wives, by refusing motherhood, may not have impoverished their own personal experience, and may not regret their choice with the approach of a childless old age. This may or may not prove true. Women must be granted freedom to experiment with regard to this question and must find out for themselves whether the supreme values that society has attached to motherhood in the personal experience of *all women* are valid or not; and whether some married women may not find rewarding substitutes for these emotional experiences.

But even if a fraction of husbands and wives agree to make their marriage a "companionate" without children in order that each may pursue a chosen profession, the difficulties are not wholly disposed of. How is the home to be kept up and meals prepared? It is probable that this hindrance will more and more be overcome in two ways: (1) by the erection of apartment houses with a central kitchen and dining-room, containing family tables; (2) by coöperative ventures in neighborhood kitchens, laundries and cleaning establishments. Already apartments with central dining-rooms, and even nurseries, are being built in our large cities, and will probably rapidly increase in numbers in response to a real demand. With respect to the second method of meeting the difficulty, signs are not so encouraging. America has been called "the grave of the coöperative movement"—and probably with justice. Within the last fifteen years, several coöperative schemes for furnishing hot food to homes have sprung up, withered and vanished. But this record of failure need not end experimentation. When married women *are pressed hard enough* to find a way out of their predicament, then experiments with various types of coöperative schemes for releasing the married woman from distasteful household work will be begun.

One further obstacle in the path of the woman who desires both a home and a career lies in the fact that, when husband and wife are pursuing different professions, there is no guarantee that their work may not call them to widely separated parts of the country. In this possibility lies a very stubborn difficulty, which husband and wife would do well to face before embarking on separate careers. Several solutions have been suggested: (1) that to the partner whose work is the more important and lucrative should be left the choice with regard to location; (2) that husband and wife go their different ways, spending vacations together; (3) that husband and wife follow the same profession. In the first case it would probably more often than not be the wife who would have to turn her back on an established profession in which she was, perhaps, attaining competence if not distinction, in order to follow the husband into a larger field of opportunity. This possibility she should take into serious consideration before marriage; and if the situation arises, she should meet it with cheerful philosophy. In the course of time she will probably find it possible to reëstablish herself in the new sphere. Occasionally the woman's salary and the importance of her work will exceed that of the man. In such instances, of course, the position is reversed, and it is for the husband to make the sacrifice.

Another way out of the difficulty might be the carrying on of their work by husband and wife in different places. This would, obviously, reduce their life together to the periods of vacations and possible week-ends. Not a few social students and writers [18] at present hold that highly individualized married couples should live apart a portion of the year in order to avoid the clash and friction of too close and continuous daily association. Instances where the plan appears to work successfully are known to the writer. In one case, the husband teaches in a Western university, while his wife is on the faculty of an Eastern woman's college. Vacations together are eagerly anticipated and enjoyed. Nevertheless this method of untying the Gordian knot will probably appeal to relatively few men and women. The comradeship of marriage, the sharing of its mutual cares and joys, the growth in understanding and sympathy on the part of husband and wife can scarcely be achieved by a life of long separations punctuated by periods of intimacy, and this comradeship in sharing is surely precious enough to be worth some sacrifice.

The third method, that of choice of the same profession by husband and wife, is advocated by Ethel Puffer Howes and others. Wherever possible, this way out of the difficulty might well be followed. No doubt cases are known to all of us where husbands and wives practise in the same

[18] See Edith Ellis (Mrs. Havelock Ellis), *New Horizons in Love and Life.* A. & C. Black, Ltd., London, 1921.

city as physicians, lawyers, teachers, architects and industrial engineers. In the last instance one recalls the comradeship of Mr. Frank Gilbreth and his wife, who after marriage, became partners in his work as industrial engineer. Since the death of Mr. Gilbreth, his wife, *who is the mother of eleven children,* has "carried on" alone, and has achieved an important and useful position as an expert in the field of industrial engineering. Obviously, however, if the interests, abilities and training of husband and wife lie in widely disparate spheres of work, no such easy solution of their problem is feasible.

What Shall Be Done for Married Women Who Desire Both Work and Children?

Despite the gloomy forebodings of eugenists and biologists to the effect that educated women will increasingly refuse to perform their fundamental social duty of recruiting the race, it is highly probable that Nature has sufficiently endowed both men and women with parental impulses and with a spontaneous interest in little children to assure the survival of the human race on this planet. To be sure, it appears likely that the birth-rate will continue to fall *among all classes,* once the prohibitions against imparting contraceptive information are removed. Nor is this a cause for alarm, since man's conquest of disease and thus of death will probably result in a satisfactory natural increase in most countries. In the future there will be fewer babies, but there is reason to believe they will be better, both in ability to survive, and in health, which is the outcome of better nurture. Human beings in the coming generations will presumably not be produced in such numbers as to be held cheap; but their social worth and efficiency may be enormously enhanced by improved education and training. Nevertheless, there will always be women who long for children, and who find their deepest joy in caring for them and guiding their first fumbling attempts to adjust themselves to the world. Such women will cheerfully resign the exacting demands of a career for motherhood, and perform a great social service with no thought of return. Yet it is probable that even these mothers would perform their duties as mothers with more skill and knowledge if they were free to choose their work and plan their lives accordingly. To quote Charles Zeublin: "Even the main function of woman, maternity . . . cannot result happily for offspring or parents, until the woman is granted the same control of her life that man enjoys." [19]

No doubt even the maternal women, if they have enjoyed higher edu-

[19] "Woman and Economic Dependence," in *American Journal of Sociology,* Vol. XIV, pp. 606-14.

cation and training, have their hours of dissatisfaction with a plethora of domesticity, and are impelled at times by an unsettling urge to try their mettle once more in skilled work that is standardized, coördinated and economically rewarding. For these wives and mothers, increasing opportunities for part-time employment, at home and outside, should be opened up. Little has been done as yet to discover what types of work the housewife can carry on in her hours of leisure. Yet signs are not lacking of a widespread interest in this question, so crucial to women. The Bureau of Vocational Information in New York City has recently published a study [20] of 100 women of training and ability who are doing some serious work in addition to their jobs of home-maker and mother. The purpose of the investigation was to find answers to the following questions: "What kinds of jobs, what kinds of families, what kinds of homes do such women have? What are their reasons for working? Are they motivated by financial necessity, by desire to enrich their contribution to the family life, by the need to provide an outlet for unused intellectual and emotional powers? What kinds of paid work can they do? Can any kind of work be done without sacrificing some of the other factors in the combination? Is the financial or intellectual return commensurate with the effort?" [21]

This is a move in the right direction, a praiseworthy attempt to abandon theories for facts, which ought to stimulate organizations of women the country over to undertake similar investigations and thus enormously increase the scope and value of the study. The findings of the study have recently been published.

The Institute for the Coördination of Women's Interests.

Within the last two years an Institute for the Coördination of Women's Interests has been established at Smith College, with Dr. Ethel Puffer Howes, its creator, as director. The Institute will be financed for three years by the Laura Spelman Rockefeller Foundation. In the words of President Neilson of Smith College, the purpose of the Institute "is to find a solution for the problem which confronts almost every educated woman today: how to reconcile a normal life of marriage and motherhood with a life of intellectual activity, professional or otherwise." [22] In the belief that the college woman of the present needs not only education for parenthood, but the "working out of a philosophy of life and a technique of living that shall include *all* her main interests," this new venture has

[20] *Marriage and Careers.* The Channel Bookshop, New York, 1926.
[21] *News Bulletin*, November 1, 1924, p. 132, Bureau of Vocational Information.
[22] From the press notice, November, 1925.

been hopefully launched. More concretely, the Institute will work to discover practical means and methods by which women may coördinate their family interests with their interest in professional work and social movements. In the opinion of the founder, what "is needed at present is a study, first of methods of releasing women from wasteful occupation in their homes and, second, of modifying present professional opportunities and opening new possibilities for productive and satisfying occupation within the limits of normal family life." [23]

With respect to the first part of the program, the release of women from wasteful home occupations, the Institute plans to discover "continuous, automatic and inexpensive (methods) adapted to modest and newly established households." Accordingly the Institute will investigate experiments in coöperative kitchens, laundries, nurseries, nursery schools, coöperative housing, service organizations connected with coöperative housing schemes and other experiments of a like nature, with a view to discovering methods, costs, causes of failure and elements of success. The results of these studies will be charted, principles will be developed and methods of procedure demonstrated.

The second part of the program involves the study of possible modifications in the professions and in the future training of women for the professions. It is Dr. Howes' belief that new subdivisions of the professions will constantly be made, such as have already appeared in engineering and architecture; and that these subdivisions will furnish opportunities for part-time work or work which women can carry on at home. In her widely read article on "Continuity for Women" already cited, Dr. Howes estimated on the basis of the "Report of Engineering Council on the Classification and Compensation of Engineers" that no less than 350 variations of engineering were possible for women in part-time work. If it be assumed that this is the way out of their difficulties for a large number of college women, obviously not only must employers be educated to the point of being willing to take on trained married women as "piece workers," but the professional training of women must be modified to meet the new situation and possibilities. This problem the Institute undertakes to examine. Ultimately it hopes to "make a comprehensive plan for the education of women in connection with this coördination of their interests."

Finally, the Institute is shortly to organize two experiments in Northampton,—a small, coöperative nursery and a coöperative organization for home assistance. These will be practical demonstrations of the fact that,

[23] *Loc. cit.*

with intelligent planning and organization, the housewife and mother can be released from some measure of her domestic occupations for more intellectual professional work. But it is no part of Dr. Howes' plan that talented wives and mothers shall be wholly emancipated from household employments. Far from this, she believes that every woman should master the principles of household management, family hygiene, child care and training and other domestic arts. To this end, the Institute is working out a comprehensive plan for the education of women, with a view to the coördination of their interests, which will make provision for the training of every woman in household arts.

All those men and women who are concerned to find a way out of her present *impasse* for the married woman have cause to congratulate themselves that, in one corner of the country at least, theorizing is to go hand in hand with intelligent experimentation. All honor to Dr. Howes and her co-workers for conceiving their problem in the concrete and for attempting a practical demonstration of how it may be solved. There is great need of experimentation of this sort, and ever more experimentation, if educated women are to achieve that integration of their interests so essential to an integration of personality. Yet the writer ventures to suggest that the Prospectus of the Institute neglects certain stubborn facts that must be reckoned with in any inclusive scheme for solving this woman problem. In the first place it ignores the fact that there is an ever-growing body of women who have no interest in housekeeping arts or in the exacting physical care and guidance of infants, who yet long for love, home and children. These women cannot be ignored or dismissed with a gesture. They dare to hope that a more adaptable economic and social order will find room for women who seek useful and satisfying lives, in which their desire for husbands and offspring shall not be penalized by the loss of full professional opportunity. In her oft-cited articles on "Accepting the Universe" [24] and "Continuity for Women," [25] Dr. Howes clearly sets forth her own philosophy regarding this dilemma of the modern woman. She maintains that there is an "antinomy" in the very nature of woman, an essential contradiction between her desire for children and her desire for full self-expression in work, that can only be resolved when the married woman refuses to compete with men in professional employments. If, however, she makes home tasks and the rearing of children her central interest, Dr. Howes believes that something can be done partially to release her from domestic duties and to give her the intellectual stimulus of

[24] *Atlantic Monthly*, April 1922.
[25] *Ibid.*, December, 1922.

congenial professional occupation for part of the day. The Institute, there-fore, is organized to find a way of resolving the feminine "antinomy" by compromise. Renunciation of a full-time job in the professions is to be compensated by provision for part-time employment in subdivisions of the work.

It may safely be prophesied that such an answer to their paramount problem will not satisfy all of the thousands of highly trained women who are seeking a way out of their difficulties. Indeed, there are not lacking so-called "radical" or "advanced" thinkers among both men and women who will be quick to point out that the Institute is really engaged in an effort to induce dissatisfied matrons to return contentedly to their ancient domestic sphere on the ground that "half a loaf is better than no bread." This vanguard of feminism may be expected, also, to point out that any organized attempt to find part-time employment for married women and to adapt the professional training of women to the restricted demands of subdivisions of the professions is in reality striking a heavy blow at all serious participation by women in professional work. From the point of view of these radicals, the Institute appears to have entered upon a cru-sade to put women back into the home, educate every one of them in do-mestic science, child care and family hygiene and give them the sop of a limited professional training to fit them for employment on the fringes of the skilled occupations.

The writer believes that the comments of these critics do not fairly represent the purposes of the Institute. Yet one criticism may justly be made of the Institute's scheme. In planning that ultimately all college women shall be trained in household arts and child care, it overlooks the fact that a large percentage of college women will never marry. Fifteen years after graduation, slightly less than half of the graduates of women's colleges in the East are married and the marriage rate is only slightly higher in many coeducational universities.[26] To require that college women who are interested in scientific research, business management or public service shall devote any considerable part of their higher education to domestic arts, which they may never thereafter use, seems a grave mistake. But this is not all. What will be the economic effect of part-time professional work by married women? The fact that they are first of all home-makers, for whose support their husbands are legally liable, would unquestionably operate to lower the scale of remuneration for their work, as it has always done in the past. These part-time workers would thus remain at least partial economic dependents, not earning enough to maintain themselves

[26] See chapter XVIII on "Individualism and the Marriage Rate."

nor sharing to a really helpful extent in the burden of family support which often falls with undue weight on the shoulders of the married man in the professions and business.

The Institute scheme may, and probably will, meet the needs of many married women who have no desire to take up serious professional work, and for that reason it should be welcomed. But it fails to take account of another group who do not accept Dr. Howes' views with respect to the fundamental "antinomy" in the nature of women. In the opinion of this group, the "antinomy" exists, not in the original make-up of women, but in the structure of society. A social order more amenable to the deep-seated desire of its members for fuller life would itself initiate experiments, or at least further those begun, with a view to helping married women out of their predicament. To overcome the obstacles society plants in the path of wives and mothers, who know they are capable of doing work of genuine social value, would demonstrate to the satisfaction of all but the most recalcitrant that the "antinomy" is social, not psychological.

There is one more aspect of this many-sided question that the Institute has not, apparently, taken into consideration in framing its plans. More and more, in the years to come, society will need the assistance of all educated and trained human beings, women as well as men, in the cure of its many economic and social ills and in the upbuilding of a social order responsive to the needs of *all* its members, not merely to those of a privileged fraction. Women, shoulder to shoulder with men, must help to build that fair city, wherein not only will individuals be worthy, but their lives will be worth living. No longer, as Dr. Beatrice Hinkle has so clearly shown, will the "eternal maternal" type of woman [27] suffice, as it so long has sufficed in the past, to meet the social need. Not only must the women of the future be tender and wise mothers, but they must find a way of combining this service to society with constructive work, covering the entire gamut of skilled employments. It is possible that men in the future will demand that their wives not only realize their conception of the maternal woman, but also their ideal of the stimulating companion with interests as wide as their own, of the co-worker in some useful sphere of the world's endeavor. Even now, not a few intelligent men are showing signs of dissatisfaction with the merely motherly woman, completely engrossed with home and children. This critical discontent will, the writer believes, increase and multiply with the passing of the years. Moreover, it is at least conceivable that, in the future, wide breaches will be made in the entrenched popular opinion that bringing up one or two children is a

[27] "The Chaos of Modern Marriage," in *Harper's Magazine*, December, 1925.

full-time life job for an educated woman. When this social dogma is once overthrown there will be found in its place the belief that society needs the services of all its members, to the extent of their gifts and opportunities and *without regard to sex*, in the establishment of a new social order, more equitable, humane and beautiful. In that day, associations will be organized for the purpose of trying out plans for the expert care and development of small children similar to that of the rapidly spreading nursery school. Also, these organizations will venture upon experiments, coöperative and otherwise, for meeting family needs for appetizing food and cleanliness. These projects will not be planned to afford *partial* release to the wife and mother, but a whole day's release, to the end that she may pursue her chosen vocation, not in amateur fashion, but with serious purpose. Any other approach to the professions on the part of women spells dilletanteism, and merely delays the time when they will make worth-while contributions to the upbuilding of a better social order.

Entering the Professions in Middle Life.

Many writers sincerely believe that women who have practised a profession before marriage will find it practicable to return to it after fifteen years or so spent in the social service of bearing and rearing children. It is held by these writers that trained women who chafe against the routine and confinement of domestic work will be cheered and sustained in its performance by the hope of returning to their vocations when their children no longer demand all their time and attention. But those men and women who have had years of experience in professional work, who appreciate the continuous growth in theory and practice characteristic of all highly skilled vocations, will be thoroughly skeptical of the possibility of women's "coming back" into the professions after years of disorganized, unstandardized employment. What chance has the woman doctor, architect, teacher, research worker of making good in these professions after fifteen or twenty years of removal from their problems, their experiments and discoveries, their new methodology? No one has summed up more convincingly than Dr. Howes the well-nigh insuperable difficulties in the way of reëntrance into skilled occupations after a protracted period of absence:

"Much has been said of the woman's 'second leisure,' as affording the desired usefulness. But there are two obstacles hardly to be overcome.

"First, the long interruption spells for most occupations a fatal weakening in knowledge, skill and energy. . . . The hand, the eye, the scientific flair have failed, as with Andrea del Sarto:

'But all the play, the insight and the stretch—
Out of me, out of me !'

"Last of all, the foothold of opportunity is lost. Chances for work of any kind depend for the most part on unbroken relations with the source of supply. These are not lightly to be renewed." [28]

In an age of scientific investigation, when members of a profession are daily immersed in its demands and can with difficulty keep abreast of its novel theories and projects, it is idle to expect women of forty or more, depleted in energy and deficient in both practised skill and knowledge, to carry on their former vocations with success. They will inevitably have lost their place in the line.

TOPICS FOR REPORTS

1. Visit a dozen or more large business enterprises in your town or city and secure from the personnel manager exact information with respect to (1) the policy of the firm regarding the employment of married women; (2) the efficiency of married women as compared with single workers; (3) the absence or tardy record of married workers as compared with single; (4) the policy of the firm with regard to granting leave of absence (say for six months or less) to a married woman to bear a child. Report on your findings.
2. Investigate the agencies in your city or town (if any) which might relieve mothers from full-time or part-time domestic work. Report on your findings.
3. How Present Home Conditions React upon the Family.
   See Charlotte Perkins Gilman's article in *American Journal of Sociology,* Vol. XIV, pp. 592-605.
4. Unpaid Home Work and Gainful Part-Time Employment.
   orine Pruette, *Women and Leisure,* Ch. V. E. P. Dutton & Co., New York, 1924.

[28] Howes, *op. cit.,* pp. 735-6.

Three Possibilities.

1. Woman's place is in the home.
2. Free choice of outside work or profession
3. Choice of motherhood or career.

CHAPTER XVIII

INDIVIDUALISM AND THE MARRIAGE RATE

CIVILIZATION AND A DECLINING MARRIAGE RATE

IT is a fairly well established fact that a positive correlation exists between a highly developed civilization and a low birth-rate; but the evidence of a similar correlation between culture and the marriage rate is not so clear. Our knowledge of ancient society in the Orient does not substantiate the theory, but there is ample evidence in its support in the case of the Roman Empire. Here the proofs are abundant and unequivocal to the effect that, hand in hand with the progress of culture, the spread of wealth and luxury and the development of higher education, in which patrician women shared, there went a continuous decline in the marriage rate. So unpopular did marriage, with its attendant family responsibilities, become in Rome that government officials were seriously disturbed by the problem and Augustus Caesar, as we have seen, penalized celibacy by statute.[1] There is no reason to believe, however, that the financial penalties which he attached to the single state accomplished the much-desired end of inducing men to seek wives. On the contrary, Tacitus informs us, nearly a century after the passage of the law, that "Marriages and the rearing of children did not become more frequent, so powerful were the attractions of a childless state."[2]

For several centuries after the advent of Christianity, there was little or no improvement in the marriage rate in Rome; probably there was a further decline, owing to the widespread influence of asceticism, with its gospel of disciplinary repression of all bodily desires, especially the sex impulse. But, following upon the successive inroads of barbarian hordes into the confines of the Empire, and the continuous decline of culture, the ideas of the Goths, Vandals, Huns and Lombards gradually came to prevail over Roman customs in regard to the duty of marriage. With the reversion of western Europe to barbarism went the loss of the accumulated knowledge and control of natural forces on which Rome had built her mighty empire. Cities decayed or disappeared, and the functions of government and law were relegated once more to the "great fam-

---

[1] See *ante*, p. 39.   [2] *Annals* (translated by Church and Brodribb), III, 25.

ily" or kinship group. Life was reduced almost to its simplest terms, and was characterized by a never-ending struggle, on the one hand with natural forces, on the other with marauding foes. Under these conditions, marriage and the bearing of offspring to recruit a constantly depleted race became a paramount social duty enforced by the tremendous pressure of public opinion and the *mores*. These sanctions, supported in later centuries by the Church, art and literature, served to keep the marriage rate and birthrate high until after the middle of the nineteenth century. But the profound economic and social changes brought about by the Industrial Revolution, the extension of educational opportunities and the spread of individualistic ideas since the eighteenth century have once more resulted in creating for modern states a problem with respect to the marriage rate similar to that which confronted Imperial Rome. The development of civilization means expanding knowledge and control of material things and forces, increase in wealth, growth of a leisure class with time and means for cultivation of the mind and spirit. With higher culture goes increased individualization, an enhanced sense of personal rights and of the value and importance of the individual life. The cultured man or woman finds on every hand stimulating interests and activities with which to enrich his days; and unless his personal education has included the development of social interests and a sense of social responsibility he may, and sometimes does, elect to live a purely individualistic life, exempt from the burdensome cares entailed by marriage and children. Hence a falling marriage rate in this group.

IS THERE A MARRIAGE DECLINE IN THE UNITED STATES?

At this point it is pertinent to ask whether a decline in the marriage rate is characteristic of the United States as it is of certain European countries. A study of the Census report for 1920 shows that there has been a small but continuous increase in the proportion of both married men and women since 1890. If we select the age-groups from twenty-five to forty-four years, and compare the percentage of males and females married in 1900, 1910 and 1920, we get the following results:

Age-Group	Percentage of Males Married	Date
25-34	65.6	1920
	62.8	1910
	60.6	1900
35-44	79.8	1920
	79.2	1910
	78.8	1900

Age-Group	Percentage of Females Married	Date
25-34	76.5	1920
	75.1	1910
	73.0	1900
35-44	80.3	1920
	80.1	1910
	79.5	1900

Clearly, the marriage rate for the nation at large is slowly increasing. If, now, we ask whether the *age* of marriage has risen during the last two decades, the Census is no less explicit in its answer. Not only were there more females married at the age of nineteen years in 1920 than in 1910 (the percentages are respectively 28.6 and 25.7), but *at every age*, from fifteen to twenty years, more girls were married in 1920 than in 1910.[3]

May we then sit back complacently and declare that there is no marriage problem in America? Not at all. Despite the undoubted fact of a steady rise in the national marriage rate and a growing increase in marriages at an early age, it remains true that America, like England, has a marriage problem. It is concerned with the falling off in the number of marriages among the so-called "superior" class, by which is meant the prosperous, intelligent, upper-middle class which recruits the professions and skilled vocations. For more than a generation, the sharp decline in both the marriage rate and the birth-rate in this social grouping has given acute concern to biologists, eugenists and social investigators.

THE MARRIAGE DECREASE AMONG COLLEGE GRADUATES

Since a large proportion of college men and women belong to the middle class, a study of the marriage rates in this selected group will prove rewarding. Numerous investigations of this question have been made from time to time during the past twenty-five years by alarmed eugenists and others, and in no instance are the results encouraging save in the single case of the state agricultural colleges. In an article in the *Journal of Heredity* for April, 1915, Sprague shows that only fifty-three percent of Vassar graduates of the classes 1867-1892 were married in 1915, from twenty-three to forty-eight years after graduation! Nor do the Wellesley records make a better showing. Of the 528 alumnæ of the early classes from 1875 to 1889, only fifty percent were married in 1915, from twenty-

[3] United States Census for 1920, Vol. II, "Population."

six to forty years after graduation.[4] Similar doleful figures have been gathered by G. Stanley Hall and Theodate Smith for Vassar, Smith and Wellesley. Smith College reveals much the same condition with respect to the marriage of its alumnæ as its sister institutions. Only 42.7% of Smith graduates of the classes 1879-88 were married in 1903, from fifteen to twenty-four years after graduation. Of the classes 1889-98, only 28.35% were married from five to fourteen years after leaving college.[5]

More recent investigations tell the same tale. In 1918, the *Journal of the Association of Collegiate Alumnæ* published the results secured by Miss Van Kleeck and others from nine educational institutions in the East—eight women's colleges, namely, Barnard, Bryn Mawr, Mt. Holyoke, Radcliffe, Smith, Vassar, Wellesley and Wells, and one coeducational university, Cornell. Of the 23,582 graduates of these colleges living in 1914, a high percentage (seventy-one percent) returned records on which the study is based. These records of 16,739 graduates show that only 39.1% were married. In interpreting this result, of course, it is necessary to keep in mind that *all* graduates were included in the study. The most recent classes are numerically the largest, and are also the ones where the marriage is lowest, since these classes are composed of the younger men and women. When the graduates of the last five classes (1910-14) were excluded, the percentage of married graduates rose to 48.2; and when all graduates subsequent to 1900 were eliminated, the percentage married was fifty-one.

At this point it might be objected with justice that the colleges thus far investigated, with the single exception of Cornell, are Eastern women's colleges where girls are pretty thoroughly shut off from the society of young men during their most romantic years. This suggests the need of an investigation of the marriage rates in the great coeducational universities. Fortunately such a study was undertaken by Price in 1916, and the results were published in the *Journal of Heredity* the following year.[6] The figures which follow furnish no ground for undue optimism on the part of those men and women who regard the low percentage of marriages among the most intelligent of our youth as a social disaster.

It will be seen that, with the exception of Oberlin, the marriage rates over a period from ten to fifty-five years after graduation (varying with

[4] *Loc. cit.*, p. 161.
[5] "Marriage and Fecundity of College Men and Women," *Pedagogical Seminary and Journal of Genetic Psychology,* Vol. X, March, 1903, pp. 375-414. Clark University, Worcester, Massachusetts.
[6] Vol. VIII, January, 1917, pp. 43-5.

Institution	Period	Percent of Women Graduates Married in 1916
Oberlin	1850-1905	65.2
Ohio State	1885-1905	54.0
Wisconsin	1870-1905	51.8
Illinois	1880-1905	54.0

the university) do not exceed fifty-four percent. Only the agricultural colleges show a high percentage of marriages. In Kansas Agricultural College, for example, 67.6% of the graduates of classes from 1885 to 1905 were married in 1916. In Iowa State College, 72.7% of the graduates of classes from 1872 to 1905 were married in 1916. This high marriage rate is, of course, explained by the fact that the young women and men who elect to obtain their higher education in these state colleges, which furnish intensive training in agriculture and domestic science, are quite frankly looking forward to marriage and farm life.

But what are the marital records of college men? It must be admitted that, although the marriage rate in this selected group has been gradually falling for many years, it is by no means so low as that of college women. A study made in 1917 of the marriage rate in Stanford University [7] showed that, of 1,000 graduates in the classes from 1892 to 1900, 670 men and 330 women, 73.2% of the men were married, and only 48.5% of the women. The Stanford rate for men, allowing ten years after graduation before marriage, is similar to the rates at Harvard and Yale, which were shown to be respectively seventy-four and seventy-eight percent. Further investigations made by Banker of the percentage of the men and women graduates of Syracuse University who were married in 1917 bear out the fact that the marriage rate among college men is markedly higher than that among college women. The figures follow: [8]

Classes	Women	Men
1862-1871	87	87
1872-1881	81	90
1882-1891	55	84
1892-1901	48	73

The sharp fall in the marriage rate of the women graduates after 1881 probably corresponds with the widening of professional opportunities for college-trained women.

It has been repeatedly charged by social investigators that the char-

[7] *Journal of Heredity*, Vol. VIII, April, 1917.
[8] *Ibid.*, Vol. VIII, May, 1917.

acter of the higher education given to women, especially in the Eastern women's colleges, is largely responsible for the small percentage of marriages among them. But this theory has by no means been established. Merely to pile up statistics of low marriage rates among college and university women does not prove that higher education must shoulder most of the blame for this state of affairs. As an astute critic has pointed out, it is quite conceivable that the type of girl who goes to college places intellectual interests above the attentions of the male sex, and, if she found congenial work, might not marry if she never entered a college hall. But this is not all. College and university education cannot fairly be indicted until the marriage rates of college women are compared with those of their sisters, cousins and friends of the same social group. To say that the percentage of college women who marry before forty-five is strikingly lower than that of women in the country at large gets us nowhere because we are comparing unequal groups. There is urgent need of a thorough, comprehensive study of the marriage rates of an equal number of college and non-college women of the same social class and age-group. Until such an investigation is undertaken it seems idle to pile Ossa upon Pelion in the matter of statistics. The author ventures the conjecture that, when this important study is made, as it surely will be, the results will show that the marriage decrease is general in the educated middle class from which most college women are drawn, although it may be more conspicuous in the college group.

Causes of the Marriage Decrease in the Superior Group.

Many discussions of the falling marriage rate among college men and women are characterized by somewhat more heat than light. There is a very general disposition to lay the onus of responsibility for the situation at the door of the woman. When it is recalled, however, that social conventions the world over forbid women to take the initiative in securing mates, and enjoin them to refrain from showing by word or look any affection for men who have not declared love for them, the matter takes on a different complexion. It is difficult to see why most of the blame should be shouldered by the sex to whom tradition assigns the passive rôle in mating. As one indignant woman writes, in response to criticisms of the small number of college women who marry, "The authors of such articles do not suggest—I have never seen one that did—that a woman cannot marry alone, nor even produce children by herself." [9] If the taboo

[9] Laura Lockwood, "College Women as Wives and Mothers," *School and Society,* Vol. III, March 4, 1916, p. 334.

against a respectable girl's taking the initiative equally with the man in the game of becoming better acquainted, falling in love and marrying were once removed, leaving no reproachful shadow behind, the curve of the marriage rate would, probably, take a turn upward. But, certainly, the prohibition will not disappear until many more women achieve economic independence and show a firm resolve to stand on their own feet, in a financial sense, after marriage. For the roots of the taboo reach deep down into economic causes. So long as the woman at marriage ceases to engage in gainful employment and looks to her husband for her support, so long as she is dependent upon him for the necessities and comforts of life, she is restrained from openly and frankly seeking him as her mate with the same freedom that he seeks her.

But the limitation put upon young women in the matter of securing husbands is, of course, only one cause of the low marriage rate among them. The fundamental cause is probably the fact that education and professional work individualize women precisely as they individualize their brothers. A talented, highly developed young woman, who has tested and proved her abilities in a chosen career, and who finds life opening up before her avenues of broadening opportunity and usefulness, will more often than not reflect twice before she marries. And this for several reasons. In the first place, she has probably formed an ideal of love and marriage based upon equality and comradeship which her suitor does not meet. A hundred years ago, or even fifty, she would have compromised with that ideal in order to escape the stigma of being an old maid, whom everybody regarded as a social failure. But in this day and generation, the social pressure pushing women into marriage is enormously lessened. Instead of lowering her standards, she can continue to work, to hope for a lover who is also a comrade and to look the world bravely in the face as only the independent human being can do.

Again, the college-bred girl who is establishing herself in a congenial profession will think long before she renounces its spiritual as well as material rewards to keep house, even for the man she loves. This may be deplorable, but it is none the less a situation which is to be met on every hand. Probably such situations are increasing in frequency with every year that opens up better vocational opportunities to trained women. A case of this kind was recently brought to the attention of the writer. A young man and woman, both members of the faculty of a state college in the Middle West, were contemplating marriage. They were deeply in love with each other and the man was eager to be married and establish a home. So, too, was the woman, but she was held back by the knowledge that, in accordance with the statutes of the college, she must give up her pleasant and lucrative position as soon as she married. Very clearly she envisaged all the consequences that her resignation entailed. She must abandon work of absorbing interest, to prepare for which she had devoted years to professional training, and must settle down in a small middle-western town to being Mr. ——'s wife. Her experience would henceforth be determined by Main Street psychology and conventions. There would be few broadening interests in her life, a minimum of stimulus and challenge to her developed powers. As she faced this situation in all its stultifying reality, she naturally quailed, and was plunged into an agony of indecision from which she could not extricate herself. Needless to say, this young woman epitomizes in her own life the difficult situation in which thousands of educated women find themselves. Surely it is not to be wondered at if some of them choose stimulating work at the expense of love and home, and refuse to marry. Until some way is found of reconciling an educated woman's desire for love and offspring with her desire for self-expressive and self-developing activity, which moreover secures her financial independence, the marriage rate among college women will be low. This is one of the outcomes of modern individualism, *i.e.,* of the sense of personal worth, personal possibilities of achievement, and a conviction of the right of every human being to conditions of life in which he or she may thrive, develop his abilities and be happy. The attitude is no more characteristic of educated women than of men—indeed it is less so, for women are still strongly influenced by the ancient *mores* which decree that home-making and motherhood are their natural sphere. Nor is this spirit by any means wholly selfish. Thousands of young women have had several years of opportunity to try their mettle in the professions, before the opportunity of marriage comes to them, and they *know* that their work as teachers, public health nurses, trained economists, personnel managers, health directors in factories and stores has positive social value.

But there are other causes at work to bring about a small percentage of marriages among educated women. College women, in their friendly contacts with men, are not slow to see that underneath all the well-bred chivalry of their male associates lurks the old idea of woman's dependence and subordination in the home. Few young men honestly look upon women as their equals, intellectually or in any other sense. Few have any real appreciation of the individuality of the girls in whom they are becoming interested, or of the women they have taken to wife. Still less are they concerned to prevent the cramping and suppression of that individuality. Women are still considered *en masse* by most men, who continue to talk and think about "Woman" and her social functions, as if no individualizing of the feminine half of humanity had ever taken place. This attitude will disappear very slowly, even among highly intelligent men, for its roots rest deep in social custom. Unquestionably, it must be reckoned with as one factor making college women cautious in entering into the bonds of matrimony. To give up not only financial independence, with its resultant sense of self-respect, but no small degree of personal independence and consideration as an individual, whose ideas, interests and projects are worthy of respect, is more than many college women are willing to do. So they turn their backs on matrimony, sometimes, no doubt, with regret, and choose agreeable work carrying with it personal independence. Even the eugenists who are most critical of "superior" women for their failure to marry admit that men need to change their basic attitudes toward women. Thus Popenoe and Johnson declare: "Men should be taught greater respect for the individuality of women, so that no high-minded girl will shrink from marriage with the idea that it means a surrender of her personality and a state of domestic servitude. A more discriminating idea of sex-equality is desirable, and a recognition by men that women are not necessarily creatures of inferior mentality." [10]

Another cause of the low marriage rate among college women lies in the fact that too often, when they take up some vocation after graduation, they find themselves in semi-social isolation, meeting congenial women, perhaps, but few men. This is a serious social problem. If it be socially desirable that women of superior intelligence and education should marry, some way must be found to increase their opportunities of meeting agreeable men of their own intellectual level. Quite commonly this question meets with indifference on the part of men and women who do not appreciate its importance, if indeed, it does not stir their risibilities. Yet it is far from a negligible or laughing matter, as many a young woman (and man as well) starting out in a vocation in a strange city has declared. It has not escaped the attention of eugenists, who urge that parents and social organizations seek by every legitimate means to bring young men and women together in friendly association under suitable supervision.

The woman's college has been charged with failure to make young women desirous of having homes of their own and of managing them efficiently. "The very proper preference in many intelligent men," write Johnson and Stutzman, "for girls trained to be efficient wives and mothers is one of the causes of the low marriage rate and late time of marriage

[10] P. B. Popenoe and R. H. Johnson, *Applied Eugenics*, pp. 252-3. By permission of The Macmillan Co., New York, 1923.

of the graduates of the women's colleges. The trained girl can and will marry a man with an income too restricted for the support of an inefficient wife." [11] Therefore the woman's college has long been the target of bitter criticism on the part of biologists for its "stubborn resistance . . . to the introduction of education for domestic efficiency, especially in the care of the infant." [12] Obviously, such comments quite overlook the fact that all women are not alike; that many girls attending liberal arts colleges are already interested in some field of work for which they are preparing themselves. To compel these young women to crowd into their college courses in sciences, economics, languages or mathematics, some of which serve as essential preparation for a profession, extra courses in the domestic arts, child hygiene and child psychology seems a procedure open to grave objection. This is not to say that these latter subjects are not valuable and important. They surely are. But in view of the fact that a little over half of college women now marry, why should the other half be forced to pursue subjects they may never use? Even if the introduction of such practical domestic courses did appreciably raise the marriage rate (which in the judgment of the writer is doubtful), it would not thereby justify making these courses *compulsory* for all women. Not only would this procedure work an injustice on the considerable proportion who will not marry in any case, but it is exceedingly doubtful whether such subjects would contribute as usefully to efficient home management and child care five or ten years after graduation, when the woman marries, as they would if taken when the need for such training is felt. Every city and town should offer well-planned, scientific courses in subjects relating to home management and the nurture of children which should, so far as possible, be free to all young women expecting to marry, and to all married women who wish to become more efficient mothers and home-makers. Such a plan has been adopted in the agricultural state of Denmark, where home economics courses are widely established and offer intensive work to young women about to be married.

As already intimated, the entire responsibility for the low marriage rate of college women cannot justly be placed on higher education. After all, college women, like others, must wait to be asked in marriage, and men have their reasons for remaining single as well as women. Neither men nor women who have had four pleasant years in college are desirous of lowering their standards of living very materially, even for the sake of living together. No doubt Americans need simpler standards of living as

[11] Johnson and Stutzman, *Journal of Heredity*, June, 1915, p. 252.
[12] *Ibid.*

a people, but exhortations will probably accomplish little in inducing young persons to live in unattractive, low-priced apartments in our large cities when they have been accustomed to cheerful, comfortable homes. This is not to say that many would not be willing to give up luxuries, such as motor cars and fur coats, in order to marry, but merely to state that, as a class, college men and women rebel against beginning life together in dingy, uncomfortable surroundings. And this is what many young persons would be forced to do if they married in the twenties on the salary most young men are earning at that age. On the other hand, if the man himself and his social group were willing to accept as a matter of course the idea that his wife should continue her lucrative employment after marriage, the difficulty would disappear. Many a man would not hesitate years to ask the girl he loves to share life with him, if he knew that she would contribute her part to the family income. If signs do not fail, marriage will more and more become an economic partnership as well as a partnership in love, in home-making and in the rearing of children. This idea is vigorously espoused by a male contributor to the *Woman Citizen:*

"The economic dependence of wives causes several great evils:

"(1) It leads to abnormally late marriages, or celibacy, because of the urban cost of living. Our rural grandmothers made dozens of food products which, in these days, must be purchased. Wives were an asset then and a liability now. 'Proposing' is a costly business. The remedy is: Two for the money and two for the show." [13]

Of course, financial considerations are not the only reasons why young men are not seeking college women as wives. They know that the conceptions of love and the marriage relation held by most of these women are high—higher than they care to measure up to. So they seek less exacting mates who have no clear-cut ideas about marriage as comradeship, as a sharing of thoughts and experiences, of large purposes and plans, as well as of emotions.

No doubt Popenoe and Johnson are correct in ascribing to men other reasons for not marrying. They mention as causes the cultivation by men "of a taste for sexual variety and a consequent unwillingness to submit to the restraints of marriage"; pessimism about women due to early and harmful sex experiences; infection by venereal disease; mental and physical deficiencies which make mating difficult; and the ardent pursuit of business or professional ends, which makes the sacrifice of freedom and money necessary to marriage seem altogether unpalatable.[14]

[13] "What Is a Good Wife?" *Woman Citizen*, January, 1926, p. 18.
[14] Popenoe and Johnson, *op. cit.*, pp. 247-8.

IS THE LOW MARRIAGE RATE OF THE EDUCATED GROUP NECESSARILY A
SOCIAL EVIL?

I. The View That Celibacy among College Women Is Not Socially Disadvantageous.

On this important question there seems to be a division of opinion among social writers. One not inconsiderable group holds the view that college women probably represent a highly intellectualized group of low fecundity, and therefore would not be fertile mothers even if they did marry. From this standpoint, society loses little, even if the marriage rate remains low in this group. This theory harks back to the view of Herbert Spencer, and a few more recent writers, that high individuation, the product of culture, is accompanied by low fertility. The theory has never been scientifically established, and its validity is positively denied by most contemporary biologists and eugenists. Moreover, a study made more than twenty-five years ago [15] of the comparative fecundity of 343 college women and 313 non-college women of the same social class showed that, whereas the latter group had borne sixty-four more children than the former, the college women had had more children *per year of married life*. That is, the non-college sisters, cousins and friends had borne one child to every 6.71 years of married life; the college-bred wives, one to every 5.97 years. Now, while this experiment obviously does not prove that college women have as many children as non-college, it *does* show that, in a given period, and so far as this experiment goes, the college women, far from being infertile, are slightly more so than their non-college relatives. The reason why the non-college group had absolutely more children is doubtless due to the fact that the average age of marriage among them was exactly two years lower, namely 24.3 years, as compared with 26.3 years for the college group. This question of the higher age of marriage of college women will be considered later.

One or two other theories which tend to minimize the social importance of a higher marriage rate for college women may be briefly suggested. Gardner suggests [16] that there "have been too many altogether lovely mothers without culture to warrant any presumption in favor of the maternal capacities of the college-bred girl." While admitting that an educated mother "can tell her child more, and teach it better grammar," the writer hints darkly that "mother love may be somewhat less intense in

[15] By Dr. Mary Roberts Smith, in *Publications of the American Statistical Association,* Vol. VII, 1900, p. 11 ff.
[16] "College Women and Matrimony," in *Education,* Vol. XX, pp. 285-91.

educated women as a class than in women of a narrower outlook [who] are apt to be wholly absorbed in their children, and to give themselves up to them with complete abandonment." He concludes that, if these considerations are true, "they go to show that society loses no more by reason of the celibacy of an educated man or woman than from that of one less favored, and that the celibacy of the cultured classes, if it exists, is not peculiarly to be deplored."

Clearly, this writer lived in a decade (1899) cheerfully ignorant of the discoveries of psychoanalysis regarding the harmful effect upon children's development of the "parent-fixations" so often induced by the "complete abandonment" of mothers to their offspring. Harmful to both mother and child, this attitude has become the target for the special censure of mental hygienists. Intense mother love, which is partly the result of the "narrow outlook" that Gardner seems to approve, and the total absorption of mothers in children are precisely the states of mind that psychiatrists deplore. Far from its being true that the divided interests of the college-trained mother react harmfully on her child, it has been pretty conclusively established that these wider concerns are positively beneficial in preventing mother-fixations that deaden initiative and make the upbuilding in the child of an independent personality difficult, if not impossible.

Finally, mention should be made of the theory that the State is not so much concerned with the marriage of its educated men and women as it is with their character, ability and achievements. From this point of view, society's chief interest is not in the question whether cultured persons add to its physical life, but rather whether they contribute fully to its intellectual and spiritual life. Indeed, Gardner goes so far as to say: "History and observation surely do not warrant the assertion that the quality of these is determined by marriage." [17]

II. The View That Celibacy among the Educated Class Is a Grave Social Evil.

The above considerations are minimized or opposed by an important group of eugenists and social investigators, who argue that the low percentage of marriages among college men and women is a serious social disadvantage, which, if allowed to continue, will result in a progressive lowering of the quality alike of the human stock and of the civilization it has built. These men are armed with facts and figures which tend to show that a good biological inheritance is of the utmost importance to every

[17] Gardner, *op. cit.*, p. 291.

human being; that intellectual and artistic ability are due chiefly to heredity, and are far more prevalent among the cultured classes than among unskilled wage-earners. Karl Pearson estimates, on the basis of investigations of the inheritance of ability in families, that "exceptional fathers produce exceptional sons at a rate 3 to 6 times as great as non-exceptional—the superior stock produces above the average at over twice the rate of the inferior stock. Pairs of exceptional parents produce exceptional sons at a rate more than 10 times as great as pairs of non-exceptional parents." [18] Pearson has also made intensive investigations of over 3,000 school children with regard to the resemblance of brothers and sisters in physical, mental and moral traits. The correlations between sister and sister, brother and brother and sister and brother for various physical traits averaged about .5, and the correlations for mental and moral characteristics were slightly higher. Commenting on the results, Holmes [19] says: "If the fraternal correlation for mental ability or temper is about the same as the fraternal correlation for eye color and cephalic index (characters not sensibly influenced by the environment) we must conclude, as Pearson argues, that correlations in these mental characteristics are due mainly to inheritance."

In his valuable studies of *English Men of Science* and *Noteworthy Families,* Francis Galton has also made important contributions to the evidence on the inheritance of mental ability. Further evidence is furnished by Schuster and Elderton in their study of the comparative scholastic standings of fathers and sons at Oxford and the famous schools of Harrow and Charterhouse. With striking regularity, the percentage of scholarship among fathers at Oxford decreased with that of their sons, while the correlation coefficients between father and son were .29 or .31, according to the method of calculation.

It is highly probable that, in all these studies, too much causative effect is attributed to inheritance, and too little to home environment and educational opportunities. Referring to the correlations of ability between parents and offspring, and between siblings, Holmes comments: "Of course association, similarity of home environment, and common training may tend to increase these correlations." But he hastens to quote the remark of Pearson that home environment "is in itself a part of the stock." Further, he cites the measurements of Thorndike on the performance of school children, associated for years in the same school, which go to

[18] *Philosophical Transactions,* CXCV. Quoted in *American Journal of Sociology,* Vol. XIV, pp. 733-4.
[19] See his *The Trend of the Race,* p. 104.

show that, under the same stimuli and training, children were quite as different in mental ability at twelve to fourteen as they had been between nine and ten.[20] In this connection it might be pointed out that, if certain children were hampered by poverty and its train of evils—bad home surroundings, malnutrition, long hours of work before and after school hours and the like—at the beginning of their school course, they might very well be so hampered five years later. In other words, the comparison was probably made of unequals.

We are still lacking in authoritative evidence of the degree in which mental abilities are influenced by environmental circumstances (including those during gestation), although Watson's experiments have done much to demonstrate the importance of these determining conditions in the case of certain emotions, such as fear. Moreover, mental ability does not appear to be a dominant trait which closely follows the Mendelian law. Indeed, the investigations of Hurst seem to prove that musical ability is transmitted as a recessive, not a dominant character; and Davenport's studies of numerous family records lead him to the same conclusion with respect to artistic and literary ability, mechanical skill, calculating ability and memory. Commenting on these facts, Holmes says: "It is not denied that Mendel's law holds for the transmission of mental as well as physical characteristics, but it is not proven that mental peculiarities are inherited in accordance with any simple Mendelian ratio. Neither is the evidence satisfactory that superior ability of various kinds is recessive to the normal conditions."[21] It appears, then, that although very able scientists declare that mental ability is inherited, most of these men are careful to add that the traits which make up mental ability are highly fluctuating, and may be profoundly influenced by environing conditions. To quote Holmes once more: "A child of good ancestry but exposed while *in utero* to the influence of malnutrition, alcohol, or the toxins of disease at the time when the delicate architecture of its brain is being built up may fall considerably short of its normal expectation in intellectual development."[22]

But while psychologists and biologists continue to disagree with regard to the relative importance of heredity and environment in determining mental ability, and even concerning the essential character of mental abilities as dominants or recessives, no competent student denies that environment does play a significant rôle in developing these abilities. The home

[20] Holmes, *op. cit.*, p. 107. By permission of Harcourt, Brace & Co., New York, 1921.
[21] *Ibid.*, p. 11. By permission of Harcourt, Brace & Co.
[22] *Ibid.*, p. 110.

surroundings of educated men and women, the social environment in which they live and move, are rich in stimuli for developing the minds and tastes of children. From their early childhood, these boys and girls are accustomed to hearing social, literary, scientific and artistic questions discussed by their parents and elders; they are surrounded by books, material for handwork, artistic copies of great works of art, all of which are quickening of dormant abilities. It is idle to ignore or minimize the fact that the offspring of such parents, reared in cultured homes and educated in progressive schools, have a tremendous advantage over the children of intelligent parents of the laboring class, and will, in all probability, make much larger contributions to the world's stock of knowledge, wisdom and beauty.

It appears, then, that even if mental abilities were not determined in large degree by inheritance (which they probably are), nevertheless society would very greatly benefit by the marriage of educated men and women because of their superior *social heredity*. Therefore, the conclusion seems inevitable that, from the viewpoint of society and its spiritual and material needs, the low marriage rate of college-bred men and women is socially disadvantageous.

HOW CAN THE MARRIAGE RATE OF THE EDUCATED GROUP BE INCREASED?

If it be admitted that college women as a group are precisely of the type who would make the most intelligent wives and mothers, the question inevitably arises: What can be done to induce more of them to marry? Eugenists are not lacking in suggestions for bringing this about. There is well-nigh complete unanimity among them that a fundamental change is essential in the character of college education for women. This education, they hold, must give them the intellectual and moral training that will incline them toward marriage and motherhood. Instead of stubbornly resisting the introduction of courses in eugenics, domestic science, the physical care of children, child psychology and child guidance, the college authorities should bend every effort toward directing women students into these courses, even to the point of making them compulsory. It is confidently believed that such a concerted reform on the part of all colleges and universities educating women would effect a sharp rise in the marriage rate of that group.

It should at once be admitted that courses in eugenics and parenthood, in the evolution, the social functions and the contemporary problems of the family, might very wisely be incorporated in the offerings of colleges and universities educating not women alone, but both sexes. These subjects have developed a rich and suggestive content that would no doubt prove interesting and valuable to college students—both men and women. Such courses might even incline a larger number of students toward matrimony and parenthood. But this latter point seems more than a little doubtful. It is not *knowledge* that impels young people to marry, but *emotions*. Ignorance of eugenics is not the real barrier to establishing a home, but rather economic conditions. If college girls were equipped with all the information now available with regard to the arts of housekeeping and child rearing, this equipment would not suffice to make college men and women marry if social and economic conditions were not favorable to such unions. It has already been pointed out, more than once, that so long as society hinders rather than helps the educated young woman in her attempt to reconcile professional interests with marriage and motherhood, a proportion of college women will not marry. And as long as our social and educational systems require years of professional training and experience of young men before they can earn a salary that makes marriage practicable, these men will hesitate to assume responsibility for a dependent wife and family. The way out would seem to lie in wholehearted social acceptance of the theory that both men and women should contribute to the economic support of their common home; and, further, in social aid and encouragement given to practical experiments to discover how this may be accomplished without sacrificing home life and children. Needless to say, the day of that social acceptance and encouragement has not dawned on the horizon, although it may not be so remote as some writers would have us think.

Another reform urged by eugenists is the extension of coeducation in colleges and universities, and (by implication) the gradual disappearance of separate colleges for the sexes. This would appear to be a wise suggestion from the eugenic standpoint. Certainly four years of life, during the romantic ages between eighteen and twenty-two, spent in the academic seclusion of the typical woman's college, does seem to incline many college girls to seek the society of their own sex for recreation, intellectual give-and-take and congenial projects of various kinds. Probably the same effects are produced in men. To make the sexes more or less independent and ignorant of each other in the most susceptible period of their lives, when they should be establishing a sound heterosexuality, seems on its face to be a colossal eugenic blunder.

This leads to consideration of a closely similar social situation that exists after graduation, when a high percentage of college men and women enter skilled occupations. If their work lies in a city remote from home, they may live through many bitter hours of loneliness, and, quite possibly have few or no opportunities to meet agreeable persons of the other sex. Thousands of educated young men and women just starting on their life work find themselves "socially marooned." It was recently estimated that, in New York City alone, there were 300,000 unmarried men and 450,000 unmarried women, a considerable proportion of whom had a very restricted range of selection of a mate. Some years ago, a newspaper discussed this social situation in an editorial, and received in reply hundreds of letters from young men and women who complained of being without social opportunities.[23] Instead of criticizing young professional workers for turning their backs on matrimony, it would seem wise for the critics to undertake surveys of the conditions in our large cities with respect to the opportunities they offer educated men and women to meet and know each other. Of this situation, and of the separation of the sexes in colleges, Popenoe and Johnson quote a woman novelist as saying:

"I'm a Wellesley woman, but one reason why I'm dead against women's colleges is because they shut girls up with women, at the most impressionable period of the girls' lives, when they should be meeting members of the opposite sex continually, learning to tolerate their little weaknesses and getting ready to marry them.

"The city should make arrangements to chaperone the meetings of its young citizens. There ought to be municipal gathering places where, under the supervision of tactful, warm-hearted women—themselves successfully married—girls and men might get introduced to each other and might get acquainted."[24]

No doubt the majority of men and women would disapprove of such municipal action, or would merely be amused by the suggestion. Probably an organized and determined civic effort to throw young people of opposite sexes together would defeat its own end, at least in the present state of popular opinion, and would meet with scant coöperation from the youths it sought to reach. But surely churches, clubs and social organizations of every sort, where young men and women meet naturally, might accomplish more than they do by way of creating pleasant opportunities for them to know each other. The Y. W. C. A. and Y. M. C. A. might well coöperate in trying out various ways and means of meeting this social problem. Indeed, it is questionable whether these useful organizations can render their greatest social service by remaining separate.

[23] See W. E. Carson, *The Marriage Revolt*, p. 416. Hearst's International Library Co., New York, 1915.
[24] Popenoe and Johnson, *op. cit.*, p. 235. By permission of The Macmillan Co., New York, 1923.

Probably eugenists are right in asserting that Christian peoples have never developed a noble conception of love between the sexes. Western civilization is even yet influenced, if not dominated, by the ascetic philosophy of the Latin Church Fathers. We are still more than a little ashamed of intense romantic love, more than half convinced that there is something reprehensible about it. Unlike the Orientals, Occidental peoples have never frankly accepted sexual love as rich in possibilities for the enhancement of life in its many phases. They have continued to be embarrassed and furtive in their attitude toward it; and, what is much worse, to indoctrinate the young with the theory that there is something indecent about the sexual act. A complete regeneration of our ideas and attitudes regarding the love of men and women, especially in its culmination in an act of physical and spiritual union, is profoundly needed in our contemporary civilization. Sexual love should be honestly faced for what it is —an emotion replete in potentialities of beauty, of spiritual as well as physical intimacy, of the heightening of all the meanings and values of life. Conversely, it should be understood as an impulse which, without enlightened guidance and control, is capable of overriding and degrading the entire nature. If young women and men had been instructed from childhood in the ideal significance of love, had been imbued with reverence for it as a culminating and profoundly enriching experience, there would probably be less skepticism and indifference in the minds of certain young people today regarding love and marriage. Educated men and women would be more apt to seek this experience in marriage, even at the sacrifice of a part of their ambition and freedom.

But even if this much-needed education were given, if college years afforded ample opportunities for the sexes to meet and come to know each other, if women were free to carry on a chosen work after marriage, there still would be superior men and women who, failing to find satisfying mates, would never marry. Individuation is accompanied by ever more exacting standards regarding the marriage relationship and what constitutes a congenial mate. Furthermore, life offers immeasurably fuller opportunities and experience to the single woman (if not to the man) than it did even a generation ago. These two causes will probably always operate to lower the marriage rate among the intellectual group of college-bred men and women. Biologically, they may accept sterility; but socially they may be abundantly fruitful in ideas and enterprises which promote the well-being of humanity.

TOPICS FOR REPORTS

1. Examine the alumnæ (or alumni) registers of as many women's colleges and coeducational universities as you can secure, and find out the proportion of graduates who are married.

2. Summarize the criticisms against the higher education of women contained in a series of articles treating of "College Women and the Marriage Rate" in the issues of the *Journal of Heredity* for April and June, 1915, and January, April and May, 1917. Comment on these strictures and try to meet them.

3. What evidence can you find in support of the theory that mental ability is inherited?

    See Samuel Holmes, *The Trend of the Race,* Ch. V. Harcourt, Brace & Co., New York, 1921.

    Popenoe and Johnson, *Applied Eugenics,* Ch. IV.

4. Eugenics and Marriage.

    Popenoe and Johnson, *op. cit.,* Chs. VIII-XI.

Death Ratio of children under 5 to every 1000 women 16-49

    1800 = 976
    1860 = 714
    1920 = 487

Too check a population increasing too fast.

1. Birth control.
2. Lower standards
3. Increased efficiency
4. Increased death rates.

CHAPTER XIX

THE PROBLEM OF BIRTH CONTROL

"To multiply the people and not increase the joy of living is the most dismal end that could be set for human striving."—Sir William Beveridge.

THE FALLING BIRTH-RATE

THE last half century has been marked by a conspicuous fall in the birth-rate [1] in the more advanced countries of Europe and in America, Australia and New Zealand. Havelock Ellis declares that, since 1905, the decline has been general throughout Europe with the exception of three countries—all backward—namely, Ireland, Rumania and Bulgaria.[2]

The birth-rate trend in Europe between 1871 and 1915 is indicated in the following table:[3]

Years	England and Wales	Scotland	Ireland	France	Germany	Austria	Hungary	Italy	Norway	Sweden	Russia	Spain	Belgium	Holland
1871-1876	35.5	35.0	27.4	25.5	38.9	39.3	42.8	36.9	30.2	30.7	50.3		32.6	36.1
1876-1880	35.4	34.8	25.7	25.3	39.2	38.7	44.1	37.0	31.7	30.3	48.4		32.0	36.4
1881-1885	33.5	33.3	24.0	24.7	37.0	38.1	44.6	37.8	31.2	29.4	49.2	36.7	30.9	34.8
1886-1890	31.4	31.4	22.8	23.1	36.5	37.6	43.7	37.3	30.8	28.8	48.7	36.2	29.4	33.6
1891-1895	30.5	30.5	22.9	22.4	36.3	37.3	42.0	35.9	30.3	27.4	48.2	35.8	29.1	32.9
1896-1900	29.2	30.0	23.1	22.0	36.0	37.0	39.7	33.9	30.3	26.9	49.4	34.6	29.0	32.2
1901	28.5	29.5	22.7	22.0	35.7	36.8	37.8	32.5	29.6	27.0	48.0	34.9	29.4	32.3
1905	27.3	28.6	23.4	20.6	33.0	34.0	36.1	32.7	27.4	25.7	44.8	35.2	26.2	30.8
1910	25.1	26.2	23.3	19.6	29.8	32.6	35.7	33.3	26.1	24.7		33.1	23.8	28.6
1912	23.8	25.9	23.0	19.0	28.2	31.2	36.2	32.4	25.8	23.7		31.5	23.2	28.1
1913	24.1	25.5	22.8	18.8	27.4	29.6		31.7	25.4	23.1		30.3		28.2
1914	23.8	26.1	22.6	18.0				31.1	25.3	22.8		29.6		
1915	21.8	23.9	21.8						23.8	21.6				

[1] The birth-rate indicates the annual number of births per thousand of the population.
[2] *The Task of Social Hygiene*, p. 136.
[3] Samuel Holmes, *The Trend of the Race*, p. 119. By permission of Harcourt, Brace & Co., New York, 1921.

A study of this table will show that, in the first five-year period, Russia, Hungary, Austria and Germany had the highest birth-rates and France the lowest—25.5. England, Wales, Scotland, Holland and Italy each had a birth-rate over 35; while Sweden and Norway showed a rate over 30. By 1915, however, a marked change had taken place. Russia still led with an *estimated* birth-rate of approximately 45.5; but in the remaining countries, the birth-rate had fallen to about 25 or less, with the exception of Hungary, Austria, Italy and Spain, where it remained above 30. During the World War, the birth-rates of all the countries involved fell sharply, as was to be expected. But in England, the rate rose from 18.5 in 1919 to 25 in 1920, and 22 in 1921.[4] The apparently low birth-rate in Ireland can probably be attributed to the facts that the country has a considerable proportion of persons of non-child-bearing age and that its economic conditions make delayed marriages inevitable. The birth-rate among women who are of child-bearing age, however, is very high.

When we turn to the newer countries, we find similar conditions. Sixty years ago, the birth-rate in Australia was about 43 per 1,000. In 1916, the birth-rate had fallen to 27 and in 1920 to 25, and it will no doubt continue to fall. In the United States, no accurate birth statistics are available for the country as a whole, owing to the fact that not all the states of the Union require a careful registration of births. The census, therefore, furnishes no such data concerning the declining birth-rate as most European countries have long placed at the disposal of the social investigator. Wilcox has compiled census data showing the steady decrease in the ratio of children under five years of age to every 1,000 women of child-bearing age (16 to 44 years) in the United States. In 1800, the ratio was 976; in 1860 it was 714; and in 1920 it had fallen to 467.[5] In 1924, in the Birth Registration Area of the United States, which comprises thirty-three states and the District of Columbia, the birth-rate was 22.6.[6]

This figure represents a fall of 2.5 points from the birth-rate in the Registration Area in 1915, which was 25.1. Clearly, the United States is proceeding along the same path as European countries.

---

[4] Harold Cox, *The Problem of Population*, p. 19. G. P. Putnam's Sons, New York and London, 1923.

[5] "The Change in the Proportion of Children in the United States," in *Publications of the American Statistical Association*, Vol. XII, 1909-11, pp. 490-9. Quoted in E. M. East, *Mankind at the Crossroads*, p. 209. Charles Scribner's Sons, New York, 1923.

[6] "Birth, Stillbirth and Infant Mortality Statistics." Bureau of the Census, 1924.

More recent figures showing the comparative crude birth-rates and the natural increase in selected countries and the United States follow: [7]

Country	Period	Crude Birth-rate	Crude Death-rate	Natural Increase
Australia	1919-24	24.6	10.4	14.2
Austria	1919-23	21.9	17.9	4.0
Belgium	1919-24	20.5	14.0	6.5
Bulgaria	1920-21	40.3	21.7	18.6
Ceylon	1919-23	38.6	31.6	7.0
Chile	1919-24	39.7	32.6	7.1
England & Wales	1919-24	21.0	12.5	8.5
Egypt	1919-23	41.6	26.6	15.0
France	1920-24	20.0	17.4	2.6
Germany	1919-24	23.5	14.8	8.7
Holland	1919-24	26.6	11.4	15.2
Italy	1919-23	27.3	17.0	10.3
Japan	1919-22	34.7	23.6	11.1
New Zealand	1919-24	23.0	9.1	13.9
Norway	1919-24	23.7	12.2	11.5
Rumania	1919-22	32.9	22.9	10.0
Scotland	1919-24	23.9	14.4	9.5
South Africa	1919-24	27.5	10.4	17.1
Spain	1919-23	29.8	21.8	8.0
Sweden	1919-24	20.3	12.8	7.5
Switzerland	1919-23	19.9	13.2	6.7
U. S. A.	1919-23	23.8	12.7	11.1

In most civilized countries, the urban birth-rate is markedly lower than that of the rural districts. The figures given on the next page have been taken from the 1926 Report of the League of Nations Health Organization,[8] giving urban birth-rates in selected cities in Europe, Asia, Africa and South America.

A cursory glance at these figures reveals some interesting facts. The birth-rate in Germany, which was relatively high before the World War, has fallen, in forty-six cities, to a level lower than that of Paris in the corresponding years; and the birth-rates in the cities of Berlin and Vienna are the lowest in Europe with the exception of the twenty-six Swiss cities. Furthermore, even in Catholic Spain, which is governed by traditions hostile to birth control, the birth-rate has fallen to a level not quite five points higher than that of New York. Only in certain large cities of South

---

[7] *Encyclopædia Britannica*, Thirteenth Edition (1926), Vol. III, p. 191.
[8] "Epidemiological Intelligence," No. 10 (for the year 1925), July, 1926, p. 148. Geneva.

America, in India, in Upper and Lower Egypt and in Moscow do birth-rates remain high.

Birth-rates in Large Cities

	1924	1925
105 English cities	19.4	19.3
London	18.6	18.9
Edinburgh	19.7	19.2
Belfast	24.0	23.6
Dublin	25.6	17.3
New York	21.7	20.8
14 Dutch cities	21.2	20.6
46 German cities	14.9	15.9
Berlin	10.1	11.6
Cologne	18.0	18.7
26 Swiss cities	6.4	12.8
Paris	15.9	16.2
49 Spanish cities	26.5	27.0
Madrid	24.5	24.8
Vienna	14.7	13.8
Rio de Janeiro	39.3	
Santiago (Chile)	30.8	26.3
Buenos Aires	24.4	24.8
Lower Egypt	45.9	44.6
Upper Egypt	55.8	53.5
Madras (India)	43.1	44.0
Delhi (India)	47.8	
Moscow	30.4	

CAUSES OF THE DECLINING BIRTH-RATE

So striking a social phenomenon as this of a steadily declining birth-rate could not escape the attention of social investigators, who have been busy for a generation looking into its causes and evaluating its effects. Probably the efficient causes are (1) delayed marriages, (2) pathological sterility and (3) voluntary restriction of births. The first condition operates, of course, to decrease the fertility of married women. A woman who marries at twenty-eight or thirty instead of twenty or twenty-two years of age obviously has curtailed the period during which she might bear children by eight years. Moreover, these are among the most fruitful years of her life. A considerable body of evidence exists to the effect that the period of a woman's highest fertility is that from seventeen years to twenty, closely followed by the period of twenty to twenty-five. Now, although the age of marriage has not risen among the working group, indeed has slightly decreased,[9] the marriage age has steadily advanced in the middle and professional groups. As we have seen, college women marry at least two years later than their sisters and cousins in the same level of life. Dr. Mary Roberts Smith's investigation in 1900 showed that the average age at marriage of 343 college women was 26.3 years, whereas the age of 313 of their non-college women relatives was 24.3.

The question whether civilized man at present is characterized by pathological sterility, *i.e.*, infertility caused by adverse conditions, has been the subject of much controversy. As stated before, Herbert Spencer held that increase in individuation, through the combined influences of higher civilization and of education, results in a decrease in fertility. But this theory is contradicted by the evidence brought together by Professor Edward A. Ross,[10] showing that, in the period between 1851 and 1865, the average number of children in English and Scotch families, where the wife had been under nineteen at her marriage, was 7.28 and 7.8 respectively. In the case of Norway, the Census of 1920 showed that the type family of surviving couples, married before 1888, the bride being eighteen or nineteen, was actually ten! These families are larger than the average among certain backward peoples. Certainly the theory that civilization is, in itself, the foe of fertility remains to be proved.

The most powerful agent in bringing about a declining birth-rate is unquestionably voluntary restriction of births by the use of contraceptive measures. These methods have been in use in France for many years, especially since 1860, but they seem not to have been practised much in England until after 1875. In most other European countries, the birth-rates fell only slightly until the opening of the twentieth century. That voluntary restriction is the chief cause of the falling birth-rate in England (and in all probability in the other countries) is proven by an investigation made by Sidney Webb in 1906. Mr. Webb made systematic inquiries concerning voluntary restriction of families among English men and women of the middle class in all parts of the country. He received replies from 316 married persons which showed that, of this number, 242, or seventy-six percent, had limited the size of their families. If marriages prior to 1875 (the year when voluntary restriction began) be eliminated from the list, there remain 236 limited marriages and fifty-seven unlimited, or eighty percent of marriages reporting voluntary restriction. In the decade 1890-99, Mr. Webb found that 107 families out of 120, or

---

[9] See United States Census for 1920, Vol. II, "Population."
[10] E. A. Ross, "How Fast Can Man Increase?" in *Scientific Monthly,* March, 1927, p. 266.

eighty-nine percent, practised contraceptive methods. Of the thirteen families that did not restrict births, five or six were childless, leaving only seven or eight unlimited marriages out of 120.[11]

The causes of family limitation voluntarily given by 128 persons to whom the questionnaire was sent show that the poverty of the parents in relation to their standard of living was the determining factor in seventy-three cases; sexual ill health, *i.e.,* the harmful effects of childbearing, in twenty-four; other forms of ill health, in thirty-eight; and the disinclination of the wife to bear more children, in twenty-four cases.

The thorough and painstaking study made by Ethel M. Elderton of the English birth-rate in the counties north of the Humber River led the investigator to the conclusion that the immense fall in the rate of births "is not due to any physiological decrease in fertility, but to a widespread and nearly universal artificial restriction of the family." The writer's investigation of the hypothesis that higher wages, pursuit of pleasure and increase of luxury had induced partial sterility in the English people led her to the conclusion that there "is no evidence whatever" to support it. On the contrary she unearthed an immense amount of evidence indicating the very general sale of contraceptive drugs and devices, as well as drugs designed to induce abortion! [12]

Behind the phenomenon of voluntary restriction of births the student of social conditions naturally looks for the motives that determine action —the psychological causes. Prominent among these is the desire on the part of husband and wife not to lower in any marked degree the standard of living to which they are accustomed. Eugenists are disposed to criticize with some asperity those educated middle-class husbands and wives who are not willing to accept cramped living quarters, plain food, out-dated garments and few recreations in order to rear large families. But the exhortations of these scientific gentlemen, and their gloomy forebodings of race deterioration, seem to have had no appreciable effect in bringing about an upward trend in the birth-rate curve, or even in staying its downward fall. Appeals to patriotism and the indefinite future welfare of society also fall on deaf ears.

This leads us to consider a second psychological cause of a lowered birth-rate. With the progress of civilization has developed a higher regard for human personality—the personality of the child no less than that of the adult. This heightened consciousness of the personal worth and per-

[11] Sidney Webb, "Physical Degeneracy or Race Suicide," in *Popular Science Monthly*, December, 1906, pp. 522-3.

[12] "Report on the English Birth-rate," Part I, "North of the Humber," p. 232. *Eugenics Laboratory Memoirs*, Vol. XVII. Cambridge University Press, 1914.

sonal rights of children has led governments to restrict the exploitation of boys and girls in industry and to enforce compulsory education laws against recalcitrant parents. Fathers and mothers, also, especially in those groups that are not subjected to heavy economic pressure, have developed a sensitive appreciation of their obligations to their offspring. They are reluctant to bring into the world more children than they can house, feed and clothe comfortably, as well as educate and prepare adequately for their life work. Thoughtful, responsible men and women are more alive today than ever before to the handicaps under which children have labored in the past, and, indeed, labor at present in the large families of the poor; and they are resolved that their little ones shall have a fair start in life, so far as wholesome home environment, sound education and training can secure it. Thus it has come about at one and the same time that children are no longer economic assets to their parents, since the state constitutes itself an "over-parent" to guarantee them against ruthless exploitation; and parents themselves have a deeper sense of parental responsibility in most instances, where the struggle for a bare living has not stifled it. Both these conditions operate powerfully among the more intelligent laborers and the middle class to depress the birth-rate.

A third motive working to the same end is the more or less conscious rebellion of women against the social philosophy that they exist primarily as *means* for recruiting the race—not as *ends* in themselves, in the same sense as men are ends. The higher education of women has opened their eyes to many things, notably to the handicaps that their historic function as mothers has laid upon them in their efforts to attain complete and well-rounded personalities. A restless dissatisfaction with continual child-bearing has long been smouldering among women, and they are becoming ever more insistent in their claims to be considered first of all as free and intelligent individuals, not primarily as mothers.

But this is not all. Refined and thoughtful women, who have a sensitive feeling for personal independence and dignity, are in revolt against the ancient theory that at marriage their husbands acquire certain definite "marital rights" over their persons. In ever swelling numbers, wives are standing upon their fundamental right to decide whether or not they will engage in sexual intercourse, whether or not they are ready to bear children. "The most far-reaching social development of modern times," says Margaret Sanger, "is the revolt of woman against sex servitude. The most important force in the remaking of the world is a free motherhood. . . . Millions of women are asserting their right to voluntary motherhood. They are determined to decide for themselves whether they shall become mothers, under what conditions and when. This is the fundamental revolt referred to. It is for woman the key to the temple of liberty." [13]

Undoubtedly, these three powerful motives are the unseen agents in bringing about voluntary restriction of offspring and a steadily falling birth-rate. It would seem that a fair, unbiased consideration of each in turn would lead to the conclusion that they are dictated by common sense, moral responsibility and a regard for personal liberty, none of which are conspicuous attributes of primitive or retarded cultures, but rather of highly civilized nations.

FALLING BIRTH-RATES AND THE WORLD'S FOOD SUPPLY. THE MALTHUSIAN THEORY OF POPULATION

For a generation past certain eugenists have been sounding an insistent warning against the steady decline in national birth-rates. Serious statements are uttered from time to time to the effect that society is embarked upon a process of self-extermination or, if not that, at least of degeneration, due to the low birth-rate among the educated classes. This is a serious charge, which deserves the thoughtful consideration of students of social conditions and, indeed, of all intelligent persons. Is it true that society is destroying itself by a deliberate artificial restriction of births?

The Theories of Malthus.

Before examining the data at hand with respect to the real growth of populations, and the relation of this growth to the world's food supply, it will be well to consider briefly the theories of population held by the renowned Englishman, Thomas Malthus. In 1798, this clergyman and economist wrote his epoch-making *Essay on the Principle of Population,* which has proven a storm center of controversy ever since its appearance, especially in the present age. In this treatise, Malthus took the position that the population in every country increased so rapidly that it was ever tending to outgrow the food supply. To this fundamental cause he attributed the misery and starvation of the poor. So long as no deliberate measures were taken to prevent the swift growth of populations, there would always be crushing poverty and an insufficient supply of food for the ever swelling millions. To quote from the opening chapter of the famous *Essay:*

[13] M. Sanger, *Woman and the New Race,* pp. 1 and 5. By permission of Brentano's, New York, 1920.

"I think I may fairly make two postulata. First, that food is necessary to the existence of man. Secondly, that the passion between the sexes is necessary, and will remain nearly in its present state. . . . Assuming, then, my postulata as granted, I say, that the power of population is indefinitely greater than the power of the earth to produce subsistence for man."

By the publication of this treatise, Malthus brought down upon himself a torrent of bitter criticism, on the ground that his theory represented a soulless condemnation of the poor to hopeless misery. But such was far from being his intention. Instead of preaching a fatalistic doctrine of despair, Malthus, at least in the later editions of his work, emphasized the importance of developing some intelligent method of restricting the growth of peoples, in the interest of the submerged portion of society. The means advocated by the writer consisted in delayed marriages and a rigid exercise of control of the insurgent sex impulse, both before and after marriage. Needless to say, contraceptive methods were unknown in eighteenth-century England; therefore Malthus was driven to espouse a means of limiting population growth, namely deferred marriages, which has grave social and individual disadvantages.

Although certain details of the Malthusian theory have been adversely criticized even in recent times, contemporary biologists are almost unanimous in declaring that, in its fundamental positions, it is profoundly true. Thus Dr. Raymond Pearl, vital statistician in Johns Hopkins University, declares that Malthus' *Essay* is "one of the greatest books the human mind has produced, so far ahead of its time that in the main his argument is truer and more significant today than it was when he wrote it." [14] With the theories of Malthus in mind, then, let us consider the facts in regard to population in various countries of the world, as well as the rate of population increase.

The Natural Increase of Populations: Ratio of Births to Deaths.

At the outset of our study, it should be understood that the actual population growth in any country is represented by the ratio of births to deaths. A country like Japan, for instance, with a birth-rate (1914) of thirty-three and a death rate of twenty-seven, had in that year a survival rate or "natural increase" of six per thousand. In the Commonwealth of Australia, where the birth-rate in 1916 was twenty-seven, and the death rate only eleven, the survival rate or natural increase of population was

[14] "The Menace of Population Growth," in Adolf Meyer (Editor), *Birth Control, Facts and Responsibilities,* p. 52. By permission of the Williams & Wilkins Co., Baltimore, 1925.

sixteen per thousand.[15] Obviously, if the mortality rate in any country were declining more rapidly than the birth-rate, the "natural increase" in that population would be on the upward curve, even though its birth-rate might be falling so conspicuously as to call forth the warnings of eugenists. Now this condition appears to exist in many civilized nations throughout the world. Professor East has prepared a valuable table of figures covering the five-year periods from 1890 to 1914 which shows the excess of births over deaths in fifteen European countries and Australia: [16]

EXCESS OF BIRTHS OVER DEATHS IN VARIOUS COUNTRIES PER THOUSAND OF THE POPULATION

Averages for five-year periods

Years	Australia	Austria	Belgium	Bulgaria	Denmark	France	Germany	Hungary	Italy	Norway	Rumania	Russia	Spain	Sweden	United Kingdom
1890-1894	19.7	9.0	8.7	9.7	11.4	0.1	12.5	9.0	10.5	13.0	9.1	12.1	3.8	10.6	10.7
1895-1899	15.4	11.4	11.1	15.9	13.7	1.3	14.8	11.4	11.1	14.8	12.9	16.6	5.7	11.2	11.1
1900-1904	14.6	12.1	10.7	17.7	14.0	1.4	14.5	11.9	10.4	14.4	14.0	17.7	8.3	10.7	11.1
1905-1909	15.7	10.8	9.0	19.0	14.3	0.6	14.0	10.9	10.9	12.5	14.2	16.1	9.2	11.0	11.1
1910-1914	17.1	10.5	7.6	18.6	13.5	0.4	12.5	12.8	12.8	12.2	17.4	...	8.9	9.8	10.0

A study of the above table will make plain that, in nine countries out of the fifteen listed, the natural increase, *i.e.*, the growth in population due to the excess of births over deaths, has been steadily increasing over a period of thirty-five years. Only in Australia, Belgium, Norway, Sweden and the United Kingdom has there been a falling off in the natural increase, and in most instances this has been slight. The enormous natural increase in Bulgaria and Rumania during the period may be explained by the fact that the birth-rates in these countries were very high before the World War; and an unexpected increase in food production, due to improved agricultural methods, kept down the infant and adult mortality rates, thus increasing the population far beyond previous rates of growth. Despite a sharp fall in the birth-rates of both Australia and Belgium during the period under consideration, the excess of births over deaths in 1914 was only 2.6 per thousand less in Australia than it had been in 1890; whereas in Belgium the loss was only 1.1 per thousand. In Norway and Sweden, where the birth-rates have been declining for many years, the loss in natural increase was only .8 per thousand; and in the United Kingdom, only .7.

[15] See Cox, *op. cit.*, pp. 21-2.
[16] *Mankind at the Crossroads*, p. 271. Charles Scribner's Sons, New York, 1923. By permission of the publishers.

Thus the student of social conditions is forced to the conclusion that, in most European countries, there has been a rise and not a fall in the natural increase of populations. Far from its being true that human numbers are waning, due to voluntary restriction of births, the opposite is the case, namely, that because of a death-rate which is decreasing more rapidly than the birth-rate, most nations will, before many generations, be faced with the serious problem of over-population. Professor East estimates that, in every country listed in the table except France, improved public health facilities could bring about so low a death rate as to result in a natural increase or survival rate of fifteen per thousand annually.[17] In Australia, the excess of births over deaths in 1920 was exactly fifteen, whereas in England and Wales, where over-population and poverty exist, the excess of births over deaths in 1921 was ten.

When we turn our attention to the United States, we learn that similar conditions exist. The census report on "Births, Still-births and Infant Mortality Statistics" for 1924 shows that in the Birth Registration Area, including thirty-three states and the District of Columbia, the birth-rate in that year was 22.6, while the death rate was 12.2, making an excess of births over deaths of 10.4 per thousand population. Clearly this excess means that in the United States, with a population of about 110,000,000, there was a natural increase of more than 1,140,000 souls [18] in 1924, without including the addition due to immigration. Surely a country which is growing in numbers at the rate of over one million a year is not in grave danger of race suicide.

During the last decade or two, not only has there been a sharp decline in most advanced countries in the general mortality rate, but the fall of the infant death-rate [19] has been most encouraging. In his presidential address to the Royal Statistical Society in 1917, the Registrar General of Births and Deaths for England and Wales gave some interesting facts concerning the decline of infant mortality in Europe. He declared that in Germany, between 1906 and 1913, the infant mortality rate declined eighteen percent; the birth-rate seventeen percent. In England and Wales, the infant mortality rate also declined eighteen percent in the same period, whereas the birth-rate fell only eleven percent. Similar conditions existed in Norway, Sweden and Denmark. In Norway, the infant mortality rate fell six percent, and the birth-rate fell five percent; in Sweden,

[17] East, *op. cit.*, p. 275.
[18] This assumes that the natural increase was not greatly different in the eighteen states and Alaska, not comprised in the Registration Area.
[19] This represents the number of deaths of infants, within the first year of life, per 1,000 births.

the infant mortality rate fell thirteen percent and the birth-rate fell ten percent; in Denmark, the infant mortality rate fell fourteen percent and the birth-rate fell eleven percent.[20] When these ratios are contrasted with those of sixteenth-century England, the gain is seen to be enormous. In that century, a Lord Mayor of London, father of Dean Colet, the famous founder of St. Paul's School, had twenty-two children in thirty years, of whom only one lived to maturity. And this is no solitary instance, as family records show. Commenting on the huge child mortality rate of this and succeeding centuries, Dean Inge says: "Parents seem to have regarded this dismal procession of cradles and coffins as a dispensation of Providence, and bore lightly the loss of children for whom there was no room." [21] Even today it is not uncommon to see working parents, who are laboring to the limit of their strength to earn a bare livelihood for themselves and their children, also viewing with calm stoicism the death of babies who should never have been born.

The Increase in the Duration of Life.

The above discussion should make clear that the rise of artificial means of restricting births has done much to prevent a high infant death-rate, while not materially reducing the natural increase of population in any country. Had not voluntary restriction of births been in operation for a generation or more, many nations of Europe would now be facing even more serious economic and social conditions bred of over-population than now confront them. If a country can successfully avoid over-population, the average human life can be lengthened, and at the same time made more worth living. Drysdale estimates that in highly over-populated countries like India, China and Russia the *average* duration of life is not more than thirty-five years. Professor E. A. Ross estimates the expectation of life at birth in India at not more than twenty-three years. Since restriction of births began, the span of life in Great Britain has risen to nearly sixty years; and it is not unreasonable to suppose that the Psalmist's estimate of "three score years and ten" may be reached by the many, if reforms in industrial conditions and in provisions for public health can be realized. In the case of Great Britain, this would probably mean a birth- and death-rate of fourteen per thousand and a stationary population.[22] During the

---

[20] See Cox, *op. cit.*, p. 115.
[21] In Marchant (Editor), *The Control of Parenthood*, p. 61. G. P. Putnam's Sons, New York and London, 1920.
[22] See Charles Drysdale's "Presidential Address at the Sixth International Neo-Malthusian and Birth Control Conference" (New York, 1925), in *Birth Control Review*, May, 1925, p. 141.

period 1781-84, when the birth-rate in France was very high (thirty-nine per 1,000), the average duration of a French citizen's life has been estimated as not more than twenty-six years; whereas at present, with a national birth-rate of about 18.5 the span of life in France has lengthened to nearly fifty-six years.[23]

The Pressure of Population upon Means of Subsistence.

There is another vitally important aspect from which the complicated problem of birth control should be viewed. This is concerned with the relation existing between the size of population in any country and the food supply. Professor East estimates, from the evidence at hand, that the population of the world increased from less than 850,000,000 persons in 1800 to more than 1,700,000,000 in 1900. This means that the entire period of human life on earth prior to 1800, which has been roughly estimated to be half a million years, was required to produce a population of 850,000,000 persons, and that only a century was needed to double that population![24] If the world population doubled every century—and an eminent population statistician of Australia estimates that the current annual increase is 1.16%, which means a doubling in 60¼ years—what would be the effect on the world's supply of land and food? East cites Pitkin's valuable study,[25] which shows that, taking the army rations of civilized nations as a basis, the average adult needs approximately 1,000 pounds of dry foodstuffs every year. At the present rate of natural increase, it follows that farmers must provide about 23,000,000,000 more pounds of food each year if the world is to be nourished. East has carefully estimated that between two and three acres of land are necessary to support each man. "Thus every season," he writes, "the tillers of the soil must prepare, plant, cultivate and harvest nearly 40 million acres more than they did the year before unless they can persuade mother earth to give up more of her bounties than has been her habit of yore."[26] Of course it must be kept in mind that not all persons are adults; a considerable percentage of any population is made up of infants and children. But even when this allowance is made, the situation is sufficiently disturbing. What is the apparent capacity of the earth to feed its teeming millions?

[23] Hardy, "The Truth about France," in *Birth Control Review*, November, 1925, p. 310.
[24] See East, *op. cit.*, pp. 66-7.
[25] *Must We Fight Japan?* The Century Co., New York, 1921.
[26] East, *op. cit.*, pp. 67-8. For the entire discussion of food supply that follows I am indebted to Professor East's excellent book.

If the land area around the Arctic Circles be excluded, the world has a territory of about 33,000,000,000 acres. The International Institute of Agriculture at Rome has investigated the proportion of cultivated land to total area in the most populous countries, and has found it to be about forty percent. This percentage is high, since the countries of densest populations are those with the most land under cultivation. Assuming, then, that this percentage is not far from representing the maximum limit of arable land, then the earth has at most 13,000,000,000 acres available for agriculture. How many people can this enormous area support? Obviously this depends upon a number of factors—a prolonged era of peace and prosperity, improved methods of agriculture, transportation and storage, and an increase in human efficiency. If all these favorable conditions are fulfilled, and if an allowance of 2.5 acres per person is made over forty percent of the arable land-surface of the earth, East estimates that a population of 5,200 millions can be supported on our globe. At the present rate of population growth this maximum would be reached in slightly over a century.[27]

This very sketchy account of the possibilities of food production throughout the world should not end without some reference to the United States. The population increase in our country has been very rapid, due chiefly to the fact that its inhabitants have been blessed with rich natural resources and much fertile soil. When the first census was taken in 1790, the population of this new republic was only 4,000,000 people; when the fourteenth census was taken in 1920, it was almost 106,000,000. Dr. Raymond Pearl has plotted the curve of growth of the population during this period of 130 years, and its probable course in the future. The curve shows a progressively diminishing increase beginning about the year 1914.[28] Not far from the year 2100, the curve ceases to rise and becomes horizontal, which means that the point of population saturation will then have been reached in this country, and the death-rate will equal the birth-rate. The maximum population will then be not far from 200 million people. According to East, however, there will be a serious population pressure, i.e., growth of population beyond the food supply and land area, by the year 1980, unless deliberate restriction of births is resorted to in preference to Nature's method of killing off the weak and unfortunate by starvation or disease.

At this point the reader may say, are not the natural resources and

[27] East, op. cit., p. 69.
[28] Ibid., p. 151. Citing Raymond Pearl and L. G. Reed, "On the Rate of Growth of the Population of the United States since 1790," in Proceedings of the National Academy of Sciences, Vol. VI, 1920, pp. 275-88.

the fertile land area of the United States very great? Unquestionably they are, but both are limited. In their interesting study of "Arable Land in the United States," published in the *Yearbook of the Department of Agriculture* for 1918, Baker and Strong examine the productive capacity of the country. The land area of the United States comprises 1,907 million acres, but 1,000 million acres of the total consists of land where the annual rainfall is meager—from zero to fifteen inches—where mountains abound, or where the soil is too barren of the necessary elements to nourish any vegetation except sagebrush. By utilizing available water sources, it is possible to add to the thirty million acres of land under irrigation another thirty million, and to recover for agriculture about sixty million acres of swamp land. To this should be added 150 million acres of forest and woodland that will probably be seized for cultivation when the demand of a growing population for more food makes it imperative. On the basis of the figures in the above study, East estimates [29] that, at the outside, there are only 800 million acres of improved land available, even when the utmost has been done ·to reclaim desert and swamp land, and 150 million acres of woodland have been leveled for tillage. To seize more than this would rob the country of much-needed timber and might act harmfully on temperature and rainfall.

How many people can this 800 million acres support? If the land reclaimed last is less fertile than that first cultivated, which is a reasonable hypothesis, it will of course be less productive. *By our present methods of agriculture,* which are not highly efficient, East maintains that only about 135 million people can be supported from the produce of this vast area. But at our present rate of growth, the United States will have a population of 175 million in 1980, and that is only fifty-three years hence. Within the lifetime of the little children of today, there will be, in Professor East's opinion, a severe pressure of population upon the country's supply of food unless methods of cultivation can be so improved that the productivity of the land can be greatly increased.

But, the reader may say, are there not possibilities of utilizing science to bring about rainfall in arid regions, to manufacture synthesized food in laboratories, to discover new food plants, to increase enormously the productivity of land? No doubt, American methods of soil cultivation can be very greatly improved. European countries and Japan have carried intensive agriculture much farther than wasteful America. For example, in the five-year period 1915-1919, the United States averaged 14.3 bushels of wheat to the acre, as compared with 31.8 bushels in the United Kingdom

[29] East, *op. cit.,* pp. 155-9.

and 22.6 bushels in Japan. Also, it raised 92.7 bushels of potatoes to the acre, as compared with 213.9 bushels in the United Kingdom and 151.6 bushels in Japan.[30] But although the arable land in this country has by no means been intensively cropped, East is inclined to believe that, even with the use of better methods of agriculture and increased man-power, production cannot be increased much beyond fifty percent of the present yield. This may be too low an estimate, but it must not be forgotten that there is a limit beyond which the most scientifically cultivated land will not increase its yield. Since the opening of the century, there have been diminishing returns in agriculture in the United States, which is only to say that a given amount of capital and labor has continuously produced less and less. It is possible that the generations to come will see deserts converted into fruitful farm lands by scientifically induced rainfall, and will eat protein tabloids and other foods prepared in chemical laboratories, but we must not be unduly hopeful on these points.

Professor East is by no means alone in holding the disturbing views of the world's population problem outlined above. Many writers have in recent years called attention to the danger of population saturation. Among these may be mentioned W. S. Thompson [31] and Dr. Raymond Pearl. The latter statistician has adduced encouraging figures to show that the curves of production of essential commodities such as coal, pig iron and cotton on the one hand, and of food on the other, have risen much more sharply than the curve of population. This means, of course, that man has been able to make the means of subsistence and the means of industry increase more rapidly than the human family. Unfortunately, this fact has been and still is a cause for complacency on the part of unthinking optimists, a complacency that Pearl believes to be ill warranted by an impartial study of all the facts. Thus he writes:

"Now a superficial view of the situation . . . is likely to be extremely complacent. Population has grown since Malthus's day. Yes, about as he said it would. But Malthus quite overlooked the powers of man to make nature do his will. As the population has increased man has made the means of subsistence increase still faster. So far from population catching up with the means of subsistence, it is plainly out-distanced in the race. *So will the unthinking interpret our charts.*

"But we are unable to convince ourselves that such complacency has any warrant. We believe that anyone who will take the trouble to read

[30] See East, *op. cit.*, p. 169.
[31] "Population: A Study in Malthusianism," *Columbia University Studies in History, Economics and Public Law,* Vol. 73, No. 3. New York, 1915.

even the present chapter carefully and will ponder over the facts it presents, rejecting if he likes everything that savors of opinion or theory, will be bound to feel some misgivings about the world's ability to go on indefinitely increasing both its population and its average standard of consumption or of living. For precisely that is what we are now doing." [32]

Again referring to the optimistic theory that there is no reason why production should not go on in the future as it has in the past Pearl comments:

"This view overlooks the fact that besides the human element involved in production, there is another of even greater importance which finally limits the process. It is, that the volume and the surface of the planet on which we live are strictly fixed quantities. This fact sets a limit, if no other does, to the indefinite projection of these straight lines of production." [33]

The foregoing discussion of the world's productive capacity is intimately related to the problem of birth control, as already indicated. Unless the countries of Europe, the Americas and Australia are ready to accept the conditions of population saturation that prevail in impoverished India, China, and to a scarcely less extent in Japan, they must not rely too optimistically upon the possibility of importing foods and increasing production indefinitely. Rather should they give serious consideration to methods of keeping down the birth-rate. In the United States the population increased sixteen percent between 1910 and 1920. At this rate of population growth, due in part to immigration, but in much greater measure to natural increase, the population of this country would double in forty-four years, and 212,000,000 persons would be clamoring for food. Such a population is far more numerous than our arable land area and agricultural methods will feed at the present American standard of living. In the words of Professor Edward A. Ross:

"We are headed straight for a world saturation which will make toil, poverty, anxiety, and low expectation of life the portion of the masses in all countries. It was some job during the War for the Allies to feed a portion of the Belgians. Well as things now are, food for two new Belgiums must be found every year [34] . . . The end of rapid expansion is in sight. Within a lifetime, we shall arrive at a nearly stationary state of population. Shall the equilibrium between births and deaths be struck by adjusting the birth-rate to the death-rate of ten per thousand per an-

[32] *Studies in Human Biology*, pp. 530-1. Italics mine. By permission of the Williams & Wilkins Co., Baltimore, 1924.
[33] *Ibid.*, p. 528.
[34] This represents the rate of *world increase* in population.

num, which we may look for before very long; or shall it be struck by allowing the growth of crowding, over-work and underfeeding to raise the mortality to 24 per thousand per annum, which is the present birth-rate?" [35]

Social Evils of Over-population.

In Professor Ross's vigorous statement, the harmful effects upon society of over-population are clearly suggested. These are such menacing evils that they deserve further consideration. Most social writers are agreed that ignorance of birth control methods is in a substantial degree responsible for poverty, overcrowding in tenements, juvenile delinquency and family desertion. Furthermore, unrestricted breeding is a serious impediment to economic and social progress and is undoubtedly one factor making for the maintenance of war in civilized societies. Overcrowded countries are ever on the lookout for natural resources and outlets at the expense of their neighbors. The relation between a high birth-rate among the poor and grinding poverty seems obvious enough. On the whole it is the ignorant, unskilled, low-paid workers who have the largest families. Skilled wage-earners who command good wages are beginning to learn about and practise methods of birth control. An examination of the family histories of the 100 neediest cases in New York City, recounted every year at the Christmas season in the *New York Times* to stimulate philanthropy, will reveal a high percentage of cases in which the size of the family was out of all proportion to the father's wages or the combined family income. In these family groups, there are from three to seven or eight children in the majority of cases, while the income would hardly support two in decent comfort. Only skilled labor earns high wages in the United States, as elsewhere. Addressing the Senate in August, 1917, Senator Borah described the economic condition of the unskilled laboring classes as follows:

"Seventy percent of the families of our country have incomes of $1,000 or less. Tell me how a man so situated can have shelter for his family; how he can provide food and clothing. He is an industrial peon. His home is scant and pinched beyond the power of language to tell. He sees his wife and children on the ragged edge of hunger from week to week and month to month. If sickness comes, he faces suicide or crime. He cannot educate his children; he cannot fit them for citizenship; he cannot even fit them as soldiers to die for their country." [36]

[35] Quoted on the cover of *Birth Control Review*, March, 1926.
[36] Quoted in Sanger, *op. cit.*, p. 39. Brentano's New York, 1920.

In this address, the liberal Senator from Idaho was not speaking in behalf of birth control, although he well might have done so. With such facts at the disposal of every intelligent person, it is difficult to see how anyone can sincerely oppose the dissemination of knowledge of scientific methods of preventing conception. To bring children into the world to grow up in dark, squalid, unsanitary homes, where the family members are crowded together in such wise as to render privacy and even decency impossible, seems on its face a profoundly unintelligent, unsocial and immoral performance. Surely society gains little or nothing from future citizens reared under such unwholesome conditions; and the children themselves, born into homes almost totally unprovided with the means of rearing them into healthy, intelligent, moral manhood and womanhood, are in many instances mute witnesses against the ignorant parents who gave them birth and the social system which encourages such crimes against childhood.

Many well-meaning people believe that this crucial problem can be solved by attacking the economic end and striving to secure for each worker a living wage that will make it possible to rear large families in decent comfort. Far be it from the writer to minimize the importance of drastic economic reforms in our present industrial society. The need for securing to every laborer a hire that makes life worth living is real and urgent. But this reform will not of itself furnish a solution of the problem. Indeed, it might result in such thoughtless and care-free breeding as materially to hasten the day when the population of this country will have outgrown its means of subsistence and we shall be facing grave problems of over-population. In the energetic words of King:

"To attempt to better the economic condition of the masses . . . without lowering their birth-rate is as hopeless a task as trying to stamp out typhoid fever while still supplying the people with water laden with the deadly germs. Within reasonable limits, a nation's permanent economic welfare, then, depends but little on whether the soil is rich or sterile, the mines productive or exhausted, but, on the contrary, it is based almost wholly on the question as to whether the masses of the people have passed over the deep but narrow gulf which separates the control of population by a standard of living from that condition in which it is limited only by the means of subsistence, *for it is the crossing of this gulf which substitutes reason in place of the animal instincts.*" [37]

The social evils of over-population do not end with poverty. Those

[37] Wilford I. King, *The Wealth and Income of the People of the United States,* p. 246. Italics mine. By permission of The Macmillan Co., New York, 1915.

who know most about the hard lives of the workers in congested areas of our great cities do not hesitate to declare that one important cause of family desertion and juvenile delinquency and the chief source of the widespread practice of abortion may be found in the ignorance of the laboring masses of methods of controlling the size of their families. The man who is carrying an economic load beyond his strength, especially if he be weak and selfish, will quail at the prospect of an addition to his family, already far too large, and will not rarely pull up stakes and slip away to some distant town, where he looks forward to beginning life anew with no encumbrances. In most of the studies of family desertion made by social investigators the fact that another baby would soon be added to a struggling family looms large among the causes of abandonment. Many times, probably more often than not, neither mother nor father desires another child to be nourished and clothed at the expense of the children whom they are striving to rear. Hence comes the tragedy of "the unwanted child," who, unhappy at home, joins the ranks of juvenile delinquents daily passing through the children's court. Perhaps no one can speak with more authority on this question than Dr. Miriam Van Waters, well known as the referee of the juvenile court of Los Angeles. In her address before the Sixth International Neo-Malthusian and Birth Control Conference in March, 1925, Dr. Van Waters said:

"For the young child the family group should be the most vital [of his interests], affording him the most comfort and security and the best place for self-expression and fulfillment. Unless he can obtain in his home these legitimate satisfactions he is driven prematurely to the streets, or if he is a solitary child he may develop outlets such as excessive day-dreaming, timidity, temper-tantrums, lying, stealing, running away, setting fires and the like.

"So often we hear lack of proper paternal control blamed for delinquency. Parents are advised in pulpit and press to use the rod, be more firm in discipline, assert their authority. How tragic is most of this advice! It misses the central point: *delinquency in young children is a symptom of deep distress*. To use blind and ignorant force against the offending child is to display adult cruelty and stupidity at its worst.

"*The fact is delinquent children are very often—unwanted children.* [An only child frequently becomes delinquent because his parents neglect him for their own interests.] So too the unwanted child in the large family where the mother can provide nothing of motherhood to the individual save its physical aspect may become delinquent. Particularly is it true that girls go wrong in such families.

"Haphazard methods of family formation that result in the birth of unplanned for, unwelcome children produce a large proportion of the stream of delinquent boys and girls that pass through our courts and correctional institutions.

"No part of the Birth Control movement is of greater importance for the prevention of delinquency than its emphasis on durable, planned marriages, and thoughtful voluntary parenthood. The concept of family formation should be taught boys and girls in early childhood. That children come because they are desired, that children must be prepared for, that they require adequate space, shelter, nurture, love, discipline, education, medical attention, religious and social guidance, that, as Douglas Thom says, 'being a parent is the biggest job on earth'—this enlarged view of family life would reduce delinquency and stop an appalling waste of childhood." [38]

The practice of abortion to prevent unwelcome births is more or less general in all countries where knowledge of contraceptive methods is denied to the masses of the people but it is shockingly prevalent in the United States. Physicians estimate that 1,000,000 abortions are performed in this country every year. To be sure some of these are therapeutic operations, performed to save a prospective mother's life, but by far the greater number are self-induced. In the view of Dr. James Cooper, these abortions "are an expression of rebellion against enforced maternity." [39] This revolt may be personal, representing the woman's intense desire for freedom from the crushing burden of continuous childbearing, or altruistic, representing her dread of bringing into the world babies who cannot possibly be given wholesome nurture. But, be the cause what it may, the mounting number of abortions in this country is a national disgrace. The laws enacted to suppress the evil have had but little effect because they have not taken sufficient account of the conditions that produce it. Probably not many physicians would disagree with Dr. Benjamin Tilton, who writes:

"The practice is most common among married women, particularly of the poorer prolific classes who already have children and cannot afford to add to their number. The mothers, on finding themselves pregnant again after repeated pregnancies, resort in desperation to this immoral and dangerous means of relief. Some women seek this means not only once but a dozen or twenty times. Some women do not live to seek it for the second time.

[38] *Birth Control Review*, November, 1925. Italics mine.
[39] Address in Carnegie Hall, December 6, 1924.

"It is no exaggeration to say that thousands of women die annually from the effects of these illegal operations and other thousands become chronic invalids or permanently sterile. These tragedies are a disgrace to our civilization and cry for prevention. They can be prevented and I believe alone prevented by the dissemination (through proper channels) of Birth Control knowledge concerning scientific, safe and sure methods of contraception. Woman has the undeniable right to limit her children to the number that she can adequately provide for and the number that is consistent with her health and strength and that of her children." [40]

The social ills described above are just so many obstacles in the path of progress toward an enlightened, humane society. Few persons will deny that poverty, with its attendant train of evils, is one of the ugliest blots on contemporary civilization; that juvenile delinquency is a deeply disturbing fact; that family desertion is all too common among the poor; that the facts adduced by physicians prove the widespread practice of abortion—yet many of these same persons will close their eyes to the connection that unquestionably exists between these evils and the ignorance of men and women concerning birth control. Social life is morally lowered and social advancement gravely impeded by these injurious conditions; and if the birth-rate is not deliberately and intelligently kept down, the evils will continuously increase as the population in one country after another approaches the saturation point.

TOPICS FOR REPORTS

1. Birth Control from the Woman's Standpoint.
   Margaret Sanger, *Woman and the New Race,* Chs. IV-IX. Brentano's, New York, 1920.
2. Birth Control and Mental Hygiene.
   Ross McC. Chapman, M.D., "Birth Control and Mental Hygiene," in Adolf Meyer (Editor), *Birth Control, Facts and Responsibilities,* pp. 105-15. Williams & Wilkins Co., Baltimore, 1925.
   Eleanor R. Wembridge, "The Seventh Child in the Four-Roomed House," *ibid.,* pp. 140-52.
3. Causes of the Declining Birth-Rate.
   S. J. Holmes, *The Trend of the Race,* pp. 143-79. Harcourt, Brace & Co., New York, 1921.
4. War and Population.
   Harold Cox, *The Problem of Population,* Ch. III. G. P. Putnam's Sons, New York and London, 1923.
   Margaret Sanger, *op. cit.,* Ch. XIII.

[40] *Birth Control Review,* March, 1925, p. 71.

CHAPTER XX

THE PROBLEM OF BIRTH CONTROL
(*continued*)

THE DIFFERENTIAL BIRTH-RATE

I N the last chapter, the social menace of national over-population and the serious evils following upon a high birth-rate among the poor were set forth. At this point, it may well be objected that the problem of a steadily falling birth-rate presents several aspects other than those discussed, and that from at least one of these viewpoints the decline in births appears to be a grave disadvantage to society. Social investigators have ample evidence to show that the declining birth rate is *differential, i.e.,* it is lowest not among the ignorant, the inefficient, the needy, but among the intelligent, the prosperous and the able. For example, a table of the comparative fertility among classes in England in 1911 shows a birth-rate of 119 per thousand married males under fifty-five years in the upper and middle class, 153 among skilled workmen and 213 among unskilled workmen. If these groups be classified according to particular professions and occupations, the contrast in the birth-rate, and also the infant death-rate, is even more striking. The table follows : [1]

England and Wales 1911	Births per 1,000 Married Males under 55 Years	Death of Infants under 12 Months per 1,000 Born
Medical practitioners	103	39
Solicitors	100	41
Clergymen, Church of England	101	48
Dock laborers	231	172
Earthenware makers	181	172
Costers and hawkers	175	196

If 100 be taken as the general population fertility of England, a table of comparative fertility, *which referred only to women of child-bearing age* would show at the top wives of coal-miners, with a rate of 126.4. Next come wives of agricultural laborers, with a rate of 113.4; of boiler

[1] From Harold Cox, *The Problem of Population*, p. 117. By permission of G. P. Putnam's Sons, New York and London, 1923.

makers, 110.1; of farmers, 100.5; while at the bottom of the scale are wives of Nonconformist ministers, 79.8; Church of England clergymen, 72; teachers, 70.3; and doctors, 64.7.[2]

In the United States, conditions are much the same. The largest families are found among the lowest income groups, where lack of economic and educational opportunities has resulted in ignorance and thoughtless, uncontrolled breeding; while the smallest families are almost invariably found in the educated, far-sighted and high-income groups. Of 454 men selected at random from those who subscribed to the *Harvard Alumni Bulletin* in 1925, only 379 were married. These men had a total of 793 children. The average income of the entire group was $18,566.74.[3] An examination of these figures shows that the married Harvard alumni and their wives are little more than reproducing themselves, and that nearly seventeen percent of the alumni are unmarried. In his study of the birth-rate among graduates of Harvard and Yale Universities, Phillips finds that the number of children per married graduate has fallen from 3.25 in the decade 1850-60 to a little over two in the decade 1881-90. Add to this the results of the study made by J. McKeen Cattell[4] of 643 American men of science. The investigation revealed that the families from which the scientific men had sprung had an average of 4.7 children, whereas the scientific men who were married and whose families were complete had an average of only 2.3 children, including all the children born, whether living or not. Needless to say these men, of marked intellectual ability, together with their wives, are barely reproducing themselves; for it must not be overlooked that death will probably claim some of the offspring before they marry and reproduce, and also a considerable proportion of the children of these scientists will not marry.

One of the most significant of the recent studies of the birth-rate decline in the educated middle class is that of Professors Baber of the University of Illinois and Ross of Wisconsin.[5] This investigation was restricted to completed American families,[6] with parents still living, and to the families of their parents. Not only college graduates, but all educational and occupational groups were represented. Embraced within

[2] See Prof. J. Arthur Thomson, "Biological Aspects," in James Marchant (Editor), *The Control of Parenthood,* p. 23. G. P. Putnam's Sons, New York and London, 1920.
[3] See the *New York Times,* January 15, 1926.
[4] In *Scientific Monthly,* Vol. IV, 1917, pp. 252-7.
[5] "Changes in the Size of American Families in One Generation," *University of Wisconsin Studies in the Social Sciences,* No. 10, 1924. Madison, Wisconsin. By permission of the authors.
[6] Those in which the mother was forty-five years of age or older.

the study were 750 families of a generation ago and 2,500 of their descendants of the present generation. The families of the older generation had an average of 5.44 children, while those of the younger had an average of 3.35. But since this study was made only of families with children, the average is undoubtedly too high in both instances. All childless families were automatically excluded from the investigation; and, in the case of the older generation, it was impossible to learn how much the average (5.44) was lowered by that fact. But the infertile families in the present generation were known, and if they were included in securing the average, it would fall to 2.81 children per marriage. Commenting on these facts the authors say:

"This is indeed startling. Five years ago a leading statistician calculated that with existing death and marriage rates nearly four children per married couple (3.7 to be more nearly exact) were required to replace the preceding generation. In this statement he has been supported by other experts, who further maintain that there has been no substantial change in the figure in the last five years. Even making more allowance for a slightly lower death rate for the people of our study than for the general population, careful figuring (including consideration of comparative marriage rates) does not seem to justify a figure lower than 3.6 as the minimum number of children per married couple necessary to keep stationary that portion of the population included in our study." [7]

As stated in a previous chapter, the graduates of women's colleges are held to be the worst offenders with regard to the birth-rate; and, indeed, there is no denial of the fact that this group of women, highly selected on the basis of intelligence, is very far from perpetuating itself. Not only is it true, as we have seen, that only about fifty percent of Eastern college women are married fifteen years after graduation, but among the group who have married there is a high proportion of sterile marriages and a low birth-rate. Thus the Smith College *Decennial Record* (1905-15) shows nearly half the class of 1905 married in 1915. But of that married group, 28.3 percent have no children, and the remaining 71.7 percent have 116 children in all, or an average of 1.6 children per marriage. Wellesley's showing is slightly lower. Of the students graduated between 1879 and 1888 only fifty-five percent were married in 1912; and in this group, there were only 1.56 children per wife. If these children were distributed among all the graduates, married and unmarried, there would be only .86 of a child per woman. A study of the graduates of more recent classes—1901-1904—disclosed that in 1912, from eight to eleven years

[7] Baber and Ross, *op. cit.*, p. 25.

after graduation, only forty-four percent were married, and only .87 of a child had been born to each wife or .37 to each graduate.[8] These figures, which seem disturbing enough, it must be admitted, lead Sprague to exclaim:

"Is the woman's college as now conducted a force which acts for or against the survival of the race which patronizes it? Whatever intellectual and moral superiority a race may have, it needs also a certain amount of reproductive impulse in order to remain on the earth. No culture, art, science or morality can save it unless it produces about three matured children per married, child-bearing couple, and any race which does not do this is doomed to extinction."[9]

But it is pertinent to inquire whether in reality these low birth-rates should be ascribed to the baneful effects of college education, or whether they do not characterize the entire intelligent middle class from which college students are largely drawn. Ross and Baber's study,[10] previously referred to, throws some light on this crucial point. It reveals that, of 1,420 men of the present generation whose families are completed, those who had received only high-school education had an average of 2.73 children (including infertile families), whereas the men of college education had 2.88 children, and the men who had advanced to graduate study had 2.79 children. In the case of 1,183 women of the present generation, the figures show slightly lower averages for the college and graduate groups, when compared with the women whose education had ended with the high school. The group who had received only elementary education reveals a markedly higher average. The figures follow:[11]

Education	Totals	Average No. of Children Born, Including Infertile Marriages
None	—	—
Elementary	451	3.49
High school	459	2.67
College	251	2.51
Graduate	22	2.31

It appears, then, that of 1,420 men, those who had had the privilege of college education and graduate study had actually a higher average of children than men with only high-school education; whereas of 1,183

---

[8] Robert J. Sprague, "Education and Race Suicide," in *Journal of Heredity,* April, 1915.

[9] Sprague, *op. cit.,* p. 160.

[10] Baber and Ross, *op. cit.,* p. 66.

[11] *Ibid.* Adapted from p. 67.

women, those who were college graduates had an average of only .16 of a child less than women whose education did not extend beyond high school. The women who had had the benefit of graduate study (only 22 in number) showed an average number of children .36 less than the average of the high-school women. These figures seem very significant; and although they do not establish the theory that a declining birth-rate is characteristic of the entire educated middle class, with or without college education, they certainly support it. Instead of hurling criticisms at colleges, especially at those devoted to the education of women, it behooves these critics to make wide investigations of the birth-rate among the middle class whose education has not gone beyond the secondary school.

Since writing the above, the author has received some support for this theory from two sources. A study [12] of the fertility of the middle class of England, with particular attention paid to the factors of age at marriage and duration of marriage, seemed, in the opinion of the writers, to furnish no justification for the current theory that college education in itself is a potent cause of limitation of families. The authors declared that "paying attention to the errors of sampling, there are no differences between the size of the family of a non-college mother and that of a college mother which cannot be explained by a difference of age at marriage and duration of marriage." Since the English group was socially homogeneous, consisting of college mothers and their near relatives who had not gone to college, the writers' conclusion seems justified that "the alleged prejudicial effects of higher education *per se* upon the capacity or inclination of women to bear children do not exist." [13]

Further support for the theory is furnished by Banker's analysis of the study recently made by Professor Holmes of "The Size of College Families . . ." [14] The conclusion of Holmes, based upon an examination of the families of grandparents and parents of students in the University of California, was to the effect that "education has a potent effect in reducing family size whether it is possessed by the male or the female parent." [15] The figures further showed that higher education of the mother "has a somewhat closer association, than the education of the father." The writer also holds that the factor of age at marriage is important. The relative youth of the common-school mothers explains in part their greater fecundity.

[12] Brown, Greenwood and Wood, "The Fertility of the English Middle Classes," in *Eugenics Review*, Vol. XII, 1920, pp. 158-211.
[13] *Ibid.*, p. 179.
[14] *Journal of Heredity*, Vol. XV, October, 1924, pp. 407-15.
[15] *Loc. cit.*, p. 410.

Using Holmes's figures, Banker brings out some suggestive points.[16] He shows that the mean number of children of high-school mothers, mated with fathers of all types of education (common-school, high-school and college), shows a far larger differential, when compared with the mean number of children of mothers of common-school education, also mated with fathers of all types of education, than it does when compared with the mean of college mothers mated with fathers of the different types. The mean number of children of the three groups follow:

Common-school mothers	4.03
High-school mothers	3.38
College mothers	3.23

It will be seen, as Banker points out, that "the decline in fecundity from the common-school mother to the high-school mother is over four times the decline from the latter to the college mother. To put it in another way, the high-school mother is 16 per cent less fertile than the common school mother while the college mother is only 4 per cent less fertile than the high-school mother." [17] There is no reason to suppose that the date of the high-school girl's marriage is materially delayed by her school course, or her fertility reduced because of it. High-school girls are graduated between the ages of sixteen and eighteen.[18] Therefore, the hypothesis of the relative youth of common-school mothers does not adequately explain the marked disparity between the mean number of their offspring and that of high-school mothers. If corrections for duration of marriage could be made, it is Banker's opinion that the slight disparity in the mean number of children of high-school and college mothers would be negligible, while the more marked and probably more significant difference between the means of common-school and high-school mothers would remain. It is, then, the group of high-school mothers that furnishes the chief problem. In view of these facts, Banker concludes that "education and especially formal, college education, has little or nothing to do with the declining birth-rate, that the correlations between education and fecundity which have been so greatly exploited are spurious or rather that they are simply mutual correlations with a *tertium quid* and are not directly related." [19] He further ventures the suggestion that if data concerning the

[16] "Education and Fecundity," *Journal of Heredity,* Vol. XVI, February, 1925, pp. 57-9.
[17] *Ibid.,* p. 58.
[18] Eighty-seven and one-half percent of women marry after the age of nineteen, according to the Census of 1920.
[19] Banker, *op. cit.,* p. 59.

income per head in these three types of families were available, we might find "an even more consistent correlation with fecundity than is now evident between fecundity and education. It is highly improbable that education in itself is sterilizing our population, and it is time we made search for other factors in the phenomenon." [20]

While cordially agreeing in the main with Mr. Banker's conclusions, the author desires to point out that it makes little difference in the eugenic result whether education *per se* causes the disparity in the mean number of children of high-school and college mothers on the one hand and common-school mothers on the other, or whether education is an indirect causative factor by raising the parents' standard of living. In either case, there would remain a significant disparity, alarming to eugenists. This is not to maintain that education *is* an important factor in bringing about this difference in living standards, but to suggest its possibility.

IS THE DIFFERENTIAL BIRTH-RATE A CAUSE FOR ALARM?

On its face the differential birth-rate appears to be a cause for grave concern, and has evoked sharp warnings from social statisticians in recent years. These men point out that, if a high birth-rate is a social desideratum, it is far more advantageous to society that large numbers of children should be born to intelligent, prosperous and responsible citizens, well fitted to nurture and educate their offspring, than to parents engaged in a struggle for existence which affords little time or opportunity to acquire even the fundamentals of intelligent parenthood. Conversely, they argue that if a low birth-rate is socially detrimental, how much more is it so when it is confined chiefly to the educated class, whose abilities are confidently held to be precisely those that should be transmitted to the next generation, while the high birth-rate among unskilled and untutored laborers quite destroys the social balance by flooding our cities with children of undesirable heredity and defective nurture and training.

Let us examine these facts and theories as impartially as we may. No thoughtful and well-informed student of the problem will, I believe, formulate a confident and definitive answer to the question: Is the differential birth-rate cause for social alarm? At first glance the situation seems menacing. But there are certain considerations to be kept in mind that are frequently overlooked by statisticians. In the first place, it is highly unscientific, even absurd, to assume that all the useful, gifted and desirable citizens are to be found in the ranks of the prosperous business and professional classes and all the undesirables within the ranks of wage-earners.

[20] Banker, *op. cit.*

There are too many instances of highly gifted individuals springing from the humblest and most crippling circumstances for intelligent men and women to adopt this easy theory. Social history makes clear that the production of the talented and the fit is not a monopoly of any class. To be sure, there is reliable evidence that a much higher proportion of gifted children come from families of the professional, semi-professional and business groups than from the groups of skilled and unskilled labor. Terman's admirably thorough and scientific study of 643 exceptionally gifted children in the California public schools showed that a great preponderance of these children came from the professional and commercial classes. Thus in the case of 560 fathers whose occupations were known, it was found that the professional fathers furnished 29.1% of the children, although this group constitutes only 2.9% of the population of Los Angeles and San Francisco. Similarly, the public service group of fathers furnished 4.5% of the children, although they constituted only 3.3% of the population. The commercial group, with a proportion of 36.1% of the population, furnished 46.2% of the gifted children. On the other hand, the industrial group (skilled, semi-skilled and unskilled labor), although making up 57.7% of the population, furnished only 20.2% of the gifted children.[21] Obviously, the laboring class is not furnishing its quota of children of exceptional intellectual abilities.

When, however, we consider the deprivations of the children of the industrial group with respect to cultured and stimulating home environment, intelligent parental guidance and wholesome neighborhood influences, and when we further consider the handicap of economic pressure, which necessitates out-of-school paid employment for many of these children, perhaps it is matter for surprise that slightly over one-fifth of the gifted children sprang from this class. Moreover, it is well to remember that no set of intelligence tests yet devised can claim to be a test of "pure" or innate intelligence apart from those environing conditions that determine behavior, attitudes, dispositions and tastes from the hour of birth; and no scientific psychologist maintains that they are accurate and entirely reliable tests of inborn abilities. The most that can be claimed for intelligence tests is that they are the best measures yet devised for determining the quality of native mental capacities. It would be, indeed, a confident believer in the prior importance of heredity in determining mental traits who would deny that greatly superior home environment, more highly educated and trained parents, better neighborhood conditions and

[21] Lewis M. Terman, *Genetic Studies of Genius,* Vol. I, pp. 62-3. Stanford University Press, 1925.

more leisure had influenced favorably the showing made by the non-industrial class in this investigation. How much these improved conditions would raise the proportion of gifted children in the industrial group no one, of course, can say. Possibly the gain would be slight, since Terman points out that the differences in the proportion of highly endowed children in the various classes extend down to the youngest groups between the ages of two and five years.[22] These small children would possibly be less influenced by unfavorable home conditions and education than would their older brothers and sisters. Yet it should not be overlooked that psychologists today are attaching more and more importance to the earliest years of life as powerful determinants of dispositions, tastes and interests, no less than of behavior.[23]

But even if it could be demonstrated that the percentage of intellectually superior children in the industrial group would not be appreciably increased by a substantial improvement in their environment from birth, yet the fact that slightly more than twenty percent of highly gifted children sprang from this class should make us pause before deciding that the present differential birth-rate is a grave social evil. This is, of course, not to say that the high birth-rate among the laboring class is beneficial either to the laborers or to society as a whole, but only to point out that this group is not wholly lacking in abilities of a high order and furnishes recruits to the more gifted and highly trained group in every generation.

Another point which it is well to hold in mind in attempting to reach a judgment concerning whether or not our present differential birth-rate is cause for alarm is the fact that, despite all public health measures yet inaugurated, the death-rate among the poor is relatively very high. If a family grows in numbers far beyond its means for food, clothing and shelter, Nature steps in and balances matters by means of poverty, undernourishment, sickness and death. The infant death-rate under such circumstances is tragically high, as the studies of the Federal Children's Bureau in Manchester, Fall River and New Bedford abundantly show.[24] However, improved public health work will steadily reduce this mortality rate, and thus remove one safeguard against a high birth-rate among the mediocre and the dull.

Finally, it should be remembered that all measures for increased control of life forces are initiated among the more thoughtful groups and gradually make themselves felt among the ignorant and relatively undis-

[22] Terman, *op. cit.*, Vol. I, p. 43.
[23] See John Watson, "What Is Behaviorism?" in *Harper's Magazine*, May, 1926.
[24] See *ante*, Ch. IX.

ciplined. History shows this to be the course of progress in all ages and all climes. That contraceptive methods are already known and used by skilled and highly paid workers is evidenced by the fall in the birth-rate in that group. America supplies little or no data on this question, but there is evidence in English records to sustain this theory. And it is reasonable to suppose that the same tendency to limit the size of families to the amount of family income is making itself felt among the intelligent skilled workers in our own country. Otherwise our sharply falling birth-rate cannot easily be explained. Moreover, it is to be hoped that in the near future the ban against furnishing safe and reliable contraceptive information to all citizens will be removed.

For the three reasons briefly discussed above, then, it would seem wise not to adopt an alarmist attitude toward the matter of our present selective birth-rate. "There has always been a differential birth-rate," says Dublin, "and a replacement of one group of people above by another, equally good, from below. In all ages men have raised themselves above their inherited station in life and have occupied the seats of the mighty, left vacant by those considered their superiors, who have neglected or have been incapable of performing their highest obligation to society, namely, parenthood. In all fairness, we must critically examine the current point of view and shift the emphasis in our population discussion from a glorification of the upper strata to a more generous recognition of the inherent worth of the great mass of mankind." [25]

There is a measure of truth in Mr. Dublin's statements, however unjustifiable they will no doubt appear to many psychologists and eugenists. Nevertheless, it seems idle to ignore or deny the fact that our present differential birth-rate *is* to some extent socially disadvantageous. If improved opportunities for living and for education could be secured to the unskilled working classes, it is doubtful if these groups could furnish to society so high a proportion of gifted leaders of thought and action as do the selected professional and business groups. But this is not all. Even if the native endowments of the unskilled laboring class were equal to those of the professional group it yet remains true, as we have seen, that, as conditions are at present, the families in the low-paid labor class can by no means surround their children with the cultural, stimulating influences that the offspring of professional families receive almost with their mother's milk. There is a social and cultural heredity, no less than a biological one,

[25] *Population Problems in the United States and Canada,* p. 15. Publication of the Pollak Foundation for Economic Research. Houghton Mifflin Co., Boston, 1926. By permission.

and in this respect the children of uneducated day laborers are largely disinherited. While our differential birth-rate may not be a cause for such serious concern as eugenists would have us believe, neither does it justify a cheerful indifference. Handicapped children, with meager opportunities to discover and develop their talents, cannot readily fill the depleted ranks of the cultured and low birth-rate groups.

SHOULD THE LOW BIRTH-RATE CLASSES BE URGED TO HAVE LARGE FAMILIES?

As suggested above, a vigorous propaganda has been launched by certain social statisticians who are alarmed about the ultimate consequences to society of a high birth-rate among the foreign-born and a steadily declining birth-rate among the native stock, which largely composes the cultured groups. These men have assembled data which indicate that the native stock in the United States has fallen from 67.8% of the total population in 1870 to 60.5% in 1910. In the New England and Middle Atlantic States, the disparity is even greater. The native white stock in New England decreased from 52.3% of the total white population in 1890 to 40.3% in 1910; whereas in the Middle Atlantic section, the native white stock decreased from 51.8 to 44.8 in the same period.[26] Stirred by these conditions, eugenists and others unite to condemn the education given to young women in colleges, which tends to direct their minds toward professional achievement, and which, they believe, too often operates to smother the maternal instincts that should be stimulated and developed. Thus Dublin writes: "The old virtues of womanhood need restatement today. Whatever else women learn in the schools they must be educated for their place as mothers, and democratic education must make efficient provision for this primary function." [27] He goes on to urge a "birth release" among healthy, normal people "as a primary national duty," a release deliberately undertaken with high, moral purpose.[28]

Is it conceivable that the writers who thus urge a "birth release," especially among the native, educated stock, are unacquainted with the important studies made by Cox, East, Knibbs, Pearl and others, all of which show that unless the birth-rate continues to decline in most countries, or production enormously to increase, there will be a ruthless struggle for survival in these nations half a century hence—a shortage of food and other necessities of life, followed in time by undernourishment, disease and death? It is possible that the conclusions set forth in these writings,

[26] Louis I. Dublin, "The Significance of the Declining Birth Rate," an address printed in the *Congressional Record*, January 11, 1918. Government Printing Office, Washington, 1918.
[27] *Ibid.*, p. 7.   [28] *Ibid.*, p. 8.

based as they are upon a solid substratum of facts, appear to these statisticians as unduly alarmist and even speculative in nature, deserving little serious consideration from intelligent men and women. The group of eugenists that is disturbed about our differential birth-rate does not fail to point out that the evils they combat are with us here and now; that the Anglo-Saxon cultured stock actually *is* giving place to a peasant stock from southeastern Europe which has failed to make any important contributions to human culture and never will, in their opinion. This suicide of superior stock being a menacing fact of the present, big with possibilities of social deterioration, the eugenists ask: Why waste time worrying over a purely speculative danger two or three generations from now? Contemporary ills have always loomed so large in the eyes of mankind as to blind them to more serious evils in the distant offing and thus have prevented such a thoughtful, comprehensive consideration of social questions as would take account of all the factors in a complicated problem.

Let us consider what consequences might follow a concerted social effort to bring about a "birth release" among the educated classes, by means of social propaganda as well as by a redirection of the education of women which should emphasize their primary functions as mothers. In the case of college education, it may be said that in the state universities solid courses in home economics have been introduced within the last fifteen years which, because of their scientific basis and many-sided consideration of the problems of home-making, have done much to break down an earlier prejudice against "domestic science" courses in higher education. Moreover, the wave of interest in more intelligent parenthood that has swept the country during the last five years has resulted in the establishment of research departments for the study of the child of pre-school age, such as the Institute of Child Welfare Research in Teachers College, Columbia University; the Merrill-Palmer school in Detroit; and the Child Welfare Research Station of the University of Iowa. Even the ancient strongholds among the liberal arts colleges for women are beginning to respond to the social pressure of this widespread dynamic interest. Witness the establishment of the Institute for the Coördination of Women's Interests at Smith College (see *ante,* p. 293), and the new department of euthenics opened at Vassar two years ago. This last venture aims to "apply scientific knowledge to the complex problems of adjustment between individual and environment, with especial emphasis on the home and the family." A recent gift from an alumna makes possible the building of a laboratory for the scientific study and demonstration of the care and nurture of little children from two to four years of age.

From the eugenists' point of view, this tendency to educate women to be intelligent housewives and mothers is all to the good, and should be extended to every higher institution educating women. These men proceed upon the theory that the inclusion in women's education of *compulsory* courses glorifying the family and stressing the social importance of high birth-rates among the superior class will increase the marriage rate among college women, and will stimulate them to bear and rear numerous offspring. Needless to say this is largely a hypothesis. It is true that the marriage rate among the women graduates of schools of home economics in our state colleges and universities is markedly higher than the prevailing rate among graduates of liberal arts colleges. But the careful statistician recognizes that a principle of selection was at work from the beginning in determining the group that chose to study for an A. B. in liberal arts, with a profession in view, and their sisters whose primary interests were in the home-making arts. As we have seen, most of the young women in state colleges of home economics are looking forward to marriage and motherhood as their life career. It is by no means certain that the introduction of home-making courses into liberal arts colleges and professional schools would raise the marriage and birth-rates in this group of intellectual and professionally minded women one point.

The reasons why intelligent people of the professional and business classes have few children are by no means wholly selfish, as was suggested in the previous chapter. This is precisely the group most likely to have a developed sense of personal and social responsibility, although this is obviously not always true. To intelligent and far-sighted parents, children will always appear as serious responsibilities not to be lightly assumed, as is the case among the unthinking and the improvident. Their nurture, education and training for vocation involve large outlays of time, energy and money, and this fact is thoughtfully considered before a new child is brought into the world. The education of women in a deeper appreciation of the problems of child nature and child nurture quite conceivably might result in more rather than less caution in assuming the duties of parenthood.

Therefore it is doubtful whether lessons in eugenics given to college women, even if accompanied by well-meaning exhortations to fulfil their so-called duty to society by bearing at least three children would ever produce the desired results. Addressing the Sixth International Neo-Malthusian and Birth Control Conference in March, 1925, Dr. Raymond Pearl expresses virile skepticism with regard to this method:

"My fourth, and final point, is that the efforts of the eugenists to correct the evils of the differential birth-rate, by endeavoring to induce the socially, economically, and in some part biologically, superior classes to reproduce more freely, as a sort of transcendental social duty, has not met with any statistically discernible success, and in my opinion is not likely to. . . . As was recently pointed out editorially in England: 'A man may be induced by patriotic motives to die for his counrty, but hardly to procreate children for her, unless he can be convinced that those children will find places to fill at least as good as that he occupies. Rhetoric about race suicide, the decline of the empire, and so on, will never be accepted by the potential parent as a substitute for an economic guarantee.' " [29]

But if educated women cannot be impelled by admonition to engage in a "cradle competition" with their less privileged sisters of the working class, is it not both possible and desirable to attack the problem of the differential birth-rate from another front? Why not set about removing the obstacles, in law and custom, which prevent giving to the burdened mothers of the poor the knowledge that would make it possible for them to limit the size of their families? The enormous benefits of the children who *are* born to parents in these low income groups, not alone in material welfare but in parental guidance and training, seem undeniable. Mothers who have only one or two mouths to feed, instead of four to eight, would find it possible to live in decency on their husbands' wages and, not being pushed into industry by economic necessity, might and probably would often prove good home-makers and mothers, especially if expert guidance were given them by visiting nurses and furnished in the maternity centers and child clinics now happily being instituted.

But, it may be argued, the working classes want large families; they would not limit the number of their offspring if they could. This statement is almost wholly speculative, with a very frail underpinning of facts. Because working men and women have numerous children, it is inferred that they always would have, no matter how much enlightened information they received. Such is not the case in France, where the birth-rate tends to be low *in all classes*. Moreover, the letters which pour in upon Margaret Sanger and the New York Clinical Research Bureau from mothers of the poor are pathetic, sometimes tragic evidence of the desire of these women for the knowledge which will set them free from being "breeding machines," and will enable them to rear a few children in decent comfort. One of these mothers, who had married at seventeen and had borne seven children in twelve years into conditions of grinding poverty, wrote Mrs. Sanger:

[29] "The Differential Birth-rate," in *Birth Control Review,* October, 1925, pp. 301-2.

"Now, Mrs. Sanger, I did not want those children, because, even in my ignorance I had sense enough to know I had no right to bring those children into such a world where they could not have decent care, for I was not able to do it myself nor hire it done. I prayed and prayed that they would die when they were born." [30] Probably no one factor has so stiffened Mrs. Sanger's resolve and energized her efforts to bring about the repeal of existing laws prohibiting the dissemination of knowledge of contraceptive methods than the hundreds of appeals she receives every year from desperate mothers pleading to be delivered from bringing another child into a struggling family.

In view of these well-attested facts, would it not seem the part of wisdom to secure to poor families the deliverance many of them crave, rather than preaching to the educated groups the questionable duty of being fruitful and over-populating the earth? But, some one may say, will this policy not eventuate in a stationary population? Suppose it does. What, after all, are the conspicuous advantages of an ever-growing populace? Probably the real cause of the opposition of most governments to birth control is the ever-present fear that some other nation, which prohibits the dissemination of contraceptive knowledge, will have a substantial advantage in numbers in time of war. Should all enlightened countries agree to remove obstacles to the spread of regulated scientific information regarding birth control, this bogy would vanish into thin air.

ARGUMENTS ADVANCED AGAINST BIRTH CONTROL

In every country where the issue of birth control has been raised, there are many well-meaning and intelligent people who are sternly opposed on moral and religious grounds to the spread of this knowledge. Needless to say their arguments deserve open-minded consideration.

The Objections on the Side of Religion.

Orthodox religious believers in considerable numbers hold the view that refusal of parenthood, or any effort to curb natural fertility thwarts the purpose of God in the marriage relation. This group believes that in reproduction "God delegates to His creatures the exercise of creative power" to be "exercised worthily for Him"; that it is possible to improve the conditions in which human beings live so that life may abound on the earth and the children of men become the family of God, growing in likeness to the divine and gaining fellowship with Him. This is God's intention in the creation of man; therefore "it is to be desired that to as

---

[30] Sanger, *Woman and the New Race,* p. 82. By permission of Brentano's, New York, 1920.

many human beings as can be the opportunity of realizing such a destiny should be given." [31]

It will be noted that the author of the above statements believes that it is possible to improve social conditions in such wise that parents may indulge in large families with reasonable assurance that their children's development will not be hindered by adverse circumstances. "We should have as many persons as possible," he writes, "even if some of them may have to put up with fewer things that there may be enough for all." [32] But when we seek light as to how this economic transformation is to be brought about, whereby the prosperous accept plain living in order that the poor may be fruitful, we learn nothing save that adverse conditions "can and must be changed" and a rising birth-rate made to coincide with a falling death-rate. Evidently the writer knows nothing of the studies made by his countrymen, Cox and others, plainly revealing population pressure in Great Britain; or, if he has read these books, they have been brushed aside as speculative and unimportant. The only worth-while question, in his opinion, is how to populate the earth more rapidly, by some method of social reform, not even tentatively outlined, so that God's intention for the race (as he conceives it) may be fulfilled. No doubt, millions of members of Christian sects hold similar views and are equally vague with respect to methods of realizing this "far-off, divine event to which the whole creation moves."

The foregoing are not the only reasons advanced by the religious group against birth control. Not only is the practice of contraception stigmatized as a deliberate thwarting of the will of God, but the Lambeth Conference of Bishops of the Anglican church went on record in 1908 to the following effect:

"The Conference regards with alarm the growing practice of the artificial restriction of the family, and earnestly calls upon all Christian people to discourage the use of all artificial means of restriction as demoralizing to character, and hostile to the national welfare." [33]

When we ask in what ways character is demoralized by the use of contraceptives, we learn that, in the first place this practice involves an interference with the processes of nature, established by God, an interference which was punished in the Biblical story of Onan by death; [34]

---

[31] See Rev. Alfred E. Garvie, "Social and Religious Aspects," in Marchant (Editor), *The Control of Parenthood*, pp. 168-73. G. P. Putnam's Sons, New York and London, 1920.

[32] *Ibid.*, p. 171.

[33] Quoted in Drysdale, *The Small Family System*, p. 34.

[34] See *Gen.* xxxviii.

secondly, limitation of families is dangerous and wrong because it removes the need for self-discipline and self-control, and opens the sluice gates to unbridled passion. It is a little difficult to treat with fair-minded tolerance the first statement of the theological opponents of birth control. Setting aside the story of Onan, as referring to the Jewish people in a primitive stage of social development and thus inapplicable to the moral ideas and customs of the twentieth century, let us consider the charge that the use of devices for restricting births is "unnatural" and therefore sinful. It cannot be denied that contraception hinders the regular course of nature and in that sense is unnatural. But, as John Stuart Mill once said, the whole history of civilized life is an attempt to redirect and control nature. Medical art and science reveal one long struggle to defeat nature's ways, and the same may be said of surgical operations. Our artificial lives in heated houses are thoroughly unnatural, as are all our efforts to harness the physical and chemical energies of nature so that they may serve human ends. This argument seems unworthy of more detailed and serious consideration.

But what of the second point, that artificial restriction of births removes all motives for self-control in sexual relations within marriage? If this charge were well sustained, it would be a serious argument against the practice of contraception. But is it? In the first place has "the fear of consequences," in other words the dread of procreating unwanted offspring, prevented gross sexual license within marriage? The history of the marital relation, ancient and modern, reveals huge families, overburdened mothers, and undesired children born every year into homes unable to provide for them. Family history must be regarded as furnishing emphatic denial of the theory of the disciplinary effect of "fear of consequences." Could the wives of the past but speak with entire frankness, what tales would they not tell of forced marital relations at any and all times! Not self-control, but license seems to have been the rule in marriage—a reproductive license not only sanctioned, but on the whole encouraged by the Church, on the theory that a married pair are under obligation to "be fruitful and multiply." Even to this day, the three largest religious bodies in Europe and America—the Protestants, the Roman Catholics and the Jews—hold that the primary purpose of marriage is procreation of children, life companionship, love and mutual help and comfort being distinctly secondary ends. In a memorandum prepared by a Committee of Bishops of the Church of England, women are urged not to "shrink from the heavy burdens which marriage may entail upon them"; and a distinguished churchman has gone on record to the effect that the "performance of the marital act *at any time* should be at the will of the woman as well as of the man." [35]

But the religious opponents of birth control, while forced to admit that large families have been the rule in the past and are still almost universal among the ignorant and improvident, urge that a fine chivalry toward women has been for centuries developing in men, a consideration for their wishes in the matter of childbearing which will be completely destroyed if devices for preventing conception come into general use. Instead of chivalrous self-control on the part of husbands, there will ensue a "purely animal relation" between the married pair which will tend to lower them to the level of the brutes. In answer it may be said that, while chivalrous conduct of men toward their wives with respect to what is very revealingly called their "marital rights" no doubt exists among a small minority of men, especially in the class that has enjoyed the influences of a refined home environment, it has never been present in the mass of men. Nevertheless, regard for the personality of women *is* gradually increasing among educated men; and hand in hand with this will go respect for women's inalienable personal rights, of which the right to choice of motherhood is one of the most fundamental. On this question, age-old tradition concerning the man's "rights" in marriage is in conflict with modern ideas of individual freedom. But this does not constitute an argument against contraception. Under a régime of birth control, "chivalry" will still be a necessary attribute of both husband and wife. Both should be taught to have regard for each other's moods and desires, and self-control enough to refuse to force marital intercourse upon an indifferent or reluctant partner. The theory that the use of methods to prevent conception would result in a purely "animal relation" of husband and wife has its roots in medieval asceticism, which has always been blinded to the essential spiritual beauty of the physical expression of love on the part of mates who truly love each other. Sexual intercourse *may* be a beautiful thing, whether or no children are desired as its outcome. That in many instances it is gross and unlovely testifies to the failure of society to hold the physical aspect of marriage in high regard and to appreciate the importance of educating youth in an understanding of its finer spiritual possibilities. Perhaps some day we shall be intelligent enough to provide for our young men and women as careful preparation for marriage and parenthood as we now furnish for business and war.

[35] See Meyer, "Social and Religious Aspects," in Marchant (Editor), *The Control of Parenthood,* pp. 143, 146-7. Italics mine. G. P. Putnam's Sons, New York and London, 1920.

Objections from the Side of Patriotism.

As populations increase in every nation, numbers tend to outstrip production. Then inevitably comes the time when governments become actively concerned in securing fresh territories blest with virgin natural resources. In defense of aggressive policies toward weak and undeveloped states; they advance plausible seeming arguments to the effect that they must have more land and access to raw materials to feed their superfluous millions, to increase production and to stave off unemployment. The economic cause of war is not the sole one, but it is the most important. Prior to the World War, the principal nations of Europe were engaged in a desperate competitive struggle to secure new lands to make homes for their people, new sources of raw materials, new markets for their goods. Within thirty years after Belgium's seizure of the Congo region about 1880, Africa had been largely carved up among Great Britain, France, Germany and Belgium. The fundamental cause of the cataclysm of 1914-1918 was the bitter economic rivalry of these nations, each of which feared to fall behind in the race for territory and resources. Cox quotes a German writer as stating in 1901: "Because the German people nowadays increase at the rate of 800,000 inhabitants a year, they need both room and nourishment for the surplus. . . . As a world power in the world market we must assert our place and make it secure in order that the younger hands may find room and opportunity for employment." [36] But Germany was by no means alone in holding this view. Great Britain, an island kingdom, with a rapidly swelling population, has during more than a century seized and held the lands that compose her "far-flung empire" chiefly because she needed outlets for a redundant population as well as means of feeding and employing her millions. The same holds true of Belgium and France.

The intimate relation between population pressure and ambitious policies provocative of war seems obvious enough. Sometimes the struggle centers around securing raw materials, sometimes around the crucial problem of obtaining access to thinly populated regions which would serve as colonies for a too numerous people. Thus we find Japan, with an area of 261,000 square miles, inhabited by 60,000,000 souls (1925), desperately seeking outlets for her surplus population in Australia, Canada and the United States. We are all aware of the animosities, dangerous to peace, that have grown out of the legislation enacted in these countries to exclude the Oriental peoples.

[36] Cox, *op. cit.*, p. 80. Quoted from *Conquest and Kultur*, p. 47. By permission of G. P. Putnam's Sons, New York and London, 1923.

It would seem as if every man and woman with a modicum of knowledge of history would clearly perceive the connection between over-population and war, and would eagerly seek ways and means of restricting the growth of peoples within the limits of territorial space and productive capacity. But such, unfortunately, is not the case. The second National Birth-Rate Commission, which presented its report to the British people in 1920, asks with anxiety:

"In the event of a war similar to that which we have just experienced, what would happen to us with a greatly reduced birth-rate? Surely all we have would be taken, and we must become slaves."

Commenting on this statement, Cox declares: "This can only mean that English people are to breed children as a protection against the danger of war. . . . But if that advice is good for the people of England, it is equally good for the peoples of other countries, and the more fully the advice is followed the more frequent must be the racial struggles for room to live." [37]

The essential truth of this statement seems only too obvious and compelling. Yet governments approach the whole question from the point of view that wars are inevitable, since human nature is as it is. Therefore the people must be reminded from time to time of their patriotic duty to breed children for national defense in future wars, as well as for national power and prestige in piping times of peace. It is a striking fact in this connection that France, which has hitherto adopted a matter-of-fact attitude toward birth control, recognizing it as a means of keeping the French population within the national means of subsistence, has been deeply concerned about her low birth-rate since the close of the World War. Actuated by fear and suspicion of Germany, the French legislature has recently enacted drastic laws against the spread of birth control knowledge.

Thus the mad race for armaments may easily be paralleled by an equally mad race to excel in man-power—and all to the end that countries may be in a position to engage in a warfare which modern scientific knowledge will make so immeasurably destructive that such a conflict may well result in the suicide of the human race. Instead of challenging each other to a competition in birth-rates, would it not be the part of wisdom for the civilized nations of the world to agree that a moral obligation rests upon each of them to restrict its numbers within the limits of its territory and its capacity to feed and employ its people, thus avoiding the chief causes of conflict with its neighbors?

"What is wanted," declares Cox, "is a League of Low Birth-Rate

[37] Cox, *op. cit.*, p. 94. By permission.

Nations, prepared to take joint action, if necessary, against any race that by its too great fecundity is threatening the peace of the world." [38]

There is another, and more personal, aspect of this question of birth control and patriotic duty that merits consideration. Upon woman, the bearer of the generations, will increasingly fall the responsibility for opposing the cutthroat competition of nations that leads to war, first, by striving to establish reasonable methods of settling menacing national controversies, and, second, by refusing to be deceived by the arguments of militaristic governments into the belief that it is a high act of patriotism to bear children for the purposes of war. When woman was a chattel, she was unable to refuse to bring children into the world to fight her lord's battles; now that she is a free person, she must not be cajoled into accepting the ancient theory that her lot is to be the mother of warriors. Margaret Sanger has vigorously expressed this thought:

"Upon woman the burden and the horrors of war are heaviest. . . . Hers is the crushing weight and the sickening of soul. And it is out of her womb that those things proceed. When she sees what lies behind the glory and the horror, the boasting and the burden, and gets the vision, the human perspective, she will end war. . . . For she will refuse longer to produce the human food upon which the monster feeds." [39]

The Moral Issues Involved.

Many thoughtful men and women are opposed to birth control for moral reasons. Some of these have been touched upon in the discussion of the views of the theological group. But there are a few points raised by the moralists that merit special consideration. In the first place they seriously object to the use of artificial devices for preventing conception on the grounds (1) that there will result a deplorable increase in sexual immorality outside of marriage; (2) "that there is a good deal of selfishness behind the empty cradle and the celibate club"; (3) that there is danger of mechanization of the intimate love that finds expression in marital intercourse to the point where men and women tend to adopt what Professor Thomson calls "a mere natural history view of marriage and children"; [40] (4) that if, for good reasons, no more children should be born into a family, continence in marriage should be practised rather than artificial restriction.

Let us briefly examine each of these points. First, there is the charge

[38] Cox, *op. cit.*, p. 98.
[39] Sanger, *op. cit.*, pp. 165-6. By permission of Brentano's, Inc., New York, 1920.
[40] In Marchant (Editor), *The Control of Parenthood*, p. 31. By permission of G. P. Putnam's Sons, New York and London, 1920.

that legalizing the free dissemination, in public clinics, by competent doctors and nurses, of information concerning the prevention of conception would greatly increase sexual immorality. In answer it may be frankly admitted at the outset that there is no certain guarantee that irregular sexual unions would not be more numerous under a régime of publicly sanctioned birth control. But in those countries—Holland, New Zealand and Australia—where contraceptive methods have long been known and practised, with no legal bar, there has been no charge brought by moralists that sexual morality is deteriorating. Moreover, persons who object to birth control on this ground can hardly be well informed with regard to the enormous amount of sexual irregularity that has always existed in society. The dread of bringing undesired children into the world has not prevented prostitution, or seduction, or voluntary irregular unions among young people, from time immemorial. It is not unreasonable to hold, as Cox suggests,[41] that if young men and women knew that they could prevent the birth of a child until they were prepared to rear it properly, more of them would marry at an early age, and to this extent sexual irregularities would be reduced.

But if it could be demonstrated that irregular sexual unions would increase with knowledge of contraceptive methods, yet, even then, it is by no means certain that the imparting of such knowledge should be condemned. The opposition takes its stand on the theory that the fear of producing illegitimate children, socially stigmatized from their birth, acts as an important check on sexual intercourse outside marriage. There is very little in the records to support this view. In the United States, where Federal and state statutes prohibit the giving of information about birth restriction and the sale of contraceptive devices, the number of illegitimate births in 1923 was 37,823, or 23.3 per 1,000 births. In 1921, the ratio per thousand births was 24.4. It should be added that these rates are materially increased by the inclusion of the illegitimacy figures for negroes, which are very high. Yet, among the white population in 1923, there were 20,518 illegitimate children born, a rate of 13.8 per thousand white births.[42] In England and Wales in the decade 1901-10, the average rate was markedly higher, being 40 per thousand births.[43]

The cruel treatment meted out in Christian countries to the innocent child born out of marriage appears to have accomplished little in preventing illicit sexual intercourse. But if the dissemination of knowledge of methods

---

[41] Cox, *op. cit.*, p. 163.
[42] "Birth, Stillbirth and Infant Mortality Statistics for the Birth Registration Area of the United States," p. 19. Bureau of the Census, 1923.
[43] Cox, *op. cit.*, p. 164.

of birth restriction were legalized, it is highly probable that the number of illegitimate births would sharply decrease, not, of course, because of a decrease in sexual irregularity, but because the means of preventing the birth of babies doomed to lives of shame would be generally known and used. Cox gives figures from the Report of the Registrar General of Great Britain for 1919 showing that the rate of illegitimate births had fallen from sixty-one per thousand in the decade 1861-70, when birth restriction was not practised, to forty per thousand in 1901-10. Not only the rate but the volume of illegitimacy fell from an average of 45,700 births in the earlier period to an average of 37,000 in the more recent. This represents a decrease of more than 8,000 illegitimate births yearly. Commenting on these figures Cox says:

"In itself this is a most powerful argument for the still wider dissemination of the knowledge of methods of birth control. For illegitimacy involves a cruel wrong to the child and a distinct injury to the nation. Fair play to the child requires that it should be a unit in a recognized family. . . . But the illegitimate child is often deprived not only of the father's influence but also of the mother's care. For the unmarried mother without means to maintain the child dumps it in a workhouse ward, or in some other institution for the care of parentless children. How gravely the illegitimate child suffers in the earliest months of its life is seen by comparing the rates of infant mortality for legitimate and illegitimate children. In London, in the year 1919, the number of legitimate infants who died under 12 months was (omitting decimals) 77 out of every thousand born; the corresponding figure for illegitimate infants was 233.[44]

"In the face of all these facts surely it is inhuman to attempt to use illegitimacy as a weapon against unchastity. It means that tens of thousands of children, who by the nature of the case must themselves be innocent of any offense, are called upon to suffer for the sins of their parents. That may be ecclesiastical law, but it is directly contrary to the spirit of English law which declares that it is better that the guilty should escape than that the innocent should be punished. It is a far less evil that a hundred women should indulge in irregular intercourse free from the fear of conception than that one illegitimate child should be born."[45]

Many, perhaps the larger part, of the readers of the last statement will disagree with it in greater or less degree. But in fairness, we should ask ourselves which is the better weapon with which to fight sexual laxity

[44] Cox, *op. cit.*, pp. 165-6. Reference here to *Registrar General's Report*, 1919.
[45] *Ibid.*, pp. 165-6. By permission of G. P. Putnam's Sons, New York and London, 1923.

—the fear of consequences, which has so conspicuously failed of satisfactory results, or the method of sound enlightenment and training from infancy, a method the race has hardly begun to try out because of an ancient taboo? Character building, grounded on knowledge, is a slow means of social improvement, but it is the only certain one.

The second objection of the moralists is to the effect that unrestricted knowledge of birth control will have the effect of encouraging selfish motives in parents and result in many childless homes. There will, no doubt, be fathers and mothers who refuse from selfish motives to procreate children. In ancient society parents of that type exposed helpless infants they did not wish to rear, or resorted to abortions. But shall information of such signal advantage to scores of millions of laborers and professional workers be withheld because a proportion of men and women are motivated chiefly by a narrow self-interest? It is pertinent to ask whether such persons would be desirable parents in any case. Furthermore, it should be kept in mind that the true motives actuating parents to have few children or none at all are not matters of public knowledge, and it is only too easy to assume that these considerations are selfish, when they may be both wise and altruistic.

The third objection against dissemination of knowledge of contraceptive methods is based upon the fear that the sexual relation would be so mechanized that husband and wife might develop a purely materialistic attitude toward what should be a beautiful experience. It is possible that there may be some truth in this objection. Yet it seems to the writer highly improbable that men and women of sensitive refinement, who deeply love each other, will gradually be transformed into crass materialists because they employ devices to prevent conception. As for the many in whose eyes sexual intercourse is merely a physical experience, mechanical devices might serve to make them more materialistic; but it does not seem probable. Not the presence or absence of artificial contrivances renders husbands and wives capable or incapable of the highest form of marital union, but the inner selves they bring to this intimate act of love.

This leads us to the final objection of the opponents of birth control on moral grounds. A very considerable number of theologians and church people are willing to admit that, in certain instances, parents of limited means or defective mental or physical health should not have large families. But this group stigmatizes the use of devices for restricting births as "unnatural" and therefore profoundly immoral. They urge instead that husband and wife observe a temporary or even permanent continence within marriage as the only moral means of preventing conception. This proposal has met with adverse criticism from physicians of high standing on the ground that the complete suppression of the sex instinct, while living in the intimacy of the marriage relation, may be, and not infrequently is, harmful in its effects upon health of mind and body. This is not to say that self-control is not a good thing, both within and without marriage. Nor does it means that sexual impulses may not be diverted into intellectual, æsthetic or social channels and made to energize worth-while endeavor with no loss to health. But the total repression of the sex urge over many years or a lifetime *may* bring about grave nervous disorders. Margaret Sanger quotes Dr. J. Rutgers, founder of birth control clinics in Holland, in his *Rassenverbesserung* as follows:

"Physiology teaches that every function gains in power and efficiency through a certain degree of control, but that the too extended suppression of a desire gives rise to pathological disturbances and in time cripples the function. Especially in the case of women may the damage entailed in continued sexual abstinence bring about deep disturbances." [46]

Again, Dr. William A. Pusey writes that "those who, like physicians, get a view of the concealed part of the motives and activities of life must realize the supreme importance to the happiness of mankind of a proper sexual life. It is society's business to see that this is attained by providing proper conditions of married life. Civilization is built upon the family, and satisfactory civilization can be built only upon satisfactory family life. I do not mean to intimate that happiness in family life is dependent altogether upon sexual gratification . . . but I am willing to say bluntly that sexual life is the elemental fact upon which satisfactory family life, as a rule, depends and that without sexual life, marital life, as a rule, is irreparably damaged. . . . In the lack of knowledge of . . . proper methods of birth control . . . in the uncertainties of the situation, penalties are put upon what should be the pleasure of proper sexual life in marriage that are so great that they often utterly destroy it." [47]

Abortion.

While the moral aspects of birth control are being discussed, it is necessary to consider briefly one of the most deplorable effects of government refusal to sanction instruction, under proper safeguards, in methods of birth restriction. As a result of this prohibition, women, made reckless by the prospect of bearing other children into already over-

---

[46] Sanger, *op. cit.*, p. 104. By permission of Brentano's, New York.
[47] "Medicine's Responsibilities in the Birth Control Movement," in *Birth Control Review*, May, 1925, p. 135.

burdened families, or convinced that they will not be able to survive another child-birth, often resort to the immoral and criminal practice of abortion. In a recent article, Dr. Benjamin T. Tilton sheds a stream of light on the prevalence of this practice:

"It is not generally known outside the medical profession and social workers, how widespread this practice is. It amounts in fact to a national disgrace. I say national because the United States leads all other countries in the number of abortions performed yearly. . . . It is no exaggeration to say that thousands of women die annually from the effects of these illegal operations and other thousands become chronic invalids or permanently sterile. These tragedies are a disgrace to our civilization and cry for prevention. They can be prevented and I believe alone prevented, by the dissemination (through proper channels) of Birth Control knowledge concerning scientific, safe and sure methods of contraception." [48]

The United States, then, has the dishonorable distinction of leading the world in the number of abortions annually performed. It has been estimated, on the basis of physicians', nurses' and hospital records, that over a million abortions occur in this country every year. Not a little evidence was laid before the First Birth-Rate Commission in Great Britain to the effect that in that country also, wives of the poorer laboring classes practise abortion, while the wives of highly paid workers adopt measures to prevent conception.

In the face of such facts as the above, it is difficult to understand how moralists can strain at the gnat of artificial means of family restriction, and swallow the camel of self-induced abortion—a practice not only harmful physically, if not actually fatal to the mother, but one which the law in well-nigh every civilized state declares to be a criminal offense. The only explanation of such a position seems to be that these well-intentioned critics are ignorant of the facts regarding the prevalence of abortion. It may be said that the women who practise this method should be taught the moral evil of their action. But when human beings are brought face to face with a serious situation, and are ignorant of a sane way of meeting it, they will feel justified in resorting to desperate measures to escape from the trap in which they are caught.

THE BIRTH CONTROL MOVEMENT

Space prevents any but the briefest consideration of the rise and development of the birth control movement. Voluntary restriction of births seems to have begun in France in the first decade of the nineteenth

[48] *Birth Control Review*, March, 1925, p. 71.

century. In that period there was a striking fall in the birth-rate, from about thirty-nine per thousand in 1774 to thirty-two per thousand in the decade 1801-10. The death-rate correspondingly dropped from thirty-seven to twenty-eight. During the entire century, both the birth-rate and the death-rate have fallen steadily and proportionately, until at the present time the French birth-rate is about 18.5 per thousand and the death-rate 16.0, making a rate of increase of 1.6 per thousand. It is a striking fact that the natural rate of increase in France is only .4 per thousand less than it was in 1774, when the birth-rate was thirty-nine and the death-rate reached thirty-seven. Despite this fact, however, the French government has been alarmed about the national birth-rate ever since the World War. Animated, no doubt, by fear and suspicion of other countries, bred by the War, the government passed an anti-Malthusian law in 1920, absolutely suppressing all practical birth control propaganda and prohibiting the sale of artificial devices for preventing conception.[49]

The first country in Europe to approach the problem of birth restriction in a scientific and broadly social spirit was Holland, where a Neo-Malthusian League was formed in 1881. Four years later the first birth control clinic in the world was opened in Amsterdam by Dr. Aletta Jacobs, who has been an enthusiastic worker in behalf of birth restriction for more than a generation. In 1925, fifty-four clinics with eight doctors and fifty-six nurses in charge, had been established in Holland, for the purpose of giving free scientific information to women concerning contraceptive methods.[50] These clinics are sanctioned by the Dutch government. It is a significant fact that the birth-rate in forty-one cities of Holland is not so low as in selected cities of Great Britain, Germany and Austria.

Other countries where information concerning artificial means of birth restriction is available to the masses are Australia and New Zealand. In both these Commonwealths, the birth-rates have fallen sharply in the last two decades, but so, likewise, have the death rates, which are the lowest in the world. In 1915, the Australian birth-rate was 27.3, and the death rate only 10.7; while in New Zealand, the respective rates were 25.3 and 9.1.

In Great Britain, Dr. Marie Stopes and others have done valiant work in recent years in an attempt to break down the prejudice of the British Government and people against the dissemination of information concerning birth control. On April 28, 1926, the House of Lords, by a vote of

[49] Hardy, "The Truth about France," in *Birth Control Review*, November, 1925, pp. 309-10.
[50] Sanger, in *Birth Control Review*, January, 1925, p. 20.

57 to 44, passed a resolution of Lord Buckmaster, former Lord Chancellor of England, requesting "His Majesty's Government . . . to withdraw all instructions given to, or conditions imposed on Welfare Committees for the purpose of causing such committees to withhold from married women in their district information, when sought by such women, as to the best means of limiting their families." [51] This has recently been enacted. Contraceptive information is now being given in maternity centers maintained by Welfare Committees in Great Britain.

In the United States, the work of the advocates of birth control has been seriously hampered by the mistaken efforts of the late Anthony Comstock, founder of the Society for the Suppression of Vice. In 1873, this well-meaning but misguided reformer succeeded in inducing Congress to pass a Federal obscenity act, preventing the circulation through the mails of vicious literature and pictures, and to include under the term *obscene* all literature or devices designed to prevent conception. Later acts of Congress made the original law applicable to all common carriers, including express companies, as well as to the mails.

Following the lead of the Federal government, many of the states of the Union have enacted laws to the same effect.[52] Therefore no important advance will be made in the direction of establishing birth control clinics in the United States until these laws are amended or repealed. Two organizations—the Birth Control League and the Voluntary Parenthood League—have worked with fine courage and persistence, in the face of hostile public opinion, to secure the amendment of the existing obscenity laws in such wise as to remove information concerning contraceptives from its present grotesque classification among things obscene. In this crusade Mrs. Margaret Sanger has been the chief American leader, and her influence has recently been extended to the Orient by means of lectures and writings. Nowhere in the world is population pressure so great as in India, China and Japan; and it should be cause for gratification that these enormously over-peopled lands are showing some faint signs of interest in birth control propaganda.[53] The movement can hardly spread far, however, so long as ancestor worship continues.

In the United States, clinics have been established in New York City, Los Angeles, Berkeley and Oakland, where knowledge concerning methods of preventing conception may be given to women *when such information is necessary to cure or prevent disease*. In the case of New York, the

[51] See *Birth Control Review*, June, 1926, p. 205.
[52] See the digest of state laws by Worthington, in the *Journal of Social Hygiene*, Vol. IX, November, 1923, p. 458.
[53] See *Birth Control Review*, January, 1925, pp. 8-9, 12-3.

State Court of Appeals rendered a judgment in 1918 that a physician has the right to prescribe contraceptives in cases where conception would entail disease or death. Six years later a Clinical Research Bureau was opened in New York City, in charge of a competent woman physician, and here women who fall under the provisions of the law may obtain the help of which they are in serious need. In less than two weeks from its opening, the Bureau had treated 900 patients. This is a small beginning, but, needless to say, all great social movements at their inception seem to the onlooker so feeble as to be almost negligible. It is, perhaps, a safe prophecy that another generation will see the battle for birth restriction won in most of the civilized countries of the Western world.

TOPICS FOR REPORTS

1. Economic Aspects of Birth Control.
    Harold Cox, *The Problem of Population,* Ch. II. G. P. Putnam's Sons, New York and London, 1923.
2. Ethical Problems of Birth Restriction.
    Ibid., Ch. VI.
3. Increasing the Marriage Rate and Birth-Rates of the Superior.
    Paul Popenoe and R. H. Johnson, *Applied Eugenics,* Chs. XII, XIII. The Macmillan Co., New York, 1923.
4. Religious Aspects of Birth Control.
    James Marchant (Editor), *The Control of Parenthood,* pp. 96-135, 158-78. G. P. Putnam's Sons, New York and London, 1920.

CHAPTER XXI

THE RISING TIDE OF DIVORCE

INCREASE OF DIVORCE: DIVORCE STATISTICS

O F the many twentieth-century problems relating to marriage and the family, none has so disturbed socially minded men and women and provoked such vigorous controversies as has the question of our ever-increasing divorce rate. The two earliest government Reports on Marriage and Divorce, the first issued by Hon. Carroll D. Wright, Commissioner of Labor, in 1889, and the second by the Bureau of the Census in 1908-09, cover the forty-year period from 1867 to 1906 inclusive. In 1914, the International Committee on Marriage and Divorce wrote the Director of the Census urging the collection of more recent statistics because of the growing demand for an amendment to the Federal Constitution conferring on Congress the power to legislate on all questions of marriage and divorce—a power which now resides in the State. The petition stated that if this proposed measure were to be intelligently considered, all the facts must be known. In 1917, the House of Representatives appropriated a sum for the collection of statistics in this field, and the Census Bureau decided to use this appropriation to secure the figures on marriage and divorce for the year 1916 and for each year thereafter. The report for 1916 was published in 1919, and since that time census reports have been issued for the years 1922, 1923, 1924 and 1925. There is available for the student of divorce statistics, then, a long record covering forty years (1867-1906) together with five annual reports published between 1916 and 1926.

A study of the earlier reports reveals a continuous, almost unbroken augmentation in the number of divorces for the period 1867 to 1906. The total number of divorces in 1867 was 9,937; in ten years, the number had increased to 15,687, an increase of 57.8%. In 1887, after another decade had passed, the number of divorces was 27,919, an increase of nearly eighty percent over the year 1877; in 1897, the total number was 44,699, an increase of sixty percent over 1887; while in 1906, at the end of the period, divorces had risen to 72,062, an increase of 61.2% over the year 1897. The report of 1916 shows little diminution in the rise of the tide of divorce. The number of divorces granted in that year was 112,036,

an increase of fifty-five percent over 1906.[1] In 1925, the most recent year
for which statistics are available, the number of divorces has risen to
175,449, an increase of 56.6% in nine years. It will be seen that, in the
sixty-year period from 1867 to 1926, divorces have increased over 1,621%,
or, to put it in another way, there were considerably more than sixteen
times as many divorce decrees granted in 1925 as were granted in 1867.
Furthermore, the increase in divorces has far outstripped the population
increase. J. P. Lichtenberger [2] has reckoned the comparative percentage
increases in divorce and in annual average population for five-year periods
from 1870 to 1905. The figures follow: [3]

Year	Percentage Increase in Divorce	Percentage Increase in Population
1905	22.1	8.7
1900	36.7	9.4
1895	22.3	10.4
1890	34.8	11.3
1885	28.6	12.8
1880	33.2	13.1
1875	28.2	15.0
1870	——	——

Thus it appears that, in the five-year periods under consideration,
the percentage of divorce has increased between two and four times as
much as the percentage of population, varying with the period. In 1905,
the population was slightly more than double that of 1870 while divorces
were six times as numerous. The census report of 1916 gives us the divorce
rates per 100,000 of the population for the ten-year periods from 1890 to
1916. Beginning with a rate of fifty-three divorces to every 100,000 of
population in 1890, the rate rose to seventy-three in 1900, to eighty-four
in 1906 and to 112 in 1916.[4] The report for 1924 reckons the divorce
rate per 1,000 of population. Multiplying by 100, we get the divorce rates
(as usually reckoned) from 1916 to 1924. (See page 374.)

Perhaps the clearest idea of the tremendous acceleration of the divorce
movement can be gained by comparing the number of divorces with the
number of marriages reported in any one year. In 1916, there was almost

[1] Report for 1916, p. 13.
[2] *Divorce: A Study in Social Causation,* p. 68. Longmans, Green & Co., New
York, 1909.
[3] The percentage of increase both for divorce and for population represents the
average for the five-year period of which the year given is the median year, except
that for 1905, which is the average of the four years 1903 to 1906 inclusive.
[4] Report for 1916, p. 14.

one divorce to every 9.6 marriages; in 1925, there was one divorce granted to every 6.7 marriages. If the divorce movement continues at its present rate, we may look forward in another ten years to a ratio of one divorce to every three or four marriages.

Year	Rate
1924	152
1923	149
1922	136
1916	113

Divorce Statistics in Geographic Division and States.

A comparison of the percentage increases in divorce in the various sections of the United States for the year 1923-24, as compared with the preceding year, show clearly enough that the highest rates of increase are found in the Pacific Coast States (14.8), and the lowest in New England (2.4), while two geographic divisions—the West North Central and the East South Central—show a small decrease. In 1922-23, however, all the sections of the country showed a marked increase in the percentage of divorces over 1921-22, highest in the East South Central States (14.3) and lowest in the Middle Atlantic group (4.2). In the number of divorces granted in 1924, per 1,000 of the total population, the State of Nevada led, with a divorce rate of 13.4. Far behind, yet with high divorce rates, were Oregon (3.53), Texas (3.06), Oklahoma (2.92), California (2.88) and Washington (2.69). It will be seen that, with the exception of Nevada, Texas and Oklahoma, the three states of the Pacific division had the highest divorce rates in the country in 1924. The lowest states (per 1,000 of the population) were New York (.42), North Carolina (.54), New Jersey (.58) and Connecticut (.80). Apparently, in the Atlantic seaboard states divorce is not as freely resorted to as in the newer commonwealths of the Pacific coast, where the free, pioneer spirit still prevails.

The ratio of divorces to marriages is highest, as might be expected, in the State of Nevada, where the law requires only six months' residence in the state before an action for divorce is brought.[5] For this reason, hundreds of discontented partners, living in New York and other states where the causes of divorce are limited, take up their residence for half a year in Nevada and then bring suit for divorce. In consequence, the divorces granted in Nevada in 1924 were 1,037, while the marriages recorded were only 1,079—a ratio of almost one divorce to every marriage.

[5] This period was reduced in March, 1927, to three months.

In Oregon, the ratio was one divorce to every 2.3 marriages; in Texas, one to 4.7; in California, one to 4.9; in Oklahoma, one to 4.1 marriages.

An Analysis of Divorce Statistics.

A study of the latest Census report reveals some interesting facts. For many years, about two thirds of the divorce decrees in the country have been granted to women. In 1924, the percentage of divorces granted to the husband was 31.5; and to the wife, 68.5.[6] Apparently the proportion of decrees in favor of the wife as plaintiff is increasing. In the ten-year period from 1887 to 1906, the percentage of divorces granted to husband and wife were respectively 34.2 and 65.8. In 1896, the percentage of decrees granted the wife had risen to 66.4; and ten years later, to 67.5.[7] The small but steady increase in the proportion of divorce actions brought by the wife may indicate a growing unwillingness on the part of women to submit to conditions in the marital relation which once they tolerated or shrank from ending by means of the painful publicity of the divorce court:

The Report for 1924 further analyzes the total number of divorces with respect to the causes for which they were granted, and the percentage of decrees granted to husband and to wife for each cause. The figures follow:

Cause	Total Divorces[8]		Granted to Husband		Granted to Wife	
	Number	Percent Distrib.	Number	Percent Distrib.	Number	Percent Distrib.
All causes	168,312	100.0	52,984	100.0	115,328	100.0
Adultery	16,932	10.1	8,263	15.6	8,669	7.5
Cruelty	62,529	37.2	11,251	26.9	48,278	41.9
Desertion	55,380	32.9	24.057	45.4	31,323	27.2
Drunkenness	2,217	1.3		0.4	2,027	1.8
Neglect to provide	6,232	3.7	190		6,232	5.4
Combinations of preceding causes	11,645	6.9	1,761	3.3	9,884	8.6
All other causes	13,377	7.9	4,462	8.4	8,915	7.7

A critical study of these figures will prove rewarding. First it should be noted that the two outstanding causes of divorce are cruelty and deser-

[6] Report for 1924, p. 20.   [7] Report for 1916, p. 15.
[8] Exclusive of 2,640 cases for which no detailed statistics were obtained.

tion. Adultery—the one cause which most religious denominations in this country recognize as valid—ranks third among the important causes brought forward in the divorce court. It is noteworthy that the percentage of divorces granted to the husband for adultery is almost double the percentage awarded to the wife. The explanation of this disparity no doubt lies in the fact that women are slower than men to make public the unfaithfulness of their mates and to endure all the unsavory publicity that attends a divorce trial for marital infidelity. The women, and in some instances the men also, prefer to bring charges of cruelty or desertion if such charges have a chance of securing a decree in favor of the plaintiff. Therefore social investigators are agreed that the figures with respect to divorces granted for adultery do not reveal the true conditions. Another noteworthy fact is that the percentage of divorces granted the wife for cruelty is much higher than the percentage granted the husband, whereas the reverse is true with respect to desertion. The number of divorces granted the wife for the cause of her husband's drunkenness has fallen from 3,381 in 1916 to 2,027 in 1924, despite a large increase in population. This is quite possibly due to the effect of the prohibition law.

Since 13,377 divorces were granted in 1924 for "all other causes," the report analyzes this caption into its component causes. The figures follow:

Cause	Number	Cause	Number
"All other causes"	13,377	Lewd and lascivious behavior	157
Gross neglect of duty	8,967	Impotency	148
Separation	626	Fraud	106
Imprisonment	525	Incompatibilty	105
Vagrancy	500	Insanity	103
Conviction of felony	487	Other specified causes	245
Bigamy	240	Cause not reported	1,168

A glance at the above figures shows that the most important cause for divorce in this group is "gross neglect of duty." Obviously this is a general term including diverse causes of complaint. It is interesting to note that only 105 decrees were granted for incompatibility; yet it can hardly be doubted that this is one of the chief determining causes of the flood of divorce cases in our courts. Incompatibility probably lies at the root of a large proportion of divorces granted for "cruelty," which is a blanket term covering many forms of physical and mental suffering inflicted by one mate upon the other.

When the student of divorce statistics turns to the section dealing with the divorces contested or uncontested, it is rather startling to learn that eighty-three percent of the total number of divorces granted in 1924 were uncontested.[9] Of the 52,984 divorces granted the husband as plaintiff, 83.4% were not contested; and of the 115,328 divorces granted the wife, 82.8% were uncontested. This would appear to mean one of two things: either that the defendant has too poor a case to contest the action of the plaintiff, or that both husband and wife desire release from a rasping bond. If we had exact knowledge of the extent to which the latter motive operates to prevent husband or wife from even attempting a defense in a divorce action, we should gain a clearer realization of the fact that marital unhappiness is commonly mutual—not one-sided.

Another suggestive analysis made by the Bureau of the Census consists in classifying the divorces granted according to the duration of the marriage.[10] In 1924, 4.6% of divorces were granted to couples who had been married *less than one year*. If we add to this the percentage of divorces granted to those whose marriage had endured one year, the percentage rises to 12.3. This figure represents a marked increase over the corresponding percentages for the periods 1867 to 1886 and 1887 to 1906, which are respectively 5.1 and 5.2. Apparently, divorces granted in cases where the duration of marriage is one year or less are between two and three times more numerous now than twenty-five or thirty years ago. Of the total divorces in 1924, 38.9% were granted to persons who had been married less than five years; whereas only 8.9% were granted to the entire group of persons whose marriage had lasted "21 years and over." Obviously, the first five years of married life represent the most critical period, when adjustment and compromise are most difficult. The percentage of divorces granted in each year thereafter falls steadily, until in the twentieth year of marriage it is only 1.3.

The classification of divorces according to whether or not children were reported as affected by the decree yields some significant results. In 1924, of the parties seeking divorce, 35.7% reported the existence of children; 53.9% reported no children; and 10.4% failed to report as to children. A comparison of these percentages with the average percentages for the twenty-year period 1887 to 1906 shows that the percentage reporting children has fallen from 39.8 in the earlier period to 35.7 in 1924, and the percentage reporting no children has risen from 40.2 to 53.9 in 1924. This is one more bit of evidence of a declining birth-rate. It is significant that children were reported much more frequently in cases where the divorce was granted to the wife than in cases where the husband

[9] Report for 1924, p. 25.   [10] *Ibid.*, p. 27.

received the decree. In 39.7% of the cases where the divorce was granted to the wife, children were reported; whereas in only 26.9% of the cases where the husband received the decree were children reported. Except in those instances where the mother is manifestly an unfit guardian, the court usually assigns children to the wife. In 1924, children were assigned to the mother in 76.3% of the cases reporting children. Consequently the father may well be more reluctant than the mother to bring an action for divorce which might cost him the society of his children. In view of the popular belief that the existence of children strongly tends to make marriage more permanent, it is a striking fact that nearly forty percent of the divorces in 1924 were granted to women with children. Formerly the percentage was even higher, being 46.8 in the period 1887 to 1906, and 42.2 in 1916.[11] Probably children do act as deterrents to divorce, but not in so powerful a degree as many suppose.

The belief is widespread that divorce is far more prevalent in cities than in rural districts. On the whole, with the exception of New York City, the census figures support this view. San Francisco, with fourteen percent of the population of California, has 19.8% of the divorces; Denver, with 27.5% of the state population, has 40.7% of the divorces; Richmond, with 7.6% of the state population, has 14.6% of the divorces; Baltimore, with 51.6% of Maryland's population, has 74.4% of its divorces. Yet it is surprising that in several large cities the percentages of population and divorce tend to approximate. Some figures selected from the census report for 1924 follow:

City	Percent of State Population	Total Divorces
New Orleans	22.0	24.8
New York	52.9	50.1
Philadelphia	21.2	21.9
St. Louis	23.5	29.6

THE DIFFERENT REACTIONS EVOKED BY THE FACTS ABOUT DIVORCE

Such facts and figures as those discussed above cannot fail to call out different responses from men and women of antithetical outlooks on life. The attitudes of two groups in particular deserve special consideration. These may be called the ecclesiastical and the sociological groups. In the first are the clergy of all the orthodox faiths and their followers, with some judges and other earnest people; in the second will be found most of those individuals who have given some study to the genesis and evolution of

[11] Report for 1924, p. 31.

social ideas and have, in consequence, what may be called the sociological point of view in judging all social problems.

The Ecclesiastical Point of View.

In the sincere opinion of the ecclesiastical group, divorce is an unmitigated evil, and every new legal cause for the dissolution of marriage is looked upon as a fresh "assault upon the marriage compact." Divorce statutes are generally regarded as "threatening the very foundations of the home" and in consequence as "undermining the very substructure of society." The Catholic doctrine regarding divorce is stated in the seventh canon of the Council of Trent, where it is declared that the "consummated marriage of Christians can never be dissolved as to the vinculum or bond, save by the death of either party." [12] In an Encyclical of 1880 Leo XIII described the consequences of divorce as follows:

"Divorce renders contracts changeable; . . . breaks up the domestic relations; sows dissensions among families; lessens and degrades the dignity of woman who is thus exposed to be cast off, after having been the slave of man's passions." [13]

The views of Protestant clerics do not differ widely from those of Rome, although most Protestant sects recognize adultery as the one valid cause for divorce. Throughout the entire history of Protestantism in America the various sects, with the exception of the Presbyterians, who recognize "wilful desertion" as a cause, remained consistent to the view that marriage can be dissolved only for "scriptural cause." [14] The alarm with which these sects—Episcopal, Presbyterian, Methodist, Congregational and others—regard the growing laxity in divorce is clearly reflected in the minutes and resolutions of Church Councils. Thus the Congregational Church Council in 1901 records in its minutes the following:

"1. We view with serious misgivings the alarming increase in divorces and the consequent deplorable result in domestic and social life.

"We regard the purity and unity of the family as cornerstones of Christian homes and Christian civilization." [15]

These statements, both Catholic and Protestant, reveal a curious confusion of thought with respect to the effects of divorce. In every instance, the idea expressed is that divorce strikes a blow at the sanctity of

---

[12] See H. A. Brau, in A. B. Wolfe, *Readings in Social Problems,* p. 587. Ginn and Co., Boston, 1916.

[13] *Ibid.,* p. 586.

[14] See *Matt.* xix, 1-9.

[15] Quoted in Lichtenberger, *Divorce: a Study in Social Causation,* p. 138. By permission of the author.

the marriage relation, destroys "the purity and unity of the family" and disrupts the home. Yet a moment's clear, unbiassed thinking should serve to convince these clerics that all these conditions *preceded,* instead of followed, divorce. As Professor Ross has pointed out, divorce never broke up a happy home nor defiled its sanctities. What "sanctities" indeed remain in a marriage made intolerable by abuse, sexual license or drunkenness? How can divorce possibly destroy the "purity" of such a home or disrupt a family life already torn asunder by bitter dissensions or mutual loathing? Obviously the viewpoint of this group is deeply colored by their conviction that marriage is a sacred institution ordained by God and made holy in each particular case *by the nuptial service,* not by mutual love and comradeship. Holding firmly to this dogma, the eyes of thousands of men and women are closed to the fact that divorce does not create disunity, but follows upon it; that divorce is not a disease, but a symptom; not a cause, but an effect. Thus in the thinking of the ecclesiastical group, theological preconceptions are responsible for the fact that the cart is all too frequently put before the horse. In his study of the evolution of morals, Lecky holds that no other branch of ethics has been so largely determined by dogmatic theology as has the ethics of marriage and the family, and none will be so profoundly affected by the decay of theology.[16]

The Standpoint of the Sociological Group.

In the view of that growing body of men and women who have learned to look upon all social problems as the product of social forces, divorce can best be understood and evaluated in the light of the economic, religious and ethical changes that have engendered it. From this point of view, divorce is not to be summarily condemned, but rather clearly understood as the essential first step in bringing about, if possible, more satisfactory conditions with respect to family stability. Since the family is subject to the same social forces as are other institutions of society, it is obvious that no intelligent action with respect to the disruption of family ties can be taken until the causes of divorce are better comprehended.

SOCIAL FACTORS RESPONSIBLE FOR INCREASING DIVORCE

Decline of the Family as an Economic Unit.

Among the chief causative factors of our ever-increasing volume of divorces is the marked decline in the economic functions of the family. A

[16] *History of European Morals,* Vol. II, pp. 371-2.

hundred years or more ago, the family was a center of production of food products, clothing and household furnishings. Its members were held together in the firm bond of mutual dependence. During the long centuries from savagery to modern times, by far the greatest part of all productive labor was carried on in the family. Every home was a hive of domestic industry, and every member, from the householder and his wife to the youngest child who could be relied upon to spin thread, had his or her part to perform in maintaining the family. All were linked together by a common need to produce sufficient goods to feed and clothe the group.

Needless to say, all this has been transformed during the last century, when domestic manufacture has steadily yielded ground to factory production. Millions of men, women and children respond every morning to the whistle that calls them from their homes to labor, perhaps in widely separated mills and factories. At night the family members meet again in the home, which thus becomes for them chiefly a place for eating and sleeping, after pursuing diverse forms of occupation during the day. It would be difficult to over-estimate the disintegrating effect of the present industrial system upon the interdependence and thus upon the unity of the family. "Incessantly," says Professor Ross, "the factory planes away the economic basis of the family." [17] Even in those cases where an adequate family income renders it necessary for only the father to work outside the home, the disintegrating effect of machine industry is hardly less felt. Set free from her ancient productive tasks, the woman of the prosperous classes frequently has too little to occupy her time, and spends it away from home in a monotonous round of teas and bridge parties. When the family lives in the modern apartment, which is so rapidly supplanting the detached home in our cities, there are few family tasks and responsibilities for the children to be charged with. In consequence father, mother and children tend to have wholly different occupations and interests.

The Employment of Women in Gainful Occupations.

But the influence of modern economic conditions does not end with the break-up of domestic industry. The employment of women for wages, which began even before the Industrial Revolution, was greatly accelerated thereafter, until, at the present time, millions of women are engaged in gainful employments in every advanced industrial country the world

[17] "The Significance of Increasing Divorce," in *Century Magazine,* Vol. 78, May, 1909, p. 151.

over. Who can doubt that this condition has had a profound reaction upon family stability? How many of the 121,333 divorces granted in the United States in 1925 to wives as plaintiffs would ever have been brought into court had women remained in the condition of economic dependency that was theirs until after 1850? No doubt, a paramount factor in the rising divorce rate is the fact that both husband and wife fully realize the fact that a woman employed before and perhaps during marriage can support herself after the union is legally dissolved. Probably the majority of divorces would never have been secured had not the industries and professions been opened to women, and had not the law guaranteed to them the separate ownership and enjoyment of property and wages.

The Trend toward Individualism.

Another factor that must be reckoned with in accounting for the increase in divorce is the movement toward freeing the individual from cramping restrictions that hamper his welfare and happiness. Ever since the eighteenth century, the "mighty forces of spiritual liberation" [18] have been at work to secure to every individual the right to "life, liberty and the pursuit of happiness." Especially in the United States, where the individualistic spirit of our pioneer forefathers is still at work, has the doctrine of the worth of personality been most strongly upheld. A logical corollary to this is the conviction that the well-being of the individual is of prior importance to the stability of the institutions that he has created. Very widespread in this country is the belief that the institution should be the servant of man's highest needs—not his master.

It is not difficult to perceive how such a spirit would react upon the family. Men and women reared in the tradition that institutions should be progressively changed to render them more responsive to the universal need for happiness and personal development will not patiently accept the contrary teaching that marriage is a lifelong union whether it be successful or not. Common sense and regard for personality alike revolt against the theory that the institution of marriage is more sacred than the well-being of those who have entered it; that the integrity of the family should be purchased, if necessary, by the misery and stultification of its members.

The doctrines of the worth of human personality, the right of the individual to the fullest development of which he is capable and the prerogative of the human being to happiness were at first, of course, applied only to men. For generations after the individualistic philosophy of the eighteenth century was born, women remained a subject sex with no

[18] On this see Lichtenberger, *op. cit.*, pp. 172-82.

personality in the eyes of the law and with no command of the purse strings such as would lead to freedom. But when economic changes made women wage-earners, and it was proved that they could stand on their own feet financially, most civilized states began that revision of the laws concerning women which has freed them from economic dependence, has accorded to them the rights of persons before the law, has granted them liberal opportunities for education and has thrown open to them most of the gates to industrial and professional opportunity. Such a revolution in the lives of women has had its inevitable effect: women have become developed personalities like their brothers, and have claimed the same individual right to welfare and happiness. Once unhappy wives meekly bore intolerable wrongs, and accepted marriage as their only vocation. Now, under transformed conditions, they bring actions to sever galling marriage bonds and cheerfully enter one of the myriad vocations open to the modern woman. The most dramatic outcomes of individualism are seen today among womankind, precisely because they were so long denied the status of free individuals, and are still in some respects in servitude to traditional ideas.

Needless to say, the spirit of individualism may well go too far in the direction of self-assertion and result in an exaggerated egotism which takes no account of social welfare, or indeed of the happiness of individuals whose lives are intimately bound up with that of the egoist himself. Both men and women at the present time occasionally reveal a ruthless determination to climb to complete freedom and so-called "self-expression" on the backs of their family members. Such evidences of single-eyed individualism are to be expected during a period of rapid transition from an old order to a new. When larger freedom is accorded to mankind, after ages of restraint, it is not surprising that some persons do not know how to use it. A prolonged period of education is essential if men and women are to learn to substitute moral sanctions of their deliberate choosing for the old external compulsions. Serfs cannot be transformed into self-directing freemen by merely striking off their shackles.

Ethical and Religious Changes Affecting Divorce.

There can be no doubt that the profound alterations in religious belief and in the popular conception of morality that have been silently taking place since the publication of Darwin's *Origin of Species* in 1859 have had a tremendous indirect effect in changing the public attitude toward divorce. As already pointed out,[19] the strongest support of the dogma

[19] See above, p. 380.

that marriage is indissoluble has been dogmatic theology. Now it is clearly evident to all intelligent persons who do not wilfully close their eyes to facts that dogmatic theology has been dethroned from the lofty seat it once so confidently occupied and has been required to reconcile, if it can, certain of its fundamental tenets with the findings of modern science, especially with the doctrine of evolution. This reconciliation it has in some instances been unable or unwilling to accomplish. The dissemination of popular education in enlightened states has tended to give the masses of the people a modicum of the scientific attitude of mind. Therefore, the citizens of modern states show an increasing indisposition to accept on authority religious teachings that do not square with the facts and the methods of the biological and social sciences.

In consequence, there exists today a widely prevalent scepticism in matters of religious belief which is bound to undermine still further the dogma that marriage is an institution ordained of God which can only be dissolved for the "scriptural cause" of adultery. In sharp opposition to this view, anthropology and history reveal marriage as a convenient arrangement worked out by early peoples as the best means of insuring to children proper care and to the husband the ownership of legitimate offspring to inherit his property. Only when Christianity had gained a firm foothold in pagan Rome was the dogma of the sacramental nature of marriage taught to the people—a doctrine for which there is little support in the teachings of Christ. Moreover, sincere Christian people are coming more and more to see that Christ's saying that a man should put away his wife only "for the cause of fornication" should be interpreted in the light of Jewish social conditions. At the time of Christ, divorce was very frequent among the Hebrews and took place for the most trivial causes. A man was permitted to give his wife "a bill of divorcement" and send her out of his home if she were displeasing to him in any way. The prophets had begun to criticize the freedom accorded the husband long before the Christian era, but the School of Hillel upheld the husband's rights to free divorce.[20] It was unquestionably this condition of license that led the Founder of Christianity to react powerfully against divorce save for the one cause of adultery.

It is not alone religious beliefs which are undergoing change. The moral ideas of the present generation have been deeply colored by the theories of evolution. Genetic study of history, of social institutions and of ethical conceptions has convinced many thoughtful men and women

[20] See W. Goodsell, *A History of the Family as a Social and Educational Institution*, pp. 67-9. The Macmillan Co., New York, 1915.

that in every age the commonly accepted moral standards and customs are the product of human experience in its effort to secure the welfare of the group. As the conditions of social life undergo change, the prevalent moral ideas tend gradually to accommodate themselves to these changes. No doubt the accommodation would be accomplished more rapidly were it not that two powerful sanctions operate to prevent the alteration of ethical codes—the sanction of custom itself, with its dead weight of inertia, and the sanction of social institutions, especially of religion, which have usually proved hostile to any modification of accepted moral ideas. When once enlightened individuals have grasped the theory of the relativity of ethical conceptions to social conditions, they are reluctant to accept a ready-made morality grounded upon tradition and custom. Moreover, the last fifty years have seen a powerful growth of humanitarian sentiment, and a wide acceptance of the theory that morality should make for human welfare and happiness—not obstruct these ends. Thus the ethical ideas of the twentieth century are being continually reshaped in the interest of a practical morality. From this point of view, human institutions exist for man, not man for institutions, and marriage is no exception to the rule. A traditional code of morals declares that it is just and righteous to chain human beings together in a wretched bondage in order to preserve the integrity of the marriage institution; public opinion holds that this code must be altered to correspond to the humanitarian feeling and the common sense of mankind.

When we are tempted to deplore our rising divorce rate, it may be well to ask ourselves whether this social phenomenon really does point to a decline of morals. In every age of social change from Socrates to the present, the cry of immorality has been raised whenever the teachings of reformers reacted upon the *mores*. Yet history shows that, on the whole, moral standards have been rising, not sinking, when viewed from the standpoint of human liberation from bonds that cripple personal development. May it not be possible that the present tendency to sever unhappy marriages that were once endured indicates a mounting rather than a falling morality—a finer conception of marriage, not a more degraded one? If marriage be regarded as a union of minds as well as bodies, a joining of mates in sympathetic comradeship and mutual helpfulness, not merely a useful social arrangement for the rearing of children and the transmission of property, divorce becomes a social necessity because human choices are not infallibly wise. In earlier times men and women married for reasons of economic and social convenience, and stuck to their bargain (with some exceptions) because the Church taught that, however unsatisfactory the contract proved, it was wrong to end it. Now, with a nobler conception of the spiritual significance of marriage as a union the very essence of which consists in loving harmony of life interests and purposes, disappointed husbands and wives seek release from a relationship that has realized few or none of these ideals.

On the other hand it is well to remember that all divorces are not sought for idealistic reasons, any more than all marriages are entered into for ideal ends. At the risk of monotonous repetition, it must be said that nothing is more needed today than the education of youth in a finer conception of marriage. When once young men and women have grasped this conception, and gained some appreciation of the preciousness of a satisfying marriage, they will be slower in forming unions that promise merely physical satisfaction and a home. This is only to say that cheap ideas of marriage are one potent cause of increasing divorce.

Professor George Elliott Howard is strongly of the opinion that divorce can in considerable measure be cured by abandoning the custom of "bad marriages." First among the varieties of these he places "light-minded wedlock," the union of a man and woman who "rush into matrimony as if it were a transient fête or a 'society function.'" Even worse is the type that Howard calls "tainted wedlock"—the marriage of the physically, mentally or morally unfit. "Is there," he exclaims, "any boy or girl so immature if only the legal age of consent has been reached; is there any 'delinquent' so dangerous through inherited tendencies to disease or crime; is there any worn out rake who cannot somewhere find a magistrate or a priest to tie the 'sacred knot'?" [21]

Who can deny the essential truth of this charge? Yet even if marriages were always entered into by competent persons with an enlightened realization of the nature and obligations of the contract, it is doubtful if divorce would thereby be cured. Marriage is so delicate and complex a relationship, and human beings are so subject to changes in feeling and in life interests, that it is highly improbable that all marriages can ever be made permanently successful and happy unions.

While our changing morality is being considered, reference should be made to the profound alteration that is taking place with regard to the double standard of morality. The Church has preached for centuries the doctrine that sexual purity is an equal obligation of both sexes without very greatly influencing popular opinion or practice. Witness the wide-spread existence of prostitution maintained by men, the infidelity of hus-

[21] "Bad Marriage and Quick Divorce," in *Journal of Applied Sociology*, Vol. VI, pp. 1-10.

bands to their wives on the one hand and the chastity rigidly exacted of women on the other, all of which social history makes plain. Now that scientists and physicians are well-nigh united in declaring that continence before marriage and self-control within it work good rather than harm to the health of young men, and now that women have risen to a place of larger influence and power, the double standard of morals has been attacked in recent times with far more effect than in the centuries of the past. Far from subscribing to a social code that demands absolute fidelity of the wife and allows liberal license to the husband, women with unfaithful husbands now uphold their belief in a single standard of morality for both sexes by securing a severance of their marriage bonds through the divorce court. Does this mean a lowered or a heightened morality?

Transition from the Patriarchal to the Democratic Family.

No discussion of the causes of our rising divorce rate would be complete which ignored the potent fact that the modern family has been undergoing a transformation from the patriarchal to the democratic form. During those long centuries of social evolution when the family was governed by its male head with an arbitrary authority that must frequently have resembled a domestic despotism, there was little chance for divorce. The head of the family could satisfy his desires outside of marriage; and the wife was so completely in his power—a power buttressed by the puissant sanctions of law and religion—that it **was** hopeless for her to free herself from a wretched or degrading union. Within the last two generations all this has been changed. No longer is the family a firmly knit unit held together by the unchallenged authority of husband and father. Rather has it become an association of free individuals, united by love and mutual aid, whose fundamental rights, including those of wife and children, are guaranteed by the law. This basic change in family organization has had a tremendous effect in making it possible for the wife not only to secure divorce for wrongs to herself but also to protect the rights of her children when these are overridden by an arbitrary father. The use to which women have put their new freedom from patriarchal power is evidenced by the fact that for more than fifty years wives have secured two-thirds and more of the divorce decrees granted by the courts.

The Popularization of Law and Education.

A final condition favorable to freer divorce is the popularization of law and of education that has been taking place over a long period of time. As Willcox has pointed out,[22] law was a privilege of the few during most of the Middle Ages. "For centuries," he declares, "legal forms of procedure continued so intricate and expensive that the benefits of law accrued only to the wise or wealthy." Hand in hand with the extension of the suffrage in modern times has gone an extension of the benefits of the law to larger and larger bodies of people once shut out from these privileges. "Whole classes," says Willcox, "have been admitted to court that were formerly excluded by the efficient practical problems of ignorance and poverty."

This statement points to another condition operating to bring about freer resort to courts of law, namely, the removal of the dense popular ignorance that once prevailed. Upon the upbuilding of free school systems in modern states has ensued an opening of new avenues of privilege and opportunity to the hitherto disinherited rank and file of the people. Through the press and the magazine, these plain folk learn that marriage need not be a lifelong yoke if it can be demonstrated to the satisfaction of the law to be a failure. Although it is probably true that divorce is not so freely resorted to by wage-earners as by the professional and business groups, yet the laboring class has made fairly liberal use of the courts to end marital difficulties, as the records of the Courts of Domestic Relations and of philanthropic organizations show.

IS DIVORCE AN EVIL?

As we have seen, many thoughtful persons at present look upon divorce as an unmitigated evil, a social disease that is sapping the vitality and threatening the very existence of the monogamic family. To their minds, divorce appears as the enemy of marriage sanctity, of wholesome childhood, of permanent home influences and settled family life. Nor is their view by any means wholly a mistaken one. The severance of marriage ties and the disruption of families which were once established with happiness and hope for the future, not only entail keen suffering upon all sensitive husbands and wives, but furnish more evidences of marital failure to a society already somewhat skeptical of the benefits of monogamic marriage. Not only is this true, but the breaking up of the home and the separation of parents cannot but react harmfully on the children. Reared by one parent to whom the court has allotted them, these boys and girls visit only at long intervals the other parent, against whom their minds may have been poisoned. Thus little ones in a home which divorce has torn

---

[22] "The Divorce Problem, a Study in Statistics," p. 63, *Columbia University. Studies in History, Economics and Public Law*, Vol. I, No. I.

asunder suffer blindly the effects of their parents' alienation and are deprived of the daily love and influence of father or mother as the case may be. Statistics of the New York Juvenile Court show that fifty percent of child delinquents come from homes broken by divorce. This percentage, however, is the highest in city records. The correlation between juvenile delinquency and divorce in other cities is considerably lower. Nevertheless, the facts justify the conclusion that if a moderate degree of harmony and contentment exists within a home, it can hardly be questioned that the influence of two well-intentioned parents is better than that of one in the upbringing and guidance of the child.

But there is another side of the question. There can be no doubt that, painful as divorce proceedings may be to men and women of refinement, a divorce decree has frequently opened the door to freedom, renewed the hope of happiness and released the caged energies of many a husband and wife whose marriage had proved a ghastly mistake and whose home was little more than a prison house for the spirit. Nor is this all. When the critics of divorce attack the practice on the ground of its injurious effects upon children, they show a human proneness to consider only those aspects of the question that will establish their case. The judges and referees in juvenile courts well know that homes where bitterness and conflict have taken up their abode are the worst possible places in which to rear sensitive children. As our knowledge of child nature grows more thorough and intimate, we become increasingly aware of the baneful effects of family jars and friction upon the mental life of children. No one is better fitted to speak with authority on this point than Dr. Miriam Van Waters, referee of the Juvenile Court in Los Angeles. This is what she says: [23] "To the maladjusted child in the family-group, life is an anxiety; it dwells under a nameless shadow of fear, often a sense of guilt and inferiority. It is forced into the domestic arena, sometimes as a participant, sometimes as silent spectator condemned to lose no matter which partner wins. Adults often imagine in domestic strife the only damage done the child is neglect, or temporary suffering, if it is deprived of a mother's physical care, or the bread-winning capacity of the father. But the damage is more extensive and may permanently destroy the child's mental health. No amount of 'patching it up' or 'returning to live together for the sake of the child' can restore the child if there is an undercurrent of hostility, suspicion and dislike between the parents. For little children are not so much influenced by words and actions of adults as by attitudes.

[23] *Youth in Conflict*, pp. 72-3. Italics mine. New Republic, Inc., New York, 1925. By permission.

. . . For welfare of the child it is best to subject it to influence of only one of the combating parents; *two conflicting attitudes are almost certain to produce break-down in the child, in health, sanity, or morals."*

This is the considered judgment of a woman who has for years come into close contact with ungovernable and delinquent children brought by parents or officers into the juvenile court of a great city. And such conclusions, based upon exact knowledge, not upon traditional beliefs or prejudice, must more and more influence the views of all intelligent persons in dealing with questions of human relationships if we are to avoid grave mistakes in social legislation and practice. Trained social workers and juvenile court officers seem to be agreed that the affectionate rearing of a child by one parent who has been divorced is far better than its up-bringing in a home where conflict and recrimination are of daily occurrence but where the husband and wife "do not believe in divorce." Statistics show that there is a much higher positive correlation between the well-being of a child and his intelligent care by one divorced parent than there is between juvenile delinquency and homes which have been broken by divorce.

Further knowledge might well force some honest critics to revise their views of divorce as a deplorable social evil. A sounder theory would seem to be that divorce is not essentially an evil, but an index of maladjustment. Social and economic conditions, scientific knowledge and religious and moral ideas have changed so rapidly within two generations that the family has not been able to adapt itself to the altered conditions. The result is conflict and misery within the home and the ever-increasing frequency of divorce. America has more broken marriages than other nations because it is still a young and forward-looking country, the essence of whose creed is the belief that everyone has the right to be happy if his happiness does not encroach upon another's rights. It follows as a logical corollary that when human beings have made grievous mistakes in their choice of mates they should be released from a yoke that has become hateful in order that they may seek (and perhaps find) happiness in a wiser choice. From this point of view, divorce is a sign of the increasing faith of mankind in the beneficent effects of the liberation of personality. Even though the extension of human freedom may cost the price of a mounting tide of divorces, some of which are secured for frivolous or ignoble reasons, society stands ready to pay the cost. For every forward step in the liberation of mankind from shackling customs has been attended by an unworthy use of the new liberty on the part of a minority.

THE MOVEMENT FOR A UNIFORM MARRIAGE AND DIVORCE LAW

The conflicting variety of state laws on marriage and divorce in this Republic has long been a matter of serious concern to a growing body of our citizens. Forty-eight states and the District of Columbia have written into their statute books such a bewildering diversity of enactments concerning legal marriage and its severance that these laws have been happily compared to a crazy quilt. In some advanced states, the laws have kept fairly well abreast of enlightened public opinion; whereas in other commonwealths, the statutes still clearly reflect medieval ideas and customs. This absence of harmony in both the spirit and provisions of the state laws has had distinctly harmful results, especially in regard to divorce.

A few examples of the conflict in state codes will help to clarify this question. In many states it is possible for a young couple to secure a license and be made man and wife all in one afternoon, while their parents and friends may remain in cheerful ignorance of this important step; whereas five or six states require the lapse of five days after the license is applied for before it is issued. The laws of the states vary widely regarding marriage prohibitions. In many states, paupers, epileptics, mental defectives and the venereally diseased are not forbidden to marry; in a few commonwealths such marriages are prohibited, but often the means for determining whether these defects exist in couples applying for a license are quite inadequate. In 1923, nine states permitted the marriage of whites and negroes; whereas in a large number of the remaining states the marriage of a white person to one having even one-eighth part of negro blood is prohibited. Again, there are a few states in this enlightened Union that still recognize as valid and legal marriages of little girls of twelve and boys of fourteen, provided the parents' consent is given. Seventeen states have omitted to fix the age of marriage by statute, hence the common-law ages of twelve and fourteen are recognized by the courts as legal ages for entering upon the serious business of marriage with parental consent. On the other hand, the majority of states require that the woman must have reached the age of eighteen and the man the age of twenty-one before they can legally be married without the consent of the parents.

The same marked differences exist with respect to divorce laws. No two states have the same grounds for divorce. These vary from no ground at all in South Carolina and one only in New York to nine in Illinois and fourteen in New Hampshire. Some states, as Nevada, permit divorce after serving notice on the defendant by publication in the newspapers of the state where action is brought. Other commonwealths require personal service of the papers upon the defendant. Again, several states issue only interlocutory divorce decrees, which require an interval of six months or a year before the decree becomes absolute; in other states, the decree requires no such period for second thoughts on the part of the couple—a "cooling-off time" which might lead to their reconciliation.

In view of the diversity of our state codes, which sometimes results in couples finding themselves legally married in one State and not married in another, or holding a divorce decree from one State which is challenged in another, a movement started more than thirty years ago to secure uniformity in the marriage and divorce laws of the forty-eight States. In 1906 the National Congress on Uniform Divorce Laws was held in Washington and Philadelphia. Almost from the first, sharp divergencies of opinion appeared among the delegates. For example, vigorous objection was made to the provisions of the uniform marriage license law submitted by the committee on resolutions. Yet the salient features of this proposed law, providing as it did for two weeks' publicity before issue of the license; for no license issue to the applicants where either is a minor, without the duly attested consent of parents or guardians; for prohibition of marriage without suitable witnesses, should have commended themselves at once to the good sense of all the delegates. Nevertheless, the Congress dissolved without taking action on this and other proposed uniform laws. Since that time, little or no progress has been made in securing uniformity of marriage and divorce legislation by action of the individual States.

Within recent years a concerted effort, sponsored by the General Federation of Women's Clubs, has been made to secure for the United States a uniform marriage and divorce law by means of an amendment to the Constitution. At present, all power to legislate in matters of marriage and divorce resides in the states, and the Federal Government can take no action to secure uniformity until this authority has been conferred upon it. In January, 1923, Senator Arthur Capper of Kansas introduced in Congress a Uniform Divorce Bill which was preceded by the introduction of a joint resolution proposing an amendment to the Federal Constitution. The amendment reads:

"The Congress shall have power to make laws, which shall be uniform throughout the United States, on marriage and divorce, the legitimation of children, and the care and custody of children affected by annulment of marriage or by divorce." [24]

[24] See *Journal of Social Hygiene*, Vol. 9, March, 1923, pp. 170-3.

The Divorce Bill, which was framed by Mrs. Edward Franklin White, Deputy Attorney General of Indiana, at the direction of the General Federation of Women's Clubs, contains thirty-eight sections designed to prevent hasty and foolish marriages and to surround divorce with certain restrictions. The marriage law contains enlightened provisions regarding the age of the parties, prohibitions upon marriage of the physically or mentally unfit, giving publicity to the application for a license, witnesses to the marriage, and its registration in the county and state where it is solemnized. The Divorce Bill provides that divorce shall be granted for the following causes: adultery, physical and mental cruelty, abandonment or failure to provide for one year or more, incurable insanity, or the commission of a felony. Under the terms of the proposed law, applications for divorce must be made sixty days prior to the trial of a case; the defendant must, if possible, be reached through personal service, so that he has full knowledge of the suit and its grounds; both parents must be given access to the children after the divorce is granted; an interlocutory period of one year must elapse before any decree becomes final; the guardianship of the child or children shall be equal if both parents are fit, but the mother shall be given custody of minor children, if she is mentally and morally suited to the responsibility.[25]

Arguments for and against the Uniform Marriage and Divorce Bill.

Since Senator Capper introduced the Uniform Divorce Bill (S. 4394), a flood of controversy over the merits and defects of the proposed amendment has been let loose. Within the limits of this chapter it is impossible to give more than the briefest summary of the arguments pro and con brought forward by advocates and opponents of a uniform divorce law. The friends of the measure lay stress upon the uncertainty of status that results from the variance among state laws. They point out that the status of divorced parties is gravely affected by change of domicile and jurisdiction. Certain states attract unhappy partners by the laxity of their divorce laws; in other states these divorced persons may, and sometimes do, find their status questioned and their right to remarry challenged or even denied in the courts. Again, some states impose upon the guilty party in a divorce the penalty of disability to contract a subsequent marriage. This penalty is easily evaded by resorting to another jurisdiction where the divorce statutes contain no such penalty. In such a case, a legal marriage may be contracted by the guilty party in a neighboring state, after which he may return to his original domicile with the assurance that his

[25] For a more detailed account of the bill, see *Journal of Social Hygiene*, Vol. 9, March, 1923, pp. 170-3.

marriage will be recognized as valid by the very courts that imposed the penalty. The failure of the states of the Union to reach any sort of agreement with respect to a uniform marriage and divorce law renders it imperative for the Federal Government to be empowered to secure the much-needed uniformity. If the states have been willing to surrender to some extent their power to legislate as to bankruptcy into the hands of Congress, in order to secure uniformity and end confusion of laws, they should be willing to give Congress by means of a Constitutional amendment the authority to end the social evils growing out of conflicting divorce laws.

On the other hand, the opponents of an amendment and a uniform law point out that, if the framers of the Constitution had thought it wise to grant power to the Congress to legislate on matters of domestic concern, they would have done so. On the contrary the early Fathers of the Republic realized the wisdom of leaving to the states, differing as they do in environments, social backgrounds and peculiar circumstances, a high degree of power to make laws in harmony with local ideas and customs. Again the opponents of the amendment insist that its sponsors exaggerate the evil of migratory divorces. By far the largest proportion of divorces—"not less than 75 per cent probably"—are granted to parties actually living under the jurisdiction of the courts granting the decree.[26] Moreover, Federal legislation might be wholly unjust to such states as South Carolina, which recognizes no cause of divorce; New York, which recognizes one; and New Jersey, which recognizes only two causes of absolute divorce. There is no widespread popular discontent with the present conditions, as evidenced by the fact that only three states—New Jersey, Delaware and Wisconsin—have adopted the uniform law. Since the "divorce evil" rests not in divorce itself but in the social conditions leading to divorce, the evil will not be remedied by a uniform divorce law.

But the most astute criticisms of a uniform divorce law were formulated by Elizabeth Cady Stanton more than thirty years ago. This pioneer suffrage leader pointed out in 1894 that, since the movement for a uniform law was inspired by people who consider our present laws too liberal, the uniformity is only a cloak for a concerted effort to narrow the existing laws. She further declared that local self-government makes possible a variety of experiments on mooted social questions: "The smaller the

[26] An estimate of Walter G. Smith of the Philadelphia Bar. See Julia E. Johnsen, *Selected Articles on Marriage and Divorce*, p. 280. H. W. Wilson Co., New York, 1925.

area over which the law extends, the more pliable are the laws"; whereas the adoption of a uniform national law would not only restrict experimentation, but might result after a period of years in the nation's finding itself bound by a law that was partially if not wholly unsatisfactory.[27]

WILL LEGISLATION CHECK DIVORCE?

America is *par excellence* the nation that is most thoroughly committed to the theory that social evils can be righted by legislation. The vast majority of our people give heart-whole allegiance to the view that the behavior of men and women can be made moral by law. Yet this dogma has been challenged again and again by social writers. Perhaps the most effective denial that legislation will cure divorce is that of Willcox in his excellent study of *The Divorce Problem*. After a careful examination of available statistics concerning the changes in number of divorces due to new legislation, not alone in the United States but in Europe, Willcox declares:

"The conclusion of the whole matter is that law can do little. Agitation for a change of law may educate public opinion. It may even be the most efficient and powerful means of education. Such effects no statistics can measure, and therefore in a paper like this the educative influences of law must be neglected, but the immediate, direct and measurable influence of legislation is subsidiary, unimportant, almost imperceptible." [28]

It is highly probable, then, that the energies that are now being expended so lavishly in securing a uniform marriage and divorce law might much more effectively be employed in trying to improve the conditions of social life and to work out in each state a thoughtful plan of educating youth for marriage.

WILL DIVORCE DESTROY THE MONOGAMIC FAMILY?

In the preceding discussion, the attempt has been made to show that the instability of the present family and the rising tide of divorce mark the fact that the family has not been able to adapt itself to changed conditions. It is not surprising that the family is in a turmoil as a result of revolutionary social changes. So are industry, religion and morals. "The whole human family," says O'Hare, "is moving out of an old, worn-out social, economic and theological house into a new one and family

[27] See the *Freeman*, Vol. 7, April 25, 1923, pp. 150-1. The arguments for both sides are presented in Julia E. Johnsen, *Selected Articles on Marriage and Divorce*, pp. 241-93. H. W. Wilson Co., New York, 1925.
[28] Doctoral dissertation, Columbia University, 1891, p. 61.

jars are bound to result." [29] Nor is there much hope of stemming the flood of divorces by increasing restraints, either legal or religious. As Lichtenberger wisely says:

"It is not only futile, but highly undesirable to seek to check the processes of evolution. To attempt to dam the stream without providing a waste-weir is only to compel an overflow, and the formation of new, and perhaps destructive, channels.

"Arbitrarily to diminish the number of divorces under existing conditions would be to increase immorality and crime." [30]

Are we then forced to believe that we must accept an ever-mounting divorce rate as a necessary social consequence of family maladjustment? It is probable that, for some time to come, divorces will steadily increase. There is no reason to believe that the peak has been reached. Indeed, sentiments of regard for the individual and his happiness, and of dislike of all coercive methods of binding couples together who no longer love each other, seem to be on the increase as the true nature of marriage is better understood. The time may come when there will be in this country one divorce for every two or three marriages. But this cannot be expected to last. The old family, based on the arbitrary authority of husband and father, will in time give place to the new democratic family held together by love and mutual interest—far more potent forces than coercion. With the development of a new and more humane economic order; with the spread of enlightenment through improved education, both intellectual and moral; with the general acceptance of the idea that no one has the right to coerce another, either within or without marriage, the divorce rate will tend to fall. "Already," says Professor Ross, "there are in sight certain influences that are likely to moderate the headlong movement. The industrial and intellectual emancipation of women will, of course, complete itself; but the old despotic ideal of the family will die out of men's minds and cease to be a breeder of family discord. . . . It is likely that the public, as it wins a deeper insight into the services of the family to society and to the race, will feel less sympathy with the wrong-doings, weaknesses and whims that shatter it. Individualism, too, is probably at its zenith. In the discussion of human relations we are likely to hear less of the radical note and more of the ethical note. In proportion as the emancipated are led to an ethical view of life, they will cease to regard marriage simply as a fair-weather arrangement with personal happiness

[29] "Is Divorce a Forward or Backward Step?" in *Arena*, April, 1905, p. 414. Quoted in Lichtenberger, *Divorce: a Study in Social Causation*, p. 213. By permission of the author.
[30] Lichtenberger, *op. cit.*, p. 213. By permission.

in constant view. They will recognize the inexorable demands for patience and self-control, for loyalty through sorrow and sickness, through misfortune and the ageing years." [31]

This is only to say that there are valid reasons for believing that the monogamic family will survive the present storms and make, in course of time, a peaceful harbor. Monogamic marriage is rooted deep, not only in the mating impulse, but in those sentiments of romantic love, of unselfish devotion to helpless young, of loyal comradeship and mutual aid that have been coming to flower through the long centuries of family history. Slow and halting as their growth has been, nevertheless these sentiments are spiritual realities today, imponderable but strong, and tending powerfully toward the perpetuation of that form of sex union which seems best to meet the deepest and highest needs of personality.

TOPICS FOR REPORTS

1. Is Marriage a Contract in the full Sense of the Term "Contract"?
   Havelock Ellis, *Sex in Relation to Society,* pp. 470-86; 503-5. F. A. Davis Co., Philadelphia, 1913.
2. Attitude of Religious Bodies toward Divorce.
   James P. Lichtenberger, *Divorce: A Study in Social Causation,* Ch. VIII. Longmans, Green & Co., New York, 1909.
   A. B. Wolfe, *Readings in Social Problems,* pp. 586-98. Ginn & Co., New York, 1916.
3. The Proposed Uniform Divorce Law in the United States.
   Lichtenberger, *op. cit.,* Ch. VII.
   Wolfe, *op. cit.,* pp. 657-64.
   Julia E. Johnsen, *Selected Articles on Marriage and Divorce,* pp. 241-93. H. W. Wilson Co., New York, 1925.
4. Education as a Preventive of Divorce.
   Marguerite O. B. Wilkinson, in *Craftsman,* Vol. XXI, February, 1912, pp. 473-81.
5. Repressive Influence of Unhappy Marriages on Individual Development.
   Mona Caird, *The Morality of Marriage,* pp. 98-137, 143-5. George Redway, London, 1897.

[31] "Significance of Increasing Divorce," in *Century Magazine,* Vol. 78, May, 1909, p. 152.

CHAPTER XXII

FREEDOM IN LOVE

THE EMERGENCE OF THE THEORY OF FREEDOM IN LOVE: ITS UNDERLYING CAUSES

THE last quarter century has seen the birth and development of a theory of love relations fundamentally opposed to that held by the Christian Church from the beginning of its history. The open advocates of this view, who speak and write in behalf of a growing freedom of the individual from the restrictions of monogamic marriage as now understood, are on the whole a highly educated group of men and women. With one voice they attack the theory, so long sanctioned by State and Church, of a lifelong union of man and woman, primarily for the propagation and nurture of offspring. With equal unanimity they proclaim the right of the individual man and woman to regulate his or her own love life in accordance with his conscience, his deepest emotional needs and his developing erotic experience. They declare, sometimes with fervid sincerity, that the permanent bonds which society fastens upon young people in marriage frequently prove to be galling chains, fettering body and spirit in a relationship that has become intolerable and subversive of the true interests of a developing personality. This group of writers points to the apparent failure of present-day monogamic marriage, as evidenced by the mounting divorce rate and the swelling army of dissatisfied critics of monogamy. They urge that social opinion should accommodate itself to a new morality which proclaims the ideal of freedom in love relationships, to the end that men and women may develop richer and finer erotic personalities, and discover in love a stimulus to the noblest thought and feeling of which they are capable.

It is not difficult to trace the causes that have given birth to this twentieth-century philosophy of freedom in love. Quite obviously it is but one expression of the struggle of the age to rid itself of what it claims to be outworn conventions that stifle mental and spiritual growth and cripple freedom. It is but one aspect of the universal movement for the liberation of mankind from laws and customs which are believed to be no longer socially useful. Hitherto the fight against hampering institu-

398

Trial marriage
a couple lives together for awhile to find
out if they can be happy together. If they aren't
satisfied, the ...

tions has been waged solely by men because women were essentially an unfree sex, held down by law and the *mores* to a subordinate position in the family and in society. But one of the distinguishing features of the present agitation for the emancipation of love from lifelong monogamy is the presence of women in the forefront of the movement. A moment's reflection will serve to make plain why this is so. Unquestionably women have been the chief sufferers from a marriage bond that has subjected them to the sexual desires of their husbands whether love was present or not. Now that greater honesty and frankness in the consideration of marriage relations prevail today, a flood of light has poured in upon the dark corners of wedlock and has illuminated a sorry array of marital sex incompatibilities and tyrannies. Because of their age-old subjection to men, because of the prevalent theory that the chaste wife should not look for pleasure in the marriage relation but only to *give* pleasure and release to her husband, many wives have been the passive victims of marital intercourse, not equal sharers in its deepest joys of body and spirit.

With the economic, legal and intellectual emancipation of women, this ancient theory has been challenged not alone by men but by women. It was inevitable that the individualization of women, their achievement in some degree of free personality, should have led them in time to voice insurgent protests against those conditions within marriage that too often deprived them of joy, of further personal development and not rarely of love itself. Although women are still not fully conscious of the reasons for their discontent with monogamic marriage, and although it must be clearly understood that probably only a minority reveal this discontent, yet here and there a woman does struggle up into full awareness of the grounds for her dissatisfaction with present-day marriage. It is this small band of protestants that are expressing not only their indictment of wedlock but their faith in a new morality for women which shall be grounded upon freer love relations and shall be the expression of ethical ideals that *women have formulated for themselves*. This is only to say that these leaders proclaim the right of women to discover, to find out for themselves, what moral standards they will accept as true and obligatory upon them. They point out what cannot be denied, that women's controlling ethical ideals in the past have been imposed upon them by men who desired above all things that their wives should come to them virgin, and should remain utterly loyal after marriage, no matter how unsatisfactory the union proved to be. Furthermore these writers declare that the demand for inviolable chastity and complete faithfulness in women was part of a dual standard of morality that regarded unchastity in woman as an unspeakable sin, while winking at the same offense in men. Underneath the whole ethical theory were originally property rights—the claim of the husband to complete assurance that his property right in his wife had not been tampered with and his further claim to assurance that at his death his property would descend to children of his own blood.

To the student of social history, this revolt of a minority of men and women against a theory of sex relations that demands of them lifelong celibacy on the one hand or lifelong wedlock on the other appears as an inescapable phase of culture development. In any advanced society, there will always be a group of highly individualized persons who will be sensitive to any social pressure brought to bear upon them which in any degree limits their freedom to explore and to experiment in every form of human association, especially of sex relationship.

THE INDICTMENT OF MONOGAMIC MARRIAGE

The indictments leveled against contemporary marriage by a growing body of men and women in every land have been touched upon above. They deserve more detailed consideration before inevitable adverse criticisms are made. First and foremost is the attack upon the coercive character of the marriage bond, its assumption that two young people, inexperienced in love and with natures not fully matured, can and should choose each other as partners for life and abide by their choice whether it prove a disastrous mistake or not. These critics point out that the more people understand their own natures, the more they will hesitate to promise love and fidelity for life. Life is growth and change, and no one can be certain that his love and devotion to his chosen mate will survive these changes in character and personality. By binding together a man and woman who have ceased to love each other, who no longer find possibilities of happiness and spiritual development in the intimacy of marriage, it is society itself that commits a sin against the sacredness of love. When love possesses individuals, it inclines them to promise eternal loyalty; but this fact does not justify State and Church in taking advantage of what may prove to be a passing attraction by clapping together its book of marriage and exclaiming, "There now, you are married and done for, for the rest of your natural lives." [1] In the opinion of these critics of monogamy, not only is such a procedure on the part of society responsible for intense unhappiness and atrophy of personal growth, but it renders impossible the selection of a more suitable mate, with whom the individual

[1] See Edward Carpenter, *Love's Coming of Age*, p. 113. Boni & Liveright, New York, 1911.

might have a deeply ennobling love experience. A perfect union must have perfect freedom as its condition.

But the critics of monogamic marriage have other counts in their indictment. They declare that the chief support of this institution has been the economic and legal dependence of women, which has made of the wife a species of serf. Not only has marriage found its strongest bulwark in the dependence of the wife, but it has been a potent factor in perpetuating that dependence. Until recent times, Church and public opinion alike have sanctioned Guido Franceschini's view of the relations of husband and wife. He addresses the court in defense of the murder of his young wife Pompilia, and declares what he expects of a wife:[2]

> "Why loyalty and obedience,—wish and will
> To settle and suit her fresh and plastic mind
> To the loyal, not disadvantageous mould!
>
> .   .   .   .
>
> With a wife I look to find all wifeliness,
> As when I buy, timber and twig, a tree—
> I buy the song of the nightingale inside.
>
> .   .   .   .
>
> The obligation I incurred was just
> *To practice mastery, prove my mastership:—*
>
> *Pompilia's duty was—submit herself,*
> *Afford me pleasure, perhaps cure my bile."*

This, say the opponents of marriage, was the abject subjection to which women were frequently reduced in the past—a subjection which they were able partially to throw off only when they achieved economic independence. Now that women in most advanced countries have been granted a large measure of freedom, it is not surprising, declare the critics, that certain of their sex have turned against the institution responsible for their serfdom. Marriage, in the judgment of these writers, is incompatible with personal freedom. When a man and woman are united for life by a religious or civil rite, the partner possessing the stronger personality will seek to subordinate the other, knowing full well that his or her mate cannot escape the yoke of marriage. The result is an increase in the number of the unmarried of both sexes, who rebel against the "mouse-trap-like structure of marriage. The instant those attracted by the bait have entered the trap, the door snaps to behind them."[3]

[2] See Browning's *The Ring and the Book,* pp. 155-6, 158. Italics mine. Houghton Mifflin Co., Riverside Press, Boston, 1894.

[3] Grete Meisel-Hess, *The Sexual Crisis,* p. 27. Critic and Guide Co., New York, 1917.

The indictment does not end here. Not only does monogamic marriage frequently prevent the finest flowering of love by denying it freedom, not only does it tend to subordinate women and keep them in a dependent condition, but it throws two human beings together in such a close and perpetual intimacy (into which no others may be admitted) that it is only too apt to result in what Edward Carpenter calls an *"égoisme à deux."* No writer has described the circumscribed and stifling character of some marriages—those which deny freedom to either partner to form warm friendships and stimulating associations outside of the domestic circle—with such conviction as has Carpenter.[4] Thus he writes:

"Marriage by a kind of absurd fiction, is represented as an oasis situated in the midst of an arid desert—in which latter, it is pretended, neither of the two parties is so fortunate as to find any objects of real affectional interest. If they do they have carefully to conceal the same from the other party.

"The result of this convention is obvious enough. The married pair, thus driven as well as drawn into closest continual contact with each other, are put through an ordeal which might well cause the stoutest affection to quail. . . . It is hardly necessary to say, not only how dull a place this makes the home, but also how narrowing [*sic*] it acts on the lives of the married pair. However appropriate the union may be in itself it cannot be good that it should degenerate—as it tends to degenerate so often, and where man and wife are most faithful to each other—into a mere *égoisme à deux*. And right enough no doubt as a great number of such unions actually are, it must be confessed that the bourgeois marriage as a rule, and just in its most successful and pious and respectable form, carries with it an odious sense of stuffiness and narrowness, moral and intellectual; and that the type of Family which it provides is too often like that which is disclosed when on turning over a large stone we disturb an insect home that seldom sees the light."

Such is the picture drawn by this English critic of the average reasonably happy middle-class marriage. But what of the unsuccessful union, in which the partners have found increasing boredom and satiety? Carpenter describes the "weary couples that may be seen at seaside places and pleasure resorts . . . their blank faces, utter want of any topic of conversation which has not been exhausted a thousand times already, and their obvious relief when the hour comes which will take them back to their several and divided occupations." He deplores "the kind of fatal

[4] Carpenter, *op. cit.*, pp. 92-3. Boni and Liveright, New York, 1911. By permission of The Modern Library, New York.

snap-of-the-lock with which marriage suddenly cuts them off from the world"; the "selfish sense of monopoly which each has in the other"; the "intense mutual ennui" which sometimes leads to covert relationships outside of marriage.[5]

The Englishwoman Mona Caird likewise decries the "walled-in existence" of married pairs which results in making life "airless and lacking in vitality." In consequence, society itself, which is largely composed of married couples, "suffers from a sort of coagulating process, whose effects we are all feeling in a thousand unsuspected ways. Life is tied up into myriads of tight little knots, and the blood cannot flow through the body politic. . . . The marital relationship of claims and restraints is, perhaps, in its vaunted 'success,' more melancholy than in its admitted failure." [6]

Nor is this all. The critics of modern wedlock do not fail to point out that monogamic marriage in its true sense has never been realized in Western Christendom. While rendering lip service to its ideal, men, and occasionally women, in every age have sought in secret, illicit unions the love life they have not found in marriage. The penalties that society exacts of those who infringe the law of marriage, or rather of those who are *discovered* in this infringement, are so heavy that individuals seek to cover up their extra-marital relations as well as they may. Bertrand Russell scores the "widespread but very flimsy hypocrisy" characteristic of social opinion at present, which closes its eyes to secret infractions of the marriage code, even when they are suspected, so long as they do not become matters of public knowledge. He believes that, subject to the necessity of secrecy in illicit sexual relations, there is today great freedom in actual practice, thus rendering the law tolerable to those who do not accept its principles. "What has to be sacrificed to propitiate the holders of strict views," he declares with ironic bitterness, "is not pleasure, but only children and a common life and truth and honesty." [7]

Finally, monogamic marriage is attacked by its critics on the ground that its hard and fast dogmas deny the joys of love and motherhood to hundreds of thousands of warm-hearted young women who have not been fortunate enough to find mates or who have had the misfortune to fall in love with men already married. Our present system of lifelong marriage condemns these young women, longing for love, eager for children, to everlasting celibacy and childlessness. Naturally it is women, at present denied the privilege of men to seek actively and openly their mates,

[5] Carpenter, *op. cit.*, pp. 94-5.
[6] *The Morality of Marriage*, pp. 144-5. George Redway, London, 1897.
[7] *Why Men Fight*, p. 189. The Century Co., New York, 1917. By permission.

that suffer most from this aspect of monogamy, and it is women that are most earnest in its condemnation. Grete Meisel-Hess declares that in Germany in 1916 there was an excess of one million women over men. Moreover she estimates that not more than sixty percent of German men marry. In 1900 the German census showed that seventy-eight percent of women eighteen to twenty-five years of age were unmarried, and sixty-six percent of the women of twenty-five to forty years were single. In view of these facts, which enforce celibacy upon millions of young women fit for procreation, she declares that those who would reform our modes of sexual life "aim at complete freedom for all those forms of the erotic life which promote racial progress; freedom, above all, for the work of reproduction in so far as this is the outcome of unrestricted natural selection." [8]

The eminent Swedish writer, Ellen Key, whose death last year was mourned not alone in her native country but in many lands where her literary work is known, also upholds the right of young women, who fail to marry and who ardently desire children, to motherhood outside of marriage. While not encouraging unmarried women to provide themselves with children without love, nevertheless she writes:

"But, on the other hand, the unmarried woman, from her own point of view as well as from that of the race has a right to motherhood, when she possesses so rich a human soul, so great a mother's heart, and so manly a courage that she can bear an exceptional lot. She has all the riches of her own and her lover's nature to leave through the child as a heritage to the race; she has the whole development of her personality, her mental and bodily vital force, her independence won through labor, to give to the child's bringing up. In her occupation she has had use only for a part of her being: she desires to manifest it fully and wholly, before she resigns the gift of life. She therefore becomes a mother with the full approval of her conscience." [9]

THE POSITIVE THEORIES OF THE ADVOCATES OF LOVE'S FREEDOM

It has seemed desirable to present as clearly and impartially as possible the negative and critical aspects of the so-called "new morality," for it is probable that the young men and women of the rising generation will read and hear much of it, and it is well to understand just what the case of the proponents of this theory really is.

[8] Meisel-Hess, op. cit., pp. 32-3. Critic and Guide Co., New York, 1917.
[9] Love and Marriage, pp. 190-1. G. P. Putnam's Sons, New York and London, 1911. By permission.

Needless to say, the advocates of a new morality do not stop with adverse criticisms of monogamic marriage. They have a positive philosophy which should be given a hearing. And first, the reader should make a sharp mental distinction between the serious group which proclaims the desirability of freedom in love and the superficial advocates of unrestricted "free love." The latter are, on the whole, a body of thoughtless or oversexed people, generally ignorant of the important rôles that marriage and the family have played in the long ages during which mankind has climbed from savagery to civilization. Callow, undisciplined and uninformed, this vocal group appears to resent all forms of social restraint that prevent the freest exercise of their sex instinct. The well-being of the race, the glorification of love as a spiritual force, and reverence for the child that is the offspring of love do not enter at all into their shallow, unthinking sex adventures.

The first point that challenges our attention in the views of the more serious group is their exaltation of true love as one of the greatest educative experiences of life, and their emphasis on its more spiritual phases which should always accompany the physical expression of love. Hand in hand with this doctrine goes the theory that the finest fruition of love cannot be attained where love is bound. Only where men and women are free to retrieve their mistakes of ignorance can they both, made wiser by experience, at last achieve the fullness of a noble, satisfying love experience. The last and hardest lesson the race has to learn, says Carpenter, is the lesson of love. Today we are deplorably untutored in its heights and depths, its possibilities for the enrichment of life. Men enter marriage with crude ideals, ignorant of the sexual psychology of women, selfishly eager to satisfy a primitive sexual urge without consideration of the finer spiritual potentialities of the act of intercourse or of the pleasure of their mates. Women are frequently ignorant of the meaning of physical union in marriage, or have only vague ideas about it. Also, they have too often been imbued with the vicious theory that there is something essentially unclean and vile about sexual intercourse, even on the part of those who truly love each other. This belief, of course, tends to develop in them a shrinking distaste for the most intimate expression of love, a prudery and unwillingness to yield themselves to passion that may well prove a reef on which the ship of marriage finally breaks. Thus between the selfish, masterful haste of the male and the ignorant prudery of the female the finest fruits of love are lost, and not rarely love itself.

For this reason, these writers advocate not only freedom to find love in its highest form but *education* in the meaning of love so that it may be understood as something more than affection, something more than a passing sex attraction. Rather should youth be taught that it is the supreme force in life, to enhance or to devastate it. The emphasis on the power of a great love, unrestrained by marriage vows or private contracts, to quicken the spirit, to heighten all the capacities for intellectual and creative endeavor is perhaps strongest in Ellen Key. Thus she writes:

"Love . . . has now become a great spiritual power, a form of genius comparable with any other creative force in the domain of culture, and its production in that region is just as important as in the so-called natural field. Just as now we recognize the right of the artist to shape his work, or of the scientific man to carry out his investigations as it seems good to him, so we must allow to love the right to employ its creative force in its own way provided only that in one way or another it finally conduces to the general good." [10]

The final clause of the quotation is pregnant with meaning. Ellen Key is far from upholding "free love" in the sense of a series of superficial sexual experiments. She expressly declares, however, that the morality of any sexual union, within marriage or out of it, cannot be determined in advance. Only by its outcomes, by its power to enhance life, should it be judged. Love must be held *"subject to the same law as every other creative force; the law of dependence on the whole for its own enhancement to its highest possible value."* [11] In Ellen Key's judgment, love is not an end in itself, to the extent of being unfruitful. "It must give life: if not new living beings then new values; it must enrich the lovers themselves and through them mankind. Here as everywhere the truth which gives faith in life and creates morality is to be found included in the experience which creates happiness; and the most serious charge against certain forms of 'free love' is that it is unhappy love; for there is no unhappy love but the unfruitful." [12]

At this point, the question will inevitably intrude itself upon the mind of the reader, "What is to prevent a succession of love adventures, of cheap and varied sexual experiences, on the part of large numbers of men and women, if all social restraints upon sexual unions are removed?" The prophets of love's freedom seek to meet this objection. In the first place, they freely admit that marriage cannot be suddenly abandoned and all social conventions and laws that bring pressure to

[10] Key, *Love and Marriage*, p. 46. By permission of G. P. Putnam's Sons.
[11] *Ibid.*, pp. 47-8.
[12] *Ibid.*, p. 47.

bear on undisciplined men and women at once removed. Thus Carpenter declares:

"The more people come to recognize the sacredness and naturalness of the real union, the less will they be willing to bar themselves from this by a life-long and artificial contract made in their salad days. . . . Ideally speaking it is plain that anything like perfect union must have perfect freedom for its condition. . . . Practically, however, since a love of this kind is slow to be realized, since social custom is slow to change, and since the partial dependence and slavery of Woman must yet for a while continue, it is likely for such periods that formal contracts of some kind will still be made; only these (it may be hoped) will lose their irrevocable and rigid character, and become in some degree adapted to the needs of the contracting parties.

"Such contracts might, of course, be very various with respect to conjugal rights, conditions of termination, division of property, responsibility for and rights over children, etc. In some cases possibly they might be looked upon as preliminary to a later and more permanent alliance; in others they would provide, for disastrous marriage, a remedy free from the inordinate scandals of the present Divorce Court. . . . In any case we think that marriage contracts, if existing at all, must tend more and more to become matters of private arrangement as far as the relations of husband and wife are concerned, and that this is likely to happen in proportion as woman becomes more free, and therefore, more competent to act in her own right." [13]

In the opinion of this group, the State has a right to interfere in the sex relations of men and women only when children are born of the union; but here its right is unquestionable. Proposals for separation of couples could only be sanctioned by public authorities when satisfactory provisions had been made for the maintenance, care and education of the children of the union. [14]

Thus a few of the leading prophets of the gospel of love's freedom (and Ellen Key is one) advocate a *gradual transition* from coercive marriage to private contract unions. It is clear, however, that the period of private contracts is intended to be relatively brief and transitional. In the end, these writers look to an era of complete freedom for love to find its mate and to grow to a higher spiritual stature than the world has often seen under monogamy. They repudiate the theory that such free-

[13] Carpenter, *op. cit.*, pp. 112-14. By permission of The Modern Library, New York.
[14] *Ibid.*, pp. 115-16.

dom would lead to the throwing off of all restraints and to an era of crude sexual experiments, as various as they were transitory. Both Ellen Key and Carpenter express their faith in the deep desire of fully developed men and women for one satisfying union, for a permanent and unitary love experience. Thus Carpenter holds that "as the spiritual and emotional sides of man develop in relation to the physical there is probably a tendency for our deeper alliances to become more unitary. Though it might be said that the growing complexity of man's nature would be likely to lead him into more rather than fewer relationships, yet on the other hand it is obvious that as the depth and subtlety of any attachment that will really hold him increases, so does such attachment become more permanent and durable, and less likely to be realized in a number of persons." [15] Woman, on her side, because of "her more limited sexual needs, and her long periods of gestation" together with her "more clinging affectional nature" can much more readily than man find her highest satisfaction in a single union if it be happy.

KEYSERLING'S THEORY OF MARRIAGE

Before passing to a critical consideration of the theories set forth above, a brief word should be said of the arresting philosophy of marriage held by Count Keyserling, founder of the School of Wisdom in Darmstadt.[16] This German philosopher looks upon the marriage state as "an elliptical field of force" with two foci, the man and the woman, which can never be merged. The ego of each partner in marriage will forever retain its essential isolation and independence and the interpolar tension created by this fact is the very essence of marriage. Consequently, the yearning of lovers to be merged utterly in the other is eternally unrealizable. Quite frankly Keyserling declares that marriage is not designed by nature to give happiness, although happiness *may* be derived as a by-product of the relationship. Primarily, marriage serves as a means of spiritual discipline, of education in the subordination of the self to the needs of the group, and especially to those of the child. Only those men and women who view marriage as the one best relationship in the cosmos for educating individuals to lift their lives to higher spiritual levels should ever enter into this state of interpolar tension. Only if the man and woman both choose their mates wisely, with the desire to rear offspring, to share a common destiny to the end, to look upon their

[15] Carpenter, *op. cit.*, p. 103.
[16] See Keyserling (Editor), *The Book of Marriage*. Harcourt, Brace and Co., New York, 1926.

union in its universal aspect, as a means of furthering the great cosmic movement toward ever higher spiritual development, should the pair accept the yoke of marriage, which is essentially tragic.

In Keyserling's judgment, marriage is by no means the vocation of all; it is a sort of "order" into which the type of mind that envisages life in its universal aspect will enter, although as the race advances, it may come to be chosen by an increasing number of highly developed persons. For others, free union, not necessarily involving offspring, will become common. For Keyserling holds that the social doctrine that the marriage relation is the best under all possible conditions is a prejudice which society must definitely abandon. In his opinion, the disadvantages of illicit unions are not so great as those of bad marriages, especially if birth control be practised.[17] This German philosopher, then, upholds, on the one hand, a conception of marriage as a discipline for those who strive to bring their lives into harmony with the universal spiritual trend; and, on the other, love unions, more or less temporary, for those who rebel against the legal bonds of wedlock. From an Anglo-Saxon point of view, the stern idealism of the author's conception of marriage stands in striking contrast to his easy, Teutonic acceptance of irregular sex relations.

A CRITICAL EXAMINATION OF THE THEORIES OF THE ADVOCATES
OF FREEDOM IN LOVE

The first criticism that the intelligent reader will inevitably bring against the philosophy of love's freedom has to do with the moral advancement attained by the average man and woman of the present generation. The sketches of married pairs drawn by the very writers who uphold freedom in love reveal narrowness, smugness, jealousy, ill temper and difficulty in adapting the one to the other. Yet, in the next breath, the authors paint glowing canvases setting forth the beauty, the dignity, the nobility of free love relations. Have the individuals who are to enter into these unions undergone "a sea-change," or are they the same plain citizens who constitute the great majority of every nation, uninstructed in the meaning of love and sex functions, muddling along as well as they can, weak, selfish, not too idealistic? Can anyone who shrewdly observes the run of humanity in the twentieth century fail to conclude that most of mankind are living on a lower ethical level than might fairly be expected after thousands of years of culture history? It may be freely admitted that, in every walk of life, there are persons who control their

[17] Keyserling, *op. cit.*, p. 43.

natural impulses in the interest of social and moral ideals and others who perform deeds of unselfishness and heroism which stir in him who sees a profound sense of admiration and faith in the possibilities of human nature for nobility and sheer goodness. But are these not the exceptions that keep alive our belief in the spiritual progress of mankind rather than the daily course of events in the lives of the masses? It has been said *ad nauseam* that this is a materialistic age, a jazz era, marked, above all, by a frenzied search for pleasure in the guise of "thrills," and by a widespread revolt, not alone against the external restraints of custom and convention, but quite as much against those inner controls that are self-imposed. If this indictment be true, it is only to say that we live in an age of social changes so rapid as to be bewildering, wherein the swift current of life has torn many people from their moorings. Perhaps the next generation will have recovered its balance, will have moved on and up to a moral level on which material possessions, physical thrills, constantly varied stimulation and intense absorption in self-advancement do not seem goals of supreme worth.

Even now there are thousands of men and women in every land to whom these ends have small attraction. By means of a happy heredity, family life and education, these people have come to perceive beautiful and enduring satisfactions having little to do with "the flesh pots of Egypt." They have struggled up to a plane of living where beauty in its many forms—in nature, art and music—makes powerful appeal; where the building of a better society is one of the most dynamic motives of life; where, above all, love appears as potentially a mighty creative and ennobling force—the mightiest in human experience. These individuals, self-disciplined and with a sense of responsibility concerning their human relationships, are, perhaps, even now ready to practise freedom in love without moral harm to themselves. For the bonds of Church and State would be substituted the regulations of their own developed consciences. In a considerable degree they have discovered the ultimate meaning of life—self-direction towards satisfying, ideal ends.

But what would be the effect of a release from all external support and authority for the mass of mankind? It can hardly be doubted that large numbers of over-sexed, spiritually under-developed people would give free reign to physical passion and enter upon a period, more or less prolonged, of cheap sexual adventures. It is true that a considerable body of men in every age of social history have lived such lives, and a few have exploited sex to satiety. Possibly a very limited number of women have done so. But the removal of all the restraints of religion, law and public opinion would, the writer believes, encourage that large group of persons in every society who are sensitive to social judgments and lean heavily upon the supports furnished by Church and law, to throw off weak inner restraints and avail themselves of freedom in sex relations before they are morally ready for it. The advocates of love's freedom maintain that this condition would be preferable to the present situation, where lip service only is rendered to monogamy while secret amours may be found on every hand. But *is* it in reality morally preferable? At present large numbers of men and women receive distinct help from more than one social source in maintaining control of that powerful sex urge which seeks to dominate human nature, subordinating all other impulses to its will and not infrequently devastating personality. In the present state of moral development, it is quite possible that under a régime of freedom millions would try one thrilling sex experience after another, only to find in the end complete disillusionment and a kind of moral nausea with regard to love and sex. *For true love, apparently, is not satisfied with mere mating* and the deepest spiritual needs of humanity are frustrated when one powerful impulse of nature leaps into the saddle and rides mankind. The profound disillusionment, the bitter cynicism of certain historic sex profligates should give us pause before we agree to remove such external supports as now exist to buttress inner control.

But there is a further objection to freedom in sex relations, although obviously this may apply only to the initial stages of the movement. It is a fact well known to physicians that a large number of young men visit prostitutes in the years between 18 and 30, and a considerable proportion of this group becomes infected with those diseases that are chiefly spread by prostitution. During the period when sexual freedom was becoming general, inevitably these diseases would be communicated to young women who acted upon the theory that they had as much right to sex experience as men. Girls excited by all-night dancing or motor trips with accompaniments of "petting," would do well to consider whether common prudence, if no worthier ideal, should not restrain them from yielding to the solicitations of their partners and "getting sex experience." It may be objected by the advocates of freedom that, bad as this result would be, it surely is no worse than the infection of wives by husbands. To which it may be replied that, with the spread of knowledge concerning medical treatment for these diseases, more young men are seeking this treatment and obtaining cures before undertaking the serious responsibilities of marriage, and this number will no doubt increase. Moreover, several states already require a clean bill of health in respect to venereal diseases of all men before marriage; and, despite the expense entailed by searching examinations and laboratory tests, it is probable that more states of the Union will add this health requirement to those already existing as prerequisites to securing a marriage license. *No such protection exists in the case of young women who embark on sex adventures before marriage.*

Another important point should be considered. In all probability, popular opinion will remain hostile, for generations to come, to freedom in sex relations. Unless all matings of this sort were designedly sterile, a considerable number of the offspring of these unions, lightly formed and as lightly broken, might well become public charges, as they are at present in the great majority of illegitimacy cases. Therefore organized society has a direct interest in serious, responsible sex unions, and its attitude toward free relations will remain antagonistic for a long time to come. As a necessary corollary, it follows that men and women who form illicit unions will be driven, by reason of the tremendous power of public opinion, to a secretiveness, a "hole and corner" existence, not only painful to all honest persons but often subversive of love itself. Every individual who is tempted to form such an irregular relationship should ask himself if he is willing to lead a life of secrecy, evasion and falsehood, and, if he is, what will be the effect of such a life upon the love that seems now so all-compelling?

But there are other considerations adverse to a reign of sex freedom. In its more lasting form, love reaches beyond the act of mating and seeks a common life and destiny with the beloved; it craves the refuge of a home that endures, amid kaleidoscopic social changes, and the happiness of offspring. Probably a fairly trustworthy criterion by which to distinguish true love from a "passing sex spell" would be the degree in which lovers desired mutuality of life—common hopes, plans, joys and responsibilities, including those that children inevitably bring. Generally speaking, true lovers seem to take "the long view" of their relationship —they look forward to life together through the years and accept the limitations upon *absolute* freedom that it imposes. For it cannot be denied that when two individuals are impelled by love to enter into the most intimate relationship of life, which they plan tó make an enduring one, they must resign to some extent, determined by the exigencies of the situation, their untrammeled freedom as separate individuals. The mutual relationship demands some concessions to the well-being and happiness of the other partner, some degree of subordination of the self to the needs of helpless children.

Nor is this all. So long as society remains unconverted to a philosophy of free love relations, the children of these temporary unions will be stamped from birth with a cruel social stigma. Such children, innocent of any offense, would suffer all their lives for their parents' light-hearted infraction of social laws. This fact should give pause to all lovers who crave both love and offspring. Are they willing to purchase what may prove to be a transitory joy at the expense of the lifelong shame and handicapping of children who did not seek to be born?

There is a final point which should not be overlooked. The psychology of the man and woman who enter into a free relationship is almost antithetical to that of the partners who look forward to a common life, to the making of a home in accord with their heart's desire, to the rearing of offspring. Under a régime of sex freedom, each mate, whether consciously or not, harbors in his mind the idea that if the relationship is not immediately and continuously satisfactory it can be easily terminated. Most women and some men expect that the romantic glamour of courtship can and should persist throughout the period of their union; that the ardor of first passion can endure. If they are disappointed in these hopes —and women nourish them far more often than realistic men—if the lover grows less thrillingly interesting, as he or she comes to be better known; if misunderstandings occasionally occur, the natural tendency is promptly to regard the relationship as a mistake, the choice of a mate a misguided one. Then, if the disillusionment is mutual, each may seek another and more fortunate experience; or, if only one partner is discontented, the other is left desolate. In the case of marriage, the psychology is quite different. The initial love may be no stronger but, in this case, it is reinforced by the desire for a permanent life together which leads to the will to make the union an enduring success. Each partner, knowing that he has taken the other with the hope that their relationship may be lifelong, seeks to make allowances for the other, to concede and adapt to this human being so intimately linked to oneself. Misunderstandings and bickerings will occur, but they will be understood as the perhaps unavoidable accompaniments of the delicate business of adaptation of one complex personality to another. Again "the long view" will be taken and this will aid love in making the necessary adjustments. If the partners win through the first difficult years of married life, they will find in the end that they have exchanged romantic glamour and flaming passion for a deep, abiding love, calmer, but none the less joy-giving, and for a comradeship based on mutual understanding that will grow dearer and more satisfying with the passage of the years. This happy relationship, which many married couples know, is not a free gift to the shallow and impatient lover; it is the hard-won prize of those mates who set before themselves an ideal of married life that transcends passion, and leads them to seek harmony of interests and purposes. Those who have once achieved this relationship of comrades, who are at the same time true and tranquil lovers, no doubt would, if they could, testify that it is the most profoundly satisfying and enriching of all human ties.

But having testified to the beauty of the marital relationship at its finest, it is necessary to add that, with the best will in the world, some couples cannot achieve it. Unsuspected incompatibilities—sexual, temperamental, intellectual—thrust up their heads after wedlock and resist every effort to harmonize them. Lovers who craved an eternity of intimate companionship before their marriage discover at the end of a year or two that they are quite unsuited to each other, and that their honest efforts to adjust one to the other meet with little or no success. Day by day, week by week the incompatibilities assert themselves more powerfully, and the rift between two maladjusted personalities widens to a chasm. Even the little mannerisms and superficial characteristics that once seemed to each lover so delightful in the other come to appear as irritating habits that serve to make their union more intolerable.

In such a state of affairs, the only course to follow, in the interest of love itself, is a permanent separation. At this point the writer finds herself in agreement with the advocates of freedom in love who proclaim that love is too spiritual and precious a force to be subjected to the degradation of a wrangling, hateful relationship. In the future it is possible that the more advanced societies will adopt the method of making divorce more easy and robbing it of its devastating features of publicity, rather than the alternative of accepting the views of the prophets of love's freedom. This larger freedom of divorce might not entail much social and individual injury *if it were accompanied by a sound, scientific and idealistic education of young people for marriage, beginning early in life*. It is putting the cart before the horse to increase the restrictions on divorce rather than to provide what is so urgently needed in our present day society—intelligent preparation for true marriage.

In another respect, the writers who advocate freer love relations have taken a sound position. Ellen Key is everlastingly right when she declares that our present moral doctrine, which affirms on the one hand the necessity for absolute celibacy before marriage and, on the other, does nothing to make it possible for warm-blooded young people to marry between twenty and thirty, is gravely defective. Our whole economic system, combined with high standards of living, throws obstacles in the way of early marriage, especially of the educated groups. What we need today is more honest, more realistic thinking concerning the sex problems of young men and women. If pre-marital continence is a fine ideal, it is time for those who advocate our present social *mores* to ask themselves how this ideal can be rescued from the lofty atmosphere of abstract thinking and made a practical reality on earth. As Popenoe points out, employers are taking it for granted that young persons will spend the best and most romantic years of their youth "establishing themselves" in a business or profession before they seriously think of marriage; and public opinion supports them in this attitude. The outcomes are long-delayed marriages, increase of prostitution, social over-stimulation of sex impulses of young people, on the one hand, with denial of the right to express them on the other, thus leading in some cases to mental disturbances and neuroses.[18] A social order that exposes youth to a stream of sexual stimuli issuing from the press, the theatre, the cabarets, the moving picture houses, should at least set itself to work to encourage and pave the way for earlier marriages. Otherwise it exposes itself to the charge of upholding a theoretical and insincere moral standard entailing pernicious social consequences. In the words of Ellen Key:

"All preaching of morality to youth which does not at the same time condemn the state of society that favors immorality, but makes the realization of youthful love an impossibility, is more than stupidity, it is a crime." [19]

Will Marriage Persist in the Future?

That an age of sharp social transitions will be accompanied by radical experiments in new ways of living, including freer forms of sex relationship, seems inevitable. But this is not to say that the institution of marriage is seriously endangered. Those who foretell the gradual disappearance of monogamy seem lacking in the historic sense. Is it reasonable to suppose that an ancient social institution, growing out of human need and experience, will yield to the first onset of a band of opponents who seek to take it by assault? No doubt in the days of Luther and Calvin there were those who prophesied that the Church could not survive the breach made in its unity by the Protestant Revolt. Many must have been the seers that foretold the destruction of all government during the Revolutions in

[18] Paul Popenoe, *The Conservation of the Family*, pp. 68-9. Williams & Wilkins Co., Baltimore, 1926.
[19] Key, *op. cit.*, p. 139.

France and Russia. Yet the Church lives on; and the governments of the French and the Soviet Republic seem as strong as they ever were. Changes there will be in marriage, no doubt, changes tending to free the personalities of husband and wife, as well as those of their children, from too suffocating a dependence and intimacy, too narrow a relationship to the world outside the family. But, in the judgment of the author, marriage itself is destined to endure because it provides the best means mankind has yet discovered for transforming passion into tender, abiding love and for guaranteeing a stable home for children, in which they may be nurtured and educated, by parents who respect their individuality, into free, self-directed citizens of a democracy.

TOPICS FOR REPORTS

1. Analyze and comment upon the view of marriage expounded by Count Keyserling.

    Count Herman Keyserling (Editor), *The Book of Marriage*, pp. 3-49. Harcourt, Brace & Co., New York, 1926.

2. The Future of Marriage and the Home.

    Mona Caird, *The Morality of Marriage*, pp. 115-27, 138-56. George Redway, London, 1897.

    Ernest R. Groves, *The Drifting Home*, Chs. IV, IX. Houghton Mifflin Co., Boston, 1926.

3. The Evolution and Meaning of Love.

    Ellen Key, *Love and Marriage*, Chs. II, III. G. P. Putnam's Sons, New York, 1911.

4. The New Philosophy of Youth.

    Ernest R. Groves, *op. cit.*, Ch. VI.

    George A. Coe, *What Ails Our Youth*, Chs. I, V. Charles Scribner's Sons, New York, 1925.

5. A Critical Consideration of the Theory of "Free Love."

    Maude Royden, *Sex and Common Sense*, Ch. III. G. P. Putnam's Sons, New York and London, 1922.

All these of these theories are based on sex. They all amount to legalized prostitution

Criticism of trial marriage.
1. Problem of children.
2. Spreading of disease.
3. Psychologically, they enter the union
   with the idea that they can throw
   it overboard if not satisfied.
4. Based on sex.

II - Freedom in love.
   There is no restriction at all. It is
about the same as promiscuity.
   It would involve state care of children.

PART FOUR

THE CHILD AND THE FAMILY OF THE FUTURE

CHAPTER XXIII

THE RENAISSANCE OF FAMILY EDUCATION

NEW INTEREST IN THE FAMILY AS AN AGENCY OF EDUCATION

THE last twenty-five years have witnessed an awakening of interest in the young child and his education that is probably unparalleled in history in its extent and sincerity. This social phenomenon bears witness to the truth of Ellen Key's statement that in the future the twentieth century will be known as "the century of the child." Not only has there been very marked advance in the knowledge of child psychology, but, in certain progressive schools, educational procedure with regard to young children has been revolutionized. Nor is the mounting interest in the child and his growth confined to educators. Parents in all advanced countries, but perhaps more especially in the United States, are showing clear signs of a quickened interest and concern in the wholesome development of their offspring into unwarped maturity. Witness the spread of parent-teacher associations, of child-study organizations and parents' clubs.

Owing to the new importance that psychologists and mental hygienists attach to the first six years of the child's mental and physical growth, attention is being focussed upon the family as the child's first school. The determining influence of family situations, of parental example and guidance, upon the entire life of the child, in its physical, intellectual and emotional phases, is clearly enough understood by psychiatrists and teachers of small children, and is gradually being comprehended by an ever-increasing body of intelligent parents. In consequence, the present age is privileged to see and take part in a renaissance of parental education that may eventuate in a new generation of adults that have escaped the warping, repressive influences of much of our parental treatment of children in the past.

UNDERLYING CAUSES OF THIS AWAKENING

Unsatisfactory Functioning of the Home.

When the student of social conditions seeks for the causes of the new interest in family education, he is confronted with the fact of the maladjustment of the home, not only to external social conditions, but to the basic requirements of the family members. That the home is not successfully meeting either the demands of society or the deepest needs of its members is evidenced by the prevalence of juvenile delinquency and crime, by outbursts of suicidal mania among youth, by the establishment and spread of child guidance clinics, juvenile courts and the probation system. Unsuccessful functioning of the family is further revealed by the alarming growth of mental and nervous diseases, culminating in nervous breakdowns. Psychiatrists now hold that the original source of these diseases is commonly to be sought in the frictions and strains of unhappy family life in childhood. The leading mental hygienists of Europe and the United States have declared over and over again that few cases of nervous breakdown have ever been brought to their attention in individuals who began life in happy, frictionless homes. Apparently the chief cause of all serious neuroses is to be found in the mistaken treatment that the patient has received in his childhood at the hands of parents who loved him, but failed utterly to understand the fundamental needs of his developing nature.

Parental ignorance is, however, not the sole reason why the family is performing its ancient functions so unsatisfactorily. The conditions of modern life in our huge urban centers are so complex that both the child and his parents find difficulty in adjusting to them. Homes consist of a few or many rooms on "shelves" of tall apartment houses. They bear not the remotest resemblance to the original homes of man—simple huts in the open, with wide stretches of earth, air, lake and river around them. Although life was laborious in some early societies, it was simple and relatively without strain. At present, both adults and children in our large cities live under conditions of hurry, noise, competition and nervous tension. There are no back yards for city children to play in, no materials with which to build things, no wide, free spaces in which a child may run and work off surplus energy, making as much noise as he likes in the process. Scarcely a home in our huge centers of population today is built with the slightest attention to the original impulses and needs of children. Scarcely an apartment house manager in most cities is disposed to welcome or even tolerate babies. It is not surprising then, that, among the well-to-do classes occupying apartments, families are small. Even so, in our five-room and six-room flats, privacy is hard to secure, and the family cannot easily get away from under each other's feet unless they go outside for amusement.

In the case of children, as we have seen, modern family life provides almost nothing that gives an outlet to original nature and interests.

In the case of parents, particularly fathers, the strain of business and professional competition is so intense that they are often exhausted by night and have nothing to give to their families except the tenseness and irritability that accompany nervous strain. Under such conditions the child develops what has been called a "protection reaction" to the unsatisfactory elements in his home environment and sometimes becomes a "problem child."

Another important reason for the fact that our homes are not successfully performing their functions lies in the defective relations of parents to each other. As has so often been said before, the freeing of women from feudal disabilities, the opening to them of almost every avenue to higher education, to the world's work and to achievement therein, has meant that some women are no longer satisfied with an exclusively domestic life. Many a married woman, who has discovered and tried out her special powers in business or professional occupations before marriage, grows restless and dissatisfied with the more or less routine, unorganized duties of home-making and the constant, exacting care of small children. Being both more frank and more honest than her feminine forbears, who perforce yielded to powerful social pressure designed to keep women contented wives and mothers in the home, the modern woman, if she be unfitted for household tasks, voices in no uncertain tones her discontent with a purely domestic career. She is not ashamed to say that her peculiar talents are not such as to make her a successful housewife and child nurse, or even the best person to guide wisely and well the developing nature of her child. Fifty years ago few women indeed would have made such an honest admission, and a century ago no woman would have dared to do so. Willy-nilly, she would have pretended to be just that loving, self-sacrificing wife and mother, wholly absorbed in home interests, that represented the social ideal of womanhood.

Now, because thousands of married women are dissatisfied with the home duties that have been allotted to them, they unwittingly "project" all their unsatisfied desires and unfulfilled wishes upon their children. Often, quite unconsciously, restless, discontented mothers use their helpless children as a means of obtaining release from their inner conflicts. What is the inevitable outcome of such an atmosphere upon a little child? Mental hygienists and psychiatrists are at one in stressing the "overwhelming effect of the parents' conduct upon the child." They declare that the "subjective relation of the child to his environment is enormous; and thus without words at all, his reactions are determined, his habits created, and all the complex impressions and motivations evoked that determine his entire future life."[1] If this be true, an enormous importance attaches to the fact that an ever-growing body of wives and mothers are in a state of mental rebellion against their domestic lot. What warps and repressions of child nature may not be traced back, step by step, to the unhappiness of frustrated mothers who, although deeply loving their children, are unfitted to be constantly with them, guiding and influencing their unfolding natures?

The influences with which the home surrounds the child are also determined by other factors. The relations of husband and wife, the sort of married life they have worked out together, determine to an extraordinary extent the spiritual atmosphere of the home. If their daily association results in nagging and conflict, in a constant irritability, which is the outward and visible sign of incompatibility of temperaments, the effects upon children are nothing short of disastrous. Almost equally harmful is the home where the casual visitor can see no overt evidences of disharmony, but where a fundamental lack of mutual sympathy and understanding, and consequently of coöperation on the part of husband and wife, produces a family spirit that is far from happy and wholesome. A perfectly normal child may react to such home conditions in unsocial ways that appear to have no relation whatever to the unhappy atmosphere of the home. For example, he may begin to develop certain undesirable physical reactions such as sleeplessness, difficulties with his food, abnormal sex tendencies. Or he may react to the situation in a mental way by indulging in temper tantrums, bullying of younger children or servants, jealousy, quarrelsomeness or a stubborn negativism. Of these unfortunate victims of family conflict, Dr. Thom writes:

"It is not surprising to find that a very large per cent of all our problems of social conduct, such as destructiveness, lying, stealing, truancy and assaults, come from the friction home. This means, then, that the friction home is the workshop which specializes in turning out children who, during the first six years of life, fail to develop habits and inhibitions which are so essential to efficiency and happiness in later life."[2]

The New Psychology.

Another potent cause of the widespread quickening of interest in the pre-school child and in parental education lies in the rapid development

[1] Dr. Beatrice Hinkle, "New Relations of Men and Women as Family Members," in *Concerning Parents*, pp. 17, 18. New Republic, Inc., New York, 1926.
[2] Dr. D. A. Thom, "The Importance of the Early Years," in *Concerning Parents*, p. 109. New Republic, Inc., New York, 1926.

of child psychology, mental hygiene and psycho-analysis during the last twenty-five years. The newer psychology, with its emphasis on *behavior*, on the child's reactions to the flood of stimuli furnished by his environment, has called the attention of educators and parents alike to the paramount importance of the stimulus-response bonds formed in the nervous mechanism of every human being by his early experiences. Likewise child psychology has stressed the significant rôle played by imitation (of parents and others) in shaping the personality of a little child in his formative period. Referring to the proneness of small children to imitate the characteristic manners and actions of their parents, Dr. Richardson says:

"The overwhelming importance of the home, and of the character of each one of its members, is due to the enormous power of this charteristic of imitation in character formation. . . . It is the constant imitation of *ourselves,* who as their parents are the ones in closest and most constant touch with them, that is responsible for the results that we have been attributing to our sage counsels." [3]

Apparently the first five or six years of the child's life are of the utmost importance so far as his capacity to receive impressions from the conduct of his parents is concerned; and of these formative years, the *first* is easily the most influential. Physicians and psychologists tell us that, at an age when it seems impossible that the child can be in any sense conscious of what goes on around him, his plastic mind registers "parental tricks and habits and mannerisms" which appear long after to dismay the parents. Indeed, imitation of parents (conscious and unconscious) may go so far in impressionable children as to result in what is known as *identification* of the child with the parent.[4] In such cases, the child may so think himself into the feelings and thoughts of father or mother, as these are revealed in the parent's characteristic reactions, that he may develop a personality, through close daily imitation, that is more or less identical with that of his model.

When confronted with such psychological facts, parents may well pause and take account of those traits of character that they have built into their personalities through habit, which serve every day as suggestive models to their children. An honest and thoughtful inventory of personal traits and habits on the part of fathers and mothers would, in many instances, lead to resolute attempts to modify, if not to eradicate them.

[3] *Parenthood and the Newer Psychology,* pp. 63-4. G. P. Putnam's Sons, New York, 1926. By permission.
[4] See Richardson, *op. cit.,* pp. 68-9.

Of the utmost significance, also, are the new theories concerning the emotional development of the child, advanced by the behavioristic school of psychologists and by mental hygienists. These specialists in mental reactions declare that the emotional patterns of the adult are laid down very early in the life of the child. Fears, dislikes, prejudices, all sorts of emotional attitudes are acquired by children in their early years as a result of experiences which the unthinking adult regards as trifling and not worthy of consideration. Only by "re-conditioning" the experiences of the child can these emotions be modified. For instance, Watson tells us of a child who fell and struck his head against the bath-tub just as he was about to be bathed. He at once developed a lively fear of water, which under ignorant treatment might have continued for years, if not into adult life. The unwise parent would insist upon his getting into the bath-tub each day in the hope of overcoming his fear. This course would inevitably lead to a violent struggle between parent and child, which might not only increase the child's fear but encourage in him a negativistic attitude. On the other hand, the informed parent would try another method. For a few days she would sponge the child off while he stood on a rug, and follow this procedure with a sponging while he stood in a basin containing a little water. The depth of the water could be increased from day to day until the child gradually lost his fear and was ready to try the bath-tub again, at first with just a little water in the bottom. Since it was a conditioned set of circumstances—the fall and striking the bath-tub half full of water—that produced the fear, it must be a re-conditioning of circumstances that removes it.[5]

One of the most suggestive teachings of the new psychology regarding emotions is the idea of "emotional fixation"—the theory that something may happen to arrest the normal emotional development of the child and "fixate" his emotions at an immature stage. This is a very serious matter, about which parents are greatly in need of enlightenment, for such fixations result in tragic consequences in later life. In the opinion of mental hygienists, they are the fertile soil from which spring those mental eccentricities, moods of depression, idiosyncrasies that may in time become serious neuroses, making life difficult for those who suffer from them and causing the victims to be burdens to their friends. Every parent should know something of these emotional fixations and how they are brought about. Psycho-analysts tell us that there are two antithetical ways in which a child's emotions may become "fixated" at an immature stage of

[5] See Article by J. B. Watson, "What to Do When Your Child Is Afraid," in *Children*, March, 1927, p. 27.

his development. If a child is prevented by parental authority or other cause from *living through* an emotional experience at the time that emotion normally appears, the child may suffer a fixation at that level. On the other hand, if a child is encouraged to *prolong* and over-stress an emotional stage, instead of being helped to grow out of it up to a less childish level, his emotion may and probably will become fixated. Thus he will be unable to experience the full gamut of the emotional life which most adults have passed through.

What are the emotional stages at which a fixation may occur in the case of love, the most powerful of all emotional forces? The first stage, say the psycho-analysts, is that of physical sensation, of pleasure in mere muscular vigor and activity, in animal sensations. Then comes the stage of self-love, called the "narcissistic stage," in reference to the Greek myth of Narcissus, who fell in love with his own image reflected in a quiet pool. There is grave danger that an ignorant and prudish mother, not understanding that a child's interest in his naked body and in muscular movements of limbs or face is a perfectly natural thing, may rebuke him and even try to shame him for such naïve self-love. By so doing she prevents him from getting from this stage all of the emotional satisfaction there is in it, so that it may be outgrown and make way, as it will in all normal children, for the next level of emotional life. Of course an uninstructed parent may do the exact opposite and exaggerate and prolong the narcissistic period by extravagant admiration of her child's beautiful little body. In either case, an emotional fixation may occur at that point. Adults of either sex who spend an inordinate amount of time and money upon their persons and show an absorbing interest in dress and adornment are examples of individuals emotionally fixated at a childish stage of development. They will never care deeply for people other than themselves; and if they marry and have families, the chances of the family members to find happiness are slender indeed. Of course there is a certain emotional "hang-over" from each of these stages that is perfectly natural and wholesome. For example, most healthy, vigorous adults take pleasure in their sense of physical well-being, although they do not long dwell on it. Similarly the emotional tone of the narcissistic stage persists into mature life in the form of a decent self-regard for one's appearance that causes men and women to dress as becomingly as they can.

According to the psycho-analysts, the next period in emotional evolution is that wherein the child develops an absorbing love of its mother. Although this, too, is an entirely natural stage, it bristles with dangers if the child is in the hands of well-meaning but ignorant parents. On the one hand, the mother and father may be too absorbed in their own affairs to give the child the legitimate amount of cuddling and affection that it deeply needs. Or they may resent the birth of another child into a family already too numerous for the family purse. Whatever the reason may be for denying to the child his due share of "mothering," the consequences may be nothing short of calamitous. For the records of orphan asylums and all public institutions for young children show plainly that emotionally undernourished babies have a high mortality rate. Even if these children survive the lack of parental love and cuddling, "there is inflicted a definite injury, whose results may, and probably will, last as long as the life of the individual." [6]

But far more common is the mistake of spoiling the child with too lavish a display of love and of binding him too closely in dependence upon the mother. In some families, the entire household revolves about the whims and tantrums of a spoiled child who has never encountered any firm opposition to his will because his mother has developed an utterly selfish, absorbed love of her child. It is one thing for a mother to meet a child's natural cravings for affection and it is quite another to submerge herself in mother love, and to seek, as some mothers do, to center their children's affection wholly upon themselves, long after it should have reached out to others. Such devouring maternal love inflicts irreparable injury upon the child. Instead of striving to hold his affection fast bound to herself, the wise mother will direct the cravings of her child for love toward others in the family and outside it. By so doing she will give her child a fair chance of attaining a rich and varied emotional life in his maturity. If she seeks to prolong the stage of mother love through which her child is passing, if she refuses to recognize that he must not always be helplessly dependent upon her, she may fixate him at the emotional level of early childhood and make him liable to some of the unhappiest experiences which a human being can undergo. The child with a so-called "Œdipus complex" is likely to be sensitive, unhappy away from home, a "mother's boy" who becomes fair game all his boyhood for his ruthless schoolmates. The same holds true of the girl. In the opinion of mental hygienists of wide experience with these cases, such an individual will be permanently crippled in his (or her) love life, forever unable to consummate a happy marriage. Doting mother-attachment on the part of a son or of father-love on the part of a daughter often renders it tragically impossible for either to "fall in love" in the mature, responsible, self-forgetting sense, or to establish a happy family life.

[6] Richardson, *op. cit.*, p. 18.

If the child passes successfully through the earlier stages of love for himself and his mother, his affection and interest will reach out toward others within the family, and later in the school and the neighborhood. As he grows older and broadens the range of his social contacts, he will find a growing number of persons, chiefly of his own sex, to like and perhaps to admire. The intelligent parent will encourage the child to form friendships outside the family circle, for these are not only the mark of his partial escape from parent dependency but also the sign that his emotional life is gradually approaching the adult level.

Then comes adolescence, the period of storm and stress in the lives of not a few boys and girls, and of some degree of emotional tension in most. Now, if all has gone well up to this time, the boy will begin to entertain romantic fancies centering about some girl or older woman. He may imagine himself in love half a dozen times before the reality comes to him, but each experience, if wholesome, will serve to prepare him for the deep and real emotion that is lasting. In the case of the girl, there is probably a period in her life between sixteen and eighteen when she "discovers" her father and tends to make a hero of him (if this is at all possible). He appears to her then as the embodiment of her budding ideals of manhood. The wise father will neither repulse nor encourage this hero-worship, but will seek to direct the interest of his daughter toward young men of her own age.

At this stage, parents will do well to allow their adolescent children a larger liberty and freer association with individuals of the opposite sex than they have hitherto enjoyed, even if the friends chosen by their sons and daughters do not always wholly commend themselves to the parents. While remaining somewhat "on the side-lines," ever ready to help and advise when they are needed, parents must accept some anxiety as their lot while their adolescent girls and boys are widening the circle of their friendships with the opposite sex and discovering for themselves that Jill is a little vulgar and selfish, and Jack is quicker with his fists than with his brain. As Dr. Frankford Williams has so earnestly pointed out, the two great needs of the adolescent are (1) to emancipate himself or herself from the family and (2) to establish his or her heterosexuality—that is, his or her capacity to fall in love with a member of the other sex.[7] Needless to say, well-meaning parents may deny both essential needs—in the one case by resisting the youth's natural desire for greater independence, in the other by preventing him or her from

[7] "Confronting the World—the Adjustments of Later Adolescence," in *Concerning Parents*, p. 138. This entire article is valuable.

forming friendships with members of the opposite sex through fear that harm will come of it. In cases where the adolescent does not succeed in freeing himself from parental control he never becomes a self-reliant person. If he never breaks away from mother-love or father-love to the extent of falling sincerely in love, it may truly be said that the very affection and concern of his parents have been stumbling blocks in the path of his development to emotional maturity.

To the mental hygienists, sex love appears as the most powerful force in the life of the individual. These specialists are daily brought in contact with men and women whose lives have been warped, thwarted or devastated by this tremendous emotion, so pregnant with possibilities for the heightening of human powers and the enrichment of human life—or the reverse. Out of the depths of their experience, these students of the unconscious motives of human action urge parents to recognize the fact that sex interest manifests itself very early in the life of the child, and must be intelligently guided from the time of its first appearance. Feelings more or less directly concerned with the sex function sometimes appear as early as the second year, and by the age of five, curiosity about sex may be quite active in the normal child. Indeed, psycho-analysts say that five is the age at which many critical experiences occur which form the material of sex repressions. By the term *repression* is, of course, meant "purposive or intentional forgetting"—the method of solving an inner conflict by thrusting impulses and their accompanying ideas into the unconscious substratum of mental life. If, for example, a child asks his parent where babies come from and is hushed up or reproved, this idea may come to be associated with the mysterious and the shameful. Many children who have met with rebuffs of this kind, especially if accompanied with the stupid parental rebuke, "Nice little girls (or boys) don't ask such questions," will push the matters about which they are curious below the threshold of consciousness and refuse to allow them to come up into the light of truth and understanding. These repressions may result in giving the child a permanent bias in life. Denied the satisfaction of his legitimate curiosity, he may never come to appreciate the beauty of the sex life in its ideal forms because he has never been able to throw off his early impressions of sex as in some way indecent, and never to be acknowledged and frankly talked about.

The first thing that parents should realize is that the more sound information a curious child receives from its parents before the sexual feelings associated with puberty appear, the better for the child. Apparently, frank and honest answers given to small children's questions do not cause any difficulty or embarrassment in their minds. There is an impressive body of evidence to the effect that a child feels no shock of surprise to learn that both a father and a mother are needed to produce a baby —or a puppy—and that both come from the mother's body. Of course, this early sex knowledge is gained in the most natural way if the child has pets—cats, dogs or rabbits. Parents should accept, as the first principle of sex instruction, that a child must never be snubbed when he shows curiosity about sex. On the contrary, the mother or father should always convey by word and manner that the child's question was a sensible and interesting one, and he or she will answer it as fully as the child's understanding permits. Those parents show true wisdom who treat the subject of sex as a part of the whole of nature and life, neither to be avoided as indecent nor talked about in hushed tones as a solemn mystery apart from everyday life. The more prompt, cheerful and matter-of-fact the information given by the parent to the child whenever it is asked for, the better.

These are only a few of the ideas that the new psychology is offering to parents. Further light is thrown on childish fears, on the desire of children to create a sensation and thus occupy the center of the family stage, on the tendency of some children to flee from a world of reality too harsh for them to bear into a world of phantasy from which they may be recalled with difficulty if they are allowed to dwell too frequently therein. When well-meaning parents are first introduced to this array of novel facts and theories about the workings of their children's minds, they are not only bewildered, but not a few tend to lose confidence in their capacity to rear and guide their boys or girls without committing one or more of the serious mistakes already mentioned. It is small wonder that intelligent parents have come to feel that they are poorly equipped —as indeed they are—to avoid the pitfalls that the new psychology has revealed as lying directly in their path.

THE RENAISSANCE OF PARENTAL EDUCATION

I. Efforts of Parents to Help Themselves.

Stirred by a sense of their own insufficiency, parents began years ago to remedy it by studying the physical and mental natures of their children. Not only have parent-teacher associations been in existence many years, as a means whereby parents might coöperate with teachers in understanding and treating the problems of their children in school, but parents have felt the need of forming an organization of their own. As early as 1888, a group of mothers organized "The Society for the Study of Child Nature," at the prompting of Professor Felix Adler. The purpose of the society was to inform parents concerning what psychologists and educators had to say about child development. Other groups were formed in various localities, each carrying on its own program of study. So vital was the impulse that led to the formation of these child-study groups, and so numerous did they become, that in 1912 the Federation for Child Study came into existence as a means of unifying the separate groups and furnishing them with the advantages of a central organization. Gradually, as the study groups grew more numerous through the agency of conferences, lectures and publications they spread from coast to coast. In 1924, the Federation was incorporated under a new name—the Child Study Association of America.

As its name suggests, the purpose of the Association "consists in devising ways to make available to parents the knowledge of child life and human nature which we have now and which is constantly being increased, so that they can meet situations in their home intelligently and effectively. Groups of mothers and fathers working together, studying authorities and discussing their problems, still remain the most important of these methods, even though other ideas and techniques have developed." [8]

In New York City, the various study groups have organized a group leaders' council which prepares detailed programs concerning children of different ages that are of the utmost assistance to the particular groups in planning their year's study. To supplement the work of individual groups, the Child Study Association offers each year conferences and lectures in which the speakers are men and women of national importance in the fields of child study, mental hygiene and nursery school education. Summer play schools have been organized in several cities for the benefit of children who cannot leave the city during the hot season. An interesting new departure has been the establishment of visiting mothers' committees, which coöperate with visiting teachers in the public schools, going into homes where children are not happily adjusted to school and home life. These mothers can often establish sympathetic relations with mothers of difficult problem children that teachers find it hard, if not impossible, to make. A Committee on Research has also been organized to keep abreast of new discoveries or novel theories concerning child life and development, to evaluate them and make reports to Association members. Manuals for group study, a magazine called *Child Study* and a series of pamphlets

[8] "Annual Program" (1925-26), p. 5. Child Study Association of America.

on such topics as Habit, Obedience and Punishment are published from time to time for the benefit of members.

It seems clear that educated parents in America are viewing their parental responsibilities in a new spirit—a spirit of frank recognition that there is much they need to know, an attitude of intelligent inquiry and exploration. This condition is rich in promise for the future, especially as all these educative activities have grown out of the parents' own sense of their deficiencies. The next step should be an effort to include the mothers of the working class in this movement. Hitherto the membership and work of the Association have been largely confined to women of the prosperous middle class. How to interest foreign-born women, coming from lands where patriarchal ideas about children still prevail, where parents are too often domestic autocrats, not yet even dimly awake to the importance of studying the physical and mental natures of their offspring—how to secure the active coöperation of these women in the purposes and activities of the Child Study Association is a problem that should challenge the attention and enlist the best energies of the leaders in the new movement.

II. The Nursery School Movement.

The profound need of small children between two and five years of age for more intelligent nurture and guidance has led to the establishment of nursery schools in England and America. In England, where the first school was opened about fifteen years ago, the movement grew out of a different situation and has developed in a different way from that in America. The first nursery school in London was established by Rachel and Margaret MacMillan in 1912 to meet the critical needs of small children of the poor who flocked to a neighboring clinic—tiny sufferers from diseases most of which could have been prevented by wholesome nurture and plenty of fresh air. Despite the poverty of England since the war, the schools have increased in number, although not to the extent that might have been expected under normal economic conditions. In these nursery schools the under-nourished, neglected children of London's poor are received and given the chance to play in open, sunshiny spaces, to make friends with flowers, birds, rabbits and other small animals, to be bathed and physically examined every day by nurse or doctor, to grow strong on a diet suited to their physical demands, even to shed their ugly clothing, "the livery of poverty," and slip into more comfortable and attractive garments. Attention is paid to speech and table manners, to the formation of habits of cleanliness, regularity of life, consideration of the rights of other children. Songs, dances, play with a variety of toys and objects, lessons in color discrimination and exercises with Montessori apparatus fill up the days with happy, developing activities.

In America the nursery school has grown out of the need of well-to-do middle-class parents first, for better nurture and guidance of their children in the pre-school years, and second, for a sounder education of the parents themselves in the new theories regarding the child's physical and mental growth. On the whole, then, the nursery schools of America, still few in number, but spreading, perhaps, more rapidly than trained women can be found to staff them, serve the needs of the educated class and ignore the poor; whereas their English prototypes confine their efforts to the most needy class and pass over children in the families of the prosperous. Needless to say, if the nursery school does promote the physical, mental and moral development of toddlers between eighteen months and five years, its advantages, already clearly demonstrated in the Merrill-Palmer school in Detroit, should be brought within the reach of all social classes. This will, in the opinion of the writer, be the next great forward step in educational progress.

The American nursery school also differs from its English model in being far better financed, and therefore more able to furnish expert nursing and physicians' care, physical, psychometric and psychological examinations and tests, the coöperation of trained dietitians, psychologists and teachers. Moreover, the nursery schools of the United States are frequently more or less intimately associated with universities, as, for example, the Child Welfare Research Station, the school in connection with the University of Iowa, the Merrill-Palmer school and the Institute of Child Welfare Research, Teachers College, Columbia University.

Now that so much is already known of the primary importance of the years between two and six in determining an individual's character and successful adjustment to life; now that a steady stream of light is being shed on the deficiencies of even the so-called "good" homes which, in the opinion of O'Shea, "are becoming unsuited to minister to the primitive nature and needs of young children," nursery schools are bound, it would seem, to grow in numbers, as their value is more thoroughly appreciated. The nursery school is constructed and equipped especially for little children, who require ample space, air and sunshine, toys and materials with which to play, to build, to express their interests, and opportunity to run, jump and make a noise without being suppressed and reproved by mothers anxious about their house furnishings. At present few homes offer these advantages to small children. To quote O'Shea again:

"We know that nine out of ten American homes are not organized or conducted with special reference to the needs of children of pre-school age. In the construction of our houses, practically no consideration is given to the question of the needs of young children. The writer has had a survey made of a large proportion of the houses in a mid-western city with a view to finding out whether in their construction any thought was taken of the possibility of young children living in them; and the number of houses which have been planned with a view to making proper provision for the care and culture of babies, as contrasted with older children and with adults, is so small as to be negligible. The investigation asked the parents why they did not consider the needs of young children at all in building their houses, and the usual response was, 'Why do babies need special arrangements which are not suitable for older children or adults?' This illustrates the attitude of the typical parent toward the nature and needs of children of pre-school age—they do not need any special arrangements in order that they may develop physically, intellectually, and temperamentally in the best way." [9]

Nursery schools will not only minister more and more to the developmental needs of small children, particularly in crowded cities, but they will serve parents in two ways. First, they will provide, by means of informal visits and well-planned courses for parents, the much-needed education which will enable fathers and mothers to escape the pitfalls that beset their path in the up-bringing of their children. Who can predict how much maladjustment to the situations of life may not be avoided by such intelligent guidance of small boys and girls! The second service rendered by the nursery school to parents consists in freeing vocationally trained mothers from the home in order that they may engage in work better suited to their special aptitudes. This will not in the least prevent those mothers who enjoy home-making tasks, including the care of children, from making this work their own. In it lie the possibilities of an interesting and challenging career for all women whose talents incline them toward it.

TOPICS FOR REPORTS

1. The Dangers of Ignorant Parenthood.
   Frank H. Richardson, M.D., *Parenthood and the Newer Psychology,* Chs. I-IV, VI-X. G. P. Putnam's Sons, New York, 1926.
2. What Psycho-analysis Teaches Parents.
   H. Crichton Miller, M. D., *The New Psychology and the Parent,* Chs. I-VI, X, XII. Thomas Seltzer, Inc., New York, 1923.

[9] M. V. O'Shea, "Pre-School Education," in *Progressive Education,* Vol. II, No. 1, p. 12.

3. The Family as the Nursery of Growing Children.

   Ernest R. Groves, *Personality and Social Adjustment*, Chs. XII, XIII, XIV. Longmans, Green & Co., New York, 1924.

4. The Child and Pre-School Education.

   See articles "Progressive Education," pp. 3-37, in the *Quarterly Review*, January to March, 1925. Washington, D. C.

CHAPTER XXIV

THE FAMILY IN THE FUTURE

TRANSITIONAL CHARACTER OF THE FAMILY

IT would reveal more audacity than wisdom to prophesy with confidence concerning the forms that marriage and family life will take on in the generations to come. Changes both in ideas and, to a somewhat less extent, in practices are proceeding so rapidly that outcomes cannot be clearly foreseen. Two generations ago the family was, perhaps, the most inflexible of all social institutions—the one that revealed the fewest changes since medieval times. Today it is the most unstable, and probably the powerful current in the direction of change has not yet reached its crest.

This is only to express the truism that the family is in an acute stage of transition from standards and customs that no longer are adapted to twentieth-century conditions to a state where it will have achieved more satisfactory adjustments to the circumstances of modern life. It would be surprising if the family were not compelled to make fundamental changes in its controlling ideas and habits, since every other institution has been forced to undergo far-reaching alterations to bring it into harmony with social conditions that have been literally transformed during the last century and a half. Government, industry and intellectual life have been largely made over since 1750. In America, frontier conditions have disappeared; a rural nation has become an urban nation; a highly mechanized and specialized industry is in the saddle; and science has literally revolutionized thought and living. It has attacked theology in its stronghold; has developed respect for facts and a sound method of discovering facts in millions of minds; has undermined loyalty to moral and religious codes, once unchallenged, by developing an insistent demand that their ideal standards be brought into accord with the realities of human nature and social life. Applied science has brought to laborers comforts and conveniences once unknown to princes and, through the medium of film plays, portraying an exaggerated luxuriousness of living, has created in the minds of many plain citizens an ardent desire for luxury by no means confined to the middle class.[1]

[1] See Groves, *The Drifting Home*, pp. 201-2.

All these fundamental changes in the social and intellectual life of America—and of the world—were bound to react profoundly upon the family. With the disappearance of the frontier went the type of hard-working, adventurous, united family life that characterized it. With the rapid growth of cities and the influx of men and women from the farms to crowded centers of industry, there has sprung up a bewildering tangle of family problems and difficulties discussed in previous chapters. With the spread of factories and machines has gone the mechanization of life, followed by a human reaction against routine and a craving for excitement. Other consequences of our present economic system have been industrial insecurity, low wages for unskilled labor and the work of mothers and children outside the home. In the midst of such a revolution in ways of living and of thinking, why should we expect that the family would escape change?

Owing to the barrage of criticisms directed against the family by judges of juvenile and domestic relations courts, by social workers, public health nurses and psychiatrists, all of whom come into intimate contact with maladjusted families, the inefficiency of the contemporary family has been brought to the attention of most thoughtful people. It follows that, for the first time in social history, change in family ideas and customs is not only rapid but *conscious*. This is a more pregnant fact than may at first appear. For if intelligent folk are aware of the alterations taking place in the family, and of the need for such changes if this basic institution of society is to effect essential adjustments, they can *in some measure* control the character and direction of the adaptations. How far intelligence can direct and modify powerful social trends has long been a moot question. But to assert that knowledge and good-will can do nothing to control these movements is to accept a philosophy of fatalism and despair.

As might be expected, the rapidity of family changes, once brought to the attention of social groups, has evoked different attitudes and constructive proposals. A considerable body of conservative persons, jolted out of a comfortable complacency regarding the family, are filled with alarm and tend to fall back on sentiment, prejudice and a censorious attitude toward everybody who advocates or participates in bringing about changes in family ideals and habits. This is the group that is vocal in deploring the good old times of our forbears, when families were unified and enduring, wives and mothers were devoted housekeepers and nurses of children, the children themselves were modest, respectful and obedient to their parents, and decent people never mentioned subjects now the daily theme of table-talk. Far from realizing that, since the family is an organic part of society, changes in the social organism demand responsive adaptations in the family member, this group urges a return to the customs and standards of our forefathers. It sincerely believes that, if they would, progressive and radical thinkers who urge a new type of family life could turn their backs on "disrupting" ideas, stop dangerous experiments and preach a return to the safe and sane ways of the past. That serious writers and social workers favor progressive changes in family relations and organization is, in the opinion of this numerous class, mere wrongheadedness, which will result in sending the family institution, even now somewhat unseaworthy, upon the rocks. Mistaken as this group may be, lacking as it indubitably is in insight into the processes of social evolution, it must not be overlooked that it serves a useful purpose in holding back changes that might occur too fast to be solidly incorporated into the living organism of social life.

In sharp contrast to conservative opinion are the views of that increasing body of sophisticated men and women who readily accept the theory that the monogamic family has outlived its usefulness and should be decently interred without undue delay. A widespread skepticism regarding the personal and social value of the family permeates much of contemporary drama, fiction and the press. Not rarely, by implication at least, the ideal of enduring monogamy is cleverly pilloried as the relic of a rigid and outgrown social system. More and more frequently the drama portrays experiments in freer sex relations, and tends to paint the husband or wife who clings to an ideal of lifelong marriage as at least faintly ridiculous. Most critics do not fail to point out that the monogamic family is chiefly responsible for the economic dependence and the resulting subordination of women, for the ownership and exploitation of children, for the development of an exaggerated respect for individual and family property, resulting in grave economic and social injustices, and, finally, for the propagation and maintenance of the theory that marriage *in and of itself* is a sacred institution ordained by God.

All these ideas, say the skeptics, are out-moded and should be relegated to the social scrap-heap. In this age, when the current has set powerfully away from an outworn social order toward a new and better one, every intelligent person should adopt a hospitable attitude toward social change, and should encourage rather than frown upon experiments in freer sex unions. Young people will inevitably try out the various expedients of trial marriage, companionate marriage and no marriage other than an agreement to live together so long as both mates are happy. This being the case, the radicals urge that it is idle for adults to oppose and condemn these experiments, especially as they have made something of a mess of marriage and family life themselves. Witness the ever rising rate of divorce, the obvious unhappiness of many married pairs who decide to remain together "for the sake of the children," the devastating effects of unwise family domination upon the personalities of little children, as revealed by psychiatrists. Furthermore the spokesmen of this "advanced" group openly challenge the doctrine that monogamy is "natural," and suggest that, if society should remove its powerful pressure and permit free sex experimentation, polygamy might be demonstrated to be both more natural and more conducive to happiness in the case of not a few men and women.

There remains a large body of reflective men and women who admit honestly and frankly the grave defects and deficiencies in the monogamic family as it exists in the present day, but who sincerely believe that progressive reforms can remedy, and indeed have already done much to remedy, the evils in marriage and family relations. This group does not fear change, because it knows that change is the mark of vitality; its fear is of stagnation, the sign manual of death. Therefore these progressives look forward with optimism and faith to continuous, gradual modifications in the organization of the family, in its controlling ideals and habits, such as will rid it of the last relics of patriarchalism. When this is accomplished, as they believe it will be, they look forward to a new type of family in which freedom and a sense of obligation and mutual love and *respect for the personality of each member* shall unite to furnish the most wholesome conditions for personal growth. Not the elimination of the family, but its reform, is the slogan of the liberals.

In the eyes of the skeptics, the faith of the progressive group in the survival of the family rests on a precarious support of sentiment and conservatism, with little solid evidence to serve as a foundation. Yet an impartial examination of the facts justifies us in a considerable degree of confidence in the persistence of the monogamic family. In the first place, anthropology shows it to be one of the earliest of human institutions, growing out of real human needs. Neither monogamy nor the family *originated* in coercive social pressure; rather, they developed as the best ways to meet the urgent instinct of sex, on the one hand, and the utter need of helpless infants on the other. It is not reasonable to suppose that an institution that has survived for thousands of years, and has more or less successfully adjusted itself to the demands of a changing civilization, will surrender to the first onslaught of hostile criticism or will break up because of experiments in new forms of sex union. As suggested above, the attacks in the past upon government, organized religion and accepted knowledge have been even more powerful than any yet launched against the family. Yet the former institutions are as strong today as ever, because they serve basic needs of mankind and because they have proved reasonably responsive to criticism and organized efforts for reform. Such, in the considered judgment of the writer, will prove true of the family. In so far as it shows flexibility and capacity to meet the novel conditions of social life in the twentieth century, so far will it reveal a vitality that ensures its survival.

Examples are not lacking of capacity for adaptation on the part of the family during the last century. Although the emancipation of women from their subordination in the patriarchal family has been tardy, it has been finally effected in most civilized states. The life of a married woman today, even with its handicaps, is vastly more free than that of her sisters a century ago; her intellectual horizon is (or may be) as broad as the universe; her property and wages are her own. Likewise the lives of children, once even more under subjection than those of their mothers, have been transformed. The law protects the small boy and girl from cruelty, from too grave economic exploitation, from ignorance, from parental neglect. Although any social system which breeds and maintains poverty cannot give to children important "natural rights," yet the lot of most children is distinctly better than in past centuries; and, in the case of many, it is enormously improved. Among educated people, children are no longer snubbed and suppressed, regarded as "limbs of Satan" for exhibiting the faults and weaknesses of childhood, harshly reproved and even cruelly punished for their misconduct. A new spirit of comradeship, of understanding and, above all, of mutual confidence, is sweetening the relationships of many parents and children—a spirit rare indeed in the oppressive atmosphere of the patriarchal family of the past.

There is another ground for faith in the survival of the family which is worthy of serious consideration. What institution could take the place of the family should it decline and disappear? The critics who would destroy the last relics of this "outworn institution" and inaugurate a régime of sex freedom are strongest when they point out the imperfections and deficiencies of the family, weakest when they sketch a plan for getting along without it. The serious student of family evolution cannot fail to be impressed with its services, not alone to society, but to the individual. It has furnished an abiding place for men and women and children apart from the excitements, the disappointments, the bitter griefs and frustrations of life—a quiet retreat where each member was understood and loved in spite of everything. In the family, if anywhere, the human being might find sympathy and joy and comfort. This is not to say that all families have been spiritual refuges for their members, but only that many have so proved themselves, and that apparently no other social institution is equipped to satisfy the human craving for love and comprehension.

The services of the family to infancy, to growing children and to adolescent youths are too obvious to need more than passing mention. With all its faults, the family has provided an indispensable nursery and school for children. Despite its too frequently repressive and censorious spirit, it has furnished a *permanent* home for children (who greatly need stability of life) where they might be nurtured with love, with some degree of understanding of their needs as individuals, with pride in their achievements and regret at their failures.

What will happen if sex relationships should ever come to be looked upon as temporary? Probably children would be the chief sufferers. No sooner would they begin to send roots down into home life than these would be torn up and they would be required to adjust to a new household and a new step-parent. There would be little stability and continuity in the lives of such children—two conditions vitally essential for peaceful growth and maturing. Parents who thus sacrificed their children, by depriving them of the circumstances best assuring their growth, would in reality be demanding the free development of personality for themselves while denying it to their offspring.

Moreover, temporary sex unions, readily dissolved if not wholly satisfying, would render it impossible for the partners to grow through patience and insight into a finer comradeship. Those who have once known the love and understanding that are the reward of mutual concessions and mutual forbearance esteem them as far more precious than the restless fever of romantic passion—infinitely more satisfying to the mind and heart. This does not mean that passion does not persist in such unions, but only that it is less urgent and masterful. As brought out in a previous chapter, the whole psychology of the man and woman who enter into a free sex relationship with the understanding that it can be ended at will is antithetical to that of the pair who desire to make their union lifelong. In the former case, the demand is insistent that the relationship remain romantically appealing and unfailingly stimulating.

> "Oh think not I am faithful to a vow!
> . . . .
> Were you not lovely I would leave you now:
> After the feet of beauty fly my own." [2]

[2] Edna St. Vincent Millay, *A Few Figs from Thistles*, Sonnet III. Harper & Brothers, New York, 1923.

How can such an attitude, all-demanding and impatient of every quality in the beloved which fails to meet exacting standards, ever make possible a successful marriage? Most of the precious things of life are bought with a price and one of the most rare—loving, utterly understanding comradeship in marriage—exacts the costly price of self-control, willingness to concede, sometimes even to suffer, that many lovers have not the moral capital to pay.

REFORMS NECESSARY IF THE FAMILY IS TO FUNCTION SUCCESSFULLY IN MODERN LIFE

Although improvement in the social environment of the home and the enactment of much-needed legislation cannot of themselves assure the successful functioning of the family, they can provide those wholesome conditions without which there can be scant assurance of family stability, freedom, and happiness. As indicated above,[3] modern government has gone far toward acceptance of the theory that the State exists chiefly to promote social well-being and happiness. Many reflective minds are asking whether the State is not inevitably moving toward a more truly socialized order in which regard for the welfare of its citizens will constitute one of the primary motives of government. Therefore, it seems timely to ask what is involved in acceptance of the spirit and purpose of such a society. In the case of marriage and the family, it would mean that the State would actively concern itself in the improvement of these institutions in at least three ways—by means of legislation, economic reforms and social and educational aids. A brief consideration of each type of assistance may be worth while.

Legislative Reforms.

On the legal side, it is to be hoped that governments in the future will enact laws eliminating certain of the worst conditions that threaten marriage at present. A few years ago, twenty-six of these United States recognized so-called "common-law marriages" as valid, while in six other commonwealths the status of such marriages was doubtful. Only in seventeen States had such loose unions been declared invalid by statute.[4] Needless to say, irregular, perhaps unwitnessed, marriage arrangements such as these make possible easy repudiation of all family responsibilities. Common-law marriages are a relic of the family individualism of the

---

[3] See p. 385.
[4] Hall and Brooke, *American Marriage Laws in Their Social Aspects*, p. 31.

medieval barbarian tribes, and should be declared invalid by statute in every State which has not taken such action.

Another evil that should and will be righted is that of child marriages. The valuable study of *Child Marriages* by Richmond and Hall, published in 1925, points out that in fourteen States, the minimum age of marriage for girls is twelve years; in nine States, fourteen years; in eight States, fifteen years; in seventeen States, sixteen years.[5] This means that, with the consent of the parents, which apparently can be secured with astonishing ease, little girls between twelve and sixteen years of age may assume the responsibilities of marriage and founding a family in all the States of the Union save one—New Hampshire, which has fixed a minimum marriage age, for girls, of eighteen years. According to the estimate of Richmond and Hall, there are about 343,000 women in the country who began their married life as children during the last thirty-six years. This is nothing short of astounding in an age when interest in and knowledge about questions of social well-being are probably more general than in any previous period of history. Apparently a thoroughgoing education of public opinion is essential before legislative reforms can be effected. The authors of this study have summarized the opinions of 113 experienced persons concerning the desirable minimum age below which no marriage license should be issued to a girl, with or without the consent of her parents. The summary shows that six persons actually favored a minimum of twelve or fourteen years (one twelve years); six favored a fifteen-year minimum; forty-seven, a sixteen-year minimum; forty-five, an eighteen-year minimum; and only nine persons, a minimum over eighteen years.[6] It would be interesting to know what conceptions of the responsibilities and psychological relationships of marriage are held by intelligent persons who advocate a marriage age minimum of twelve to fifteen years.

Eugenic marriage laws, *i.e.,* legislation designed to improve the stock by preventing the transmission of physical and mental diseases, have been powerfully advocated by biologists but have not yet won over public opinion. In 1925, seven States had enacted laws requiring that male applicants for a marriage license should secure a medical certificate declaring them free from any venereal disease.[7] Because of the expense and time involved in giving thorough laboratory tests to determine the presence of syphilis, the operation of these laws has been difficult and imperfect.

[5] Mary E. Richmond and F. S. Hall, *op. cit.,* p. 45. Russell Sage Foundation, New York, 1925.

[6] *Ibid.,* p. 49.

[7] These states are Alabama, North Carolina, Indiana, North Dakota, Oregon, Wyoming and Wisconsin.

Especially has controversy centered about the working of Wisconsin's law, passed in 1917. In a valuable study of the results achieved by the law,[8] Hall quotes the opinion of various physicians, most of these to the effect that, although the statute has almost certainly not prevented the marriage of some men suffering from syphilis in an active or inactive form, it has proved of very great value in educating popular opinion in the State. An increasing number of men, knowing that they are infected, either postpone their marriages or put marriage definitely behind them until they are cured. Probably further experience in the operation of the law will convince these seven pioneer States and others that will, it may be hoped, follow in their footsteps, that a higher fee must be granted to the examining physician for making exacting tests, this fee to be paid by the State in cases where it is beyond the means of the applicant.

Another form of eugenic law sponsored by a group of eugenists today is that concerned with sterilization of the unfit—of those persons who, by every known test, are physically or mentally unsound. These persons would be likely to have an abnormal number of children, unhealthy in body or mind, and thus incapacitated to meet the ordinary demands of modern life. Twenty-three States had, up to July 1, 1925, enacted laws permitting sterilization, or had actually performed operations for sterilization, upon a varying number of men and women held to be totally unfit for parenthood.[9] California leads the way with 2,355 operations performed upon men and 1,596 performed on women in the State hospitals for the insane up to January 1, 1927.[10] At the other extreme are the States of Idaho and Washington, with one operation each, and six States which apparently have never made use of the provisions of the law.

Very few advocates of *compulsory* sterilization to eliminate unhealthy stocks can be mustered at present. Although this method is espoused by a number of eugenists, public opinion is far from sanctioning it as a wholesale device. However, voluntary sterilization of criminal and mentally defective types, or even occasional compulsory sterilization where it is clearly necessary, will no doubt continue and increase. The difficulty in committing States to this policy lies in the fact that the laws of heredity with respect to the inheritance of mental and physical defects are by no means thoroughly established and generally accepted. Until they

[8] F. S. Hall, *Medical Certification for Marriage*, pp. 41-5. Russell Sage Foundation, New York, 1925.

[9] Harry H. Laughlin, *Eugenical Sterilization* (1926), p. 60. Quoted in Groves, *Social Problems of the Family*, p. 254. J. B. Lippincott Co., Philadelphia, 1927.

[10] Paul Popenoe, "Eugenic Sterilization in California," *Journal of Social Hygiene*, May, 1927, p. 258.

are, popular opinion will not support legislation designed to weed out defective stocks by compulsory operations for eugenical sterilization. Nevertheless education can do much to awaken public sentiment to the importance of eugenics as a factor in successful marriages. Likewise education can dispose defective persons to submit to voluntary sterilization in cases where competent physicians and psychiatrists are agreed that such persons should not have offspring.

Social experience does not justify great confidence in legislation as a means of improving family welfare. Yet it seems not unreasonable to believe that the prohibition of common-law marriages and child marriages would at least eliminate two grave evils that threaten family life at present, while the education of the mass of men and women in certain fundamental eugenical ideas and practices would tend appreciably to improve the human stock, even if such a policy did not accomplish all that has been claimed for it by enthusiastic eugenists.

Economic Reforms.

A fully socialized society would not stop with the enactment of a few laws righting grave abuses. It would attack the problem of poverty with its full resources of scientific knowledge and good-will. To this evil in our midst may be traced in large measure an appalling number of the ills from which the families of the laboring, and not rarely the small-salaried, classes are suffering. As indicated in previous chapters, poverty, with its twin brother, ignorance, must bear heavy responsibility for the existence in our midst of ugly, unsanitary tenements, bad home conditions, juvenile crime and delinquency, family desertion, prostitution and child labor. If a society should grow up in the future which put the health, happiness and welfare of its members *above every other end,* the present economic system would be transformed. In such a society everyone would work, so far as possible, at tasks adapted to his capacities and individual aptitudes. Payment for that labor—were it manual or mental—would be sufficient to secure decent, comfortable homes for every family, and to drive fear of pauperism from the door, especially if the ban upon the spread of sound contraceptive information were removed. Indeed the State would make the housing problem its own, and, recognizing that society has no right to expect that healthy, intelligent, socially-minded children should come from dark, overcrowded homes, would see to it that these physical and moral pesthouses were replaced by attractive, sanitary dwelling places. If to the reader this plan seems unduly Utopian or "socialistic," he should recall that several European countries—England,

France, Belgium and Holland, to mention a few—have already attacked the problem of the housing of their laborers with a will. In ten years there will be no unsanitary tenements in Holland, and in thirty years none in England,[11] if the good work keeps up.

A more socialized society would also concern itself with providing for young people such economic opportunities as would make early marriage a sane possibility, not a foolish risk. It would attack the economic props of prostitution, and by securing to young workers a wage that makes life worth living would remove at least one inducement to vice —the longing of young women for a few of the pleasures and pretty things with which the lives of the privileged seem to abound. It is not the judgment of the author that lax sex relations will disappear with the removal of poverty. But it seems reasonably certain that the barter of their bodies by ill-paid girls and women in return for good times, money and attractive clothes will practically cease when these young persons earn sufficient wages to supply a reasonable amount of material "goods" and recreational· pleasure for themselves.

The society that sets as its primary task the job of securing to workers, both men and women, good homes, wages that will ensure moderate comfort for themselves and their children, some recreation and leisure, and the abolition of child labor will reap its inevitable reward in more wholesome family life, better upbringing of children, a sharp decrease in the huge public appropriations for dependents, delinquents and criminals. With the wiping out of child labor should and will go more opportunities for schooling and vocational training for *all* children to the extent that they can profit by them. Child labor means ignorant, untrained labor, and children so exploited swell the ranks of unskilled, low-paid workers. In all probability, the families they rear in adult life will live like themselves in dirty tenements, will be insufficiently nourished, clothed and educated. These children, in turn, will become child workers with little hope for the future, while their parents will probably join the army of dependents whom society carries on its back. If no other motive operates, enlightened self-interest alone will more and more dictate to modern States the necessity for getting down to the fountainhead of a great many social and family evils in economic conditions.

Social Reforms.

But a humane society will not have completed its task of promoting individual and family well-being even when it has brought about economic

[11] The estimate of Edith Elmer Wood, expert on housing, made to the author.

reforms. There still remains the great work of planning and putting into operation constructive educational and social programs, definitely designed to raise the level of family life and to promote the health and efficiency of family members. Before such plans can be conceived, however, society will be forced to abandon a heavy luggage of old ideas and customs regarding the nature and sphere of women, the limited functions of the State and the importance of leaving to individual initiative a large area of vital human concerns. When once society has outgrown these age-old notions, it can attack with an open mind certain questions of far-reaching importance to family life. In the first place, social acceptance of complete sex equality, not merely theoretical but practical acceptance, would mean social coöperation in meeting the crucial problem of married women— how to harmonize marriage and parenthood with gainful employment. Perhaps, in the future, towns and cities will be almost as much concerned in helping the working mother solve practical questions of food preparation, household management and child care as they are beginning to be in the conservation of child health. Who knows but the next generation will have community kitchens; apartment house and neighborhood nurseries, managed by experts in child care; coöperative or public house-cleaning service, all furnished at moderate cost to mothers who can give their best service to society outside the home?

Provision of recreational facilities in convenient localities to meet the need for sports and relaxation of the masses of our industrialized society will proceed apace and will, in course of time, result in ample playground space for all children and adults, within reach of their homes. In the years to come, teachers of organized games and sports, supported from public funds, may vie in importance with teachers of grammar and history. The enormous benefits, both to the family and to society, of adequate provision for health-building, out-of-door recreation can hardly be exaggerated. A recent study of one of the most troublesome boy-gangs in Brooklyn led to a report in which the collaborators united in the opinion that the total lack of play space for these boys, other than the street and the docks, was the most important factor in their growing lawlessness. The fathers of these boys were mostly stevedores, who frequently slept in the daytime, and the boys were told to go out and keep away from the house in order to secure unbroken sleep to their fathers.

Not only will society in the future provide ample play space for youth, but it will make the supervision of commercialized amusements its serious concern. Dance halls, cheap movies and cabarets, steamboats, amusement parks and other forms of recreation will be required to conform to standards of decency or close up, and the youth that resort to these places will be more carefully supervised and protected from powerful temptations to vice. The cities and towns of America may even enter into competition with commercial amusement places and furnish to youth satisfying outlets for their love of pleasure and adventure which are free from vulgarity and vicious suggestions.

On the educational side there is much for a socially-minded society to do, even though much has already been attempted. Probably the laws against giving contraceptive knowledge, either privately by physicians or in clinics under public supervision, will break down before many years. Maternity centers in the next generation will be greatly multiplied and will offer to expectant and nursing mothers not only expert prenatal and postnatal care, but educational assistance in the nurture and guidance of their children which will be available to *every mother* who is in need of it. Many maternity centers will probably, like the East Harlem center in New York, see fit to engage in educational campaigns throughout a whole district, to interest foreign-born and native mothers in the maternity center and in the various forms of assistance which it offers them. Such a crusade in the East Harlem center, over a period of four years, resulted in educating fully four-fifths of the mothers to give up recourse to ignorant midwives and to make increasing use of the valuable facilities of the center. In the years ahead, maternity centers, public health nursing associations, behavior clinics, public schools and universities will tend in ever-growing numbers to employ the services of mental hygienists in order to discover in time evidences of mental strain and abnormality in children and youths. So far as possible, they will redirect these tendencies and forestall grave unhappiness and maladjustment in the lives of the victims of these disorders and in the families which they may establish in the future.

The writer is also inclined to be optimistic with respect to another educational question. At present the State provides equality of educational opportunity to children only so far as elementary education is concerned. To be sure, the high schools are free to all, but economic disabilities prevent scores of thousands of children from making use of their offerings. Perhaps, in the generations to come, the State may accept responsibility for giving every boy and girl as much educational opportunity *as he can profitably use,* together with that type of vocational guidance and training which will discover and develop his special aptitudes in work. Such an enlightened policy would result not only in securing greater well-being and happiness to individuals, but even more in promoting the progress of society. At present we do not know what proportion of the army of children that leaves school every year at fourteen or fifteen to go to work is capable of profiting by further education adapted to their particular capacities and interests. Certainly the few tests we have show a preponderance of merely average or below average ability in this group.[12] But that a proportion of these children could profit greatly by further study and training seems an inevitable conclusion. In his *Genetic Studies of Genius,* Terman found more than twenty percent of his highly talented children in the laboring class. If such youths, far above the average in mental ability, could be selected and educated according to their individual gifts, they would be saved from recruiting the ranks of lower paid workers, would achieve an independent economic status and would, in all probability, establish better homes and rear their children with greater intelligence than would be the case had they entered unskilled or semiskilled trades at the earliest age the law permits. The need of childhood for the nurturing and protecting care of the State does not cease at fourteen years.

CHANGES WITHIN THE FAMILY

I. Complete Economic Emancipation of Women.

So far as the family itself is concerned, the student of its long historical evolution has every reason to believe that the last vestiges of patriarchal power and privilege are bound to disappear. The emancipation of the wife and mother, not alone from property and legal disabilities, but from the restraints which the husband can still put upon her complete liberty as an individual will, in all probability, be accomplished in a generation. Social and economic currents are unmistakably moving in this direction. No doubt, the movement would be materially hastened by the fading out of certain stubborn ideas concerning woman's sphere and functions which still dominate the minds of men and women. It is these persistent notions, heirlooms of a long past, that dictate the upbringing of girls, their education and their preparation for gainful employment. Neither parents on the one hand nor the public on the other take the work of women in business and the professions with much seriousness. Back in the minds of both is the idea that the true work of all women lies in the pursuit of their ancient tasks in the home. Therefore the vocational training of girls is not held to be of great importance, since, of course, they will marry in a few years and become home-makers. The most powerful impulse toward the complete liberation of women will

---

[12] See Helen T. Woolley, *An Experimental Study of Children,* The Macmillan Co., New York, 1926.

come when it is taken for granted that *every unmarried woman will earn her own living,* no matter how large is her family's income, and that every married woman who elects to work outside her home shall be helped, not hindered, in realizing her purpose. When that happy day arrives, the vocational training and employment of women will be taken seriously; then married women will achieve a degree of economic independence enjoyed by relatively few at present. Every woman who is a financial dependent is to a considerable extent unfree. Such is the writing of social history on the wall. Slaves, children and women have been held in complete or partial subjection because they were compelled to look to another for the means of subsistence.

When women have broken their last chain—the economic one—they will become full-fledged human beings. Several generations will probably pass before the plain man on the street *takes it for granted* that married women shall choose for themselves whether or not they will continue in gainful employment and contribute to the family income. When that transformation of public opinion is accomplished, we shall see wives and mothers dividing their time between work and home much as their husbands do. No doubt there will be fewer children in such families and they will not have so exclusive a claim on their mother's time and attention as was true in the past. But that situation may prove by no means so calamitous as appears at first glance. For, if the psychiatrists are to be believed, the suffocating devotion of many mothers has been more of a bane than a blessing to their children. As we have seen, it has all too frequently resulted in binding the boy or girl to the mother with cords of steel so that he or she could never become a self-reliant person capable of falling in love and founding an independent, harmonious home.

Not only is it true that emotional dedication of mothers to children, followed by selfish demands upon sons and daughters for a corresponding exclusive devotion, has resulted in "mother fixations" which stunt development, but it is also a matter of common knowledge that children intellectually outgrow mothers whose exclusive interests are home-making and mothering. As it is at present, when matters of public concern or challenging intellectual problems begin to arouse the interest of youth, it is not to the mother, who has been tied to the home, but to the father, who has had wider social and intellectual contacts, that older children turn. Many a self-sacrificing mother must have realized with bitter regret that she was no longer an intellectual companion to her children, who had outstripped her. Conversely, there is already some testimony, offered by married women employed outside the home, to the effect that they have noticed an agreeable change in their children's attitude toward mother's information and views on social topics under discussion. Once their boys and girls turned only to the father for enlightenment on any subject outside family and neighborhood concerns. Now they seem as interested in mother's experience and ideas as in father's.

Although the children of gainfully employed women will not receive so large a part of their mother's attention and physical care as in past generations, they may, nevertheless, be very well nurtured by trained child nurses, and start their education under wholesome and happy conditions in a nursery school. No normal mother or father will fail to take deep interest in his or her children, or to seek every opportunity to stimulate and guide their developing minds and characters. More and more, as the child grows older, the mother will find occasions to be companionable with him (or her), to observe carefully his individual traits and aptitudes and to establish between herself and her child that rare spirit of mutual confidence which must exist if she is to be a guide and help in his formative years. Recently a little girl whose mother is a professional woman was naming her best friends to a visitor. Among them was her mother. When the caller expressed mild surprise at this inclusion of the mother among loved companions, the little girl replied: "Oh, yes, she is one of my best friends." The gainfully employed mother who is a comrade to her children and has their confidence, has surely not failed as a parent.

In the years to come, married women will increasingly contribute from their earnings to the family income. This will mean that earlier marriage will be possible for the salaried middle class in which the marriage rate is relatively low. A man will not hesitate for years to ask the woman he loves to marry him if he knows that she expects to contribute her share to the maintenance of their common home and children. Then will disappear our present inequitable situation, which no doubt leads heavily burdened professional men seriously to raise the question whether the economic burden is fairly apportioned between husband and wife. Society should be greatly benefited by the services of a growing body of trained women, married and unmarried, whose most valuable contributions will probably be made in those fields of economic and social life that are most concerned with human welfare. When the majority of women are engaged in gainful work, the semi-parasitism of so disturbing a number of married women at present will inevitably meet with increasing social disapproval. A prominent social investigator recently declared in a college address that parasitic women should be compelled by the State to go to work. Probably such action will be long deferred, if indeed it is ever undertaken. But that such a policy should have been publicly advocated seems to the writer a straw showing which way the wind blows. Idle married women, who have no regular employment within the home or outside it, and who are content to be maintained in indolent comfort by overworked husbands will more and more fall under a social ban.

II. Education of Husbands and Fathers.

Among the fundamental changes in family life that are apparently on the way is one involving husbands and fathers. Until men are educated to a different point of view regarding their wives and their homes, stubborn obstacles will remain in the path of family improvement. As has been pointed out more than once, relatively few men are sincerely convinced that their wives are as truly *individuals* as themselves, with special talents of genuine social usefulness. The majority of men still think of women in the mass as potential or actual wives and mothers. Few indeed are the men who can separate women from their biological and historic functions and look upon them as personalities capable of rendering skilled and perhaps even unique service. Only when men come to regard their wives first as individuals, and only secondarily as bearers of children, can women hope to achieve their purpose of a free, self-directed life in which continual mental growth is possible. Husbands, by lack of sympathy or by open antagonism, can make it difficult, if not virtually impossible, for their wives to find a solution of their present knotty problem of combining home and children with stimulating work. The way out lies in the whole-hearted coöperation of husband and wife in meeting the difficulties that inevitably arise as soon as the plan is attempted. Numerous instances exist, even now, of generous assistance rendered by not a few men to their wives who are struggling with the combined demands of home and career.

When men really *believe in* and are even proud of their wives' achievements outside the household, when they recognize that the addition made by the wife to the family income is a very acceptable, if not indispensable, increment, then these husbands will view their own personal relations to their families in a different light. They will look upon the founding of a home and the rearing of children as a *mutual responsibility* of the man and the woman who maintain that home. When the antiquated idea of man that household cares and the nurture of the young are wholly "woman's work" is gradually transformed into the conviction that these duties constitute the common job of husband and wife, then indeed a revolution will take place in the daily life of the family. The gainfully employed wife and her working husband will divide their household tasks. If their combined income permits the employment of a trained domestic helper, their chief care, before going to work in the morning and after their return, will be bathing, feeding and coming to know their children. Marketing, household oversight and cleaning and preparation of the family budget will be equitably shared tasks. It will not be easy to work out a satisfactory scheme of coöperation because the new arrangement will demand sacrifices of the husband which he has been taught to think should not be expected of him. But love and a new conception of the relations of husband and wife when both are free, developing individuals will help him to effect the necessary changes in personal habits. He will be aided, too, by the realization that his wife is a happier, more effective human being than she ever could be if held down solely to domestic tasks. A university professor, who recently addressed a group of his colleagues on the theme "Women and Careers," declared that every husband who wished to escape the menace of a nervous, dissatisfied wife, showing clear signs of becoming neurotic, should encourage her to find congenial employment suited to her abilities. This gentleman had practised what he preached, for he had encouraged his wife, when their two children were past babyhood, to study medicine and psychology and to fill the very useful social niche she now occupies as a child specialist.

The benefits derived by the wife from this new point of view on the part of her mate will be no greater than those accruing to the children. It has long been a matter of regret on the part of educators, psychiatrists and social workers that the upbringing of children is so exclusively left to mothers. Men have pretty completely shaken off responsibility for shaping the tastes and characters of their offspring, in order to leave themselves free to become engrossed in business or professional interests. The results have by no means always been fortunate. In the first place, fathers have different points of view regarding the meanings and values of life to give to children than have mothers. The life experiences of the two parents have not been the same, and their interpretations of life experience are bound to vary. The child needs both outlooks on life. Then, too, it not infrequently happens that the father has more instinctive sympathy with and understanding of child nature than has the mother. It is a commonplace that the mother who bears a child is not always the person best fitted to rear and develop it. Mother love does not imply mother insight and wisdom. The loss of its father's daily care, guidance and companionship is a serious deprivation to any child and especially is it so if the father has that rare, spontaneous understanding of child nature and needs that may be lacking in the mother.

In the family of the future, the writer has the optimism to believe that both father and mother will be *educated parents,* availing themselves of the opportunities furnished by the nursery school and by public schools of parenthood to become wiser companions and guides of their children from infancy. The parents of the coming generations will learn how to avoid crippling or stunting their offspring by unwise parental action and how to hold in check their own selfish demands for the exclusive devotion of their boys and girls. In this new and enlightened parenthood, the father will share equally with the mother. Who can tell how much greater happiness and liberation of power may not be the assets of the rising generation when parents have been set free by knowledge from ancient errors!

EXPERIMENTS IN NEW FORMS OF MARRIAGE AND SEX UNIONS

In any period of profound transition from an old order to a new, there is bound to be exploring, experimenting and radical theorizing. There can be no renaissance in thought or institutional life without these accompaniments. History shows that social change is always attended by expression of opinions and by experiments in new ways of living that seem radical and even dangerous to thoughtful men and women. Sometimes these novel ideas and customs are incorporated into the life of society and come to be accepted as commonplaces. Witness the widespread freedom of thought and of conscience that intellectual "radicals" have brought about, the universal franchise rights that social leaders have fought to realize, the just claims that organized labor has made good in its protracted struggle for higher wages and better working conditions. On the other hand, history also bears witness to not a few movements designed to overthrow or radically alter old institutions and thought systems which did not entirely accomplish the ends in view. Voltaire and the young atheists in the ardent group of French Encyclopedists did not succeed in destroying the Church—*"L'Infame"*—but they did change public opinion by making it more tolerant and humane with regard to religious questions. The Russian Communists have not overthrown the State; they have only substituted one form of dictatorship for another. The daily lives of millions of citizens have been profoundly altered by the Fascist revolution, that in a few years has deprived the Italian people of political, economic and (to a considerable extent) personal liberty. But what student of history believes that the Fascist régime will persist? Ancient institutions, customs and habits of thought are rarely permanently overthrown by a minority, no matter how able and powerful.

This is only to state once more the writer's belief that, despite the attacks made upon it, despite the experiments in freer sex relations that are unquestionably going on, the monogamic family will survive. Yet even on this point it is well not to be overconfident. In the words of the liberal pastor of the Community Church of New York:

"Marriage as we know it in our part of the world—namely the monogamic relation between men and women—is regarded as the fixed and final, indeed, as the only thinkable solution of the problem of the sexes. What is the use of discussing what is already settled for good and all? But *is* it settled for good and all? . . . at whatever hazard of misunderstanding at this time I want to lay down the proposition that no question is ever settled, no institution finally and irrevocably established. . . . The changes may not be great; they may never be made at all. But the way must always be wide open for experimentation. Not otherwise can progress be assured." [13]

The way is partly open today for experimentation, and some men and women are availing themselves of the opportunity. Society will probably be more familiar in the future with companionate marriages, trial marriages and other forms of tentative exploration into the field of freer sex relations. Companionate marriages have in all probability come to stay. The union of men and women for companionship and with the definite intention of preventing the birth of offspring, already far from rare, will doubtless become more common. As Professor Groves predicts, this type of marriage, allowing as it does for freer comradeship, for the joys of love and home without their responsibilities, will persist, at least until certain family evils are righted, and will prove an aggressive rival of the family with children.[14]

To be sure, some of these companionate unions will be transformed into conventional marriages, voluntarily or involuntarily, by the advent of a child, and in such cases parents may develop as strong an affection for their children as if they had formed no initial purpose to remain childless. But many companionates will end as they began—childless marriages. Probably Groves is right when he declares that such unions would have been formed ages ago by men and women who did not desire offspring had they known how to prevent their conception.[15]

What will be the effect of the companionate upon the conventional family? Who can say that it may not prove a stimulus to the removal of antiquated ideas and handicaps that stand in the way of the happiness and successful functioning of the family with children? Challenged by a

[13] *Birth Control Review*, May, 1927, p. 135.
[14] See *The Drifting Home*, pp. 212-6.   [15] *Ibid.*, p. 212.

successful competitor for the favor of men and women, the historic family of parents and children may be impelled to set its house in order, to remove causes of friction and to lift ancient burdens from the shoulders of fathers, mothers and children.

On the other hand it is doubtful whether society will ever place the stamp of its approval upon companionate marriage, since, from the biological point of view, it is a failure. Sociologists tell us that at least three births are required to replace each married pair. This is true despite a steadily falling death-rate; for not all children, under the best conditions, grow to maturity and perpetuate themselves, and not all marry. Since companionate marriage is not self-perpetuating, it seems bound to be restricted in every age to a minority of individualists who care less for the enriching experience of parenthood than for so-called "self-expression."

Not much is known of the extent to which experiments in so-called "trial marriages" have gone. These unions are by their nature private, entered into by the partners concerned in order to "try out" living together and to discover whether they are happily mated, not only sexually but psychologically. "It is these psychic necessities," says Dr. Beatrice Hinkle, "which have put the old marriage relation out of joint." [16] And it is the difficulties that two individualized persons encounter in effecting happy adjustments to each other which are primarily responsible for the emergence of the idea of trial marriage. Such private unions can be easily dissolved if they prove unsuccessful and if there are no children. If they remain happy under the acid test of prolonged daily association, some at least of these irregular relationships may result in permanent and conventional marriages. Long ago Elsie Clews Parsons pointed out to an indignant and outraged society that, since monogamous marriage seems best fitted to promote health and intellectual and emotional development in individuals, and since such marriages are long delayed because of economic circumstances, it might be well, in order to avoid the evil of prostitution, which is an accompaniment of delayed unions, to encourage early trial marriage. In this much criticized proposal, Mrs. Parsons was by no means suggesting that society sanction sexual license, for she expressly stated that the relation should "be entered into with a view to permanency," but with the privilege of ending it if it were unhappy. *If no offspring were born,* such unions should not, in her opinion, meet with sharp public condemnation.[17]

On the basis of his long and intimate experience with the boys and

---

[16] "Changing Marriage," in *Survey Graphic,* December, 1926, p. 289.
[17] *The Family,* pp. 348-9. G. P. Putnam's Sons, New York, 1906.

girls of Denver, among whom, he believes, there is far more loose sexual commerce than ever comes to light, Judge Lindsey is inclined to believe that if public opinion could be brought to tolerate some form of companionate marriage, permitting youths "a free, normal and decent exercise of their sexual cravings," much secret and unlovely sexual intercourse would be done away with. Birth control knowledge may, he thinks, result in two kinds of marriage contracts, the one permitting the birth of children and encouraging permanent marriage, and the other prohibiting conception in the case of the unfit and permitting only cohabitation. The latter unions might easily be dissolved if they proved unhappy. The honest realism of Judge Lindsey has met with a storm of hostile criticism, indicating that society is not yet ready to face with frankness the actual sexual laxity in its midst. In course of time, when public opinion is more soundly informed, it may be brought to sanction companionate marriage and divorce by mutual consent *in the interest of a finer sexual morality*. But such a revolution in popular thinking lies in all probability far in the future.

The greatest hope for the improvement of marriage and family life rests upon the spread of enlightenment and a finer idealism in regard to sex relations and functions. The American people have long been distinguished for their passionate faith in the possibilities of popular education. Yet they have never brought that faith to bear upon one of the most critical of all social problems—how to make marriage and home life satisfying and developing. Although the educated class is gradually being converted to the belief that harmonious adjustments within marriage and the family cannot be brought about without sound, scientific education, infused with honesty and idealism, average men and women remain in Egyptian darkness regarding this social need. A large number of unsuccessful marriages are due, if we may believe the psychiatrists and physicians, to sexual incompatibilities, a considerable proportion of which could have been prevented by the right kind of sex education from the earliest years to adult life. When shall we awaken as a people to the urgent importance of this instruction, not alone to give information when it is needed, to establish hygienic sex habits and to develop dynamic ideals, but to prevent those sex repressions and misunderstandings which are so inimical to happy marriage?

Obviously, education for marriage and parenthood includes more than sex knowledge, or even sex idealism. Young people should be instructed in the leading part the family has played in social life, the causes of its present unsuccessful functioning, the reforms that are essential if it is to prove satisfying to its members, the indispensable services it has rendered and may increasingly render to society. If the social organism is not to be disrupted by violent change, it must increasingly rely upon the extension of scientific knowledge and the development in youth of sincere ideals, both of which youth is taught to apply to contemporary problems. In education rests the chief hope of far-reaching improvement in the family as in every social institution. This should not be interpreted to mean that new forms of marriage and family relationships will not be tried out but that, with widespread education, they will tend to be intelligent and socially responsible experiments, not mere selfish, personal revolts against convention.

If knowledge and practical idealism unite in facing squarely the many inadequacies of the present-day family, its suppressions of personal freedom, its conflicts and unhappiness, there will emerge in the generations to come a finer, more satisfying, and therefore more enduring family life than is at all general today. This family of the future may combine the unity and permanence of the old-time family with sympathetic comradeship and deep emotional satisfactions that give joy to life and in which too often the family relations of the past were lacking. Not authority but comprehending love will prove the cement of the family that is to be.

TOPICS FOR REPORTS

1. Contemporary Criticisms and Proposals with Regard to the Family.
   Survey Graphic, December, 1926. Woman's Number.
2. Legislation and Education as Factors in Reconstructing the Family.
   George E. Howard, History of Matrimonial Institutions, Vol. III, pp. 201-59. University of Chicago Press, 1904.
3. Is Society Becoming More Socialistic?
   Arthur W. Calhoun, A Social History of the American Family from Colonial Times to the Present, Vol. III, Ch. XIV. Arthur H. Clark Co., Cleveland, 1919.
4. The Future of the Home.
   Dr. Ernest R. Groves, The Drifting Home, Ch. IX. Houghton Mifflin Co., Boston, 1926.
5. Companionate Marriage: A Critical Analysis.
   Judge Ben B. Lindsey and Wainwright Evans, Companionate Marriage, Chaps. VII, VIII, IX. Boni and Liveright, New York, 1927.

Justification of Monogamy.

I Biologically.
In general 105 boys to 100 girls born into world.
As the sexes nearly equal it is impossible to have polygamy on a large scale.

II Socially.
Monogamy makes possible the greatest number of social groups. Children have association of mother & father.

III Historically.
From the beginning monogamy in all groups of people has been the prevailing form of marriage.

IV Individual or Emotionally
It satisfies more than any other type.

V Economically
more or less it fits into all economic systems of the present time, Only the rich could support many wives,

Suggestions for IMPROVING Family.

1. Education
2. Recognition of parenthood.

Finis.
Jan. 22, 1930.

INDEX

When woman get their hands on money, becau